D0991995

A Murder in Wartime

More advance praise ...

"A *Murder in Wartime* is one of those exceptional pieces of reporting that reads like a superb novel of intrigue and suspense.

"A *Murder in Wartime* has a 'You Are There' feeling for time, place, and people, evoking both nostalgia and unsettling memories. As a former Army infantry officer who knew one of the accused, I was absolutely fascinated by Stein's exposé of the 'other war' that raged in the back alleys and government offices of Vietnam's besieged cities.

"After two decades, Jeff Stein blows away the fog of war and reveals the world of double agents and double crosses, of clandestine meetings and political assassination. A truly eye-opening history of the things you never saw on the nightly news.

"A very good read."

—**Nelson DeMille,** author of *Word of Honor*

A

The Untold Spy Story

MURDER

That Changed the Course

IN WARTIME

of the Vietnam War

JEFF STEIN

St. Martin's Press   New York

For the Timps

Editor: Jared Kieling
Production Editor: Mara Lurie
Copyedited by Diane Hess
Design by Judith A. Stagnitto

Library of Congress Cataloging-in-Publication Data

Stein, Jeff.
    A murder in wartime : the untold spy story that changed the course of the Vietnam war / Jeff Stein.
        p.   cm.
    ISBN 0-312-07037-3
    1. United States. Army. Special Forces—Trials, litigation, etc.
2. United States. Central Intelligence Agency—Trials, litigation, etc.   3. Courts-martial and courts of inquiry—Vietnam—Ho Chi Minh City.   4. Trials (Murder)—Vietnam—Ho Chi Minh City.   5. Vietnamese Conflict, 1961–1975—United States.   I. Title.
KF7642.U55S74   1992
343.73'0143—dc20
[347.303143]   91-39002
                                                                CIP

First edition: June 1992
10 9 8 7 6 5 4 3 2 1

Contents

All arrogance will reap a rich harvest in tears. God calls men to a heavy reckoning for overween-ing pride.

—HERODOTUS

Other people had unhappy childhoods. We had Vietnam.

—MICHAEL HERR

Acknowledgments

A t six o'clock on the night of February 4, 1990, I boarded an Amtrak train in Washington for Georgia, setting out on the first leg of what would become a much longer journey than I expected to track down the major participants in this story. Supplemented by hundreds of telephone calls and letters, the trip would eventually take me to twenty-five states where the men caught up in the Green Beret drama had once lived or where they had scattered to since 1969.

Many people helped me along the way. This book could not have been written, or at least written with understanding and detail, without the important contributions of several key people. First among them is former Green Beret Colonel Robert Bradley Rheault, who was the commander of the 5th Special Forces Group at the time of the events recounted herein. His constant efforts to dissuade me from writing this book must be noted if only to underscore his generosity in spending time with me and giving approval to his former men, who hold unswerving allegiance to him, to talk to me.

The former defendants and their families were extraordinarily generous in sharing their reminiscences with me, as well as their scrapbooks, pictures, and letters saved from the period. I am particularly indebted to Dorothy Boyle and Mary Boyle O'Hara, wife and sister, respectively, of late Warrant Officer Edward Boyle, for letting me see his letters home from the Long Binh stockade. The same goes for Bob Marasco and Budge Williams, who took me into their homes and spent hours explaining, and reexplaining, various aspects of a difficult period in their lives many years after the event. Tom Middleton and Alvin "Pete" Smith, respectively, were also unflagging in their courteous responses to my pestering questions and intrusions. To Phyllis Middleton, especially, I give my thanks for recounting an important episode that she has kept secret all these years. To Bob Marasco and his wife, I give thanks for a hearty dinner and grocery bags full of mementos. To all the countless friends, relatives, wives, and ex-wives of the Green Berets, I give my deep appreciation for their kind help to a stranger.

Among the many lawyers involved in both sides of this case, two were critically important to whatever measure of success I've achieved in telling the legal side of this story. First was George Gregory, who in July 1969 answered the call of his friend Tom Middleton, locked in solitary in the Long Binh stockade, to come to Vietnam and help him out. Gregory became my friend and guide in my early floundering days of research, pointing me this way and that, opening his house in South Carolina to my visits, and providing me with boxes of his personal records, which turned out to include everything from Saigon hotel chits to hand-typed legal motions and scrapbooks of yellowed clippings from now-defunct local newspapers. I am eternally grateful to both him and his wife, Debbie.

Former U.S. Army captain Steve Berry, at polar opposites from George Gregory in his strategy for defending the Green Berets, was also an enthusiastic, serious, and generous contributor to this project, sharing many hours of telephone conversations and letters full of advice, encouragement, and explanations of the case to which he was so deeply and passionately committed. His personal account of his Vietnam service, *Those Gallant Men*, included a chapter on the case that was an invaluable starting point for my own research.

Of the other military defense laywers who shared their time and recollections with me, I particularly want to thank Richard Booth, Bill Hart, and Marty Linsky, each of whom supplied different pieces of the legal puzzle. Whatever misinterpretations have crept into my account of the defense lawyers' strategies are, of course, only mine.

On the other side of the ledger, former Army detectives Frank Bourland and Bob Bidwell contributed extraordinarily detailed and often poignant recollections of their investigation. Without their invaluable guidance, I would not have been able to even begin deciphering the real meaning of the investigative documents in the case.

The leadership of the United States Army was widely denounced, even ridiculed, for its handling of the Green Beret case, but I am grateful for the time and cooperation that many of its members gave me. In particular I want to thank former secretary of the Army Stanley Resor for his hours of recollections and efforts to piece together the missing pieces of the prosecutorial puzzle. Former defense secretary Melvin Laird also provided valuable insights and commentary, as did Generals William Westmoreland, Bruce Palmer, Bill Potts, Dick Rossen, and the late George Mabry. Harold Seaman, Wilton Persons, and Bob Jordan, each of them with different legal responsibilities for the Army, provided interesting anecdotes and insights on key events in the case.

Writing anything about the Central Intelligence Agency presents a special challenge. Even the agency's own documents are often deliberately misleading or fail to tell the entire story. The problem is compounded by some officials who, by habit or statute, are reluctant to confide the facts of an episode in which the CIA's role remains largely classified. Thus, some of the former CIA officers who helped me understand the agency's role in the Green Beret affair must remain anonymous. Of the many officials I talked to, however, I can single out Dean Almy, John Greaney, Sam Halperin, and Joe Lazarsky for special thanks. To the rest of you, many thanks.

For the White House end of the story, I must especially thank former presidential counsel John Ehrlichman and former Nixon chief of staff H. R. "Bob" Haldeman. Alexander Haig, Kissinger's military assistant at the time, was also prompt and generous in corresponding with me.

The perceptions of the Saigon press corps as it picked at the Green Beret mystery was another key element of the story. To whatever degree I accurately reflected their thinking, I must praise Robert Kaiser, Kevin Buckley, Terence Smith, and James Sterba, all of whom I have quite unfairly singled out to give readers an understanding of how a competitive press corps goes about trying to decipher a spy story—especially one the government desperately wants to hide. Last but hardly least, Vu Thuy Hoang deserves belated special acknowledgment. As Bob Kaiser's Vietnamese assistant in the Saigon bureau of the *Washington Post*, Hoang scored one of the real scoops of the spy murder mystery, identifying the name of the victim. In 1990–91, employed in the paper's library, he helped me write and translate correspondence with the victim's family in Saigon.

This book could absolutely not have been written without access to previously classified and hard-to-get documents. My first thanks goes to the Freedom of Information Act of 1976.

But close on its heels is the staff of the U.S. Army Criminal Investigations Records Depository in Baltimore, Maryland, particularly Barbara Parker, who patiently and even cheerfully handled my many requests and queries concerning the hundreds of pages of documents I received from the CID, which included all of the Army detectives' case interviews. Lt. Col. Rex Bragaw of the U.S. Army's Criminal Law Division also facilitated my review of thousands more pages of documents relating to the case.

A task of this kind renews one's deep appreciation for able research librarians. I thus want to give heartfelt thanks to the staffs of the U.S. Army War College library, the Center for Military History, the Presidential Papers division of the National Archives, the John F. Kennedy Memorial Library, the U.S. Senate library, the Boston Public Library, and the Martin Luther King, Jr., Library in Washington, D.C. Thanks also to H.D.S. Greenway for access to the morgue of the *Boston Globe*.

The staffs of regional newspapers in the home states of the eight accused Green Berets were also swift and courteous in responding to my requests for clips and other information. I particularly want to thank the Athens (Georgia) *Daily News*, the Cedar Rapids (Iowa) *Gazette*, and the Duncan (Oklahoma) *Banner*.

* * *

No author is an island. The support of friends and family is an irreducible part of completing a book.

Words cannot adequately convey the debt I owe my sister Susan and her husband, Bruce Timperley, for their unflagging support for this project. There was money in a pinch, a warm place to stay, good food and drinks and challenging conversation, but much, much more. I am eternally grateful. I also want to thank Dr. Warren Platt, my uncle, for giving me a lifelong appreciation for books and good writing.

The idea for writing the Green Beret story would never have reached paper had it not been for my friend and agent Gail Ross. A lawyer herself, Gail saw the real contours of this story years ago when I first mentioned it to her, goaded me into writing a proposal, and stayed with me to the end. Thanks also to her assistant, Elizabeth Outka.

The proposal wouldn't have become a manuscript, and the manuscript a book, if it weren't for Jared Kieling, my kind and talented editor at St. Martin's Press. His formidable assistant, Ensley Eikenburg, also deserves praise, as does Paul Sleven, St. Martin's able lawyer. Jared was what every writer should have: a patient, brilliant man who can turn the semblance of an idea into a completed thought. My gratitude also to proofreader David Graf. Whatever errors remain on these pages are entirely my fault. I probably wore him out, as they say in Maine.

Adequately acknowledging the role of friends in these pages is impossible. Good ideas spring from a multitude of sources. First among these was Gigi Wizowaty, whose tireless enthusiasm, concern, and generosity carried me over many mountains. I thank her from the very deepest pockets of my heart.

Ben and Gabriella Forgey were also dear friends, always available for timely relief, good cheer, and challenging ideas. So, too, Nick and Joan Ludlow, Bob Manning and Jan Austen, and John Dinges. Valerie Strauss, no slouch as a foreign news editor for the *Washington Post*, gave selflessly of her time and talent at a critical moment in this project. Many of her suggestions are in this story. Jay Ross, my fine editor at UPI, and his wife Kathy buoyed me with their hospitality and good cheer. Louis Toscano, another former UPI colleague, helped me shape the tough, early parts of the book. Lorraine Gray offered constant encouragement, important criticism, and enthusiasm at difficult times. I also want to thank Nicholas Von Hoffman and Asa Baber for their timely praise and help, but I must especially single out Myra MacPherson, the author of *Long Time Passing: Vietnam and the Haunted Generation*, for encouraging me to go back to the roots of my journalistic passions and tackle this story.

Many others played timely roles in moving this from an idea to paper. My thanks to: Shelley Broderick, Charlie Clements, John Connell, Carter Cornick, Anne Groer, Denis James, Kathy Johnson, Kitty Kelley, John Marks, Ralph McGeehee, Brendan Murphy, Tim O'Brien, Thomas Powers, Peter Range, Barbara Raskin, Molly Roberts, Mike Sager, Shelby Stanton, Rick and

Carol Swett, Louis Sorley, Evan Thomas, Mary Travers, Patricia Vasquez, Michael Welzenbach, Kim Willenson, Catherine Williams, and Bill and Irene Weidenhamer.

The book also would never have been completed without the generous loan of a house near Sugarloaf Mountain, Maine. And so I end with thanks to C.C. Hamilton, Joann Grenier, Bruce Auclair, Kevin Caswell, and all the other good folks of Kingfield and Carrabassett Valley. You know who you are.

A Murder in Wartime

PART I

American

Boys

1

NHA TRANG, SOUTH VIETNAM

Late on the moonless night of June 20, 1969, three men in unmarked camouflage uniforms backed a small boat out of a slip and turned down a dark slow river toward the South China Sea.

Under scudding monsoon clouds, the men smoked, alone with their thoughts, as the whining engine pushed them past the mouth of the river into rising swells of the warm-water ocean.

Thick steel chains, two iron wheel rims, and a bulky sack the size of a small man were piled at their feet.

Near midnight, the boat slowed to a drift. An island lay ahead, jutting out of the dark horizon. Hon Tre was where the strong coastal current turned north, away from shore, a place where the sharks gathered to chew on the war's messy waste.

The boat bobbed sideways in the swells, the engine at idle. Years later, they would remember that the moment had a surrealistic feel to it, as if they were watching themselves in a spy movie.

A warm, salty wind rose from the east. They took a compass reading and then slowly trolled ahead in the darkness.

A few minutes later, they came to a stop. This would be the place. They cut off the engine and prepared for their task.

Suddenly, a groan arose from the bag on the floorboard.

The men stared at each other. How, they wondered, had it ever come to this? None of them had thought of themselves as assassins.

2

CHERAW, SOUTH CAROLINA

July 31, 1969

D ear George," the letter began, and George Winfield Gregory propped his feet up on the desk, sipping his first cup of morning coffee.

"I find myself in one of the worst situations I have ever been in, and I need your help, or your recommendation for help. . . ."

George Gregory smiled. The letter was from his boyhood friend Tom Middleton, now a Green Beret major in Vietnam. What'd that hell-raiser get into now? he wondered.

Gregory took another sip of coffee. The air conditioner, struggling with the swelter of inland South Carolina in late July, shuddered in the window. He lifted his portly frame, walked around the desk, and looked out on Cheraw Town Hall. The sidewalks were empty. Most people were inside drinking iced tea and watching the pictures of the astronauts on the moon.

The letter was scrawled in pencil on USO stationery, its red-and-blue motto, *A Home Away From Home*, streaming across the top. Middleton probably needed a new will, Gregory thought, resuming his reading. Or was it a divorce?

"I am currently located in the stockade at Long Binh, Vietnam," it continued. Gregory frowned and flipped to the last page again to look again at his friend's signature, then went back to the top. It was dated July 23, a week ago.

"I cannot for security reasons discuss the details of the offence of which I am accused and involved," the scrawl continued. "It is a question of following orders from my CO, who has also been relieved from duty (Col. Rheault, West Point). Another major, three captains and a warrant officer are also involved."

Gregory leaned forward and put his cup down, reading faster. All that rank in jail? The commander of all the Green Berets in Vietnam? Didn't make sense. What could be the charge?

> I am still hoping the charges against me will be dropped, because I am the middle man in the operation and had nothing to do with the actual incident. I was offered immunity at one time, and I stupidly declined because of loyalty to my CO.
>
> George, it is a very serious charge and I am a little scared of leaving my future in the hands of military lawyers. I thor-

oughly believe I am innocent of the charges and to tell you the truth, I am scared to death. I keep thinking of my wife and kids and how it will affect them and their futures and mine.

Gregory raced through the rest of the letter. Near the end, Middleton begged Gregory for help.

"Would you consider defending me, and could you come over? If not, do you know any lawyers in the ACLU?"

That made him smile. Gregory couldn't imagine Middleton even being polite to a civil-liberties lawyer.

"George, I don't think I need to remind you of the seriousness of this matter," the letter went on. "I do not desire word of this letter and the situation I am in to spread to any of my relatives or anyone other than you. The whole thing could be dropped tomorrow for all I know. In any case, keep it discreet. . . ."

Gregory gently put down the letter.

A "middle man in the operation," his friend had written. "An incident." That sounded like something to do with intelligence work—that's what Green Berets did, didn't they? The dirty work?

Why would he be put in jail for that? Weren't those things authorized?

Gregory hadn't thought much about Vietnam lately. Like most people, he was exhausted by reading, thinking, and certainly arguing about it. It affected his conscience, but not his own life. He'd done his own time in the Army. Now Vietnam was like a cancer that somebody else had. It was just a newspaper story or something he saw on TV.

Sometimes, he had to admit, it was riveting. Like the time when the CBS "Evening News" showed marines taking out their Zippos and burning down a hamlet with all the peasants yammering and crying and begging the GIs to stop. Or the time when some officious major famously explained how they bombed the shit out of a village "in order to save it." Or last year during the big surprise attacks at Tet when the Viet Cong ran right into the American embassy and starting shooting. That was pretty damn exciting—and hilarious when General Westmoreland said it was a huge "allied" victory. Who was he kidding?

The war was supposed to be over after that. Walter Cronkite said so; he stood in front of the camera as Vietnam burned and said the war was lost, over. The generals had oversold the thing, and now nobody believed them anymore.

That was a year and a half ago. Gregory wondered why it just didn't stop. You didn't have to be a goddamned Communist to see the thing was all wrong. But Vietnam was so big you couldn't do anything about it. He'd tried, going to the Democratic National Convention as a delegate for Eugene McCarthy, the only candidate pledged to stop the war as soon as he was elected. That went down the drain with the nomination of Hubert Humphrey and the spectacle of Chicago police cracking the skulls of demonstrators in front of his hotel. Only the extremists flourished now, he concluded, the bomb-'em-back-to-the-Stone-Age types on one side and the burn-baby-burn Marxists on the other. It was all politics now, people living out their fantasies. The Vietnamese were incidental to the whole thing. They were just a sideshow.

After the convention, George Gregory forgot about ending the war, went back home to his wife and two kids, and concentrated on his law practice. His aims became more modest. He did feel good about helping end segregation in the local schools. It was too expensive, he argued. Hell, we could build a new road with that money, or a new sewage line. And he won. He'd never said segregation was wrong—that was impossible in Cheraw.

George Gregory was learning something: Never argue principle when you can argue cost.

The air conditioner shuddered as the temperature outside the tiny office spiked into the nineties. Gregory's face was slick as new paint. His black-framed glasses kept slipping down his nose.

He studied Middleton's letter. Its frightened tone was out-of-character with the swaggering boy he grew up with. Their families had been friends for generations in the hardscrabble cotton and watermelon country of central South Carolina, which once supported vast plantations and thousands of slaves, but was desolate now. Tom's father owned the general store down the road in Jefferson, population eight hundred, hardly more than a railroad crossing. By the 1960s it was no place to get ahead without inherited money or a knack for shrewd investments, both of which Tommy Middleton lacked. His interests were racing hot rods on the blacktop, a pack of Luckies rolled up on his shoulder, drinking beer, staying out late. He was a good kid, his father said, in with "a wild crowd."

In fact, Gregory remembered, Tommy was a little bit crazy. One day when they were kids, Tommy climbed up on the roof of the store and started ripping shingles off to build a cage for his rabbits. When his mother ordered him to come down, he refused, sitting up there grinning from ear to ear. The afternoon turned to evening. It became a contest, and the neighborhood kids gathered around. Finally his father told them to throw rocks at his son until he came down. Shortly afterward, his parents shipped him off to a military school in Virginia.

At Staunton Military Academy, Tommy Middleton found he was far behind the other boys. On his first day in English class the teacher asked the students to write "a theme on what you did on your summer vacation." Middleton was stumped. "What's a theme?" he asked. Twenty years later, he was still embarrassed by it.

But he was good at the military things: marching, saluting, twirling rifles, polishing shoes. His reading and composition skills slowly improved. By his senior year in 1957, a military career looked attractive. He enrolled at Presbyterian College, a small school in South Carolina where he could virtually major in ROTC. In 1961 he graduated as a second lieutenant in the U.S. Army. It was a typical southern story.

*　　*　　*

George Gregory didn't think much of military life. He did his duty when his draft number came up in 1963, enrolling in the Army's Judge Advocate General Corps after graduating from the University of South Carolina Law School. It was a cushy way out. Assigned to Fort Knox, Kentucky, he defended a parade of sad-sack AWOLs and deserters, barracks thieves and rapists, pitiable young men whose plights persuaded him that the Army's recruiting posters fell far short of their promises. You couldn't "make a man" out of somebody if the raw material wasn't there; most people didn't change that much no matter what you did. Supplying guns to empty young men and telling them they're special, then putting pinch-minded martinets in charge of them, was nearly criminal—the dumb ones started to believe the things they were told.

But George Gregory made the best of his time, opening an office off base and making a few bucks on the side.

"Melvin Belli and Lee Bailey and all these big lawyers," he would crow to a newspaper reporter later, "write books about their cases. I'm going to title my first volume 'Gregory's Guide to the Preparation of AWOLs, or How to Handle Forty Cases a Day and Still Have Time for a Part-Time Job.'"

With his bulging torso and short flapping arms, Gregory also had to figure out a way around the Army's physical training standards. He had flunked the test for push-ups and pull-ups twice, which threatened to cost him a promotion to captain. On the third try he altered his scores with a red marking pencil.

"I changed all the 30s to 80s and sailed right through," he explained cheerfully. "The instructors were very proud of my progress."

A fun-filled guy, George Gregory, chortling at life whenever he had the chance, his jowls and glasses bouncing all over his face when he laughed, which was often. Slow-smart, as they said in the South, a lot smarter than he looks.

George Gregory put down Middleton's letter and drank the dregs of his coffee. He thought about it: Stockades were generally for enlisted men, not for the commander of the Green Berets and his top officers. That part really puzzled him. Officers were put behind bars only for serious crimes. Even then they'd be out on bail pretty quick.

Obviously this was more serious than drunk driving.

Why were all these Green Berets penned up like criminals, he wondered, in a war zone? The possibilities tumbled through his mind like the pieces of a lock.

He sat and thought.

The caseload had been pretty slow lately. Routine, to tell the truth. Boring. He had been a state representative once. He missed the time at the statehouse fooling around with the guys, being in the limelight. And something else was churning deep in his chest, undigested thoughts about the Army, and Vietnam. He grew angry.

Gregory picked up the telephone and dialed information for Washington, D.C. He wanted to track down a friend at the Pentagon.

*　　*　　*

Five hundred miles north in New Jersey, Denise Marasco pulled a letter from her mailbox. She immediately recognized the military post office number and didn't look forward to reading it.

It was from her husband, Bob. Two years ago he had been a successful young insurance agent, a draftee who had enlisted in Army intelligence to avoid the infantry. Now he was a gung-ho Green Beret officer, and she hated Vietnam. They were on the verge of splitting.

"I don't know exactly how to tell you what I now must," the letter began. "I have never had to write anything as horrendous as this or even ever considered it. . . ."

She raced through the four pages. The letter was full of jargon about "an operation," things her husband liked to brag about, but this time there was trouble: He was in jail, charged with murder, along with a colonel, two majors, three captains, and a warrant officer. He said he didn't know why he had been arrested, because "the proper coordination had been made. This was a military operation."

"The situation is too unbelievable to comprehend," the letter went on. "There are things involved here which would have international implications and could affect even the Paris Peace Talks."

Denise quickly went to the telephone and called her father-in-law.

Frank Marasco had already gotten a letter from his son.

"I can only apologize for any disgrace I have brought you," Bob had written, full of grief. But he insisted they were victims of a frame-up whose exact contours he could not fathom. He asked his father to contact Rep. Peter Rodino, the local Newark congressman.

Frank Marasco finished the letter and again wished his son had followed him into the family insurance business. Vietnam was bad; it was turning the country upside down.

The next day he made a copy of his son's letter for Congressman Rodino as instructed. On second thought, he made more copies. One was for Rep. Thomas Helstocki, another New Jersey congressman. Two more were for the state's United States senators, Harrison Williams and Clifford Case. He put them all in separate envelopes and prepared a covering letter.

"Just as a background of my son's character," Frank Marasco wrote, "he is 27 years of age, married, and has a home in Bloomfield, New Jersey. To my knowledge, he is the recipient of three Bronze Stars, Commendation Medal, and the Good Conduct Medal. He volunteered to serve in Viet Nam and was not drafted.

"I bring all this to your attention so that you know that my son, Robert, is not a troublemaker, but a highly dedicated young man who is trying to serve his country and serve it well."

On July 29, Frank Marasco put all four envelopes in the mail, special delivery to Washington, D.C.

In Athens, Georgia, Frank Williams hid his son's letter in a drawer, not wanting to alarm his wife.

Budge was in jail! He was stunned. His son's assignments in Panama and Bolivia and a previous Vietnam tour had gone off without a hitch. He was a decorated intelligence officer serving with the Special Forces. Now he was penned up in a solitary five-by-seven cell, "treated like a dog," as he said in his letter.

My god—these were Green Berets, the very best. His son had been the youngest Eagle Scout in Athens, Georgia. Why would the Army lock him up? His son didn't say. What the hell was going on in Vietnam? It had to be politics.

George Gregory was on the telephone to the Pentagon, listening with quiet disbelief. The voice at the other end of the line was insisting that nobody in Washington knew anything about the arrests of any Green Beret officers in Vietnam. Checks had been made, the general assured him.

But that was impossible, Gregory retorted. He repeated the facts: a full colonel, two majors, three captains, and so on? All arrested for murder? And nobody in the legal section of the Pentagon knew about it?

"You know, at Fort Knox," Gregory said drily, "a presentencing report on a captain arrested for drunk driving would rocket right up the chain of command. Everybody'd know about that."

"Well, things have changed," the general responded. "It's a war zone over there, and we just don't have the same type of information or controls you'd have in the States."

Gregory grunted.

"But we'll get back to you," the general said. "You can be sure of that." He hung up.

Pretty strange, Gregory thought, making a note of the conversation. The man he'd talked to was one of the Army's top legal officers, a two-star general. He should know what's going on.

Gregory called his partner David Trice, who had also been a military lawyer. They agreed something wasn't right.

"Well, hell, George," Trice interjected. "You know what to do. Call the A.P. or something. They can check it out in Saigon."

The news media—*of course*. But why not go right to the top? He needed somebody who could cut through the bullshit. He decided to call James Reston, the prominent columnist of the *New York Times*.

He got as far as an assistant. Gregory told her who he was and why he was calling.

"Mr. Reston wouldn't have much interest in that kind of story," she assured him. Didn't he know the columnist's position on Vietnam? He was against it. He wouldn't be interested in taking up the cause of soldiers arrested for killing somebody.

Gregory said he wasn't calling to start a defense fund.

"Look, lady, you've got a full colonel—a West Pointer—two majors, three captains, and so on, in a Vietnam stockade. That's highly unusual. Don't you think somebody'd be interested in that?"

The woman politely demurred. She would take down the information, she said, and get back to him.

The next day, his phone rang. The Saigon bureau of the *Times* had checked out the information, the assistant said. The military command in Vietnam had denied there was anything to it.

"Nothing to it?" Gregory fumed. "Lady, I've got a letter from a defendant here. Do you really think it's a prank?"

"No, I don't think it's a prank," she shot back. "But what do you want us to do?"

Gregory was exasperated. "I don't know. I just thought it was a good story." He hung up. Something, definitely, was wrong.

Where the hell was Tommy?

He picked up the telephone and called Western Union. He wanted to dictate a telegram, he said, to the commander of the U.S. Army in Vietnam.

He was entering the case on behalf of Maj. Thomas C. Middleton.

The Digital Information Relay Center was one of the Pentagon's most highly kept secrets. Its warren of basement offices housed the communications center for the Joint Chiefs of Staff. Access was severely restricted and enforced by armed civilian guards.

At 10:54 on the night of August 5, a cable began clattering out of the DIRC's teletype machine with a special "back-channel" message from Saigon. It was classified "Secret—Limited Distribution on a Need-to-Know Basis Only" and addressed to the chairman of the Joint Chiefs of Staff from Gen. George L. Mabry, commander of the U.S. Army, Vietnam.

> SUBJECT:
> ALLEGED MURDER: INVOLVING COL ROBERT B. RHEAULT, MAJ DAVID E. CREW, MAJ THOMAS C. MIDDLETON, CPT LELAND J. BRUMLEY, CPT ROBERT F. MARASCO, CPT BUDGE E. WILLIAMS, CW2 EDWARD M. BOYLE, SFC ALVIN L. SMITH, JR. (SUBJECTS). VIETNAMESE NATIONAL CIV MALE (VICTIM).
> IT IS ALLEGED THAT DURING THE PERIOD 15–20 JUNE 1969 SUBJECTS CONSPIRED TO KILL A LOCAL VIETNAMESE NATIONAL WHO THEY SUSPECTED WAS AN NVA AGENT AND THAT ON OR ABOUT 20 JUNE THE VIETNAMESE NATIONAL WAS KILLED. THE EIGHT SUBJECTS HAVE BEEN CHARGED WITH PREMEDITATED MURDER (ARTICLE 118, UCMJ) AND CONSPIRACY TO COMMIT MURDER (ARTICLE 81 UCMJ).

The message further stated that secret proceedings had opened on July 31 to weigh the evidence. Two days later they had been recessed to "determine the availability of certain defense witnesses."

Both the arrests and hearings had been kept hidden from the news media, the cable went on to say, but recent inquiries from the *New York Times* had sparked rumors among other reporters. As a result, a limited announcement of some sort would have to be made.

The cable was slugged BLUE BELL, indicating it contained news of a military development with sensitive political ramifications, to be quickly circulated to a small circle of White House officials and key figures on Capitol Hill.

Gen. William Knowlton, secretary of the U.S. Army's General Staff, fielded the message, translated the military's cabelese into plain English, and prepared a substitute memorandum for the president's national security adviser, Dr. Henry Kissinger.

"One of the officers concerned has written to a law firm in the United States, asking that the firm represent him," Knowlton added. "Apparently as a result of that contact, the *New York Times* posed a press query on 4 August about the case."

Knowlton took care to delete the cable's specific reference to the victim as a suspected North Vietnamese agent.

"There is an intelligence connotation to this case," he wrote instead, "which may result in part or all of the case being handled on a classified basis. For that reason, press queries are to be handled in Vietnam by the U.S. Army Vietnam, rather than the United States."

Knowlton advised the White House of General Mabry's decision that, in the face of snowballing media interest, there was no alternative to releasing the bare facts of the arrests. All of the other details of the case, however, would be kept in the strictest secrecy.

George Gregory was packing for Washington when his ear caught the fragment of something familiar on the local news.

". . . arrested for the murder of an unidentified Vietnamese male. One of the defendants is a South Carolina man, Major Thomas C. Middleton of Jefferson. . . ."

"Goddam!" he whooped. "That's it!" He hurried his packing.

Down the road in Jefferson, South Carolina, Phyllis Middleton ran to the telephone hoping that it was someone from the Army. She had learned about her husband's arrest from a reporter only the night before.

She picked up the telephone. It was another reporter, this time from the *Charlotte Observer.*

"I've been waiting patiently for some word . . ." she said, her voice cracking.

"I heard about it over the eleven o'clock news," she blurted out. "That's why I'm very bitter, especially when they're going to plaster his name all over the papers."

She quickly recovered. She'd never talked to anyone from the press before. "How did you get my number?" she asked. She had thought their lives were completely private.

Dorothy Boyle sat surrounded by friends in her office at a Baltimore trucking company. She was still in a daze.

The night before, she'd heard something on TV about some Green Berets being investigated for something in Vietnam. Since her husband, Eddie, was an investigator of some kind with the Special Forces, she figured that's why she hadn't heard from him. He had been due home last week.

Then the telephone started ringing. The news is *about* Eddie, her friends said. Didn't you see it? He's been arrested for murder!

All her friends crowded around now, comforting her. They all knew Eddie and liked him. They asked about him all the time. They all knew the war stunk, but that didn't keep them from supporting their friends who had to be there.

Dorothy was worried sick. She'd called the Pentagon, but nobody could tell her anything.

In Duncan, Oklahoma, Karen Brumley, her dark hair swept back in a Kennedy-style bouffant, picked up the telephone. It was 10 P.M. Tuesday, an unusual time for anyone to be calling in the bleak oil country of south-central Oklahoma. It was a reporter from the Associated Press, calling for a reaction to her husband's arrest.

"A reaction to what?" she asked. He told her: "Murder."

"I cannot really believe it is true," she said. Her mouth hung open. She had nothing more to say.

Nan Rheault was bending over her garden, deep in her thoughts. The gulls wheeled and screeched over the saltwater lagoon behind the gray shingle house on Martha's Vineyard. Under a bright sun and clear blue sky, a slight cool breeze tugged at wisps of her blond hair.

There was a clamor in the front yard, and she stood up hearing her name called out. Peering around the corner, she saw a throng of reporters, cameras, and sound booms crowding at the front door.

She steeled herself and stepped out in front of the jostling crowd of reporters. There were so many of them, she thought, then remembered the Kennedy accident at Chappaquiddick the week before.

No, she hadn't had any word until just last night, she said, when a reporter called. No advance notice. There was absolutely no word from him, she answered to another shouter.

Why was he arrested? they wanted to know. Could she give them any details? Col. Robert Bradley Rheault, a few of them had learned, was no ordinary officer. He had worked in a covert-operations section of the Joint

Chiefs of Staff. He was West Point, Phillips Exeter Academy, scion of a wealthy Boston family.

Nan Rheault lifted her chin, her blue eyes giving away nothing. Really, that was all she knew, she said. She was as eager for news as were they, she said, a brittle smile parting her lips.

"If you have anything to say about his family," she added, "you can say they are very proud of him.

"My husband has had a long and honorable career in the Army. Whatever he does has always been in defense of his country and for the protection of his men."

She smiled coldly and slipped back into the house.

There was much more to the story, she knew. Much more.

In Malibu, California, a disillusioned former government official lay in bed, reading an account of the Green Beret arrests on the front page of the *Los Angeles Times*. Something stirred in him, and his intense blue eyes bore down on the print.

Daniel Ellsberg had spent most of the past decade trying to understand Vietnam, first as a U.S. marine, then as a high-level expert with the State Department and Pentagon. He had just finished compiling a secret history of the war at the direction of the Secretary of Defense. What he had found in the locked vaults had deeply upset him, and the Green Beret case, he knew, was part of something much bigger. If only the American public could be let in on the secret, he believed, it could change the course of the war.

3

George Gregory sped along the country blacktop early the next morning, roaring past the signs for Red Man tobacco, pit barbecue, church suppers, and RC Cola, heading for Charlotte, North Carolina, and an Eastern Airlines flight to Washington. The radio screeched with preachers and hellfire. He snapped it off.

Gregory could mock that part of the South. He knew it was often intolerant and bigoted, backward and superstitious, a fool for faded glories. *The Green Berets*, starring John Wayne, still played to full movie houses in the South. Barry Sadler's "Ballad of the Green Berets," the number-one song in America in 1966, was a stock item in southern juke boxes. A year after Tet.

Clinging to the past, however, had its practical aspects. One of them was honoring its men at war.

But nothing had been harder to honor than the cause in Vietnam. It had ripped the country to shreds: young versus old, fathers versus sons, soldiers versus students, draftees versus career men, liberals versus conservatives, North versus South. Five years after troops landed in force, even hawks seemed to be at a loss to defend a policy that lacked a clear plan for winning. Vietnam was a war for people with double vision, someone had said, fought against a two-faced enemy, using two kinds of combat, one open and orthodox and the other clandestine with very few rules.

Which was where Tommy Middleton came in, Gregory was thinking as he settled into his seat for the flight to Washington. His friend was just an average guy, thrown into the middle of hopelessly complicated Asian guerrilla war, dressed up with a fancy hat that convinced him he was an expert.

Gregory unfolded his copy of the *Charlotte Observer* and saw the headline in the middle of the front page.

BERET CHIEF, 7 AIDES CHARGED IN VIET KILLING
SAIGON (A.P.) The U.S. Army uncorked a military mystery today by charging the commander of the Green Beret forces in Vietnam and seven of his staff—including three intelligence officers—with murder and conspiracy to commit murder.

The eight are charged in the shooting of a Vietnamese man June 20 near Nha Trang, headquarters of the 5th Special Forces, 200 miles northeast of Saigon. But the U.S. command gave no details.

Gregory wondered if there was any significance to the "three intelligence officers" singled out. What did that mean? Weren't they all involved in intelligence work? Beyond listing the defendants' hometowns, the story had no new details.

What was the Pentagon holding back? he wondered. Prosecutors usually laid it on thick when they unveiled a big criminal case.

Something else was odd, Gregory noticed: The victim was unidentified. Who ever heard of a murder case brought without announcing the victim's name?

The Boeing 727 banked over Virginia and began its approach into Washington over the Potomac River, gliding past the Lincoln, Washington, and Jefferson memorials, clearing the 14th Street Bridge on its final descent to the runway.

Gregory deplaned into a gray and unseasonably cool day. Thick sooty clouds raced across the horizon, the tail end of a vicious storm that had ripped through the area the night before, felling trees and power lines and filling the swollen river with stumps, trash, and runoff oil. The airport was crowded, unusual for Washington in August. But Congress was still in session, debating a Nixon proposal to build an antiballistic missile system to ward off Soviet ICBMs. The president had also just returned from a foreign tour that had included a stop in Guam to announce U.S. troop withdrawals from Vietnam and a triumphant motorcade through Bucharest with Nicolai Ceauşescu. For the first time, the papers noted, Air Force One had flown under Soviet air control.

Gregory headed toward the gate. As he passed into the concourse, he heard his name called out. A man was querying each passenger.

"Mr. Gregory? Mr. Gregory?"

The lawyer walked up to him.

"I'm Mr. Gregory."

"Juan Vasquez, *New York Times*." He said Gregory's secretary had told him what flight he would be on. "I'd like to talk to you about your client in Vietnam. Can I give you a lift into town?"

Gregory smiled and shook hands, scanning the crowd. "I'm supposed to meet Congressman Gettys's aide," he said. Tom Gettys was a pal from their days together in the South Carolina legislature. A young man soon scurried up and introduced himself as a member of the congressman's staff. Turning serious, Gregory asked him to wait a minute. This was a correspondent from the *New York Times*, he said.

"Maybe we can talk here a minute," Vasquez suggested, "and then we can get together later." He had a deadline to meet. "What can you tell me about this Green Beret case?"

Well, Gregory said, he didn't have much more than had been reported. That was the problem. He had called all over the Pentagon and they said they didn't know anything. It annoyed him. He was a lawyer for one of the defendants. The Army was violating basic standards of law not to give him any information.

"It's a shame that I have to learn what my client's been charged with by reading the newspapers," he said. "I'm getting a runaround. The Army won't tell me the exact nature of the charges."

Vasquez asked him a few more questions, but Gregory said he had told him all he knew. Maybe he'd learn more during the day, he added. They agreed to meet for dinner.

Outside, Gregory and the young congressional aide stepped into one of the beaten-up taxis that were a feature of Washington's main airport and told the driver to take them to Capitol Hill.

Congressman Tom Gettys greeted Gregory with a big smile and backslap and led him into his inner sanctum. They were country boys making good. Gettys was "New South," cautiously progressive on race and the war while minding the powerful conservative committee chairmen who decided his rank in Washington. For that reason, he said, he didn't want "to get involved" in the Tommy Middleton case—at least not yet.

The best idea was to get Mendel Rivers involved, when the time came. If the chairman of the Armed Services Committee, a South Carolinian, couldn't do anything for Tom Middleton, then no one could. But they had to have the facts first, Gettys said. No one could do anything until then. He'd have to wait until he heard more about it himself. Hell, he told Gregory, he didn't want to find out Tommy Middleton had shot some innocent little boy. That's possible over there, you know. Mistakes do happen. Vietnam is an awful mess.

How else can I help you otherwise? he asked Gregory. The lawyer told him he had to get papers for Vietnam—a passport and security clearance.

No problem, Gettys said. He picked up a telephone and told an aide to clear Gregory at the Pentagon.

A few minutes later, Gettys escorted Gregory to the front of his office. A reporter from NBC, Bob Goralski, was waiting in the reception area with a camera crew. The veteran correspondent introduced himself and politely said he'd like to ask Gregory a few questions about the Green Beret case.

Jesus, network television, Gregory thought. First the *New York Times*, now this. Tom Gettys couldn't hope for this in a lifetime.

He straightened his tie and smiled wanly, suddenly feeling nervous. What did Goralski want to know? Gregory asked.

The correspondent smiled and used his usual gambit to relax an anxious subject as the equipment was set up.

"What's capital of Nebraska?" he asked with a laugh, moving in with a microphone. Gregory was still trying to think of the answer when the lights went on.

George Gregory walked up the gray cement steps of the Pentagon. The steel and glass doors gave way to a small shopping mall with a dry cleaner, shoe shop, sandwich nook, and tobacco stand. It was a surprising first sight for most visitors to the heart of America's war machine. A crowd of sightseers gathered at a desk where tours departed on the hour. Gregory spotted a bank of telephones on a far wall and walked over.

A few minutes later an escort arrived and took him through the security gate, where he signed for a visitor's badge. Then they walked down the wide linoleum corridor, passing through a swirl of admirals, generals, and colonels, and headed for the office that would grant him travel papers and a security clearance. The vetting would be no problem; he had had a clearance when he was in the Army.

Gregory also wanted to use the opportunity to sniff around the offices of the judge advocate general, headquarters for all legal activities in the system, for any facts on his case. Now that the charges had been publicized, he felt certain there had to be more details available.

An hour later, he gave up. Even his former instructor from JAG school, a general, had turned up his palms and insisted they didn't have anything on it. It was all being handled in Vietnam, he said. Top secret.

It was very strange, his friend had to agree.

George Gregory awoke in his hotel room at 6 A.M. with an immense hangover. He limped to the bathroom, drank a couple glasses of water, and then started to run a hot bath.

He'd stayed up late with Juan Vasquez. They'd gone to an ornate restaurant on the Senate side of Capitol Hill called The Forum. Vasquez insisted it was where the senators took their girlfriends, but Gregory had a hard time believing it. Impatient waitresses took their orders for tough steaks and bad scotch. He somehow expected more.

Vasquez said the *Times* had picked up an interesting tidbit. Somebody with a friend in Vietnam had called the paper with a tip that two U.S. Navy ships had been sent to Nha Trang Bay, where the Green Berets were headquartered, to drag for a body. They didn't know any more at this point. The Saigon bureau was checking.

Interesting, Gregory said. The Army was still refusing to identify the victim, wasn't that odd? He hadn't learned a damn thing about the case himself. He told Vasquez about his letter from Tom Middleton, their boyhood friendship, the meeting with Congressman Gettys, and the blank looks he got at the Pentagon.

"Do you think you have enough to write a story?" he asked the reporter.

"I sure hope so," Vasquez laughed, "because I've already written it."

Before they parted, Gregory asked a question: Did Vasquez think the *Times* could help him out in Saigon? Maybe pick up his hotel tab in exchange for an exclusive? It was an expensive trip, you know.

"I'll see what I can do," Vasquez said evenly. "I'll sure let them know you're coming."

Now Gregory soaked in the tub, thumbing through the *Times*, starting from the back. That's where he figured the story would be, if at all. He didn't expect much. It was just a story about some country lawyer getting a runaround from the Army, hardly worthy of the *New York Times*. Happens all the time.

There was a short item on page 24 that caught his eye. Antiwar pickets at a movie theater in Paris had denounced the opening of *The Green Berets* as "an apologia for barbarism." Included in the story was a comment from a Viet Cong spokesman that the arrests of the eight Special Forces officers on murder charges this week showed that the protesters' views were obviously correct.

Jesus, Gregory thought, this case is really taking off. *Paris.*

There was more war news toward the front of the paper. Viet Cong guerrillas had slipped into an Army hospital at Cam Ranh Bay and run wild through the wards, tossing dynamite, killing two patients, and wounding ninety-nine more. It was one of the worst terrorist attacks of the war.

Elsewhere U.S. and Communist forces had fought four separate battles, with a body count of eighty-two North Vietnamese killed by heavy artillery and air strikes. The Saigon command reported only two U.S. soldiers had died. In Washington, meanwhile, the Justice Department announced it was dropping plans to appeal the acquittals of two protesters, Dr. Benjamin Spock and Michael Ferber, on charges of conspiring to counsel draft dodging.

The war was still on in its patch quilt, zany way, Gregory thought. Funny how he hadn't thought much about it until now, but why would he have? He hadn't been involved.

Seeing nothing else, Gregory dressed quickly and went downstairs to meet Tom Gettys for breakfast. The congressman was waiting for him.

"Well goddam, George," Gettys grinned as Gregory walked up to the table. He waved a newspaper. "I can't believe it. You're on the front page of the *New York Times*." Gregory snatched it from him. It was a later edition than the one delivered to his room.

"Green Beret Case Stirs A Complaint," the headline said. "Lawyer Says He Can't Get Facts From the Army." His quotes seemed to burn on the page.

"Well, there's no turning back now," he said to Gettys.

The lights in the Pentagon were still burning Friday night as a TWA jet lifted off the runway at National Airport, carrying George Gregory on the first leg of the thirteen-thousand-mile trip to Saigon. The lawyer sat back and ordered a cocktail, savoring his appearance on network TV and quotes in the *Times*. Life in Cheraw would never be the same.

The Joint Chiefs of Staff had also taken close note of Gregory's activities in Washington. A message was prepared for urgent transmission to Saigon, addressed to Gen. George Mabry, commander of the U.S. Army in South Vietnam. It was classified SECRET-NOFORN.

"There have been certain developments since the initial press release in Vietnam that you may wish to bring to the attention of General Abrams," the cable said, referring to the commander of all military forces in the war theater. Creighton Abrams was, in military parlance, COMUSMACV, Commander-in-Chief/Military Assistance Command—Vietnam. Abrams ran the war while General Mabry administered the U.S. Army as his deputy. It was a close fit: They had come up through the ranks together in World War II.

"The New York Times of 7 August has run an article on Mr. George Gregory, a lawyer engaged by Major Middleton," the cable reported, and went on to explain:

> Gregory says he received a letter from Middleton on 31 July asking for legal aid. The tone of the article is accusing the Army of failure to provide Gregory with the facts of the case. In actuality Gregory's prime concern appears to be that the government will not finance a flight for him to Vietnam. The indications are that we can expect more publicity to be sought by Mr. Gregory.

"Another development is more complicated," the cable went on. The Joint Chiefs had obtained a copy of a letter that one of the accused Green Berets, Capt. Robert Marasco, had written to his wife. Marasco's father had sent a copy to New Jersey senator Clifford Case, the cable said, and Case had supplied it to the Army.

"It has not yet hit the press but could at any moment," the cable warned, with unforseeable implications for the Army and the CIA. The cable went on to quote from the operative parts of the letter.

"When I got back here from leave, my operation had been compromised and they had just taken one of my people to headquarters under suspicion of being an NVA agent," Marasco wrote. "Many of the details I cannot go into, because they are classified, but suffice it to say that we determined his guilt and had to decide what to do with him."

It continued, "We went through all the channels, to include civilian intelligence agencies. There were numerous reasons why we could not let him go, so the powers that be decided to do away with him."

> It was up to us to come up with a plan and execute it. We followed through with it thinking that the proper coordination had been made and that this was a military operation. The result: One colonel, two majors, three captains and one warrant officer are presently in jail, charged with conspiracy and murder.
>
> The situation is too unbelievable to comprehend. We felt we were doing something that was approved and in the best interest of the war and the country. There are things involved here which would have international implications and affect even the Paris Peace Talks.
>
> For some unknown reason the generals over here are pressing this thing and they think they can make it a classified trial without any publicity.

"If Mr. Marasco releases to the press," the secretary of the Joint Chiefs concluded, "I shall notify you."

Marasco's threat was obvious: He and his fellow prisoners might not go quietly into the night.

4

N ha Trang was lovely once, a sleepy beach resort for French planters and well-to-do Vietnamese. A strip of bright white sand fronted one side of the village. Across an emerald harbor, dark green mountains rose into the mist. Its quiet, palm-shaded residential streets were lined by the high ocher walls of secluded villas. Long ago, late in the afternoon, waiters in starched white linen scurried through the sidewalk cafés with trays of iced citron and lobsters the size of toy trucks.

But most of that was only a memory now. The war had turned most of the sedate cafés into raucous honky-tonks crowded with soldiers. Bored prostitutes hung by the doorways, smoking Kools and hailing GIs. Trucks and jeeps filled the streets. The beaches had turned brown with the waste of a stream of refugees forced off their land by the war.

Two miles from downtown, on a slight rise over the Cua Be River, was the headquarters for the 5th Special Forces Group, a sprawling compound of low-slung buildings surrounded by steel fences and rolls of barbed wire, nerve center for the far-flung Green Beret network in South Vietnam. Alongside was the military camp of its Vietnamese counterpart, a Green Beret base augmented by thousands of wives and children in temporary shelters.

Late on the afternoon of August 7, Bob Kaiser, a poker-faced young reporter for the *Washington Post*, stood outside the gates of the Vietnamese camp, scanning the passing soldiers. He was looking for a recent widow—one in particular—or at least somebody with a shred of information about the anonymous victim in the Green Beret case.

"Speak English? *Parlez français?*" Kaiser asked. A parade of tough-looking soldiers passed by, ignoring him.

Kaiser hadn't had time to hire an interpreter. A flurry of cables had rained down on the Saigon bureau of the *Post*, as well as every other news organization in Vietnam, from editors demanding fresh information on the Green Berets. All the elements were there for a world-class sensation: spies, murder, and bureaucratic intrigue, a police story with a spicy twist. To some it also held the promise of lifting the lid on the secret war in Vietnam, a dark theater of frontier justice whose violent particulars had been overshadowed by the main clashes of North Vietnamese and American forces. Added to that was the whiff of intrigue in high places: the secret removal of the top Green Beret in Vietnam. Also driving the tempo was the surging demand of hundreds of hometown newspapers and TV stations for the human angle on all the highly decorated suspects. Who were they? Where were they? Why were they hidden from view?

Kaiser was dispatched to Nha Trang, where the victim was said to have been killed. "Talk to the Vietnamese," his editors said. "The wires are only talking to the predictable Americans." Even those knew little or nothing; the investigation was being tightly held at the highest levels of the American command.

"Speak English?" Kaiser tried. *"Parlez français?"*

Finally a Vietnamese Green Beret stopped. "What do you want?"

As Kaiser quickly found out, the man had exhausted his vocabulary. Using Pidgin English and sign language, Kaiser tried to explain what he was looking for: information on a Vietnamese man killed by American Special Forces. He tapped at the soldier's headgear and drew a finger across his throat: Dead man, killed by Green Berets.

Ah, the soldier said.

"What can you tell me?" Kaiser asked.

The soldier said he didn't know anything himself, but he could take the reporter to see another man who was sure to know something. He patted the seat of his three-wheeled Lambretta. Hop on, he told Kaiser. They sped off into the twilight.

A half hour later the soldier dropped him on a deserted street, pointed to a dark house, and sped away.

Kaiser looked around; there was obviously no one home. With the sun going down, the reporter hiked back to where he had begun.

"So it goes in Vietnam," he thought.

✳   ✳   ✳

Terence Smith felt betrayed and angry. The Saigon bureau chief of the *New York Times* had asked the Army about the tip from George Gregory and the Army had lied. "Nothing to it," they said, and he had gone back to a weekend piece on the political fallout from President Nixon's trip through Asia.

Smith's inquiry, however, had prompted the Army to issue a brief press release, which, when it clattered across the A.P. wire in New York and ended up on the paper's front page, severely embarrassed the bureau. The *Times* was the *Times*, after all, the best newspaper in America. On a story like this, it should never have been beaten. The Saigon bureau had fumbled an exclusive that the top leadership of the Special Forces was in jail just up the road. Now there was hell to pay. Demands for fresh information crashed on the Saigon bureau like so many pianos thrown from a window. Smith dispatched one of his reporters to Nha Trang and made plans to buttonhole George Gregory when he arrived in Saigon. The *Times's* foreign editor had instructed Smith to pay Gregory's hotel bill.

James Sterba was Smith's chosen legman. When he arrived at the airport, he found Kaiser on the same plane with *Newsweek's* Kevin Buckley. At first they were all in a competitive frame of mind.

Saigon was a star factory for bright young reporters on the rise, as well as the final curtain for older correspondents closing out their careers. A generational fault line loosely divided the press corps, like the military ranks they covered. The older correspondents who had covered World War II and Korea tended to trust the brass and accept its excuses and failures as the timeless price of war. But Vietnam had spawned a new era of reporting, prompted in some measure by the persistent ability of the Viet Cong to upset the military's upbeat forecasts on the war. The younger men also gravitated to the "muddy boots" school of reporting, spending more time talking to the grunts in the field and getting a grim picture of the war in and around the villages. As a result, they began to turn a tin ear to the antiseptic accounts of body counts, search and destroy sweeps, and surgical air strikes proffered by the immaculately tailored Army briefers in Saigon.

Kaiser and Buckley were friends from college, having worked on the *Yale Daily News* in the early 1960s. When Buckley graduated into the fast track with the Associated Press and then *Newsweek*, he passed the baton of campus correspondent for the *New York Herald Tribune* to Kaiser, who eventually joined the *Washington Post* and began his own rapid ascent through a succession of tough domestic and foreign assignments. Only in their twenties by the time they were awarded the prize Saigon assignment, both were well primed to cover the increasingly complicated war.

Buckley was as effusive and intense as Kaiser was phlegmatic. With the advantage of hindsight, Buckley was sure neither he nor Kaiser would have taken the Army's denials at face value. They gave Sterba a little ribbing about the *Times's* discomfort when he arrived on the plane.

Sterba's hard-bitten, blue-collar style belied his anointment as one of "Reston's boys," one of the bright young men taken under the wing of the powerful *Times* columnist. In fact, he was as much in the breed of intellectually minded younger reporters covering the war as Kaiser and Buckley, despite his studied, young Spencer Tracy kind of nonchalance.

Terence Smith expected Sterba to play his cards close to the vest, hewing to a strict competitive posture vis-à-vis Kaiser and the *Washington Post*, which, four years into the hard-driving management of executive editor Benjamin C. Bradlee, was challenging the *Times* as the country's preeminent newspaper. Especially since the *Times* had gotten late out of the gate, Smith was determined to beat the competition. The reporters were of a different mind. After coming up empty-handed after a day in Nha Trang, Kaiser, Sterba, and Buckley quickly and discreetly agreed to cooperate. They were, after all, friends.

Buckley made the rounds of the local U.S. command while Sterba and Kaiser searched together for "knowledgeable Vietnamese." First, however, they needed an interpreter, neither of them able to speak the language. Kaiser had noticed a sign advertising a "College Français" the day before, and they headed out to find it again. The school turned out to be located in one of those charming shaded compounds so common in Nha Trang, a few low buildings in a beautiful garden surrounded by loose-needled pine trees. The acting principal, a witty Frenchman who had been there since 1946, came forward to meet them. With the advice of his secretary, he recommended a parent of one of his students for the job and sent the reporters off with the school gardener leading the way on an ancient bicycle with thick red tires. Kaiser and Sterba followed in the local version of a taxi, a pedicab with the passenger in an armchair in front and the driver on a high seat behind. They bounced along the bumpy dirt streets of Nha Trang.

Eventually they found the man, who said he already had a job and recommended his daughter, who he said would be back later in the day. They agreed to return at three.

Back in the pedicabs, they decided to continue on to the Nha Trang police station on the droll assumption that the local authorities might know something about a murder in the neighborhood, even though the Vietnamese had long ago ceded criminal jurisdiction over Americans to U.S. authorities.

The police commissioner appeared smoking a pipe and wearing French spectacles, looking, Kaiser thought, like he'd just walked out of the 14th arrondissement. The chief had indeed been trained in Paris a quarter of a century ago, it turned out. He invited the reporters to sit.

Mais no, he knew nothing about the crime, the commissioner said, except what he'd heard on Voice of America. But he was curious about it himself. What did they suspect?

Kaiser and Sterba said that's what they had hoped to learn from the police; there were no new leads in the case.

With a flourish, the commissioner began calling his sources and dispatching underlings to follow up. One of his friends was in charge of all the Vietnamese who worked with the American Green Berets, he confided. He had saved the man's life once, so he was sure he would tell all.

The friend, as it turned out, knew nothing. Nor did the chief of security for all Vietnamese Special Forces, nor, as the afternoon went on and the commissioner worked the telephone and barked orders, did any of his precinct captains.

When he had exhausted his list, the reporters thanked him and left. The day was rapidly disappearing.

Kevin Buckley spent the morning interviewing the top American official in the area, the senior American adviser to the chief of Khanh Hoa Province, which encircled Nha Trang. A former FBI man, the adviser had proffered a tale of high-level conspiracy so convoluted that Buckley found it incomprehensible, and incredible. The Vietnamese, Kaiser wryly observed in his notes later, have American advisers at every level, from platoons up to the Presidential Palace, but it was the Americans who really needed the advice in Vietnam.

Next the three reporters tromped back to 5th Special Forces headquarters. They wanted to talk to Col. Alexander Lemembres, who had replaced the mysteriously vanished Colonel Rheault.

Lemembres greeted them from his bed, where he was recovering from a broken ankle suffered in a hastily arranged parachute jump to qualify for the Special Forces job. It was odd, they noted, that General Abrams had rushed a replacement to Nha Trang who was not even airborne qualified. Was it a deliberate insult? Did it suggest any reasons for the unprecedented arrests?

Lemembres was bright and affable, a modern military bureaucrat on a smooth path to the Pentagon. He easily fielded their skeptical questions, even welcoming a congressional inquiry—"Congress has the right to know what we do"—and scorned the logic of a conspiracy among so many different ranks of soldiers.

"There is no way these people could work together," he said of the accused men. "It's highly unusual that you'd have a full colonel working together with majors and captains. You don't get a cross-section like that." He said he was curious himself to know what really had happened.

With Lemembres a washout, the reporters took a last-ditch tour of the bar strip in Nha Trang with the idea of trolling for tips among the beer-guzzling Green Berets.

"Yeah, isn't that something?" said one. The others ignored them. The hunt was a bust. Nobody knew anything or wouldn't say. At the end of a long two days in Nha Trang, the only story to be filed was that at the site of the alleged crime, nobody knew anything. The reporters looked forward to getting back to Saigon. George Gregory, Esq., of Cheraw, South Carolina, was flying in "from the world."

George Gregory sat back in his seat, drink in hand, bubbling at his good fortune as the Cathay Pacific jet cleared Honolulu control and headed east through the starry night toward Hong Kong. A strike at Pan Am had forced a one-day detour.

A spy scandal, front-page interviews in the *New York Times*, TV crews meeting him in Los Angeles and Hawaii and hanging on his every word—whew! He had polished and trimmed his spiel into a sharp instrument: his client as a wronged hero, the Army unlawfully keeping information from him, etc., etc. He stared out the window.

The thought of actually having to try a murder case flitted through his mind and a shiver ran up his spine. *Don't screw up,* he said to himself.

The fact was, he knew a lot about homicide, about men who did it and why, sometimes for good reason. He had grown up with a case close to home. It was part of the Gregory family lore. His own father had killed a man in cold blood.

It was the depression in Chesterfield County. A man named Hoss Nicholson had been trying to run the Gregorys out of the county and corner the grain business—a local version of the Hatfields and McCoys. Nicholson and his men had shot the Gregorys' mules and burned down their barns. Gregory Senior was up against the wall, facing terror and ruin, his fortune and family at risk.

One morning he decided to bring the harassment to an end. He and his brother walked into the drugstore in Jefferson and shot Hoss Nicholson dead. Both were tried, convicted, and sent to the state prison for life.

Before long, Gregory's father befriended the prison warden and became his driver. Not long after that, with a few well-placed favors, he and his brother were out of jail. With Hoss Nicholson dead, George Gregory, Sr. led the family back to prosperity. He even became a powerful member of the South Carolina state legislature. Governor Strom Thurmond came to his second wedding.

Justice, George Gregory lectured his son, was measured in many ways. But results were what counted.

The Cathay Pacific jet touched down in Hong Kong on Saturday, August 10, local time. Gregory took a cab into the city, found a hotel room, and went out for some sight-seeing with a construction engineer he had met on the plane. Along the way they stopped at one of the mass-production tailors for which Hong Kong was famous, and Gregory bought fourteen new suits. Dinner and a long night of drinks followed.

Just after dawn, the telephone rang in his room, waking him from a deep sleep. It was a reporter from Reuters, the British news agency. Could Gregory comment, he wanted to know, on the story about the Green Beret case in the *Washington Post*?

Gregory was in a fog. How was he supposed to know what the *Washington Post* said? he asked. He was in Hong Kong.

The reporter apologized again for the early hour. The story was reprinted in the *International Herald Tribune*, he explained. It should be available at the hotel. He started to read the text.

Gregory, his mind clearing, told the reporter he'd get a copy first and call him back after he'd read it.

Downstairs in the morning, he found a copy in the hotel lobby. The lead story caught his eye and compelled his attention, although it was not the one he was seeking: Actress Sharon Tate and a group of other Hollywood figures had been stabbed to death in a gruesome Beverly Hills murder. He read through a few paragraphs, wondering what the hell was going on back home.

Finally, he scanned the rest of the front page and found the story he'd been looking for.

KILLING APPROVED, BERETS BELIEVED
Victim Considered a Spy
By Richard Homan
(WASHINGTON, AUG. 11) The Green Berets suspected of killing a Vietnamese in their unit believed the act had the full approval of their superiors, it was learned today.

Reliable sources also were told that the killing threatens to explode into an international incident that could hazard the Paris Peace Talks.

Jesus. He read on.

The story said the charges stemmed from an incident in Nha Trang on June 20. The victim, it said, was a double agent employed by the Communists.

There is evidence in Washington, informed sources said, that the Vietnamese man was killed only after considerable discussion by Green Beret officers and civilian intelligence officials in Vietnam.

"Civilian intelligence officials." Tommy Middleton had written something about "following orders," Gregory remembered. Is that what he meant? Orders from the CIA? The story gave more background on the decision to kill the man, without any attribution from sources.

The focus of these discussions was what should be done with the "plant" Hanoi had placed in the Green Beret unit. The conclusion was that the Vietnamese agent knew too much about the clandestine operations of the Special Forces to make it feasible to release him.

The story reviewed some of the previously reported details and then veered into a titillating avenue of speculation.

While no one talks about it in public, torture and murder are part of the clandestine activities of the Special Forces, established as an elite group by the United States government. In this sense, the tactic of assassination as a legitimate part of war is under challenge.

The pending murder case has focused world attention on that ugly part of American activities in Vietnam. And there are no signs that all the efforts at secrecy are diminishing international interest in the case. The arrest of Rheault and his seven comrades-in-arms has thus put the Army on trial.

"Any full-blown public trial," it concluded, "is likely to uncover not only the activities of the Special Forces, but Central Intelligence Agency operatives as well."

Well, Gregory thought, the finger-pointing has already begun. Good. That can only help dig out the details.

But who, he wondered, were the sources of the story? Where did it come from? He noticed it had a Washington dateline, not Saigon.

The slant made it obvious the story came from someone trying to put the best spin on the case for the Green Berets, and someone with a close knowledge of what had happened. Maybe another one of the accused men had written to a lawyer. There was obviously a self-serving leak somewhere. The sides were lining up.

He scanned back over the story. An idea began to form in his head, like his slow awakening to a long-ringing telephone. It was something so big, and so simple, that it had escaped him until now. How could he have missed it?

He found the quote: "the tactic of assassination as a legitimate part of war is under challenge."

Everyone, he thought to himself, considered assassination and torture so routine as to be legitimate. It had been the stuff of movies and books so long that it had the ring of reality.

But was it *legal*? Was it legal even in wartime, carried out by a U.S. government agency?

More to the case at hand, had government-sanctioned assassination ever been examined in a courtroom? Could the practice *be* put on trial? And what would be the result?

At midday, Gregory's Cathay Pacific jet lifted off from Hong Kong and turned southwest toward Vietnam.

5

George Gregory walked down the gangway of the Cathay Pacific jet at Saigon's Ton Son Nhut Airport decked out in a new blue seersucker suit jacket and a white polyester shirt, smiling and pink-faced in the broiling sun. He was still wearing his old black wool trousers. The tailor had welshed on his promise to have the new ones ready to go.

A throng of reporters and camera crews stirred on the broiling airport tarmac and began to poll the disembarking passengers, asking each one if their name was George Gregory. They had been expecting him for the past twenty-four hours. In the eight days since the first announcement of the arrests, almost no fresh news had come out of Vietnam on the case. The lone exception was a story that day by James Sterba, who had slipped back to Nha Trang and reported that the Navy was dragging the waters for "a canvas bag believed to contain the body of a slain Vietnamese intelligence agent." The victim was "reported by informed sources in Washington to be a double agent working for both the U.S. Special Forces and also for the enemy," Sterba wrote.

The *Times* story had been picked up by the wire services and had quickly circled the globe. In its superheated competition with the *Washington Post*, the *Times* was finally back in the lead. Kaiser's editors were eager for him to match it or more.

Gregory stepped onto the airport apron and walked slowly toward the crude concourse looking for Terence Smith, who Vasquez said had booked him a room. Just then, a proprietary arm came forward out of the crowd of reporters.

"George Gregory?" the man said, smiling confidently. "Terence Smith, *New York Times*. I've got a car outside." He started steering Gregory around the crowd toward the exit.

"Wait a minute," Kevin Buckley yelled. "What the hell's going on?" He and Kaiser and the other correspondents quickly surrounded Smith and his quarry in a circle of microphones, cameras, and note pads.

"Do you have some sort of special relationship here with the *New York Times?*" a reporter asked, dripping sarcasm and eyeing both men. Smith shifted on his feet, looking chagrined.

"You're the only story we've got," another said, only half joking.

The lawyer stopped, smiled, and raised his hands. Smith stood back.

"Don't worry," Gregory chortled, his face turning deep pink, "I'm big enough for all of you." Everybody laughed. They were delighted to see him. He was the only one who would talk.

But first, Gregory said, turning serious, he wanted to make a short statement.

"My client, Major Thomas Middleton, is an honorable citizen," he declared. "The treatment the Army has given this honorable man to date is deplorable." He explained how they had known each other for twenty-eight years, growing up together in Jefferson, South Carolina. He knew Middleton's family. His mother taught him in school.

His client, his friend, was "surely innocent." He should, at the very least, be out on bail.

Now he would take questions.

How had Gregory become involved in the case? a reporter asked. What did he know about the facts? another asked. "Start from the beginning," shouted another. Patience was wearing thin.

It began with a letter from his client in late July, Gregory explained.

"I figured he had something he wanted done with his will—considering the business he was in," he said, drawing chuckles. But he was shocked to learn that Middleton was in jail and charged with murder along with seven other high-ranking, decorated officers.

Officers are never treated like that, Gregory said. Even in the Army, he added sarcastically, you're innocent until tried and found guilty, especially if you're lucky enough to be an officer.

It was the Army's harsh treatment that convinced Middleton he needed civilian counsel. He didn't trust the Army to handle the case fairly.

And why should he? Gregory asked, considering the Army's performance so far.

"They aren't going to sacrifice one of these good South Carolina boys, you know," Gregory said. "We love foreign relations and that sort of thing, but, you know, everything must have its limits."

There were more questions. Was his client working for the CIA? Was the victim a double agent as had been reported? Why did he think the Army was prosecuting the Green Berets?

Gregory acknowledged that he'd read the story about Communist spies, double agents, and so forth. It was all very interesting. He had something to say about that.

"If in fact he was in any way involved in killing a Viet Cong spy, as the rumors have it—and I'm not in any way stipulating here that he was involved in anything like that, you know—then it seems he and these other boys should be given medals, shouldn't they?

"I mean, isn't that what this war's all about? Killing Communists, and so on? Body counts and all that?"

The reporters furiously scribbled in their notebooks.

Gregory stooped to pick up his suitcase. He had to go now, he said. He'd look forward to talking with them again when he had more information.

That's one of the problems so far, of course, he added. The Army wouldn't tell him anything in Washington. Well, he hoped to change their mind now that he was here. He began to walk off with Terry Smith to the car and then turned back to the crowd.

"We're going to have a lot of fun with this one," he grinned, waving good-bye, "no matter who gets hurt."

6

George Gregory looked out the car window as Terry Smith drove away from the airport, joining the flood of traffic heading downtown. Like most first-time visitors to Saigon, he didn't really know what to expect. At home on TV, Vietnam was jungle death, soldiers firing into distant tree-lines, wounded men rushed to waiting helicopters. But Saigon, Gregory quickly discovered, was a bustling Asian metropolis with one foot in a sleepy colonial past, the other in a hustling wartime present. A huge billboard just outside the airport gate announced, "You Have Friend at the Chase Manhattan."

The traffic was another surprise. The main boulevard from the airport was officially one-way, but two thick streams of vehicles blew by in the other direction. New Fiats, old Citroëns, and Honda motorbikes with whole families slabbed on the back flanked each side of the avenue, cutting in and out at will. On pedestals at the intersections, mean-looking little Vietnamese cops in oversize military hats and dark glasses, their hips weighed down by heavy revolvers, conducted an invisible symphony to indifferent drivers.

Prefab cement office and apartment buildings topped with billboards for Sony, Pioneer, Philco, and Seagrams banked the dusty avenue. As Gregory and Smith approached the center of the old city, the concrete widened to a quieter boulevard graced with tall royal palms and deciduous shade trees. Vietnamese men in white shirts and ties strolled along the sidewalks. Delicate Saigonese women floated through the shimmering heat in scoop-neck silk dresses slit at the hip over shiny black pants. Boys and girls in their blue-and-white school uniforms, miniature leather briefcases in their tiny hands, skipped among the sidewalk vendors.

Here the vast American presence was more discreet than the raw bases carved out of the countryside. A few officers meandered along the sidewalks with Nikons slung around their necks, but the face of the U.S. military was mostly hidden behind the tall stucco walls of the old French forts. Here were the headquarters of U.S. Army, Navy, and Air Force intelligence, as well as the various departments of the Central Intelligence Agency and the many branches of the military command and the pacification program. The old fort doors swung open as plainclothes Americans and Vietnamese in unmarked sedans, invariably wearing their aviator sunglasses, entered and left.

Smith decided to stop at his house for a while and talk to Gregory alone. As they drove downtown, the fin de siècle architecture, with its rococo balustrades and elaborate stone-carved portals, became more pronounced. Just past the nineteenth-century Catholic cathedral, the grand old Post Office, and the former headquarters of the French opium monopoly were a scattering of flower stalls, ice cream parlors, and fashionable bistros where the international press corps gathered each evening to drink and gossip. "Radio Catinat," they called the bars, after the old French name of the street.

They swung around a traffic island with a huge iron statue of two Vietnamese soldiers in a heroic combat pose, the first obvious reminder that Saigon was a city at war.

George Gregory had heard about Saigon's varied attractions, but the shock of seeing them for the first time excited him. The anxiety he felt on the flight path into the war zone had evaporated. He was having a hell of a good time.

Smith swung into a quiet, residential street and pulled up at a three-story, white stucco house.

The bureau chief had brought his wife, Ann, and their one-year-old daughter to Saigon, which in many ways was safer than New York. But the neighborhood, home to many of the city's temporary foreign residents and wealthy

Vietnamese, was a synthesis of the war's many paradoxes. The ubiquitous military patrols and household help gave them a sense of security and comfort, but their proximity to the presidential grounds and other government offices also made them a collateral target for Viet Cong rockets.

Smith led Gregory inside and poured drinks. The two men sat and talked about the long trip across the Pacific, Gregory's now-celebrated dealings with the Pentagon, and his stint as an Army lawyer at Ft. Knox. The lawyer eventually remarked that he'd like to get in touch with his client.

Smith picked up the telephone, got an operator on the line, and made a swift connection to the stockade at Long Binh. Both men silently wondered why it hadn't been done before.

The duty officer responded respectfully to Smith's identification of himself and said he'd fetch the prisoner from his cell. In a few minutes, Middleton came on the line, and Smith handed the telephone over to his guest.

"Don't you worry about a thing, Tommy," Gregory yelled. "I just got here and I'm loaded for bear."

Middleton was shocked. He couldn't believe Gregory was actually in Saigon. Hadn't he gotten a telegram telling him to stay home until the smoke cleared?

No, Gregory said. It must've arrived after he left. Anyway, he was here now and he'd get him out of jail fast. Just keep calm, he said. He'd be out to Long Binh as soon as he could.

"Okay, George," Middleton answered weakly. "I hope so."

Far away, in the bare administrative office of the Long Binh jail, Tommy Middleton slowly put the receiver down. His mouth went dry. He turned to the MP guarding him and signaled that he wanted to go back to his cell. Outside, he walked deliberately across the dusty compound, wondering what he'd tell his jailmates. He'd sent a telegram to Gregory on August 8, telling him to stay home for awhile. Apparently it had arrived in South Carolina when Gregory was already in the air heading to Saigon.

Middleton's mates in the stockade had been heaping abuse on him ever since Gregory's complaints about the Army had exploded on the front page of the *New York Times*. They way they saw it, Gregory had backed General Abrams into a corner. Their best hope lay in keeping everything quiet until pro–Special Forces allies in the Army came to their rescue and talked sense into Abrams. Their leader, Colonel Rheault, had assured them this would happen, and he had a lot of connections. Gregory was fouling everything up.

Middleton entered the stockade and walked down the narrow row of cells, past the metal doors. His fellow prisoners—all except Rheault, who was sequestered in a nearby trailer in deference to his rank—sweltered in the heat of the tiny, nearly airless enclosures.

"What was that all about?" somebody hollered. "You turnin' state's evidence now?" Everybody laughed. More cracks were made. Their eyes were pressed against the slits in the doors.

Middleton stopped at the entrance to his cell and turned around. He face was drawn.

"That was George, fellas," he said, taking a deep breath and talking slowly. "He's here. He was calling me from his hotel in Saigon."

A thick silence filled the jail as Middleton entered his lockup. The door clanged behind him.

"Middleton," said Budge Williams, "you are the dumbest white man I've ever known."

Terry Smith pulled up to the Caravelle and parked in front of the art deco glass doors. A bellboy rushed forward to take Gregory's luggage. Before they were inside, a caravan of cars filled with the other correspondents swerved into the driveway.

Smith had reserved Room 414 for the lawyer, a comfortable two-room suite with a shady interior balcony. A louvered door opened into a spacious living room with an overhead fan. A sideboard bar was amply stocked with liquor and beer. Gregory had barely set down his luggage before the herd of other reporters caught up to them and crowded their way inside.

"Drinks are on me," the lawyer hollered. The reporters laughed. They were pretty sure it was Terry Smith's liquor.

Gregory rose early the next morning and took breakfast on the palm-fringed hotel veranda. An orange sun rose over the Mekong River. An ancient waiter delivered a pot of chicory coffee and two plates of croissants with fresh butter. He wordlessly set them down on the thick white tablecloth, straightened the silverware, and drew away.

The patio was cool and secluded. Only a block away, Tu Do Street was awakening. At Mimi's, the Wild West, and Playboy, the doors were already opening for soldiers on a one-day pass. The first quarters dropped in juke-boxes, the first bottles of "Buzz-wie" were popped open, and scratchy waves of "Hey Jude" and "Devil with the Blue Dress On" filled the street. Sleepy-eyed bargirls lounged in the doorways, combing their hair, smoking Kools, and listlessly hailing the first forays of nervous GIs. On the sidewalks, conical-hatted peasants set out their PX booty on cardboard mats—Seiko watches, Nikon cameras, Ivory soap, Crest toothpaste, boxes of Tide and Marlboros, new jungle boots and stacks of second-hand *Playboys*—and smiled through black teeth at the passing soldiers.

Morning stripped Saigon of its makeup. Behind the modern billboards, elegant hotels, graceful women, and the flood of new cars, it was a raw, nervous city shivering on the brink of collapse. A million refugees ringed the outskirts in wooden huts, taking cholera, yellow fever, and malaria from the polluted brown river. Hamlets just outside the city were infested with Viet Cong. The nightly artillery booms and B-52 raids were moving closer, mea-sured by the tinny vibration of empty hangers in hotel closets.

Around the corner from Tu Do Street, the shaded, manicured grounds of the Presidential Palace, the National Assembly, and the huge U.S. Embassy held reminders that the war could suddenly and violently erupt in the midst of all the apparent security, like a knife-wielding mugger leaping from an alley. The walls of the buildings still showed bullet pocks from the Tet attack eighteen months ago. Many of the hundred-year-old cypress and palm trees that had graced the parks had been cut down after Communist sappers used them as cover. Now a rubble of ugly stumps and foxholes blighted the park, symbols that the regime would do anything to stave off defeat but little to win.

Shortly before 8 A.M., George Gregory finished breakfast and returned to his room to fetch his briefcase. Downstairs a few minutes later, he met CBS television correspondent Gary Shepard, who offered to give him a lift to the Long Binh stockade. They drove back through a slow-moving grid of morning traffic toward the airport, turned right, and then passed over the heavily guarded Newport Bridge onto the main highway to Long Binh.

The dusty two-lane road was crammed with Army trucks and jeeps, armed personnel carriers, old Citroën taxis coughing smoke, and motorized pedicabs with passengers holding handkerchiefs over their noses and mouths. Peasants hustled along the road with bamboo poles on their shoulders, baskets on each end loaded with rice, vegetables, pineapples, chickens, rabbits, or even small pigs. Soup vendors squatted in the dust with their customers, ladling out fast-food bowls of *pho*. The whole mélange was enveloped in a great brown haze of diesel exhaust and dust as far as the eye could see.

Barren fields, "security zones" burned out of the jungle by aerial defoliant, flanked the highway. Only a few peasant huts stood in lonely clusters in the fields. As Gregory and the correspondent approached Long Binh, a refugee shantytown began to appear, rickety shelters built from foraged sticks of wood, flattened Coke and beer cans, and the discarded cardboard boxes of tape recorders and stereo sets. As their car slowed to a crawl in the line of traffic, dirty waifs swarmed around begging and cajoling in broken English, sticking their hands through the open windows. Gregory was warned to be careful about his watch. The kids could be off with it before he knew what happened.

Gregory stirred at the pathetic sight. He hadn't been in Vietnam long enough to grow cold.

It was late morning by the time they pulled up in front of the gate at Long Binh. In the center of a wooden arch over the entranceway was the green-and-black emblem of the U.S. Army in Vietnam, a sheathed dagger.

Gregory alighted from the car and thanked Shepard for the ride. He had made another good contact among the reporters, who he thought would make good allies. Instinctively he was beginning to feel they were on his side. They shook hands and the correspondent drove away, leaving him in the dusty entranceway.

The lawyer walked forward, sweating in his white drip-dry shirt and dark slacks, carrying his briefcase. The sprawling USARV headquarters spread before him as if Fort Dix, New Jersey, had been picked up and airlifted whole to Vietnam. Beyond the gates a grid of hard-packed dirt roads intersected a vast maze of warehouses, two-story wooden office buildings, and barracks. Platoons of marching soldiers filled the streets, some in crisp new fatigues, newly arrived from the States, others haggard and grim, shuffling toward C-131 transport jets heading home.

If Saigon was the brains of the war effort, Long Binh was its belly. USARV was the supply depot and administrative center for some four hundred thousand Army troops in Vietnam, the font of paperwork, bullets, boots, ponchos, ice cream, shoelaces, and body bags. The Marine Corps had its own version, the Navy its, the Air Force its own. Long Binh kept the Army fed, supplied, and disciplined. It was where the Army processed its legal affairs. It was the home of the Long Binh Jail, in short, the LBJ.

A sandy-haired young Army captain was waiting for Gregory at the sentry gate and stuck out his hand. Richard Booth, the military counsel assigned to Tom Middleton, smiled and told Gregory he had been expecting him to arrive that morning. Actually, he gently joked, he had heard Gregory coming all the way across the Pacific Ocean.

They chuckled. Gregory recognized Booth's accent. In a pure coincidence, it turned out he was from Conway, South Carolina. The two lawyers quickly slipped into home talk as they passed through the gates and headed for the USARV legal office.

Booth said he had been amused by Gregory's antics so far. He had really riled up the Army. His airport press conference had been front-page news all over the States, he said. All the South Carolina papers were full of sympathetic features about Middleton's wife and young children, Booth said. Everybody at home was mad as hell at the Army, his wife had told him on the telephone.

As they walked to the staff judge advocate's office, where Army lawyers and records were headquartered, Booth brought Gregory up-to-date on the case.

The Army had wrapped everything in unusual secrecy, he said. The defense lawyers had been ordered to sign a secrecy agreement that even prohibited them from referring to their clients by anything other than numbers. When they went to the stockade, in other words, they had to ask for their clients by numbers, "Prisoner Number Six," and so on.

In addition, the Army still hadn't given him access to their criminal reports. Another thing: His files had been tampered with. The whole situation was ridiculous.

Gregory raised an eyebrow. "Your files had been rifled?" Booth nodded.

There was another thing, Booth said, stopping. The phone has been ringing off the hook in the JAG lawyer's office the past few days. Strange calls, he said.

"They say they work for something called Operation Phoenix."

Gregory listened.

"They're reluctant to say exactly what it's about, but they say they're calling because of the 'Green Beret thing,' " Booth continued. "They say they've been reading about the case in *Stars and Stripes*. They say they do that kind of thing everyday."

"What kind of thing?" Gregory asked.

"Well, 'take out' Viet Cong, one by one. Assassination. They say that's their job over here. They want to know what the hell the Army is doing. They wonder if they're going to be arrested, too. They're asking for legal advice."

Gregory and Booth walked along the street in silence. Gregory was factoring in what Booth had just said with what he had read in the *International Herald Tribune* about assassination being commonplace in Vietnam, about the CIA and the Green Berets having some sort of special relationship. He didn't quite know what to make of it yet, how he could use it. For now, he tucked Operation Phoenix into the back of his mind.

"Well, Richard, let's see if we can make some progress here," he said as they arrived at the JAG office.

Lt. Col. Lloyd Rector, the legal officer in charge of administering the case, greeted them coldly. He nodded to Booth and gave Gregory a chilly handshake.

"You'll have to sign a security agreement," he said. He slid the one-page statement to Gregory.

"Fine, no problem," Gregory said. He signed it and pushed it back to Rector.

"Now, where's the file?"

Rector sat back and eyed the lawyer. "We're fighting a difficult war here," he started to say. "This case involves secrets that could seriously jeopardize the war effort if they were released. So it's the duty of the civilian attorneys to not undercut our fighting men here. . . ."

Gregory sat as politely as he could and listened to Rector's lecture. Finally, he broke in to ask again for the file. Reluctantly, Rector shoved it forward, thick manila folders with over a hundred pages of interviews conducted by detectives of the Army's Criminal Investigation Detachment.

Rector resumed his security lecture, noting that the file was classified "Secret-Noforn," meaning No Foreign Dissemination, including the South Vietnamese government. *Especially* the South Vietnamese government. Gregory pawed through the file as the colonel talked. His eyes fell on the index, and he noticed that a number of the accused men had given statements to the Army's detectives. That was a bad sign; he was anxious to read them. When Rector paused, Gregory mumbled thank you and then turned to Booth.

"Let's have a look at this stuff and see what we can do about it, Richard."

They started to rise, but Rector wasn't finished. He signaled them to sit and repeated that divulging any classified information from the case would result in criminal prosecution. Then he again launched into a theme of patriotism and protecting the lives of American soldiers in Vietnam.

Gregory had heard enough. "Look, Colonel, if this is what I think it is, all you have to do is turn my man loose and I'll be on the next plane out of here. And you'd be smart to do it."

Rector glowered. "You just don't know enough about the case to make a comment like that."

"Oh, yes I do," Gregory said. "The way I've been getting a runaround, I know there's a lot here that doesn't meet the eye. But I can assure you, Colonel, that in very short order I'll know this case from A to Z, and as far as I'm concerned, my only obligation is to my client. I didn't come over here to run the war—that's your business. But it seems to me that this is a matter that should be handled administratively.

"So just remember," he said, "if you get hurt on this and the war effort is hurt—and I am patriotic whether you believe it or not—then all you have to do, at any time, is to turn my man loose."

Gregory stood. When he reached for the files, Rector put his hand on the pile.

"That stays here," he said. "Nothing leaves this office. You can come back here and read it later."

Gregory thought of objecting, then let it go. He would challenge control of the files later. The first thing was to get his man out of jail. Without further word, the two lawyers left the office and headed for the stockade.

The Quonset hut holding the special prisoners was in the far corner of the stockade compound, surrounded by its own cyclone fence, topped with barbed wire, and guarded by MPs with K-9 dogs.

Gregory and Booth entered the outer office and were asked to sit down by an officious-looking lieutenant. He left, they sat, and the seconds turned to minutes. Sweat trickled down his cheeks. More minutes passed. The delay was just harassment, Gregory fumed.

Finally, the officer came back and led them through a narrow dark corridor where the men were held. They stopped at number two, and a solid metal door was swung open. Tom Middleton was sitting on his bunk.

"Goddam, George, I can't believe your ass is here!" Middleton exclaimed, jumping up. He looked pale and thin, like a bantamweight off the training schedule. The old friends embraced and shook hands.

"Well, how the hell are you?" Gregory asked. Middleton looked sheepish. The lawyers looked around. The closed cell was only five feet wide and seven feet long. A dim light bulb burned above a wire mesh ceiling. The air was fetid and sour. It looked like—it was!—a Conex container, one of the large metal bins the Army used for trash. It had been made into a jail cell.

Gregory and Booth didn't want to talk until they had more privacy. They waited until the MP led them from the lockup into an adjacent room where the three men sat down.

Gregory reached out and gripped Middleton's forearms. "We're gonna get you out of here as soon as we can, Tommy. Don't you worry now." He smiled confidently.

Gregory told his client what little he knew about the case and the Army's lack of cooperation. He had just now seen the file, he said. He needed to study it first.

Middleton blamed the case on General Abrams, who he said was "out to get" the Green Berets.

"I was offered immunity," Middleton said. "They're trying to pressure me to make a statement."

Gregory didn't say anything.

"Richard told me not to do it," Middleton continued, nodding at Booth. "He said I don't have to tell them any goddam thing—fuck 'em."

Gregory still didn't react.

"You'll tell them the same thing, right, George?"

Gregory shook his head. He formed his thoughts carefully and then glanced at Booth.

"Look, Richard, I like you," he said to his cocounsel. "But Tom," he said, turning back, "if they offered me the chance to be a witness instead of a defendant, I'd be the witness."

A cloud of doubt passed across Middleton's face.

"Well, I started to," he finally said. "You know, Colonel Facey did, but we don't like Facey, he's a turncoat."

"Who's Facey?" Gregory asked. Booth quickly explained that Ken Facey was Colonel Rheault's executive officer. Facey had given a statement to Army detectives implicating the others in discussions to execute the Vietnamese.

Gregory considered that. "Well, I'll look at that later," he told Booth. Then he looked back to Middleton.

"Well, you know, Tommy, there's things in life besides being popular all the time. You gotta realize these commanders have a right to information. They don't have a right to get it from a defendant, but if they give you immunity. . . ."

"Now George, don't you say anything!" Middleton erupted. "Our other lawyers, these JAG guys, are telling me you're trying to fuck up everything."

"Tom," Gregory countered gently, "I'm trying to get you free, to get you out of it." He let that rest for a moment. "And you, and these guys, have not done too good a job so far. So whatever I fuck up, I can't do any worse than you already have."

Middleton smoldered. Despite his anger, he seemed to be considering the logic of what Gregory had just said. The lawyer sat and watched him, let it sink in.

Weakly, Middleton offered that all the men had solemnly sworn not to cooperate with the investigators. They had made a pact.

"Well, hell, Tom," Gregory said, "I've just looked at the files. It looks like everybody's given a statement but you. How can they bitch at you if they've spilled their guts, and now you spill yours?"

Middleton's face turned down. For a moment he looked completely confused.

"Well," he finally said to Gregory, "don't say anything more for now. Cool it, just cool it."

Middleton was a long way from being a poster version of a Green Beret now, Gregory thought. He was a small-town country boy, in way over his head, trying to bluff a serious situation.

"We're gonna get you out of here real fast, Tommy," he repeated. "Don't you worry." He reached for his briefcase. "We're gonna file a release petition right away. An officer of your rank shouldn't be penned up like this. But first, Richard and I need to read through the whole file." He got up to leave. "We'll be back tomorrow. Don't worry. You just leave everything to me."

Middleton smiled wanly and got up. They walked back to the cell.

"Is there anything you need, Tom?" Gregory asked. "Anything I can get you?"

Middleton brightened. "Yeah, some books," he said. "I've finished these." Gregory saw a small pile of paperbacks on the floor, all of them spy thrillers. He was tempted to make a crack but held back.

"Okay," he said with a smile, "I'll get you some more." He put his arm around his friend and patted him on the back.

The two lawyers walked out of the stockade and back to the judge advocate general's office where they asked for the case files. After a few minutes' wait, a sour-faced sergeant brought a large file box into the room and set it on the table in front of them. It was all classified secret.

George Gregory sat down with Booth and started reading.

PART II

The

Gamma Papers

7

Twenty-five miles west of Saigon, the Mekong River splinters into a thousand tributaries, watering a vast plain of palm trees, marshes, and impenetrable thick forests. Four thousand years ago, Chinese tribes wandered south into the sweltering bogs and, over the centuries, tamed the forbidding delta with a network of dark-water canals that became the engines of rice and prosperity.

With wealth came envy. The peasants of southern Vietnam were soon engaged in a perpetual struggle to defend their land. First came waves of imperial Chinese armies, and after a brief period of independence in the seventeenth and eighteenth centuries, French colonizers. Soon followed French armies, to exploit and discipline a new class of indentured workers in the factories and rubber plantations. By the twentieth century, the people of the delta had slid inexorably into starvation, misery, and desperation. The effluvial Mekong, once so hospitable to rice, began to sprout rebellions.

Most of them failed, but a permanent underground inevitably took root, nurturing a culture of clandestinity. Secret brotherhoods and political organizations, religious sects, and private armies flourished. As nationalist fervor spread, dozens of splinter parties vied to lead an anti-French revolt. At the end of World War II, an enigmatic northern revolutionary, Ho Chi Minh, welded them into a loose confederation. After nine years of struggle, the guerrilla forces of his Vietnam Independence League challenged and crushed a dug-in French Army at Dien Bien Phu, a hundred miles northwest of Hanoi. Vietnam was divided in two, with Ho's Communists ruling the North and a new U.S.-backed government installed in the South. A plan for countrywide elections in 1956 was scrapped.

In late 1960, the National Front for the Liberation of South Vietnam was formed with the not-so-secret backing of Hanoi. Supplies began flowing south through Laos and Cambodia on a network of jungle trails. By mid-1961, the trails were dirt-packed highways.

The newly elected American president, John F. Kennedy, was alarmed. Humiliated by a disaster at the Bay of Pigs, confronted by Russian threats over Berlin, lectured like a schoolboy by Soviet Premier Nikita Khrushchev in Vienna, and faced with what seemed a global Marxist challenge in Latin

America, Africa, and Asia, Kennedy was determined to draw a line against communism somewhere.

"Vietnam is the place," he told his advisers, after a negotiated settlement in neighboring Laos fell apart. But "massive nuclear retaliation," the main strategic defense doctrine of the Eisenhower years, was clearly inadequate to the task. Kennedy encouraged his advisers to come up with a more flexible strategy. "Counterinsurgency" quickly became an administration fad, and its sharp edge, the U.S. Army's Special Forces.

A relic of the sabotage and intelligence teams created in World War II, the Special Forces had become a minor player in U.S. military doctrine by the late 1950s. Postwar missions with the CIA to ignite resistance networks in the Soviet Union and Eastern Europe had failed. When Kennedy came into office they had been relegated to training German border units and endlessly practicing behind-the-lines operations in the event of a Soviet invasion of Western Europe. Only a few teams had been scattered to Vietnam and other third world boiling pots, and the effort was halfhearted. For the most part, the Army establishment kept them on the shelf, apprehensive about their connections to the CIA.

Kennedy was fascinated with the guerrilla fighters, the closest thing America had to a French foreign legion. Its officers were often colorful nonconformists, unable or unwilling to adapt to a peacetime garrison army. The ranks were full of outcasts, loners, soldier-of-fortune types. Some of its recruits were drawn from among Baltic émigrés who had joined the Nazis to fight the Soviet Red Army. It was a rough, tough, and often undisciplined group of guys in a traditional Army sense, but to its devotees, it represented the spirit of the American Revolution.

Organized into teams of experts in sabotage, intelligence, communications, foreign languages, and psychological warfare, the Special Forces units could be deployed behind the lines or in advisory roles in any kind of climate. Most were skilled skiers, parachutists, mountain climbers, and frogmen, but first and last they were infantrymen.

They were fast, light, and lethal, reflections of the image the Kennedys had of themselves: smart, bold, ruthless. They were the flip side of the Peace Corps: They could kill in a dozen languages. It didn't hurt their cause in the White House that they were outlaws within the Pentagon establishment, often borrowed by the CIA to work on special missions. Kennedy thought they were just what he needed, a force that could wield the tactics of Marxist guerrillas in a twilight war for democracy.

After a trip to Fort Bragg, Kennedy awarded the Special Forces their distinctive headgear, which the staid Pentagon brass had always resisted. The Green Berets quickly became the first team at the White House, a Harvard among Michigans. Just to make the point, the young president kept a beret on his Oval Office desk. Favored soldiers began flying into Hyannisport for weekends of touch football with the Kennedy family clan.

On May 6, 1961, Kennedy dispatched four hundred Green Berets to Saigon to "expand present operations in the field of intelligence, unconventional warfare, and political-psychological activities," which included the creation of a forty-thousand-strong army of Montagnard tribesmen, funded by the CIA and led by the Green Berets. A year later, twelve thousand more were sent. Until the president's death in November 1963, Vietnam would remain nearly a CIA–Green Beret show.

The ascension of Lyndon Johnson to the presidency changed all that. The American military commitment was dramatically expanded to blunt the threatened collapse of South Vietnam. The North Vietnamese responded in kind, bolstering their secret battalions in Laos and Cambodia, as well as in South Vietnam. In a matter of months the guerrilla war had been eclipsed by the extended clashes of American and North Vietnamese army units.

The mission of the Special Forces had expanded as well. The Green Berets became the principal means for building reliable spy nets in neutral Cambodia, forward headquarters for the North Vietnamese army, and for bringing back American POWs. By the end of Johnson's presidency, the 5th Special Forces Group was the largest single command in Vietnam.

On October 15, 1968, a new sergeant took up his duties at a Special Forces camp on the edge of Muc Hoa, a delta hamlet a few miles from the Cambodian border. With his wiry physique, darting gray eyes over a rakish mustache, and jaunty beret, Sgt. Peter Sands was a slight cut above the hundred or so other Special Forces troops assigned to Muc Hoa, most of them members of a mobile strike team that set ambushes in the area.

And his duties were indeed different. Sands was nominally assigned to Special Forces Detachment 142, which worked on civilian projects with local villagers, such as helping clear canals and finding better ways to get their produce and fish to market. But his actual mission was espionage, and his real name was Alvin P. Smith. All the rest was just cover. His control unit was buried deep inside the headquarters of the 5th Special Forces in Nha Trang. It was called B-57, code name Project Gamma.

At forty-one, Smith was an intelligence veteran with a resume in unconventional operations that stretched back to the Korean War. For his mission in Muc Hoa he was expected to set up nets of agents in Cambodia and keep them completely secret from the intelligence services of the Saigon government.

U.S.-only, or "unilateral" intelligence operations were routine in any allied country. But in South Vietnam they were mandatory because the Saigon intelligence services had become riddled with Communist spies. The United States went through the motions of working with its ally, but recruited its own spies for the best, or at least the most trustworthy, information.

By day, Smith carried out his cover job, consulting with the Muc Hoa hamlet chief on local economic projects. The palm trees and lacework of delta canals reminded him of the Florida Everglades, where he'd once temporarily retired, and he began to enjoy the work. Soon he was spending more time at his cover job than his mission. Five months after arriving in Muc Hoa, he had managed to recruit only two agents, both of them duds.

Recruiting well-placed, long-term, and loyal spies was an art in the most advantageous and familiar surroundings, but it had proved nearly impossible in Vietnam. The multiple and crisscrossing allegiances of Vietnamese with family members on both sides of the conflict was forbidding. Knowledge of local customs and language, a useful barrier to confidence games and enemy infiltration, was nearly nonexistent among Americans in Vietnam, who had to guess and gamble in their operations, with predictable results. The younger military intelligence officers especially, often college dropouts rushed through spy courses and dropped into a civil war they knew little about and cared about even less, were unprepared for the task.

A spy operation usually began with the search for a suitable "principal agent" who could in turn recruit informants in Communist political organizations and combat units, or who at the very least resided in a Communist-controlled village. The principal agent might be found working for an American company as a bank official, construction boss, oil refinery manager, or labor adviser. He or she might be running an import-export company, supplying building materials, medical supplies, or transport trucks to outlying villages. What was indispensable, in the jargon of the trade, was "access" and "placement"—a rational, explainable reason to meet with an American, on the one hand, and spies close to the Communists, on the other. In Vietnam, that wasn't hard to find, since the locals commonly played both sides against the middle. For an American spy handler, the challenge was finding someone who would remain loyal to him.

Muc Hoa, a palm-tree-shaded hamlet of pineapple farmers and river fishermen on the edge of the delta, provided a tiny recruiting pool for suitable agents. After three months, one of Alvin Smith's recruits was a Vietnamese Protestant missionary, the other a small-time smuggler, both of whom were employed in his civil affairs projects as cover and crossed into Cambodia regularly.

The results were dismal, Smith ruefully discovered. The agents seldom reported in, failed to recruit any informants, and never saw more than a few NVA soldiers firsthand, those usually buying rice from local Cambodian villagers. Despite Smith's occasional threats to cut off the cash, the situation remained unchanged into the new year. Soon, they stopped reporting at all. After five months, Smith's Muc Hoa efforts were barren.

And the timing couldn't have been worse. Project Gamma was feeling reverberations from the Nixon administration's new emphasis on Cambodia. Heavier intelligence requirements were flowing from Washington, and sometimes from the White House itself, on the political situation inside Cambodia.

One of Gamma's principal missions was to confirm or elaborate on photos taken by U.S. satellites and U-2 spy planes streaking over Cambodia; its spies were given miniature cameras to photograph supply trains running north from the Cambodian port of Sihanoukville. But agents were also dispatched to put wiretaps on telephone lines to gather evidence of collaboration between supposedly neutral Cambodian officials and the North Vietnamese. Something was obviously in the works.

The feeble trickle of Smith's intelligence soon became unacceptable in Nha Trang. Warning memos were coming down the line from B-57 headquarters in Nha Trang. If production didn't improve, he'd be out.

He was a stout young Vietnamese man with a quick, friendly grin and engaging manner, the only good thing to happen to Alvin Smith in the past five months.

His name was Thai Khac Chuyen, and he had arrived in Muc Hoa just after Alvin Smith's posting, looking for a job. With his unusually good command of English and American slang, he was quickly hired for the Civil Affairs office.

The chubby interpreter made the gloomy sergeant's sinking fortunes tolerable. As time went by, they spent longer days together in the rudimentary wooden office, talking politics and history, war and peace, America and Vietnam. There hadn't been much else to do what with Smith's bankrupt spying operations.

Smith was awed by Chuyen. His English far surpassed that of the interpreters he had encountered at the other Special Forces units. But there was more than that. Chuyen never asked for anything special, never wanted a handout. He was articulate and reflective. He came to work each day in neatly pressed cotton slacks and a sport shirt, always on time. He looked Smith straight in the eye, carried out his duties without question, even volunteering to help translate intelligence reports when the other interpreters were absent. He seemed, to Smith, more American than Vietnamese.

No, better than that, Smith quickly decided. Chuyen was a cultured, sophisticated man, an independent thinker like himself. While the Green Berets assigned to the nearby Mike team hung out at the crude enlisted men's bar each night, Smith went less and less, preferring to spend his time with his interpreter, talking books, politics, and history. Soon he and Chuyen were dining together and sharing late-night drinks.

Only one thing nagged at him: With such a good array of skills, what was Chuyen doing in a backwater place like Muc Hoa?

Chuyen's father, Smith learned, had been a minor bureaucrat in North Vietnam, a Catholic who sympathized with the anticolonial struggle and only reluctantly fled south when the Communist designs of Ho Chi Minh became evident. A man of books and culture, he had had to forfeit his large library when he departed with the family in 1954.

Their fathers were much alike, Smith reflected. He shared his memories of Saturday afternoons at the movies in Washington, D.C., watching newsreels with his father. Afterward, they would talk politics.

"Yes, yes," Chuyen would say, his flat black eyes agreeing, "we are very much the same." He made the sergeant feel better about his plight in Muc Hoa. He told Smith he deserved better than such a dead-end assignment.

Chuyen said he had hoped to go to college but had failed to graduate from high school after many tries. Instead, seeing more and more Americans arriving in Vietnam in the early sixties, he studied English. Eventually, he found work as a combat interpreter with a few Special Forces units in the northern part of the country. Usually they sent him deep into the jungle on missions, which he admitted he hated—it was too dangerous. He didn't want to go back to the Ashau Valley, and, of course, his wife had moved to Tay Ninh. He needed to be close to her. They had two children now.

But the Green Berets, he said, smiling and mocking the local peasant English, were "number one"—the very best. He blew movie smoke from a cocked finger. "John Wayne," he said. "Number one." They laughed.

As the days passed and their relationship grew closer, Chuyen also revealed his fears of dying for a corrupt and unworthy government. Cautiously, he even denounced the succession of official tyrants in Saigon.

Far from provoking Smith's disapproval, the story evoked the sergeant's admiration. He liked Chuyen's pluck and irreverence. He confided he didn't care much for the Saigon government either and sometimes wondered why the United States continued to fight in Vietnam. Chuyen said he wondered, too.

The red lights that had gone on in Smith's mind when they first met changed to yellow. He realized how little he had going for himself in Muc Hoa; how, once again, a promising new assignment was slipping from his grasp. And it was *not his fault*. He felt like he was lashed to a car that was driving off a cliff.

What would happen if he were taken out of Muc Hoa? Bad as the Delta was, it was better than typing up reports as a sergeant at headquarters. He was an operative, a professional case officer; he couldn't let himself sink to the level of a clerk.

Finally, during a night of brooding, he looked at Chuyen anew. The answer to his problem was sitting right there in front of him. Back in the office the next morning, Smith drew Chuyen close and offered a deal: How would he like to be more than an interpreter?

Chuyen was skeptical. Would it be dangerous? Smith dismissed his worries with a wave. He *would* have to go into some delicate areas.

"Where?" Chuyen asked.

Cambodia.

The chubby young man considered the offer, then said slowly he'd be delighted. He'd like to help his new friend out in any way he could.

Alvin Smith threw himself into his new project. On March 3, 1969, nearly five months after he had arrived in Muc Hoa, he sent an official request for a name trace on "Chu Yen Thai Khac"—the correct order of family and given names had been a bugaboo for Americans from the beginning of the war—to the Source Control office at MACV intelligence headquarters in Saigon. There, computerized files held the records of Vietnamese employed by U.S. forces in Vietnam, as well as a "burn list" of undesirable former intelligence agents cross-checked with the CIA.

A few days later, the response came back: "No record." That was odd,

Smith thought, considering Chuyen's past employment by Special Forces up North. But there was no time to worry about computer glitches now. He would check back again later.

Next he filed an "Operational Interest Plan" to Detachment B-57 head-quarters in Nha Trang, declaring his intent to recruit Chuyen. Copies were again sent to Source Control and the Office of the Special Assistant to the Ambassador, or OSA, a euphemism for the CIA. A week later he was given official approval to recruit Chuyen by both the 5th Special Forces intelligence section and the CIA.

On March 8, Chuyen was fingerprinted, photographed, and registered as Agent No. SF7-166. There wasn't time for a polygraph.

8

The column of droop-winged B-52s rolled down the runway, lifted into the air, and roared over the white sand, heading east from Guam. Below, a pair of Russian trawlers bristling with antennas floated in a turquoise sea. The ships always seemed to be stationed at the end of the runways when the bombers took off. The pilots had no doubt of the trawlers' electronic spying mission relaying flight information to Hanoi. But sophisticated scramblers on-board the B-52s, they were sure, prevented any leakage of their destination.

Reaching their cruising altitude at thirty thousand feet, the crews set their course and then settled into a regime of naps, reading, and snacks for the long trip to Indochina. Their destination was five hours away. There was nothing to worry about but storms over the Philippines and a midair refueling.

At midnight, the bombers approached the dark southern coastline of Viet-nam and came under the control of ground radar. A coded message was flashed to the crews: a change in targets. The navigator in one of the crews finished plotting the new coordinates and spoke into his intercom: "Hey boss," he told the pilot, "Guess what? It's Cambodia."

There was silence in the hissing headset. After a moment, the pilot clicked his microphone twice, signaling acknowledgment. The B-52s swung north-west. Each plane carried up to thirty tons of bombs.

From the ground along the Cambodian border, the rapid yellow flashes on the western horizon looked like heat lightning. Then a deep rumble rolled out of the jungle and traveled along the ground. As far away as Tay Ninh, glasses tinkled on bar tops. It was March 18, 1969. The bombing of Cambodia had begun.

In secret.

Richard Nixon had made it clear that Cambodia would no longer be off-

limits to American bombers. Ten days before moving into the Oval Office the
president-elect sent an order to his new national security adviser, Dr. Henry
Kissinger.

"I want a precise report on what the enemy has in Cambodia and what, if
anything, we are doing to destroy the buildup there. I think that a very definite
change in policy toward Cambodia should be probably one of the first orders
of business when we get in."

Adding Cambodian territory to the target list meant expanding the bombing
only five or ten miles west from where B-52s had been pounding triple-canopy
jungle for years. But the two-digit change in a bombardier's computer had
immense ramifications for domestic and international affairs.

The bombing was no secret to the North Vietnamese army, or to thousands
of innocent Cambodian peasants vaporized without warning in the blockbuster fireballs. The secrecy was aimed at critics of the war in Congress, on
campus, and in the media, sure to be outraged by the bombing's extension
into Cambodia—officially neutral in the conflict—at a time when the war was
supposed to be winding down. Exposure of the bombing, Nixon knew, would
reinvigorate the antiwar movement, which had driven Lyndon Johnson from
office. It might even spur a call for his impeachment—especially if the me-
chanics of the bombing were known: The "Failsafe" system for nuclear-
capable B-52s had been breached.

The existence of the B-52 missions was held tightly by a small circle of
White House officials, a handful of Air Force and Army generals, and a
necessary few targeting officers. Operation Menu was classified at a level far
higher than top secret, with a special clearance for access to the information
granted on a case-by-case basis by the White House.

But doubts soon cropped up. Air Force targeting officers in Saigon, who
were out of the security loop, watched the flights fly off the radar and became
curious.

At the Pentagon a few colonels who found out what was going on became
alarmed; the "Failsafe" system of the Strategic Air Command was a cornerstone of U.S. nuclear-weapons policy. Loosening control over B-52s, whose
main function was to deliver H-bombs over Moscow and Beijing, was akin to
religious heresy. The very idea of nuclear bombers in the hands of a few White
House officials and their generals was the stuff of *Seven Days in May*. What
would the Soviets think if they found out? What would the Congress do?

But that was not Nixon's prime concern. He wanted the war to end, and the
way out, he believed, was through Cambodia.

Cambodian leader Prince Sihanouk, Nixon believed, tacitly approved of the
secret bombing because it held the promise of weakening Hanoi's longtime
occupation of his eastern provinces while allowing him to maintain a studied
neutrality in the conflict. But a public scandal about the bombing would be
politically lethal.

Sihanouk, meanwhile, walked a diplomatic tightrope. He had kept Cambodia out of the war, but any official acknowledgment of the bombing would
force him to take sides. Repudiating the American escalation would harden
the hands of pro-U.S. generals conspiring behind the throne to overthrow

him. Acquiescing in the bombing, however, could prompt Hanoi and Red China to add fuel to a sputtering Communist insurrection, the Khmer Rouge.

To Nixon, the pitfalls were worth it. Destroying the sanctuaries in Cambodia was the key to getting out of Vietnam on American terms. The Communist base camps, only forty miles from Saigon in heavily bunkered jungle, had been the staging ground for the surprise attacks at Tet in 1968 and still posed a threat to the capital. In practical terms, the bombing was meant to buy enough time to get U.S. troops safely out of South Vietnam without provoking the collapse of the Saigon army. Despite billions of dollars in U.S. military and economic aid and the lives of forty thousand American soldiers, the Army of the Republic of Vietnam had shown no sign that it could stand on its own. Cambodia was the last, desperate card.

The U.S. command anticipated that rumors of the bombing would spread quickly inside Vietnam. On the eve of the campaign, Gen. Earle Wheeler, chairman of the Joint Chiefs of Staff, cabled his commander in Vietnam, Creighton Abrams, with a carefully worded advisory on how to handle questions from the press:

> U.S. spokesmen will confirm that B-52's did strike on routine missions adjacent to the Cambodian border but state that he has no details and will look into this question.
>
> Should the press persist in its inquiries, or in the event of a Cambodian protest concerning U.S. strikes in Cambodia, U.S. spokesmen will neither confirm nor deny reports of attacks on Cambodia but will state it will be investigated. After delivering a reply to any Cambodian protest, Washington will inform the press that we have apologized and offered compensation.

As an added deception, Nixon ordered a last-minute message sent to Ambassador Ellsworth Bunker and General Abrams announcing that feasibility studies for the B-52 raids had been called off. Although the message was classified top secret, it was sent through regular military channels, assuring that it would be shared widely in Saigon. Nixon then sent a back-channel cable to Abrams—but not to Ambassador Bunker—telling him to ignore the first message.

At MACV headquarters, Abrams and a small staff privy to the bombing began to file false targeting data into Air Force computers and then sent the real bombing results back to Henry Kissinger at the White House. Each night through March 1969, the B-52's came again and again on official flight orders for Vietnam and were diverted to Cambodia.

It soon became apparent that the missions weren't producing the expected results, however, despite their awesome power. Secondary explosions were signaling direct hits on ammunition dumps, and hundreds of North Vietnamese soldiers were being shredded in the raids, but the enemy seemed to be able to take the blows and bounce back.

One night a Green Beret reconnaissance team assigned to assess bomb

damage found that out firsthand. The team had been inserted across the border by helicopter, assured that only craters and body pieces would await them. Anyone unfortunate enough to survive would be found wandering dazed and bleeding.

Instead, a North Vietnamese ambush hit them like a swarm of angry bees. Only a few soldiers escaped to tell the horror story.

The Green Berets refused to go back on a second mission a few nights later. Their commander threatened a court-martial, but the men stood their ground.

"You can't try me for refusing to go where we're not supposed to be," one said. The Army backed down. It was a lesson many soldiers were learning in the ever-expanding secrecy of Vietnam.

Bob Marasco was in charge of B-57 intelligence operations in the Cambodian border area. One day the swarthy young captain took a prop-driven airboat down the river from Thanh Tri to Muc Hoa to talk with his sergeant and get a personal feel for his new agent. He was hoping Smith had finally gotten something going after the past dismal months with the missionary and the smuggler.

Marasco wasn't in Muc Hoa for long before he began to feel something was wrong. To the uncomplicated former life-insurance salesman from New Jersey, Smith and Chuyen quickly came off as an odd pair. As they shared a few beers, Smith seemed eager to impress Marasco with a vague history of derring-do and special operations. He had worked "for the company" in the Middle East, he said, after some "wild stuff" in Korea. He had also been with the Special Forces in Germany. When Marasco pressed, Smith changed the subject. Marasco also thought it odd that Smith had brought along his interpreter for a beer with them. He grew uncomfortable with the open shoptalk.

At twenty-three, Marasco had little experience in intelligence work. Three years ago he had been inducted into the Metropolitan Life Insurance Company's "Million Dollar Roundtable" for selling a record number of policies. When he came home from a convention in Miami, his wife handed him his draft notice.

What little he knew about Vietnam came from *Life* magazine. All he knew was that it was jungles and death. Instead of gambling with the draft and certain assignment to a two-year infantry hitch, and probably Vietnam, he volunteered for a three-year assignment with Army counterintelligence. He'd grown up on biographies of J. Edgar Hoover, the great G-man. Maybe he would be an investigator. Off he went on the bus to boot camp with the other boys from Newark, "half my high school class." At least he wasn't going where they were.

At Fort Holabird, something clicked when he heard about officers' candidate school. Always a spiffy dresser and student leader, he liked the idea of an officer's rank and uniform. He signed up and graduated with honors. Then he heard about airborne training. Suddenly a passion for danger and excitement

was aroused in him. He volunteered for that, too. Sure enough, he soon landed in Vietnam with the 101st Airborne Division, not just a draftee.

It wasn't good enough. When he heard about the Special Forces, he just had to have the green beret. In 1968, he extended his tour to join the 5th Special Forces. They put him in their spookiest unit, Project Gamma. He was in heaven.

Marasco didn't know what to think about his aloof, tight-lipped sergeant, and the clandestine atmosphere of B-57 didn't encourage him to ask questions. There were lots of guys like Smith, he found, forty-year-old soldiers with hundred-year histories. After a few months with Gamma, he thought, anything could be true: The unit was drenched in a James Bond–like intrigue.

And he liked it. "First you have to volunteer, then we'll tell you what we do," they told him when he asked. "If you don't like what we tell you, and you change your mind, you go directly to the United States—your tour is over, finished that day."

He was assigned to Thanh Tri, a palm-fringed hamlet in sight of Cambodia, under a new name, Capt. Robert A. Martin. His mission was to run Detachment 142 and recruit his own spies to keep track of Cambodian officials. He crossed the border several times in an unmarked uniform, carrying no identification and armed with a Russian AK-47, to meet with his agent.

Packets of mail arrived in Thanh Tri with his real name and military address cut off. His paycheck was deposited for him in the United States, and money for operations was delivered by plainclothes couriers in unmarked helicopters. As far as he knew, he worked for somebody in Washington, maybe the CIA. He couldn't be sure, and he wasn't supposed to ask.

As he listened to Smith's vague history, Marasco didn't press for details. Nor later, when he returned to Thanh Tri, did his curiosity about Smith provoke him to request the mysterious sergeant's personnel file from Nha Trang. He doubted he would be allowed to see it anyway; information was dispensed on a "need-to-know" basis, and it wasn't necessary to dig up Smith's past to get the job done in Cambodia. If he looked at Smith's file, he thought, how could he be sure the truth was in there anyway? As far as he could see, everything in the intelligence world was based on deception.

Actually, it was fine with him. He motored back to Thanh Tri.

Alvin Smith was also having his problems with Chuyen. His reports were getting weaker and weaker. One described a major NVA hospital complex in Cambodia, which turned out to be a wild exaggeration; the follow-up raiders, pumped up by Smith's praise for his agent, found only a temporary clinic with a few rolls of bandages and a box of French medicine.

Under Project Gamma's mission, Chuyen was also supposed to be going deep into Cambodia, ideally to develop contacts with village-level Cambodian officials and recruit them as subagents; regular border coverage was the task of other combined U.S.-Vietnamese units. Yet Chuyen never seemed to roam far from Muc Hoa for long.

Smith's reports were also badly written and wordy, with little useful information, Marasco complained to headquarters. "They tell me everything about Cambodia except what I need to know. In the time someone else turns out ten reports, Smith is still working on one. He always goes into the history of the region—some of his reports are so long they are totally worthless. I can't break him of that."

Something else bothered him: "They aren't the reports of a man who's supposed to have his background"—meaning the CIA. Marasco was growing impatient with the sergeant who intimated a vast experience in espionage but was producing so little. Something nagged at him about Chuyen, too.

"He's heavier, chunkier than most Vietnamese. Absolutely fluent in English—he could've worked for an American corporation. He's too smart, too educated, almost as if he had studied English at a university.

"Smith told me he has worked for all the right places, all over the country. But we're not getting good stuff from him. Sometimes my agents report from the same area as Smith, and his information is different."

Marasco advised headquarters: "It's not adding up."

Alvin Smith sensed something more dangerous.

His other agents had resigned. They weren't even showing up for money anymore. Asked why, the agents would only say they were afraid to work any longer and nervously asked not to be contacted again.

Something worse happened. One night a recon team was ambushed. Chuyen was one of the few Vietnamese agents who had known about the mission in advance.

To Marasco, it seemed like termites had invaded their operations. He radioed Nha Trang for permission to transfer Smith out and put Chuyen on ice for a while until he could figure out what to do next. That way they could keep an eye on both of them. With staff changes going on in Nha Trang, it took a few weeks for the approval to arrive.

In was mid-April by the time Marasco motored down the river to Muc Hoa and told Smith he was needed for an important job in Nha Trang. Chuyen, he was told, would be put back into his old job as an interpreter in the civil affairs shop in Muc Hoa.

Marasco left, hoping his problems were over. The problems in Cambodia, however, were only beginning.

9

NHA TRANG

May 10

The darkroom technician poked at the negative one more time, flipped it over, then lifted it out of the tray of chemicals and hung it up on a string to dry. It was the last picture from a roll of captured Viet Cong film.

Alvin Smith dawdled in the darkroom, sifting through the other prints as the technician worked. Although he rationalized it was a serious part of his duties, sifting through enemy film was one of his favorite pastimes. Ever since his transfer to the B-57 headquarters a month ago, his days had become long and boring, spent turning raw agent reports into finished product. About a dozen men worked in the team house—radio operators, code clerks, translators, and intelligence analysts, whose job was to make sense of the inchoate mix of reports, photographs, and stolen documents supplied by spies in Cambodia.

The agent reports sometimes came in via radio. More often they were scratched out on rice paper two or three times weekly and planted in tree hollows, walls, and bridges in a Cambodian village—"dead drops" to be serviced by other agents.

The spies' reports on North Vietnamese units were usually no more than three or four paragraphs. They gave a unit's name, location, and troop strength, the kind of weapons it carried, its foodstocks, its plans of attack, and occasionally the names of its officers. Since many of the units had been operating in the same areas for years, the reports varied little, like the day-in, day-out line up of a baseball team over a season. Only the experienced intelligence analysts took interest in the little blips—a new lieutenant, a change in diet, a new tack in the lectures by political cadres, a different color uniform—that signified an important change in the pattern. But experienced analysts were rare. Few stayed long enough in Vietnam to get a feel for the rhythm. The official tour was 365 days, then home.

Alvin Smith thought the job was beneath him. To while away the time, he wrote up proposals for new operations—he had an idea for putting an agent into North Vietnam—or hung around the photo shop.

Smith flipped idly through the captured pictures as they came out of the developing tray. Most were of North Vietnamese soldiers wearing olive green khaki and pith helmets, assembled in a jungle clearing for some kind of a political rally or welcoming ceremony, surrounded by revolutionary banners.

The film had been captured after a battle at Bu Gia Map, a sparsely settled region in Phuoc Long Province northwest of Saigon. A date on the frame read 1964.

Suddenly, one picture caught Smith's attention. He stared at it intensely. It showed rows of North Vietnamese soldiers assembled like classmates. One chunky man in the front row, wearing the floppy black hat of a Viet Cong cadre and smiling widely between slightly large ears, looked eerily familiar.

Incredible, the sergeant thought to himself. *It can't be.*

Smith pawed through the other prints on the table. Gathering up a handful, he scurried from the darkroom.

Smith stayed in his room for hours, pacing the floor, concentrating on the picture. His mind whirled like a slot machine.

He thought back: Chuyen's unusual facility with English, his out-of-place appearance in Muc Hoa, the mysterious fact that all the other agents had quit after Chuyen came to work.

He cursed himself and began to wonder: How deep did the penetration go?

Budge Williams, the B-57 operations officer, was cautious after seven years on Special Forces teams. At twenty-eight, after assignments in Bolivia, Panama, and an earlier tour of Vietnam, the airborne ranger thought he had learned at least one lesson: Be careful of who you depend on; the wrong person could screw you up good. But all that went out the door in Vietnam; men were rotated in and out so fast you hardly got to know their names.

Williams peered at the photograph Smith had brought him. The stocky captain from Georgia could definitely see a resemblance between the Vietnamese man in the group picture and the somber face in Chuyen's ID photo. But it could go either way—all "gooks" looked alike to him.

"I dunno," Williams said with a shrug, shoving the photograph forward. "It could be him. Maybe not."

He considered the fidgeting sergeant. What did he know about him? Alvin Smith had been transferred to headquarters by his predecessor. Williams hadn't had the time or reason to look into it; transfers went on all the time. All he knew was that the sergeant was a trained case officer and at forty-one had many years in the Special Forces behind him. Usually that was enough to inspire trust, but something in Smith made him pause. He asked the sergeant to come back the next day after he'd had time to study the dossier.

That night, Williams leafed through the papers. He found Smith's initial evaluation of Chuyen, the forms for Chuyen's clearance from Source Control and OSA and their responses of "no record" for the agent. There was Smith's request to make a recruitment pitch, the approval from headquarters, and the operational plan for Chuyen's use in Blackbeard, the overall code name for collecting intelligence in Cambodia. There was the assignment of Chuyen's agent number.

Williams thumbed through the dossier again. Something was missing.

The polygraph report—the man hadn't been put on the box. *Oh God, save me from Vietnam*, he thought. Looking back through the file, he now noticed there also had been no further assessments of Chuyen, or more background reports on him since he had been recruited.

Well, shit, he thought. Let's at least get a polygraph right away. Then we'll decide what to do.

He thought about Smith again: not a very thorough piece of work, after all, for a guy with all that experience.

Odd.

The difference between 1967 and 1969 was night and day, Budge Williams thought, comparing his two tours. He was appalled by the decline of the Green Berets, who were being diluted by inferior officers and stretched too thin by the war.

In his first week as operations officer for B-57, Williams toured Project Gamma's offices in the hamlets along the Cambodian frontier and came back disgusted. Cover for most of the intelligence teams was pathetic.

"They were supposed to have civil action cover, and they were supposed to have their projects going," he wrote later. "But when I went out to inspect them, I found only two or three who were actually doing it. The rest of them made no pretense as to what they were doing. Everybody in the goddam camp knew what they were doing. Every interpreter, every swinging dick, every VC in the whole goddam area knew exactly what they were doing, and they probably knew their true names."

The decline of intelligence standards matched the decay of the Green Berets as a whole, he thought. There were too many men being rushed through airborne training and doled into the units to meet the expanding missions of the war. The esprit de corps was gone. Drinking was a problem. The camps were running whorehouses, and weapons were left to rust.

With his piercing eyes and barrel chest, Williams exuded the casually malevolent air of a South Georgia teenager on Saturday night, cruising for action in his pickup truck, hound dogs in the back, shotgun racked in the rear window. He had no patience for the "hearts and minds" programs of the war. He came to kill Cong.

"I'm not here to solve social problems," he'd say. "I'm here to kill gooks"—or "slopes," or "dinks," or "zips," in the parlance of the grunts. He was an airborne ranger, a fighter. And as far as he was concerned, *our gooks were worse than theirs. Let's kill them all!*

The liberals who said the U.S. was too rough in Vietnam ought to spend time with "our allies," he sneered. During his first week in 1967 he had watched a squad of Vietnamese Green Berets drag a Viet Cong suspect out of his house and beat him to death in the street, laughing and smoking their cigarettes all the while. Right there in the street, smashing skulls with their rifle butts. It hardly softened the spectacle to learn later that the VC had assassinated the hamlet chief and his family the night before.

He loved war, Budge Williams did, he loved goddam war. But he couldn't stand this kind of stuff. He wished he'd been born a century earlier.

*   *   *

Bob Marasco returned from an emergency leave in the last week of May and passed through Nha Trang on the way back to duty. The curly haired captain went into Budge Williams's office, dropped his bag, and slumped in a seat. One look at Marasco's troubled face told Williams that his team chief in Thanh Tri hadn't had a good break.

He was getting divorced, Marasco confided. His wife had recently enrolled in college. Now she was leading antiwar demonstrations on campus! She said it was a healthy thing for her to do.

Williams laughed. What more could be said? Vietnam didn't make any sense, but it was the only war they had.

"Okay bubba, take a look at this and tell me what you think," Williams said. "You know this guy, right?" He shoved the picture forward.

Marasco leaned forward over the desk. He stared at the photo for a moment, gave Williams a puzzled look, and then looked down again.

"Jesus," he whispered.

"What do you think—is it him?"

"Where'd you get this?" Marasco asked. Williams filled him in, then went to the door. He hollered across the adjoining operations room for Smith.

The sergeant ambled in.

Marasco looked at the picture again and then said he thought it was Chuyen. Smith nervously smiled and started to offer his theories about the agent, but the two captains cut him off—Smith had created the problem.

Williams and Marasco thought about what to do next. A penetration in Cambodia was a serious development anytime, but right now it was worse with the secret B-52 bombing at full steam and whispers of an invasion in the works. They could not have a flap.

Another problem was that the guard was changing in Nha Trang, with three new key officers just coming on board.

Colonel Rheault had just arrived to take over the group, but he was already off on a countrywide inspection tour and wasn't expected back for a few days, when he'd officially take command. Taking it to Colonel Aaron, who was on the way out the door, wouldn't make sense.

Maj. Tom Middleton, the new 5th Group intelligence officer, had also just arrived. Middleton had done a previous Vietnam tour and should know the ropes. Williams liked him; he was a "good ole boy" from South Carolina. But he hadn't settled in yet either.

Then there was the new chief of B-57, Maj. David Crew. He had just arrived, too, and it would be another two weeks before he even found his way to the latrine. Crew looked like a pussy, Williams confided. Strictly a staff type, paper-pusher, no crease undone.

A whole new team, Williams complained. Bad timing. U.S. combat units hadn't been in Vietnam five years, two million men had gotten their tickets punched for a year each time! He decided to stall until all the new men were fully on board.

Williams decided he could get the paperwork started and take a few precautionary steps. He told Smith to write up a "Suspect Source" report for the outgoing B-57 commander, Bob Thrasher. Then he told Marasco to get back to the delta and write up a report on other operations that might have been contaminated: Who did Chuyen know? What did he know about other agent nets? A polygraph would have to be arranged and a warning bulletin sent to the CIA with a copy of the agent's registration.

Two days later, Smith turned in his report on the captured photograph. It was stamped SECRET-NOFORN in red at the top. It referred to Marasco by his cover name.

"One of the VC appears to be CHUYEN, Thai Khac," Smith wrote. "The photograph was shown to CPT MARTIN, who has associated with CHUYEN and he corroborated this impression. It is the opinion of CPT MARTIN and the undersigned that if the photo is not of CHUYEN, it is of a person very similar to him."

Smith's concluding paragraph struck a note of equivocation.

"If it can be proved that CHUYEN is innocent of these allegations, it is the opinion of the undersigned that he should be moved to another area and his talents exploited. Professionally, he is one of the best trained individuals the undersigned has observed and, if innocent, capable of great contribution to the collection effort."

Thrasher read the report and examined the photos but was far less certain they were the same man.

"Definite similarities appear in the facial features," Thrasher noted in his memo of May 19. "The earlobes seem different, however. Due to the draw string on the hat, a complete view of the ear is obscured."

Thrasher concluded, "While the photo does not establish proof that Chuyen is a VC, it definitely requires further investigation." He recommended an immediate polygraph and bringing the counterintelligence experts into the case.

The thickening dossier was shuffled upstairs for his successor. That was a good way to leave it—for the next guy. Thrasher was on his way home—"back," as they put it, "to the world."

10

The dust had hardly settled from his predecessor's departing helicopter when Col. Robert Bradley Rheault decided to put his stamp on his new command. Stomping into the commander's bedroom, he grabbed the soft, queen-size mattress, dragged it out the front door, and ostentatiously tossed it into the dust of the 5th Special Forces Group compound. In its place, he ordered a plain canvas cot set up in his office.

Next he posted a short bulletin: The separate canteens for officers and enlisted men were over. From now on they would all watch the nightly movies together.

At forty-three, with gray-flecked hair, crinkled blue eyes, and an occasional cheroot stuck in the corner of his mouth, Bob Rheault looked like Clint Eastwood's version of a Green Beret officer. But his resume went deeper than Hollywood, starting with Phillips Exeter Academy, to West Point, the University of Paris, a master's degree in international relations, and fast-track duty on the Joint Chiefs of Staff. His French was flawless. He was as comfortable in the straps of a parachute as in a graduate-school classroom.

Commanding all the Green Berets in Vietnam was the pinnacle, the best, the highest he could go. The general's star that followed would surely be an anticlimax. He could never be more happy than with men in the field. He hated stateside duty. He had to be in the mountains or jungles leading a small team of guerrillas. The hotter or the colder, the more uncomfortable or the more dangerous, the better. Men who watched him closely during his first Vietnam tour in 1964 thought perhaps that Bob Rheault, taking long trips alone into Viet Cong territory, deliberately put himself in danger.

"Nothing is worth having," he would lecture his own children, "unless it's hard to get."

Now at the top, Rheault could survey it all. The 5th Special Forces Group was a pyramid of teams, the biggest operational command in the war zone, scattered across the entire length of Vietnam. Not even a general with his own division could boast of overseeing forty-five hundred men and a forty-thousand-strong Montagnard mercenary army with its own payrolls, weapons, and supply systems. More special units conducted long-range reconnaissance on the Ho Chi Minh Trail, snatching North Vietnamese officers, East German, Russian, or Red Chinese advisers for clandestine interrogations and then dumping them back in the jungle. Others teams sent spies into Laos, Cambodia, and North Vietnam—or to ports around the world from which Communist supplies for Hanoi might be moving. And in almost all of its work, the 5th Group enjoyed a special relationship with the CIA—which for Bob Rheault was a great satisfaction; it gave him some independence from the Army chain of command.

On the morning of June 3, en route to take over his new post, Rheault had paid a courtesy call on the commander of the U.S. Army in Vietnam. Gen. George Lafayette Mabry, fifty-two, ramrod straight, his uniform stiffly starched, welcomed the charismatic colonel to his empire in Long Binh. The sound of marching troops passed by the window, a reminder of the general's immense power and responsibilities—four hundred thousand soldiers in the country. He fed them, clothed them, armed them, kept up their files, and if they died, boxed them up and shipped them home. He supplied ice cream on the Fourth and turkey on Thanksgiving and ran the Army's jail. Gen. Creighton Abrams ran the war, and George Mabry ran the Army for him.

To Rheault, the visit was mostly protocol. In the Army's table of organization, the 5th Special Forces Group occupied a unique and independent niche, reporting only to Creighton Abrams and bypassing the Army's regional chain of command. And it was not unusual for the Special Forces to get missions directly from the Pentagon's Office of Special Activities as well as from the CIA.

Respect, however, had to be paid. George Mabry was a legend in the autumn of his career, the winner of every combat award from the Bronze Star, Silver Star, Purple Heart, and Legion of Merit to the Medal of Honor, the nation's highest military decoration.

The citation was explicit: Leading a company of riflemen across France in 1944, young Major Mabry and his unit were pinned down by withering German automatic-weapons fire. He crawled forward through a mine field and explosives-rigged barbed wire, raced up a hill, knocked out a machine gun, killed three enemy soldiers in hand-to-hand fighting and captured nine more. Then he dashed on to a second, and then a third bunker, and repeated his heroics. His valor opened the way for the U.S. Army's assault across the Cologne Plain, which had hung in the balance at the Battle of the Bulge.

"Major Mabry's superlative courage, daring, and leadership in an operation of major importance," the citation read, "exemplify the finest characteristics of the military service."

The campaign also left him a stickler for discipline. During the Nazi retreat his troops were inflamed by evidence of tortured American prisoners. One day a junior officer retaliated, executing a group of German POWs. The lieutenant was a West Point graduate. Mabry, the son of a minor-league baseball catcher with an ROTC commission from Presbyterian College in Clinton, South Carolina, broke the man on the spot.

"You fight like hell during the battle," he lectured the assembled men, "but when it's over your enemy is due the privileges of a prisoner, just as you are. I will not countenance the murder of a POW and will immediately relieve any other officer I suspect of carrying it out." The atrocities ceased.

Mabry went steadily up the ranks and became an expert in combat training and operations, volunteering for a commission to study Army discipline in Vietnam. He was a firm traditionalist, and his reputation for playing by the rules was unsurpassed. In April 1969, he had begun his second Vietnam tour.

As Robert Rheault sat before him, Mabry praised the bravery of the Special Forces and remarked how impressed he was by the young colonel's service record. But there were problems with the Green Berets, he added, and brought up an example that "really got under my hide." It was one of the reasons he had requested a man of Rheault's caliber to run the Special Forces, he said. A few things had to be straightened out—mostly a matter of attitude—but they would not be tolerated as long as he was in charge.

Some soldiers in a Green Beret outpost had actually *sold* bottles of Coca-Cola to thirsty U.S. Army troops passing by on patrol, he said. *Sold* drinks to thirsty American soldiers! And at exorbitant prices!

Rheault was relieved. He thought it might be something important. Green Beret troops always thought they were superior, he knew, and threw their weight around. It was one of the things he accepted, even reluctantly liked, but he knew it galled the hell out of the Army.

But the tensions were inevitable. The troops were stationed for long periods in remote jungle camps with food, supplies, and mail erratically delivered, and they were under constant pressure from North Vietnamese; military discipline was lax. The Green Berets often ignored reveille, drank heavily, and grew their hair long. Some were on their third tour in desolate Montagnard villages, raising their own armies to track the Viet Cong, living in the bush and eating monkeys, taking wives and fathering children, painting their faces with native inks and adopting headbands, beads, and mystical amulets—becoming the enemy in order to defeat him.

Rheault admired the warrior spirit, even if he knew that some had gone off the edge. But to the regular Army, such behavior was intolerable. Military envoys from Saigon with their neat haircuts, starched fatigues, and pale faces often got a rude reception when they dropped in on the resentful troopers. The grunts thought of them as slackers. "REMFs," they were called. "Rear-echelon motherfuckers." The Green Berets in the boonies often cheered the sight of Viet Cong rockets raining down on a rear-lines Army post.

Mabry was going on about the Coca-Cola. Well, the general was saying, clenching his teeth, there was no place in his United States Army for that kind of behavior. He expected Colonel Rheault to clean it out.

Rheault got the message and gravely nodded.

"I will do that," he said. Privately, he knew the Special Forces needed to be whipped into shape.

Mabry smiled and rose to his feet. He felt good about the new man. They shook hands.

"I'm only a telephone call away," he said. "You call me if you ever have a problem."

"I certainly will," Rheault answered. In fact, he had plenty of problems on his mind, but George Mabry was not the man to share them with. He flew back to Nha Trang.

Robert Rheault's path to Vietnam began improbably behind the high walls of a forested estate in Dedham, Massachusetts, on October 25, 1925. It was the heyday of the Roaring Twenties and two years before Charles Lindbergh flew the Atlantic. The Rheaults were immeasurably rich, and fixtures of Boston society, but it was his mother's side of the family that owned the silver spoons. His father was a fish out of water, a former corporal with the Royal Canadian Mounted Police.

That story began with the outbreak of World War I, in 1914, when Charles Rheault was on police duty in the Arctic Circle. He signed up with the Royal Canadian Dragoons and shipped out for Belgium. His future wife, Rosamunde Bradley, soon met him in Flanders, where she had gone to serve as a Red Cross nurse.

The disparity in their stations could not have been greater. Charles Rheault was a gruff enlisted man, she, a soft-spoken, shy, thirty-year-old heiress to a vast fortune in timber and mining, her family a pillar of the Boston establishment. Romance rooted slowly; only some years after the war, when he was assigned as a guide to one of her father's hunting expeditions to Canada, did their relationship resume.

Charles Rheault had not rejoined the Mounties. "It would have meant going back into an organization and working for people that had been his subordinates," his son said years later. The Rheaults settled in Dedham, where Charles assumed a position as a supernumerary in the family businesses, and they began to raise a family.

Robert was the youngest of three sons, educated in the traditional manner of well-off New England youth: first Brooks School and then Phillips Exeter Academy. He was a B student, handsome and popular. His sports were rifle and crew. But the silver spoon was beginning to gag him; he was his father's son, after all. In the attic, a trunk load of old sabers, Eskimo and Indian gear, and Sam Browne belts had left their impression. At sixteen, he ran off to Wyoming to be a cowboy. He would make his own way, he said, be his own man.

The shadows of another war were falling on America. The Nazis had overrun Poland, France, and the Low Countries and were bombing London. Young men of his class were volunteering to fly for the RAF.

Rheault was itching to do something, and the war held promise. In any event, the life of a ranch hand had turned out to be less than romantic. The pay was terrible, but worse than that, the most he could look forward to was chasing cows and mending fences.

He flirted with joining the Marines after the attack on Pearl Harbor. Eventually he accepted an appointment to the U.S. Military Academy arranged by Sen. Henry Cabot Lodge, a family friend. At sixteen, he was the youngest cadet in his class.

Despite an accelerated wartime schedule, he graduated in 1946, too late to be a hero. He and his classmates felt "a deep sense of embarrassment having missed the big war," he recalled. "Things were different then." Now he faced occupation duty in Germany.

Caroline Young, the vivacious Vassar art student he had been dating, put down her foot. She wouldn't wait around for him to come back, she said. It's now or never.

Okay, he said, let's get married. His father, a rigid Roman Catholic, boycotted their wedding, a grand Episcopal affair at St. John's Cathedral in New York.

From the standpoint of a young man in a hurry, the slow pace of postwar promotions was intolerable. Garrison duty in Germany and then Korea was miserable. He stalled at the rank of captain and sleep-walked through a series of stateside assignments. He hated the Army—it was so plebeian. To escape the humdrum he even took on a stint teaching French at West Point. Finally, in 1960, he was introduced to the Special Forces.

It was love at first jump. "I've finally found my niche," Rheault wrote to a friend. "This is what I like to do."

The conventional wisdom was that an officer should not stay long with the irregular warfare unit if he knew what was good for him. Rheault rejected the advice: "To hell with my career."

Special Forces not only extricated him from the dullards of the Regular Army brass, it was fun. Assigned to the 10th Special Forces Group in Germany, he skied with the Norwegian home guard, went scuba diving with the

Greek raider force on Crete, roped up rock cliffs with West German mountain troops. His unit was flung around Europe and the Middle East, training the Jordanian parachutists, the Pakistani rangers, the Iranian special forces, and medics for the Tunisian army. Other missions took him to Turkey, Saudi Arabia, and even the Himalayas to reconnoiter Chinese positions during the Sino-Indian border war of 1962.

"We had people going left, right, left, and sideways," he would remember fondly, looking back at kinder days, "and anytime there was a mission, people wanted to go. We skied, scuba dove, we sky dived. It was always with some sort of dim, distant military justification, but a lot of it was just allowing people to indulge their sports at Army expense."

Special Forces doctrine rested on small highly trained teams to operate behind enemy lines at the outbreak of war. Each team included experts in explosives, communications, intelligence, and psychological warfare. There were medics and language specialists. With the rising threat of Wars of National Liberation in remote regions of Africa, Latin America, and Asia, specialists in pig-breeding, fishing, and farming were added to their groups. At the bottom line, however, all of the soldiers were infantrymen, the best.

In Germany, Rheault's team was responsible for sabotage and stay-behind agent nets in Czechoslovakia. They regularly played hide-and-seek with the Communist border police. Another favorite pastime was war games against the 7th Army, the main U.S. battle group in Europe.

For the Green Berets, the exercises really were games. On one exercise Rheault's band of guerrillas slipped into the quarters of a sleeping 7th Army general, painted a thin red line across his throat, and pinned a note to his pajamas: "You are dead." At another time they disguised themselves as MPs and waved convoys of Army fuel trucks off into the mountains.

The Special Forces were to the Army establishment what Jesuits were to the Catholic church. They shook the Army up. The Special Forces allowed men who loved soldiering to do it. And it afforded an escape from the growing consensus that nuclear weapons had made war unthinkable. In the era of ICBMs and massive nuclear retaliation, the commandos were throwbacks to an earlier ideal of noble warriors, killing only when it was necessary, honorable, and personal.

"Unfortunately, the 7th Army and the Army as a whole did not learn how helpless they were against a guerrilla force," Rheault would write later, years after Saigon had been lost. "All of their high-tech gear—armored personnel carriers, aircraft, helicopters, sophisticated communications, and powerful weapons—were useless against the guerrillas."

The hand-painted green beret on a wooden sign over the doorway in Saigon was the only clue to what was going on upstairs. An attractive receptionist sat at a desk near the door, and people wandered in thinking it was a restaurant.

It was 1957. The Special Forces mission to Vietnam had begun as a quiet intelligence and training project housed in the nondescript apartment building in the Chinese section of Saigon. Behind the receptionist was a room full of machine guns, automatic rifles, and crates of ammunition. Upstairs, the rooms were packed with CIA agents and Special Forces men in civilian clothes.

The units were a burr under the saddle of the U.S. military mission and the Saigon government.

Its main task was to create a local Special Forces counterpart to carry out sabotage and intelligence missions in Laos and North Vietnam. But the Vietnamese Special Forces (the Luc Luong Dac Biet, or LLDB) were quickly expropriated by presidential cronies and deployed as private guard forces for their factories and plantations. They also made good agents to spy on the Americans.

Another cause for friction was the Green Berets' relationship with Montagnard tribesmen in the Central Highlands. With CIA money and supplies, the Green Berets were organizing the villages into militia strong enough to repel the Viet Cong. The program soon was a victim of its own success. The Saigon government, which had always viewed the natives with contempt and fear, was inflamed by the creation of a foreign-controlled army on its soil; it moved to reassert its authority over them. Many Montagnard units revolted at the betrayal, running amok and executing some of their U.S. advisers. Such developments did not endear the Green Berets to the American military mission in Saigon, which had long bristled at the free-wheeling style of the Special Forces and their CIA godfathers. The Montagnard program, in any event, had outgrown the spy agency's ability to manage it with discretion. It was turned over to the Pentagon.

But close links between the CIA and Green Berets necessarily remained in place, particularly in intelligence collection. Few of the CIA's civilian agent handlers, after all, could be stationed in remote jungle camps without drawing attention to themselves. And only Special Forces teams were adequately trained and equipped to operate in Laos, Cambodia, and occasionally, North Vietnam. The CIA defined the missions; the Green Berets, leading teams of locally hired Chinese-ethnic mercenaries, or "Nungs," carried them out.

The covert nature of such operations required the Green Berets to keep the CIA's clandestine bookkeeping practices intact: Weapons, uniforms, and food for special missions were drawn locally or from secret CIA suppliers in Okinawa. Funding came from "black budgets," CIA money laundered through other Pentagon programs or, conversely, Defense Department money funneled through the CIA. The code name for the financial deception was Parasol Switchback.

It was during this gray era that Bob Rheault arrived for his first Vietnam tour as deputy commanding officer for operations and intelligence with the 5th Special Forces Group. Basically, he said, he was a troubleshooter.

"I would go out to a camp, put on a tiger suit and get rid of my insignia because I felt that was the only way you could find out what was going on," he would recall. Billeted in Saigon, dining in French restaurants with CIA agents and diplomats from the embassy, his was a beau geste kind of duty with its "moments of sheer panic and terror and then back to a relatively civilized environment." With CIA agent Edward Lansdale, Lt. Col. John Paul Vann, and former marine Daniel Ellsberg, Rheault had joined a succession of counterinsurgency experts who were obsessed by the unfolding tragedy in South Vietnam.

A pillar of their belief was that doom awaited entry of the large U.S. ground units into the war. A disaster was in the wind. Success would come only from the painstaking process of "winning hearts and minds," a euphemism for the carefully calibrated application of sugar and sticks. By day there would be aid projects, by night, counterterror doled out to the Viet Cong. The trouble was, the strategy nearly all depended on the government in Saigon.

"In the final analysis," Kennedy had said in the fall of 1963, "it is their war. They are the ones who have to win it or lose it." The president was prophetic. Saigon's endemic corruption and resistance to change was giving him second thoughts. In October he signed an order to remove one thousand troops from Vietnam. Covering his bases, however, he gave a provisional go-ahead to the CIA to remove Ngo Dinh Diem from power.

Lyndon Johnson was a blunter man. With Diem assassinated on November 1 and Kennedy dead three weeks later, the withdrawal order was quietly rescinded. Less than a year later, the bombing of North Vietnam began, followed by the dispatch of U.S. ground units. The "body count" became the principal device for measuring progress: If they were dead, they were Red.

Rheault's contempt for the Regular Army mushroomed with each escalation. The Green Berets were "being diluted by expansion," he complained. "I noticed the quality of officers going downhill. They were young, inexperienced and untrained in many cases." When he left Vietnam in late 1964, "I swore to myself I was going to come back and command that group, and that I would be the first guy to command it that had 'carried the rucksack.' "

Washington in 1965 was on a war footing, stimulated by the Vietnam buildup as well as trouble in Brazil, Panama, and the Dominican Republic. China was slipping into the chaotic Cultural Revolution. Moscow was rattling its missiles and stoking "Wars of National Liberation." Cuba was an open sore.

Rheault arrived in Washington impatient with people who knew or cared little about Vietnam. He was assigned to the Army War College in Carlisle, Pennsylvania, an hour and a half from the capital, but he also arranged to enroll at George Washington University for a simultaneous master's degree in international relations. His thesis compared the Kurds of Iraq to the Montagnards of Vietnam.

The Pentagon's money for counterinsurgency was peaking, fueled by the budgets of the Kennedy years. When Rheault finished his master's, he was assigned to counterinsurgency and special activities in the Joint Chiefs of Staff. His duty was to coordinate "black" cross-border operations from Vietnam into neighboring Laos and Cambodia with the White House, State Department, and CIA.

Official policy maintained that there were no U.S. units operating in Laos and Cambodia, nations officially neutral in the Vietnam conflict. The cross-border teams were stripped of U.S. insignia and carried Soviet and Chinese rifles; they were expected to die rather than be captured and paraded as trophies. In earlier years the fiction was of little concern; Ho Chi Minh and Cambodia's Prince Sihanouk each found reasons to let the "secret" go unchallenged. In "neutral" Laos, the CIA was running its own guerrilla war against North Vietnamese troops with the help of the Green Berets. In America, as domestic support for the bottomless war evaporated, pressure to keep the activities secret from Congress and the public mounted.

At the Joint Chiefs, knowledge of particular clandestine operations was increasingly restricted as fears of a leak deepened. Rheault was among the insiders. His access often infuriated senior officers outside the loop.

"Colonel," a general complained one day as Rheault rushed by with a classified folder, "I've got clearances you've never seen."

"I'm sure you do," Rheault retorted, "but you don't get to see this one."

His rounds included the offices of Walt Rostow at the White House, George Ball at the State Department, William Colby at the CIA, and Cyrus Vance, the deputy secretary of defense. There were trips to Pearl Harbor, hurried flights to Saigon. As the political sensitivity of the operations grew, the president was less and less informed about agent drops or reconnaissance behind enemy lines. Lyndon Johnson, the military men believed, didn't want to know; he wanted to be protected in case of a flap.

"You are not going to ask the president to approve a mission where two Americans and four Montagnards are going ten miles across the Laotian border," Rheault believed. "It was an education in how the government works."

At forty-one, in 1966, Rheault made full colonel and a general's star was within sight. Once again, friends counseled him not to stay in "black ops" too long—too far out of the mainstream, they worried. His career would be frozen or chewed up in some flap.

But the Regular Army was not for him, he answered; he was never going back. The full colonel's eagles "meant to me was that I was doing very well in spite of not taking the mainstream." He began angling to head the Green Berets in Vietnam, the world's best command to a man of his persuasions. The first stop was Okinawa, heading the 1st Special Forces, responsible for covert activities in an arc extending from Taiwan to Indonesia.

Then, in May 1969, the call finally came: Nha Trang, commanding the 5th Special Forces Group, all the Green Berets in Vietnam. He rushed off without taking leave.

11

Lee Brumley studied Thai Khac Chuyen's dossier with his flat brown eyes. The twenty-six-year-old captain, head of counterintelligence for the Green Berets, was a specialist in the war's most thankless task, rooting out Viet Cong spies.

Brumley's stolid personality was perfectly engineered for the bottomless task. His ancestors were native Americans who had roamed the Oklahoma plains for centuries. In the early 1900s his maternal grandfather, a Chicasaw scout, battled Pancho Villa in Arizona and rode with the U.S. Army's punitive expeditions to the gates of Mexico City. Other military careers weaved through the family. His father and his uncles had fought in both world wars, seen action in Korea, been posted to West Germany. The Brumleys had been going off to war for a hundred years.

Growing up in Duncan, Oklahoma, in the 1950s, Lee devoured fiction for young boys like *The Santa Fe Trail, Thirty Seconds over Tokyo*, and *The Bridges of Toko-Ri*. During high school in the Kennedy years, he picked up the fad for Ian Fleming and John le Carré, sacked groceries after school, and earned an Eagle Scout badge. At sixteen there was dating and cars, an ordinary teenage life. At Oklahoma State, he enrolled on an ROTC scholarship, married his high-school sweetheart, Karen, and in 1966, he arrived in Vietnam, a freshly minted lieutenant.

What he would remember the most was the noise and smoke—the sharp, ear-splitting blast of bombs and the acrid clouds that filled the air—nothing like the movies. The 173rd Airborne Division squared off against battle-hardened North Vietnamese units in a series of battles and clobbered them. It was the set-piece campaign the American command had been relishing, but much to its surprise when the smoke cleared a year later, the Communists were still taking the country.

Lee Brumley left Vietnam convinced that good intelligence was the missing factor. Up against American firepower, mobility, and control of the skies, the Communists shouldn't win. But the enemy was doing a better job. It understood the American side's strengths and weaknesses. It could predict the movements of U.S. and Saigon troops before their orders were dry. Its spies were everywhere. Like termites, they had gotten inside the house. When Brumley returned from Vietnam he signed up for counterintelligence, six months of learning how to get them out.

His courses buzzed with a topical practicality. Kim Philby, the former British liaison to the CIA, had recently surfaced in Moscow, revealing himself as a long-term Soviet mole. American intelligence was still in shock, particularly since Philby's regular Washington lunch partner in the early 1960s was James Jesus Angleton, the CIA's chief of counterintelligence.

Few students failed to daydream about being at the center of such events. A career in intelligence was alluring. But Brumley's war was in Vietnam, not

Moscow or Berlin. Hanoi was his target, and the elusive Viet Cong. He had seen Americans die. He yearned to get back.

Counterintelligence included instruction in the traditional tradescraft of espionage: finding, recruiting, and running foreign agents. There were classes in surveillance, radios, dead drops, and invisible writing. There was photography, microdots, lockpicking and electronic bugs. But the focus of the course was on learning how to prevent enemy intelligence from penetrating U.S. forces.

Graduating in late 1966, the compact captain looked forward to trying out his new skills on the Viet Cong. But the Army had a new enemy in its ranks, and it said it needed him stateside. It assigned him to Fort Sill, Oklahoma, with orders to destroy an antiwar group on base.

Using the techniques he had learned from his counterintelligence studies at Fort Holabird, Brumley penetrated a group of antiwar GIs with wiretaps, bugs, hidden cameras, and informants recruited from the stockade. Its members were arrested, court-martialed, and sent to jail.

Another stretch at Fort Holabird now followed, a career course that broadened and deepened his familiarity with the wide range of global U.S. intelligence operations. Then it was time to go back to Vietnam. Now twenty-six, Brumley requested assignment with the Special Forces. Army intelligence, he knew, was being diluted by the war, filling Fort Holabird with apathetic draftees avoiding the infantry by enlisting in his specialty. He was a professional; he wanted the real thing.

Brumley arrived in Nha Trang in mid-1968, posted as counterintelligence officer for the 5th Special Forces Group. He threw himself into the work. At night, when the other officers found refuge at the bar, blotting out the war with beer and whiskey, Lee Brumley studied the files.

And they were the worst kind of files, the ones that stripped away the upbeat rhetoric about Vietnam. Here were glimpses deep inside the political struggle, reports from his own spies that showed that America really had two enemies in Vietnam—the Communists, and their immense web of collaborators inside the Saigon army and government.

Brumley would snort when he heard the virtues of the Saigon regime extolled. American officials could praise the virtues of our heroic ally all they wanted, but he didn't have the luxury. Like any other American intelligence officer in Vietnam, he operated on the assumption that a friendly South Vietnamese officer could be his enemy as much as the Viet Cong; in many cases they were the same thing.

By the morning of June 9, when Budge Williams handed him the dossier of Thai Khac Chuyen, Lee Brumley was already hyperalert to treachery of all sorts. One of his investigations had revealed that top South Vietnamese Green Berets were selling their U.S.-supplied arms and equipment to the Viet Cong. He had also learned that the general heading the South Vietnamese Green Berets was trying to infiltrate Project Gamma with his spies. Now, as Brumley studied the file, it occurred to him that Chuyen could be a triple agent, working for the South Vietnamese as well as for Hanoi.

Something new had been added to Chuyen's dossier since May 19, he noticed, the date when the outgoing Major Thrasher had forwarded Smith's report with the captured photos to his successor, Major Crew. One of Project Gamma's Vietnamese informants had reported that a "new chubby interpreter" working in Thanh Tri was "asking pointed questions about SF personnel and duties." That could only be Chuyen, whom Marasco had transferred to his own office. Rumors were also circulating among other Vietnamese agents that the same interpreter was a Viet Cong spy who had a female collaborator in Muc Hoa.

Brumley also noted with impatience that background checks on Chuyen still hadn't come back from Saigon. It had been almost three weeks. He fired off a classified cable to a friend at the 5th Special Force liaison detachment in Saigon, asking him to expedite a records check on Chuyen with "utmost discretion." No South Vietnamese intelligence clerks, he emphasized, should be alerted to the problem with Chuyen.

Next he noticed that Chuyen had still not been scheduled for a session on the lie detector. Every day that went by with the agent at large, he worried, increased the vulnerability of their operations. He placed a call to a polygraph operator he knew.

Finally, there was Sergeant Alvin Smith. A curious bird, Brumley thought. Williams had told him that Smith was an experienced agent handler, that he had made allusions to once working for the CIA.

As Brumley thumbed through Chuyen's dossier, it didn't add up: Smith's reports were poorly prepared; his written assessments of Chuyen were wordy and vague; he had learned almost nothing about Chuyen's employment history or family. It was a curious lapse, since Chuyen had admitted he had brothers in North Vietnam.

Since joining counterintelligence, Brumley had experienced a disconcerting set of surprises, such as encountering stateside GIs who were not merely against the war but openly sympathetic to the Viet Cong. Why wouldn't they be in Vietnam just as well? he wondered. Suddenly, he wanted to know a lot more about the strange Sergeant Smith. He made a note to request Smith's classified personnel file.

"The problem is," Budge Williams was saying, "we still need that dumbass to get Chuyen in."

Across from his desk, Lee Brumley sat listening.

"There's no damn way around that," Williams went on. "Smith is the only one he'll trust to come to a meeting at this point."

There was a knock on the doorway and David Crew came in. With a quick, bashful smile, the darkly handsome colonel quietly took a seat. The task at hand, Williams went on, was to find a way to get Chuyen to come to Saigon without creating any suspicion so they could polygraph him. If there was a way to do it without Smith, he'd like to hear it.

Crew wanted to know what the problem was.

Williams and Brumley brought him up-to-date. They reviewed their apprehension about Smith and their worries about involving him with Chuyen any longer. After all, they said, the sergeant had created this problem. Their dilemma was how to get Chuyen to come in without using Smith.

Crew appreciated their caution, he said softly, but wasn't Chuyen really the more immediate, and frankly, more likely threat? Go ahead and use Smith, he said. Anyone else might make the agent suspicious.

Williams and Brumley locked eyes. Then Williams got up, opened the door, and hollered across the adjacent room.

Sergeant Smith walked in and was offered a seat. His mustache was neatly trimmed, his blue eyes alert. He was still wearing his cover nametag, "Sands."

Appearing to take him into his full confidence, Williams explained the plan: Smith was to arrange a meeting with Chuyen in Saigon, at which time he would tell the agent that he was being considered for a very important mission. But first, he would say, Chuyen had to submit to a polygraph examination. If the test went all right, he would get the job. If he didn't want to take the polygraph, he wouldn't be considered for the job. Simple as that.

Smith should emphasize to Chuyen that it was a very important mission, Williams said, ultra top secret. That should bring him in, whether he was working for the VC or not. The examination would be in Saigon on June 12. They ordered him to get in touch with Chuyen right away.

Smith quickly left the room but returned after only a few minutes. Chuyen, he had just found out, had quit his job the day before and left word he'd gone to Saigon.

Williams shook his head. Get down to Saigon, he ordered Smith. Find Chuyen and track him until you're told to bring him in.

Back at his desk, Brumley rolled a pad of white paper and three carbons into his typewriter and began tapping. He marked some of the paragraphs secret, the others confidential.

9 June 1969
MEMORANDUM FOR THE RECORD
SUBJECT: "Possible NVA/VC Penetration of USASF De-

tachment B-57, Muc Hoa Site."

1 (S) On 9 June 1969, the undersigned was informed by Major Crew, Commanding Officer, USAF Detachment B-57 that A-414 had received an intelligence report that Thai, Khac Chuyen, was a VC agent. This report originated from the "A" Detachment Intelligence net, which is separate from the B-57 net. This report stated that the interpreter for S5 was a VC agent who worked with a woman in Muc Hoa.

2. (C) On the above date, a meeting was held with the Commanding Officer, Operations Officer, and former Case Officer of B-57 to determine a course of action to apprehend the subject. The apprehension would allow the subject to be interrogated and polygraphed. At the conclusion of the meet-

ing, it was agreed that subject would be contacted and told to report to Saigon for a job interview with SGT Sands (Case Officer). When Chuyen reached Saigon, he was to be met by Sands and polygraphed.

3. (C) Future actions or extraction to Nha Trang will be based upon the results of the polygraph examination.

Brumley signed his name at the bottom, dropped it into a folder stamped "SECRET-NOFORN," and filed it under the Ts for "Thai, Khac Chuyen," as it had been written in the report. Years into the war, keeping Vietnamese names straight was turning out to be a major hurdle for Americans, even the counterintelligence officers.

As Brumley was typing his memo, Williams and Crew were parting for the night outside the B-57 office.

They had a rescheduled meeting with the CIA in Saigon tomorrow, Crew reminded Williams. Maybe they should bring up the Chuyen problem with them.

Why not? Williams thought. They're supposed to be the pros.

12

The Central Intelligence Agency occupied the top three floors of the new U.S. Embassy in Saigon. Designed by Edward Durrell Stone and completed in 1968, it was a six-story steel box wrapped in a white concrete sunscreen, making it look like a Holiday Inn girded for battle. It replaced a colonial-era building down by the river that had been demolished by a Viet Cong car bomb the year before.

David Crew and Budge Williams arrived at the embassy gates at 9 A.M. on June 10, showed their identification—Williams was still traveling under his longtime cover name of Ben Wells—and proceeded to the sixth-floor CIA executive offices.

Williams knew his way around the CIA offices from his first tour in Vietnam, having picked up fake IDs, radios, cryptography equipment, and silencer-equipped pistols from the agency tech support shop. Its linoleum floors, pale green walls, government-issue desks, and the middle-aged men wandering the halls in their short-sleeve white shirts suggested nothing more than a typical federal office.

Williams had nothing but loathing for the CIA. The bureaucrats sat safely in air-conditioned comfort, he thought, while the Green Berets did all their dirty work.

The Saigon station was home office for some seven hundred CIA employees in Vietnam—intelligence specialists and police advisers, labor-union organizers, political experts and economists, interrogators, linguists, lockpickers, wiretappers, photo technicians, pilots, radio operators, personnel and payroll clerks, secretaries, drivers, guards, cooks, and psychiatrists. It was the largest CIA operation in the world outside of Washington. Even its regional offices in the five war zones of the country were bigger than most of the CIA stations in Africa.

Most CIA officials carried identification as State Department diplomats, employees of the U.S. Agency for International Development, or officers in the Navy, Army, Air Force, or Marines. But there was a myriad of other covers as well, inside and outside the government.

Inside the bureaucracy, the CIA's name was the Office of the Special Assistant to the Ambassador, or OSA. In the provinces, the agency often hung out such shingles as "Combined Studies Detachment," "Joint Technical Advisory Group," or "Studies and Observation Group," a joint military enterprise with specially selected Green Berets. Inside the so-called intelligence community—which included the swollen Army, Navy, and Air Force intelligence bureaucracies—and on documents and in casual cocktail conversation, the CIA was simply called CAS, which people thought might stand for Combined American Sources, but which had been synonymous with the agency for so long that its precise etymology was forgotten.

Various commercial airlines whose CIA ownership was lightly concealed—Air America, Air Asia, and Southern Air Transport, to name a few—gave refuge to the agency's pilots and operatives. Scores more worked undercover in the large American firms doing business in Vietnam, such as RMK-BRJ, the huge Texas-based construction firm; Ford Motor Company; and the U.S. banks with branches in Vietnam—Chase Manhattan, Wells Fargo, and City Bank of New York.

The CIA's mission had expanded so dramatically during the 1964–1968 buildup that its headquarters staff had overflowed to a half dozen offices around Saigon. It even had its own downtown hotel, the Duc, which came complete with an acceptable restaurant and a rooftop bar with a panoramic view of the nightly firefights and bombing.

The CIA's appropriation of so many U.S. government agencies for cover had sometimes blurred the distinction between them. The largest was CORDS, or Civil Operations/Revolutionary Development Systems, the so-called hearts-and-minds pacification program set up as an independent entity. CORDS was also commonly used as cover for the officials running the Phoenix program.

Publicly launched with great fanfare in 1967, Phoenix was touted as little more than an aggressive police program to identify, locate, arrest, and prosecute members of the "Viet Cong Infrastructure," or underground cadre, as if they were common criminals. It was a massive, bureaucratic, and belated response to the kidnapping, terror, and assassination the Viet Cong had practiced for years. Phoenix offices were quickly established at the province and district levels to gather and sift intelligence on Viet Cong personalities. Quick reaction teams called Provincial Reconnaissance Units, or PRUs, were set up to either "neutralize" the VC or bring them in.

But the program quickly ran afoul of incompetence, corruption, and treason. While some Phoenix directors carefully built solid bases of intelligence on the Viet Cong underground through the skillful use of defector interrogations and double agents, others dispatched their hunter-killer PRU teams as soon as suspects were fingered and assassinated them on the spot. In such an environment, Phoenix became ripe for manipulation. Vietnamese informants learned to use it as a protection racket, squeezing bribes from villagers to stay off the death lists. The corruption created resentment and alienation, which, in turn, opened the Phoenix teams to infiltration.

Phoenix was the logical compromise between the counterinsurgency emphasis of the Kennedy years and Lyndon Johnson's massive escalation, between the CIA and the Pentagon, between "hearts and minds" and "search and destroy." But its abuses were a tightly held secret inside the CIA, except to Green Berets who were borrowed for the program.

Many didn't care. It was all part of the war. "When you got 'em by the balls," the sign in the offices of many Phoenix operatives said, "their hearts and minds will follow."

Crew and Williams neared the end of the corridor and found the office they were looking for. Two men were inside talking.

Both looked like retired military officers, Williams thought as he walked in and shook hands. He was half right.

Bruce Scrymgeour, with gray hair and Norwegian blue eyes, was a former Navy captain who had served on ships in both the Atlantic and Pacific in World War II. In the mid-1950s he had transferred to the CIA and developed a speciality in Arab languages and the Middle East. He had been called out of retirement to work in Saigon as a CIA liaison to U.S. military units.

The fleshy man sitting at the desk in clear plastic glasses and an unmarked tropical U.S. Army uniform looked like a retired colonel. Clement Enking had been loaned to the CIA by the Air Force during the Korean War and had never really gone back. After subsequent tours with the CIA in the Philippines, Japan, and Vietnam, he was indistinguishable from a regular CIA officer—except to career agency professionals, who looked on such hybrids with disdain.

To outsiders like Crew and Williams, however, the distinction—had they known about it—was irrelevant. They were there to do business with the CIA. Enking and Scrymgeour sat just outside station chief Ted Shackley's office. They were, in fact, his liaisons to U.S. military units. They were the CIA.

The Green Berets sat down and exchanged light banter with the CIA men. The flight was fine, they said, lots of changes in Nha Trang recently. Things were looking up, a new CO with a great reputation, a West Point man with a previous Vietnam tour. A real Special Forces kind of guy, not another bureaucrat.

Crew and Enking quickly discovered that they had met before in Korea. Scrymgeour added that he had met Bob Rheault at the U.S. Embassy in Paris in 1963.

There were a number of things they came to talk about, Crew said, getting down to business. First of all, they wanted to discuss the possibility of running an operation into North Vietnam. They had an agent available, he said, who might be able to pull it off. After all, there was a need for agents on the ground to help downed pilots and locate POWs.

The CIA men sat back and shook their heads. They had plenty of assets up there, Enking said, smiling. Williams smiled back. He knew it was a dodge, a gentle way for the CIA men to say they didn't want the Green Berets screwing around in their territory. It was common knowledge that almost every agent the Special Forces had sent up there had been rounded up or doubled by the North Vietnamese. Williams also knew the CIA hadn't done much better on its own. They moved on.

Cambodia. Crew reviewed the situation with Project Gamma, noting that they had been getting some good photographs of trains running north from the port at Sihanoukville to Communist base areas in Cambodia. They'd also had some productive wiretaps on Cambodian government telephones, he said. The evidence was solid: The North Vietnamese army was getting as many supplies by sea through Sihanoukville as down the Ho Chi Minh trail from North Vietnam. Royal Cambodian Army officers, he added, were also funneling weapons to the NVA and still turning their backs on Communist occupation of the border areas.

The program to get pro-U.S. Cambodian units to fire on the collaborating units was showing some promise, Williams added. They were also making progress with the anti-Sihanouk units they were training at secret bases in the Central Highlands.

Scrymgeour and Enking nodded their approval. Good work. Everyone in the room knew that intelligence from Cambodia was a "hot button" of contention between Army intelligence and the CIA, whose analysts were convinced the Ho Chi Minh Trail was the main Communist supply route, not the port at Sihanoukville. The Air Force, responsible for bombing the Trail, backed the CIA.

Crew opened a new topic. They had an agent on their hands who might be a VC, a double agent.

The CIA men leaned forward, showing concern. Crew turned to Williams and asked him to summarize what they knew.

Williams started with the operations in Muc Hoa and Chuyen's employment three months earlier. Opening a folder, he took out the captured photo and placed it on Scrymgeour's desk. Then he put Chuyen's ID picture next to it. As the CIA men studied the photographs, Williams went on to explain that nobody had become excited about the pictures at first: The case officer who handled Chuyen, he said, tended to be a little jumpy. But an independent report had come in saying that "the new chubby interpreter" in Thanh Tri—significantly, the source did not know Chuyen's name—"was asking too many questions" and was rumored to be a Viet Cong spy.

What they were doing now, Williams said, was remedial work on the case. They planned to polygraph and interrogate Chuyen right away. Based on the results, they would decide what to do next.

That's where the agency came in, Crew said.

"We need to put this guy on ice somewhere until we figure out what's going on. We can't give him to the Vietnamese—that would be like turning him right over to the Viet Cong."

"And to Congress," Enking added softly.

That was the damndest thing, Williams thought. Some goddam allies, some goddam war. Can't even trust your goddam ally, because they're all corrupt or fucking Viet Cong spies. He had seen more than one senior Green Beret officer transferred home because he blew the whistle on his Vietnamese counterpart's stealing.

What did Scrymgeour and Enking think? Crew asked. Did the CIA have an island somewhere they could stash this guy? At least for a little while?

The two CIA men listened sympathetically. Unfortunately, they said, they couldn't offer any help. The CIA didn't have any islands—didn't, in fact, really have any of its own jails in Vietnam. The National Police controlled all the jails.

Anyway, Scrymgeour said, it was too expensive to fly him out of the country, to Okinawa or Panama, where they occasionally "cooled off" a big fish.

The Green Berets listened.

They could understand their problem, the CIA men said. The Cambodian stuff was too sensitive to risk a flap. The Foreign Relations Committee would go nuts if they found out what was going on there. But the guy they were having a problem with seemed like small change.

"Well, what do you think we should do?" Williams asked. He liked to get to the point.

The CIA men hesitated, smoking their cigarettes.

Finally, Enking exhaled and looked up through his plain glasses.

"Well, you know," he said, "the most effective course of action may well be to get rid of him."

The remark floated in the room. The Green Berets weren't sure what they had heard. Was it a suggestion? Some kind of indirect approval?

"We can't sanction anything like that, of course," Enking quickly added. "Officially, we can't approve anything like that."

Crew and Williams listened. It was sinking in.

A wink and nod, that's how it was done. He ran it through his mind again: "We can't officially sanction it, but getting rid of him might be efficient."

They got it. They didn't need a flashing neon sign. They looked at each other, then rose to leave.

The CIA men were studiously quiet.

Williams and Crew said good-bye. They had their answer: If their agent was a problem, just get rid of him. Kill him. What's the big problem?

They walked down the hall, put on their berets, and walked out into the tropical heat.

13

Alvin Smith finally had an address. It was a house in one of Saigon's maze of smokey alleys down near the river, Phan Thanh Gian Street. It took him hours to find it. Now, as he stood at the top of the dirt passageway, dressed in his felt beret and green fatigues, he was suddenly aware how far he was from another American.

A stream of Vietnamese swirled around and past him in the twilight. His skin grew cool and moist. He walked forward warily.

Westerners were rarely alone in Saigon. Thousands of U.S. soldiers and civilians walked the capital's streets, drank in the bars, stayed in the hotels, went to the movies, or just went sight-seeing, cameras in hand. After a few days in the city, most Americans learned to relax. It was almost like a night out in Chinatown; the Vietnamese faded to a backdrop.

A few blocks off the mainstream, though, the other Saigon appeared, the world of the "Orient," forbidding, exotic, closed in. The street signs were foreign, the people unsmiling, the smells unfamiliar. Alvin Smith was just far enough off the main drag, a few blocks where "round-eyes" were rare, to feel vulnerable. The dusty alley suddenly became forbidding, even frightening. He wondered whether someone might be watching him from behind the shuttered windows. He was sure he had been followed earlier in the day.

He took a few steps forward. The pungent smoke of fish sauce and charcoal assaulted his nose. At the corner, peasant women lit joss sticks in prayer boxes, clasped their hands and jabbered in a rocking motion. Other women, sweeping their stoops, seemed to be eyeing him warily. There seemed to be no men around.

He pulled a slip of paper out of his pocket and checked the address again. He resumed his walk ahead, looking for number 53/1/46.

Finally, he saw it, a one-story cement house. A thin young woman stood on the porch with a child on her hip, talking to a neighbor. Chuyen's wife, Lien, he guessed. Smith walked up and pronounced her husband's name with a question mark at the end, "Thai Khac Chuyen?" Somewhat flustered, she nodded, called inside, and then led him through the door.

Chuyen came into the living room looking happily surprised to see his former boss. He and his wife exchanged a low staccato of Vietnamese, and Lien padded off to another room. A moment later she returned with tea and a small plate of sweet cakes, placing them on a low table in front of the couch. As the two men sat, Lien's eighteen-month-old child crawled across the polished tile floor and tugged at Smith's cuffs. The sergeant leaned down and tussled the boy's hair, but Lien scooped him up and quickly left the men to talk.

When she had gone, Smith got right to the point. There was new work for him, he said quietly, a very good job.

Chuyen looked eager. That was good, he said. Muc Hoa was a bad place. He had to pay bribes to the Vietnamese Special Forces captain to get in and out of the area. He wanted to work for only the Americans now, no Vietnamese.

That was good news, Smith said, because he had a very important, very sensitive job for him. Chuyen brightened. But first, Smith resumed, he'd have to answer a lot of questions. He'd have also to pass a very stiff test, a lie detector examination, to reaffirm his loyalty.

"No problem," Chuyen quickly said. He was eager to prove himself again. Good, Smith smiled. He was very happy to hear that. He was sorry they hadn't been able to work together in Muc Hoa anymore, he missed their conversations. Nha Trang was desk work, he chatted on, he didn't enjoy it much. Quickly, the conversation petered out. Smith gave Chuyen directions to the Special Forces liaison detachment and told him to be there tomorrow at 9 A.M.

They talked awkwardly for a minute more, then Smith rose to leave and moved toward the door. He gave Chuyen the time and place one more time, shook his hand, then exited the house. He hurried out of the alley.

The executive jet pivoted at the top of the runway in the gun-gray dawn, its dual rear engines revving into a high whine. The pilots waited for a signal from the control tower. When the first rays of the sun painted the runway, the jet began rolling down the concrete. Quickly accelerating, it lifted steeply into the air, roaring over a passel of fishing boats bobbing on the bay of Nha Trang. It was just after 6 A.M. on Thursday, June 12.

The aluminum jet banked south and streaked toward Saigon in clear skies. A bright yellow glow filled the cabin. Alvin Smith, wearing his old name tag "Sands," sat back in his seat, fidgeting with his thoughts. He had raced back from Saigon after finding his agent and had given his briefing.

Chuyen bought the story, he reported. He would come in for a meeting.

Now, flying to Saigon, he felt a foreboding. Had he done the right thing? Was he really sure about the picture? Had he jumped to a conclusion just to get back into action?

Events were moving fast. He was torn by ambivalence. He felt like he had betrayed his friend. After all, he had set the trap. One thing for sure, it was getting late for second thoughts.

Across the aisle sat a heavyset civilian in thick black glasses, polygraph operator Vincent J. Driver. Next to him sat a thin young sleeping Vietnamese man, Ta Xuan Cuong, Driver's interpreter. Like most Vietnamese who worked with Americans, he was given a nickname, "Joel."

In the front seat was a sandy-haired young man in plain green fatigues, reading a magazine and rapping his palm on the arm of the seat. Warrant Officer Eddie Boyle, twenty-seven, was Lee Brumley's deputy for the first interrogation of Thai Khac Chuyen, scheduled for that morning.

Boyle, a wise-cracking Irishman from the Bronx, had been involved in scores of interrogations since arriving in Vietnam a year earlier. Sometimes they ended neatly with a confession, sometimes they didn't.

He wasn't in favor of the war, he told his sister before leaving for Vietnam; he thought it was a waste of lives and money. But he planned to make the Army his career, so he had to go. Counterintelligence training at Fort Holabird, followed by a year in Washington as a special agent on security investigations, and then a year at Vietnamese language school in Texas, had prepared him as well as anybody. He was ready.

And he was proud. Boyle's grandfather had been a patrolman with the Irish constabulary. Coal miners, railway workers, and farmers, first in Ireland and England and then in frontier America, filled out the family tree.

His father, who settled in the Bronx, was a car inspector for the New York Central. After Eddie graduated from Cardinal Hayes High, he was expected to be a working stiff, too. College was out.

"Look at me," his father would rage, his brogue thickening in anger. "I did fine without it. Why do you need it?"

They fought over it all through Eddie's senior year of high school, his mother and sister taking his side. Finally, the three of them won, and in 1960 Eddie went off to Fordham. After all the fighting, however, he found it boring and quickly dropped out.

He tried his hand as a draftsman. He got bored again. Finally, the only thing left was the Army. He signed up for three years, went off to Germany in an artillery unit, but when his time was up, walked away. Back home in the Bronx, he tried selling insurance. That didn't pan out, so he found work as a roofer. Seven months later, he was back at the enlistment office. The recruiter offered something new: training as a special agent with the counterintelligence corps, a profession. He was gone the next week.

It was September 1964. Civil-rights protest was in full swing. A movement against Vietnam was heating up. Professors were calling for draft resistance, and Malcolm X for revolution. Students were going off to Cuba to pick sugarcane. Marijuana had moved from the ghettos to the campus.

Protest groups provided full employment for Army counterintelligence agents, who helped the FBI with wiretaps and surveillance. The work suited Eddie Boyle; it put him at the center of world events, and far from the Bronx.

He met a nice girl in Baltimore who worked for a trucking company. They married, and by all accounts became the happiest, most popular couple in their circle. Finally, he had found something he liked and was good at.

His wife Dorothy's friends worried when he went off to Vietnam in 1968. They would crowd around her desk at work when she brought in his letters. Eddie was always light-hearted, at least when he first arrived in Saigon.

"Things are great so far, considering I am in a war zone," he wrote. "No uniforms, I am in civilian status. Housemaids galore, TV in room. Movies in club every night. Air conditioned office, air conditioned room soon. Hot water. 'O' club on compound. Security is great all over town."

He was assigned to the 525th Military Intelligence Group, headquartered in an old French fort off the main road from the airport. The agents living there had rehabilitated its old saloon and dubbed it the "Ponderosa."

"Now for the bad news," he wrote. "Hot, humid. Cigarettes are mildewed.

Mosquitos are thick. Saigon is dirty, filthy. All the natives look shifty. Traffic is unbelievable. People crap in the streets. The smell is unbearable and nauseating. I am breaking out in a heat rash. The monsoon is starting. Rain every day. The rain makes it hotter."

In a letter to his sister, Mary Boyle O'Hara, he turned down her husband's offer to send him a pistol.

"I am armed to the teeth," he cracked. "I have a .45 grease gun, a .45 pistol in my room and office. I have an M-16 and M-60 machine gun for air travel."

Mary laughed when she read that. Eddie could never hurt a fly, she thought. Later, when he wrote home about being inducted into a Montagnard tribe and having to take a sacrificial slice off a live bull's leg, he said he threw up. But he did it.

His family worried about him as time passed. He was developing a hard side from his time in Vietnam. He wrote that it was impossible to tell the civilians from the Viet Cong. All the South Vietnamese were out for themselves. They just wanted Americans for the money.

But he hadn't changed completely, they were glad to find out. He had risked his life running into a burning apartment building to save a Vietnamese family.

That was her Eddie, Mary Boyle thought, tough on the outside, soft on the inside. Still, she wanted him home. One reason was "the dream."

It had started coming to her every night in the spring of 1969, waking her up, and always, always the same—she kept seeing him in jail.

She couldn't figure out what it meant. Why would Eddie be in jail? she asked her husband.

Lee Brumley stayed in Nha Trang while Chuyen was brought in for interrogation. Nixon and Thieu had just announced the beginning of U.S. troop withdrawals, setting off a collective nervous breakdown among his agents. Fearing abandonment, they were signaling requests for emergency meetings by making chalk marks on the walls around Nha Trang.

"It looks like they're playing tic-tac-toe out there," one case officer joked, coming in from his daily drive around town.

The titters masked a genuine nervousness: No one knew what was coming next. Politicians had talked about ending the war for years but no one had ever actually started to do it. Who knew what would happen? Would we just leave? How fast?

The Vietnamese agents searched the faces of their American case officers, looking for reassurance. What would they do when the Americans left?

There was another matter holding Brumley's attention, the dossier of Sgt. Alvin Smith. Inside the official 201 file, with its wad of orders, health records, and fitness reports going back to 1944, was a seven-page single-spaced essay.

It was an autobiographical sketch, he discovered. Smith had written it in 1965 at Fort Holabird as part of his agent handler's course. Large red block

letters were stamped at the top: SECRET-NOFORN. Maybe it wasn't supposed to be there.

From the first sentence, Lee Brumley was intrigued. By the time he had
finished, he was alarmed.

The twin-engine Volpar jet touched down at Ton Son Nhut airport in
Saigon at 8 A.M. and taxied to the Air America terminal. Floyd Cotton, one
of the few black counterintelligence warrant officers in Vietnam, picked up the
party after waiting an hour at the wrong terminal. The five men—Cotton,
Alvin Smith, Ed Boyle, Vincent Driver, and his interpreter—then drove
through downtown Saigon to a former French police station, headquarters for
the 5th Special Forces liaison detachment. Driver and his assistant lumbered
inside with their bulky polygraph equipment, along with Boyle. Smith and
Cotton walked to the tall iron gates and waited for Chuyen.

At exactly 10 A.M. Chuyen walked up, dressed in freshly pressed slacks and
a white shirt, freshly bathed and smiling, his thick black hair neatly combed.
Smith identified Chuyen to the sentry, who directed him to sign the registry
before allowing him inside, and then introduced him to Cotton.

Chuyen seemed nonchalant as they walked across the small compound.
Eventually they reached a two-story wooden building that housed the counterintelligence office. Waiting for them inside was Ed Boyle, who gave Chuyen
a wide smile, extended a friendly handshake, and introduced himself as "Mr.
Bee."

14

I t has been said that a man is the sum total of his experience," Alvin
Smith's essay began.

It was June 1, 1965. The thirty-seven-year-old sergeant was sitting in a
hot shuttered classroom with rows of other enlisted men at the Army Intelligence School, typing his autobiography.

Outside, America was moving toward the summer of love, the British
invasion, dope and hippies in Haight-Ashbury. Inside the gates of Fort Holabird, situated in a gritty industrial section of Baltimore, hundreds of U.S.
Army men were training to be spies.

A cluster of red brick dormitories and old wooden classrooms, the fort was
derided as "the College on the Colgate" after the foul-smelling creek at the
bottom of the hill. The school taught the fundamentals of espionage and
counterespionage in a wide variety of courses. Area Studies, the innocuous
name for the foreign intelligence-gathering course, covered the recruiting,
managing, and "termination" of spies. Specialty classes covered writing with
invisible liquid, "flaps and seals" (opening mail without detection), preparing

microdots, inventing codes, losing surveillance, and most important, managing a false identity, or "cover."

All of that was about to be taught to Alvin Smith.

Classwork alternated with practical exercises. Students spent days wandering through Baltimore's parks, shopping centers, and department stores practicing dead drops (hiding messages under benches, in books, etc.) or live drops (passing messages to other agents) and learning the tricks of surveillance and countersurveillance. At the end of the six-month course came a final exam employing all the novice spies' skills, a countrywide simulated espionage mission behind the iron curtain, all the while chased by the FBI.

Before the first week was out, the instructors made sure the students understood that espionage often required the deliberate violation of U.S. and foreign laws. Mail would be opened, telephones tapped without court order, embassies burgled. It was the only course in the Army curriculum, the instructors said evenly, that a student could quit for moral reasons. No one raised a hand, no one quit.

Alvin Smith reveled in the prospect of beginning life again after several false starts. He was a buck sergeant on his fourth military enlistment since World War II. Rolling a sheet of red-bordered paper into a typewriter, he began his classified autobiography, a requirement of every student in the area studies course.

"The undersigned was born in Washington, D.C., the fifth of December, 1927," Smith typed. "His father was employed by the U.S. government in the Fire Department of the District of Columbia." Their home was in an all-white middle-class part of the city near Walter Reed Army Hospital. It was "a stable economic environment through the chaotic days of the depression," he wrote.

Alvin was the only boy of the family, with four sisters. His father was "a firm believer in Victorian gentlemanly manhood" and "interested in international affairs." On Saturday afternoons they often went together to the nearby Trans-Luxe Theater, which showed only newsreels.

"The Russian breach of the Mannerheim Line, the bombing of the Panay, the fall of Poland and the Maginot Line were . . . more important than a secondary education," Smith remembered. "From 1932 until December 1941, undersigned followed the rapidly deteriorating world situation which precipitated World War II."

The mobilization after Pearl Harbor was "dramatic, hectic, and fascinating," he typed. "The deadly horror of a possible air raid was an exciting thing." During blackouts, the fourteen-year-old raced through the streets on his bicycle carrying civil-defense messages given to him by his mother, the neighborhood air-raid warden.

On his seventeenth birthday in 1944, he joined the Naval Air Corps and "learned something of aviation ordnance, air bombing, aerial gunnery, and the opposite sex." He never saw action before the war ended, however, and was mustered out in July 1946.

After an indifferent stab at college, Smith joined the Army and was commissioned a lieutenant, he wrote. But within six months, he "elected to return to civilian life."

Married now to Mary Frances Morrow of Columbus, Georgia, he spent the following year selling encyclopedias door-to-door, first in Washington, then Houston. Then, in 1950, the Korean War began, and he was called to active duty again. His unit, the 187th Airborne Regimental Combat Division, was pulled back to Japan within a month of his arrival.

But he longed to prove himself in combat.

"Despairing of a long tour in Japan," Smith typed, "he called the commanding officer of the 8086th Miscellaneous Group," a commando outfit in Korea. He "volunteered as an airborne demolitions man." His taste for danger, he thought, was "a reaction to the fervor of World War II and international affairs [that] helped mold a personality that was peculiar to his times." In the commando group, he spent eight months as "the only Caucasian with a group of fourteen hundred [Korean] guerrillas."

Years later, he would recount the difficulties, terrors, and privations he encountered in the unit. But in his essay in 1965 he said they were "too dramatic for inclusion in this sketch." Instead, he posed a series of rhetorical questions that suggested a deeply troubled experience.

> It's been said that courage is a sum diminished by expenditure. How was the undersigned's expenditure made? What is his balance? What was his reaction to the sight of a captured enemy agent being tortured? What did he do when the head of a rival intelligence unit sent word that he would shoot the writer on sight? How did he get rid of the Korean guerrilla leader to gain control of the group?
>
> These were typical of local problems calling for local solutions and not facts to be found in a personnel file. In this setting of grim reality, the writer matured.

Reassigned stateside, his field promotion to lieutenant was soon rescinded. In 1952, after eight years of military service, he had already been a Navy recruit, Army private, Army lieutenant, and now he was an enlisted man again.

"I had been happy-go-lucky, but when I came back from Korea I was completely changed," he wrote. "I'd seen the real thing—blood, danger, gore."

He wanted more. Using his contacts from Korea, he wangled an interview with the fledgling Central Intelligence Agency in Washington and was hired.

"When I went to the Agency, I was as motivated an individual as you could find," he typed. "We were the defenders of the country."

The first stop was the CIA training camp in rural Virginia for classes in sabotage, subversion, agent handling and the other facets of paramilitary warfare. His instructor was an Army major and Korean War hero, John Singlaub.

Lee Brumley, reading Smith's essay, stopped. He recognized Singlaub's name as the former head of cross-border operations in Vietnam. He continued reading.

Upon completing the CIA course, Smith wrote, he was sent to Washington with the civilian grade of GS-11, ready for a covert assignment to "a non-Asian country." But after only a few months, he suffered another reversal. His son's severe asthma forced him to drop out of the CIA and move to Arizona.

In Tucson, he sought a job with Air Force intelligence at the nearby air base. But the unit "was too small to support the grade of undersigned," he recounted, so he couldn't be hired. The commander gave his name to the Tucson police chief, who also headed the local Office of Naval Investigations reserve unit.

In a series of secret meetings in city hotel rooms, Smith wrote, "the undersigned was approached and recruited by narcotics specialists of the police force and Treasury Department, Narcotics Division."

The ambitious undercover agent chose Tucson's tiny Chinatown for his first investigation, convinced that a Tong gang was turning the sleepy desert resort city into a major transshipment point for Mexican heroin.

He had "unexpected success in cultivation of a Chinese source," he wrote, but his boss apparently didn't share his theories; to his "surprise," he was demoted to investigating small-time bookies.

"Naturally," he wrote, "I resigned."

Next, at Hughes Aircraft, Smith found a job "starting at the bottom of the plant security force." Despite his lowly position as a night watchman, he quickly spotted lapses in security, which he called to his boss's attention. Saboteurs could gain entry to the defense plant, he warned.

"The head of security, a former FBI man, was not impressed by this writer's opinion of existing security controls," Smith typed. "To more forcefully demonstrate the weaknesses of the system, undersigned started from the border with a simulated explosive, traveled to Tucson, illegally entered the Hughes plant, gained access to the generators and rocket assembly area, and successfully escaped. A report was then written detailing the illegal entry and the ease with which one saboteur could disable the plant.

"A tragic event occurred," Smith wrote, "before reaction to the submitted report was received."

One afternoon, while he and his wife talked as their three-and-a-half-year-old son took a bath, "the sudden cessation of splashing noises caused him to rush to the bathroom, only to find his son face down in the tub." He tried artificial respiration and called a doctor who lived next door, who gave the boy an injection of Adrenalin. They failed to revive him.

"The doctor listed the cause of death as drowning," Smith wrote, "but, privately, expressed his belief that heart failure, caused by abnormal growth from previous severe asthmatic attacks, was the true cause of death."

Not long after, the couple returned to Washington.

A month later he was rehired by the Central Intelligence Agency. In September 1957, Alvin Smith arrived in Port Said, Egypt, a CIA agent posted undercover as the new American vice consul.

Port Said, situated at the northern mouth of the Suez Canal, was one of the most strategically sensitive postings in the region. The French-British-Israeli invasion of the Sinai had just failed, Egypt's Nasser was tilting toward Moscow, and a civil war was looming in Lebanon. Iraq, Syria, and Iran were all churning with plots and revolutionary cells.

Smith's cover called for him to attend the usual round of diplomatic cocktail parties and ribbon cuttings, but his actual mission was to recruit and manage spies and keep an eye on shipping through the canal.

A French-language newspaper in Cairo helped him bolster his cover.

"Thirty Minutes with M. Alven Smith [sic], United States Consul," the headline said. In a profile, the paper gushed over the "young and dynamic" new diplomat, "with attentive gray eyes and a thin mustache that underscore a simple and courteous attitude."

"M. Alven Smith has a relaxed and straightforward manner," the paper went on. The ersatz vice consul returned the compliment, praising "the sophisticated pleasures of Cairo" and predicting that Egypt could expect "a bright future under the leadership of President Gamal Abdel Nasser."

The twenty-nine-year-old operative was extremely happy.

"It has been said that the test of ideal employment is that vocation one would pursue as an avocation," Smith typed in his Army autobiography eight years later.

"This writer . . . would have worked for subsistence wages. He had served as case officer, principal agent, action agent, support agent, trainer and instructor."

Within months, however, his Egyptian mission was cut short.

"His wife was a reluctant volunteer in his operations," Smith explained. "She was operationally flexible and could be counted on for a good show, whether it was required to associate with drug-addicted musicians or to give a formal dinner party for fourteen."

But she tired of the double life, he said. He had to quit.

"In the naive belief that they could return to America and settle down to an existence with no surveillance, no opposition, and no clandestine effort, the undersigned resigned."

He soon found that he had also been passed over twice for promotion in the Army Reserve, so he was forced to resign that as well. The couple moved to Florida, where the ex-spy and diplomat took a fling at selling real estate. It was a boom market, but he found himself "incompatible with the unreal, martini circuit of Naples." The Smiths moved back to Washington once more, where he took a job selling encyclopedias again door-to-door.

Even this bottom-dwelling existence, banging on doors with his heavy briefcase of books, he insisted, had its secret pleasures: "Each of these sales was, in the final analysis, based on deception."

He sold "twenty-one sets at an average cost of four hundred dollars per set" in the first month. But he soon developed a bad conscience about the job, which undermined his talents, he wrote.

"Psychological manipulation of a person's mind in the achievement of national objectives is one thing, and exploitation for personal profit another," he wrote. "Unfortunately, persons least able to afford these excellent reference works are, for the most part, the intended market. The undersigned's inability to sell this product resulted in the loss of his income. As 1958 came to a close, this writer decided to reenter the Army."

He would start again as a private.

The timing, at least, was fortunate. The cold war was creating openings for operatives in Berlin, Cuba, the Congo, and Southeast Asia. There were jobs everywhere for experts in guerrilla warfare and intelligence. Smith, now thirty-one, headed off to boot camp.

He trained in flight operations and was ordered to Germany with an aviation company of the 2nd Armored Calvary Regiment. A year later, he requested a transfer to the 10th Special Forces Group in Bad Tolz. Finally, he was back in intelligence.

It was September 1961. President Kennedy was planning to award the paramilitary soldiers their long-sought green beret, making them the first string on the cold war team.

"Come on in," Smith remembered his commander saying. "We need someone with your background."

One of his superiors was a dynamic young major, Robert B. Rheault.

Lee Brumley closed the dossier, leaned back, and closed his eyes.

His mind drifted to something that Smith had said earlier in the day, which he now saw in a new and unsettling light.

The sergeant had called in to report that Chuyen had shown up on time for the interrogation. Then, lowering his voice and using a quasi-code language over the crackling line from Saigon, Smith said he thought he had been followed.

The call only bothered Brumley then, but it worried him now. Was Smith for real? If there was surveillance by North Vietnamese agents, there really was cause for concern. Could he trust Smith to know?

Still, they had Chuyen in custody. If the situation were handled correctly, they could take care of it. They would bolster security and not let Chuyen go if there was any sign that the cover story of his employment test was breaking down. After all, to the North Vietnamese employing him as a double agent, Chuyen had good reason to associate with Smith. If they were following him, it was just a good idea. But Brumley just wanted to make sure the VC didn't blow him away—at least not yet.

What really bothered him was Smith. The man was clearly erratic. What accounted for his incredible pattern in and out of intelligence? With such a background of failure and rejection, how could he have succeeded in gaining such sensitive assignments again and again?

And again?

Brumley noted that Smith had spent two years with Special Forces in Germany and then returned to the regular infantry in 1962. After six months at Fort Benning, Georgia, he applied for Chinese language school but was sent instead to a year-long course in Burmese. After that he won entry to the case officer course at Fort Holabird, where he wrote his bizarre essay.

After Holabird, the record continued, Smith was posted to Hawaii for a counterintelligence assignment. After a few months he was on to Bangkok, where he stayed for a year as an agent handler under civilian cover with the Department of the Army. Then it was Vietnam.

Maybe he was still working for the CIA, Brumley pondered. It wasn't unknown for the CIA to place spies in the other services.

He ruminated on the possibilities.

Smith, a CIA plant. Smith, a Viet Cong sympathizer. He thought about it.

No, that was ridiculous. It couldn't be either. The sergeant was too goofy.

Vietnam was killing the Army, Brumley thought. Really killing it. Somebody was going to have to pay for that before the war was over.

15

E ddie Boyle walked into the room and faced Thai Khac Chuyen for the first time at 10 A.M., June 12. Alvin Smith was already sitting with his former agent at the far end of the green wooden table, preparing him for the interrogation.

Vincent Driver was humming as he set up his equipment. Next to him sat his interpreter Joel, silently waiting to begin.

The room was quiet. This interrogation would be far different from frenzied questioning in a rice paddy with fire and death all around when enemy soldiers were dragged forth, slapped and beaten, water poured down their noses, their genitals wired to field radios and given a quick crank, pistols cocked at their foreheads.

Away from the battlefields, trained American interrogators worked in cool, quiet rooms, subjecting their quarry to markedly different techniques. Facing hardened North Vietnamese officers and longtime spies, they used prolonged questioning, sleep deprivation and truth drugs, and rarely lifted a hand. The routine, which could last weeks, months, or even years, was designed to break the prisoners and turn them into defectors. It often worked.

Eddie Boyle was acquainted with both techniques. He had seen prisoners mutilated and shot on the battlefield. He had also seen them broken and turned into enthusiastic collaborators, fingering their former comrades in the Viet Cong underground. He had participated in both; as a professional interrogator, as a human being, he preferred the latter.

Boyle's immediate goal this morning was to extract preliminary signs of Chuyen's treachery. His principal weapon would be Vincent Driver and his polygraph machine.

Technically polygraphs didn't detect lies. The machines only recorded "blips" on a chart, which were triggered by a subject's changes in breathing, pulse, and sweat in response to a series of questions. Recorded by a belt strapped across the chest and electrodes attached to the fingers and forehead, the answers turned into "blips" etched by a stylus on a continuous roll of paper.

In the hands of a skillful, patient interrogator and his polygraph man, a subject's false responses "indicated deception." In lesser hands, especially in the hands of men in a hurry, the blips could really mean nothing: evidence of general stress and anxiety, even heartburn.

The polygraph machine was another technical innovation that the Americans believed could deliver success where the Chinese and French before them had failed. Like the electronic sensors on the Ho Chi Minh Trail, the spy satellites, and chemical defoliants, the polygraph was designed to flush out the Viet Cong from the civilian population.

Ordinary Vietnamese subjected to the machines were nearly always terrified. They knew what the bottom line of the exercise was: to find out if they were Communist, or had Communist connections. But after thirty years of war, every Vietnamese knew who the Communists were because they had all grown up together or had them in their own families.

The clan and family came first, despite the long and bitter struggle. Even the highest Saigon government security officials were protecting relatives on the other side, as everyone knew. On the eve of the Tet offensive, some were dining with their Viet Cong relatives who had slipped into the city to celebrate the holiday before the surprise attacks.

The polygraphs could quickly pick up a person's "sympathy" for the revolution, too, and that could terrify a subject. It was common to see valor in the Viet Cong's fight against foreign domination and corruption, even in those who, having fled the North, despised Ho Chi Minh and his Communist methods.

The real spies were trained to beat the machine by confessing to something less: a loathing for the corrupt Saigon government and the boorish Americans who had invaded their country, or too close contact with relatives in the Viet Cong. Brazen lying was fatal.

Theoretically, every Vietnamese agent employed by U.S. intelligence in Vietnam underwent an initial polygraph examination and tests at regular intervals. But the constant pressure to set up intelligence nets overnight, to win the war by every Christmas, meant that many agents weren't polygraphed until well into their spying duties. Chuyen was just another example.

To Vietnam novices the lie detector was the frontline defense against enemy penetration, as reliable as a tripwire. But those who had spent more than a one-year tour in Vietnam knew the machines were just another empty exercise: By 1969, there were twenty thousand, maybe even thirty thousand enemy agents inside the Saigon government and American spy services—nobody really knew for sure. Many of them had been cleared, of course, by polygraph tests.

As Eddie Boyle stood by, Alvin Smith turned to Joel and asked him to make sure that Chuyen understood the procedure.

He would be asked many questions about his work and family, Smith said as Joel translated. Some of the questions would seem rude and question his loyalty. But he had to remember that he was being considered for a very sensitive job.

Lie detector tests were used for everybody's benefit, to keep Viet Cong spies out of their operations, Smith said. They protected everyone from danger, including him. If there were any problems with the test, he would be just outside the door.

Did he understand?

Yes, Chuyen said.

And that taking the test was voluntary?

Yes, he answered. But no test, he smiled, no job, right?

Smith nodded and looked at Boyle. Then he patted Chuyen on the arm, stood up, and left.

To Vincent Driver, Chuyen seemed no different than the hundreds of other Vietnamese he had been testing at a rate of two a day for nearly a year. He routinely explained the procedure. They would attach some wires to his thumb, chest, and forehead, girdle his chest with a strap, and ask some basic questions. They would write the answers down, then ask the questions again. The machine would tell if he was lying or not. It was as simple as that. If Chuyen told the truth, he had nothing to worry about.

Driver turned on the machine. An air conditioner vibrated in the bottom of a single boarded-up window. Over the table, a light bulb cuffed by a dark green shade hung from the ceiling.

Chuyen smiled nervously and whispered to Joel, prompting the interpreter to explain to him that the wires *khong co dien*—"don't have electricity." Chuyen shifted in his seat.

Now they were ready. Driver turned on a tape recorder then lifted a pen to mark Chuyen's responses on the polygraph paper.

"Where were you born?" he asked, adjusting the dials. A thin metal arm with a pen-like point at its tip began scrawling a wave of red ink on a roll of white paper.

"North Vietnam, 1938," Chuyen answered.

"What are your parents' names?"

"Thai Thi Luc, my mother. Thai Khac Qui, my father."

For the next half hour, Boyle and Driver took Chuyen through a series of simple questions—age, names of relatives, length of employment, residences—designed to get a consistent reading of Chuyen's breathing and pulse rates. The responses would allow them to measure "peaks of tension" when the harder questions came.

The calibrations set, Eddie Boyle then asked Chuyen to explain his family's background and how they came down from North Vietnam. If there were indications of deception here, Boyle would know where to bear in later.

Chuyen began his tale.

When the Imperial Japanese Army landed in Hanoi in 1941, Thai Khac Chuyen was just learning to ride his first bicycle. His father would steady the two-wheeler as the boy took his first pedals around the small courtyard in

Thanh Hoa, a small village in the Red River Valley, just outside Hanoi. Chuyen's father, a thin bespeckled man with a large private library, was a minor local bureaucrat in the French colonial government.

Many Vietnamese regarded the Japanese soldiers with awe. The only rulers they had known for more than a half century were white Europeans, particularly the French who had claimed Indochina as their colony in 1887. Now yellow-skinned Asians like themselves were in charge. The Japanese had succeeded, moreover, by hardly firing a shot. With the French government defeated at home by Hitler, the Vichy colonial troops put up no resistance. The Japanese Imperial Army permitted them to govern local matters under their guidance.

But the Japanese occupation also put new fire into the independence movement led by Ho Chi Minh, whose left-wing guerrillas had been waging an intermittent campaign against the French for a decade. Ho made a marriage of opportunity with the American secret services, who relayed Roosevelt's pledge to end colonialism with the defeat of the Axis powers. Money, guns, and supplies began to flow to Ho's "Viet Minh" guerrillas from U.S. intelligence bases in southern China.

His father, Chuyen said, secretly supported the Viet Minh but remained wary of their Communist leanings. When the defeated Japanese shipped out of Vietnam under an American flag in 1945, the French attempted to regain control with President Truman's blessing, but the Viet Minh had gained an unshakable foothold. It took nine years, but the French finally succumbed at the epic battle of Dien Bien Phu, and a peace conference at Geneva divided the country in half. With two million other Catholics, Thai Khac Qui decided to pack up his family and move south into the Western-controlled zone.

Only half the family decided to go, Chuyen said—his mother and father, one sister and a brother. Three older brothers and two sisters had their own friends and wanted to stay in the North.

The polygraph needle twitched.

In the spring of 1954, Chuyen and his family boarded the refugee ship Mirabelle and waved good-bye from the docks of Haiphong. Three storm-tossed days later, they steamed up the Mekong River and disembarked in Saigon. Chuyen was sixteen years old.

Compared to Hanoi, the capital was a beehive of prosperity and postcolonial sophistication, Chuyen remembered, its markets jammed with prosperous peasants and overflowing with fresh vegetables, fish, and meat. The hotels bustled with aging French planters and tourists, wealthy Saigonese politicians and generals, and the new wave of American technicians. A fragile charm gilded the old colonial city, the "Paris of the Orient." But Saigon seemed to be holding its breath, waiting for the inevitable war to resume.

It was all very exciting for the young man, who looked forward to a new home, life, and school. His father moved the family to Dalat, a resort area in the piney Central Highlands, where he quickly found a job again as a government public-works official. It was peaceful, but antigovernment sentiment was growing in the area, especially among the Montagnard tribesmen.

Within three months the family was broken up again, Chuyen said, when his mother decided to return to North Vietnam and try to bring her other children south. On her way back, while crossing the Ben Hai River dividing North and South, they were stopped by Communist border troops. She never tried to come back again, he said, and eventually his two older brothers were drafted into the Peoples Liberation Army.

Driver and Boyle listened without interruption. The stylus on the polygraph twitched occasionally as Chuyen discussed his boyhood—that was to be expected. But when he described his mother's journey north and brothers' enlistment in the army, it began to jump more dramatically, leaving sharper peaks and valleys of red ink on the paper. Driver put a check mark on the side of each fluctuation.

Chuyen continued his story. At sixteen he moved a few miles north to Ban Me Thuot, enrolled in high school, and went to work in a pharmacy that his older brother Canh had opened. But he didn't like it there, he said, and moved to Saigon for school. Within a year he was back in Dalat, but soon after moved back to Saigon again. Two years later he returned to Dalat, again taking classes because he still hadn't graduated.

Now nineteen, handsome and talkative, with his ink-black hair brushed across a wide forehead, Chuyen returned again to Saigon for more classes but again failed to earn a diploma. Finally, after two more years of school, he quit for good and found a job back in the Central Highlands with a huge American construction company, Root-Morris-Knudsen, known as RMK-BRJ.

It was now 1963, a time when antigovernment protest was sweeping the country but was especially strong in the Central Highlands. Driver noticed that the needle jumped again, which he interpreted as an attempt at deception. Boyle thought there might be other reasons to make the needle quiver: The captured photograph that Smith identified as Chuyen was taken near Ban Me Thuot sometime during 1963–1964.

Chuyen said he resigned his job with RMK-BRJ after only three months for a higher paying job with a U.S. Green Beret unit in Da Nang. He was assigned to the Ashau Valley as a combat interpreter, he said. The valley, spiked by steep cloud-covered mountains and shrouded by triple-canopy jungle, was also a major infiltration route for the North Vietnamese army. Although the job paid more money, Chuyen said, he soon quit "because the Ashau was bad for my health." A few days later his outpost was overrun.

For the next three years, Chuyen bounced from one Special Forces unit to another, usually volunteering for any duty at first but then quitting within a few weeks when heavy combat broke out.

At noon, Boyle called a break.

Outside, he and Driver smoked and discussed the morning session. Either Chuyen was a rank coward, Boyle said, or he was using his brief assignments to spy on Green Beret recon units. There seemed to be a correlation between where Chuyen showed up to work and the pattern of combat activity. When antigovernment protests broke out in Ban Me Thuot or Saigon, he added, Chuyen was there; when the NVA threatened the Ashau Valley or delta, he was there.

Boyle asked Driver and Cotton to check out Chuyen's employment history. The 525th Military Intelligence Group operated the Source Control office, where the centralized agent files were kept.

They returned after lunch. Amazingly, not a single trace of Chuyen was on file in the metal cabinets save for his sign-on with Alvin Smith a few months earlier, they reported. Chuyen's driver's license "checked out," they said, but not his parent's home address. Can the system be that sloppy? they wondered, or was there another explanation?

Boyle resumed the interrogation with greater intensity.

They were back in 1963.

"Have you ever been to Bu Gia Map?" Boyle asked, probing about the captured picture.

"No," Chuyen said. The needle swung wildly, and Driver made a mark.

Boyle then bore down on Chuyen's employment in 1966. Chuyen had said he was working for a Special Forces B-team in Tay Ninh.

"Did you work for anyone other than B-32?" Boyle asked.

"No."

Suddenly, the needles jumped again, scratching sharp vertical lines of red ink on the paper.

"Did you work for anyone else?"

Chuyen started to answer, then stopped. The tape recorder's reels turned silently.

"Did you work for anyone else?"

Silence. Chuyen stared straight ahead. The lines twittered and scratched as the paper rolled forward.

"Who else did you work for in Tay Ninh?"

"I am not to say."

"Who did you work for? You must tell the truth."

"I don't know."

"What do you mean, you don't know?"

"I cannot say. I signed paper saying I would never say."

"You must tell the truth. Who did you work for?"

"An American intelligence organization. Maybe CIA."

"How did you start work for this organization?"

Chuyen hesitated again.

Boyle signaled Driver to turn off the polygraph machine.

"You do not have a choice of what questions to answer, Chuyen," he said evenly. "You work for U.S. intelligence, and must answer all the questions we ask you if you want to continue working for us." Joel, with prompting from Boyle, translated the statement in full.

Chuyen said he understood.

Boyle told Driver to start the paper rolling again.

"I'll ask you again. How did you start work for this other organization?"

"The S-2, Major McBride, bought me several drinks and he asked me if I would work for another agency," Chuyen answered. "So I was taken to the 25th Division in Tay Ninh where I met Mr. Ginger."

Ginger was a cover name, Boyle surmised.

"When did you begin work for Mr. Ginger?"

"1966."

"What was your job?"

Again, Chuyen was silent.

"What was your job?"

"I translated messages which were left in the dead drop by the agent handler."

Dead drops were used to transfer information between case officers and their agents without personal contact. A crack in a bridge culvert, a hole in a wall, a book in a library—they were particularly necessary in a small city like Tay Ninh, where meetings between a lone American and a Vietnamese would surely be noticed. Two or three times a week, the agent would scratch a chalk mark on a prearranged wall or stick a piece of tape on a lamppost. That was the "load signal" to indicate he had information to pass. Chuyen would then be dispatched on a motorbike to a prearranged spot "to service" the drop.

"What was the agent handler's name?"

Chuyen hesitated. "Huynh Son," he finally answered.

A Vietnamese case officer working under Ginger's supervision, Boyle thought. That didn't sound like a CIA operation, though he couldn't be sure.

"What organization did Mr. Ginger work for?" he asked.

"I think he worked for JTAD." It came out "jay-tad."

Boyle thought the acronym stood for Joint Technical Advisory Detachment, the cover name for a military intelligence unit. He wasn't sure.

"Why do you think he worked for JTAD?"

"He drove a jeep with JTAD bumper markings," Chuyen answered simply. "Also, since I worked in S-2, I saw the JTAD reports when I placed reports in the S-2 boxes."

Jeeze, Boyle thought, some security. Chuyen could just paw through the in-box.

"I don't know if JTAD was a cover name," Chuyen added. He went on to explain a total security lapse in the unit.

"In 1966 there were many intelligence agencies working in Tay Ninh City. Someone found out who one of the agents was, and that he worked for the Americans. The person who found out told the ARVN S-2 and the agent was arrested and beaten. He told the S-2 everything about the net—who Huynh Son was and that he was working for Mr. Ginger. When Mr. Ginger returned from Saigon I told him and he took the agent to Bien Hoa, where he was polygraphed. The test showed that he had told the S-2 everything. When Mr. Ginger returned, he talked to me and Huynh Son and then his organization made him leave Tay Ninh."

So Ginger's operation was blown. "How did you know," Boyle probed, "that the ARVN S-2 had the agent?"

"Because I worked in S-2 and we were in the same compound," Chuyen said.

Boyle was appalled. He made a note to talk to Brumley about the compromise of a U.S. operation to a Vietnamese intelligence officer. Another compromise.

He prompted Chuyen to continue.

Chuyen related how he looked for work in Can Tho, the largest city in the delta, where his younger brother was assigned to a South Vietnamese army psychological warfare unit, a branch of intelligence. For a few weeks he was unemployed, he said, but he soon latched on again with the Green Berets. This time it was Special Forces Team B-40, which was conducting recon operations around Viet Cong strongholds in the Co To Mountains, which rose sharply out of the delta. But he quit after only a few weeks, he said, because he "didn't like Nui Co To." Again the needle twitched wildly.

After that, he said, he went to Muc Hoa.

"Why did you go to Muc Hoa?"

"I met a friend, Lieutenant David, who took me to see Mr. Cox at Phoenix. You know, they have PRUs, CIA."

Boyle shook his head again. Chuyen knows *everything.*

"Why did he take you to see Mr. Cox?"

"Because he knew I had worked for S-2."

"Why didn't you go to work for Mr. Cox?"

"He offered me twenty-five thousand piasters but he would not fix my papers. When I asked him to fix my papers, he shouted, 'What papers?' I didn't like him. He was very impolite."

Boyle didn't believe the story. Chuyen's language talents would give him a pick of jobs—unless there was something else wrong. The CIA must have picked up something derogatory about Chuyen, but they obviously failed to tell anybody else. So much for team play.

"Where did you go when you left Mr. Cox?"

"Back to Muc Hoa, to B-41."

"What did you do at B-41?"

"I worked for the S-5, civil affairs, intelligence." Alvin Smith.

Boyle had to pause. He signaled Driver to stop. He needed a break.

What Chuyen had told him meant that the CIA had interviewed him, rejected him, and then failed to put him on the "burn list." By his own count so far, Chuyen had worked for a handful of U.S. intelligence units for six years, and yet his name hadn't shown up in the files.

He was astounded. Jesus-fucking-Christ, how could you win the war this way?

Since it was 5 P.M. Driver said they might as well take a recess. Outside, he assembled Boyle and Smith.

Chuyen changes dates and places so often it's hard to get a clear story, Driver said. The results were showing a high general level of stress, quite likely due to attempts at deception. Still, he said, the subject appeared to be unusually calm and cooperative for a likely enemy agent. And bright, Driver noted. A few more sessions would be needed to pinpoint the areas where Chuyen was lying.

When they went back inside, Chuyen announced he wanted to go home. He had been questioned all day, he said, and wanted to see his wife and children.

Boyle asked him to wait a moment and left the room to find Smith.

In the corridor Boyle and Smith considered what to do next. They faced a dilemma. They couldn't very well hold him against his will, not yet—they didn't have a plan for holding him. That would lead him to suspect something was wrong and spook his wife. They both might try to run.

Smith suggested they tell Chuyen he was doing well, but that more questioning was needed. They'd take him home so he could tell his wife he'd be away for a few days on "a mission." Boyle agreed.

At 7:30, Cotton, Smith, and Joel got into a plain black jeep with Chuyen to take him home. Chuyen turned to Smith and said he really didn't like the interrogation. The wires scared him. The questions were very hostile. "Mr. Bee" acted like he didn't believe him, he said.

Smith half-laughed. "Naw, it's not a lot of fun," he said, smiling and patting Chuyen on the back. "Everyone goes through it, though. You'll be fine."

Cotton nosed through the camp gates and stopped. Although he knew the city well, including Chuyen's street, he decided to ask the Vietnamese for directions.

"Go right," Chuyen said, and they swung into the stream of twilight traffic. After ten minutes, Cotton noticed that Chuyen had been taking them in circles. Was he setting them up for surveillance, he wondered, or worse? After Cotton had driven randomly for a few minutes more, Chuyen suddenly issued specific instructions that led them directly to Phan Thanh Gian Street. When Cotton came to the corner, Chuyen told him to pull to the side and stop. It was nearly dark.

"You wait, I will be back in ten minutes," he said, jumping from the jeep.

Smith touched his arm. "I'll go with you," he said, nodding to Joel to come along. "Until this examination is finished," Smith explained, "I'm afraid we have to accompany you everywhere." Chuyen nodded assent, and the three of them then walked down the street to the narrow dark alley and turned in. Thin gray shapes glided by, peasants on rubber sandals. Joss sticks smoldered in votive boxes.

Reaching his house, Chuyen led them onto the cement porch and then through the bead curtain to the main room inside. An elderly couple sat at a table eating out of small ceramic bowls, eying the American warily. Two small children scurried around the floor. Lien rushed forward to her husband, relief and anxiety on her delicate face. Glancing at Smith, she mumbled a few words to her husband, who quickly whispered an answer, then turned back.

"This is my father-in-law," Chuyen announced, "and my mother-in-law." The old man stood slowly and extended a hand.

"*Comment allez-vous?*" he said with a slight smile.

As they shook hands, Lien took her husband into the back room. As he left, Chuyen waved at Smith's nervous glance, assuring him he'd be back.

Smith stood there, nervous and uncomfortable. The old man introduced his wife, who nodded blankly from her chair. Smith greeted her, then turned to one of the children who crawled toward him. He bent to pick him up, raised him in the air, and gently bounced him up and down, cooing and clucking. The child gurgled and laughed.

In a minute, Chuyen returned, and Smith set the child down. When they reached the doorway, the Vietnamese turned and kissed his wife good-bye.

At 8 P.M., the interrogation resumed.

Boyle and Driver took Chuyen through the same questions again, which had been reshuffled to segregate answers that indicated deception from the ones with a flat response. Then they began to bear in on his specific answers relating to a possible affiliation with enemy intelligence.

The answers were not good, they quickly found. An hour and a half later, they recessed again and left Chuyen in the room.

Standing in the courtyard, Driver told Smith and Boyle that deception was now strongly indicated on certain questions. The agent had blown the worst of them all, "Are you working for North Vietnamese intelligence?" Red ink all over the chart.

As they spoke, Cotton walked up with a startling piece of news: Two women had come to the gates of the camp that afternoon asking for Chuyen. The guard, not understanding Vietnamese and nervous about terrorists, had forced the insistent women to leave, but not before they thrust a piece of paper into his hand.

Cotton gave it to Boyle. He saw two names on it. One was Chuyen's wife, Phan Kim Lien. The other name was Miss Lam Hoang Oanh, a "sister-in-law." Oanh had also written down her office telephone number and place of employment: the Saigon office of CORDS, the U.S. pacification agency.

It was an incomprehensible complication. Smith, his nerves already stretched taut with layers of deception and intrigue, pondered what to do. It was important to maintain Chuyen's cooperation, he argued, to persuade him he was passing the test and to assure him that he, "Sands," was his friend. He thought Chuyen still might be useful, but he needed time. If Chuyen was lying, they would need to find out why. If Chuyen was being blackmailed by the Viet Cong or was a true double agent in the employ of North Vietnamese intelligence, Smith said he would try to "double him" again, play him back to the Communists as a triple agent.

All these options could be derailed if Chuyen and his wife suspected he was in deep trouble, whether he was innocent or guilty. They couldn't afford to make them flee.

Chuyen, Smith said, had to be sent home with the same story that his employment test was continuing. Everybody keep cool.

"They tell me you're doing fine," he said to Chuyen when he was brought out.

Chuyen nodded.

"I'm really going to be looking forward to working with you again, Chuyen," Smith proclaimed. "Real soon."

Chuyen smiled slightly.

"You can go now. But," he added, as if it were an afterthought, "I need you to come back in the morning to sign some forms, okay?"

"Sure, Sands. I be back," Chuyen said.

A jeep pulled up driven by two stocky Nungs, Chinese ethnic mercenaries regularly employed for security jobs by the Special Forces. Smith signaled Chuyen to get in and waved him good-bye.

Chuyen showed up exactly on time again the next morning in a clean white shirt, dark blue slacks, and with a nervous edge to his smile. His prompt arrival came as a slight surprise to Smith and Boyle, who had half-expected him to run. After all, Chuyen could have no doubt about the direction the questioning had taken.

Why was he here? Could he be bouncing the polygraph like this and still be innocent?

They were surprised again when Chuyen volunteered that his wife had come looking for him the previous afternoon, worried about him.

What was his game? Smith wondered.

At 8:45 A.M., Vincent Driver flipped a power switch on the side of the polygraph machine, attached the electrodes and chest strap to Chuyen, and started the paper moving forward. Across the table, Ed Boyle asked the first question of the session, and as Joel translated, the metal arms began to twitch on the paper.

"Are you involved with another intelligence agency?"

"No."

"Are you involved with North Vietnamese intelligence?"

"No."

"Is the information about your employment correct?"

"Yes."

The needles had swung to a high pitch on the first question and stayed there.

"Are you trying to conceal any information about your background?"

"No."

The needles swung higher.

"Were you unemployed during part of 1963 and 1964?"

"Yes."

The needles quivered again.

"Did you leave Saigon during that period of time?"

"No."

The needles stayed high.

"Have you ever voluntarily helped the VC?"

The metal arms shuddered at the top of the paper roll, even before the answer came . . .

"No."

. . . and stayed there.

"Do you have an intelligence target in South Vietnam?"

"No."

"Were you unemployed during 1963 and 1964?" Boyle was bearing in again on the dates of the captured photograph.

"Yes."

"Did you leave Saigon during that period of time?"

"No."

The stress reading remained high.

"Have you answered all the questions truthfully in this test?"

"Yes."

The needles jumped.

"Were you married in Saigon?"

"Yes."

"Is your wife involved in intelligence activities?"

"No."

"Are you being forced to work for North Vietnamese intelligence?"

"No."

The needles had stayed high.

That was it. Driver smiled at Chuyen, disconnected the wires, and called a recess.

Outside, the examiner said Chuyen was lying.

It was time to move him out, but how? They needed to talk to Nha Trang on a secure telephone.

At 11 A.M. Smith and Boyle jumped into a jeep and sped across the steamy wet streets, out the jammed main boulevard toward the airport, and three miles later pulled to a stop at the gates of the Military Assistance Command–Vietnam, the sprawling complex at the edge of Ton Son Nhut.

It was as if they'd gone into a tunnel and come up in Disneyland. MACV looked like a high-rise apartment complex with its Sears-size PX, commissary, tennis courts, bowling alley, swimming pools and billets for officers, called Dodge City. Neatly uniformed soldiers strolled around with shopping bags, flirting with the nurses from the nearby Third Field Force Hospital, making plans for dinner and drinks in the city. Others were in their swimming trunks and sandals, heading for the pool, or carrying tennis rackets under their arms.

No wonder the grunts resented the Saigon desk jockeys. Smith and Boyle lurched past the big MACV-HQ sign and darted into a parking spot outside the main building. The headquarters itself was a hulking four-story cement and glass rectangle with nearly a thousand people sitting inside, Army, Air Force, Navy, and Marines. They called it Pentagon East.

Its normally placid pace had quickened from an upsurge of combat outside Saigon. Over the past forty-eight hours, the Communists had mounted assaults all along the central coast and rocketed a U.S. Army hospital, killing the first American nurse to die in Vietnam. Fighting was also heavy northwest of

Saigon, in the delta, and along the Cambodian border. B-52s were flying waves of bombing missions against NVA positions near Tay Ninh. Radio Hanoi had said once again that American pilots shot down over North Vietnam would be tried and punished as war criminals.

Boyle still couldn't believe there wasn't a trace of Chuyen anywhere in the files. Making his way to the second floor intelligence section, he decided to make one last stop at the Source Control office to see for himself. In a few minutes, the clerk came back and told him: Nothing.

Walking down the hall to the MACV J-2 office, Boyle identified himself and Smith to the duty officer and was directed to the scrambler telephone. After a few minutes, he got Crew and Brumley on the other end of the line. The scrambler made their voices sound like they'd gulped nitrous gas. He wasted no time getting to the point.

"He's an NVA-controlled agent," Boyle declared, summing up the interrogation. "Maybe his wife as well." As he recounted some of the "blips" Driver had recorded during the polygraph questioning, he had to admit the test wasn't entirely conclusive. Chuyen hadn't cracked or confessed.

"Why don't you show him the captured photo," Crew suggested, "and see how he reacts?"

Brumley gently resisted. It would tip their hand to Chuyen, he explained. Then he would have no doubt why they were questioning him and what evidence they had. Crew relented.

Then Boyle told them about the visit of Chuyen's wife and sister-in-law to Camp Goodman.

Crew and Brumley hesitated. They hadn't thought through the particulars or implications of Chuyen failing the test. Now they had to factor in his wife and family.

The first objective was damage control, they decided.

Bring him up here, Brumley told Boyle. Don't let him know the real reason. Don't alarm him. Keep the cover story going. Tell him it's just more of the job test. Major Middleton, he added, will arrange for an aircraft to be in Saigon tonight.

There was more unsettling news when Boyle and Smith returned. While they were away, Driver had tested Chuyen on the question of whether he had disclosed anything about the interrogation to his wife or anyone else. The result showed that he had told his wife and some other unidentified person about the ordeal. Confronted with evidence of his lying, Chuyen had dug in his heels and insisted he had told no one about his interrogation.

That was a bad sign, they all agreed. Added to the other evidence, it meant Chuyen might be trying to contact his NVA control.

It was time to move him out.

Boyle asked Cotton to get a medic; they needed to administer a sleeping potion to Chuyen, he said. The black warrant officer, hesitating, went off to find one.

Smith went into the interrogation room. His agent was sullen and restless,

he found. He wanted to go home. He was tired of the questions. He feared
they thought he was disloyal.

Smith raised a palm. You've done well on the test so far, he said in a soft,
fatherly manner. Now it's time for the mission itself.

Chuyen seemed surprised.

But for that, Smith said, he had to be taken to another site. And the
destination was so secret he had to be put to sleep for the trip so that he would
not know where he was going. They'd give him some harmless sleeping
potion.

Chuyen listened without reaction. Boyle walked in and joined the meeting.
After a moment of hesitation, Chuyen agreed to go along.

He had one request, however. He wanted to write a note to his wife telling
her he would be away for a few days and not to worry about him.

Smith looked at Boyle, who nodded. They agreed to let him write the note
and left the room.

Outside, they agreed to take precautions. They would read the note before
sending it on and then polygraph Chuyen once again on its contents, asking
whether he had put any secret coded messages in it. If he passed the test, it
would be delivered to Lien after Chuyen had been evacuated from Saigon.

Meanwhile, a security detail was being rounded up to transfer Chuyen from
Camp Goodman to the airport in the back of a truck.

Chuyen finished the handwritten note and gave it to Smith, who walked out
and showed it to Joel. It appeared to be innocuous, the interpreter said, a
simple excuse for going away for a few days.

At 3:30 in the afternoon, Driver and Boyle hooked Chuyen up to the
polygraph again to quiz him on the letter. It was a useless exercise, Driver said
after a few minutes: Chuyen's anxiety level was so high he couldn't get an
accurate reading. After discussing the matter, they decided to let the note go
anyway. To withhold it would just raise more suspicions.

In an adjacent office, Sgt. Stanley Shank, the unit's medic, was arguing
with Cotton about using drugs to knock out Chuyen for the trip. Thorazine
and sodium pentathol were not designed to be used over a long period of time,
he said; if they weren't closely monitored, they could kill a man.

Cotton insisted; the risk was necessary for an important intelligence operation, he said. He had gotten approval from Lieutenant Colonel Weil, the
detachment commander, who had checked in with the CIA and briefed them
about Chuyen's interrogation.

Unhappily, Shank gave in, gathered up his equipment, and went with
Cotton to the interrogation room.

The medic sat down and took Chuyen's pulse. Then he inserted an intra-
venous needle into Chuyen's wrist and hooked up a saline solution. Next, he
drew 2 cc's of thorazine into a syringe. He then injected the dose into the IV
tube. After a few minutes, Shank picked up a vial of sodium pentathol, drew
a few drops, and injected that into the apparatus. Ten minutes later, he added
another few drops, and five minutes later, another dose. After a half hour, 5
cc's had been fed into Chuyen's vein. His head was slumped on his chest in
a deep sleep.

Shank and Cotton then lowered Chuyen onto the floor, wrapped him in a green plastic poncho, and slipped a blindfold over his eyes.

A small truck backed up to the office. Chuyen was carried out and placed in the back. One soldier was at the wheel, another rode shotgun. Two more Green Berets climbed in the back, heavily armed. As the truck started up, Boyle told Shank to get in the back and monitor Chuyen's condition.

Boyle, Smith, and Cotton, accompanied by another armed Green Beret, mounted an unmarked black jeep. At ten minutes to six, the caravan pulled out of the gates.

"Are you superstitious?" the soldier asked Smith, leaning forward and smiling. The jeep was inching slowly through the early evening city traffic. A drizzle fell over them as a stream of motorbikes and pedestrians brushed by in each direction.

"Why?"

"Because it's Friday the thirteenth," he said. Smith did not smile. He was always wary of portents, and tonight he was stretched tight as a piano wire. His gray eyes darted around the traffic, looking for signs of an ambush.

Twenty minutes later, they swung into Ton Son Nhut and drove to the Air America terminal on the far corner of the airfield. An unmarked two-engine jet waited on the tarmac. The truck swung up in a short arc, jerked to a halt, and backed up to the cargo door. The guards jumped to the ground, rifles at the ready, while the transfer was made.

Smith's nerves pinged with anxiety. He noticed a Vietnamese man sitting in a battered old car about thirty yards away. Ton Son Nhut was not a U.S. base, and Vietnamese civilians were common around the terminals. But the coincidence that one should be sitting there at this exact moment rattled him.

He slid from the jeep, stepped forward, and lifted his M-16 to waist level. When the man reached behind the seat, Smith lifted his barrel and clicked the M-16 onto full automatic. Suddenly, the man noticed the Green Beret aiming at him and froze. Slowly, he lifted his hand. It was only a dust rag. He waved it at Smith, smiling weakly. The sergeant lowered the rifle and waved it, a signal for the man to leave. The Vietnamese started his car and quickly drove away.

Two soldiers lifted Chuyen out of the back of the truck and loaded him into the jet. One by one, Smith, Boyle, and Cotton clambered aboard. Shank asked to come along, to monitor the drugs, and hopped in. A crewman swung the door shut behind them and sealed it.

The jet's engines began to turn over with a whine. Chuyen was laid out on the metal deck, his eyes closed, still wrapped in the poncho. The jet lurched forward and slowly taxied away from the terminal. A few minutes later, it was racing down the runway.

Behind them in Saigon, a motorbike turned into an alley off Tran Nhat Duat Street and stopped at the modest house at number 38 Phan Thanh Gian. The messenger went to the door, asked for Phan Kim Lien, and then wordlessly handed her a note.

"To my darling and to my cherished children," she read, as the messenger motored away. "I have to go on a mission for a few days. Don't worry. I want to wish all of you good health and happiness. Kisses."

Lien put down the note. Why did her husband use such stiff and formal language, wishing her "good health and happiness"? Something had to be terribly wrong.

Twenty-five thousand feet over the South China Sea, halfway to Nha Trang, Chuyen stirred, pulled at his poncho, and mumbled about the cold. Smith went forward and had the heat turned up. Chuyen flew the rest of the way in silence.

An hour later, Nha Trang came up in the distance. The jet banked northeast over the ocean, waiting for the sun to sink deeper into the horizon. Below, little sticks bobbed in the slate gray water, fishing junks setting forth for the night. Slowly, the jet continued its arc, now heading west into an orange glow from the Cambodian horizon. In ten minutes, the last edge of the sun had wobbled into the jungle, and the equatorial darkness came swiftly. With one more circle, the plane banked again, swiftly descended, and touched down on the barely lit runway. As it taxied sleekly to the 5th Special Forces terminal, the runway lights went out.

The jet's engines were still whistling when a truck pulled up and stopped. Two soldiers in green berets jumped out and received the bulky poncho from the cargo hatch. In a few minutes the truck had arrived at the B-57 team hutch at 5th Special Forces headquarters. Chuyen was unloaded and laid onto a canvas cot in a bare room. Cotton was assigned to sit with him.

As the door closed, Chuyen slowly sat up and shook the cobwebs from his head. He asked for a cigarette.

"I was awake—whole time," he said, smiling groggily. To prove it, he recounted how he was lifted from the office at Camp Goodman, driven through Saigon, placed on the plane, and flown what he assumed to be northeast for an hour and a half. Was that right? he wanted to know. He was right, wasn't he? he smiled.

Cotton nodded wearily. "You're right, Chuyen. You're very smart."

"Because I not sleep with many women, I stay strong," he said, pumping his arms like Charles Atlas. "I am very strong."

16

Lee Brumley sat at his crude office desk and listened as Thai Khac Chuyen was stored in the room down the hall. The stocky counterintelligence chief was freshly showered and fed, prepared for the long night ahead. In a few minutes he would begin the interrogation.

Cambodia was coming to a head, and he wondered if Chuyen was connected to other developments. One of his agents reporting on corruption in the Vietnamese Special Forces had been exposed. The commander of the Special

Forces, Major General Quang, was now planning to double Brumley's spy back to penetrate B-57's operations in Cambodia. If General Quang learned that they had targeted Cambodia's Prince Sihanouk for special attention, Brumley reasoned, it could provoke an international incident.

Brumley typed up his findings before facing Chuyen. If Quang's plans were successful, he wrote, it would "result in the death of our operatives and a break in diplomatic relations between the U.S. and Cambodia, which are just being restored." As he walked down the hallway, the future of the war floated through his mind. Not just B-57's operations were at stake now; a complex web of diplomatic relations depended on handling Chuyen right.

And fast. They couldn't keep Chuyen forever. Within sight of the interrogation room was Detachment B-55, composed of tough Vietnamese Rangers led by American Special Forces officers. The unit, Brumley knew, was riddled with spies reporting to Saigon, the Viet Cong, or both. Word of Chuyen's presence would inevitably leak.

Jesus, Brumley thought, how can you fight a war under these conditions?

He opened the door to the interrogation room. Chuyen was sitting alone on his cot.

Brumley hit the first vein a little after midnight. Standing over the agent, his voice was firm, slightly threatening. Chuyen sat in a chair at the end of the plywood table, his weary head in his hands. In the corner, beyond the light, Boyle sat on a reversed folding metal chair. A tape recorder's spools turned slowly in the middle of the table.

Brumley had been methodically leading Chuyen through his job history, taking him over dates, places, and names again and again, plumbing for evidence of Chuyen's contamination of other operations and personnel. For this session, they had decided to do without an interpreter.

"Did you know of other people who worked for Martin or Sands?" Brumley asked, using the names Chuyen knew Marasco and Smith by.

"Yes."

"Who?"

"Phan, a Cambodian. He worked for Martin."

"How did you know he worked for Martin?"

"A friend of mine who works in B-41, S-1 front office, told me."

Brumley briefly hesitated.

"How did he know Phan worked for Martin?"

"He lives with Phan."

"When was the last time you saw Phan?" Brumley continued, pacing the room.

"Last Sunday."

"What was Phan's cover job?"

"He didn't have one."

Brumley hesitated again.

"Did anyone ask questions about Phan?"

"The LLDB captain, who is executive officer of the camp."

Brumley privately groaned. Another leak.

"Why did he ask questions?"

"Phan was seen in the marketplace with a Honda, and a pistol, and money. But he doesn't work."

Brumley decided to stop and send a bulletin to Muc Hoa. The operations had been thoroughly contaminated, even if Chuyen was not an enemy agent. Was the executive officer of the Vietnamese Special Forces a spy? he wondered. Likely, but for whom? Viet Cong or South Vietnam? Or both?

What really disgusted him was that the most elementary principles of keeping operations and personnel segregated had been violated. Hell, Marasco's principal agent *lived with* an agent from a different outfit! Didn't Marasco know that? Whether he did or didn't, he had screwed up royally. Wasn't this supposed to be a top secret operation, with all sorts of diplomatic ramifications to a security flap, etc., etc., etc.?

And Smith! Chuyen said that "Sands" often brought him along on visits to "Martin's" camp!

Brumley returned to his office in the middle of the night and typed up a damage report. Subject: the security mess in the delta.

"The above questions disclose that Principal Agent Phan was disclosed to SUBJECT by Tran Trong Thu, S1 interpreter at B-41, Muc Hoa. Questions 19 and 20 disclose that the LLDB Executive Officer at Muc Hoa may have knowledge of Phan's activities."

He ripped the last page out of the typewriter, locked the report in his safe, and walked back to the interrogation room. It was 4 A.M., June 14. The questioning had just begun.

"Did your mother live with your father in South Vietnam?"

"Yes."

"How long did she live in South Vietnam?"

"Three months."

A new phase of the interrogation had begun. Brumley intended to keep Chuyen awake and wear him down with a drumbeat of repeated questions, gathering string to entangle him in his conflicting answers. Eventually he would immobilize Chuyen in a weave of carefully elicited contradictions.

Inside the smoky, harshly lit room, Chuyen slumped as Brumley circled him. The temperature soared even though the sun had barely cleared the ocean.

"Where did she go when she left your father?" Brumley droned on.

"She went back to North Vietnam to get my brothers."

"Was she held in North Vietnam?"

"Yes."

"How was she detained?"

"When she tried to cross the Ben Hai River into South Vietnam, she and my brothers were captured by the NVA and put in jail."

"How many brothers do you have in North Vietnam?"

"One older and two younger."

"Have you been contacted by them?"

"No."

"Have you received letters from them?"

"No."

"Has anyone contacted you concerning your brothers?"

"No."

Brumley again ran through Chuyen's early years as a student. On the twenty-third question, he noted a conflict. Chuyen had said he never left Saigon during 1957–58.

"Are you certain?"

"Yes," he said wearily, fading from lack of sleep.

"Where did you live in Saigon?" Brumley pressed.

"At thirty-three Bui Nhut Xuan, the student house."

"Did your brother and sister live in Saigon at this time?"

"No."

Chuyen closed his eyes and put his head down on the table. Before, Brumley noted, Chuyen had said he lived with his sister and brother in Saigon. Brumley jerked him up by the chin. Once more, he took him through his student years. Then he pressed Chuyen with questions about his wife.

"Does she work for the VC?"

"No."

"Does she know anyone who is a VC?"

"No."

"Have you ever been asked to help the VC?"

"No, never."

"Have you ever known anyone who joined the VC?"

"No, never."

That was impossible.

"Not even a friend or classmate at school?"

"No."

Chuyen slumped again. Brumley ordered him to sit up. He decided to play his trump card. He placed a picture on the table in front of Chuyen, the captured photo of the North Vietnamese officers taken in Phuoc Long Province in 1964.

Chuyen peered groggily at it. He looked up at Brumley, then back at the photo. His face dropped with complete and utter exhaustion, and nothing else.

"Is this you?"

Chuyen looked up. "Me?"

"Is this you?" Brumley tapped the face in the picture.

"Me? No, not me."

Brumley withdrew the photo. Having planted a seed, he would come back to it later.

"Has your wife ever visited Muc Hoa?"

"No."

"Do you have a woman friend in Muc Hoa?"

"No."

"Did you talk about an intelligence operation with Phan?"

"No."

"Did Phan talk to the interpreter in S-1 about intelligence operations?"

"Possibly. He lived with him. I don't know, Phan is very quiet."

"Did you know Martin prior to coming to Muc Hoa?"

Chuyen's chin fell to his chest and his eyes closed. Brumley repeated the question. After a moment, Chuyen answered, his eyes still closed.

"I might have seen him in Tay Ninh."

"Who was Martin's boss at Moc Hoa?"

Chuyen's eyes remained closed. He was drifting off.

"I don't know. He was the boss."

Brumley asked another question, but there was no response. After a moment, Chuyen began to mumble something about recruiting for Cambodia. The only words Brumley could understand sounded something like "Mike Force" and "C and C." Finally, Chuyen's head went down on the table and he lapsed into a deep sleep.

Brumley stood over the Vietnamese. He could go no further, but that was all right. He would give Chuyen just enough time to recover. But only slightly. Then he would begin again, this time with sodium pentathol.

At 8 A.M. Saturday morning, Chuyen was shaken awake. He had been dozing for a half hour.

A group of men stood around him.

One was Maj. Stanley C. Allison, chief physician of the 5th Special Forces Group. The doctor watched as Chuyen opened his eyes and focused. Then he wrapped a rubber tourniquet around Chuyen's biceps, pumped it a few times, and took his blood pressure.

It was normal. Next he felt Chuyen's pulse, timing it with his watch. That too was normal.

Chuyen was still in a daze. Allison asked him to lie down on the cot. Then he swabbed the back of his right wrist with alcohol, slid an IV needle into his vein, and attached it to a tube flowing from a clear plastic bag. A saline solution with two grams of sodium pentathol began dripping into Chuyen's blood at a rate of ninety drops per minute.

Allison stood by monitoring the flow of drugs as a tape recorder was turned on. Brumley leaned over Chuyen and began asking questions again.

"Has anyone ever talked to you about your mother in North Vietnam?"

"Negative," Chuyen snapped. Then, after a pause: "One time. My younger brother, right now he's an NCO, Psywar Battalion Forty. He invite one Hindu. Come to see me at the house. I ask him when he come to North Vietnam, can he drop a letter to my mother and send to family. He say no. He work CII."

"Who?" Brumley asked.

"CII."

Brumley turned off the tape recorder and with a few questions figured out that Chuyen had inverted the initials for the International Control Commission, a UN unit set up in 1954 to monitor the North-South cease-fire. Despite long ago losing any real function, its staff regularly traveled between Hanoi and Saigon. Chuyen's "Hindu," Brumley figured out, referred to one of the Indian delegates on the ICC.

Brumley turned on the tape recorder and began again.

"Is that the only time you tried to send a letter to North Vietnam?"

"No. I don't want to forget that. I don't want to remember that because when I remember that, make me fed up. I think everybody of my family left there maybe die, maybe they get sick . . ."

His next words trailed off into babble. Maybe the sodium pentathol wasn't such a good idea, Brumley thought. Chuyen was nearly incoherent.

"Did your brothers come to South Vietnam?" he pressed.

"Who?"

"Your brothers."

"Yes, 1957, twice."

"Why did they come to South Vietnam?"

"They look for freedom."

"Did you see them in 1957?"

"Yes."

"Where did you see them at?"

"When I see them?"

"Where did you see them? What place did you see them at?"

"Down there. I Corps."

"What were they doing in I Corps?"

Silence, then finally: "I have the front office bring your name and everything to S-1, B-41."

Brumley was growing frustrated. He went back to Chuyen's contact with his brothers. "How long did your brothers stay in I Corps?"

"Two . . ."

As Brumley waited, Chuyen's words tailed off again.

"Where did they stay in I Corps?"

Nothing.

"What were they doing here?"

Nothing, again. Chuyen's eyes were closed.

"Are your brothers members of the North Vietnamese army?"

Chuyen suddenly came awake.

"Negative."

"How did they come from North Vietnam in 1957?"

"I say negative. Why you know they come North Vietnam, South Vietnam?"

"How did they go to I Corps?"

"Who?"

"Your brothers."

"Work for who?"

"Were your brothers in I Corps in 1957?" Brumley's frustration was complete.

"No."

"Who did you see in I Corps in 1957?"

"American in North Vietnam . . ." He mumbled a string of words, then, "Not good."

"Where were you in 1964?"

"I have been in Ban Me Thuot."

"Were you in Ban Me Thuot in . . ."

"1954."

"Where were you in 1964?"

"mmmmm . . . Saigon. . . ."

"What city were you in in 1964?"

"1964 . . ."

"Where were you in 1964?"

"Where have I been? Saigon."

"Did you stay in Saigon all of 1964?"

"Yes."

"Have you ever been in Phuoc Long Province?"

"Negative."

"Did you recognize the picture you saw last night?"

Chuyen, fading in and out, now closed his eyes.

"I try teacher . . ."

"Did you recognize the man in the picture last night?"

"No."

"Was that you in the picture last night?"

"My picture?"

"Was that your picture last night?"

"Last night? I have come here this afternoon. You say last. Where you show me last night? Last night I sleep at home with my wife. Why you ask me last night? Last night I was still at Saigon, not here. The picture this morning, just this morning you show me."

"Did you recognize the man in the picture this morning?"

"No, negative. I tell you one thing. If I see anywhere, anytime, the VC cadre or VC combat or North Vietnam in South Vietnam, I kill them immediately. Because Communist in North Vietnam or South Vietnam, they are special enemy of my family. If had a Communist right now I am not here, I am not at Pa-ree."

Brumley stared at Chuyen, on the verge of quitting. The drugs were useless. Or was Chuyen being purposefully vague?

"Does your wife know," he resumed, "that you work for an intelligence agency?"

"For who?"

"Does she know that you have worked for an American intelligence agency?"

"But for who?"

"Did she know you worked for Ginger?"

"Yes, because I love my wife too much. I love my wife. I trust my wife. All time she stay home. When she market, she ask the neighbor woman buy for him. She don't go out because I was must prevent. Tay Ninh very dangerous, small, small city. If my wife go out VC can kidnap."

"What did you tell your wife about Ginger?"

"What?"

"Was your wife at your house when Ginger came for meetings?"

". . . mmmmmm . . ."

"Could your wife have told anyone else that you were working for Ginger?"
Chuyen's eyes were closed again. He was silent.

"Did anyone in your family tell someone that you were working for Ginger?"

Chuyen slept.

"Did anyone in your family tell someone that you were working for Ginger?" Brumley asked again.

Chuyen stirred, but his eyes stayed closed. "I feel interest there. . . . American come back here," he mumbled.

Brumley tried yet again.

"Did your wife know you were meeting Ginger in Saigon?"

"No, negative. My wife is good woman, a good woman, good mother, good wife. I love too much. I trust her and not enough education, so she . . . tell everything she thinks."

"She tells everything she thinks?"

"Yes."

"Did she tell someone you were working for Ginger?"

"No. Not until asked for him and for me."

Brumley had heard enough to alert MACV that "Ginger's" operation had been compromised. Safe houses, dead drops, and radio frequencies would have to be shut down and other agents connected with the operation terminated. "Ginger" would have to get out of Vietnam.

"When you left Saigon, you gave your wife a letter . . ." Brumley resumed.

"Right now my wife and me love themself," Chuyen blurted out. "Love too much. Keep every, every letter. Yes. . . ."

He faded off again, then back. "I buy for her . . ."

The sodium pentathol, dripping from the clear plastic over the cot, was about two-thirds gone. Dr. Allison had long ago left.

"Was there a warning in that letter?" Brumley persisted.

"No, my wife don't have anyone friend."

"Do you have a girlfriend in Muc Hoa?"

"Negative, negative, absolutely negative. Anywhere I don't have girlfriend because I love my wife too much. I love her."

"Have you ever met a contact in Muc Hoa?"

"In Muc Hoa?"

"Have you ever met a female contact in Muc Hoa?"

"Negative."

"Have you ever worked in Thanh Tri?"

"Have I worked for Thanh Tri?"

"No, have you ever worked in the town of Thanh Tri?"

"Thanh Tri?"

"A team, Special Forces?"

"Yes."

"What type of job did you have there?"

"Sometime Thanh Tri doesn't have interpreter and S-5 job. That easy job. So I assigned Thanh Tri for two, three, or four days, maximum three days."

Jesus, Thanh Tri would have to be disinfected now, too, Brumley swore. Every agent, code book, the names of everyone Chuyen had come in contact with.

"Have you ever talked to anyone about intelligence at Thanh Tri?"

"Negative. I hate the LLDB too much. During eight years I have been working with Special Forces, I know this. The first of the LLDB. Negative, negative."

"Did the LLDB have questions about Phan?"

"Yes. The captain, the camp commander before at Thanh Tri, he is XO at Muc Hoa now. He ask me, 'What is Phan doing for U.S.? I don't see him work for camp.' I answer him, 'Negative, negative, I don't know.' "

Brumley groaned to himself again. The Vietnamese Special Forces had figured out Marasco was using Phan.

"What is the LLDB captain's name?"

"Chieu. Nguyen Chieu. I spell, you write down. N-g-u-y-e-n. C-h-i-e-u."

"Did Captain Chieu ask questions about Sergeant Sands?"

"Never."

"Did he know what Sergeant Sands's job was at Muc Hoa?"

"Funds officer."

We'll have to polygraph Chuyen more on that, Brumley thought. Chuyen might be trying to protect his own operation.

"Who took you to see Mr. Cox at Muc Hoa?" he now asked, probing Chuyen's contacts with the CIA.

"Mr. What?"

"Who introduced you to Mr. Cox?"

"Lieutenant David, because . . . I forgot the . . ." He was drifting off again.

"Did you ask Lieutenant David to introduce you to Mr. Cox?"

"Ask what?"

"Did you ask Lieutenant David to introduce you to Mr. Cox?"

"No, negative."

"For what agency does Mr. Cox work?"

Chuyen's chin was on his chest. He started to snore.

"Who does Mr. Cox work for?"

Chuyen didn't respond.

". . . I know him," he suddenly mumbled.

"Why didn't you go to work for Mr. Cox?"

"Why?" Chuyen slowly lifted his head.

"Why?"

"I don't like him," Chuyen said. "He is an impolite man. Excuse me, but Americans poor education. The first time . . ." Suddenly, he drifted again. ". . . Even Vietnamese speak English, you know, must talk, talk, talk. . . ."

The answer petered out. On a hunch, Brumley decided to probe another area.

"Did you and Ginger ever talk about C and C?"

"Yes."

Holy shit, Brumley thought. The Command and Control group was the most secret intelligence organization operating in Vietnam, a contemporary Dirty Dozen. C & C roamed the world on special missions, snatching Communist officers off the Ho Chi Minh Trail, including Russians and Chinese advisers, dropping behind the lines for special sabotage missions, and seeding North Vietnamese supply dumps with exploding ammunition. Some C & C teams were dispatched to Europe and the Middle East to intercept and foul shipments of surface-to-air missiles to North Vietnam.

C & C was a project of MACV's Special Operations Group. Its personnel were recruited from all the military services—Navy SEALs, Marine recon units, Army Special Forces and Air Force special ops wings. Even Coast Guard crypto specialists played a role.

"What did Ginger tell you about C and C?" Brumley asked.

"He ask me to recruit seven men, brave, strong, single, who like to go to VC area."

"Did you recruit men for Ginger?" Brumley asked.

"No . . . not yet."

That was a break, Brumley thought, if it was true.

"Is Ginger still in South Vietnam?"

Chuyen's answer was unintelligible again. Brumley tried again with the same results, then tried another tack.

"Did you tell your wife about C and C?"

"My wife . . . negative. . . . My wife . . . very, very good. Only take care of children."

"Did you tell anyone else about C and C?"

"Negative, but sometimes I hear they talk themselves about C and C. I think they joke, they lie."

"Who talked about C and C?"

"Interpreter."

Another security breach. Jesus.

"Which interpreter?"

"B-40 and B-41 at Can Tho. Before that, he work for C and C. . . ."

"Do you know his name?"

"Yes, for sure."

"What is his name?"

"Thu Linh . . . Ninh."

Chuyen fell again into a deep sleep.

Brumley, too, had reached his limits. Boyle could take over for awhile. He called for Allison and told him to remove the IV.

Chuyen would break soon, Brumley thought, watching the needle come out. He had to.

17

H ave you ever received training in North Vietnam?" Brumley asked
again, standing over Chuyen in the stale room.
Outside it was 10 A.M. on a gray rainy day. Rain pelted the tin roof.
Inside, the room was dark except for the funnel of light that fell on the table.
Cigarette smoke filled the cramped space.

Chuyen looked half-conscious from his interrupted sleep and a sodium
pentathol hangover. But he had worn out his interpreter. Brumley had brought
in a new one who was sitting at the table, alert, waiting for cues.

Time was becoming important. Word had inevitably spread that B-57 had
a problem on its hands. At some point soon they would have to decide whether
to shift tactics and confront Chuyen with their certainty that he was an enemy
agent, that there was no hope, that his life hung in the balance, that only a
confession could save him.

But that, too, would expose their weakness.

Brumley asked the question again.

"Have you ever received training in North Vietnam?"

"No."

"When you worked for Ginger, did you receive training at an intelligence
camp?"

"No."

"When you worked for Ginger did you receive any intelligence training?"

"I mostly see him at Twenty-fifth Division at night. He taught me map
reading, cover, how to determine true and false information, how to use radio
to direct aircraft and how to mark targets."

"Did you ever go on penetration missions for Ginger?"

"No, but I work with his people."

"Have you been to Vung Tau?"

"For what?"

It was a stab in the dark. Vung Tau, an old French beach resort on the
South China Sea, was the official in-country R & R spot for GIs and ARVN
troops. Unofficially, Viet Cong cadres changed out of their uniforms and
rested there, too. Making things more interesting, the town also hosted the
Saigon government's intelligence school. The inevitable intrigue that enveloped the resort made it Vietnam's Casablanca.

"During 1963 and 1964, did you go to Vung Tau?"

"Yes. I went with a friend for a seven-day vacation."

"Did you go to an intelligence school at Vung Tau when you worked for
Ginger?"

"No. He sent other persons but not me because he needed me in Tay
Ninh."

"When Huynh was compromised by ARVN security, did he ask anyone to
go to work for ARVN intelligence?"

"No."

"Did MSS," Brumley probed, referring to Saigon's FBI, "ask you to work for them?"

"No, never. They wanted to have only their own people, not North Vietnamese like me."

Not a bad idea, Brumley thought, though it probably didn't make a difference.

"Did they interrogate you?"

"Never."

"Did your wife know you worked for JTAD?"

"Yes, because Ginger came to my house. He often talked to my wife."

"Did your wife know that you were going to work for Sands?"

"No, I told her I was only working for a good man."

"Did anyone else in your family know you were working for Mr. Ginger or Sands?"

"No, but my mother-in-law knew I was working for a good man."

"Did your mother-in-law ask you questions about your work?"

"Never."

"Did your father-in-law ask you questions about your work?"

"Never. But he is not really my father-in-law. He is my wife's stepfather. He speaks Chinese."

Brumley made a mental note to follow that up. Chinese-Vietnamese controlled most of the money in Saigon and were heavily involved in gold smuggling and currency manipulation.

"Have you ever met your wife's real father?"

"No. He is dead."

"How long has your wife lived in Saigon?"

"Since 1960."

"Did she live in Tay Ninh?"

"Yes. She lived there three years. She left in 1969."

Brumley went back to what Chuyen knew of American intelligence tradescraft.

"Have you ever learned secret writing?" The technique used classified chemicals for agents and their case officers to write in "invisible ink." Brumley wanted to know if Chuyen could have compromised the chemicals to Hanoi.

"Not yet. Ginger gave me a radio because my house was about two kilometers from his house. At 1200 and 1800 hours I would make a call. I also called if I picked up dead drop and found a message that said Tay Ninh would be mortared."

Great, Brumley thought, Chuyen was not only servicing the dead drops, he was reading Ginger's messages.

"Why did you leave Tay Ninh?"

"Ginger said he didn't need me anymore. . . ."

In the middle of the war? Brumley privately scoffed.

"He made me sign document promising never to mention his name or say what I did. Even if I see him, I not supposed to show I know him. Every week

I also go to a place and see if there is a mark on the wall. If I see mark, then I go another place and meet him."

"Have you ever talked to Ginger since then?"

"Yes, I saw him once in Saigon, in a restaurant, early this year."

"What information did you discuss?"

"He wanted to put me in C and C."

"What is your name?"

"My name is Chuyen. Thai Khac Chuyen."

Brumley stood over Chuyen again. The hours had become countless. His legs were rubbery, his head foggy with the repetition of questions.

Chuyen had still not given in, so the doctor was called again. At two o'clock in the afternoon of June 15, he inserted another IV in Chuyen's arm and started the drip of sodium pentathol.

"Did you see your brothers at Muc Hoa?"

"Who?"

"Your brothers. From North Vietnam?"

"No, never see them. They in North Vietnam."

"Does anyone in your family work for the U.S. government?"

"No."

"Do you have a sister-in-law who works for CORDS?"

"Yes, young sister-in-law."

"What does she do for CORDS?"

"She is a clerk. . . . She is a clerk."

Brumley remembered to ask a routine counterintelligence question.

"Is she planning to go to the United States?"

"Yes. Very soon, maybe July. . . ."

Brumley was startled. He hadn't expected that answer. It added another liability to the case. North Vietnam, like any other Soviet ally, was assumed to have close relations with the KGB.

"Why does she want to go to the United States?"

"Because an American there, he is adviser in Saigon, he like her. He look for a long time and also give money for four years to go to university in U.S. Miss Oanh name of my sister-in-law. She agree to that and twice I saw the American there. One time he come to my house take dinner, and one time go to his house take dinner. I am the brother-in-law of her so I must protect her. Maybe the U.S., some U.S. man not good for her. We go to movie, *The Good, the Bad, the Ugly*. You know that. After discuss I think he is a good man. He divorce his wife. He have two sons in the army, one at German air force and one at infantry, he come to Vietnam before. Now my sister-in-law go to U.S. for learning the economic political program."

Chuyen's answer alarmed Brumley. He decided to take one more tack on Chuyen's family before ending the session and deciding what to do about this latest security threat.

"Have you seen your brothers who live in North Vietnam?"

"I see?"

He was fading again.

"Have you seen your brothers recently?"

"North Vietnam?"

"Yes!" Brumley shouted.

"When?"

That was all he could get for now. It was just as well. He was exhausted. He left the room and asked Allison to disconnect the IV.

18

At four o'clock Tuesday afternoon, June 17, the polygraph operator switched off his machine, turned to Lee Brumley, and shook his head. It was useless, he said. Chuyen was too burned out for the lie detector now. His heart and pulse rates were all over the chart. No way to get an accurate reading anymore.

Chuyen lay on the cot in the fetid room, eyes squeezed shut, his body crusty with old sweat, his black hair plastered to his scalp. Six days of sodium pentathol, sleep deprivation, longer sessions with the lie detector, and rotating teams of rested inquisitors had knocked him out. Their drone was relentless, numbing: Where were you born? When did you come south? When was the last time you saw your brothers? Where were you in 1964? Have you ever been in Phuoc Long Province? Is this you in the picture? How long have you worked for North Vietnamese intelligence? Who else knew about your operations?

Chuyen had bent, wavered, and collapsed in exhaustion. As time wore on, however, he began to curse his tormentors.

"You will lose in Vietnam," he screamed at Brumley. "You Americans are stupid. You know nothing, nothing about Vietnam. You will lose."

To Brumley, Chuyen's outbursts were more evidence of his true allegiances. At one point, he also admitted going to meet his brother once in the northern reaches of the jungle. Consistently, the polygraph showed that he had lied about his employment, his whereabouts in 1964, contacts with his family in North Vietnam, and links with the Communist intelligence service. But the problem was that Chuyen had not given him the biggest prize of all: a confession.

Without a confession, their options were starkly narrowed. Without a confession, there could be no certainty of his guilt. Ironically, in fact, they would have to investigate whether the machine was faulty, or whether some other factor had contaminated the results. It was common, after all, for Vietnamese families to have members on both sides of the war and to maintain discreet contact with the Viet Cong. Without a confession, they could not begin to learn anything about the Communist intelligence apparatus that they were sure had recruited and targeted Chuyen against them. And without a confession, they had no base from which to begin rebuilding Chuyen into a triple agent, sending him back against his Communist controllers.

To a skilled interrogator, a confession was the juice that could be squeezed from the hardest orange. Chuyen had been squeezed, but he had given nothing of substance. Even worse, instead of locking shut the case against Chuyen, the last polygraph had been actually useless. Horton found a typewriter, rolled in the correct blank form, typed up his conclusion, and left it with Brumley as he packed up to leave: "The subject showed no deception on the relevant questions." It was the last recorded summary of his interrogation, Tuesday afternoon, June 17.

Brumley was in a quandary. Sleep deprivation, round-the-clock interrogation, confronting the subject with his contradictory answers, showing him the squiggly lines on the polygraph paper and evidence of lying—these were the tried and true methods of interrogators in Moscow and Washington. Rank brutality had long ago been discarded by the most sophisticated interrogators. Beatings, cigarette burns, electric wires to the genitals were the stuff of amateurs, or sadists. Brumley would never do that; he considered himself a professional.

The Chinese in Korea and the British in Malaysia had shown what could be done without laying a hand on a captive. The Pentagon had been astounded when GIs paraded before the cameras denouncing American imperialism. Their methods had been studied in the intelligence schools for years.

Brumley had used all these techniques to little avail. After six days, he held only the promising charts of the polygraphs when Chuyen clearly "blipped" the questions on his loyalty and possible affiliation with North Vietnamese intelligence. His guilt could only be inferred. Now, Brumley sat down to summarize the results of his interrogations, defeated. The "subject," he lamely concluded, "has possibly assisted the VC."

If so, what next? The Americans had everything in Vietnam except what Brumley now needed, a place to put Chuyen away. The United States had its own weapons, bases, troops in Vietnam, its own air force, navy, mess halls, and even its own swimming pools, movie theaters, and bowling alleys. But it did not have its own jails.

He carried the report to Major Crew. The men sat back and considered the alternatives. They couldn't keep Chuyen, and they couldn't just let him go. Handing him over to a South Vietnamese jail was equivalent to giving him to the Viet Cong, they thought. From their vantage point, the South Vietnamese were just as much the enemy. Chuyen would surely be tortured until he spilled everything about the Cambodian operations and the Americans he worked with. The Vietnamese weren't shy about that.

They needed some advice.

The CIA office in Nha Trang was secluded behind a mustard yellow wall on the beach road just outside of town. Antennas bristled from its red-tiled roof. Through the palm trees, the pale blue waters of the South China Sea sparkled to the far horizon.

Nha Trang was the base for CIA operations in II Corps, which belted central Vietnam from the coastal plains to the Cambodian border. Three major towns anchored the coast from Qui Nhon in the North to Nha Trang in the middle and Phan Kiet in the South. As one of only five regional offices, the Nha Trang CIA station was an important step on the CIA career ladder.

The North Vietnamese army controlled the jungle, nearly impervious to intelligence probes. U.S. radio intercepts, the statements of deserters driven from the forest by B-52 raids, and low-level spies in hamlets controlled by the NVA were used to fill the gaps. On the coast, far from their supply lines, Communist military activities were confined to scattershot guerrilla raids and underground proselytizing.

The CIA had little success in penetrating North Vietnamese army units west of the Central Highlands, conceding the mission to Army intelligence nets or Special Forces recon units. Instead, the CIA concentrated on pacification projects, Phoenix operations, and holding the hand of the National Police, a ruthless apparat that managed the regime's infamous prisons. Whatever the police lacked in competence, it was rumored, they made up for in enthusiasm for corruption and torture.

Crew and Brumley pulled up to the double steel gates and beeped their horn. A Vietnamese sentry jumped from his post and pulled the gates open. They drove through and parked among the International Scouts and Ford Broncos that filled the compound.

Harold Chipman, a husky man with a pistol strapped to his belt, met them in the foyer and took them upstairs. The operations chief was the number three CIA official in Nha Trang, a protégé of Ted Shackley from their days together in Berlin and Miami. Sitting down, he got right to the point. He had heard about their problem from people in Saigon, he said. How was it going? What did they want from him?

Crew and Brumley reviewed the problem from the beginning, starting with the captured photo, the agent reports fingering Chuyen as an enemy spy, and the past six days of interrogation. Crew reviewed the meeting with Enking and Scrymgeour in Saigon on June 10 and again raised the notion of the CIA taking Chuyen off their hands.

Chipman shook his head. No way, he said. They didn't have the room.

Crew went back to what Enking had said, that "elimination" might be the only way out. But it worried him that the agency could never give an official approval. If something went wrong they'd be out on a limb.

Chipman shrugged.

"What do you think Ted Shackley's attitude would be toward eliminating the guy?" Crew asked.

"Are you kidding?" Chipman said slowly. "He won't have any objection to this, considering all the people that disappeared when he was in Laos."

Brumley and Crew smiled. They knew Laos was still a CIA show where all the rules were off.

What else? Chipman asked, taking notes. There was another problem, Brumley said. Chuyen had a sister-in-law going to the States. She could be dirty, too.

The CIA man frowned at that. Communist agents in the States was not a good idea.

Bring back all the interrogation reports and polygraph charts, he told Brumley. He'd be glad to take a look at them.

It was early evening when the two Green Berets left. A fragrant breeze blew off the bougainvillea as they drove along the ocean. But the moment lay heavily on them. A problem that had been merely theoretical in May, even an interesting counterintelligence exercise, was narrowing to one grim alternative.

They decided it was time to meet with Colonel Rheault.

Bob Rheault sat behind his desk fiddling with paperwork as the men filed into his office at 6:30 P.M. Reports from around the country, generated by a week-long inspection tour and an upsurge in combat, had piled up while he was away. He was glad to be here, the best command of his life, but the pace had been extreme. He'd hardly settled in when the North Vietnamese army launched a string of stinging attacks in the Ashau Valley, overrunning some Green Beret camps. Apparently Hanoi was trying to consolidate its grip on the jungle as the Paris Peace Talks entered a new phase. There were also heavier than usual requirements for collection on Cambodia, a reflection of the stepped-up secret bombing. General Abrams put a premium on the operations.

The men took their seats on folding metal chairs: Crew and Brumley, plus Tom Middleton, the group intelligence officer, and Lt. Col. Ken Facey, Rheault's executive officer. To Rheault, all the men but Facey, whom he had known in Germany, were strangers. He had been in charge for only a week.

Crew opened the discussion, outlining the history of their problem with Chuyen. Rheault signed documents, occasionally glancing up as the officer touched on one or another point. Brumley then reviewed the interrogation and polygraph reports, listing the pluses and minuses of letting Chuyen go. Middleton listened quietly in the corner.

The problem was that Chuyen was now angry as hell, Brumley added. He could very well go to the Saigon security services out of revenge and spill everything.

Rheault wrapped up his work and began to listen closely.

"What about your visit to Saigon?" he asked. He knew the CIA's attitude would be critically important to their decisions, even if the CIA had no official place in the chain of command. Cambodia was mostly a CIA show. During 1967–68, when Rheault was assigned to the "special activities" office of the Joint Chiefs of Staff, his job was to coordinate CIA and State Department approval for activities in Cambodia, missions that were carried out by the Green Berets under CIA supervision. Lyndon Johnson, faced with a public souring on the war, was obsessed with keeping them secret. Nixon had no less a reason for keeping them hidden; the cornerstone of his war strategy

was convincing Americans he was on the way out of Vietnam, not en-
tangling them in another Indo-Chinese country. When Rheault arrived
in Vietnam, he was amused to hear President Nixon declare that "Cambodia is one place where our hands are clean." Rheault had been supervising operations in Cambodia from a distance; now he was running them
himself.

Crew told Rheault what Clement Enking had said at the CIA meeting in
Saigon: that "the CIA could not sanction it, but killing Chuyen might be the
only way out." Enking had been offhand about it, Crew said, but had also
made it clear that they were on their own if there ever was a flap.

"Plausible denial" was something they all understood. It was part of their
work.

Lee Brumley summed up their talk with Chipman in Nha Trang and
relayed the CIA man's crack that Shackley wouldn't mind them killing Chuyen
because so many had been zapped on Shackley's watch in Laos. They were
due to go back again during the week, he said, because Chipman was going
to review their interrogation and polygraph charts and enlist the CIA to help
with background checks on Chuyen's family. Hopefully, since there was no
place to put him on ice, they could peddle Chuyen to the CIA as a possible
counterintelligence asset.

Rheault cut off the discussion. It was his habit to give his men responsibility.
He turned to Major Crew. It was his unit, his problem.

"What do you recommend?"

Crew paused, and cleared his throat.

"Well, there are various options," he said. "We can keep him on as an
agent, isolating him in do-nothing missions where we can closely control him.
Nothing in Cambodia. We can't let him go back to Muc Hoa."

"Or," Crew continued, "we can also fire him. Give him a cash payoff, keep
him on a leash with small regular payments after that. Warn him to keep quiet
and stay away from Muc Hoa."

"Or," Crew concluded, clearly uncomfortable, "we can terminate him."
He paused. "Get rid of him."

Rheault was listening intently. It was all right so far, but he wasn't going to
let Crew off the hook.

"Okay," he said with a dry smile, "what do you think we ought to do?" He
scanned the room. These were all his intelligence officers, his experts, sitting
in front of him. He wanted an answer from them. He wanted them to take
responsibility. That had always been his style.

"I think we ought to get rid of him," Crew said finally.

Rheault looked at him.

"Okay," he finally said. "Make up a plan." The room was silent. Rheault
told them to get a clear line of guidance on it from the CIA. "I'd like to know
more what they think. Then we'll decide."

With that, the meeting was over, and the men started to get up and leave
the office. Rheault turned back to his paperwork.

"Wait a minute," Ken Facey suddenly said. The executive officer had been quiet throughout the meeting. "I think we ought to think about this some more."

The others hesitated.

"I think we ought to research every possible alternative before going through with something like this," Facey said, still sitting. "I'd rather build a cabin and keep him here until the end of the war."

The men turned to Rheault for their cue. Facey was, after all, the number two, the commander's deputy.

"I just am not sure this is the right way to proceed," Facey plunged ahead. "One thing, it might be smart to get MACV's approval on this."

No one said anything. Finally, Rheault spoke up.

"Nothing's been decided yet, Ken. We're going to get some more information." He nodded at the men, and they took the signal to move on. Facey had said his piece.

Rheault remembered why he hadn't liked Facey before when they served together in Germany. He was wishy-washy, a thumbsucker. He'd give him something else to do for a while, get him out of the way.

At three o'clock the next day, Crew and Brumley went back to see Chipman with the interrogation reports and polygraph charts. It was June 18.

There was no word yet from Saigon, Chipman told them. Nothing about the traces.

We're running out of time, they told him. Something has to be done.

Have patience, Chipman said. I'll send another cable.

When they returned to B-57 headquarters, two of the sergeants assigned to guard Chuyen said the prisoner was getting out of control. He had been banging the walls and yelling. At one point, they had had to tie him up and handcuff him to keep him quiet.

The entire headquarters group was getting jumpy, Crew and Brumley knew. Chuyen was taking up all of their time and involving too many people. Now there were clerks, radio operators, and pilots involved, plus a handful of people in Saigon. The whole thing was ballooning way out of proportion. Something had to be done to get Chuyen out of their hair.

The discussions had already started.

One idea was for Lee Brumley and Eddie Boyle to drive out into the woods with Chuyen and put a bullet in his ear.

Another plan was to fly him to Taiwan and turn him over to the Nationalist Chinese secret police "for safekeeping." He'd never be heard from again.

They talked of dropping him from a plane.

They debated the comparative merits of knives, garroting, poison, pistols, and Swedish K's.

The men were in the serious final stages of dealing with Chuyen's fate now. Their options, as they saw it, had run out.

There was an irony to the debate as the nights and the interrogations went on: For all the killing in Vietnam—the bombing and artillery, the "free-fire zones" and "harassment and interdiction fire," the men were turning themselves inside out for the sake of a "single gook." Why was it such a big deal?

"How the hell do we do this?" Marasco asked, breaking up one of the meetings. "I mean, is there a manual or something?"

What were they waiting for? Were they going to do something unique?

There were the Phoenix hunter-killer teams, and the Kit Carson Scouts (Communist defectors dressed in black pajamas who slipped into villages to assassinate their former VC comrades). There were the SOG teams who prowled North Vietnam, Laos, and the Ho Chi Minh Trail looking for POWs or taking a few. Killing in quiet was common in this war, almost routine. They all knew about the "tiger cages" where South Vietnam kept some prisoners. Life was cheap.

Everybody knew "the mere gook rule," from the generals on down, as in "the only good gook is a dead gook." And there was the joke that every newcomer heard about the three-step program for winning the war: "One, remove all the Vietnamese and put them on ships. Two, pave the country over. Three, sink the ships."

There was Gen. George Patton III, son of the famed World War II tank commander, who was infamous for keeping a VC skull on his desk. Ear collections were not unknown. Villages suspected of harboring VC were razed.

Why, they began to wonder, were they worrying so much about "their gook?" The war was measured by body counts, wasn't it? So here was one more body, one more gook. Big deal.

Yet something held them back: They weren't Nazis, they were American boys.

Budge Williams made a last stab with his idea of paying Chuyen off. It was rejected.

What were the rules in Vietnam, they asked themselves, for killing an enemy spy? None of them knew.

The VC don't have any qualms about it, somebody said. They bump off hamlet chiefs every night. Look at the Hue massacre during Tet. Thousands taken out and executed in mass graves.

But what if they were caught? someone asked. But by whom? the others clamored. Who was going to take the time to investigate them for killing a VC spy?

Who would *want* to do that?

Crew and Brumley went back to Chipman again Wednesday night. There was no time left, they said. They wanted an answer.

What would the agency think if they "took him out on patrol?"

Chipman got their drift, Brumley was sure. On Thursday morning he called again. No answer yet. Chipman told them he would send a cable to Saigon asking for a priority response.

More than a week had passed since Crew and Williams had asked the CIA for advice. They wondered about the agency's foot-dragging. Or was it a deliberate silence? The more they thought about it, the more they began to conclude that the delay was intentional. After all, hadn't they been told twice that "eliminating Chuyen might be the best option"? What else did they need, a singing telegram? The CIA was maneuvering to distance itself from the problem, building a case for "plausible denial," they concluded. The CIA obviously wanted to be able to say they had no involvement in Chuyen's execution.

Another factor, Brumley thought, was Chipman's dismissal of their idea to squirrel away Chuyen on a CIA island. That, too, must be a tactic to close out their options. He was sure the CIA had one island in the Pacific and another facility in Panama where renegade agents could be "cooled off."

Let's face it, he told the others, the CIA is never going to say "kill him." That's not their way.

The CIA's way is silence.

19

On Thursday afternoon, June 19, a secretary walked into a conference room at the U.S. Embassy where senior CIA officials were meeting, and handed Dean Almy a message. The head of the Nha Trang CIA office was surprised. By consensus, the meetings of the top CIA field officers in Vietnam were almost never disturbed. Ted Shackley didn't permit it. There was too much to do.

Almy, a patrician New Englander, excused himself and privately scanned the cable. It was from Harold Chipman, whom he had left in charge in Nha Trang when he left for Saigon earlier in the week.

The cable was marked "Urgent." It concerned the problems some Green Berets in Nha Trang were having with their agent.

Why the hell would Chipman bother me with that? Almy wondered. What does that have to do with us? We don't get involved with run-of-the-mill Green Beret operations. The first warning signal went down his spine.

The second came when he read through the text. Chipman summarized how he had been trying to help the soldiers figure out whether they had a double agent on their hands. He had asked the Saigon station to do traces, but nothing had come back. Now the Green Berets were planning to "take him on patrol." They weren't asking permission, they wanted the CIA's help—perhaps an aircraft to fly their agent to Cambodia. There was no doubt what they intended to do with him. Chipman said he needed guidance.

Almy was alarmed. Chipman was supposed to be able to handle things himself. From what the cable said, he had not only failed to handle a routine problem, he had made it worse.

This wouldn't happen if his deputy Ed Splain was on duty, Almy groused to himself. But Splain was on leave, forcing him to leave Chipman, his operations chief, in charge. That always made him nervous.

Chipman was touted by Shackley as a top-flight agent recruiter from his assignments in Moscow, Berlin, and Miami, but Almy didn't share the admiration. Chipman talked a good game, but his reports were late and usually full of jargon. His judgment could be screwy, too, Almy thought. And he had a phony tough-guy attitude that annoyed the hell out of him.

Chipman's predilection for the company of Vietnamese bargirls also bothered Almy. The current flame was a thin little wraith at Streamers, "Chichi." She couldn't weigh more than sixty pounds soaking wet, Almy thought. At the same time, Chipman was romancing a CIA secretary in Saigon whom he said he was going to marry. That kind of behavior could leave him open to coercion or blackmail. Almy didn't want to be a bluenose, but he thought Chipman needed to be reined in. The problem was that the operations man was a protégé of Ted Shackley.

"Shack," Chipman called him, as if the icy station chief were a close pal—"I just talked to Shack," or "Shack and I talked about this and that." It grated on Almy to no end. Nobody talked to Ted Shackley like that, certainly not a subordinate, no matter how close they were.

Chipman's cable was the first Almy had heard about the Green Berets. He couldn't believe it had gone so far. Why hadn't Chipman just told them to get lost—"Sorry, boys, we can't help you." That's all. Why get the CIA involved?

In his nearly two years in Vietnam, Almy had seen a parade of Green Berets come knocking on the CIA's door for help with their various schemes. Sometimes they asked for an aircraft to drop someone out of, sometimes a boat. They were always looking for advice on "knocking off" somebody, as if the CIA were a bunch of thugs for hire. They read too many spy novels.

Almy knew a few things about how things worked. He came from a long line of secret agents. As far back as the American Revolution an ancestor was helping smuggle British textile machinery to Rhode Island. A great-great-grandfather was a spy for the Union at Vicksburg. A younger brother also worked for the CIA.

Almy joined the Marines at sixteen in World War II and chased the Japanese across the Pacific in island-to-island fighting. He ended up in China with the OSS. After the war he took a fling at newspapering in Fredericksburg, Virginia, but it bored him. The CIA came along and offered to send him to graduate school in Southeast Asia studies at Cornell and Yale and then to Indonesian language training. It was the depths of the cold war, and Almy was off on a career as a CIA case officer.

The next decade took him to Sumatra, Korea, the Philippines, and before coming to Vietnam in November 1967, Laos. He knew the ropes in Asia, where conspiracies and plots were a way of life. He was certainly not naive. He knew double agents got killed in wartime, and more than the usual number in Vietnam. If you wanted to put a fine point on it, sure, you could call it murder. But what for? There was a war going on, a political war.

Murder was not an American policy. Phoenix was something different, he would admit. It was brutal, but it was nothing more than the Viet Cong did every night. Yes, there were "excesses." And yes, the CIA turned its head when the "locals" played rough. What else could they do? It was their country, wasn't it?

But you had to be careful what you said when "the locals" were listening. Almy got a lesson in that when he was running agents by boat into North Korea in the early 1950s. At one meeting with South Korean intelligence, the CIA chief complained loudly about a certain Korean agent. Couldn't someone get him "out of his hair?" The next night Almy noticed the South Koreans were digging a grave for the guy down on the beach.

It was an education. But as far as Almy knew, the CIA never killed guys on their own payroll. Not its own agents, he was sure of that. He remembered a CIA man in Indonesia who casually suggested such a thing during a meeting one day. He was on the next flight home.

It just wasn't done. Of course, if you turned a bad apple over to the local police . . .

Why didn't the Green Berets do the same thing? If they didn't have the same rules, Almy thought, they should. *Especially* the Green Berets.

In general he thought they were okay. Nice guys, well-meaning, well trained . . . in certain things. The problem was they took their own press clips too seriously. They thought they were global thinkers. Case in point, the Montagnards. The Green Berets loved them. One night Almy got into a long discussion about them with some guys from 5th Special Forces. The beer was flowing, talk was loose.

If your Montagnards are so great, he said, how come they're still running around the hills in loincloths and eating monkey brains and using bows and arrows? How come it's the Vietnamese who have the best real estate in the country, a great culture, a body of literature and poetry?

How come? he laughed. How come the Montagnards still live in the hills on slash-and-burn agriculture if they're so smart? Tell me that.

You picked the wrong guys, he told the Green Berets. You like the Montagnards because they're honest, and simple, and straightforward—just like you. They've lived off the land for two thousand years, but now you've trained them to shake hands and salute. They look you straight in the eye, just like Americans, not the average Vietnamese. They're your mirror image, that's why you like them.

Give me a shifty-eyed Vietnamese any time, Almy said: You might not like him, he may even steal you blind, but he's the guy who's going to win. He's the guy who's going to save the country from the Communists. Your little Montagnards will be smiling and saluting right up to the minute the Communists take over South Vietnam and kill them all.

The Green Berets admitted he might be right. But they had a question: Who started funding the Montagnards in the first place? Whose idea was it to send us over here to train them?

Almy got up and excused himself from the embassy meeting. He had to unravel Chipman's mess. It wasn't the Green Berets' fault, he knew, it was really Chipman's. He should have turned them off. Anybody who needs the CIA's help to handle a low-level Vietnamese agent should have been shown the door.

Almy walked down the corridor and turned into Ted Shackley's office. Shackley's secretary, Dana Meggs, told him her boss was in a meeting. He couldn't be disturbed.

Almy explained the problem: There was an urgent message from Harold Chipman that required a swift response. "I'm tied up all day," he said. "This is something he has to deal with."

Of course, it was something he wanted to dump in the station chief's lap anyway. Let "Shack" handle it.

Meggs reached forward to take the envelope. "I'll make sure he gets it," she said. "Gits it," it came out. Meggs was from deepest North Carolina.

Almy hesitated. "It's very important," he said.

"I said, I'll make sure he gets it," Meggs repeated. *Gits it.* It was the voice secretaries use with their boss's underlings.

Almy stepped back, holding the envelope. He ducked his head back through the doorway. He could see Bruce Scrymgeour and Clement Enking working at desks in the outer office. They had been listening to the exchange, obviously. He smiled half at them, and half at Meggs.

"Okay, everyone can see this," he said. He ceremoniously handed over the envelope. Meggs smiled, took it from him, opened her left-hand drawer, raised the envelope in the air, and with a flourish, placed it inside.

"Done." She slid the drawer closed.

Almy smiled and left the room.

Brumley and Crew were anxious. Nine days had passed since the Chuyen problem had been brought to the CIA, nine days since Clement Enking told them "elimination was efficient." They had been cautious, prudent they thought, waiting for some kind of green light or other solution from Chipman.

But now Chuyen was impossible to hold any longer. He was making a racket, banging on the door, yelling, cursing. He wanted out—out of everything. He never wanted to work for the Green Berets, or any Americans, again.

Now everyone on base seemed to know they had someone important locked up in that room. It wouldn't take long for the South Vietnamese Green Berets next door to find out, and that would be tantamount to telling the Viet Cong.

Crew called Chipman at 10 A.M. Thursday, June 19, and again at three in the afternoon. There was still no word from Saigon, Chipman said, nothing on the traces. Yes, he understood their problem. He had cabled Saigon again, asking for a priority response. There was nothing more he could do.

The two soldiers listened. Something wasn't right, they agreed after they hung up. The CIA's silence must mean "go." Chipman was just giving them blather. It was time to make plans.

Alvin Smith pleaded for one more chance.

"Let me try it," he said. "I can turn him around."

Crew, Brumley, Williams, and Marasco had been debating what to do about Smith all week. The sergeant had hovered outside Colonel Rheault's office during the meeting to discuss Chuyen's fate. When they came out and told him it looked like Chuyen might be executed, he had been nearly hysterical. He had pleaded for a chance to turn him into a "triple agent."

"I can do it," he said. "He trusts me. Let me give it a shot."

It was too late for that, they said. Chuyen was alienated; he'd never be trustworthy.

Smith's emotional plea jolted them enough, however, to assign Marasco to sit down with the sergeant and talk to him.

"Nothing's been decided," he told Smith. "Maybe we'll give your idea a chance."

After that they'd debated whether to involve Smith at all anymore. Brumley and Williams argued that they should cut him loose. The sergeant was too nervous and unreliable, a weak link in the chain if they had to get rid of Chuyen.

Crew objected. Smith knows everything now, he argued—it's too late to just send him away. Anyway, they could use him for the cover plan—to get Chuyen's signature on a new employment contract. Better to keep him in close.

Smith was in.

At a little after 7 P.M. Thursday night, Brumley, Williams, and Marasco backed the Boston whaler out of the slip and headed downriver. Williams had brought along his Swedish K, an automatic pistol with a retractable metal stock and built-in silencer.

It was still twilight. Gliding through the sluggish water, they agreed it was too early, too much light for the real thing. They would start an hour later if they had to come back the next night.

A few hundred yards downriver, the boat jarred to a stop.

A sandbar. Cursing, the three men slipped into the water, got their footing in the muck, and began hauling the boat over the sand. That was another thing to remember, they agreed, the tides.

They pushed and pulled the boat off the sand and continued downriver.

Suddenly, automatic weapons crackled from the far bank, the unmistakable bang-bang-bang of AK-47s. The firing came closer, along with Vietnamese voices. The captains jumped out of the boat as rounds began to slap at the water around them. They pulled the boat to the bank, using it as a shield. Then came the chatter of M-16s, somebody in pursuit. More shouts. Huddling in the dark, carefully peeping around the hull, the three Green Berets were spectators—all they could see were muzzle flashes.

Quickly, the clash moved off somewhere in the darkness. The voices faded, and the night became still again. The captains waited a few minutes more and then climbed quietly back into the boat. They resumed their journey, giddy with the rapture of survivors. By 10 P.M., they had arrived in the open waters. Hon Tre Island rose on the horizon.

A gentle wind came up, nudging the boat sideways in the swells. It was dark and calm, far from shore, no one around.

This would be the place.

The next morning, David Crew pulled up to the CIA compound on Beach Road and honked his horn. This is the last visit, he decided. There was no way to keep Chuyen any longer. Something had to be done.

Crew was tired of dealing with the CIA. Did they mean what they said, or what they didn't say?

Ten days had gone by, ten days of CIA stalling. This had to be deliberate, he thought, the CIA's way to get us to shoot Chuyen without ever actually saying "do it." They had been naive to expect any more. Scrymgeour and Enking said it was "the most efficient" thing to do. What were they waiting for? He parked the jeep and walked upstairs to Harold Chipman's office.

The CIA man was glum. He had been studying their interrogation reports and polygraphs, he said. Chuyen wouldn't be of interest to the agency as a double agent. Too low level.

Crew's patience was thinning. Did the people in Saigon know what was going on up here? he asked Chipman. Did the Saigon station know they were out of time?

Chipman shrugged and turned up his palms. He said he'd send another cable to Saigon making it clear exactly what was going on in Nha Trang, with a request for a priority response.

Crew started to leave.

"You can try again later," Chipman said, but it was too late. Crew was already walking out the door.

Brumley listened to Crew's recounting of the meeting without interruption. And it wasn't just because Crew outranked him. Something still wasn't right.

"I want to hear it for myself," he finally drawled. They hopped in the jeep and sped back across Nha Trang to Beach Road. It was Friday afternoon. A gun gray sea shimmered through the palms as they turned into the CIA compound and parked.

Dean Almy was upstairs in Chipman's office talking to his operations chief. He looked upset. Crew and Brumley stopped at the doorway.

"Look," Almy said, without introductions, "there's nothing we can do to help you." He smiled slightly, but his tone was firm.

Brumley stood his ground, disgust for the CIA wrestling with his desire to get some kind of official authorization to do away with Chuyen, something on paper.

"Did you see Shackley? Did Shackley get the message?" he asked.

Almy nodded. "Shackley has the message." His tone was preemptory.

Of course, he could be sure only that Shackley's secretary had the message. If Shackley had seen that last message, Almy was certain, the station chief would have turned off the Green Berets—fast. Could Dana Meggs have forgotten it?

He moved toward the door. "There's nothing we can do for you," he repeated. "I'm sorry."

Brumley, Almy observed, was tightly wound. "Have you talked to the MSS?" he asked gently, meaning the Vietnamese security service, Saigon's FBI. "Maybe they can take this guy off your hands."

"Jesus Christ!" the stocky captain exploded, shooting a glance at the hapless Chipman. "I thought we had been through all this."

Chipman turned to Almy and quickly summed up Brumley's fears that the Vietnamese were trying to penetrate the Green Berets' Cambodian operations.

Almy sighed. "Well," he said to the soldiers, "I'm sorry. That's all I can suggest. I can't help you more than that. There's nothing I can do." He side-stepped toward the doorway. Brumley and Crew got the message. They walked out of the office.

"Really, I am very sorry," Almy repeated, watching them stomp down the stairs.

Crew and Brumley drove across town, reviewing the events of the past ten days.

The important thing was that the CIA hadn't ever said no, they agreed. Almy and Chipman had had their chance right there. If the CIA had wanted to rescind Scrymgeour and Enking's suggestion, they had had plenty of time. Crew and Brumley had filled the CIA in on everything. They had given them the interrogation reports. They had told them their fears about Cambodia and the LLDB efforts to penetrate Project Gamma. According to Chipman, all their reports had been sent to Saigon with specific requests for traces and guidance. And then a demand for an emergency response.

They ran all the factors through their minds, from the June 10 meeting with Enking and Scrymgeour to the unnerving silence from Saigon. Chipman, they remembered, had joked that Ted Shackley certainly wouldn't object to the killing of one more Vietnamese. Hardly.

The last thing was a green light from Colonel Rheault. They had to have that. If he said no, they'd go back to the drawing board.

Bob Rheault had hardly spent a full day in Nha Trang since his stiff meeting with General Mabry on June 4. He had been in the air most of the time, winging around Vietnam on an inspection tour, dropping in on Special Forces outposts from the Central Highlands to the Mekong Delta. What he saw pointed out the enormity of the task before him. The Green Berets were a mess.

He had naturally sought out men whom he knew, mostly the old master sergeants who were the backbone and history of the Special Forces, the grizzled veterans who had joined the Green Berets at its birth.

The outfit had gone soft, they told him. The new guys hardly knew a parachute harness from a garter belt. They were three-week wonders, rushed through jump school to get their wings and fancy green hats. The officers, even the lieutenants, were just here to get their tickets punched. It stunk.

Group headquarters, they had to tell him, was the worst of all, with its plush clubs, air-conditioned billets, gift shops, handball courts, massage parlors, even a Tastee Freeze. They couldn't imagine anything like that in the old days in Germany. Whatever happened to living out of the rucksack? What the hell was going on? Since when was the Special Forces a sit-on-your-duff outfit?

Rheault assured them that was history; they were going back to the old ways—lean and mean. Every available man was going to be in the field or out of the unit.

They believed him. Word had spread quickly of the incident with Colonel Aaron's bed and dismantling of the officer's canteen. They also knew Rheault had trimmed a score or more officers from do-nothing jobs at headquarters and put them in the field. Most had been assigned as advisers to Mobile Strike Force units, which made the old sergeants laugh. Working with the Vietnamese Green Berets was about the sorriest goddam duty you could get.

They asked about rumors that General Abrams had put 5th Special Forces at the top of the list of units to be withdrawn under Vietnamization.

That was true, Rheault said. You know Abrams—he's one of those old tankers who sees red when a Green Beret crosses his path. But he said he was working to turn Abrams around. He'd do his part, he said, but in the meantime, they all had to be perfect. Nothing could go wrong.

The Chuyen problem was just one more thing that annoyed Bob Rheault about the state of the 5th Group. The problem could have been dealt with before he even came on board. They had had plenty of time. Instead they had diddled and dawdled and passed it to him.

It wasn't his style. Things were simple, black and white, good and bad. He had little patience for philosophical discourse. Why nibble a problem to death?

Late on Friday afternoon, Ken Facey told him that Crew and Brumley were outside and wanted to see him again.

Tell them to come back later, Rheault said. He had a million other things on his desk.

It annoyed him that they were taking so long to deal with this one agent. He had been following the situation from afar, getting an occasional word from Crew and Middleton on the progress of the case. He knew Chuyen was stashed next door, and that things weren't looking good. He knew that Brumley and Crew had been staying in touch with the CIA office in Nha Trang. He knew the guy might have to be aced. But he hadn't really focused on it—he had the whole 5th Group to get under his control, over four thousand men and countless operations. *There was a war going on!*

Why were they involving him so much anyway? One thing he had learned in Washington was that you didn't have to tell your boss things he didn't need to know. He had put guys "over the fence" into Cambodia and Laos for two years before the Joint Chiefs went to President Johnson for authorization, and Johnson took another year to put it in writing. That's how it worked. It was the basic principle of clandestine activities—if they were strictly illegal, keep the top guy out of the details. To Bob Rheault, that's what "plausible denial" was all about.

But Crew was insistent. At 6 P.M., he was back with a demand for a meeting. Rheault reluctantly told Facey to show him in.

It took Crew fifteen minutes to go over the case step-by-step, from the beginnings in Muc Hoa through the captured photograph to the last unsatisfactory meeting with Chipman and Almy. He summed everything up. Their alternatives, he told Rheault, had narrowed down to one: getting rid of the guy. They couldn't keep him any longer. The CIA wouldn't take him off their hands.

What else could they do? Chipman's advice was that Shackley's response meant it was a go.

Rheault listened attentively. Crew just wasn't his sort of guy. He was soft. His eyes were all watery.

You're the expert, Rheault said. You're the intelligence guy, you're the chief of B-57, and you've obviously stayed on top of the case.

Rheault's hands were in the air. He was obviously impatient. What's the problem?

Crew nodded, slowly got up, and started to leave.

"Just remember," Rheault said. Crew turned around.

"My eagles are riding on this." He went back to his work.

Crew walked back to the B-57 offices. As far as he was concerned, they had their orders.

At sunset, Bob Marasco requisitioned tire rims and heavy chains from the motor pool, routinely signing chits for both. Then he walked over to the 5th Group Marine sea ops detachment and arranged for the delivery of a dark green Boston whaler and outboard motor at 8 P.M.

Marasco was feeling relieved as he walked back to his room and retrieved his M-16. Not happy—he was just glad they were going to get it over with. It had gone on too long.

Alvin Smith alone was enough to make any man want to kill, he thought. They should be taking him along with Chuyen.

Smith had gone nuts when they let him in on their final plans Friday morning, pleading for Chuyen's life, saying if he couldn't get Chuyen turned around he'd shoot him himself. He was hysterical, spouting some gibberish from Shakespeare. Said it was from Macbeth, something about murder coming back to haunt its authors. He begged for another chance with his agent.

Too late, they said. Chuyen's got to go. *You* know that. You started this whole goddam thing!

At a quarter to eight, Marasco met Budge Williams at the water's edge. They sat in the growing darkness and smoked, waiting for the delivery of Chuyen. Williams fiddled with his weapon, the same Swedish K from the practice run the night before.

A few minutes later, a sergeant drove up in a jeep with the boat on a trailer. He backed it into the water, hitched it to the dock, and started up the forty-horsepower Evinrude.

In the interrogation room, Brumley and Ed Boyle were preparing Chuyen for his last, fatal trip.

Boyle held Chuyen down on the floor while Brumley gave him a second shot of morphine. In a few minutes, his eyes rolled back. His breathing was heavy. He seemed to be in a deep sleep.

Next they taped his mouth shut. Then they tied his wrists behind his back and rolled him into a standard green poncho. Next they lifted him onto a canvas litter. A light truck had been backed up to the door. Ed Boyle was at the wheel.

At eight o'clock, the truck rumbled down the hill and pulled to a stop at the river. Brumley and Boyle jumped from the cab and walked to the rear of the truck. Brushing aside a heavy canvas curtain, they reached inside and tugged at the poncho. Chuyen, in a deep sleep, was dragged out. They carried him to the boat and with the help of Williams and Marasco laid him on the floorboards.

It was time to go. The radioman on the beach waved okay. The three captains boarded the boat, threw off the ropes, and backed from the slip. The bow turned slowly down the dark river.

The men tensed, prepared for a repeat of the previous night's encounter with the Viet Cong. Marasco pulled out a cigarette and prepared to light it. Brumley slapped it away.

Tonight there were no sandbars. The boat puttered forward on the higher tide, cutting smoothly through the dark water.

As they passed the river's mouth, a new moon slid between thick monsoon clouds. Now, in the open water, they began to relax. The boat plowed forward, picking up speed, hammering against the swells and fresh wind that came up to meet them.

Suddenly, a low soft groan came from the poncho. The morphine was wearing off. Brumley looked at the others and lifted a .45 caliber pistol from his holster. Holding it by the barrel, he delivered a swift, murderous stroke to the side of Chuyen's head. The sound was snuffed out.

Near midnight, the boat slowed to a drift. A warm salty wind rose from the East. Hon Tre Island rose on the horizon, a sharp jagged figure in the night.

Williams and Brumley dragged the lumpy poncho into the middle of the boat. Marasco reached for the pile of heavy chains. Together, they slowly rolled Chuyen's body in the iron coil, then fastened the two heavy tire rims to it. Then they lifted Chuyen's body to the edge of the gunwales and dipped his head over the edge.

One end of the poncho was loosened, allowing Chuyen's head to flop into the breach. Brumley handed Marasco the gun.

The dark-haired captain stared at it. It was a long-barreled .22 caliber pistol with a built-in silencer, manufactured by High Standard of Ohio for the CIA and stockpiled in Okinawa. Brumley's predecessor had given it to him. It was not listed in U.S. Army official inventories.

Marasco gripped the pistol by the handle and stared at Chuyen's head. The boat rocked in the breeze.

"Are you going to do it," Brumley asked, "or do I have to?" He was annoyed.

"I'll do it, I'll do it," Marasco said. He snicked the top of the barrel back and forth, chambering a round. Steadying himself in the rolling boat, he leaned forward and pressed the tip of the silencer to Chuyen's jet black hair. He squeezed the trigger.

Nothing happened—the gun had jammed. Marasco looked up, his eyes wide.

Brumley snatched the pistol out of his hand, disgusted. He quickly broke it down. In a minute, he had cleared the chamber. He handed the pistol back to Marasco.

Now they were ready again. Brumley and Williams again lifted Chuyen to the gunwale and bent his head over the water.

Marasco again pointed the muzzle at Chuyen's ear. Once more, he squeezed the trigger.

Poof.

With the sound of a tire puncture, Marasco remembered later, the agent's head blew apart. Blood, skull, and bits of brain splattered the soldiers. Bright red blood flowed into the water.

Marasco stood still. Ignoring him, Williams and Brumley lifted Chuyen's body to the lip of the rocking boat, steadied it briefly, and then rolled it gently over the side into a swelling gray wave, where it sank, trailing a chain of small bubbles.

An hour later Brumley, Williams, and Marasco motored into the slip on the Cua Be River. Ed Boyle and Don Knutson, a counterintelligence sergeant, were waiting on the beach. They helped the three captains with their gear, tossing their rucksacks in the back of the truck, then pulled the boat onto the sand.

It was Knutson's first acquaintance with the bloody solution to the Chuyen problem. He saw that the floorboards were splattered with blood; the boat would have to be washed out. The life preservers would have to be scrubbed clean, too; the supply sergeant would never take them back in that condition. He put them in the truck.

Together, Boyle and Knutson pulled the boat from the water and tipped it over, letting the crimson rivulets wash onto the sand. Knutson came forward with a hose, and they cleaned out the hull and interior. In a few minutes, the boat was hitched on the trailer. It was nearly one o'clock in the morning. Boyle slid behind the wheel of the truck and the three captains hopped in the back. They drove up the hill to their office. Crew was waiting inside along with Alvin Smith.

"We'll have to burn all the clothes—he bled all over the place," Williams drawled as he walked into the office. He quickly pulled off his fatigues and began stuffing them into a parachute bag.

Crew looked queasy. Smith, who had waited with the major for the men to return, suddenly smiled at Williams.

"Is this the first man you've killed, *dai ui?*" he asked, using the Vietnamese words for captain. It sounded like a sneer.

Williams stopped and turned to the goofy-looking sergeant.

"It's the first one I've murdered," he said, glancing at Crew and Brumley. He turned back to his bag. The room was silent. Marasco lit a cigarette. Brumley watched the scene, changing his clothes.

"That's not murder," Smith said flippantly. "You had to do it."

Williams kept packing, then looked up.

"It's still murder," he said.

Wade Ishimoto was mystified. At 5 A.M., the Japanese-American clerk-typist put on a set of black-and-tan camouflage fatigues and, as ordered, walked over to the B-57 motor pool. A few minutes later, Budge Williams pulled up in a jeep and they drove to the airfield.

Part two of the plan was kicking into gear. Unknown to him, Ishimoto was supposed to be Chuyen. They were on their way to Tay Ninh, backstopping the story to explain Chuyen's disappearance. Ishimoto would be Chuyen going on a mission.

Williams was aware the operation was becoming more complicated by the hour. So many people had become involved with or at least knowledgeable about Chuyen's interrogation and removal that more and more stories were being made up to explain his disappearance.

The first step had been to create a paper trail. Williams wrote a detailed plan sending Chuyen on a mission to Cambodia, which he dubbed with macabre humor Operation Bent Axle. Then he had ordered Smith to see Chuyen and get his signature on three blank pieces of paper. Over the signatures Williams typed employment contracts. Then he logged them into the operations file, assigning them a control number. Everything replicated the steps for a regular mission.

Next he drafted Ishimoto, a second-generation Nisei from California, to fly to Tay Ninh, the first step before the faked crossover into Cambodia. He also gave Ishimoto a radio with which to contact Nha Trang—a PRC 25, which as it turned out didn't have the range to reach headquarters. The idea, though, was that the transmission would be logged by an unwitting communications clerk. That way there would be a radio record of Chuyen's passage through Tay Ninh and insertion into Cambodia.

The last cog was Major Middleton, whom they'd needed to arrange for an aircraft. He'd balked at first. To get him over the edge, they'd had a solemn ceremony, as Middleton had insisted, where they'd all stood in a circle with their hands linked like medieval knights and pledged a vow of silence.

Now, as Ishimoto and Williams sat near the runway watching the bleaching eastern sky, Middleton pulled up in his jeep. He seemed momentarily confused when he saw Ishimoto.

"Is that one of ours?" he asked Williams, nodding at the Nisei. Ishimoto gave him a long, hard look. Apparently, white people did think all Asians looked alike.

"Oh, right," Middleton said, and shut off his engine. They waited together.

At 6 A.M. a twin-prop Air America plane was rolled out of a hangar and started up with a noisy cough. It taxied over to the gate and lowered its back door. Middleton, Williams, and Ishimoto got in, and took seats behind the two pilots. A few minutes later the plane was airborne into the cool dawn, heading west.

David Crew finally gave in to his insomnia and swung his feet to the floor. It was 5 A.M. His mind was a jangle of nerves wrung out by half-sleep dreams. The last violent seconds of Thai Khac Chuyen's life flashed through his head. The execution was not something he had been prepared for by the war college or intelligence school.

At breakfast, he learned that the cover flight with Ishimoto had taken off as scheduled. He ate little and returned alone to his office. Through the first half of the day, he shuffled paperwork, playing and replaying the last twenty-four hours in his mind.

At three in the afternoon, Harold Chipman called. There was a message from Saigon, he said. He couldn't talk about it on the telephone. He told Crew to come over and read it. He sounded serious.

The major thought it was a little late for CIA guidance. And he was tired of being dicked around by the spooks. Chuyen had been taken care of anyway. Chuyen was *fini*, as they said in Vietnam. Finished, done.

Dead.

An hour passed before he drove to the CIA compound on Beach Road. The compound was packed as usual with green Ford Broncos and blue International Scouts. Chipman was waiting upstairs with Dean Almy in the base chief's office.

There were no preliminaries. Chipman tossed a telex from Saigon on the desk for Crew to read.

He slowly picked it up.

    1. ADVISE SPECIAL FORCES WE HAVE NO CI INTEREST IN THE REFERENCED CASE.
    2. CONTACT MAJ. CREW AS SOON AS POSSIBLE AND TELL HIM THIS IS NO SOLUTION TO THE PROBLEM, THAT IT IS IMMORAL AND HAS THE HIGHEST FLAP PO-TENTIAL.
    3. UNLESS YOU CAN GET HIS ASSURANCE NOTHING WILL HAPPEN TO THIS AGENT, AS OF MINE AND YOUR CABLE, THEN WE WILL HAVE NO ALTERNATIVE BUT TO

BRING IT TO THE ATTENTION OF THE COMMAND LEV-
ELS IN MACV, INCLUDING GEN. ABRAMS AND AMBAS-
SADOR BUNKER.

The message was signed "SHACKLEY."

Crew stared at the piece of paper.

"It's too late," he finally stammered.

The CIA men waited for more.

"He's on a mission in Cambodia, a radio mission," the major recovered. "We can't contact him. He has to contact us."

Almy studied Crew's face. Finally, he leaned forward and retrieved the cable.

"All right," he said. "We'll let Shackley know."

20

T heodore Shackley read the response from Nha Trang with disgust and dismay. He didn't believe for a second that the agent was roaming Cambodia for the Green Berets, dodging B-52 bombs without a radio or commo plan.

The CIA station chief kept a tight grip on his seven hundred underlings. Small mistakes could send him into a cold fury. A potential flap was intolerable.

With his thick forearms, platinum hair, and black-framed glasses, Ted Shackley presented a formidable persona. And his reputation preceded him: after a brilliant start in Berlin, he had successfully managed two of the agency's most intricate assignments, as station chief in Miami and later Laos, and now, at thirty-nine, he was poised to go right to the top of the operations division.

Shackley's career, unfortunately, was peaking at the end of one era, or the beginning of another—old CIA hands could not be quite sure; the struggle against global communism was seemingly eternal. But Vietnam was an unfortunate place to be earning one's stripes. It was one thing to keep Western Europe out of the hands of Hitler and Joe Stalin; it was another thing altogether to save—*what? Laos?*—from Asian Communists. Let them have it, many thought, the effort's not worth it. In Vietnam, even the ancient pottery had been looted long ago; now vandals ran the government. But Saigon was the largest CIA station in the world in 1969, the biggest career prize of all. And for Theodore Shackley, it was last hurdle before arriving at the gates of the CIA's sanctum sanctorum, the directorship of the clandestine services division.

Shackley had become an expert in playing all the angles inside the CIA, where, many agents conceded, dirty tricks were as much a habit as a profession. His mentor was Bill Harvey, a hard-drinking, gun-slinging former FBI agent whose exploits in Berlin and Miami were so legendary that John Kennedy ordered him produced in the Oval Office to see for himself. The young president, an Ian Fleming fan, had heard Harvey touted as America's own James Bond.

Harvey waddled into the White House with his thick waist, bulging eyes, and splotchy complexion, looking as much like Bond as a duck does a swan. He had to be stripped of his pistols just outside the Oval Office door. In the early 1960s, he had been given the job of carrying out the job of getting rid of Fidel Castro, and he took Shackley with him to the CIA's forward command post in Miami. Shackley administered the station, which quickly became the CIA's largest with eight hundred agents, while Harvey contracted with mobsters to rub out the Cuban leader.

Harvey operated on the principle that the fewer people in on a hard job, the better. Best of all, you did it yourself. One night he and Shackley rented a U-Haul truck, filled it with five thousand dollars worth of explosives, detonators, rifles, handguns, radios, and radars, and dropped it off at a Miami parking lot. Harvey then sent Shackley across the street with the keys for Johnny Rosselli, a Chicago gangster picked for the plot against Castro. It was only one mission of the new "Executive Action" assassination unit, code-named ZR Rifle, set up in Langley under Harvey.

Shackley quickly became a bright star in Miami, untangling groups of bickering Cuban exiles and overseeing a huge real estate empire of safe houses, warehouses, airfields, and marinas. Despite the immense scale of the effort, the exact range of its activities would stay secret for years.

In 1966, he was rewarded with the CIA station in Laos, responsible for ten thousand mountain tribesmen who had been organized into an "armée clandestine" and thrown into battle against hardened North Vietnamese Army and Communist Pathet Lao troops. His tenure there would earn him a reputation inside the agency as a tough, even ruthless field general, but it also won him the spurs for Vietnam.

In Saigon, the CIA's "war in the shadows" combined two competing strains in the agency, intelligence-gathering and paramilitary warfare. To make a dent in the Viet Cong, a station chief had to have the patience of a spy handler and the daring of an operator. No less important, he had to hold his own in the quicksand politics of the American command. Under Bill Harvey, Shackley had learned not to leave fingerprints when mistakes were made.

Although his name was unknown to the public, Shackley was one of the four most powerful Americans in Vietnam, equal to pacification director William Colby (another former CIA Saigon chief) and subordinate only to MACV commander Creighton Abrams and, at the top, U.S. ambassador Ellsworth Bunker. Together, they made up "the country team." The CIA served them all, but a succession of Saigon station chiefs had kept their own pipelines to Washington open.

Shackley loved the perquisites of power, roaring around town with an armed motorcycle escort, looking every bit the proconsul. They called him the Blond Ghost.

Even old hands tried to stay out of his way. The staff was convinced he had planted spies among them. "He always seemed to know what I was doing," one CIA agent marveled. At the same time, different sections were prohibited from talking directly to each other. Analysts were ordered not to talk to field operatives.

He could be coldly dismissive when he read a subpar report, tossing it contemptuously on an employee's desk and walking wordlessly out of his office. A production-line system was introduced. "For example," said one agent, "X number of intelligence reports about X number of penetrations with X number captured and X number killed was how he liked to see things submitted."

But Shackley's defenders thought that the CIA's Vietnam staff needed to be taken by the neck and shaken. After all, they pointed out, hadn't the CIA failed to predict the Tet offensive, the biggest U.S. intelligence disaster since Pearl Harbor? The CIA had gone soft on the plush life in Vietnam, they said, and Shackley was turning it around.

Shackley quickly reminded his staff they were in the midst of a war. The top three floors of the embassy were soon packed with guns. A military atmosphere permeated the station. There would be no more Tets, he warned them, no more mistakes of any kind. "Recruit, recruit, recruit" he exhorted them, and the number of agents soon tripled.

Shackley was no stranger to the Green Berets, who had landed with Cuban exiles at the Bay of Pigs and trained the CIA's "secret army" in Laos. Under CIA direction, its SOG teams were parachuted into North Vietnam and Cambodia, carrying mayhem right to the deepest bases of the Viet Cong and NVA. He knew they were good at slitting throats, jumping out of airplanes, and organizing the locals in all manner of guerrilla warfare.

But they were not very good at the nuances of intelligence operations, he knew. That, after all, was not their speciality. The matter of Thai Khac Chuyen was a case in point.

That the Green Berets were recklessly impulsive was not a surprise. But his own officers had now compounded the problem, exposing the agency to an unnecessary embarrassment. As a seasoned operator, Shackley knew how little mistakes could become big problems. Now the CIA was vulnerable to somebody else's mistakes. And if the agency was vulnerable, of course so was he.

Enking and Scrymgeour should've turned off the Green Berets when they first came calling. Slammed the door, said, "Sorry, boys, we can't help you." In the CIA's way of thinking, if the Green Berets needed advice in eliminating one low-level penetration agent, God help 'em—they probably weren't the ones to do it. Where had these guys been? That kind of stuff was done on a jeep ride with a single bullet. No meetings, no advice. No borrowed CIA airplanes.

No cables back and forth. Enking and Scrymgeour should have booted them out of the embassy.

Chipman had made it worse, Shackley gave when he gathered all the cables together. He could see right away that this Chuyen was only an itinerant intelligence peddler, not a true double agent. Chuyen was a common character in Vietnam, where U.S. intelligence agencies had recruited all manner of riffraff as spies. As a result, many of them were just paper mills, manufacturing "intelligence" for anyone who was in the market. As far as Shackley could tell from the documents, Chuyen was a drifter, maybe trying to work both sides, maybe just keeping in touch with his brothers in the NVA. Why the alarm, the melodrama? He was certainly of no interest to the CIA.

Why Chipman took seriously the Green Berets' offer of Chuyen as a CIA counterintelligence asset was beyond understanding. Even the Green Berets said he was a lousy spy, according to the reports. Why would he be any good to the CIA?

Shackley knew they had killed him. No one could swallow Major Crew's story that the agent had been sent on a mission and couldn't be contacted. Bullshit—you always had a way to recall an agent. With all the bombing in Cambodia, you at least had to be able to get an agent out of the way of your own B-52s.

This agent was dead—that's why the Green Berets couldn't contact him.

Shackley's career had acquainted him with the practical uses of violence. The agency was all over the place when he was coming up—going after Lumumba in the Congo, Trujillo in the Dominican Republic, Arbenz in Guatemala, restoring the shah of Iran. Hell, in Miami the CIA was helping out just about anybody with a boat and a pistol who could get to Cuba. But the termination of an agent, no matter how modest, was a matter to be considered with the utmost care: Even low-level informants had wives, children, parents, friends, lovers—people who might know of an agent's connection to the organization and who might ask embarrassing questions if a person vanished from sight.

As a management technique, murder was messy.

Thai Khac Chuyen was a good example. His sister-in-law was making a ruckus at CORDS.

Shackley moved quickly. With his last telex ordering the Green Berets to deliver the agent, there was a paper trail putting him on record against the suspected execution. But that wouldn't be enough. Now he had to cover his other bases. Just as he had threatened in his last cable, he would drop the problem in the lap of the Army, where it belonged, away from CIA.

On the afternoon of June 21, the station chief picked up the telephone and called Ambassador Ellsworth Bunker. Under the "country team" protocol, Shackley, Abrams, and Bunker kept each other apprised of important contacts among them. He asked the ambassador for an appointment and minutes later walked downstairs to Bunker's office on the embassy's third floor.

"Here's my dilemma," he said, settling into a chair. The white-haired, patrician diplomat waited patiently for Shackley to continue. He sat in his high-backed leather chair, the official seal of the United States behind him on the wall.

Shackley described the mess in Nha Trang and the inept effort to help the Green Berets with their problem. The road to hell, he seemed to be saying— good intentions and all that.

"I can't be a party to this action," he wearily concluded, meaning a premeditated execution. The CIA couldn't sweep it under the rug for the Green Berets. He wouldn't be a party to that. He had to take it to Abrams.

Bunker, listening stoically, agreed that was the thing to do. It certainly had nothing to do with the State Department or Embassy. The dead man was a bureaucratic item between the CIA and the Army—nothing new—which he was confident Shackley could handle. By all means, he said, take it to General Abrams.

It was late Saturday afternoon by the time Shackley walked back upstairs to his office. He picked up the secure red telephone and called General Abrams at his MACV headquarters; he said he needed to see him right away.

"I'm really hung up right now," Abrams answered. There had been heavy fighting around Tay Ninh, with combined U.S. Army forces taking on hardcore NVA units moving in from Cambodia. B-52s had been flying raids around the clock, adding an immense burden to the shuffle of paperwork that kept the Cambodia bombing secret. "Can you come by my quarters later?" he asked.

That evening, Shackley and his retinue drove out Cach Mang Street and rolled into the MACV compound where Abrams lived in a plain stucco bungalow. A bodyguard was left alone with the car. At the door, he could hear the loud strains of classical music as the general relaxed, cigar in hand, a stack of popular history books on the table, waiting for his CIA chief to arrive.

Shackley was shown into Abrams's study and took a seat.

"What's it all about?" Abrams asked, typically direct. He squinted over his cigar, waiting for the answer.

The CIA chief outlined the problem. Some Green Berets running an intelligence operation in Cambodia had come to the CIA for help with problems about an agent they suspected of working for Hanoi. Apparently they had run out of patience with the guy because they were talking of "taking him on patrol." Shackley said he had gotten worried and told the men to produce their agent in person. But now they said the guy was in Cambodia on a one-way mission and couldn't be contacted.

"What I'm hearing doesn't jibe," the CIA man said. He was certain the agent had been executed. "I've talked to Bunker," he said. "It's your decision what to do with it." He waited for Abrams's response.

Abrams digested the story. His first instinct was to filter everything through the prism of "Vietnamization," the main agenda Nixon had assigned him. Would this incident help or hurt the program of getting American troops out of Vietnam?

Since Nixon and Thieu had dropped their June bombshell that U.S. troops were leaving, relations between the allies, from the field to senior staff levels, had been stretched tight as a bowstring. There were increasing reports of friction between ARVN troops and GIs, on the field and off.

The U.S. command had managed to sweep such incidents under the rug. But the situation had become extraordinarily volatile; the Vietnamese were more fearful and sullen with each new announcement of Americans going home.

Some Saigon politicians were jockeying to take advantage of the discord. Aides around President Thieu were accusing the United States of a sellout; left-wingers, many pro-Communist, were also quick to exploit incidents of U.S. brutality. Word that the Green Berets had taken it on their own to execute a Vietnamese citizen, and that the Army had approved it, could swell into a cause célèbre, further complicating a withdrawal.

Abrams was amused by Shackley's concern for one dead Vietnamese. The old tanker admired Shackley, but he was not one of those who were enamored with the Phoenix program, its techniques, or its results. He thought the United States should get out of programs that the South Vietnamese could, or should, do for themselves. And a lot of those involved Green Berets. The CIA's willy-nilly use of Special Forces troops had bothered him for years. It just reinforced the Green Berets' view of themselves as accountable to somebody else.

But the fate of this one agent was the least of his problems. There was a much bigger controversy coming down the road: A secret Pentagon team was already looking into a reported Army massacre in a hamlet called My Lai. One incident could be a tripwire to public exposure of the other. A flap with this agent could also lead to inquiries on other operations in Cambodia, and not just the bombing. The invasion plans were nearly complete, and under the tightest possible wraps.

Shackley had been quick to say it was purely an Army problem. That was clever. Both men knew that B-57 was an Army intelligence unit squirreled inside the 5th Special Forces, but it was funded, equipped, and often directed by CIA requirements. The CIA was quick enough to use B-57 for its own purposes, Abrams knew, but now it was more than convenient for Shackley to say it was all his problem. As he considered Shackley's information, his determination to wrest the Green Berets from CIA affiliation grew.

"This guy Rheault is a very good officer," Abrams finally said. "I'll get ahold of Colonel Rheault, and talk to him, and get to the bottom of this thing." He rose and began to show Shackley to the door. There wasn't anything more to say for now.

"I'll get back to you," the general said kindly.

"Don't bother," Shackley answered casually, waving off the gesture. "You don't have to get back to me. It's your problem now."

Abrams went back inside, sat down, and called his aide to his quarters. He felt like relaxing. Maybe they'd do some group singing tonight, he said. Maybe they could round up Townsend and Rossen. "You know that song 'He's Got the Whole World in His Hands?' " The aide did. It was one of his favorites, Abrams said. They could all sing it together.

Bob Rheault leaned back in his chair, hands clasped behind his head, listening to Crew's worried account of the meeting with Almy and Chipman. Suddenly, his orderly knocked at the door.

"Sir, it's General Abrams calling on the scrambler phone."

Rheault tilted forward, rose, and wordlessly left the room. In a minute, he was back. Without comment, he sat down and asked Crew to continue.

The major resumed the story, but the orderly knocked again.

"A Mr. Chipman here to see you, sir," the sergeant said.

Rheault leaned forward again, rose, and asked the orderly to show his visitor in.

Chipman, his thinning blond hair glistening on his sweaty forehead, walked into the office, shook Rheault's proffered hand, and found a seat.

"I understand you have a cable instructing us to return Chuyen to duty," Rheault said.

"Yes, that's correct," Chipman answered.

Rheault turned to Crew. "He's been sent on a mission, isn't that correct?"

Crew cleared his throat. "Yes, sir, he's out for a few days and can't be contacted."

Suddenly, the orderly knocked again and poked his head around the door. "It's General Abrams calling again, sir."

Rheault frowned. "Excuse me," he said and briskly walked from the office, leaving Crew alone with Chipman. Neither spoke.

When Rheault returned, he turned to the CIA man. "Well," he said with a brittle grin, "it seems that General Abrams is interested in this agent, too." He turned to Crew. "Get your papers together. They're sending a plane. I'll be leaving for Saigon in a short while." He stood up and offered Chipman his hand, a signal that whatever had brought the CIA man to see him was now redundant.

"Thanks for coming over," he said, showing Chipman the door. He turned back to Crew.

Rheault was packing for Saigon when Ken Facey found him in his quarters.

Facey was aware that Rheault didn't care much for him. They and their wives had occasionally socialized in Germany when both were with the 10th Special Forces Group—officers' cocktail parties, that kind of thing—mandatory attendance. They were very different men.

Rheault was electric, Facey thought, a scintillating leader with the aura of a Lawrence of Arabia. His men were fanatical about him. Rheault was one of those rare officers with the kismet, perhaps, for true greatness.

But on a personal level, Facey found, they couldn't relate. Rheault was aloof and distant, uneasy with idle chatter, impatient with differing opinions. And like many from West Point, he thought, Rheault was a snob.

Rheault would not have chosen him as his deputy, that was for sure. Facey was strictly blue collar, an orphan who had been abandoned by his teenage mother, who had started in the Army as a private and worked his way up. But Rheault could choose his own man soon when Facey left in August. In the meantime, he thought, Rheault had been generous and thoughtful in keeping him out of the deliberations on Thai Khac Chuyen.

Now, however, he sensed a disaster in the works. As Rheault shoved papers into his briefcase, the shy, amiable executive officer considered gently raising the idea of telling Abrams the truth.

"What does Abe want to see you about?" he inquired.

Rheault continued to gather things for his bag. "I don't know," he said.

"Does it have anything to do with Chuyen?"

"I don't know."

"If he asks you about it, what will you say?"

"I'll tell him the guy's in Cambodia," Rheault said, standing up, clearly impatient with his deputy.

Facey plunged onward. He was pretty sure Chuyen had been killed.

"You know," he offered cautiously, "commanders usually like to have all the facts, even unpleasant ones."

Rheault went back to gathering his things, but Facey continued anyway.

Abrams would probably like all the facts so he could decide what the best course was, he said. Maybe he knows something we don't. Maybe you should let Abrams in on the truth, even if it looks bad. That would get everybody off the hook. Covering up could be dangerous.

"I don't take my problems to my commanders," Rheault said briskly. "I take care of my own problems."

With that, he shut his bag and exited the room.

Now Facey sat in the silence. He could feel an ill wind blowing. The cover-up wasn't going to work. He knew it. Maybe he should go to Abrams himself.

But what would he say? That he "suspected" a Vietnamese agent had been killed? Where's the proof? he'd say. Where's the body?

He didn't have the answers. In fact, Facey didn't know much at all, for the very reason that Rheault had done him a favor. So he didn't know exactly who had killed Chuyen or where, even though he was sure of what had happened.

What generals would welcome hearing about it anyway? he mused. It was a war of body counts. The mission of the Army was to kill the enemy, as many and as quickly as possible. Now one more Viet Cong, a low-level agent, a mere gook, dink, slope, was dead. Who would care?

Rheault was a hell of an officer, Facey brooded, but he was a rich man with a rich wife and connections in high places. He'd be sure to have his bases covered. When his charges fell flat, Rheault would run him out of the Army, and he couldn't take that. The Army was his whole life.

He decided to go to bed.

Rheault sat back in the executive jet winging through the night sky toward Saigon. He knew he was about to make the most important decision of his career, and maybe his life.

Rheault had learned the nuances of lying in Washington, where deception was played as a professional sport. There were lies for all occasions: the weapons procurement lie (lowballing the cost of an airplane); the tax lie (promising never to raise them); the political lie (the White House and Congress blaming each other for their failures); the campaign lie (never intending to deliver on promises); and of course, the personal lie (screwing someone else to advance your own career).

And then there was the diplomatic lie, with which Rheault was fully acquainted. When he was sending agents over the fence into Cambodia and Laos, usually a couple of Montagnards led by a "sanitized" Green Beret, the first thing everyone understood was that if a political or diplomatic scandal erupted with the capture of a team, somebody would have to fall on their sword. The White House, the State Department, and the Pentagon would all deny they had issued orders.

That's the way it worked. A career might be sidetracked, a promotion deferred, there might even be personal embarrassment and a temporary withdrawal from government life, but nobody would go to jail. He wouldn't be charged with a crime just because a mistake had been made in the pursuit of the national interest. The national interest, after all, was the reason for which he failed. In Washington, scandals were high theater with everyone expressing outrage. The fall guy was expected to go quietly with the unspoken understanding of a later reward, perhaps a quiet, eventual rehabilitation.

All those ingredients, however, were missing in the present emergency.

General Abrams was not an understanding superior with whom a lie and a wink would work, Rheault knew. The general had not called Rheault down because he needed to go through the motions for an irate Vietnamese widow. It was not a show for public, or political, consumption, ending with a rap on the knuckles and then back to work. Abrams wasn't that kind of man. Nor did he have any interest in protecting the Green Berets.

In sum, Rheault knew he could not whisper the truth to the general and expect to be protected. The general was out for blood, he suspected, and would use the incident as an excuse to kill off the Green Berets—his beloved Green Berets.

It wouldn't be the first time they had met, which was part of his problem. The last time they'd talked was a disaster. Rheault had taken the occasion of a trip to Saigon before he took over his command to lobby the general against putting the 5th Special Forces Group on an accelerated withdrawal schedule from Vietnam.

As Abrams puffed his cigar, Rheault made the case that since the Special Forces were the first in, they should be the last out. The Green Berets were the essence of Vietnamization, he argued. They were pure advisers, that had always been their primary mission in Vietnam. Lyndon Johnson's escalation had skewered their original purpose and put them into more of a direct combat role.

If Nixon wants to get U.S. troops out of the fighting, Rheault argued, why not take out the Regular Army combat units first? Leave the Special Forces to clean up and get the Vietnamese ready to go it alone. That's what we're good at. That's what we should be doing.

His presentation was a bust. Abrams just pulled on his cigar, listening, Rheault thought, with obvious cold disdain.

"Thank you for your views, Colonel," he had said, and sent Rheault on his way like a cadet.

Now, as the general's jet carried him over Saigon's lights to a moment of truth, Rheault made up his mind.

Why entangle the top commander of all U.S. forces, a four-star general, in the execution of a low-level agent? he asked himself. Why should General Abrams be exposed to a flap over the routine elimination of a Viet Cong spy? If Abrams knows only the cover story, he can say he didn't know anything about it. If a flap comes, he'll be grateful: Rheault can take the fall.

That would be his decision: Stick with the lie, the cover story. In the meantime, he could only hope that all the other loose ends were tied up.

It was nearly 11 P.M. by the time the general's escort dropped him at MACV headquarters. Col. Robert Bradley Rheault tucked his green beret down smartly on his head and strode purposefully into the building, his boots buffed to a dull luster, silver eagles on his shoulders, master parachute wings on his chest.

A freshly pressed junior officer met him at the stairway and escorted him to the second floor. They walked down the brightly lit, polished hallway and stopped at the door of Gen. William Potts, Abrams's principal deputy for military intelligence, the J-2.

The elfish bald-headed general stood up as Rheault arrived and greeted him with his typically effusive warmth. As they sat down, Potts began to engage Rheault in small talk, telling him what "a wonderful job you boys are doing up there in Nha Trang."

"Now, we're going to wait a few minutes for General Townsend and General Rossen," Potts said cheerily, sounding as if they were waiting for a ceremony to begin. "They're upstairs with Abe right now. He wants us to talk to you first."

Townsend was Abrams's operations chief, Rossen, Abrams's deputy. At that moment, both were closely involved with the bombing campaign in Cambodia. Townsend's staff had designed the cover story to keep the bombing hidden from the public and all but a few members of Congress. They also made sure Nixon put the bombing order in writing.

Rossen was an Abrams favorite, a blunt, tough soldier who had once headed the Army's Special Warfare program. In the early days of the war he had set up the CIA–Green Beret program to organize the Montagnard tribesmen. Rossen, more than anyone in Saigon, knew the pitfalls of the Green Berets' partnership with the CIA and worried how it could work after the massive Vietnam escalations of 1964 and 1965, which brought the Regular Army in force into the war. Abrams trusted him deeply, a rare accolade from the general who was supposed to "hate the Green Berets." Abrams had called Rossen after Shackley's visit and asked him what he thought.

"Sounds like a bunch of cubs playing with their pricks," he snapped, which had made Abrams smile.

Now, Townsend and Rossen marched down to Potts's office and greeted Rheault evenly. It was late in a long day and they were tired.

Rossen told Rheault that General Abrams wanted them to talk to them first.

They quickly decided to go next door to the large MACV briefing room where there was more space and a large map of Indochina on the wall. It was also secure; Potts had it swept for Communist bugs every day; South Vietnamese of all ranks frequented the room.

Sitting down, Townsend wearily asked Rheault to explain what had happened.

Rheault was practiced at briefings. But tonight, more than ever in his life, he knew he needed to project a crisp commander's confidence.

Recently, he began, his men had brought a problem with one of their agents to his attention. The agent was employed by Project Gamma, the cover designation for B-57's unilateral intelligence collection operation in Cambodia. Sometime in May—he didn't have all the details, of course, because he was busy running the entire 5th Special Forces Group, which he had just taken over—his men began to distrust the agent's reports. Then a roll of captured film was developed, and some of his men were sure this man, Chuyen, was in the picture with other NVA officers. So with the advice of the CIA, they brought the agent in for interrogation.

Apparently—again, he didn't have all the details—the interrogation was inconclusive, so they decided to send him on a test mission in Cambodia, setting it up in such a way that they'd know if the agent carried it out as instructed. Rheault said his men had also told him that they planned to polygraph the agent again when he returned. Until then, there was no way to contact him because he carried a one-way radio. He was expected to check in in a couple of days. There was no way to be sure, of course. He was deep in NVA territory; he could be killed along the way.

"So the report we have from Shackley," Townsend asked, "that your men might have executed this agent—that's wrong?"

"Yes, sir. He's been inserted into Cambodia. We should hear from him in a few days."

"Colonel Rheault," Potts gently interjected, "could you show us on the map where the agent was sent?"

Slowly, Rheault rose and went to the huge green-and-white chart of Indochina.

"You can use my pointer," Potts added helpfully as Rheault looked at the map. Rheault reached to his side and lifted the wooden stick. He was still staring at the map.

"Why don't you show us first where he was sent across the border?" Potts said softly, making a few notes in his diary.

Rheault tapped at a place near the Parrot's Beak, where Cambodia sharply angled into South Vietnam.

"I think it was here."

"And what's his mission? Where's he going?" Townsend asked.

Rheault hesitated. He tapped at an area further inside Cambodia. "He's to report on NVA logistics. Right around in here."

Silence filled the room like an expanding balloon.

"Okay, Colonel, thank you," General Townsend said. "You can sit down." There was an officious edge to his voice.

Rheault took his seat.

"Colonel," Townsend added, "are you telling us the truth, and the whole truth?"

Rheault looked him squarely in the eye. "I am," he said thinly, twisting the West Point ring on his finger. "It's all just a misunderstanding. We expect to hear from the agent in a few days."

"I swear to it," he added.

"All right, then," Townsend said slowly, looking at Rheault. "That's it. You may go, but we want, of course, to hear from you as soon as that agent turns up. Send a report to General Potts on it every day. I believe you're going to see General Abrams now?"

Rheault nodded. "Yes, sir, that's right."

They all stood. Rheault stepped back and saluted; the generals casually returned the gesture. The colonel turned sharply and marched from the room, his beret gathered tightly in his fist. It was nearly midnight.

Townsend and Potts watched Rheault go. When the door closed, the two men got up and ambled slowly across the room.

"You know, Bill," Townsend said, "I don't believe him. I think he's lying." He shook his head in amazement.

It was long after midnight when Creighton Abrams arrived back at his bungalow. His aide, Maj. James Anderson, was waiting.

Abrams walked slowly into his study. He selected a classical record from his collection, put it on the turntable, and slumped into his leather chair. He lit a cigar, looking tired. Violins filled the room.

Anderson quietly retrieved a bottle of brandy and two glasses as he expected the general would want. They would often sit together late at night discussing the day's events and tribulations. Anderson, a former lacrosse player at West Point, was Abrams's sounding board.

The general was unusually pensive tonight, Anderson noticed, lost in his private thoughts. They sat together in silence, smoking cigars and drinking their brandies, listening to the music.

Abrams finally stirred.

"You know, he lied to me," he said, his gaze still distant.

Anderson was momentarily confused.

"Sir?"

"Colonel Rheault. He stood there and told me, face-to-face, that this did not happen." He turned to Anderson with a look of utter astonishment on his face.

Anderson now remembered seeing the late appointment on Abrams's calendar with the Green Beret commander. He knew what the subject was.

"He said they did not kill this man," Abrams went on, "but I'm sure he was lying."

They sat for another moment. Then Abrams spoke again.

"This is murder, you know. That's serious—" he chuckled sarcastically, and let the rest of the thought float in the air.

"But, you know, the whole military system is at hand here."

Anderson knew that Rheault, like Abrams and himself, was a graduate of the academy. It was a club that took its rituals and traditions, its honor code, its "long gray line," very seriously.

He watched Abrams's face shrink and contort, and he knew, right then, that the wrath of God was about to descend on Robert Bradley Rheault and the entire U.S. Special Forces.

21

L ow monsoon clouds rolled in from Nha Trang Bay Sunday morning, wrapping the 5th Special Forces compound in a thick white haze. In his tiny office, Lee Brumley was quickly thumbing through his files, purging them of evidence that Chuyen was an enemy spy.

Some of the tapes and transcripts of the interrogation were put in rough stacks for disposal—the ones showing Chuyen's treachery. Down the hallway, Ed Boyle gathered up Chuyen's clothes, wallet, watch, and his Special Forces ID card and put them in a box.

In the place of the purged material, Brumley typed up memos that would show he had reason to suspect Chuyen's treachery but found no proof of it after extensive questioning. The faked documentation would buttress the cover story of dispatching the agent on a test mission to Cambodia.

An uneasy quiet had enveloped the unit, like the eye of a hurricane. Word of Shackley's strange cable had raced through the team raising fears of a double-cross. What had prompted the CIA kiss-off? If the CIA hadn't approved of killing Chuyen, why did they remain silent for ten days after Enking and Scrymgeour had first encouraged them and Chipman had helped them along? Had they misread the signals all this time?

No, it had to be something else, they thought, maybe Chuyen's widow asking questions. Shackley was covering his bureaucratic ass and flushing them down the toilet.

They put their faith in Colonel Rheault—they had to, but the unmistakable specter of a noose tightening around their necks was in the air.

"I wonder how much time they'll give the guy who drove the truck?" Ed Boyle had cracked when Rheault was in Saigon bluffing General Abrams. When Rheault came back he passed the word through Crew that Abrams had bought the cover story "hook, line, and sinker," but no one was persuaded.

Budge Williams thought that trying to snow Abrams was a big, big mistake. Cover stories were designed for the Viet Cong, he said, not their own generals. Abrams wouldn't stay fooled for long if he wanted to get to the bottom of it.

He and Brumley and Marasco thought they should come clean—hadn't they carried out a legitimate military operation?—but now they were in a corner.

Rheault had made it clear he expected them all to stick with the story for the sake of the 5th Special Forces. Middleton, for one, said he would honor his pledge. He reminded the others that they had all taken a solemn vow of silence and said that he had personally given his promise to the boss.

Alvin Smith pooh-poohed the danger. He bet Marasco that Rheault would eventually tell Abrams the truth and they'd all be busted and reassigned to Okinawa. The spectacle of the two men arguing over the crisis made Williams want to kill them both.

On Sunday afternoon, Brumley and Boyle packed up the files and Chuyen's personal belongings and stowed them in the small truck. The closest place they could get rid of the stuff without anyone finding out, they figured, was "Indian country."

On Sunday afternoon, they grabbed their weapons, hopped into the truck, and drove west to Dong Hoi, a forested area inland from Nha Trang that was a VC stronghold. Off the dirt road they found a clearing. They stopped, emptied the truck, doused the bags with gasoline, and put a match to the pile. One part of Thai Khac Chuyen's life story went up in flames.

As Brumley and Boyle were burning the evidence, Bob Rheault was calling General Potts, as instructed, with his first report on Chuyen's mission.

There was no contact yet, he said. Potts listened without comment, then asked Rheault to put his subsequent daily messages in writing. At dawn on Monday, as ordered, Rheault sent Potts a telex. This one was devised to buy him some more time.

SECRET
NOFORN

0 230435Z JUNE 1969
FM COL RHEAULT CO 5TH SFGA
TO BG POTTS J2 MACV
1. PER OUR CONVERSATION 21 JUN AND TELCON 23 JUN THE FOLLOWING INFORMATION IS SUBMITTED:
   A. SCHEDULED RADIO CONTACT 2000–2400 23 JUN—NO CONTACT.
   B. NEXT SCHEDULED RADIO CONTACT 2000–2400 24 JUN.
   C. PLANNED EXFILTRATION TO TAKE PLACE NIGHT OF 25 JUN.
   D. PLANNED MEETING UPON EXFILTRATION—AFTERNOON OF 26 JUN.
   E. ALTERNATE MEETING—AFTERNOON OF 27 JUN.
2. POSITIVE CONTACT WILL BE PASSED TO YOU VIA THIS CHANNEL WHEN RECEIVED.
3. NEGATIVE CONTACT CAN BE ASSUMED IF YOU RECEIVE NO OTHER WORD.
4. WILL KEEP YOU ADVISED.

On second thought, Rheault made a copy of the telex for Harold Chipman and sent it off by messenger to the CIA office on Beach Road with a hand-written note on top: "Sorry for the misunderstanding." The danger seemed to have passed.

Each day passed slowly, and the gloom began to subside. With no more queries from Saigon, the incident seemed far behind them. Marasco returned to Thanh Tri to repair the mess from Chuyen and resume his operations. Brumley went back to working with his own agents, burrowing into corruption and treason in the Vietnamese Green Berets. Williams and Crew resumed their review of collection efforts in Cambodia. Middleton caught up on his paperwork. Only Smith continued to fidget and worry and rethink the case.

For David Crew, there were a few loose ends to repair. The phony O-plan that Williams had written to record Chuyen's exit on Friday, June 20, for example, didn't jibe with Saturday morning's flight log recording the movement of Sergeant Ishimoto-as-Chuyen to Tay Ninh. Flight logs could not be altered, so Crew asked a clerk to change the O-plan date. Having done that, he remembered that the new date wouldn't synchronize with the one Rheault gave the generals in Saigon. Hell, there was nothing that he could do about it now.

Rheault, meanwhile, was increasingly buoyed by the silence. On Friday, June 27, he flew to Saigon for a routine intelligence meeting with other American commanders. Afterward, he dropped by the office of General Potts. Not finding him there, he left a note on a yellow legal pad.

SECRET—EYES ONLY

Memorandum for BG Potts

Since I was in MACV today, I tried on two occasions to see you and give you an update on the matter we discussed the night of 21 June. However, as you weren't there, I am leaving this note as an update.

1. No radio contact was made.

2. The agent failed to make his physical contact 26 June in Tay Ninh city.

3. The alternate contact is today.

Should he fail to make contact (which I now rather expect), we will institute discreet surveillance of his family and other locations where he might show up. To be frank, however, I doubt that these steps will bear fruit. It is my guess that he either decided not to make the mission or was killed.

In either case, I doubt we will see him again. I also consider him no great loss, and no great threat to the security of the program.

"CIA has apparently lost interest in the case," Rheault concluded, "now that the misunderstanding has been cleared up, so that I trust this matter will now die a natural death."

Rheault flew back to Nha Trang, convinced the storm had passed. No one had questioned the cover story. He had made the right call by bluffing it out: Nobody wanted to know the details of a North Vietnamese spy's demise.

22

A lvin Smith was obsessed by the tapes.

He listened to the interrogation sessions again and again, stopping when he heard certain phrases, hitting the reverse button and sending the tapes spinning backward. Then he'd play the section again.

There had to be some explanation, Smith thought, for what had gone wrong, some missing piece that explained why Chuyen had chosen Muc Hoa, why he had chosen Smith to befriend, and how he had been able to penetrate their operations. It had to be something they had all missed, something beyond his own mistakes.

Why, he wondered, was Chuyen's name not in the Source Control files in Saigon? Could it be that Chuyen had help inside MACV intelligence headquarters? He played the tape again and cocked his ear to a blurry phrase he thought he heard Chuyen mumble under the influence of sodium pentathol. The phrase came in response to the question, "What was your mission?"

"Contact Sands, Muc Hoa," Chuyen seemed to be saying. The voice was hollow and slurred, disemboweled by the bad acoustics and the effect of drugs.

The excited sergeant summoned Budge Williams and Bob Marasco to hear the segments he had flagged. He played the tape. They listened without reaction. He played it again.

"Can't you see?" Smith said. "The question Brumley asked him was, 'What was your mission in Muc Hoa?' And he answered, 'Contact Sands, Muc Hoa.' "

Williams and Marasco didn't follow.

Smith was impatient. "Can't you see?" He played the tape again. Chuyen *had* to have help on the inside, he said. Somebody must've pointed Chuyen at him, someone inside MACV who gave the Communists his cover name.

Williams and Marasco stared at Smith, trying to see the wheels turn in this conspiracy. They didn't get it.

Anything was possible, of course. The government was riddled with VC spies. In 1969 the 525th MI Group had closed down every one of its unilateral agent nets in northern Vietnam because of enemy infiltration. Every GI learned that the smiling little boy offering a bottle of Coca-Cola could've mixed it with battery acid. Teenage girls laid mines for the Viet Cong. Seldom did a U.S. infantry unit enter a hamlet without thinking their plans had been tipped off in advance. The Viet Cong rocketed U.S. bases with inexplicable accuracy, making all the maids and kitchen workers suspects. Under every little conical hat was a potential VC spy.

Smith pressed his theory as Williams and Marasco hesitated. Why wasn't Chuyen on file in Saigon? he challenged them. Was there a VC spy inside the headquarters of Army intelligence? Perhaps an American?

It was possible. Why not? If millions of Americans were against the war, why couldn't one of them be a GI in Vietnam actively helping the Communists from right inside U.S. intelligence? He insisted that Williams and Marasco listen to the tapes again.

Smith spun the reels back and replayed the muddy section.

"Contact Sands, Muc Hoa." They could barely make it out. With Smith's prodding, they grudgingly allowed it might say what Smith thought it did. But they had been down this road with Smith before. Budge Williams had a nagging feeling that Smith might have talked himself—and everyone else—into believing Chuyen's face was in the captured photograph.

He was fed up. Smith's theory was just too bizarre. "What other goddam name would Chuyen have known you by?" he asked. " 'Contact Sands' could've just meant Chuyen had heard about you from somewhere else."

The two captains shook their heads and left. For once, they would keep it simple.

Smith was rattled by their angry dismissal. All week he'd been getting dirty looks. It made him a little queasy. The matter of Thai Khac Chuyen was far from over, he expected, and somebody was going to be set up for blame. He was not only Chuyen's case officer, he was the lowest ranking man of them all, the only enlisted man. He was the only one, he thought, to protest the killing. He *had* to protect himself.

He was certain he could. Despite Williams's rejection, he was buoyed by his discoveries on the tapes. If he could put together an investigation to uncover the ring of treachery inside Source Control at MACV, he could turn from goat to hero overnight. It would explain why everything went wrong.

Now the more he rolled the tapes over in his mind, the more he felt like celebrating. Late Saturday afternoon, he went to the NCO club. It was a simple place. A jukebox played in the corner. *Playboy* centerfolds and a huge movie poster of John Wayne stared out from the walls. He ordered a chilled martini—up, no ice—a taste picked up during his days as a diplomat-spy in Port Said. He sat savoring the cocktail, warming to his new prospects. Imagine uncovering a VC spy net right inside MACV headquarters!

As the bar filled, some other sergeants came in who invited him to join their table. Smith was glad to have company. He enjoyed himself. Later, after steaks and beer, they took in the night's movie. Afterward, turning down another round of drinks, Smith parted company and strolled back to his billet where he went to bed and quickly fell into a deep, satisfying sleep.

The next morning he was up early for a big Sunday breakfast. It was his day off, which he planned to spend at the beach, swimming, working out, and relaxing in the sun. He went back to his room to get his things and on the way ran into Richard Cruse, one of the sergeants from B-57.

Cruse had guarded Chuyen Friday night and helped line up the boat and truck. He had supplied the litter on which Chuyen was carried from the room—en route to Saigon, he was told.

The sergeant smiled and, in a conspiratorial way, looked around to make sure nobody would overhear them.

"Who are your friends after now?" he asked.

Smith was caught off guard. He asked Cruse what he meant.

"Oh, come on," the sergeant shot back. "On Friday your friends took special weapons out of the arms room. Late last night they did it again. Dressed in tiger fatigues, they left in a weapons carrier, went to the boat dock, and went out in a Boston whaler. They didn't get back until just before dawn."

He waited for Smith to answer, but Smith was noncommittal.

"I just want to know what's going on," Cruse said.

Smith didn't know how much Cruse knew about Chuyen's fate, and he was confused by the sergeant's question. He said he didn't know what "his friends" were doing, or even who Cruse was talking about.

Cruse shook his head and walked off, leaving Smith with a tingle creeping up his back. Was there another killing in the works? If so, who was next?

He decided to double-check Cruse's information. Within an hour, he had talked to the NCOs who ran the arms room and boat detachment, and they had confirmed the story: Williams and Boyle, fully armed, had taken out the boat late last night.

Was it another dress rehearsal? For him?

He thought about it.

The logic of it swirled through his mind: He was the only person who knew all the details and players firsthand. And he had opposed Chuyen's execution. And, he had seen the three captains return after the killing, blood all over their uniforms. Williams had even called it a "murder" to his face. Finally, by placing the bet with Marasco, he had insinuated that Colonel Rheault was wrong in lying to Abrams.

Which meant, in their minds, he thought the truth should come out.

He was a marked man.

With the sun going down, Smith reasoned that he might have only a few hours left before he was sleeping with the sharks. He had to be careful, think clearly.

Act normal, he told himself. Stay calm. Follow your normal routine.

He went to the club for a drink, his habit at this time of day; somebody would notice him there. Again, he ran into a few friends who invited him to join them for dinner. Smith hesitated; probably a good idea to stay around other people for a while, he thought, until he knew what to do. He agreed but said he first had to go on a short errand. He returned to his room, picked up his pistol, and tucked it into the small of his back. Armed, he rejoined his friends and sat down at the table. No one thought it odd.

Smith fidgeted through dinner, only half listening to the conversation, watching the doors. He knew there was no way he could sleep in his own bed tonight. After dinner, the friends left, and he decided to stay for a drink.

He was sitting at the bar, deep in thought, when a communications clerk came in. The man sat down next to Smith, ordered a beer, and complained that he was on the overnight shift again.

The clerk's remark gave Smith an idea. He waited for him leave, then walked out of the bar alone.

Think, he told himself. First, make sure no one is watching. He decided to check for surveillance by walking aimlessly around the compound, stopping to tie his shoelaces or light a cigarette—right by the book. Eventually, sure that no one was on his tail, he stalked out of the area. Dodging through the shadows, he made his way to the radio room. Inside, he casually told the clerk that he had loaned his bed to an out-of-town visitor. Could he borrow a bunk for the night?

No problem, the sergeant said. Take it.

Smith walked slowly back to the billet, again stopping from time to time to check whether anyone was watching. Finally, he found his way to the room, locked the door, turned off the light, and lay down on the bed.

Curled up in the dark, still in uniform, his back to the wall, pistol in hand, Smith grew certain that the same men who killed Chuyen would soon come for him.

He lay on the bed. Terrifying visions filled his mind: the sound of boots in the hallway, the door swinging open and burly arms around him, the shot of morphine in his arm, the suffocating poncho, the truck ride to the dock, and the long, helpless ride to sea. Finally, as the boat bobbed in the swells, they'd wrap the iron chains around his body and put a cold, thin silencer at his head.

He bolted upright, gasping.

In the morning, he would run.

PART III

Process
of Elimination

23

SAIGON

July 1, 1969

The phone rang, shaking Army detective Frank Bourland out of his reverie.

Stacks of manila folders were piled on his desk, the product of ten long months of police work. He had been poring through the files, remembering the good cases. Only two months more and he'd be out of this hellhole and back home in rural Illinois.

Bourland had the K-Mart look of a small-town detective: a short-sleeve plaid polyester shirt, khaki slacks, white socks, and black oxford shoes. His sandy hair was short and neatly combed. His clear frame plastic glasses were standard issue. So was the .38 police special on his thin leather belt.

Frank Bourland's beat was the sleaziest city in the world. He was a warrant officer in the Army's Criminal Investigations Detachment, in charge of investigating the crimes of American soldiers.

Hundreds of American deserters had gone underground in Saigon, fueling a bustling criminal enterprise. Some had gotten rich on the Laotian opium coming down in CIA planes from Vientiane, but there were plenty of other opportunities for scams. Saigon had a bottomless appetite for contraband, from PX stereos and Budweiser beer to soap and cigarettes. Even tanks, trucks, and guns were up for sale. Black deserters had set up their own "Soul City" in the heart of Cholon, Saigon's Chinatown, like a tropical Detroit ghetto, exotic and impervious to Army control.

A dozen other detectives worked at their gray metal desks on the four floors of the 8th CID headquarters near Ton Son Nhut airport. Like most cops, they spent most of their time reacting to crime, chasing down reports of assaults, rapes, stolen trucks, a missing crate of M-16s, counterfeit money orders.

Lately there had been a rash of shootings between Americans and South Vietnamese. An ARVN colonel had walked into a bar just that week and emptied his pistol on a bunch of MPs. A soldier from the 101st Airborne Division had sprayed his M-16 on a Vietnamese family, including a three-year-old girl.

Bourland made the collar on the killer GI. The guy was so nonchalant Bourland nearly pummeled the soldier himself.

Something was falling apart, he thought. He'd seen war in Korea, but Vietnam was different. The Army had changed.

His own boss had upbraided him one morning for not spending time helping build a new bar on the CID office roof. "That's not my job here," he said softly, and the colonel backed off. But in Bourland's view, corruption started just like that, with the little things.

It gave him another reason to stay away from the office, working the streets. He had tired of being reactive to crime. He and his partner donned sergeants' uniforms, hung out in the bars, and began eavesdropping for the chatter of obvious deserters. One night they busted a place, backed up a truck to the door, and hauled about seventy-five away. The bargirls and gangsters just stood there and laughed.

When the telephone rang on the morning of July 1, the genial detective was just trying to draw some solace from doing a conscientious job in a bad situation. He looked forward to putting Saigon behind him. Vietnam was too big for one man to solve.

"You need to get over to MACV headquarters right away," he was telling him. There was some urgency in his voice.

"What's it about?" Bourland asked.

"There's been some kind of killing involving the Green Berets," the colonel said. He didn't know any more than that.

That explained the colonel's odd tone, Bourland thought. He hoped it wasn't another "fragging." That was one of Vietnam's worst new inventions, enlisted men killing their officers for making them go out and hunt the Viet Cong. More than two hundred had done it in 1968, and the record would be broken by the end of 1969.

By the way, the colonel added, it's not just any office at MACV, it's General Abrams himself. Report to General Potts, he said, General Abrams's intelligence aide.

Bourland's curiosity was quickly overcome. He inwardly groaned at the prospect of a complicated case.

One more thing, the colonel said. "You'll be working with Bob Bidwell, out of the Bien Hoa office. He's a lot younger than you, but he's in charge because he has more time in grade."

Bourland said he didn't mind that. He could work with anybody, as long as they played it straight.

"He's kinda wild," the colonel added with a chuckle. "We're counting on you to keep him in line."

*   *   *

Bob Bidwell was already running under the whack-whack-whack of the helicopter blades, his beat-up briefcase in hand, heading for Saigon.

"This case is being handled on a top secret need-to-know basis," his boss had just told him. "Tell no one about it unless they're specifically cleared."

Bidwell, a thirty-year-old warrant officer, couldn't keep his smile down as he left the office. Green Berets, murder. Huh. It sounded like fun.

The helicopter swerved into the air over Bien Hoa, once a charming little town famous for its delicate pottery, ten miles north of Saigon. Now Bien Hoa was engulfed by a sprawling, noisy complex of Army and Air Force bases.

The chopper darted across Saigon's suburban clutter, across the Mekong River and its wretched refugee shanties. The high-rise headquarters of the U.S. Military Assistance Command came into sight near the airport, a seven-story poured cement tower among adjoining low buildings. It looked as if it had been airlifted whole from Washington, D.C., and propped up on the edge of Saigon. Inside the air-conditioned complex were movie theaters and a bowling alley. Coke machines filled the corridors.

One thousand well-groomed officers and enlisted men worked here in twelve-hour shifts, directing the war with their charts and computers and briefings. From the rooftop at cocktail hour, off-duty officers with drinks in hand could see some of their planning. Forty miles west on the Cambodian frontier, the horizon rumbled and flashed on many nights not unlike a distant summer thunderstorm, the B-52s delivering their awesome cargo.

Bidwell dashed from the chopper as soon as it had settled in front of the headquarters. He presented his CID credentials to the MPs at the busy gate and took the elevator to the second floor, where the MACV J-2, or intelligence section, was located. The door opened, and as Bidwell stepped inside, his eyes swept the room.

One general stood at a map with a pointer, talking. Three more generals sat around a horseshoe-shaped table, listening intently. Off to the side of the room sat a lanky man in sport shirt and slacks, a revolver on his belt. That had to be Frank Bourland, he thought. Bidwell tiptoed across the room and took a seat beside him. They nodded hellos.

Gen. William Potts lowered his pointer and with elaborate courtesy asked the detective to introduce himself.

"Robert Bidwell, Eighth CID."

"Thank you, Mr. Bidwell," Potts said softly as the detective sat down. Potts said he would recap the meeting. A row of clocks hung at the front of the room. Local time was a few minutes after 10 A.M., July 1.

Potts explained that a Special Forces sergeant by the name of Alvin Smith was now in the office of the Central Intelligence Agency in Nha Trang. He has asked for "asylum," Potts said, based on an astounding claim: that he is the target of a murder plot by members of his own unit.

Potts picked up a piece of paper and began reading from it. "According to the CIA report from Nha Trang," he said, "Sergeant Smith says his fellow soldiers want to kill him because he opposed their decision to execute a suspected Vietnamese double agent.

"Now let me give you some background on this," Potts said. "This is not the first time we've heard of this. On June twenty-first, we had Colonel Rheault, the commander of the Fifth Special Forces Group—and one of our most highly regarded officers—come down here to explain a problem with a Vietnamese agent under the control of his unit.

"The reason we called him in," Potts went on, "was that General Abrams had gotten a CIA report that the Special Forces might have been planning to kill one of their agents whom they suspected of working for Hanoi as a double agent." Potts considered, then dropped, the idea of explaining espionage to the detectives.

"The CIA," he continued, "said the Green Berets had asked the CIA for advice and that the CIA had advised them to let the man go. Then the agency became worried that those Green Berets had killed the man."

General Abrams immediately called Colonel Rheault on the telephone, Potts continued, and asked him about it. Colonel Rheault assured General Abrams that there had simply been a misunderstanding, that the agent had been sent on a mission into Cambodia.

But, Potts explained, General Abrams was concerned enough about what the CIA had told him to call back Colonel Rheault and ask him to come to Saigon for a fuller explanation.

Colonel Rheault came down and briefed us, General Potts said. He was asked to show exactly where he had sent his Vietnamese agent.

Picking up his pointer, Potts moved to the huge wall map of Indochina.

Colonel Rheault seemed to have difficulty finding the spot where the agent was inserted, Potts said, tapping at the Cambodian border region.

"In fact, his hand was shaking," he added dryly, drawing a chuckle from the other generals.

"Some fucking Green Beret," one of them cracked.

Potts paused like a scolding schoolmarm and then resumed for the detectives. Colonel Rheault, he went on to explain, subsequently reported that the agent in question had disappeared and may in fact have died in Cambodia. He drew a circle on the map.

"Now," he said, "we come to Sergeant Smith."

General Abrams is very upset by the sergeant's allegations, he said. No one need explain that the murder of a Vietnamese citizen by American soldiers could have terrible repercussions, particularly at this time. Relations with our ally are delicate, he said, because of the U.S. troop withdrawals President Nixon has just announced. The murder of a Vietnamese citizen could play into the hands of our many enemies, here and at home.

"So General Abrams would like you two gentlemen to go to Nha Trang right away, retrieve this Sergeant Smith, and find out if he's telling the truth."

The two detectives nodded briskly. "Yes, sir."

"You'll have all the resources you need," Potts added.

The detectives prepared to leave.

"One final thing. You will report to only me or General George Mabry, who's waiting for you at USARV in Long Binh." That was the headquarters of the U.S. Army, twenty miles east of Saigon, one of the three military services under MACV control.

"Your superiors," Potts continued, "have been notified that the investigation is secret and is being kept out of regular CID channels. So talk to no one about this, including them."

"Yes, sir," Bourland and Bidwell chimed back.

"Give us your report on Sergeant Smith," Potts said, dismissing the two detectives, "as soon as you have it."

24

B ourland and Bidwell waited until they were beyond the MACV gates before comparing notes.

They traded astonished grins.

"Thank God for you, Frank," Bidwell said, driving along the street and dodging the foot traffic.

"Whatdya mean?" Bourland asked.

"Well, you're older, you've got a college degree. You've been around."

Bourland chewed his lip. There were at least four generals in that room. He wasn't feeling all that confident himself.

What are they all upset about? they wondered together. The possibility of one smoked Vietnamese, a Communist spy? It didn't make much sense. Something else was going on. They were holding something back.

The sergeant in Nha Trang sounded like a nut, too. What kind of sergeant accuses his boss, a full colonel, the head of all the Green Berets, with murder? And then says there's a plot to murder him, too!

Bullshit. And the CIA. What's it doing in all this? From what Potts said, Bourland reflected, it sounded a little bit like the CIA had ratted on the Green Berets. Why? Something sure had all these generals riled up.

Bidwell wondered why, first of all, he and Bourland were assigned to the case. Sensitive investigations were normally handled by detectives from Detachment A, veteran agents who had been around for a while. Maybe the generals didn't understand what they were getting into, the younger man started to say, then dismissed the idea.

Bourland wondered what his new partner meant.

"Naw, they know what it's about," Bidwell added, maneuvering through the thick traffic of midday Saigon. "But we don't."

Bidwell's heart was nearly pounding. It was spooky—Green Berets, CIA, and so on. He bounced along the road, excited with the prospect of a career-making assignment. If only his father could see him now.

The last thing Bidwell wanted growing up was to be a cop. His father was a deputy county sheriff in rural Ohio. He'd seen enough of that. He wanted to get out of Ohio. He'd volunteered for Army paratrooper training as soon as he graduated from high school in 1960. But in Germany he was transferred into an MP unit and he liked it. Soon after, he applied for criminal investigations school, and a few months later he was a special agent, a tough little airborne-qualified detective.

Maybe, he told Bourland, that was why he was selected for this case. He had done some duty with the Green Berets.

Bourland listened without comment. When he didn't know what to say, he just listened.

Training duty in the Middle East, Bidwell went on, jumping into Iran and Turkey, training local police.

The older man was impressed. He'd been an ordinary rifleman for a long time, and at one point his highest ambition was to be an MP, basically a traffic cop. Then he earned his high school equivalency degree and a CID badge. Now he was eyeing a college diploma. He was proud of that. Gangly and modest, he had the low-key personality of a Texaco service-station manager. Sometimes, people were surprised he was a detective. He didn't seem the type. But he knew how to listen, and that seemed to be a good asset in this business.

But this case was already feeling strange. He didn't know anything about Green Berets and the CIA, and, in fact, he didn't care about not knowing. Already, he didn't like the feel of this thing. It smacked of politics. There was already too much of that in the war.

They nudged through the thick, dusty traffic by Bien Hoa and headed on up the road toward Long Binh. The two-lane concrete highway was clogged with pedicabs, motorbikes, and Army trucks. Peasants squatted along the roadside with their portable soupstands, waving flies away with their conical hats. Bidwell told a story.

One night the Viet Cong attacked Bien Hoa and started advancing on the CID office, he said, coming at them with automatic weapons and mortars. The VC seemed hell-bent on taking the office, and Bidwell couldn't figure out why; the CID had no military significance.

As it turned out, he was the only detective with combat training, and he had climbed up on the roof to man a .50-caliber machine gun. Even as he blasted away, though, he kept trying to figure out why the hell the VC were attacking the building. Then it came to him: They must be mistaking the MP office for the prisoner-of-war camp up the road.

He scrambled down off the roof and commandeered a fancy stereo system and a Vietnamese interpreter. Turning the speakers toward the attacking VC, he plugged in the microphone, handed it over to the interpreter, and told him to tell the marauding Viet Cong: "We are *not* the prisoner-of-war camp. You are attacking the wrong place. This is only an office. Repeat, this is *not* the POW camp, this is only an office. . . ."

Bourland chuckled. He knew a real war story from a phony one. They pulled into Long Binh.

Maj. Gen. George L. Mabry stood straight-backed and starched behind his desk as the detectives entered his office. The chief of staff of the U.S. Army in Vietnam looked exactly like they expected: thin and austere, a war hero at the Battle of the Bulge.

He sparely welcomed them to his office and without preliminaries requested a report on their meeting. Three aides stood off to the side, silent as the detectives recapped their briefing at MACV. One of them, watching Mabry's face tighten, knew of the general's strong feelings about the handling of enemy POWs: He believed absolutely in the Geneva Convention, that any enemy in American hands should be accorded formal prisoner-of-war status.

It was a point of view sharply at odds with that of younger officers who had come of age battling Communist guerrillas in the hamlets of Vietnam. Two generations, one that had cut its teeth on the plains of Europe against German tanks, the other battered by Vietnam's "dirty war," had little in common. In Vietnam, the Army was at war with itself.

When the detectives finished, Mabry directed one of the colonels to arrange for a jet to fly the detectives to Nha Trang that afternoon and take the sergeant into custody. When they had left, he asked an aide to connect him to Colonel Rheault at the 5th Special Forces Group headquarters in Nha Trang. In a few minutes, Rheault came on the line. Mabry wasted no time getting to the matter.

"You missing a sergeant, Colonel?"

Matter of fact, he was, Rheault answered.

"Did you make a report of it?" Mabry asked.

"Not yet," Rheault answered. "Smith is a bit strange. He might have just wandered off for a night." The colonel said he expected Smith to show up any moment. Nothing to worry about.

"Don't worry about him anymore," General Mabry said, "we've got him."

The line went silent. Mabry then asked Rheault to transfer the sergeant temporarily to his command. The paperwork had to be done.

Rheault hesitated. "What's it all about?" he asked.

"I don't know yet," Mabry barked. "We'll let you know if it turns out to be anything."

Mabry said good-bye and hung up. He knew damn well what was going on.

25

A sleek executive jet, fueled up and ready to go, was waiting in a corner of the Long Binh airfield for the two detectives. "Air America" was painted in bright blue script along its gleaming white hull. As soon as the two men were aboard, a crew member wheeled the door shut and the jet taxied to the head of a queue of other aircraft. Without waiting, it took off and rose sharply into the air.

Bourland and Bidwell looked around the cabin; they were the jet's lone passengers. They were impressed; red-carpet treatment. No doubt, they agreed, this one was coming from the top.

I can get used to this real fast, Bidwell joked.

The flight to Nha Trang took less than an hour. The jet touched down on the 5th Special Forces airstrip and glided to the Air America terminal where a jeep was waiting for them.

Their first stop was the CIA compound on Beach Road to retrieve Sergeant Smith. They pulled up to the closed front gates, beeped their horn, and a sleepy-looking Vietnamese sentry jumped up from a nap to open the gates. The detectives drove through the entrance and parked among a fleet of blue-and-white International Scouts and green Ford Broncos.

Dean Almy introduced himself at the door, showed them to a rear room, and quickly left. Smith jumped up from the bed as they entered. The two detectives greeted Smith calmly, showed their credentials and, with a routine manner of all cops, told him they were taking him back to Saigon to make a statement.

Smith seemed surprised. Why couldn't he just return to his unit now? he asked. He had blown the whistle on the murder plot, the secret was out of the bag, so now he was safe.

The two detectives stared at the mustachioed, gray-eyed sergeant: He was a strange little man, all right. He certainly didn't sound like someone who had just fled for his life.

They decided to cut short the discussion and get him back to Saigon, where they could take his statement under controlled conditions and then double-check it with a lie detector test. As casually as they could, they announced these plans to Smith—"just standard procedure." Oddly, the sergeant immediately agreed and walked with them to their jeep.

Smith chattered all the way back from Nha Trang about spy nets and double agents, the CIA and the Green Berets, top secret missions to Cambodia, orders straight from Washington. The story tumbled out in a kind of semaphore; Bourland hadn't the slightest idea of what Smith was talking about—intelligence operations were something he had never had any experience with and no need to know about. If the Army wanted to clue him in, that was fine; otherwise he would stay away from it. His duty was to investigate a homicide, not what the Green Berets were up to in Cambodia.

Smith's main message seemed to be that he was surrounded by nincompoops, amateurs. Bob Bidwell listened to Smith's rambling without comment. By the time they approached Saigon, he had formed an opinion that the sergeant was paranoid. Smith would soon be locked up in the loony bin.

Alvin Smith volunteered to type up his own statement the next day, Saturday, July 2. Late the next afternoon he proudly handed it to the detectives to read.

It was eight pages long, single-spaced with narrow margins. There were almost no typing errors. He had obviously prepared it with great care. The detectives sent Smith off to dinner with an escort and sat down to read.

The essay began with Smith's arrival in Muc Hoa, his discovery of Chuyen in the captured photograph, and the puzzling resignation of other B-57 agents in Muc Hoa. It wound through a detailed account of Smith's mission to find

Chuyen in Saigon, the suspect's interrogation in Saigon and removal to Nha Trang, and Smith's nervous encounter with the taxi driver while they loaded Chuyen on the aircraft at Ton Son Nhut airport. Smith then recounted his valiant efforts to save his agent's life, the meeting in Crew's office when the three captains came back from the murder party, his analysis of the interrogation tapes, and his own flight for protection to the CIA.

A hell of a yarn, Bourland thought. It was written like a spy novel.

Bidwell thought it was bullshit.

But there were facts to circle.

The plan to murder Chuyen was concocted during a "closed-door session" on June 18, Smith wrote, in the office of Maj. David Crew and attended by three captains—Bob Marasco, Budge Williams, Lee Brumley—and a warrant officer, Ed Boyle. Smith said he strenuously objected to the decision when it was announced to him immediately afterward.

"I said there was no reason to kill Khac, that he could not compromise our operations, and I did not believe he would cause any trouble," Smith wrote. "I said I was experienced at sweating out 'crimes' after a war was over (Korea), and there was no statute of limitations on murder."

The detectives were taken aback. Why in hell, when he was giving a witness statement about a murder plot *against* him, would Smith volunteer he had been involved in "war crimes" in Korea? Damn right there was no statute of limitation on murder!

But that was only the beginning.

"I even quoted Shakespeare's words," Smith wrote, describing how he tried to persuade his comrades not to kill Chuyen, " 'That we but teach bloody insurrection, which being taught, returns home to plague the inventor. This even handed justice recommends the ingredients of our poison chalice to our own lips.' "

No wonder they didn't listen, Bidwell joked.

Smith then went on to describe how he pleaded for the chance to turn Chuyen into a double agent. Crew appeared to relent, Smith wrote, and told him "nothing is definite." But then they tricked him into getting Chuyen's signature on three blank pieces of paper . . . which turned out to be the documentation for the cover story of sending him to Cambodia.

At that, red warning lights went on in the detectives' minds. Smith's statement was veering close to admitting complicity in a crime. At some point they would have to decide whether to treat him as a witness or a suspect. If he was a suspect, they would have to stop everything now and tell him he could have a lawyer.

"It was the first time I had seen him since June 13th in Saigon," Smith wrote, recounting his visit to Chuyen's cell during a break in his interrogation. "He said he was not an agent and was almost out of his mind with worry. I feigned ignorance of my knowledge of the results of his interrogation and said that I would check the interrogations and come back to talk to him.

"The idea was that, as the 'soft' approach, I would show him the hopelessness of his case, that there was a conclusive case against him, and show him a way out (to become a double for us), and, of course, with the knowledge that he was going to be killed if he didn't cooperate. As an intelligent man, sincere in his patriotism, etc., I was of the opinion that I could induce him to switch sides."

But instead, Smith said, Chuyen was taken away and executed. He saw Williams, Marasco, and Brumley return with bloody hands and clothes later that night. He had joked with Captain Williams about it being his first kill, he said, but Williams said it was "the first one I've murdered."

The three captains then turned on him, Smith wrote, because they sensed his disapproval of the murder. They even practiced killing him like they had Chuyen.

"I was the only one in the group that offered any threat to them," Smith wrote. "I was not involved in the killing, yet knew all the details. It would have been easier to cover my disappearance than it had been Khac's."

The detectives noted something else that was strange. Smith kept using different names for his agent; sometimes he called him Khac, sometimes Chuyen, sometimes Thai. Which was it? They didn't know themselves; they weren't intelligence agents. But it seemed odd that Smith didn't know.

"I believe that sometime on the night of the 29th I was to be called to go somewhere outside," the statement went on. "I was to be put in a jeep, tapped on the head, taken to the boat, taken out to the 300-foot depth, killed, weighed down, and dropped over. In the unit, it would have been said that I had gone to meet Khac."

Bidwell and Bourland turned the pages, occasionally trading raised eyebrows.

"The idea that an American officer could kill a U.S. subordinate," Smith rushed on, "is so incredible that it would not even have been believed. . . . In short, I came to the conclusion that if I stayed in my room the night of June 29, I would have been killed and disposed of."

But "what to do about this conclusion was something else," Smith went on. "Under the circumstances, I didn't want the story of the murder to get out."

The detectives circled the statement.

"I thought of telling the sergeant major and master sergeant the story and then telling Crew I had told them. I rejected this on the basis that it was all hearsay and the two could be transferred and the murder still effected."

Smith's prose rushed on, justifying his decision to seek "asylum" at the CIA.

"If I had gone straight to the local CID, they would have called the unit to come pick up their quote-nut-unquote," he wrote. "The only place that could guarantee that the story would be believed, and could keep the case quiet, was the CIA."

The detectives finished Smith's account, put it down, and then sat for a moment wondering where to begin.

They decided to call Smith in to plug a few holes in his story. Later, they decided, they'd go back over the whole thing, weed out any inconsistencies, and set up a session with the polygraph man. For now, they would continue to treat him as a witness, milking him for every detail. After all, they quickly decided, Smith's statement was voluntary.

Bourland rolled a blank witness form into his typewriter as Smith was brought into the room. They sat him down and said they wanted to fill in a few blanks suggested by his statement.

"To the best of your knowledge," Bourland asked, "is Colonel Rheault involved, or does he have knowledge of this incident?"

"I really don't know," Smith answered cautiously. Bourland sensed a dodge. Smith, for some reason, was trying to protect Rheault. He typed the answer but decided to lessen the stakes.

"You know, Alvin, this is probably just a cover-your-ass thing from General Abrams," he said. "Apparently the South Vietnamese are unhappy about this thing and Abrams just needs to give them a good explanation." He let that sink in. It was legal to say just about anything to get a witness to talk.

"Probably nobody'll ever go to jail," Bourland continued. "I can't imagine it." That was true. Bourland couldn't imagine anyone going *to jail* for killing a suspected North Vietnamese spy in the middle of the war. Fired, maybe, but not put in jail. It was a question of judgment, not a crime.

Smith was listening closely. He seemed relieved.

"Isn't it possible," Bidwell asked, turning back to Smith's fears of being killed, "that your reasoning concerning the murder of you by Williams and Boyle was in error, and a logical explanation exists for their acts?"

Bourland typed the question.

"Yes," Smith calmly responded, "but I was reasonably sure that they meant to kill me."

Well, that was hard to argue with. "Just because I'm paranoid," Smith seemed to be saying, "doesn't mean someone's not trying to kill me."

Smith wasn't dumb after all, they were concluding. Weird maybe, but not dumb. If he wasn't paranoid, he was obviously filled with resentment for his bosses and coworkers. To Bidwell, though, it still didn't add up. He couldn't believe the Special Forces would recruit a man like Smith and give him such responsibility. He was stumped.

Later, after Smith was returned to his room, Bidwell turned to his partner. "This is bullshit," he said. "No way."

Something was way off kilter, he said. "A Special Forces NCO is a *totally* different breed, a hard-core twenty-year pro, nothing like Smith."

Bourland said he was sure his partner was right. He couldn't say for sure, himself.

And something else didn't add up, Bidwell went on. "Officers like Rheault rely totally on their NCOs. Rheault would turn to his sergeant major and say, 'I got a problem, a double agent,' and the guy would figure out some way to solve that problem, and that would be the end of it. Rheault would never get involved in all the details."

Bidwell was certain about that. Smith might as well have told him the sky had fallen.

"I know that he's wrong," he went on. "There's just no way this could happen—not the way Smith said it did anyway. There's something wrong with his story."

Tomorrow's polygraph examination would soon clear it all up, they agreed. Then they'd have him locked away.

"They've got Smith," David Crew said grimly.

Brumley wasn't really surprised. He had spent Thursday night racing through the bars of Nha Trang and Friday morning checking the hospitals. He had a foreboding that Smith might have run and that the roof was about to cave in on all of them.

Maybe, he thought, it was time to come clean. First Abrams's questions, now this. There was no way out.

He, Williams, and Boyle implored Crew to go to Rheault with the facts. To their unease, Crew came back with the colonel's order: It's too late. Stick with the cover story.

"I guarantee you my eagles," Crew quoted Rheault as saying, "that we'll get through this all right. Just hang tight."

Brumley wasn't as confident. And he thought the whole turn of events bizarre. What was it exactly that they were taking such pains to conceal from the Army—that they had executed a Communist spy? Wasn't there a provision for that in the Geneva Convention? Weren't they engaged in a war? Didn't they have assent from the CIA *and* their commander?

Suddenly Brumley wished he hadn't destroyed the interrogation tapes and transcripts. Now he not only had no record of Chuyen's guilt, the files were filled with phony reports undercutting their suspicions of the agent. He was stuck with the rapidly evaporating cover story, and something equally sickening: his own growing disgust for the politics of Vietnam—everything he once thought worth dying for.

On Saturday afternoon he flew off to Saigon to see "Tommy the Cambodian," a monk who had led him into the corruption of the Vietnamese Special Forces. He was one of his best agents, a man whose admiration, even reverence, for the United States was so sincere. He would be hard to fire, but Tommy was the last man Brumley wanted to put in jeopardy, not with everything blowing up around them. Too many people knew they had some sort of a relationship. If Brumley's cover was blown, it wouldn't be long before Tommy was dead.

They met in the shadows behind the altar of Saigon's main pagoda. The flickering candles cast dark shapes on the vaulted ceilings. They talked softly lest their voices echo to unseen listeners.

There had been a complicated turn of events, Brumley whispered. He couldn't go into the details, but he had to bring an end to their relationship. As the young captain spun out the explanation, his agent's ageless smile wavered and then evaporated. He was angry. Hadn't the information been good? Yes, it had been excellent, Brumley drawled, excellent. That wasn't the problem, it was a security matter. Something had happened in another operation that could expose this one too, and he didn't want to jeopardize the agent's life. There would, of course, be a large payment for his troubles.

"If I were you," Brumley finally concluded, his voice dripping with disgust, "I would not get involved with the United States like this again. If anyone like me ever comes up to you and suggests you do work like this again, I would walk as fast, and as far away, as I could."

The agent looked perplexed.

"It's time to get out of Dodge," Brumley added. The monk started to ask what it meant.

Brumley waved his hand. "It's just a saying."

With that he shook his agent's hand, told him to stay there for a few moments, then walked back through the shadows, out of the pagoda, and into the sunlight. He had just walked away from the best intelligence agent he had ever had. And, he guessed, the last one.

Bob Bidwell was astounded.

Smith, the polygraph man said, was telling the truth. There was "no deception indicated."

C'mon, he jeered. You're kidding. Bullshit.

Worse, the polygraph man went on, Smith now indicated that Colonel Rheault was party to the murder conspiracy after all.

Bidwell searched for an alternative explanation. He was convinced no senior officer in his right mind would do what Smith was describing. Maybe, he said, it's possible Smith is *so* paranoid that he believes his own delusions. It had happened before.

Bidwell knew something about the Special Forces, he volunteered, and what Smith was saying didn't jibe. He'd been through the Green Beret interrogation course himself, been on operations in Iran and Turkey, worked with them in training exercises with police departments in the States. The Green Berets didn't go in for "wet terminations," he scoffed—the term Smith used to described the execution of the agent. He'd never heard such a term, Bidwell said. Smith's too full of spy novels.

"That's not the way they operate," he insisted.

"This is not the Special Forces I know," he repeated, pacing the office. "You tell me that Colonel Robert B. Rheault, a full colonel, promotable to general, did this, and I'm going to laugh you right out of my office."

Laugh all you want, the polygraph man said. It's true.

Bidwell telephoned General Mabry with the news on Sunday afternoon.

Holy Jesus Christ, he said to himself, waiting for the general to come on the line. *What have I got myself into? If we're wrong about Rheault I can kiss my ass good-bye.*

26

General George Mabry put the receiver on the hook. He was astounded. *Why didn't Rheault come to me?* he marveled. *I told him if there ever was a problem, come to me.*

This was probably his last war. It was not the way he wanted to go out.

Well, by God, it was too late now. He wasn't going to be part of any damned murder committed by any gang of U.S. Army officers. *The Army's not big enough to approve that kind of thing and keep me in it.*

Years ago, at the Army War College, George Mabry had written his thesis on the personality of men in combat—why some fight, and why some don't. Why some are natural fighters, why some only fight in a group, and why some men never fire their weapons in combat. In the end, he decided that the performance of a soldier was determined long before he picked up a rifle.

What was it with Rheault? he wondered. *Why had he gone out on his own?*

Hell, he didn't have time for psychoanalysis. He'd seen military officers try to ingratiate themselves with the CIA before, and here was another case of it.

Damn the CIA! During the planning for the Bay of Pigs, the CIA had tried to recruit him, too, as a secret agent right inside the senior Army staff. He told them to go to hell.

There seemed to be two American armies in Vietnam, George Mabry thought, and that was the problem. There was the Pentagon's army, and the CIA's army, and the Special Forces fell somewhere in between.

But the Green Berets had taken advantage of it. They thought their clout with the CIA put them above the rules. Now somebody had to rein them in.

George Mabry was a straight-shooter. He remembered when his father was umpiring a baseball game, right after his career as a player ended. It hadn't been much of a career to start with, mostly semipro ball in South Carolina. His dad was a catcher, five feet eleven, two hundred pounds, huge hands. He'd made it to the Washington Senators for a few games, then it was over.

He was behind the plate, umpiring a Fourth of July doubleheader. A man in the crowd jeered him. He turned around and put his mask down. "Anyone who doesn't like the way I'm calling this game," he said, "come on down." One guy did; Mabry's father flattened him with a single punch.

That's exactly the way George Mabry was. If anybody didn't like the way he was about to hammer the Green Berets, all they had to do was "come on down." And General Abrams, he knew, felt exactly the same way.

Mabry picked up the telephone and called Bob Rheault. He wanted to see him in Long Binh.

"When?" the colonel asked.

"Tomorrow morning," the general said. The Fourth of July.

* * *

George Mabry cut right to the bone as Rheault sat before him. Two aides stood at the edge of the room.

"Allegations have been made that some members of your organization murdered a male Vietnamese," he said, sitting erect behind his desk.

Rheault began to speak. Mabry raised his hand.

"It's an allegation only," the general said. He just wanted to question some of Rheault's men "to determine the validity of the allegation."

Mabry then gave Rheault a list of the names of the men who were to be questioned: Major Crew, Major Middleton, Captains Brumley, Williams, and Marasco, Warrant Officer Boyle, and a handful of sergeants.

Rheault again tried to speak, but Mabry stopped him.

"You are not to inform these individuals," the general said. "You are to keep the list of names on a close-hold basis. I do not want the word to be widespread if there is nothing to the allegations."

Rheault took the list and examined it.

"Don't concern yourself about having the individuals staying close by, or waiting to be called for an interview," Mabry added. "If a certain individual is in the field, we can interview one or the others on the list or wait for the return of the one we would like to question."

Rheault finished reading the list and once more started to say something. Mabry cut him off.

"Colonel Rheault, I don't want to discuss the case here. I want to have the individuals on that list interviewed to determine the validity of the allegations."

Rheault nodded. He then asked if the men on the list should get lawyers.

"If they desire legal counsel before or during the conduct of the interview," Mabry drawled, "their request will be granted immediately, and the interview will be terminated until counsel is made available. Those are the regulations."

Rheault looked at the general, then cautiously took another stab at starting a dialogue.

"If a murder has been committed," he began slowly, "I'm sure those involved will say that they were executing a mission in furtherance of the war effort."

Mabry shook his head.

"I do not want to discuss the case here, Colonel," he repeated. "I am merely trying to determine the validity of these allegations and making plans to interview the men whose names appear on the list."

Rheault sat still.

"You're dismissed, Colonel Rheault."

Rheault stood, saluted, and left the office.

Mabry watched him go. You learn a lot, he thought, when the rubber hits the road.

Floyd Cotton sat at his desk staring at the slip of paper the new lieutenant had just handed him.

This thing was getting all fucked up, the black counterintelligence agent thought. First Colonel Weil tells him to take Chuyen's name off the Camp Goodman visitor's register. Then he says the CIA's asking questions.

Now this.

"Does the name look familiar to you?" the lieutenant asked.

"No, sir. Doesn't ring a bell."

In fact, the slip of paper burned in his hand. The name on it was Thai Khac Chuyen.

Cotton shook his head. "What about it?"

"I've got a couple women in my office asking about this guy," said the lieutenant, Allan Becker. He was a new guy.

As far as Cotton knew, the lieutenant was in the dark about everything. "One of them says he's her husband and works for us. She says she hasn't seen him since June thirteenth. She says she's worried about him." The women were waiting for an answer, he said. They were very upset.

"I'll try to get something for you," Cotton said. He turned away and picked up the telephone. When he turned back around, he was surprised to see Becker still there.

He quickly got a connection to Nha Trang. Lee Brumley came on the line.

"Captain Brumley, sir, I have a lieutenant here with a note in his hand saying that a woman is here claiming to be the wife of a man who works for us. His name is"—he looked at the note—"Thai Khac Chuyen. She says her husband works for us, and she's here looking for him. She wants to talk to him."

There was silence on the line.

"Can you give me any guidance on this, sir?"

Brumley listened intently. Events were moving too quickly. He asked Cotton who the lieutenant was.

"Lieutenant Becker, sir, the new adjutant. He just signed on here last week."

Stall, Brumley thought. "Tell Becker," he said softly, "to tell the woman that he couldn't find anyone who knows anything about her husband's whereabouts."

Under stress, Brumley's easygoing Oklahoma twang was reverting to rough military vernacular. "Get them out of the compound right-goddam-away," he added, "but get a description from Becker of what they look like. Use some sort of excuse."

"Okay, sir. Will do."

"Send a report to me on everything that happened," Brumley added.

"Okay, sir." He hung up and turned back to his visitor.

"We don't have anything on him right now, sir. There's no one around who knows him, but we'll notify her as soon as we find something out." He calmly handed back the slip of paper.

"One more thing," Cotton said. "If you can, sir, it'd be a good idea to get them out of here right away since this is a secured area. Also, we don't have any real proof of who they are, so it would be good if you could check their IDs and give us a good description of the women for our files. Never can tell."

When Becker left, Cotton quickly grabbed a sheet of paper and began typing up a report for Brumley. Ten minutes later he was walking down the hallway when he saw the lieutenant coming out of his office with the women. He ducked out of the corridor and slipped outside through a side door.

Becker returned with a note for Cotton later. It had the name and address of Phan Kim Lien along with that of Lam Hoang Oanh. Lien, Cotton knew, was Chuyen's wife. Oanh, who said she was Lien's sister, had also written down her place of employment: CORDS/SCAG, 158 Pasteur Street, Saigon, telephone 922-5708.

Cotton immediately recognized it. It was the acronym for the Saigon office of Civil Operations–Revolutionary Development Systems, the pacification program that was connected to Operation Phoenix.

Jesus, Cotton thought, was Chuyen's sister-in-law connected to the CIA? *Holy shit.*

"There are security implications to this, sir," Cotton quickly told Becker. "I'd like to request that you not discuss the women's visit with anyone."

As soon as the lieutenant left, Cotton sent a message to Brumley in Nha Trang. Things were unraveling fast.

27

Lee Brumley raced downtown in his jeep and pulled to a sliding stop at Streamers, a gaudy bar on Nha Trang's GI strip. He was looking for Ed Boyle. His eyes scanned the smoky room. A few Green Berets were quietly drinking beers at the bar. It was still early. Boyle wasn't there, but Gina, the head bargirl, was.

"Hi, Lee, you have a beer with me?"

"Not now, Gina, I'm looking for Ed. Have you seen him?"

Gina was dolled up the way Vietnamese girls had perfected to please young American soldiers—tight skirt, tank top, blue mascarad eyes and bright lipstick. But not too much, not overdone.

Gina was bright, spoke passable English, and, most importantly, knew her customers. It was a smooth operation. Streamers had become a Project Gamma watering hole as well as a favorite of the CIA. Harold Chipman was a regular, Brumley had noticed. The counterintelligence captain had put Gina through a security check and recruited her as a casual informant. One of the more interesting tidbits she came up with was Chipman's relationship with a local girl.

"No, not today," she said. "You stay for awhile?"

"No, listen. When you see Ed, you tell him to stay low. You know, hide.

Tell him to stay out of sight for awhile, okay? Tell him not to come back to the office for at least a day."

Gina had learned not to ask questions of the Green Berets, and especially of Lee.

"Okay, Lee."

"You tell him I'll get back in touch with him tomorrow night, okay? Just make sure you tell him not to go back to the office."

"Right," she smiled. "I will take care of him."

Brumley stalked out of the bar and sped off. His next stop was to find Donald Knutson, the sergeant who had helped them with chores connected to the interrogation. Knutson, Brumley had learned, was at the top of the witness list General Mabry gave to Rheault, which Rheault had turned over to Crew as soon as he got back from Long Binh.

Boyle was number two on the list. The rest of them would surely follow, right down the drain, unless Boyle and Knutson could put up a solid wall right from the start.

Over the weekend, Brumley had also begun to develop his own sources at MACV headquarters, friends from the career officers intelligence course back at Fort Holabird who gave him reports on the CID investigation. Soon after Smith's "defection" Brumley had gotten a report on Smith's statement to the CID. According to his sources, the detectives told Smith that they were only conducting a "cover-your-ass" probe for General Abrams in response to an inquiry from the South Vietnamese government. Apparently, Chuyen's widow had made a complaint to South Vietnamese politicians and it had been relayed to the U.S. Embassy.

Brumley's spirits brightened. If no one in Nha Trang talked, he reasoned, the detectives would have to fold their investigation. After all, there wasn't a body. They were only suspicions. Chuyen was three hundred feet deep, wrapped in chains. If nobody talked, they might ride the thing out.

Brumley finally found Don Knutson at midnight in his quarters. He had been out drinking. Brumley fixed the hulking blond NCO intently with his flat brown eyes. "Can we trust you?" he asked.

Knutson nodded.

"Good. Tomorrow morning, some people are going to ask you about obtaining a boat on a certain night in June.

"Now, what I want you to say is that you obtained this boat for myself and Warrant Officer Boyle, okay?"

Knutson nodded. He looked like he was trying to remember exactly who went out in the boat.

"What's going on?" he asked.

"You remember that thing with the Vietnamese guy? Abrams knows all about it. And the criminal guys are conducting an investigation. But it's just a cover-your-ass thing. They think Smith's nuts.

"Boyle and I have a reason to take the boat out," Brumley explained, "because we've been conducting a CI operation on Hon Tre. So we're going to tell them that Boyle and I went out in the boat on a regular operation and that Smith's got it wrong." And so did the CIA.

Brumley continued, "Without corroboration, they'll continue to think that Smith's got it all wrong, and they'll just put him away. And that'll be the end of it. Abrams just needs an answer to give the South Vietnamese anyway."

Knutson nodded again. "Cover your ass," he repeated. "You mean a white-wash."

"Right."

"Okay," Knutson said. "You and Boyle took the boat out."

Brumley nodded, got up, and slipped out the door.

28

B ob Bidwell leaned back in the seat of the Air America jet and turned to his partner.

"You know, Frank, I don't care what Smith's polygraph shows. I still cannot believe Colonel Rheault is involved in this thing."

Bourland peered out the cabin window as his partner groused. From twenty thousand feet, Vietnam looked like one of those Caribbean paradises that Bourland hoped to take his wife to someday. A bright azure sky arched from horizon to horizon. Lazy puffballs of white clouds drifted by them, throwing shadows on the lush green rice paddy below. A baby blue sea lapped on a ribbon of white beach. Out the window to their left, the Annamite mountains rose sharply in emerald splendor. Only the pockmarks of bomb craters hinted at the terrible violence that had marched up and down the string of hamlets along the shore.

"It doesn't seem right to me either, Bob," Bourland said earnestly, turning to his partner. His long legs stretched under the seat. He didn't mean that he thought soldiers were incapable of bad judgment, or extreme cruelty. War was war. People do things they'd be locked up for at home. Certainly he'd seen enough men with bright military futures go wrong in Vietnam—rigging slot machines, hijacking PX goods, dealing drugs, and the worst, selling American weapons on the black market. He'd seen too many shootings of innocent civilians.

But someone with Rheault's background, he agreed, a rich man with all the advantages, would not get involved with his subordinates in an execution. People like that didn't involve themselves with, well, what he really meant was, people like him. Ordinary people.

Bidwell was getting worked up. "This is bullshit. No way. I know Smith is wrong." He kept it up all the way to Nha Trang.

The two detectives pondered the best approach to Rheault. The fact was that Smith's statement about the colonel's involvement with Chuyen was all secondhand, culled from others like Crew and Middleton. Both General Potts and General Mabry, moreover, had emphasized that they were only investigating allegations, that Rheault was due deference because of his rank and record.

"We have no evidence whatsoever," Bidwell said in his Ohio twang, sounding like he was trying to persuade himself, "that Rheault knows anything about what his men did with Chuyen."

The first test would be the cover story, they agreed: Smith had predicted that all his former comrades would line up behind the story that Chuyen had been sent on a test mission. The detectives thought that if they could crack Sergeant Knutson, who Smith guessed knew about the killing but wasn't directly involved himself, or Sergeant Ishimoto, who flew to the cover mission to Tay Ninh, then they'd have a hammer to crack open the others.

The jet circled over the South China Sea, dipping its wings over the outer harbor where Chuyen's body lay in fifty fathoms of water. Descending to Nha Trang, Bourland and Bidwell agreed on two approaches to Rheault.

First, they'd be very respectful of his rank and reputation, if only for practical reasons. The CID was littered with broken careers—detectives who'd been too diligent probing high-ranking officers. If Rheault turned out to be wrongly implicated, he'd have their asses.

They'd project an attitude that they didn't believe he was involved in the murder and that they'd like to dispose with that right away, through a lie detector test. If Rheault was clean, he'd jump at the chance.

If he balked . . . Well, they preferred to think about that later. In the meantime, they had to be very, very careful.

Bob Rheault was making coffee when they arrived at his office a little after 9 A.M. The skin around his slate blue eyes was pinched and wrinkled, and his angular cheekbones were unshaven. He looked like he had just gotten up from the canvas cot in the corner.

He offered the two detectives cups of coffee and they sat down in front of his desk. Bidwell placed his brown leather briefcase next to him on the floor. Bourland put on his glasses, opened his black Army-issue briefcase, and fished through the messy pile of papers. He found Smith's eight-page statement and took it out, placing it on the desk. Rheault reached forward and picked it up.

"CAS told me all about Smith's allegations," Rheault said, projecting both indifference and contempt. He began to read the document.

Bidwell sized him up, impressed that Rheault was already name-dropping, invoking the CIA's light cover name to suggest that he was aloof from their investigation, maybe even untouchable.

Bourland, still fishing through his papers, leaned over toward his partner.

"CAS?" he mouthed.

Bidwell mouthed the initials back, "C-I-A."

Bourland nodded.

"Sir," Bidwell began, "We're here to investigate the suspected murder of a double agent."

"Yes, I know," Rheault said, continuing to read Smith's statement.

"We're here to take a statement from you, and technically you are a suspect in the investigation. So if you want a lawyer, we can stop at any time for you to get one."

"I don't need a lawyer," Rheault said, still reading.

Bourland pulled a piece of paper from his briefcase.

"Sir, this is the list of the people we'd like to interview," he said, politely placing it on the desk. Rheault picked it up, gave it a quick scan, and then returned to Smith's statement. He read it to the end.

"Well," Rheault said when he finished, "I have to assume he's telling the truth. But, of course, I don't know. I assume if they did do away with the agent, that they did it because they felt it was to protect their intelligence operations, and in the furtherance of the war effort."

"Sir," Bidwell said with deference, going back to the game plan, "we have to make sure that you understand that, officially, you are a suspect. But we'd like to get this behind us right away. So if you could make a statement, you know, disclaiming all knowledge or involvement in this, then we can give you a quick polygraph and be done with it." Rheault considered the gambit.

"We'd like to turn the supervision of the investigation over to you, in fact," Bidwell continued, "because you are the best person to convince the others to tell the truth."

Rheault got up and took a couple paces behind his desk. There wasn't much room to walk.

"Well, I will give you a statement and can tell you what happened as far as I know it, but I won't take a polygraph test."

Bidwell sensed danger. He told Rheault that Smith had taken a polygraph and passed it.

Rheault waved off the detective. "Well, if the Army won't believe my statement, then it's high time I got out of the Army." He continued to pace. The detectives were surprised by his vehemence, and disappointed. They'd seen suspects pull this act before. Suspects who turned out to be guilty.

"Well, okay, sir," Bidwell said. "Why don't you just tell us what happened, and we'll go from there." He and Bourland pulled out yellow legal pads to take notes, noticing that Rheault's hands were slightly trembling.

Overhead, the fan spun slowly.

During the afternoon of June 20, Rheault began, a meeting was held at his office to discuss the disposition of "Khac," who was suspected of being an enemy agent.

"Who was at that meeting?" Bourland softly asked.

"Colonel Kenneth Facey, Major David Crew, and Major Thomas Middleton, Jr.," Rheault said. The detectives wrote it down.

Various courses of action were suggested and debated, Rheault continued. They decided they could not let the agent go free, because he knew too much. Nor could he be turned over to South Vietnamese intelligence. If they, or the general public, became aware of certain operations, Rheault explained, it would be detrimental to the war effort.

The detectives listened, noting that Rheault's mouth now seemed to have gone dry.

"Of course, I had no authority to authorize a killing," he said, "and I told them that." Crew could back that up, he added.

He continued, "It was decided to send the agent on a mission to test his reliability."

Pausing, he added offhand, "If Major Crew had him killed, it was not with my knowledge or approval."

The detectives scribbled.

"If he did have the agent killed," Rheault said, "I'm sure it was for my protection."

The two detectives hesitated, puzzled by the statement, but decided not to pursue it for now. It was an opening they could probe later. Instead, they asked Rheault again if he could help their investigation by persuading Crew and the others to talk.

Rheault considered it and then reluctantly agreed.

"I don't think they'll talk if they think they're liable to criminal prosecution," he said. "There's no evidence that they killed Chuyen anyway, no body."

He fixed the detectives with his eyes.

"I'm going down to see General Abrams and see if some sort of deal can be worked out," he said. "Maybe they'll talk if there's a guarantee they won't be prosecuted."

This was new territory for the detectives, and they were momentarily thrown off. They'd never heard a suspect talk cavalierly about making "a deal" over their heads. At least not right in front of them.

From what they'd heard, General Abrams wasn't in the mood for "a deal" anyway. He was looking for blood.

Rheault suddenly stood up, the busy commander with better things to do. The detectives put their notebooks away.

"I'll get you mess passes," he said, suddenly gracious. "You can use a room next door to work. And if you need a driver, just say so."

Tightly smiling, he showed the detectives out the door and closed it behind them.

29

Bourland and Bidwell ambled across the dusty compound in their sport shirts and slacks, police revolvers on their belts, briefcases in hand. Clumps of Green Berets eyed them warily from doorways and windows. The detectives felt like federal marshals riding into town in a bad Hollywood western.

Bidwell was enjoying himself. His briefcase was packed with the usual Louis L'Amour paperbacks. He chuckled to himself and Bourland. This is interesting: the CID versus the Green Berets, the Green Berets versus the CID, the CIA versus the Army, the Army versus the CIA. *Funny.*

Bourland wasn't amused. The meeting with Rheault had been jarring. Long before he was a detective he had been an infantryman, in battle. With all its blemishes, the Army had been good to him. He respected the institution and felt it had to be held to high standards. The tone was set at the top. He was disappointed with Rheault.

Bidwell read his partner's face.

"You know," he mused, calming down, "Rheault's response was perfectly in character with somebody who's been expecting to be questioned, somebody who's rehearsed his answers." He considered an analogy.

"It's the difference between a person getting hit by a truck that he hasn't seen and a truck he's been watching since it came into sight, coming closer and closer and closer."

Bourland sadly nodded. If Rheault were innocent, he said, he'd be outraged at any suggestion of his complicity in the murder. He'd be eager to clear himself. He'd demand a polygraph on the spot.

"This thing about 'The heck with them if they won't take my word' is an old trick," he said. "It's an excuse made by people trying to cover up something."

Rheault's stonewalling had thrown their game plan out the window. Now they'd have to try another angle. When they found their temporary office, they threw their briefcases on the table and sat down to think.

Why not let Rheault *think* they were letting him in on the progress of their investigation? Bidwell suggested. Play along with him. That way they could keep in close contact and not spur him into doing something rash—like destroying evidence or trying to go over their heads. Rheault also seemed quite brittle and just might confess.

That would be their plan.

"It is still likely," Bidwell jotted in his case notes, summing up their encounter with Rheault, "that either he ordered the murder of Khac, and possibly the attempted murder of Smith, or that he has knowledge and is protecting those involved."

"So you're the boat man," Bidwell said.

Sgt. Donald Duane Knutson nodded, "Yup."

He yawned.

Bourland and Bidwell smiled. The burly blond soldier slumped in a chair across the table from them, arms folded, looking bored. He was a special agent in the counterintelligence section, he said, and worked most of the time with the Vietnamese Special Forces. But he was also the 5th Group property manager and controlled the boat detachment.

"Did you sign out a boat for anyone from detachment B-57 last week?" he was asked.

Knutson raised his eyes to the ceiling, as if he were trying to recall some long-ago event.

"Friday night," he finally said. "Mr. Boyle asked for a boat."

"Any other times?"

"Maybe Thursday, too, and Saturday, come to think of it."

The detectives jotted down his answers.

"Who went out in the boat?"

Knutson thought again. "Captain Brumley and Warrant Officer Boyle," he finally said.

For the next several minutes, the detectives led Knutson through his carefully rehearsed answers, writing down the approximate times of the boat trips by Brumley and Boyle and Knutson's account of how he had gotten clearance for the missions from the Nha Trang fire-control center. There would be records there, he said, hesitating before giving the detectives the names of people in charge.

No, he said, he had no idea why Brumley and Boyle went out in the boat. No, he didn't see any blood in the boat when it came back Friday night. He quivered as if appalled by the thought.

The detectives listened without the slightest betrayal of doubt or suspicion. Knutson began to relax.

Yes, he said, he was aware of the interrogation of Thai Khac Chuyen—he had questioned the agent once himself. He didn't know if "Khac" was a Communist spy; he didn't hear the man admit to that. In fact, if he seemed to "bounce" the polygraph every time the VC were mentioned, it was "probably because he hated them so much."

More of the cover story.

The last time he saw "Khac" was on June 16, Knutson said. Then a couple days later, Boyle told him the agent had been sent back to Saigon. The sergeant sat back and relaxed, smoking his cigarette.

"Could you show us the boat?" Bidwell asked.

"No problem," Knutson said. He lifted to his feet. "I'll go get us a jeep. It's a ways from here."

When he left, the detectives smiled to each other: They were reeling Knutson in. In a minute, he was back.

The sergeant slipped back into his seat and leaned forward.

"Say," he smiled, lowering his voice, "is Abrams directing this investigation?"

"That's right."

Knutson's mouth crinkled in another smile.

"So they just want to hear this story, and that'll be the end of it?"

The detectives were silent.

"Because I'm just telling you," Knutson said, "what I've been told to say."

"What do you mean?" Bourland asked, casually.

"Well," Knutson said, "I was told that everything that was done was done with the approval of CAS and the CO, Colonel Rheault."

He waited for a signal from the detectives. It didn't come.

"You know, totally legal. And that the investigation, you guys, are just here to take care of the Vietnamese, who made a stink to Abrams about the man disappearing."

"Was Khac killed?" Bourland asked casually, as if he didn't know.

Knutson withdrew. "I don't know anything about that."

"You know about Sergeant Smith, right?" Bidwell asked.

Knutson nodded. Bidwell looked him straight in the eyes.

"He's told us everything."

Knutson sat still.

"You've told us a lot, too," Bourland interjected, "but we don't think much of it's true."

Knutson looked confused. The tables had been turned too fast.

Bourland added, "We can type up your statement, of course, and you can sign it."

Knutson weighed his situation.

"Don, do you know what the penalties are for perjury?" Bourland asked softly.

Knutson bolted from his chair. "I don't know anything about it." He walked to the corner of the small hot room.

"This is not a whitewash," Bourland said softly. "This is a serious investigation." The two detectives sat at the table, waiting for Knutson to come back.

"We are going to examine every boat in this facility," Bourland explained. "There will be a microscopic examination and lab test of the boat, the one that the three captains took out—we know who took it out—which will prove beyond a shadow of a doubt what happened in that boat."

"And we know you saw them go out and come in," he added.

Knutson stayed in the corner, his back turned. The detectives let him think.

"Look," Bourland said softly, "you've been put in a bad situation, by commanders who should know better. They're letting you be a scapegoat. They don't give a damn about you, obviously. They're going to let you lie and get caught and go to jail."

Bourland shook his head.

"Wouldn't it be something if they got away with it somehow and you went to jail for perjury?"

Knutson returned and sat down.

"Hell, you're not even involved, really," Bourland continued. "You didn't kill anybody, did you? Why should you go to jail?"

Knutson sat silently, his chin in his hand. A long minute passed. Slowly, his face grew red. He shook his head and closed his eyes.

"Oh, shit."

Bourland put a fatherly hand on his shoulder. "Don't take a fall for those guys," he said quietly. He watched Knutson struggle with his conscience. Disgust welled up from some deep spot inside. *What a strange war this is*, he thought to himself, *to do this to this fine young man. How crazy it is.*

Knutson finally lifted his head.

"I really don't know what happened to him," he said. "Brumley told me to tell you guys that he and Boyle went out on the boat and that Abrams knew the real story but everybody just wanted to cover it up."

"Who went out on the boat?" Bidwell asked.

"Marasco, Williams, and Brumley," Knutson said, sniffling.

"They took Khac with them?"

Knutson nodded.

"What did you see when they came back in the boat?"

"I just saw that the bilge was tinted red. They tipped the boat over. We had to wash the floorboards and the life jackets."

Now they were moving. For the next hour, the two detectives drew out Knutson's story: how the guys in B-57 suspected "Khac" of spying for Hanoi, how the plane brought him from Saigon, how he was locked in the room, Knutson's role in the interrogation, how he signed out the boat to Brumley and Marasco, watched them load a bulky poncho into the boat on the night of June 20 and waited for the men to return, all the while keeping in touch by radio.

It was a rambling account that skipped back and forth, but the detectives listened respectfully. When he finished, the sergeant had implicated Crew, Middleton, Williams, Brumley, Marasco, Boyle, and Smith in the plot to kill Thai Khac Chuyen. He had also supplied the names of a half dozen other potential witnesses.

He had had no contact with Rheault, Knutson said, but it was "inconceivable" that Middleton and Crew didn't discuss the matter with him.

Knutson also added another batch of possible felony counts to the list: the unauthorized injection of Chuyen with sodium pentathol by the 5th Special Forces Group doctor, Major Stanley Allison. Knutson was positive that the drug's use had to be specifically approved by the U.S. Army Intelligence Command in Baltimore.

After two hours, the detectives took a break. Bourland remarked how radically Knutson had changed once he decided to talk: He had become completely cooperative. It augured well for their investigation, he said, because all of the suspects probably were just like Knutson and really didn't think they had done anything wrong. They were lying to cover it up for some other reason.

Most of Knutson's statement was circumstantial, but Bourland thought there might already be enough to detain Williams, Marasco, and Brumley, and possibly Boyle, on suspicion of murder.

"Why did you decide to talk to us?" Bourland asked the sergeant. His legal pad was filled with notes.

"You guys are professionals—you really mean it," Knutson answered. His voice stiffened. He had the appreciation of one professional for another. "We all thought this was going to be some kind of cover-up investigation." He seemed to have an unspoken bitterness toward his comrades.

Bidwell suddenly had an idea. He tugged at his partner's sleeve and suggested they go outside for a talk. Knutson was left alone in the room.

When they returned, Bidwell had a proposal for the sergeant. The detective leaned forward.

"How about working for us now?" he asked.

*   *   *

It was nearly sunset when the detectives unpacked in their hotel room on Beach Road on the edge of Nha Trang. The days's results were far beyond their expectations. Their big break was obviously Knutson, but they had a long way to go.

Getting the murder weapon would be useful to the case. Knutson thought Williams had probably shot Chuyen with a silencer-equipped Swedish K automatic rifle, which he guessed was kept in a safe in the counterintelligence section. That tracked with what Smith had told them, the detectives said. Could he get it for them?

Knutson said he'd try.

Be careful, the detectives said: There was one body too many in the ocean already.

When Knutson looked worried, they gave him a number to call at the local CID office in case he was in danger.

Now they had their own spy.

When he got back to his hotel room, Bidwell made a note about the new operation in his case file. "Knutson is an accredited counterintelligence agent and shouldn't have any trouble. Local CID were briefed to be on the lookout and to rescue Knutson if necessary."

With that, the two detectives left for dinner, taking care to set a few traps to tell them if their room was entered while they were away.

Downstairs in the hotel dining room, the Vietnamese maître d' welcomed them with a sweeping smile and insisted they sit at a table by the window.

"The view, monsieurs, the view."

They took their seats and ordered drinks. They looked out through the palm trees to a slate blue sea. Beyond was the jagged peak of Hon Tre island, rising like a tombstone on the horizon.

30

A boy stands on the sidewalk, watching the soldiers march by. It is the summer of 1946. He waves the tiny American flag in his hand. A band is playing "The Stars and Stripes Forever." People are cheering wildly. Pretty girls run into the street with flowers, kissing the laughing GIs. His mother smiles and squeezes his hand. The soldiers are coming home to Woodlawn, Illinois, every one of them a hero.

Frank Bourland had never forgotten that scene. He carried it with him to Korea, to an air base in North Africa, to stateside duty and then to Vietnam. The memory of glorious American soldiers marching through his rural Illinois hometown had stuck with him for years. It had probably been the main reason he left high school in the 1950s to join the Army. That, and the poor prospects for welders, his father's trade. Now the memory made him sad. There would be no parades when he came home from Vietnam. A million men had already "sneaked off to Vietnam in the middle of the night and come home with their collars up," as one congressman put it. There were no parades for soldiers who were called war criminals.

Bourland took new notice of the Green Beret sergeant sitting across the table giving a statement to his partner. Bob Bidwell was taking notes on a yellow pad. It was ten minutes past eight, Monday morning, July 7.

"I didn't pay any attention to what was going on," Sgt. Richard Cruse was saying. "Because of my previous knowledge that Khac was in the room, the events of the evening led me to believe he was being moved."

"To where?" Bidwell asked. One of these days he was going to have to get that name nailed down—Thai Khac Chuyen, Chuyen Thai Khac, Khac Thai Chuyen—whatever the hell it was. It was embarrassing not to get the victim's name right in a police report.

"Saigon," the sergeant said.

Was that part of the cover-up? The detectives weren't sure, but it tracked with what Smith said they would hear. If it was, all the better. Let the soldiers run with the line. Pile up perjury counts for future leverage. When the suspects began to realize that the detectives had figured it out, Bidwell mused to himself, they'd think they were brilliant. But Smith had told them everything. The suspects didn't have a chance.

Everything was working so far. They had decided to play dumb, "like hicks who didn't know a hell of a lot, who were kind of awed by the whole thing, way out of our element," Bidwell recalled later. "We were gonna sir 'em. We were gonna dumb 'em. Frank's good at that, so I decided we had a good thing going. We pretended we were there just to document the cover story and get the hell out."

Bidwell drove that home to Sergeant Cruse with his last simple question. "Do you have anything else to add concerning the investigation?"

"No. I have no further knowledge of the incident," Cruse said.

"Thank you, sergeant. You can come back later to sign your statement."

The detectives made check marks on the interview list. They planned to run as many people through the cramped plywood room as possible, mostly witnesses on the periphery of the case who could establish the time of Chuyen's removal, the use of a boat, and the identity of the murder weapon. And where the corpse might be.

At 8:30 came Jack Harper, a grizzled master sergeant and twenty-year radio man. As he sat down, the detectives explained who they were, why they were there, and asked him if he knew anything about the disappearance of a Vietnamese agent from Detachment B-57.

"Not exactly," Harper said, smiling wryly.

The detectives perked up.

Harper went on. About ten days ago, he said, Major Crew told him to monitor a certain radio frequency out of Cambodia, starting on June 22 and continuing to the end of the month. But then just yesterday, he said, Crew came back and told him that if anybody asked him about it, he was to say that he hadn't picked up any signals.

Harper sat back and let the detectives draw their conclusions. The detectives smiled back.

"Did you hear anything, top?" Bidwell asked.

"I didn't figure it was on the level," Harper shrugged, "so I didn't listen all that much. I was short of people and too busy working."

The detectives smiled again. They asked a few more questions, but the master sergeant had told them all he knew.

"Thanks," Bourland said. Harper waved a lazy salute and left.

Next up was Ross Potter, a rugged young sergeant who was in charge of the weapons room. The investigation was running like a cannery, with the fish coming down the conveyer belt and being gutted. With more testimony like Harper's, they would bust open the case early. It was only 9 A.M.

Again they explained who they were and why they were there. Potter did not seem surprised. The detectives quickly cut to questions about the murder weapon, which Alvin Smith said was probably Budge Williams's Swedish K.

Williams did use a Swedish K, Potter said, but it was not part of the regular 5th Special Forces inventory; it was—he searched for the right phrase—Williams's "personal property." In mid-June, he said, Williams also borrowed a silencer from him and had not returned it.

Did he have documentation for that?

The silencer was not in the inventory, either, Potter added hazily. "I got it from a friend who is no longer in Vietnam."

Bourland was getting an education.

One more thing, Potter said: Williams also picked up a heavy chain from the supply office. He didn't know what he did with it, but it hadn't been returned.

Yes, he did have a receipt for that, he answered.

Well, Bidwell laughed privately, there's at least one charge they can nail Williams with. Theft.

Had Potter heard anything about an execution of an agent? he asked.

Nope. Nobody said anything to him about that, Potter said. He had been told that "Khac" had been returned to Saigon.

Had he been coached on what to say this morning? the detectives asked. No, Potter answered blankly.

That was it, they told him. He could come back to sign his statement the next day.

Sergeant Robert Clegg, an operations clerk in Detachment B-57, was next. To the detectives' surprise, he quickly chiseled another chip from the suspects' defense.

Completely at ease, Clegg explained how Crew had ordered him to back-date a document called Operational Concept—Special Operations, which included a section on "Use of Person."

Changing the O-plan date was complicated, Clegg explained, because it also required him to alter a TWX number that was catalogued when the original plan was sent to the CIA in Saigon, where all their operations were routinely reviewed.

Without interrupting, the detectives each stored that little fact in the back of their minds. The CIA role in this thing could get complicated.

He had done it as ordered, Clegg said, but only an hour ago Crew had come back and asked him to restore the O-plan's original date.

"Crew had heard you people were up here investigating. I got the impression that Crew had decided not to pull anything, just to do everything right," he said. But the major apparently changed his mind. "He asked me to keep quiet about the matter and not discuss it. In fact," Clegg added, "he asked me to lie about it to you."

Bourland and Bidwell again noted a schism between the older sergeants, who were not involved in the spy-versus-spy stuff, and the spooks of B-57. They were playing it straight, telling what they knew. They were showing disdain for Crew and the others, especially Sergeant Smith, who, Clegg snorted, "gave the impression he was a 007 type."

"I'm too old a hand to fall for that," he said.

Clegg was their first big fish; they had the hook in, now they needed to set it.

"He asked you to lie." Bidwell made it a statement.

"Yep," Clegg said. "He wanted me to lie."

The detectives tried not to smile. It was one of those moments detectives savor—when the first hot piece of information floats within their grasp. Some investigators swear to having heart palpitations, dry mouth, even tunnel vision at that moment. They remember it forever.

This was one of those times. Clegg's statement gave them a hammer to use on Crew: subornation of perjury. And once they were through wringing him out—the specter of a broken career and, oh, ten to twenty years in Leavenworth should do it—Crew would lead them to Rheault. Not lead, carry.

Bang!

Things were moving nicely. They thanked Clegg and invited him to return the next day. Bidwell's initial opinion of the U.S. Special Forces was being vindicated.

After lunch, Wayne Ishimoto came in.

The sergeant had a story to tell, he told the detectives, but he was conflicted about it. He wanted General Abrams to understand that everything that was done was done in the interests of their country. There weren't any criminals in Project Gamma. He wanted General Abrams to understand that; they'd done their duty as best they knew how.

Bidwell said solemnly that he understood. He was sure General Abrams would like to hear what Ishimoto had to say. The detectives would try to arrange it. Now, what did Ishimoto have to say?

All right, the sergeant began.

"He was pounding on the walls. . . ."

Ishimoto went on to tell the long story of Chuyen's incarceration, what he knew about the night of the execution, and his role in the cover flight to Tay Ninh. He obviously thought the team had acted honorably; he wanted no part of a criminal cover-up. His statement gave the detectives another piece of the case—motivation. The suspects had killed Chuyen because he was making a lot of noise.

The boys from B-57 obviously hadn't picked their helpers very carefully, the detectives thought. They invited Ishimoto back to sign a statement.

There was one other thing, Ishimoto wanted to add.

"Last week, Captain Brumley recommended himself for the Combat Infantryman's Badge." According to the citation Brumley wrote for himself, the vaunted decoration was for "actions against a hostile force on a water operation."

For killing Chuyen? the detectives wondered. Ishimoto thought it was for that. Maybe they took some gunfire on the trip.

31

Bob Rheault stayed up late Tuesday night drafting a careful statement on a yellow legal pad.

The situation struck him as incredibly bizarre. *My God, assassinating double agents was as old as time!* In this part of the world, it was a way of life. What kind of war did Abrams think he was fighting? He had to know that Viet Cong suspects were being popped daily by Operation Phoenix. Infantry units had their own hit squads to take out collaborating village chiefs. Snipers were a hot new commodity in the Marine Corps. Battalion commanders dropped napalm on a hamlet, for God's sakes, just to dislodge a few guerrillas. He didn't defend all of that, necessarily; it was just the way it was. The knife or silencer, in fact, were a hell of a lot more useful than B-52s in this war.

Bob Rheault was not an amateur at this. *Show me another man with better credentials to run the Special Forces in Vietnam,* he thought. Who knows more about what's going on out there in the hamlets and villages than me? Who knows more about his men? Certainly not the generals sitting on their asses in Saigon, watching the war from rooftops at cocktail hour.

Bob Rheault knew what the rules were. At least he thought he did. But were the rules changing? Is that what was going on here? His men had come to him for an answer to their problem, and he gave it to them based on long, long practice in Indochina.

The origin of his problems, he was convinced now, was Creighton Abrams. A tanker, a man thoroughly unacquainted—ignorant, really—about the kind of war they were fighting in Vietnam, the kind of tools needed to get the job done. Abrams had always hated the Special Forces and always would. He was just another one of those generals who couldn't stand the Green Berets running circles around the Army in Germany, one of those generals who were still fighting the last war, tank to tank on the fields of France, one of those generals who blundered into Vietnam with their high-tech equipment and thought they'd teach the Viet Cong a lesson. What else could be expected of General Patton's protégé?

How long the investigation would go on, how deep, he didn't know. He needed time to rally allies. He didn't know if Abrams wanted to prick his skin or drive in a dagger. Common sense told him Abrams wouldn't be allowed to indulge his rage forever, to risk all their operations, set off a scandal, drag the Green Berets into the mud, just to make a point. The CIA wouldn't stand for it.

He needed time. There were a few levers to pull, friends from West Point, allies of the Green Berets. William Westmoreland, for one, an old paratrooper himself; Dick Stillwell, who was running special ops at the Pentagon; Al Haig, Rheault's friend at West Point, now working for Kissinger in the White House. Maybe Henry Cabot Lodge and the Bundy brothers, the old Jack Kennedy crowd. They were men who understood what operations were about, and what Abrams was trying to do.

Things would work out. Everybody would see that Abrams was just indulging his famous rage, scratching an old itch.

It was after midnight when Rheault finished his statement. At ten o'clock in the morning, he called the detectives to his office, poured them coffee, and handed the statement over.

Frank Bourland picked up the six handwritten pages, softly reminding Rheault that he was still officially a suspect in the investigation. A lawyer was available, he added. Did he understand? They could stop right now. The detective's tone was respectful, almost apologetic, but his voice, his partner noticed, had a firmer edge than three days earlier.

Rheault offhandedly said he understood his rights. He didn't want a lawyer. What did he have to hide?

Bourland scanned the statement with Bidwell looking over his shoulder. Rheault wrote in a clear, aggressive script, royal blue ink on yellow paper. Halfway down the first page, Bourland stopped.

"Various alternative courses of action for disposition of the agent were discussed. These included," Rheault had written, "firing him from the program; attempting to have the individual taken out of the country and held; eliminating him; or continuing to use him in a carefully compartmented and closely watched role."

Bourland wasn't experienced in intelligence, but here was a pattern he understood. The suspect was giving in a little, hoping to gain credibility for his denial. "Elimination" was discussed after all, Rheault had conceded.

By tucking it in the middle of his list, Bourland wondered, did Rheault think they wouldn't notice it?

The statement went on: Major Crew, Major Middleton, and his deputy, Colonel Kenneth Facey, came to him again on June 20, "with the recommendation that the individual be committed on a classified mission," Rheault wrote. Chuyen, he guessed, was dispatched to Cambodia. He really didn't know.

Then, the next day, Crew told him that the CIA had ordered the agent returned to duty. That, of course, was impossible, because "the individual had been dispatched on the mission and could not be recalled."

"I was at that time convinced that this had been done," Rheault wrote, "—nobody was killed." But Sgt. Alvin Smith's allegations, he said, had filled in some blank spots. Maybe the agent *was* killed.

"It became apparent to me that it was possible that persons under my command did eliminate the agent, although definite proof was lacking."

A careful statement, the detectives thought, a plausible denial. That might be enough for an intelligence inquiry, but not for deflecting a homicide investigation. Unwittingly, perhaps, Rheault had opened daylight between himself and his men, the first step police hope for in breaking down a conspiracy. His statement continued:

> If this is the case, it should be recognized that these men were taking an action that they considered to be in the best interests of a highly important intelligence operation, and of the U.S. effort in Vietnam.
>
> If the act was carried out as Sgt. Smith alleges, these men risked their lives and careers in the furtherance of what they believed to be the mission.
>
> The individual that they could be accused of eliminating must have been in their minds an enemy agent whose presence threatened the lives of U.S. and allied intelligence operatives as much as a VC/NVA soldier with a rifle in his hands.

These men. They believed. Their minds. Rheault was sloughing it off in good style. Bourland's stomach tightened as he read through the colonel's cascade of excuses.

> If they acted without my authority and knowledge, they undoubtedly did so out of a desire not to involve my headquarters or MACV and to provide a plausible cover story.

Well, he's either sending them down the tubes or counting on their silence. "I am not in a position to know if the allegations of Sgt. Smith are true, or if the mission was carried out as I reported it," Rheault continued, "but if the agent was eliminated, the men who did it did so, not out of criminal intent, but as soldiers carrying out a difficult and dangerous mission in a wartime situation."

Bourland came to the last paragraph. Its irony startled him.

"Finally, as a commander," Rheault wrote, "I fully realize my responsibilities for everything that takes place under my command."

Sure, Bourland thought. He put the statement down. In the awkward silence that followed, there was only the sound of the fan turning overhead.

Don Knutson was worried. He requested an emergency meeting in a corner of the hotel parking lot.

"Watch out for bugs," the sergeant warned Bourland and Bidwell. "The CI section bugged the colonel's office once. It's in the overhead fan."

"Jesus Christ," Bourland muttered. What had they said in Rheault's office that could hurt them? He turned to his partner.

Bidwell laughed. The suspects were about to get a rude shock, he said. Wait until they heard Rheault's selling them out.

The detectives thought they were the object of the bug, but they were wrong. Brumley had installed it during his probe of corruption in the high command of the Vietnamese Green Berets, who he had learned were selling American equipment to the Viet Cong. They were frequent visitors to the office of Rheault's predecessor.

A counterintelligence team didn't need permission to bug their commander's office. A huge cache of Viet Cong weapons captured during the battle of Hue in 1968 had fallen into the hands of a 5th Special Forces master sergeant and mysteriously disappeared. Nothing had come of the investigation, but Brumley would go wherever an investigation took him: Corruption, after all, was a security problem.

Neither Bourland nor Bidwell was surprised by the bug. They had been shadowed, if clumsily, since they arrived in Nha Trang. Their hotel room had been entered, they were sure. Whoever did it wasn't very careful, blowing all the traps they set on the door, on their suitcases, and on their files.

There were other obvious signs of surveillance. One night the maître d' at the hotel became flustered when they didn't take their usual place by the window, making it obvious the table was bugged. During an interview one morning, a counterintelligence sergeant posing as a private first class showed up and announced he was their new messenger. He even used his real name—didn't they know the detectives had the 5th Group personnel roster?

"Jones couldn't make it today," drawled Billy Bob Maness. "I'm your new helper." The young yokel telegraphed his mission with all the subtlety of a small-town pool shark. One day he offered "to watch their stuff." The detectives had a hard time not laughing. Another time they heard the floor creak outside the door. Somebody was obviously trying to eavesdrop on an interview. Bidwell tiptoed over and yanked the door open. There was Billy Bob, holding his wallet in his hand, stuttering that he had stopped to count his money.

"They must think they're dealing with some not-too-intelligent people," Bourland remarked. He seemed upset.

Bidwell looked at him and cracked up. His partner was so earnest. "God, Frank."

But Bidwell did take security seriously. At night he slept with his arms around his briefcase, rolled up against the wall. He took it into the shower with him, placing it just outside the stall with the curtain drawn partway back. Never, ever, was it out of his reach.

Bidwell cracked jokes about the case to stay loose, he told his partner. Otherwise he'd go nuts. Laughing about it helped him get serious when he needed to. It was going to be a long haul.

Bourland just wanted to get the case wrapped up and go home. He was amused by some of the things that were happening, sure. But overall, the case sickened him.

He hated to see the destruction of a man like Rheault, he told Bidwell. Under different circumstances, he'd probably be glad to saddle up and follow the colonel. Rheault was a fine man, he said, a good leader who knew his Green Beret business. He was caught in some kind of political ploy.

Bourland didn't understand it. He'd rather chase stolen jeeps on the black market for the rest of his life than drag a man like Rheault into the mud. Harassing American soldiers for killing a Viet Cong spy wasn't right. But Rheault wasn't guiltless, either. It looked like he was letting his men take the bullet.

There were no good sides to the case. It troubled him. He had his duty to do, and he would carry the case to its end. But Frank Bourland had just one question: How did prosecuting the Green Berets for murder fit into winning the war?

The detectives faced Rheault with some discomfort after reading his statement. All three of them knew it was untrue It bothered them.

It wasn't the caution they had first felt about challenging the colonel. That had evaporated. The generals at MACV were clearly behind them now.

It didn't matter that they were only warrant officers and Rheault was a full colonel; they had the authority to do it. All they had to do was show their badge. Rheault couldn't be sure of their rank anyway; Army detectives wore civilian clothes—or fatigues with silver "U.S." bars—to stifle the impulse of high-handed officers to blow them off.

Rheault wouldn't try that now, they decided. He was in too deep with the cover-up, just as Smith had predicted.

Bourland picked up Rheault's statement and started to put it in his briefcase. He'd give the colonel a little more time to think over what he was doing.

And let the line stay in the water. See how far the fish ran with the bait.

"We'll get this typed up," he said. "Then we'll bring it back for you to sign."

32

The wheels of the Air America jet touched down on the rain-slick Saigon runway with puffs of blue smoke. Bidwell and Bourland clamored down the gangway in a driving monsoon storm and headed for MACV, the headquarters of the U.S. Military Assistance Command.

They had quickly moved far beyond their initial expectations. Less than a week ago they had assumed Sergeant Smith would be locked in a psychiatric ward and the case closed. Now they were circling a suspect at the top of a homicide conspiracy they had hardly thought possible.

A new factor had crept into their calculus: the Central Intelligence Agency. What was its role in this thing? The way the generals had told the story, the CIA had blown the whistle on the Green Berets. Now it was looking more complicated than that. Smith had tied the CIA to discussions on disposing of Chuyen. And then there was the question of the murder weapon: Swedish Ks and pistols with silencers weren't standard issue in any arsenal Bourland had known.

After interviewing Colonel Rheault Wednesday, they had visited the CIA compound on Beach Road and asked to see the man in charge. Their question was simple: What did the Green Berets tell the CIA about their plans to kill Chuyen?

A man named Harold Chipman gave them a curiously chilly reception. The base chief, Dean Almy, was out of town, he said. And he had been instructed to say nothing. Then he quickly escorted them out the door.

The detectives were puzzled. Why the cold shoulder? What did the CIA have to hide?

As they drove through the gate at MACV, they decided they had to be careful. The case was moving into deep waters.

Frank Bourland and Bob Bidwell walked into the J-2 briefing room. Maj. Gen. Elias Townsend, Abrams's operations chief, and Lt. Gen. William Potts, the head of Army intelligence, were already there, along with a new man, Col. Wilton B. Persons. Persons was introduced as the MACV staff judge advocate, General Abrams's legal representative in the case.

The officers took their seats. Potts asked the detectives to summarize their investigation to date.

Flipping open his case notebook, Bidwell outlined their progress in Nha Trang, bearing in on the interviews with sergeants Knutson, Potter, Clegg, and Ishimoto, all of whom generally confirmed the initial statement by Sergeant Smith.

From the statements taken so far, Bidwell said, there was good reason to believe that three captains—Leland Brumley, Budge Williams and Robert Marasco—had taken Chuyen out in a boat and disposed of him.

The commander of Detachment B-57, Maj. David Crew, had supervised the operation. A fifth man, Warrant Officer Edward Boyle, had helped load the victim into the boat and stayed close to Brumley throughout the incident, according to their information. The interviews also left no doubt that there was an attempt by Major Crew and assisted by Major Thomas Middleton, the 5th Group S-2, to cover up the incident.

That led to the role of Col. Robert Rheault in the affair.

Rheault had prepared a statement conceding that the "elimination" of the agent was discussed, Bidwell said. But the colonel had maintained that "to the best of his knowledge" the alternative was rejected. If Chuyen was killed, Rheault said, it was part of a necessary operation taken in good faith by his men.

From the other statements they had gathered, Bidwell carefully said, it would appear that Rheault's statement was false.

Their report was greeted with glum silence.

"What do you propose to do next?" General Townsend finally asked.

Bidwell hesitated. The CIA connection zipped through his mind.

After a few seconds, he decided not to say anything. A room full of generals was not the place for a junior warrant officer to speculate. He'd be way out of line saying, "Well, General, here's what I think about this, or, here's what I think about that." Noooo . . . generals didn't go in for that. He was there to report the facts, just the facts.

He and Frank needed more time to find out who all the players were, if there were invisible strings at work in the case. Maybe the generals had their own agendas.

"We propose to interview Warrant Officer Boyle," Bidwell finally said. "He can implicate Brumley, Williams, Marasco, and Crew."

As soon as he left the meeting, he typed up his notes on the discussion.

Ed Boyle had been on the run all week, hiding with the help of Gina and the other women at Streamers.

With his long Irish cheeks and protruding ears, the twenty-four-year-old's face utterly failed to disguise a black humor about his predicament. His sister Mary always said "he loved excitement and danger." The fact was, he was enjoying the cops-and-robbers game with the CID. All he needed was time—fourteen days until he was due to go home.

If the detectives caught him, he'd keep his mouth shut, no question. He "never ratted on his friends when they were in trouble," his sister said, even as far back as St. Luke's grammar school in the Bronx. And he was never one of the lads to get caught. The cops on Cypress Avenue pinched his friends, but they never got Eddie. And by now, after five years of counterintelligence duty in Washington, West Germany, and Vietnam, Eddie knew something about escape and evasion. With Brumley's help, he had kept one step ahead of the detectives. Fourteen more days, that's all he wanted. Out of sight, out of mind, that's the way the Army worked.

Bourland and Bidwell arrived back in Nha Trang on Friday and announced they wanted Boyle for questioning. Brumley, who was in the office, offered to help. The detectives decided, *Okay, we'll play along; an obstruction-of-justice charge will be useful later on.*

As they patrolled downtown Nha Trang, Boyle watched from a distance, wondering if his boss was pulling a fast one. Late that night, when the detectives had gone back to their hotel, Boyle met Brumley in Streamers. They took a back table in the dark and smoky room where they could talk safely under the raucous noise of other soldiers and the booming of the jukebox.

"What the hell are you doing?" Boyle said in a hoarse whisper. "You turning on me?"

The stocky captain chuckled.

"Naw, I'm taking them on a wild goose chase. Can't you see that?"

Boyle stared at Brumley, then slowly relaxed.

They sipped from their beers. Unknown to them both, the detectives had stopped back at 5th Special Forces before turning in.

Tom Middleton was the duty officer.

"I'm Robert Bidwell, CID," the detective announced. He flipped out his credentials. So did his partner.

Middleton stood there like a cigar store Indian.

"I want you to have Warrant Officer Edward Boyle here at seven-thirty in the morning for questioning."

"All right," Middleton said meekly.

The detectives smiled and left. The game was over.

33

Eddie Boyle was taken into custody early Saturday morning, July 12, for questioning in connection with the murder of Thai Khac Chuyen, a Vietnamese national.

The penalty upon conviction was life in prison, or death.

The detectives led Boyle from the cramped plywood office as the clerks and junior officers of the headquarters staff silently looked on. The bracing effect was intended.

Tom Middleton watched them leave from inside his office. David Crew stayed behind his closed doors.

The flight to Long Binh took less than two hours. The Air America jet descended through the thick dark clouds and swept low over the sprawling base, touching down just after noon. A jeep was waiting on the moist hot tarmac. Bourland and Bidwell rushed their prisoner through the muddy streets to a wooden building near the stockade, a CID interrogation room.

For the first hour they sat around a table eating sandwiches. But it was very much a part of the detectives' interrogation.

They reviewed the events of June, weaving their facts and suspicions into a seamless, steel-hard case. The situation was hopeless, they told Boyle. They knew everything. Did he want a lawyer? Once he got a lawyer, of course, there was nothing they could do for him. He had to know that.

Boyle remained impassive. A practiced interrogator himself, he had listened to the detectives' spiel all the way back from Nha Trang, gathering intelligence for his defense. Now, he said, he wanted to see their file; then he'd decide what to say, if anything.

The detectives were happy to oblige. They shoved forward a pile of manila folders, the statements of Smith, Knutson, Clegg, and Ishimoto, a paper trail of evidence linking the boat, chains, and morphine to the disappearance of Thai Khac Chuyen on the night of June 20.

The young warrant officer thumbed through the documents as the detectives continued to make their arguments for his cooperation. His name seemed to sparkle on the pages. Occasionally he looked up, said nothing, and went back to reading. Twenty minutes later he had finished and pushed the folders aside.

Boyle looked at the detectives. He was slightly less confident than before, they sensed. Perhaps Brumley had let him in on what the bug in Rheault's fan had picked up.

"Look, Ed, we sympathize with you," Bourland said, adopting his fatherly tone. "Anyone else faced with the same circumstances would probably have done the same thing."

On a legal pad in front of him was a list of questions, with enough space between them to record Boyle's answers verbatim.

Boyle remained silent.

"I'm sure you were convinced that elimination of the agent was the safest method to protect your mission, to protect the Army, and to protect your country," Bourland added. "I want you to know I understand that." His sincerity was genuine; he liked the young man.

Bidwell restated his partner's argument: War is certainly hell, just like they say. Hard decisions have to be made, sometimes the right ones, sometimes the wrong ones. There are good reasons for bad decisions. The higher-ups in this investigation, who have been in combat, understand that. But they're the ones who have to judge.

"Unless you tell the whole truth," Bourland added, "no one will be able to see what your motive was. If you say nothing, no one will be able to know your side of the story."

Boyle still wouldn't talk. The detective figured that the trained interrogator was waiting for them to reveal more of their line of questioning. Bidwell decided to go right to the weak spot.

"You know, and I know," he said, bearing down, "that Colonel Rheault had to know what was going on. Only Colonel Rheault could execute the order to put this chain of events in motion, and he will be held ultimately responsible. Yet here you are, the one being interviewed."

"I've been in combat before," Bourland spoke up. "I know it is important for you to believe in your commander. Your life rests upon his decisions. You expect your commander to stand up for you through thick and thin.

Boyle stared straight ahead.

"But where's Colonel Rheault right now? He's up there relaxing in Nha Trang while you're down here trying to protect him and the other members of the unit."

For another hour, the detectives hammered at the scapegoating theme, blaming Boyle's bosses for putting him in danger. They blamed the U.S. government for waging a no-win war with worthless cheats as allies. They blamed student protestors for undermining the war and calling them criminals while they sat on the sidelines. It was unfair that American soldiers were held to different standards than the Viet Cong, the detectives said. But that's the way it was; the law was the law.

The political situation in Vietnam was tricky, they conceded. The guys who pulled the trigger on Chuyen might end up as "war criminals." Boyle didn't want to be part of that, did he?

The young soldier's mouth turned down. His brown eyes drooped. The detectives knew they had hit a nerve, some deep moral tendril planted by the nuns back at St. Luke's.

"No matter what situation you were faced with," Bourland said softly, "no one in the United States Army really has the unilateral right to order an execution." He circled behind Boyle.

"You guys know it was morally wrong. To admit that is the first step in any rehabilitation. They're going to look favorably on any admission you make that what you did was wrong."

The detectives paced outside. The interrogation had gone on for hours. Boyle had been valiant. He was a good kid. They admired his loyalty to his friends. He was in a tough spot.

It *was* a confusing issue, damn it. But Bourland had his own duty, and that was to break this case no matter who was pulling the strings. The rest was up to the generals. After a half hour they went back inside, confident they were near a break.

Boyle looked chagrined. "Look, this was not done with any criminal intent," he began.

The detectives sat back, ready to listen, pens in hand, notepads open.

"It was sanctioned by the CIA," Boyle said.

Bourland reached for his briefcase, pulled out a clean legal pad, and slowly slid it in front of the prisoner.

"Write out everything that happened," he said. "When you finish we'll come back."

He put a hand on Boyle's shoulder. "It's not easy, but it's the right thing to do."

Bourland turned to leave, then looked at his watch. It was 6:45 Saturday night.

"Do you want to break for chow first?"

"No," Boyle said, disconsolate. "I want to get this over with."

The detectives closed the door behind them, leaving him alone. Outside, they briefed an armed guard to be on his toes.

Keeping Boyle in wasn't their worry. Keeping any other Green Berets out was.

The detectives finished reading Boyle's confession late that night. Bourland pulled a typewriter forward, rolled in a blank DA Form 2820, and he and his partner began to explore areas Boyle had dodged or left vague.

"Who gave the order?" Bidwell asked.

The young warrant officer answered in a barely audible voice.

"As far as I know, the plan was approved by Rheault."

Bourland typed the answer.

"Specifically, who participated in planning the killing of Khac?" They had settled on Khac for now.

"The five of us—Crew, Brumley, Marasco, Williams, and myself."

Bourland took it down.

"Did you believe that the CIA authorized it?" Bidwell continued.

"I believed they had nothing against it," Boyle stated.

Bourland typed out the next question. "Did Rheault attend the meetings to determine the disposition of Chuyen, and if so, what instructions did he give or imply?"

"When we met in Crew's office," Boyle answered, "there were the five of us. Anything that came out of that meeting was taken to Rheault."

For the next several minutes, Boyle described the preparations for the execution; he admitted to injecting Chuyen with morphine, delivering his body to the boat, and waiting for the boat's return.

Then Bourland, as he had promised, let Boyle describe how he and the others felt about the crime, for the record.

"What was Crew's attitude toward killing Chuyen?"

"He really felt bad about it."

"Brumley?"

"Same."

"Williams?"

"Same."

"You?"

"I feel pretty bad about it, too."

It was a "good statement," in the parlance of investigators—as far as it went. Unfortunately, though, Boyle could not tie any one person directly to the shooting. He just saw the boat go out and come in, minus Thai Khac Chuyen.

"On June twentieth," Bourland pressed, "when the three captains returned to the launch site, did you hear any discussion pertaining to the killing of Chuyen?"

"No," Boyle answered. "Except someone said, 'I hope I don't have to go through that again.' "

Bourland recorded the answer.

"During the meetings held prior to Chuyen's killing, did you voice your opinion as to eliminating him?"

"No, I just went along with what was agreed upon," Boyle said, going on to describe the cover story they concocted and their attempts to mislead the detectives when they arrived in Nha Trang.

"We all wanted to come out and tell the truth in the first place," Boyle had explained in his written statement, "but we thought it was against the colonel's wishes. On the day Crew found out about the investigation, he recommended to Rheault that they tell the truth. Rheault said it would be best if we stuck to the cover story. He said he was sticking to the cover story and we could do what we wanted, but if the story does come out and implicate him, he would deny it."

A flicker of disgust pulled down Boyle's long face. "We were all under the impression that Rheault knew something we didn't know, or had an 'in' in Saigon who would whitewash the investigation."

Bourland sat quietly looking at Boyle, sharing disdain for Rheault's conduct. Finally, he typed all of their names at the bottom of the report and pulled it from the carriage. He slipped the carbons from the set of documents, stapled the five sets of interview reports, and assembled them in a pile. He showed Boyle where to sign each copy.

The young warrant officer's face sagged as he picked up the pen. The detectives watched him sign each one.

When he finished, it was near midnight. Boyle stood up. A guard stood by to take him into custody. At the door, his eyes reddened, and he turned around.

"I would like to see a priest," he said softly.

Bourland's heart skipped a beat.

"Sure," he said, full of sympathy. The polygraph could wait until tomorrow.

34

A cool gray drizzle fell on Cach Mang Boulevard as Bourland and Bidwell drove to MACV headquarters.

The congested stretch, connecting Asia's busiest airport with the nerve center for the war, was always clogged with throngs of PX shoppers, beeping Army jeeps and trucks, fuming taxi drivers, and prune-faced old men steering their ancient pedicabs through the clouds of blue exhaust.

Cach Mang was the gateway for the billion-dollar Saigon economy. Each morning hundreds of Vietnamese queued up at the gates of MACV and nearby Ton Son Nhut, clutching their ID cards, waiting to be checked against a list of names so they could get into their jobs. Nearly every MACV office had its complement of Vietnamese officers, interpreters, translators, and clerks. And in the barracks and billets even the lowest-ranking soldier could hire a woman to make his bed, wash and iron his uniforms, and set out his polished boots each day. The officers' clubs needed bartenders, dishwashers, and janitors; the bowling alleys, swimming pools, tennis courts, and gym needed repairmen and clerks. The Communists condemned the crass display of servitude but found it to their advantage: Each employee was a potential spy.

Saigon was a curious dichotomy: a lost crusade and an endless, booming future. Caskets going home passed architects arriving with plans for new hotels. The stores bulged with Japanese consumer goods while war refugees slept in the streets. On the surface, the war seemed won, and by the numbers it was: The Communists had been pushed back to the jungles. Only the hard realists in Hanoi and Washington, and the old Chinese money traders in Cholon, knew differently. Gold was moving to Hong Kong with every departing battalion.

"We had our monthly mortar attack the other morning," Ed Boyle joked in an April letter home. "About 5 A.M. at the airfield. I heard the first one come in, looked at the clock, and went back to sleep."

Now Boyle was sleeping in a guarded room in Long Binh. The detectives were happy to have him. He had laid out the whole thing. But from a legal standpoint, his confession was marginal; it only went to the edge of the water. Boyle saw the boat go out with Chuyen's body—he even helped load it—and come back without it. He had named Brumley, Marasco, and Williams as the triggermen.

But he was not with them when the shooting took place. As for the involvement of Colonel Rheault, both Boyle and Smith had offered only hearsay. The sergeants they had interviewed knew even less.

Major Middleton, as far as they could tell, had been relegated to the periphery for most of the period, ushering people in and out of Rheault's office, arranging for aircraft, helping with the cover-up. Mostly errands. That left Crew; Crew was key.

Detectives, like prosecutors, liked to build their cases from the bottom up, the outside in. They'd done a pretty good job of that so far. What they wanted now was a bridge to the men in the killing party. With Crew, they could go straight to Rheault.

The real evidence, meanwhile, was paltry. The crime lab had analyzed scrapings taken from the boat in Nha Trang. There was blood on some wood chips, but not enough to determine its type. They also found a few filaments of black hair, indeterminate in origin. In any event, the boat had been used since June 20 by a Filipino commando team attached to the Green Berets. Who knew what they had done? The evidence was useless.

The detectives still felt ambivalent about pursuing Rheault. On one hand, the case would destroy his brilliant career. On the other hand, he had passed on the chance to level with Abrams. It was out of their hands now.

"Where do you get a weapon like that, Bob?" Bourland asked his partner. They were close to MACV now, closer to deciding whether to bring up the question of the CIA.

"You mean a Swedish K with a silencer?" Bidwell said. His eyes were twinkling.

Bourland glanced over at his partner. They were reading each other's minds pretty well now.

Bidwell would rather have his tongue cut out than divulge a military secret. But his partner had a need to know. From his Green Beret experience in Iran, Bidwell knew the CIA and Special Forces were tight, very tight. In such areas as foreign police training and paramilitary operations, the Green Berets took the field and the CIA supplied the weapons. The same with cross-border forays into Laos, Cambodia, North Vietnam, and even Red China. The CIA didn't have the kind of people to do the job, he explained. The Green Berets were the CIA's secret team.

The same with the Green Berets' guns and money. They had to be "washed" through secret accounts to disguise their end use. The Army didn't want congressmen asking the Army what they were for. Most likely, Williams's Swedish K came from a CIA weapons depot in Okinawa.

Bourland and Bidwell weighed the CIA's involvement in the case with growing apprehension. They had been able to avoid it so far because what the CIA did or did not advise the suspects was basically irrelevant. Bartenders can give advice, too, tell a man he should kill somebody. That didn't make them accessories to a murder. The real question was what authority the CIA had over the unit, whether its advice amounted to an order.

It was intriguing: From the way the Green Berets talked, the CIA was in their chain of command. Was there some operational link between B-57 and the CIA that the detectives didn't know about? If so, would that make the CIA's advice material to their case?

What if the murder weapon came from the CIA? Would that make a difference?

The possibilities spun through their minds. The CIA was not just a bit player in the war. The first American to die in Vietnam was an OSS agent on a secret mission to Saigon at the close of World War II. Lt. Col. Peter Dewey was mistaken for a Frenchman, ambushed, and shot—right after he wrote a report advising the United States to stay out of Vietnam.

There were a few new faces in the MACV briefing room at 10 o'clock on the morning of July 13.

The detectives immediately recognized General Townsend, General Potts, and General George Mabry, huddled near the huge map of Indochina. But off to the side was a husky civilian in black plastic glasses talking to a compact middle-aged man in plain military khakis.

Potts brought the detectives across the room and introduced them to Ted Shackley, the CIA station chief. Standing next to him was an aide, Clement Enking, "from CAS," Potts said offhandedly. Enking wore the stitched clusters of a U.S. Army lieutenant colonel on his collar, the detectives noticed. Otherwise, his uniform was without decorations or name tag.

Bidwell and Bourland took their seats, trying to decipher the situation, what the presence of Shackley and his sidekick meant.

Potts cut into their private ruminations and asked them for an update on the case.

Bidwell briskly summed up the results of their past two days, highlighting the confession of Eddie Boyle against the background of continued resistance from Rheault. A few questions and answers were then bantered back and forth about their prospects with other witnesses and timetables for solving the crime.

Then, taking a plunge, Bidwell decided to bring it up. His voice was flat and casual, the universal dialect of a homicide detective.

There had been allegations, he began, that two officers from the CIA in Saigon, and perhaps two more in the CIA office in Nha Trang, had offered counsel to the suspects in the killing of Thai Khac Chuyen.

In fact, he said, *they may have given the suspects encouragement; they may have, in fact, told them to do it.*

The room was silent. Potts and Townsend slid glances at the CIA men. Shackley was stolid, statuelike. Enking finally cleared his throat.

"I did discuss Chuyen with Major Crew," he said.

Bidwell assessed him with steady eyes, waiting for more.

Enkins continued. The meeting requested by the Green Berets on June 10, he said, related to problems with their agent. A series of options was explored, all of them unsatisfactory to the Green Berets. Eventually, Major Crew brought up the idea of an execution.

All eyes fastened on the CIA colonel.

"I advised Major Crew," Enking said, "that eliminating Chuyen could not be approved. However, I did say it was the most efficient course of action."

No one spoke. Potts and Townsend shifted in their chairs, scratched their arms, looked around. Bidwell immediately jotted down the startling statement.

It was obvious that Enking's admission was entirely unexpected. It was as if, Frank Bourland thought, somebody had just passed gas in the room.

Bidwell finally broke the silence. He turned to Enking's boss.

"Well, Mr. Shackley," he said respectfully, "would this be a convenient time to interview you and Colonel Enking, or could we talk to you after this meeting?"

The CIA chief's face was set. "I'm not being interviewed by a military policeman," he declared. "I'm not in your jurisdiction."

Bidwell stared back. Bourland sat off to the side, watching the showdown. The generals seemed to have melted into the walls. It was as if just Bidwell and Shackley were in the room, facing off.

"One," Shackley continued, "these are operational matters. Two, it involves the names of CIA officers. These matters are kept secret.

"Three, we will claim executive privilege.

"Four, it involves privileged communications, which are defined by the UCMJ"—the Uniform Code of Military Justice.

The detectives would have to look that one up. The CIA man looked as hard as a bullet.

"Five," he continued, "there is a precedent, in that McCarthy case, the Green Beret who had been convicted of shooting his agent. It even involved the same unit. He wanted to drag us into his defense, too. The court ruled we were irrelevant to his case."

Bidwell was puzzled by that. He'd have to look it up. Shackley was apparently finished with his statement and, it appeared, his involvement with this matter. He seemed ready to leave.

Bidwell figured the CIA chief was at least a GS-18, a supergrade civilian. No way he could win a pissing contest with the head of the CIA, at least not now, not in this setting. And he couldn't read the generals, either. What did they want to happen? He couldn't tell. He didn't know *what the hell this was all about*.

"Okay," he said as calmly as possible, a slight drawl in his voice. "I may not be able to interview you, but I know I can interview the person next to you, who's wearing a United States Army uniform."

Bidwell wasn't going to be pushed around. He had a badge. He was an officer of the law. He gestured at Clement Enking.

"I know I can interview him, and I will interview him," he said.

The generals stared at the floor, uneasy with the confrontation. Bidwell stood his ground, waiting for someone to break the impasse. No one did.

"We'll see," the CIA chief said. With that, he signaled Clement Enking it was time to leave. They walked out of the room. The door closed behind them.

Bidwell felt like the earth had moved under his feet. He looked at Potts. The general smiled kindly.

"Go over there tomorrow, Bob," he said softly. "See what you can do."

Early the next morning, Bob Bidwell drove alone to the U.S. Embassy. He was pissed. If the Green Berets weren't above the law, then neither was the CIA.

Arriving at the CIA office on the Embassy's sixth floor, he asked the receptionist for Lt. Col. Clement Enking. She picked up a telephone. The detective paced.

In a few seconds, she put down the phone. "Colonel Enking is not here," she smiled.

Bidwell was weary. It was going to be hard to find time to come back later.

"When will he be back?" he asked.

"I'm not sure," she said. "He's no longer in the country."

Bidwell wasn't sure he'd heard it right.

"What?"

"He's no longer in the country."

"No longer in the country," he repeated.

The detective was steamed.

"Some colonel," he muttered, stomping down the corridor.

*   *   *

Gen. Creighton Abrams was pleased. Those young men at the CID had done a hell of a good job.

He enjoyed seeing Colonel Rheault squirm, that son of a bitch.

He didn't mind Shackley quivering a little either. Ted Shackley was a good intelligence man, but he wanted the CIA chief to get one thing straight: There was only one COMUSMACV in Vietnam, and his name was Abrams.

Jesus, Abrams chuckled to General Townsend, that CID fella really put Shackley's nose out of joint.

Townsend and his other officers had been supplying him with regular updates on the case. Now it was time to let Washington know the guillotine was about to drop.

Abrams called in an aide and dictated a message. It was addressed to Gen. Earle Wheeler, chairman of the Joint Chiefs of Staff, Adm. John McCain, commander in chief of the U.S. Navy–Pacific, and Gen. William Westmoreland, the U.S. Army chief of staff.

> SECRET-NOFORN, ABSOLUTELY EYES ONLY
> CID WILL APPREHEND MAJ. CREW TODAY (14 JULY) AND TAKE HIM TO LONG BINH FOR INTERROGATION.
> CPTS BRUMLEY, MARASCO AND WILLIAMS WILL SUBSEQUENTLY BE APPREHENDED AND INTERROGATED AT LONG BINH.
> LATER THIS WEEK COL RHEAULT WILL BE TAKEN TO LONG BINH FOR INTERROGATION, AT WHICH TIME WE PLAN TO RELIEVE HIM OF COMMAND OF THE 5TH SFG, UNLESS SUBSEQUENT EVIDENCE DISCREDITS THAT ALREADY OBTAINED.
> THE EMBASSY AND CAS ARE BEING KEPT FULLY INFORMED

The message left Saigon on the back channel at 9:11 A.M., signed by General Abrams.

Had Robert Rheault seen it, all his fears would've been confirmed: It looked like Abrams was calling the shots.

35

A conspiracy investigation is like sport fishing: at some point you've got to hook the trophy fish and get him on board.

The detectives picked up the pace in Nha Trang. Early Monday morning, July 14, they walked into the dayroom of the 5th Special Forces and directed the duty sergeant to produce Maj. David Everett Crew.

Crew was out of the area, the sergeant said, sounding bored.

"Get him," Bidwell said firmly. The sergeant started.

They were tired of the Green Berets' clumsy obfuscations. He told the sergeant to have Crew report in civilian clothes, packed to travel for "an indefinite period of time."

As they took their seats, Bob Rheault ambled out of his office. The commander seemed surprised to see the detectives. Recouping, he invited them into his office for coffee.

They were jolted by Rheault's appearance. His face was sallow. Dark pools had formed under his watery eyes. His gestures seemed mechanical as he poured coffee and handed them cups. Sitting down, his hands slightly trembled, they noted. He dully asked if formal charges been lodged yet against Boyle.

"No, not yet," Bidwell said.

Against himself?

"No."

Casually, Rheault asked if his own statement had been typed up. He'd like to "proofread" it before signing it.

"We don't have any plans for typing it up right now, sir," Bidwell said. "Not yet."

Rheault nodded. The detectives sat quietly, sipping their coffees.

What about the other interviews? Rheault asked. Who had they talked to? What kind of progress were they making? He leaned back in his chair, apparently making a great effort to be hospitable.

Bidwell gently lifted a hand.

"Sir, you'll have to talk to General Bowers at USARV about that," he said. Bowers was General Mabry's adjutant. "We just can't get into it with you at this point."

Crew suddenly arrived in the doorway dressed in slacks and a sports shirt and carrying a small flight bag. The detectives stood up right away. They were relieved at the interruption: Rheault was paddling against the current, being swept downstream. It was a terrible thing to behold. Nothing had to be said. All of them were just playing out their roles now, moving inexorably toward a final, tragic resolution.

Bidwell told Crew that they were taking him to Saigon for questioning in connection with the death of Thai Khac Chuyen on June 20, 1969. Then the three men walked out, leaving Colonel Rheault alone with his thoughts.

As they drove away, Bidwell jotted a note in his case file. Rheault "might be thinking of taking some action, possibly against himself."

Jesus, he hoped nothing like that happened. Nothing they might achieve in this case was worth that.

David Crew sat stolidly in a metal folding chair, calmly smoking a cigarette, fingering his black mustache, as Bob Bidwell circled him asking questions.

"You say then," Bidwell asked, "that there is a possibility that Chuyen is still alive?"

"I certainly hope he is still alive," Crew said. "It's been set up for Sergeant

Smith to meet Chuyen at the Continental Hotel in Saigon on 24 July, when he returns from the mission."

Bidwell continued pacing. Frank Bourland took notes at the table. The interrogation was going slowly. Crew was sticking to the cover story.

At the detectives' invitation, Crew had volunteered to write a narrative of the events. In an elegant longhand, he began with the origin of the problems in Muc Hoa, moved through Smith's identification of the captured photo, and described the meeting with Enking and Scrymgeour at the CIA office in Saigon.

"I brought up the Chuyen matter, that maybe he was a double agent," he wrote, "and asked if CIA could get him out of the country. Enking said this was impossible because of manpower, and I volunteered the people. Enking then said it would cost too much money.

"We also discussed the feasibility of turning Chuyen over to the MSS, South Vietnam's counterintelligence service," Crew went on.

"Elimination of Chuyen was also discussed. Colonel Enking officially stated that Chuyen could not be eliminated, but took the unofficial stand that elimination 'may be the only way out.' Enking desired to be kept informed."

They were going to kill Chuyen, Crew then admitted, but changed their plan at the last minute. There were all sorts of reasons, but the main one was Alvin Smith's noisy objections. His caterwauling about Chuyen and absurd theories had bent everybody out of shape.

So they decided to let Smith *think* Chuyen was dead, with the idea that he would then just drop the whole thing.

"On Friday evening," Crew said, "Chuyen was taken out of the room by Williams and Marasco to train for the mission. He was taken out under the ruse that he was going to be eliminated. Boyle and Brumley put him in a three-quarter-ton truck, and drove him to an intersection in a road outside Nha Trang, where myself, Marasco, and Williams were parked. Then he was smuggled aboard the plane."

The detectives read carefully through Crew's essay. It was pretty good, they thought. He had accounted for the eyewitness accounts of Chuyen's removal *and* the elaborate cover story that had been written up.

Interesting. Crew, they surmised, might have been tracking their investigation and knew what other witnesses had spilled. The Green Berets must have bugged more places than the room in Nha Trang where they did all their interviews.

Crew had done a good job, but there were still a few big holes in his story.

"What about the boats?" Bourland asked. "The captains took them out on both Friday and Saturday nights."

That's easy, Crew said. Friday night was a dry run for the execution ploy. "We were playing games with Smith's head." On Saturday he wasn't sure. "They were probably out checking a dead drop."

About the flight logs, Bidwell said: The logs showed a flight on Saturday morning. "Why, then, was he taken out of his room Friday night?"

"It was to train for the mission," Crew quickly said.

That was a pretty good response, the detective thought.

He tried a new tack.

"Why did you tell Clegg to backdate the operations plan dispatching Chuyen on the mission?" he asked. "And then why did you subsequently tell Clegg to disregard it and change the log date back to the date it should have been logged?"

Crew calmly drew on his cigarette. "I told Clegg to backdate this document as part of the cover story. I did not tell him to change it back to the original date."

That was pretty good, too, they thought. They took careful notes.

Bourland intervened. "Why did you ask Clegg to make *a false official statement* regarding the change of the log date?"

"I never asked Clegg to submit a false official statement," Crew declared.

He certainly knew exactly where to deny and where to explain, the detectives thought.

"Why did you ask Harper to report that no transmissions were heard over a certain frequency?" Bidwell asked.

"I instructed Harper to listen for certain frequencies," Crew said, looking offended, "but I never told him what to say concerning what he heard."

"What about the chains Williams requested?" Bidwell asked.

"I don't know anything about that," Crew said.

Bourland scribbled a note on his pad and slid it toward his partner. *If we get him pissed off, he won't make a sworn statement.*

Bidwell nodded. They didn't want him to walk out or call for a lawyer yet. Playing it cool, Crew had waved off the offer of a lawyer.

Bourland sat down beside the major.

"You've done a real good job with the cover story," he said respectfully. "It's mostly truthful."

He smiled. "But it's false on an important point. We know, for example, that Chuyen was murdered. Other people have told us that." They knew all about the cover-within-a-cover story, too.

Look, he told Crew, come clean, get it over with. You'll feel better afterwards.

"You shouldn't try to hide behind or protect Colonel Rheault. If killing Chuyen was a military decision, it was made by senior military officers who should be willing to justify their decision."

Bourland let that sink in. Studying Crew, he thought he detected small cracks in his resolve. He sensed they were hitting the mark. He tried another appeal.

"A man with your background, experience, and rank," he went on softly, "should not have to lie concerning a military decision that he participated in, and an operation he helped carry out."

Crew started to say something. Then, suddenly, he shook it off.

"I'm sorry, I'm not going to answer any more questions," he said politely. "I'd better talk to a lawyer."

Bourland deflated. He looked at his partner.

It would be much harder now, they knew. They had failed to crack their most important suspect. They would have to go head-to-head against the three captains. If they failed to crack any of them, they were through.

36

Viet Cong rockets had pockmarked one of the runways in Nha Trang overnight, delaying the detectives' landing. It reminded them of the inanity of their investigation. The troops were chasing Charlie, and they were chasing the troops. And what did it all add up to? Vietnam would be no different when they left than when they arrived, minus a couple of hundred thousand people or so. Each side would just keep adding to the body count.

Bourland and Bidwell both went through cycles of depression. Crew had slammed the door on their plan to move on Rheault and wrap up the case cleanly. Only when the leader's resistance collapsed, they believed, would everyone else's. Then the case would be closed, a clear-cut victory in their own little war.

It wasn't a triumph to savor. It would be like shooting a racehorse that had broken its leg.

Potts had congratulated them again. "General Abrams," he had confided, "thinks you're doing a wonderful job."

Bourland found that disconcerting. Why didn't Abrams just call Rheault in and bust him? Rheault gave the order. Why get all those other fine young men wrapped up in it?

For Christ's sake, the charge was going to be murder in the first degree. These men didn't deserve a firing squad or life in prison. They thought they had killed one Viet Cong and done a damn fine job of it.

But one thing did bother Bourland about Rheault, and it bothered him deeply: Rheault wasn't stepping forward and taking the blame. He wasn't taking responsibility for his men.

That should have been his job as a commander, Bourland believed. Instead, he was letting his men suffer. That was wrong.

Nor was Rheault forthcoming about whatever role the CIA had played in this thing. If Rheault felt justified in making the decision to kill Chuyen because of the CIA's approval, why not say so?

Something didn't add up. It was as if he were looking at two different men. His whole career bespoke an officer who had spent his life in the field with his men—as the Green Berets put it, "carrying the rucksack." His personnel jacket listed the Distinguished Service Cross, Silver Star, Legion of Merit, Croix de Guerre.

Bourland couldn't figure it out, couldn't reconcile the two images—Rheault the soldier's soldier, Rheault the military bureaucrat.

Unless . . . There had to be something else. Was the colonel trying to protect something else?

The detectives called for Bob Marasco.

The dark-haired, one-time life-insurance salesman surprised them. Smiling, he said he had been expecting the detectives. He confided that he knew it was just a "cover-your-ass" investigation. He went along easily and flew back to Saigon, chatting along the way, enjoying the trip.

It was obvious to the weary detectives that Marasco wanted to be treated as a fellow professional who, like them, had been caught up in one of the war's most sensitive and important operations. Marasco indicated he expected they could dispose of the questioning quickly, keep the generals happy, and all go back to work. When they sat down together around the table in Long Binh, the captain lit a Marlboro and volunteered to type up his own statement.

"Be our guest," Bourland offered.

Over the next two hours Marasco constructed a dramatic saga of Project Gamma, starting with the high appreciation of their operations on the part of the State Department and White House and continuing through Chuyen's betrayal of "one of the largest producing stations in B-57." He recounted the consultations of Crew, Williams, and Brumley with the CIA and ended with a denunciation of Sgt. Alvin Smith.

Along the way, he described in detail how he helped to kill Thai Khac Chuyen.

> About 1700 hours, we got the word from Rheault through Crew that "It's a go." I had already picked up four, ¾-ton truck wheels, and we had also gotten a 20-foot chain.
>
> I put the wheels and the chain in the truck. I put on tiger fatigues and got my equipment ready. Brumley was going to take care of getting Chuyen doped up. We felt this was very important, to drug him, because it would be more humane.
>
> Williams, Crew and I left in a ¼-ton truck and drove to the launch site next to the A-502 outpost. Knutson was to meet us there with a boat, which we put in the water. . . .
>
> Chuyen was wrapped in ponchos and put in the boat. I had an M-16, Brumley had an M-16, and Williams a Swedish K. We also had a .22 pistol with a silencer.
>
> We went out to the designated area, which took about two hours. Chuyen was still unconscious. Brumley and Williams wrapped the chains around Chuyen, and attached the wheels to him with the chain. He was already tied with parachute cord. Brumley and Williams held him to the side of the boat so he wouldn't bleed inside the boat.
>
> I shot Chuyen in the head with the .22 pistol. The gun

jammed. Brumley fixed it and I shot Chuyen again (in the head). Williams and Brumley then threw him overboard. We sat around the area for about a ½ hour to make sure he did not come back up.

Marasco then indulged some introspection about the killing.

> We had not been involved in anything like that before, but all knew that it might happen as part of our duties.
>
> Everyone did a lot of soul-searching, and no one liked the position we were in, but we were caught in the middle.
>
> Some of us it affected more than others. Outwardly, Williams was very upset; inwardly, everyone, including myself, was upset.
>
> Remorse—actually we had no remorse. We felt that it was part of a military operation and that eliminating this man was the same as eliminating "Charlie" in an ambush or search-and-destroy mission. We all felt that this man was the enemy.
>
> There is always the moral question about killing, but this was part of our duty. We had grave reservations about it, as it was not something a normal individual could do without grave reservations. It should have been taken out of our hands and done by CIA, the "professionals."

Marasco finished his statement at midday and handed it to Bidwell. After reading it, they praised him for his thorough and vivid writing style. The captain blushed in appreciation. He always enjoyed writing and history, he said.

There were a few more questions, the detectives said. Bourland rolled a sheaf of blank interview forms with carbons into his typewriter.

"What happened to the .22 pistol and silencer?" he asked.

"I gave it back to Brumley, as it belonged in the CI branch."

Bourland typed it up.

"Did you ever hear Rheault admit that he had ordered or approved the elimination of Chuyen?"

"No, all information pertaining to his instructions or approval was related to me by Crew or Brumley," Marasco said. "Mostly by Crew."

Tap-tap-tap.

"Were you aware of any conspiracy to eliminate Smith?"

Marasco was indignant. "This is the most absurd thing I have ever heard, and under no circumstances were any such actions being considered." The detectives were coming to the same conclusion. The boat trip that alarmed Smith, they surmised, was to make sure that Chuyen's body was securely anchored to the bottom of the sea.

"Who was present at meetings prior to the elimination?" Bidwell asked.

Marasco counted his fingers. "Williams, Brumley, Crew, Middleton, Boyle, and Smith. For most of them. And I."

The detectives wrapped up the interview and stapled together five different sets for Marasco to sign.

Then, to Marasco's apparent shock, he was led off and placed under guard in a nearby trailer.

That was the best statement yet, the detectives agreed. Better than Boyle.

It was a hell of a yarn, Bidwell joked. Like Louis L'Amour.

He blew smoke off the tip of an imaginary pistol.

Bourland chuckled.

37

B udge Williams and Lee Brumley sat together in the empty B-57 team room cracking Death-Row jokes. Everybody else had been taken off for questioning. One day Boyle was gone, then Crew, then Marasco, and just that morning, Middleton. Nobody else was left but them. And the good commander Rheault.

"Place is like a morgue," Williams said.

"A morgue," Brumley smiled. They started to howl, banging the chairs. Arrested for killing a Viet Cong? What would they get—the electric chair? Maybe they should be thrown from a helicopter.

Waiting for the detectives' footsteps, they began to swap stories.

It was 1966, Williams recalled, when he first arrived off Vietnam on a troopship full of Marines.

"We arrived at Vung Tau and they told us we were going over the side on nets into landing craft. They said if we got hit on the beach to just stay there and medics would find us. We said we didn't have medics. Hell, we didn't even have real guns. We had unloaded thirty-eights."

Brumley was smiling.

"About the time we were getting ready to go over the side, here comes this Fletcher-class destroyer pulling by us doing about thirty knots, really churning it out. And he opened up with those five-inch guns. He must've fired about two hundred shells—bloom! bloom! I thought, 'My God, we're going into a hot place with unloaded thirty-eights.' "

Brumley was chuckling.

"In the channel was a buried liberty ship that had been sunk the night before. I think to myself, 'They've got shore batteries! Shit.'

"So we went over the side. You know, you couldn't see much going in. So we charge up the beach like John Wayne, and I drop my duffel bags and pull out my pistol. I look to my side . . ."

Brumley was already laughing. He knew the punchline.

" . . . and here's this guy sitting there and oiling up with sun tan lotion."

They howled some more, then settled down. Jesus Christ, they thought.

Two former Eagle Scouts. What would their families think? Lee Brumley had a wife and daughter to confide in. Williams had a younger sister in the Army. His father, the Athens High School football coach, was a local icon. What would he say? His son was a war criminal? Could they have visitors at Leavenworth?

Brumley and Williams soon tired of sitting around. In the resounding silence, they began to wonder if the game plan was changing.

They decided to go see Colonel Rheault. They walked across the compound.

Ken Facey intercepted them outside his office. They told him they wanted to see the boss, to find out "whether we should get lawyers, go to Laos and hide, or what?" Williams said.

Facey took their request into Rheault's office and closed the door. They waited outside. A few seconds later he was back.

"He doesn't want to see you right now," Facey said.

Their faces drooped. What in hell were they supposed to do? What were their marching orders?

The executive officer looked sympathetic.

"Everything is going to work out for the best," he said. As the two captains slowly walked back to their office, Williams looked over at his stubby comrade.

"Looks like we're fixin' to walk down the plank on this thing," he said. "You know, left out to dry."

A cloud darkened Brumley's face. The game was over. He knew what the overhead microphone in Rheault's office had picked up, the blame he was shifting to them. The boss was saddling up and deserting them. There was some irony in that, he thought. The bug had been put in the fan to uncover corruption.

They were on their own now.

Well, Brumley thought, I haven't been in the Army that long, five years. It seemed like a long time since he had left Duncan, Oklahoma.

What went wrong? He had studied hard, applied himself, read every book on Vietnam he could find before coming here. The base library had them all. Bernard Fall had made the biggest impression. What was the title? *Street Without Joy*. That about sums it up.

He thought of his grandfather riding with General "Black Jack" Pershing through Mexico, his father and uncles in World War II, raising flags over Iwo Jima. Even Korea had been better than Vietnam. He wanted to be a hero, too. He wasn't a goddam criminal.

Vietnam, what a shithole.

Well, he thought, there's still time to start over on the outside. The only thing to do now, he told Williams, was to come clean. Completely clean. Tell the whole truth, everything, no cover stories. Get with the program.

They had nothing to hide. Killing Chuyen was a *military operation*, carried out on the legal order of their commander, along with the advice of the CIA. They had to emphasize that. How could they go to jail for that?

"I dunno," Williams drawled vaguely. "I can't imagine it."

In fact, he couldn't. Maybe they were in trouble, but going to jail? For killing a gook?

Suddenly it sunk in: The penalty for first-degree murder was death. They went back to the office and waited.

The detectives came back in the afternoon and summoned the two captains.

Bourland sent a message through Middleton's assistant for Williams and Brumley to present themselves. He told Brumley to bring along his .22 caliber High Standard pistol, with silencer.

Tom Middleton sat back and folded his arms over his chest. The detectives had been questioning him since noon. Brumley and Williams were sequestered in a nearby building.

"Hey, y'all got some beer here? I've been talkin' alot. I'm kinda dry." He smiled.

Bourland grinned back. *This guy is good.* Every time he wavers, he catches himself and changes the subject. Or asks for a beer. Or says he's hungry.

The detectives thought they had Middleton nailed when they showed him the statements of Marasco, Williams, Smith, Brumley, and Boyle. Middleton's eyes narrowed when they watched him read through the pages, but now he was back in control.

"You guys wanna get a sandwich?" he was saying again. "I'm kinda hungry, aren't you?" It had been going like that for hours. The major was sticking to the game plan, the cover story. All he would say was that Chuyen had been picked up, interrogated, and then sent out on a training mission.

"He's due back any day now," Middleton said. " 'Course, he might not make it, either," he snickered.

The detectives chuckled back.

Middleton was hewing to the drill in the old belief that the whole investigation was a farce, they decided. The major thought he was stumping the rubes from the CID.

But it was just a matter of time. After another hour of chasing him around the tree, the detectives called it quits and shipped him off to the trailer under guard.

The next morning, they dangled immunity from prosecution if he played ball. Middleton started to bend, then caught himself again.

"Say, I'm getting hungry," he said. "Aren't you?"

Bidwell told him the game was over. He was being put back in custody and charged. He led Middleton outside to a waiting jeep.

"You a gamblin' man?" the detective asked as they bumped along the street toward the stockade.

"Yup," Middleton said.

"Well, I will lay you even odds," Bidwell said, "that you will talk."

Middleton smiled. "Oh, no, buddy. You got that wrong. Not me."

They were both chuckling as Bidwell swung up to the guarded trailer. An MP came forward and the detective signed the prisoner over. Middleton disappeared behind the wire-mesh door, still smiling.

*   *   *

Not long after he arrived in Vietnam, Ken Facey sent a packet of photographs home to his children. They showed Montagnard kids before and after operations to correct their harelips, a deformity common among the hill people. Facey had helped establish a medical clinic. He wanted his children to understand why he had gone back to the war zone for a second tour, leaving them with their mother in southern California.

"Perhaps you could take these pictures to school and show some of your friends that the war in Vietnam is not just killing an enemy," he wrote. "If I can just help just a few of these unfortunate children, wouldn't that make up for the time we spend apart? You and I are talking about a few months apart. Almost all of these children have lost their fathers forever."

Facey was intensely dedicated to the humanitarian side of the Special Forces program. In a sense, it made him a throwback to an earlier era when village civil affairs projects were considered a vital part of the war effort. After the violent escalations of 1965–1968, though, body counts had largely overtaken "hearts and minds."

But Facey's medical clinic had attracted the notice of John Wayne's producers. Wayne was thrilled when he heard about Facey. That was exactly what he wanted to show, he said, the side of Vietnam that nobody knew about. That would silence the war critics. The clinic was written into his film, *The Green Berets*.

Three years later, Facey happened to be stationed at Fort Benning when the movie was being made. Talking with the screenwriters one day, he pointed out an obvious error in the script. It had Wayne, playing the role of full colonel and head of all the Special Forces in Vietnam, leading his men into combat against the Viet Cong. That was impossible, Facey said; the commander of the Green Berets, a full colonel, wouldn't be involved at that level, he'd be managing the battle from a distance.

The writers protested. John Wayne always leads his men, he always fires a rifle. He's *John Wayne*.

Fine, Facey said; how about putting him in a helicopter over the battle and having it crash? Then he can crawl out of the wreckage and lead his men from there.

Perfect. As a token of gratitude, Facey was given a small part in the movie as the nervous young officer who briefs Wayne when he arrives in Vietnam.

Three years later, waiting for the inevitable call of the detectives, Ken Facey reviewed the events of the past four weeks, going back to the first day Chuyen's fate was debated. He had objected to the killing, and then he had tried to dissuade Rheault from lying to General Abrams. Then, loyally, he had kept his own counsel.

But where did his loyalties sit now? If he lied to the detectives, he would be part of the cover-up, part of the crime. If he told what he knew, he would send his boss to jail.

Either way he was finished. As the week went on, he sat in his office paralyzed, unable to make up his mind.

On July 20, the detectives made up his mind for him. He was summoned to Long Binh.

With a polygraph operator standing close by, Ken Facey stated that Colonel Robert Bradley Rheault did give the order to kill Thai Khac Chuyen.

Then he broke down and wept. The life the Army had given him was over.

The secret cables were flying back and forth between Saigon and Washington.

Gen. Earl Wheeler finished reading the latest back-channel telex from Creighton Abrams and picked up the telephone. The chairman of the Joint Chiefs of Staff was part of a small group to whom Abrams had sent regular updates on the Green Beret investigation, including Adm. John McCain at Pearl Harbor and Gen. William Westmoreland, the Army chief of staff. Abrams had been Westmoreland's deputy in Vietnam, but he was running a different campaign, to all appearances, supervising the American withdrawal.

The question for Wheeler was whether it was time to let Melvin Laird, the secretary of defense, in on the case. Wheeler and Westmoreland, like most service chiefs, were loathe to wash dirty laundry in front of their civilian bosses, Laird in particular. Laird was a politician, close to the anti-Vietnam crowd on Capitol Hill, which was why Nixon appointed him. The former Republican congressman had never missed a chance to put daylight between himself and the services at the hint of a scandal.

Wheeler and Westmoreland were apoplectic at the thought of a leak. Westmoreland, in particular, was hoping they could persuade Abrams to drop the matter and forever bury it in the files. A paratrooper himself, he was certain of Abrams's long prejudice against the Green Berets. He thought that was driving the investigation. Wheeler thought the same. The chairman of the Joint Chiefs had hoped there would be some way out, but Abe had been like a rock on this thing, unmovable.

Wheeler got Westmoreland on the phone at 6 P.M., July 23. His secretary listened in as usual, taking verbatim notes.

"Westy," he said, getting right to the subject, "regarding that back channel from Abe to you, Jack McCain and me . . ."

". . . Yes."

". . . referencing an earlier message of 14 July on a Special Forces subject." He didn't want to be more specific on an open line. The Soviet embassy, located on a hill across the river in Washington, had its rooftop antennas locked on the Pentagon.

"Do you intend to inform the secretary of defense," Wheeler asked, "or do you wish to handle it through service channels?"

"What do you think?" Westmoreland said. "Should I tell him?"

"I've told Secretary Resor," Wheeler grunted, speaking of the civilian head of the Army. "I haven't shown him the message yet but I intend to."

Neither of the generals needed to articulate their distaste for dealing with Stan Resor, a Yale man and Wall Street lawyer who they knew would just look up the regulations and go by the book. They hadn't told him about the first cable from Abrams nine days earlier.

"He can handle it with the SecDef," Wheeler went on, referring to Resor. "It's an Army matter and follow-up will be an administrative affair."

"Fine," Westmoreland said. "Go ahead and let Stan handle it." He hung up the phone.

Time was running out, Westmoreland thought, for him to derail Abe on this thing.

38

Gen. George Mabry stood with his hands akimbo at the front of the MACV briefing room, challenging the detectives like a bantamweight fighter inviting them outside. Around them sat a circle of men with stars on their khaki collars, shifting in their seats and staring into the distance.

Frank Bourland was mortified. A month ago he couldn't have imagined arguing about a case with a general, much less a room full of them. Now here he was, suggesting to the commander of the U.S. Army in Viet Nam that his next step in the Green Berets case was all wrong. His mouth was dry.

Mabry had just announced that he wanted to put all the suspects in solitary confinement. Frank Bourland was shocked, even alarmed. He thought it was a big, big mistake, although he didn't put it that way. When word got out, he suggested in the most respectful voice he could summon that it would backfire, maybe hurt their case.

Mabry would have none of it.

"We've been puttin' soldiers in the stockade for smoking marijuana," he declared. "Why shouldn't these critters go in there too?" *Critters.*

Well, Bourland said softly, it could hurt their case. Normally an officer with no arrest record is released on his own recognizance. . . .

Mabry cut him off.

"These men have killed one of their own agents, somebody on their own payroll. And they've threatened to kill one of their own sergeants. They've lied and covered up." He flung another challenge at Bourland. "What if they kill somebody else?"

Bourland had long ago dismissed Alvin Smith's fears of being assassinated as unfounded. But he knew he wasn't expected to answer Mabry's question.

No, Mabry continued, these men have to be kept in solitary confinement until all the facts can be ironed out. They can't be left free to roam around. Maybe they'll try to kill *another* witness!

Slowly, Bourland drew himself up. Cautiously, he decided he had to make his point. Something deep inside him said a terrible mistake was about to be made. But it was more than an issue of tactics, he just thought it was wrong. With a quick glance around the room—Potts, Townsend, Rossen, and Bowers were there, virtually all of General Abrams's top staff, plus a few colonels standing off to the side whom he didn't recognize—the detective softly offered his rebuttal.

"I don't think the American people will stand for putting these soldiers into the Long Binh stockade," he said politely. "Especially solitary. These men aren't hard-core criminals. They are highly decorated soldiers, with no criminal records."

He struggled to keep his voice under control. With no response, he was emboldened to continue.

"Supposedly, these men are the most elite troops the Army has. Why not release them—at least until the preliminary hearings are over? Jailing them could invite a backlash, a wave of sympathy that might damage the case."

General Mabry listened, impatient, and shook his head. If the men are being charged with first-degree murder, why shouldn't they go to jail? he asked. "The stockade is filled with other soldiers," he repeated, "charged with much lesser offenses. Why should they stay in jail and these others be free to walk around?"

This case began, he reiterated, gathering anger, when an American soldier became so fearful of his life, so afraid that his own officers would kill him, that he ran for his life. Now those same officers say the CIA gave the orders. So, here's another factor we have to take into account: Don't we have to consider that somebody might now want to kill *them?*

The room filled with a stunned silence.

Mabry went on. These men are also experts in escape. Ordinary soldiers have busted out of the LBJ in the past. It would be a piece of cake for these damn Green Berets to get out.

No, it was too dangerous to let them go, he said. Those men had to be held "in close confinement," solitary, at the LBJ, the Long Binh Jail.

The generals looked uncomfortably at each other. They didn't like where the case was going either, the detectives sensed. But if George Mabry wanted it, then Abe must want it, too. The deck was stacked. They certainly couldn't take a warrant officer's side over a fellow general's. At least not here.

"Close confinement," the general repeated. The orders were sealed.

"There's a change of location," the MP said, standing in the doorway with a clipboard under his arm.

The five suspects—Brumley, Boyle, Marasco, Williams, and Middleton— looked at each other. For the past forty-eight hours they had been housed in a comfortable air-conditioned barracks, watching television, lying around and wondering about their fates. Bob Marasco even seemed to be enjoying himself, remarking more than once on how much more comfortable the barracks was than his rudimentary camp at Thanh Tri.

The MP told them to gather their things. Then he led them out of the barracks. More military policemen in white helmets, armed with M-16s, were waiting next to the jeeps. The men were told to get in.

Suddenly, the reality of what was happening dawned on Marasco. The dark-haired captain stopped in his tracks, his mouth opening. Until this moment, he was confident they would never be jailed.

"Where'd you think you were going?" Lee Brumley cracked.

Off they drove to the Long Binh Jail.

It was July 21, 1969. The world was watching the astronauts on the moon.

The Long Binh Jail was a foreboding complex of tin-roofed cement buildings crammed into a remote corner of the sprawling post. A high cyclone fence topped with rolls of barbed wire surrounded the grim structures and dusty yard area. German shepherds trotted around an enclosed path ringing the fence. Tall wooden guard towers anchored the corners, manned by soldiers with submachine guns and search lights. Only a month earlier, race riots had rattled the stockade. There were heavy casualties. The warden was taken hostage. Given the unfathomable circumstances of their arrests, it occurred to some of the Green Berets that they were not necessarily expected to survive this ordeal.

The LBJ was a good name for it, with its perfect, cynical symmetry: LBJ—Lyndon Baines Johnson, the man who had sent them to Vietnam, to a jail, to death.

Marijuana smokers were indeed locked up in the LBJ, as Mabry had said, along with GIs who had used their weapons on targets other than Viet Cong. When the Green Berets passed through the gates, they joined a dozen prisoners in pretrial confinement on charges of murder.

One was an NCO whose problems stemmed from sleeping with a pistol under his pillow. Shaken awake from a drunken stupor, he had blasted a man in the face, killing him, the charges said. It might have been excusable except that it was the second time it had happened.

Another soldier was charged with firing a full clip into a bordello where his favorite girl was sleeping with another GI, killing the woman and wounding the man. Yet another inmate had allegedly rolled a hand grenade into a tent, lethally ending an argument with two of his buddies. There was also a gang of three soldiers charged with robbing, shooting, and stabbing two Vietnamese women in a Saigon alley. Yet another GI was awaiting trial for firing a stream of tracers on a group of peasant women washing clothes on a riverbank.

The remaining murder suspects were mostly young men from small towns who had shot, stabbed, or beaten to death their fellow soldiers over petty or imagined slights. The rest of the inmate population ranged from colonels to privates locked up for a variety of offenses from stealing jeeps to dealing in heroin. None of them, however, had been accused of crimes that were classified secret.

*   *   *

The Green Berets were ordered to take off their belts and shoelaces. The five men hesitated and looked at each other as guards searched through their bags and shaving kits. The men felt like they were slow-walking through an old movie, *The Big House,* maybe, or *The Birdman of Alcatraz.*

Then they were led past the regular pens to the rear of the compound. A separate warren of solitary cells made from steel Conex storage bins had been built especially for them. There, they were assigned numbers. The MPs guarding them, they were told, did not know their names. They were ordered to answer by numbers. The doors closed behind them, and the dim, fetid corridor fell silent.

Lee Brumley heard a quiet sobbing from a cell in the rear. He listened for a moment, then, by a process of elimination, figured out who it had to be.

"Is that you, Alvin?" he heard Williams yell. There was a sneer in his voice.

The sniffling continued. Finally, a voice from the back.

"I didn't know this was going to happen," the sergeant said, his voice thickening. "They told me nobody would go to jail."

Lee Brumley turned away, disgusted. Then, carefully, he scouted his cell, checking the door, the lock, the thickness of the walls, the wire-mesh ceiling, the corners of his room, the frame of his bunk.

The reconnaissance complete, he reached down into the lining of his pants. Slowly, he teased out the thin steel blade he had stripped from the razor in his shaving kit.

He knelt down and hid it in his bedpost.

At 9:30 A.M. on July 21, Col. Robert Rheault walked into a plain beige room at MACV headquarters in Saigon on the order of detectives Bourland and Bidwell. They had tired of the trips to Nha Trang. It was time to bring the play-acting to an end.

In his smartly tailored uniform and beret, Rheault appeared to have re-bounded from his haggard condition of a few days earlier. The thousand-yard stare was gone.

The detectives looked at him. A last pang of regret went through their chests, then quickly evaporated as Rheault crisply asked to see the file.

As he read, the detectives formally pronounced again that he was a principal suspect in the conspiracy to murder one Thai Khac Chuyen. They again asked him if he wanted to amend his statement of last week. If he wished, counsel could be provided.

Rheault waved them off. He didn't want a lawyer, he said. In a few minutes, he finished reading, closed the folder, and looked up with a look of calm defiance.

Bourland tried one last time to break through. He spoke slowly.

"You know, Colonel, I was in combat in Korea. I am a hawk on this war, too."

He waited to continue. He doubted he'd make a connection, but he wanted to try.

"You must know that I am sick at heart at the thought of having to investigate activities of this type. This is a different kind of warfare than I have ever encountered."

He paused.

"There are apparently lots of things that I don't know about."

Rheault remained silent.

"But I always thought," Bourland continued, "that it was basic that a commander live up to his responsibility, that the men in the field have to be able to reckon that they will be backed up by their commander a hundred percent."

The detective opened his palms.

"I cannot understand why you are letting your men be arrested one by one, put in a five-by-seven-foot cell in Long Binh while you are still denying everything and more or less living the good life up in Nha Trang."

He shook his head.

"Isn't it your responsibility to come down and say, 'Hey guys, I'm the one who ordered this execution. I'm the one that told these people what to do. If there's any blame to be assigned, I'm the one to get it'?"

Bourland waited for a response, but none came. Rheault looked straight ahead.

Bourland went back at him, his voice now rising in the face of this last roadblock. The reluctant colonel, the confounding war, the incomprehensible Army—all of it flowed together in a torrent of frustration.

"I don't understand why you didn't make all this plain to General Abrams— why you didn't make that plain to the CIA, to us, or anyone who asked."

Rheault looked up.

Bourland was standing up, nearly trembling. Bidwell started to intervene. Rheault finally decided to speak.

"I would do all these things, Mr. Bourland and Mr. Bidwell, if I thought it would help my men any. If I thought that would get them out of jail—sure I'd do that, I'd confess."

He sat back. *The detectives couldn't possibly understand what was really at stake here*, he thought.

Bourland then reached into a folder, extracted Rheault's statement from the previous week, and slid it in front of him. He turned to the last page and told him where to sign.

The colonel glanced at it.

"I don't think a lawyer would advise me to sign that," Rheault said. He left it on the desk. The detectives stared at him.

"I would admit to ordering the killing," Rheault repeated, "if it would help the situation—even if it isn't true—if it would make it easier on those who carried it out."

Bidwell noted Rheault's statements on his legal pad.

Bourland was disgusted. They already had the evidence that he had ordered the killing, he told Rheault.

"Hey, look," he added, any pretense of respect evaporating with Rheault's cold response, "any statement we get from you is going to be based on the truth, not whether the information you give us is going to help other people."

The negotiating was over.

Bidwell stirred. "What's it going to be?" he asked.

Rheault shifted in his chair. The seconds ticked by. Finally, he said, "I'll see a lawyer now."

Bourland got up and went to the door. Col. Frank Brandenburg, commander of the 8th Criminal Investigations Detachment, was waiting outside. Bourland waved, and the top military policeman in Vietnam walked in.

"You're under arrest," he told the Green Beret.

"What for?" Rheault said, slowly rising.

"For murder."

Tom Middleton was worried. In his own cell, behind another thick metal door, so was Bob Marasco. Midway through their third night of solitary, the minutes and hours were ticking by slowly. The isolation and darkness were unnerving. If they had been thrown into a cave, they'd know how to get out. Crossing jungles, mountains, fast rivers, and deserts was their specialty. But a CIA frame-up was something new.

Brumley and Williams had set up a dead drop in the latrine to exchange messages. One reported that Rheault was being held in isolation somewhere else on the post. Another had Gen. William Westmoreland, Abrams's predecessor and a patron of the Special Forces, steering the case into administrative channels. But the arrest of their commander had deflated their hopes.

On the night of July 23, Middleton and Marasco each made an important personal decision. They asked their guards for paper and pencil. They began writing letters home.

PART IV

Military

Justice

39

C ol. Harold D. Seaman tapped his gavel, bringing the hearing to order. "As you gentlemen know, I have been appointed as the investigating officer under Article 32 of the Uniform Code of Military Justice . . ."

At a table to his right, a group of young military defense lawyers exchanged papers and last-minute whispers around their eight clients, who sat dully waiting for the hearing to begin. Facing them across the room, a half dozen Army prosecutors waited for the call to present their first witness.

The Long Binh Chapel, a plywood bungalow, had been converted into a sealed chamber for the hearing. The windows had been nailed shut and painted black. A temporary red cardboard sign tacked to the front wall announced the proceedings were classified SECRET-NOFORN. An MP was posted at the door, and two more were outside. Through the walls the guards at the nearby stockade could be heard ordering prisoners to courts-martial and work details.

An early morning tropical sun pounded on the tin roof, baking the cramped rectangular room with a moist heat. Two metal floor fans labored on each side of the presiding officer, occasionally lifting the corner of documents piled on the tables of the defense and prosecution. The attorneys wiped their hands on their fatigue pants and dabbed at the drops of sweat that had dribbled onto their yellow legal pads.

The clock at the front of the room showed a few minutes after 9 A.M. as the presiding officer continued his opening remarks. A stenographer jabbed at his keyboard in the corner.

"I am responsible for investigating certain charges against the accused in the death of Chu Yen Thai Khac," the colonel said. "Copies of the charges have been provided to you earlier. I understand they are in the hands of all the accused. . . ."

The charges were murder, Colonel Seaman announced, and conspiracy to murder, both capital crimes.

The defendants sat on metal folding chairs, their berets placed in a neat column along the table. But the suggestion of collective defiance was an illusion. Three of the accused men had just met their commander for the first time. Bob Marasco, Budge Williams, and Eddie Boyle had never spoken to the alleged leader of the conspiracy. Crew, Middleton, and Brumley hardly knew him.

Marasco, the wiry captain charged with pulling the trigger to kill Thai Khac Chuyen, had eagerly shaken hands with his stoic commander at the entrance to the hearing room, as had Boyle and Williams.

"I'm sure we'll get through this all right," the colonel said softly to his assembled charges, an offhand sentiment that was welcomed by the anxious men.

Inside, at the far corner of the defense table, sat Sgt. Alvin Smith, who only a week earlier had been accorded the privileges of a prosecution witness, billeted in a private room, visiting the mess hall and PX, trading daily confidences with the detectives. To the bitter satisfaction of his comrades, he, too, was now a suspect facing charges of murder.

Bob Rheault was not a little embarrassed to be among such company, to be leveled like a chairman of an oil company dragged into court with gas station owners on a price-fixing charge. The proceedings were a sham, he thought. But the system worked both ways. Soon the right levers would be pulled, and the general's fun would be over.

The Army would not stand for it much longer, he was sure; the price was too high. Did anyone seriously think Chuyen was unique? Bob Rheault had traveled on edges of the shadows for a long time. "The execution of a double agent is as old as history," he would say. The CIA would have much to hide. Certainly, protecting intelligence operations in Cambodia would be part of a defense, and the lid would be lifted on the secret bombing.

Did the Army think it could keep all this quiet? A spy scandal would bring it all out. No one would go quietly, not with their lives on the line. Someone—all of them—would eventually talk. Hanoi would have a propaganda holiday. The world would feign outrage.

"Prior to continuing the investigation," Colonel Seaman was saying, "I would like to hear from Captain Latsons, representing the Assistant Chief of Staff, G-2 USARV, as to whether the required statement of nondisclosure has been completed."

A young officer stood up. "Yes, sir. The statement is merely a formality for this court, so that anything that goes on in here as far as pertains to the security classification should not be divulged outside this court or hearing."

A defense lawyer, Capt. John Stevens Berry, lifted himself from his chair, an ample belly pushing at his green fatigue shirt.

"Sir, are we on the record at this time?" Berry's frayed collar and scuffed black boots gave away his nonchalance toward Army decorum, making him and his client Lee Brumley the odd couple of the defense camp.

All the defendants had finally been assigned Army counsel after their incarceration in the stockade. The lawyers weren't exactly welcomed by the defendants after the events of the past month. How could they be trusted? Brumley counseled. Who made out their checks?

Brumley was especially wary when Steve Berry arrived at the door of his tiny cell. The counterintelligence officer sized up his appointed counsel's untied bootlaces and wrinkled fatigues and figured that the lawyer was just another part of the frame-up, either a rank novice or a plant. He deflected Berry's first inquiries about the facts with shrugs and silence.

The burly lawyer took a detour. From the file, he knew that Brumley, like himself, was from the midwestern plains. He talked about growing up in Onawa, Iowa, where his father operated the town lumberyard. Slowly, Brumley began to share details about his own boyhood in Oklahoma, about the grocery store in Duncan, his mother the school teacher, making Eagle Scout at fifteen, the sweetheart he married. Over the next hours and days they traded pictures of their wives and children. They had much in common, Berry remarked. He had volunteered for Vietnam, he added.

Eventually Brumley began to lay down his cards. When he had finished after a period of days, Berry was convinced his client and his comrades were being framed. A united defense, he was also certain, was their only salvation. That, and the lack of a corpse.

Steve Berry hitched his pants and quickly put the presiding officer on edge.

"Regarding the security briefing on behalf of my client," Berry said, "I want to make it clear at the outset that by signing this certificate, I don't intend in any way to waive our right to a public trial guaranteed by the Sixth Amendment, or waive our right to consult or employ civilian defense counsel. . . ."

The first defense missile had been fired.

"And further, in our signing this," Berry went on, "nothing herein shall be interpreted as a waiver of our vigorous defense of this case as provided for by the Constitution, and I want to be on the record as saying this, sir, in case the issue should ever come up."

The next salvo went off.

"Sir, I want to join in this, too," said Richard Booth, rising to his feet in defense of Tom Middleton. The other defense attorneys quickly followed.

"I would like to join in that motion, sir."

"We would join in it also, sir."

"We join in the motion, sir."

"We would also agree to this, sir."

"We concur, sir."

"I join in Captain Berry's motion, sir."

The attorneys politely withdrew.

Berry stayed on his feet. He had made his point, too. He had not only fired a flare over the government's position, signaling that the case would be long and troublesome, but bucked up the defendants. He glanced behind him. They were smiling tightly. It was the first time they had all been in one room together with their lawyers, the first time they had all had advocates since their troubles began.

Colonel Seaman expected the lawyers to be difficult. Not that he had experience with cantankerous defense counsel, not that he had any legal experience whatsoever. To the contrary, he was not a lawyer, and not a judge, and had never conducted a legal proceeding in his life, not even a traffic court. Neatly barbered, a classic inside man, Col. Harold D. Seaman was, however, the secretary to the General Staff of the United States Army/Vietnam, which was commanded by Gen. George Mabry, who in turn had been appointed by Gen. Creighton Abrams.

An Article 32 investigation was the military's version of a civilian preliminary hearing and grand jury rolled into one. At its heart was the notion of "peer review." Theoretically, the presiding officer of an Article 32 hearing was randomly chosen from a pool of available officers, and anyone could be nominated. His mandate was to hear testimony, summon witnesses, and send his report up to the staff judge advocate, the top military lawyer for the U.S. Army in Vietnam. That officer in turn made his recommendations to General Mabry. Mabry, officially, had the final word whether to dismiss the case or proceed to courts-martial.

Theoretically, no one interfered in the process, which was strictly prohibited by the statutes of the Uniform Code of Military Justice. But the appointments and careers of all the reviewing officers were tied to the officers above them. It was a hierarchy descending directly from Gen. Creighton Abrams, surely the Army's next chief of staff, and there was no doubt in anyone's mind what Abrams's position on the case was.

The system was rigged by its very nature; no one had to interfere. As the hearing opened on the last day of July, the bottom links in the chain of command had landed with a thud in the converted chapel at Long Binh.

Capt. Richard Booth, defending Thomas Middleton, had his own reasons to think the process was skewed. Chunky and amiable, Booth had debriefed his client and opted to take a few days off in Hawaii before the hearings began. When he returned to Long Binh, however, he discovered that his files had been rifled.

Booth had conducted a discreet investigation and cornered a master sergeant from the staff judge advocate's office who had been seen nosing around his office. The sergeant admitted to going into the lawyer's files but innocently insisted that he was only looking for a document he had misplaced.

Booth was frustrated. He could possibly wring a delay from the incident, maybe more, probably not. He decided to let it go. There were plenty of other obstructions to surmount, as it was turning out.

The defense lawyers assigned to the Berets, for example, had at first been instructed not to consult with each other. Instead, they were offered a "supercounsel" from the staff judge advocate's office—the same body responsible for prosecuting the men—to coordinate their cases. Secrecy agreements, meanwhile, bound them not to discuss the case with anyone else.

Next they were told that the names of their clients, and the fact of their incarceration at Long Binh, were classified. When arriving at the stockade, they were ordered to ask for their clients by number only.

The closed and obstructionist nature of the proceedings was an outrageous assault on the right to an open trial, the lawyers quickly decided. Their first job was to brush aside the clutter and put the Army on the defensive.

"Sir, on behalf of my client, Captain Marasco," said Thomas Young, a military lawyer from Hawaii, "I would ask the government to bring forth the following individuals. I will say their names phonetically. I don't know how to spell them, but there is a Lieutenant Colonel Enking. Also, a Captain Scrymgeour, who is a Navy person. And a Mr. Shackley."

Colonel Seaman asked where they could be found.

"In the embassy in Saigon, the U.S. Embassy," the lawyer said.

Seaman scribbled, but Young continued.

"Also, I don't know whether you got this down, but a Mr. Chipman and a Mr. Almy, both with the CIA in Nha Trang. I feel that these witnesses are necessary." He sat down.

As the colonel continued to write, Berry lumbered to his feet again and, hitching his pants, seconded Young's requests and added his own list of subpoenas. He wanted all the case records of the Criminal Investigations Detachment, he said, and "also the Bravo 57 case file, containing, but not limited to . . ."

"Would you identify that?" Seaman interjected.

"Sir, the Bravo 57 case file, containing but not limited to the intelligence reports of the alleged victim, a name trace report on the alleged victim, and an operational interest report on the alleged victim. . . .

"And I would also like, sir, a complete list of all agents at Muc Hoa—that's M-U-C, H-O-A—that are in any way affiliated with Bravo 57 or the CIA. Also, sir, a complete list of agents at Thanh Tri."

During their investigation of Chuyen, the Green Berets had learned that the ship carrying his family from North Vietnam had been salted with Communist agents. Berry thought it would be useful to know more about that.

"In addition, sir, I would like a passenger list of all the people who came from North Vietnam on the Mirabelle in 1954, and a complete report as to the NVA or VC affiliation of any and all these people."

The lawyer paused. He had a long shopping list.

"In addition, sir," he said, "I think that the inquiry may require the testimony of Brigadier General Potts, who is the J-2 at MACV, and Major General Townsend, chief of staff."

Berry was enjoying himself; he liked to attack. His colleagues joined in, rising one by one to echo his request.

"We also concur," said Steven Shaw.

"As counsel for Warrant Officer Boyle, I also concur and request the entire CID report of investigation," said Myron Stutzman.

"Sir, as counsel for Major Crew, I will concur in the requests," said Bill Hart.

"Sir, as counsel for Major Middleton," said Richard Booth, "I vigorously concur and agree with counsel as far as the information requested."

"As counsel for Colonel Rheault, I join in the requests of Captain Young and Captain Berry," said Martin Linsky.

Colonel Seaman seemed to be distracted. The pace of the hearings had apparently accelerated past his checklist of things to do. Did the accused approve of their appointed counsel? he asked.

Each attorney then rose to state his client's satisfaction—inserting a proviso that, of course, his client retained the right to hire civilian counsel at any time. The attorneys suppressed their smiles. The hint of unruly civilian counsels joining the case would get the Army's attention.

Berry stood again. He had a few more stabs to make, based on rumors Brumley had passed on of a meeting at the U.S. Embassy between Bob Bidwell and the CIA.

"Sir, I have one more request to make. I am sorry I omitted it. I would like a complete list of any memos that have passed between the CID and the CIA regarding the case now under investigation.

"I would also like available from the Vietnamese government any files of its Military Security Service regarding the alleged victim."

Colonel Seaman finished his notes and then faced the defense table.

"With respect to the availability of these witnesses and documents, I will ascertain this information and provide you with this data at a later date," he said. "In the meantime, I propose to go ahead with the investigation while this determination is being made."

The attorneys sensed trouble. As they considered a response, a reminder of where they were intruded into the courtroom. A sudden downpour began to hammer the tin roof, making it difficult to hear anything. A recess was called.

Outside in the monsoon showers the Green Berets were suddenly jubilant.

The endless preoccupation with Thai Khac Chuyen, the ambiguous consultations with the CIA, the startling flight of Alvin Smith, the hounding by Army detectives, seemed suddenly, even if temporarily, lifted from their shoulders. Now they had advocates, somebody in their corner. They began to pour out a stream of details to their lawyers, suggesting new questions and provocative routes of attack.

They weren't common criminals, goddam it, and they were going to start fighting back.

At 10 A.M. the session resumed.

"Sir, are we back on the record? I am Captain Berry. The counsel and accused join in making an additional request after a brief consultation among us. We request a dossier on the alleged victim, any dossier on him and any member of his family, including a sister who works for CORDS and has gone to the States, and his wife.

"We further request any messages from Nha Trang to Saigon or Saigon to Nha Trang regarding this case file."

Seaman was busy scribbling again. He looked up.

"Can you identify that a little more precisely?" he asked. A slight defensiveness had crept into his voice.

"The CIA messages, sir, and regarding the CIA, any operations involving the alleged victim."

Berry loved the sound of the words, "alleged victim." Was the Army ever going to come up with the body of Thai Khac Chuyen? No corpse, no case.

"We also request any statements made to the CID by Colonel Enking or Captain Scrymgeour," he continued. "We request the presence of Mr. Shackley and Mr. Chipman, the CIA worker at the Combined Studies Detachment, Nha Trang."

Plunging deeper into the prosecution's nerve ganglia, Berry then probed Cambodia. He wanted copies of the operational plans used by Detachment B-57, he said.

Cambodia, the magic word.

Leaning forward, he then stuck the stiletto to its hilt.

"We also request," he intoned, "a list of all terminations with extreme prejudice in bilateral operations since 1961. Similarly," he added, "we request a list of all terminations with extreme prejudice in unilateral operations since 1961. . . ." He leafed through his notes. "Including a list of all terminations with extreme prejudice in the Provincial Recon Unit."

Colonel Seaman looked up. He appeared to be confused.

"Would you identify that for me, the type of thing you are talking about? What kind of document is it?"

"Sir, termination with extreme prejudice has to do with various means of getting rid of agents who have outlived their usefulness."

He let it sink in. Seaman nodded vaguely.

"We would like to request a list of all instances in which that has been done here by the United States or our allies," Berry said.

Glancing at his clients he added, "This information should be available from the CIA."

Few military lawyers got a peek under the cloak of clandestine operations. The usual caseload ran the gamut from AWOLs to desertion, theft, rape, drugs, charges of homosexuality, and the violence common among GIs in a war zone. The stalemate in Vietnam, infected with hopelessness and futility, had added a new twist to the annals of GI crime. It was called "fragging." Hundreds of soldiers, balking at the prospect of dying for a pointless cause, had begun to roll hand grenades under the beds of their officers. More than two hundred convictions had been obtained in 1968 alone.

Few criminal cases involving espionage came to trial: The United States preferred to settle allegations of financial corruption or homicide outside the courtroom. Steve Berry was getting an education in how things were handled.

Brumley, Williams, and Crew led Berry through their consultations with Enking, Scrymgeour, and Chipman at the CIA. "The most efficient course of action," they insisted, were code words for a green light to kill Chuyen. What else could it have meant?

Look, they said, the CIA is running death squads all over the country. *This is no big deal. This is nothing.* Check out Operation Phoenix.

Phoenix? Berry asked. The Provincial Reconnaissance Units of Operation Phoenix, the killer teams known as PRUs, they told him. Phoenix had gotten out of hand, Brumley explained. In the beginning the idea was to gather information on the "civilian" Viet Cong apparatus, identify the key agents, and then send in the PRUs to arrest them. Optimally, they would be broken down by the Phoenix interrogators, retooled, and "played back" to their old comrades as double agents.

It was a tricky game, Brumley explained. Time-consuming. It demanded knowledge of Vietnam's politics, history, and language, its ethnic and religious rivalries, its regional clans and family feuds. It required first-class intelligence nets at the village level, vast personality indexes, expert interrogators, and deft agent handlers. And patience, most important, patience.

But patience was one commodity unavailable to Americans in Vietnam. Four presidents, starting with Truman, had sent money, ships, planes, bullets, bombs, and soldiers to South Vietnam. The troops had ice cream, *Playboy* models, plastic surgeons, Christmas turkeys, stereo sets, radio stations, medical clinics, Bob Hope, and one-year rotations. But they never had the luxury of patience. The war had to be won every year.

The Phoenix program also depended on close cooperation with the South Vietnamese government, which doomed it from the start. The government was riddled with spies. So the Phoenix people ran out of patience, too, Steve Berry's clients told him. The PRUs began kicking ass and taking names. The situation had gotten so bad that a memo had been issued by William Colby, the head of Phoenix and a former CIA station chief himself, reminding his operatives that assassination was prohibited. What was the difference, Brumley wanted to know, between the authorized killing of civilians under Phoenix and the execution of Thai Khac Chuyen?

Berry listened and saw a possible defense forming in his mind. It was innovative, but risky. It was called the "theory of disuse."

The theory asserted that any statute not regularly enforced was no longer valid. Successful application of the theory depended on persuading a jury that the authorities had deliberately overlooked enforcement; the law had, therefore, fallen into "disuse." Following the theory, counsel for a prostitute could argue that the exchange of sex for money was no longer illegal if police had stopped making arrests. If, in other words, they willfully overlooked the law.

Such a defense would be immeasurably strengthened if proof could be unearthed showing that the police had not only abandoned their enforcement activities but opened their own brothels.

In the issue at hand, the question was whether the United States had abandoned the Geneva Convention and deliberately countenanced the murder of civilians.

With the help of the defendants and their inside sources, Berry hoped to show just that: He would demonstrate that murder was being tolerated in Vietnam by the CIA, godfathers to the Green Berets.

Colonel Seaman nodded to the prosecution.

"You may call your first witness," he said.

40

W ould you identify yourself for the record, please?"

"Lieutenant Colonel Kenneth B. Facey, formerly the deputy commanding officer, 5th Special Forces Group."

Ken Facey fidgeted in the witness chair. His eyes looked like the dark pockets of old baseball gloves. In the ten days since his detainment by Army detectives, his mind had been running like an all-night movie, replaying the events of the past month from a thousand different angles. Had he done the right thing by not reporting his boss? Should he have objected more strongly? Could he have stopped the killing? Could he have persuaded Rheault not to lie to General Abrams?

All these things had whirled through his mind in the past month. What, he wondered, *was* the right thing for a deputy commander to do? Where was his allegiance, to his boss or the Army's Code of Conduct?

Facey had tried to go the middle course with Rheault and had failed. He felt he had gone as far as he could with his boss. Now he had to look out for himself: In a few days he would be eligible for promotion to full colonel. On the night the detectives picked him up and put him in their vise, he quickly gave in.

"The Group Commander, Col. Rheault, gave the decision that the individual would be eliminated," his signed statement said. "Subsequent discussions revolved around the methods in which this would be accomplished."

He was unequivocal: "The decision was made by the Group Commander and was carried out by Major Crew."

Facey also fingered Middleton and Brumley as participants in meetings to discuss Chuyen's fate and to design and carry out a cover plan. The statement loomed as the cornerstone of the prosecution's conspiracy case.

But Facey soon had second thoughts. Late into the night, he played back the scenes from different angles. The events began to fade from clear focus. Maybe he shouldn't have been so certain of who said what. He summoned the detectives again.

"I was emotionally upset, quite naturally," he now said, "and not thinking too clearly. As I recall, I may not have made it clear that I did not attend any meeting wherein Colonel Rheault said words to the effect that such-and-such a plan would be executed."

A "plan" was not a killing, he emphasized. He actually had no idea whether it had been carried out. He asked to make a new statement, signed it, and handed it over.

The next day, his promotion was flagged by General Mabry.

Colonel Seaman referred to his notes as he began questioning Ken Facey on the afternoon of July 31.

"During some period between the fifteenth and twentieth of June," he asked Facey, "you participated in a series of meetings concerning the compromise of a certain agent from the depth of B-57 operations, is that right?"

"I was present, yes, sir, at two meetings—three meetings."

Seaman asked him to explain what happened on June 17.

"To your knowledge, was any particular course of action recommended at that meeting?"

Facey was sweating. "There was a course of action, to my knowledge, for planning purposes, selected whereby the agent would be eliminated."

"Was any decision," Seaman asked pointedly, "or mission assignment made as a result of that meeting?"

"There was no mission assignment made," Facey said. "It was just a general discussion on the fact that this would be one of the best courses of action to select at that time."

Seaman pulled out a chart and asked Facey a few questions about his place in the chain of command. Then he continued, "Now, following this initial meeting, were there other meetings that took place?"

Facey struggled.

"There was another meeting. Again, I don't know if it was the next day or the day after that, which Colonel Rheault, and myself, Major Crew, and Major Middleton attended."

"What transpired at that particular session?"

"I believe there was a point where Major Crew was trying to read back to the group commander his outline for an operational plan, one that Colonel Rheault, during the initial meeting, said would be required."

"What specific plan was that?"

Facey struggled again to navigate down the middle of the road. "The plan was one in which the agent would be eliminated," he said. His eyes flicked to his former comrades. Most of them were staring straight ahead.

"Did you attend any other discussions," Seaman went on, "where murder was discussed?"

"The only one that I recall vividly was one in which Major Crew and Major Middleton entered my office," Facey said. "It was the day after the second meeting. They were in a position to offer the final details on the plan, plus a recommended date for implementation. At that time, I advised Major Crew of my position concerning this matter, as I had done in the first two meetings—that I didn't agree. My position was that they would have to go to the group commander to receive the final approval of the plan . . ."

"You then had no further discussions with the CO of the Fifth Special Forces concerning the matter?" Seaman inquired.

"To the best of my knowledge," Facey answered flatly, "we had no discussions per se concerning the matter that I can recall."

Seaman's face registered impatience. "Was there an indication to you," he asked, "that a plan had been carried out?"

"There was indication to me about two possibilities. One was that possibly the plan had been carried out. And there were also indications that the agent had been sent on a mission."

Seaman frowned again. He made a note, then turned the elusive witness over to the prosecuting attorney, Captain Roger Nixt.

Nixt assessed Facey from a distance. The witness was fidgeting intensely with his hands.

"What were these plans?" Nixt asked, straining to recapture something from his witness. "Do you recall anything about it?"

"No," Facey shook his head. "I do not vividly recall. No."

"I see." Facey was a disaster. "Were any names brought up that were not present at these meetings, who were also involved in the scheme or plans?"

"No."

Nixt assessed the witness. His conspiracy case was folding already. That was all he had for now, he told Seaman.

Steve Berry rose. He felt pity for Facey. He could see the anguish in his eyes, the tension in his sweaty hands. He could see that Facey was torn between trying to be a good soldier and loyalty to his comrades. In another time and place, Berry might have sympathized with Facey. But now Facey was his weapon. The Army's witness had dissolved in a cloud of ambiguity, like a retreating squid. Now Facey was trying to help his former buddies. Berry would give him an assist.

"Can you tell us why the open disclosure of Bravo 57 would cause international problems?" Berry asked.

"Primarily," Facey said, "because we were operating unilateral U.S. intelligence operations from a sovereign nation, Vietnam, without consulting— into Cambodia without their knowledge."

The statement rippled across the courtroom. Even the defendants were amused by hearing it uttered so plainly, so openly. The Cambodian operations might be a widely shared secret *inside* their fraternity, but they were never, ever discussed with strangers.

Technically, Facey had misspoken. Everyone knew the United States had to have intelligence operations in Cambodia; it had them everywhere in the world. What was missing was public knowledge of the exact missions, places, and personnel, objects of particular interest to the Viet Cong and the Saigon security services. Otherwise the silence was a diplomatic condominium shared by Washington, Hanoi, and Phnom Penh. The real secret was not getting caught.

At the defense table, Bob Rheault imagined the alarms going off around the

Joint Chiefs of Staff, CIA, and White House when they heard about Facey's testimony. And he would make sure they did. It was only the start.

"Would it be correct to say then," Berry continued with the compliant witness, "that it was considered to be in the interest of the United States that the government of Vietnam not know that we were conducting unilateral operations into Cambodia?"

"I would make an assumption," Facey said, "that that is why it became a unilateral operation to begin with. They didn't want them to know."

Berry circled in front of the witness.

"Do you know whether or not it is unusual," he asked, "to discuss the possibility of eliminating an agent?"

Facey considered the question and hesitated to answer. Berry waited. Finally, Facey spoke slowly.

"In the business or field of intelligence it is not unusual to discuss this."

Berry paced again.

"When an agent is eliminated," he continued, "is it usually considered to be a military necessity to eliminate him?"

"In my opinion, it is," Facey said.

"You don't know of any instances in which any agents were eliminated when it wasn't considered militarily necessary for them to be eliminated?"

"I have no personal knowledge of it," Facey said.

The evasion was all right with Berry. The opinions of Facey, with a dozen years in Special Forces, would likely be given some weight.

Berry next decided to fish for responses showing that the CIA had the authority to approve an execution. That was to get Rheault off the hook. *Someone* had to approve it, and it certainly couldn't be Colonel Rheault.

"Would it be correct to say," Berry asked Facey, whose spirits had brightened considerably during the last line of questioning, "that if the CIA knew that a man was going to be eliminated, and they did not in fact preempt, would this be a form of a go-ahead by the CIA, as a practical matter?"

"To the best of my belief," he said, "I would say yes, it would be a full go-ahead."

Berry returned to the defense table. "Thank you, sir," he said, backing into his seat.

"I'm sorry, I have one more question." He bounced back up.

"Do you know whether or not the Central Intelligence Agency funds the Special Forces operations, provides funds for them, documents and so forth?"

"They are involved in our funding program," Facey said.

Berry paused for a moment, then asked, "Do you know of any CIA agents who are in the Special Forces at this time?"

"I have no knowledge," Facey said.

"Thank you," Berry said, sitting down.

Captain Myron Stutzman, representing Eddie Boyle, now took his turn with Ken Facey. Young and aggressive, the military lawyer had his own reasons for exploring the relationship between the Green Berets and the CIA.

According to his client, they were virtually one and the same. Establishing that would help cement the validity of CIA advice.

"Are you extremely close to the CIA in your operations, your special intelligence operations?" Stutzman asked.

"The answer is yes." Facey said.

"Thank you. That's all."

Richard Booth followed. "Does the name Mr. Almy mean anything?"

Facey thought about it. He shook his head.

"What about Mr. Chipman?"

"Yes, that's a name I recall," he said.

"Is that an individual you saw at headquarters?"

"To the best of my knowledge he was, yes. Rather heavy, a little bit on the plump side."

Booth then elicited the fact that the CIA had long funded a Montagnard mercenary army, known as Civilian Irregular Defense Forces or CIDG, that the Green Berets led.

"They revised the funding system and it went through the Department of the Army," Facey stated. "But when moneys come in-country, they go into a bank in Saigon. I am not intimately familiar with it, but I understand there is some connection between funds we use in-country and the CIA. . . ."

An Army captain assigned to monitor the hearings for secrecy violations began to object. Colonel Seaman raised a hand, permitting Booth to continue.

"Who pays the agents for B-57?"

"We do, from our CIDG funding system," Facey said. That meant money to pay the agents originated with the CIA, an important marker to establish CIA authority on the disposition of Thai Khac Chuyen.

Next Booth moved to pluck his own client from the wobbling conspiracy charges.

"Do you have any personal knowledge of whether Major Middleton," he asked, "knew anything at all about any op-plan, as far as preparing details, et cetera?"

"I do not."

Booth nodded.

"In your opinion, did he have any part in preparing the plan?"

"In preparing the plan?"

"Yes, sir, personal knowledge."

Facey appeared to consider the question carefully. "In my opinion," he said, "he did not."

Middleton slapped the defense table and broke into a wide grin.

Booth turned slightly, shooting a glare at his smiling client. "In your opinion," he continued, "from the meetings you had, observing Major Middleton, do you think that he actively pushed the elimination, or that the B-57 commander was just using him to get through to Colonel Rheault?"

"In my opinion, I don't believe he actively pushed it," Facey said. "Major Middleton appeared to be rather quiet and reserved during the times that we had these meetings."

"What do you mean, quiet and reserved?"

"Well, he didn't say much."

"He just sat there without doing much of anything, is that a correct inter-pretation, sir?" Booth asked.

Facey nodded. "I would believe it would be a correct interpretation."

"Thank you very much, sir," Booth said, turning from the witness.

"No further questions." He walked back to the table, straight into his client's gaping grin.

It took Maj. Martin Linsky, Rheault's lawyer, only one question to finish off the conspiracy question.

"Okay," he asked Facey, "and you were at no meeting where any decision was reached?"

"I was not."

"No further questions."

Roger Nixt studied his one-time star witness from the prosecution table. He considered his redirect examination, and rising from his seat, now decided to treat Facey as hostile.

"Do you know for a fact, or only suspect, that this agent was in fact a double agent?" he asked.

"I suspect."

"Suspect. At this time, one of the alternatives was to put him under close supervision because they did not know for sure if he was a double agent, is this true?"

"That is true."

"And this is the reason this alternative was chosen? Is this why this plan, or alternative, of putting him under close supervision was chosen, because they weren't sure?"

Facey squinted. "Run that by me one more time."

"Sure. Let me rephrase it," Nixt said. "Perhaps it would help you under-stand it." His patronizing tone was obvious.

"One of the alternatives was to put this agent under close supervision," Nixt explained, "and the reason for this was . . . because they were not in fact sure he was a double agent?"

"I don't know," Facey said. "I can't answer what the reason was."

Nixt, defeated, sat down.

Berry popped up again.

"Isn't it a fact that most intelligence work is something less than absolute?" he asked Facey, trying to beat back any suggestion that the defendants had acted rashly. "You do the best with what you have available, isn't that gen-erally how you have to operate?"

"Yes."

"Isn't it also true that this 'suspicion' was more than a casual suspicion, that it was based on the fact that the man had been put under a lie detector, isn't that right?"

"Yes, this is what was reported to us."

"Isn't it true also that under sodium pentathol, certain information came out that indicated he was VC or NVA? Isn't it a fact that the 'suspicion,' as Captain Nixt uses the term, was based in part on the results of the test under sodium pentathol and extensive interrogation with and without sodium pentathol?"

"This is what I was told."

"Isn't it also true that this suspicion had to do with some compromises in some nets that this individual had been involved in?"

"Yes, sir."

"Wasn't this suspicion also brought up by some photographs," Berry went on, "in which a VC agent was seen to be the same one as the alleged victim?"

"Yes, sir."

"Sir, based on this," Berry asked, moving to the side of the defendants, "would you say that this was something stronger than a mere suspicion that he might be a VC agent?"

Facey answered evenly, "In my opinion, they had a basis for being concerned about the individual, yes."

"Thank you, sir," Berry said, as the rain began pounding on the roof again. *Basis for being concerned*—That was pretty good stuff. That and the CIA's "failure to preempt" the killing.

Seaman called for another recess.

41

A warm afternoon wind rippled across Nha Trang harbor as Frank Bourland climbed aboard the U.S. Navy minesweeper. A pale sun slipped through a bank of clouds as the ship backed out of its berth and headed out the river. Soon the ship was slicing through the sparkling gray swells toward Hon Tre island.

The detective walked the deck, enjoying the salty breeze. The excursion was a welcome release from his office, his cranky Royal typewriter, the cigarette smoke and overused coffee cup. Bourland had churned out countless pages of interviews, case notes, and progress files in the past month. His fingertips were smudged from handling carbon paper every day. He had spent hundreds of hours with suspects and witnesses and had flown back and forth between Saigon and Nha Trang at least a dozen times. Now it was all coming to a head at the secret hearings in Long Binh. His job was nearly done.

But one piece of the case was missing, a piece which had brought him to the ship in Nha Trang Bay: a corpse.

On July 23, the Navy command in Saigon had sent an emergency request to 7th Fleet headquarters at Pearl Harbor, asking for assistance in "a highly sensitive underwater recovery operation in the Nha Trang area."

Two previous requests for help had been turned down by the Navy, which could not see the point of sending a minesweeper seven thousand miles across the Pacific Ocean at a cost of hundreds of thousands of dollars to drag for the body of one suspected North Vietnamese double agent. The Navy didn't mount efforts like that for their own downed pilots.

General Potts, however, finally made it clear to the Navy that the request came from Creighton Abrams. Abrams wanted the head of Thai Khac Chuyen, or at least the chains and tire rims that had dragged him to the ocean floor.

The Navy cable to Pearl Harbor was classified SECRET-NOFORN, Top Priority.

> DEPTH OF WATER IN SEARCH AND RECOVERY AREA IS FROM 100 TO 150 FEET. REQUEST SERVICES OF A SALVAGE SHIP, EQUIPPED WITH A DECOMPRESSION CHAMBER, TO CONDUCT SEARCH AND RECOVERY OPERATIONS.
>
> THE NATURE OF THE RECOVERY MISSION IS NOT ONLY HIGHLY SENSITIVE, BUT PERISHABLE. THE EXPEDITIOUS ASSIGNMENT OF SALVAGE FORCES IS REQUIRED IF SUCCESS IS TO BE ACHIEVED.

"This recovery project," the message emphasized, "has the interest and concern of higher command."

That did the trick. Seven days later, a World War II–era minesweeper, the USS *Woodpecker*, arrived in Nha Trang.

As Bourland got his sea legs, the ship's skipper, Lt. Victor Reiling, joined him on deck. They sailed in silence for a while, enjoying the freshening breezes. The lanky Ohio detective had never been to sea except on troopships to England and Korea. Now, as the minesweeper plied away from shore, Vietnam faded away.

Reiling finally turned to the detective, probing for an explanation of the unusual mission.

Bourland smiled apologetically. "Sorry, but it's classified."

After a moment, the detective turned to Reiling. "It's a homicide," he said. They had to find a body that had been weighted down with tire rims and thrown in the water somewhere out there near those islands on June 20.

Reiling studied the horizon. He didn't want to interfere, but the odds against finding a corpse in these waters, he told Bourland, were "ten to one." The body had been in saltwater nearly six weeks. A strong current rushed through this area, making it likely that whatever was left had dragged its anchor. The search area was too large anyway, he added, two-and-a-half square miles. And it was infested with sharks.

Bourland understood. But he had little choice, he said, gazing out toward Hon Tre. The case was a big deal in Saigon. "General Abrams," he added, raising his eyebrows.

The *Woodpecker* cut a wide arc, scanning the bottom with sonar and staking out the area for a hard-hat dive. Bourland walked the deck. The breeze had shifted around to the southwest and picked up moisture. More monsoon.

He thought about the dead man somewhere down there. The Army had spent how many thousands of hours, and God knows how much money, investigating his death. And now the Navy, too.

Crazy, crazy case.

Bourland had also begun to wonder exactly why Chuyen had rated so much attention from the Green Berets. Some of the people he and Bidwell interviewed said they didn't know why Chuyen was such a big deal to Lee Brumley and his pals. One of the curious was a master sergeant who worked in the counterintelligence section. He had guarded Chuyen at one point, and from time to time talked to Brumley and the others about their prisoner. As far as he knew, he told the detectives, they had never found proof that the man was an enemy agent.

Then there was Horton, the polygraph man, whose report said the last time he examined Chuyen there was "no deception indicated."

Odd. It was hard to figure.

Who was this man who had preoccupied everybody's attention, who had thrown the whole Army command out of whack? As far as Bourland was concerned, none of the Green Berets had been able to explain, at least to him, exactly what Chuyen did that was so valuable.

He and Bidwell had talked about it one night over beers.

"It wasn't like he was sitting at Ho Chi Minh's elbow or something," Bourland said. "You know, it wasn't as if he was whispering in Ho's ear." Bidwell just shook his head; he couldn't really figure it out either.

The *Woodpecker* sliced through the sea, sending down its sonar pings, listening for an echo of tire rims and chains. Bourland walked the deck, wondering what the case was really all about.

In Long Binh, the Article 32 hearing was entering its evening session.

A new problem had suddenly popped up. Wayne Ishimoto, the sergeant who was cast as Chuyen during the cover flight to Can Tho, had been called as a prosecution witness. He was accompanied to the hearing room by a Maj. Peter Kane, apparently his lawyer.

Richard Booth matched the face to a scene the week before. He jumped up to register a strong protest.

"Sir, I would like it to be known, and put on the record, that the staff judge advocate specifically informed this officer, me, that Major Kane was to be made available to all defense counsel as a 'supercounsel'—meaning that we would be allowed to go to him for any advice on any legal matters or factual matters involved."

He moved around the table to address Seaman directly.

"Several days ago I went to Major Kane, and I asked his knowledge concerning this case. He said that he had not read the file . . .

"About two days later, I went back to him, and hit him with a legal question that may have affected a legal move I might have made here. I'm sorry, I don't remember the question, but I know it had something to do with a case I had read concerning this."

The Army had appointed Kane to work with the defense team, Booth pointed out. Now, suddenly, Kane had shown up as a lawyer for a prosecution witness.

"Kane can't work both sides of the street," Booth said. Angrily, he took his seat. The Army's conduct from the beginning of the case had been outrageous.

Steve Berry now lifted his ample frame from his seat, joining in the fray.

"One more thing in reference to Captain Booth's remarks. I was with Captain Booth in Major Kane's office recently. Major Kane asked me if this Article 32 was going to take very long."

He raised an eyebrow, walking around the table.

"He said, 'I know Captain Booth is scheduled to go on R and R Saturday. He's made financial arrangements. Will it be possible to get out of here?' So I just briefly stated what my strategy in this case was going to be."

His mouth taut, Berry returned to his seat and sat down. Now there were two instances of a tainted counsel. The room fell quiet as the attorneys at both tables waited for the presiding officer's response.

Seaman shuffled and patted his papers. "I am not so sure that he has Major Kane as his counsel," he said, referring to Ishimoto. The defense attorneys were confused. "I appreciate your remarks being included in the record. I will let somebody look at it that knows more than I do about it, to see whether this has any bearing on the case."

Seaman nodded at the prosecution. "We will move ahead now," he said. The defense counsels were befuddled.

The diver was hoisted from the water on a thick steel cable and dangled over the deck like a dripping suit of medieval armor. A minute later the diver was down on the deck, and his helmet was lifted off.

The conditions were impossible, he said. He had sunk up to his knees in mud. Visibility was only about seven feet. Forget it.

Bourland listened. He argued for another try. It was important, he said. When Reiling looked doubtful, the detective took him aside.

Look, he said, General Abrams wants this.

Skeptically, Reiling finally agreed to another effort tomorrow. The ship left a marking buoy before heading back to Nha Trang.

The next morning broke dark and wet with driving rain and choppy seas. The *Woodpecker* slashed through the stormy swells to the search area near Hon Tre. The midwestern detective wasn't used to the roll of the boat and was soon green around the gills. The novelty of the excursion began to fade.

The ship boxed the area, its sonar pinging the muddy bottom, its radar sweeping the sea for any sign of enemy boats. There was an engagement on the distant shore. A pair of Phantom jets swooped down through the sky, canisters of napalm tumbling from their wings into a thicket of trees. A huge orange-and-black fireball exploded behind them as the jets streaked into the clouds and disappeared.

Reiling and Bourland swung their binoculars around, peering through the rain for the buoy they'd hitched to a two-hundred-pound anchor the night before. Finally, in late morning, they found it. The strong current had pulled it one hundred yards north overnight. In the six weeks since June 20, Chuyen could have been swept halfway back to Hanoi.

Or anywhere. They were not going to find him.

"Sergeant Ishimoto, you initially made your statement to Mr. Bidwell, didn't you?"

"Yes, sir."

Steve Berry sounded like a school principal impatient with a student prank.

"And to get you to make this statement, he made certain promises, didn't he?"

"Yes, sir," Ishimoto replied.

"And will you tell us what those promises were?"

"Sir," said Ishimoto, following Berry's movement around the hearing room, "I was told at the time I made the statement that anytime in the future I could see General Abrams concerning this matter."

Berry nodded. "You didn't realize at the time that Bidwell was lying, did you?"

"No, sir."

"When did you find out Bidwell was lying?"

"This morning, sir."

"Would it be fair to say, from your experience this morning," Berry went on, "that Bidwell intentionally suckered you into making this statement? Do you think that is correct? That is, he frauded you, induced you, promised you something to get you to talk?"

"Yes, sir, because of the other statements he made at the time of the initial interview."

Berry suppressed a slight smile. It was only the beginning of the ordeal he planned for both detectives.

"What were some of the other statements?" he asked Ishimoto.

"Some of the other statements were, sir, that, one, I would have, I repeat, have, to take a polygraph examination concerning the statement I made."

"This would be compulsory?"

"Yes, sir. He also indicated, secondly, that at that time I was not charged with any offense, and therefore I was not required to have counsel. However, should I refuse to cooperate, I might be considered a suspect in the investigation."

"So, then," Berry said, circling to the Japanese-American's side, "your statement was made after he threatened you with a polygraph examination, threatened to bring charges against you, and promised you that you could see General Abrams, is that right?"

Ishimoto turned. "Yes, sir."

"Anything else?"

"Not right offhand, sir."

Berry nodded. "Okay, thank you, and if you think of anything else, feel free to contact any of us or the investigating officer."

Ishimoto happily nodded, and Berry returned to his seat. He had gotten really good stuff for the defense.

"Your witness," he said. Nixt rose slowly.

Bob Bidwell was waiting outside when Wayne Ishimoto came out of the converted chapel five minutes later. The sergeant hesitated, then lowered his eyes and walked on.

Bidwell proceeded into the humid room, raised his hand for the oath, and then settled in his seat. After Seaman and Nixt had Bidwell identify his stack of interviews for the record, it was the defense's turn again.

Capt. H. Thomas Young stood at his seat. His almond-shaped eyes suggested an intense intellect.

"Mr. Bidwell, how long have you been a CID man?" he asked.

"Since January of 1966, sir."

"This may appear to be a frivolous question," he continued, "but nevertheless, how would you, more or less, consider yourself as far as your caliber? Would you consider yourself a good, very good, or an excellent CID man?"

Bidwell shifted in his seat. The stocky detective answered in his easygoing Ohio twang.

"I don't know, sir. If there were forty-some others that said it, I would say I would probably be pretty good."

Young paced deliberately, appearing to weigh each answer carefully.

"Being a CID man, you are school-trained, is that correct?"

"Yes, sir."

"I assume, as part of your school training, you people are educated or instructed that there is such a thing as undue influence, or coercion, or making promises with respect to making statements?"

"Yes, sir."

"And these things should be highly avoided, correct?"

"Yes, sir."

"Isn't it a fact, that you, in the course of eliciting a statement from Captain Marasco, told him that if he made a statement, that this matter would never go to courts-martial?"

Bidwell was ready for the question. The lawyer had phrased it wrong.

"No, sir, I didn't."

"Did you not say that, if he made a statement, the whole matter would be

The captured photo that started all the problems. Members of the secret intelligence unit B-57 were convinced that the man in the floppy hat, standing among high-ranking North Vietnamese officers, was their own spy, Thai Khac Chuyen. Others who compared the picture with Chuyen's Special Forces ID photo (inset) weren't sure. Chuyen was brought in for interrogation to find out if he was a double agent. *(U.S. Army photos)*

Thai Khac Chuyen, the secret agent at the center of an international scandal. Chuyen's wife supplied this picture to lawyer George Gregory and asked him to help find her missing husband. The Green Berets said he was on a mission in Cambodia, but he was already at the bottom of the South China Sea with a bullet in his head, wrapped in chains and tire rims. *(Photo courtesy George W. Gregory, Jr.)*

Robert Bradley Rheault, head of all the Green Berets in Vietnam and scion of a prominent Boston family. The news of his arrest stunned everyone. *(Henry Groskinsky,* LIFE MAGAZINE © *Time Warner Inc.)*

Major David Crew was the commander of B-57, the unit tasked with collecting intelligence from deep inside Cambodia. All the defendants wore the green beret, but in reality most of them were Army intelligence officers working closely with the CIA. *(Photo courtesy George W. Gregory, Jr.)*

Warrant Officer Ed Boyle relaxing off duty. Boyle was the first to interrogate Chuyen during a secret session in Saigon, and found evidence that the agent was spying for Hanoi. Later he helped deliver Chuyen to the boat for the fateful ride into Nha Trang Bay. *(Photo courtesy Mary Boyle O'Hara)*

The CIA office on Beach Road in Nha Trang, where the Green Berets sought advice about their agent Thai Khac Chuyen. They left thinking the CIA had given them a green light to "terminate" him "with extreme prejudice."

Captain Budge Williams and the other Green Berets decided they could not turn Chuyen over to the Vietnamese Military Security Service (MSS) because it was infiltrated by communist spies. Williams argued that Chuyen should be paid off and kept under close surveillance, but he lost. *(U.S. Army photo courtesy Budge Williams)*

Captain Robert Marasco of New Jersey was charged with pulling the trigger of a silenced pistol that ended Chuyen's life. As part of the ultra-secret Project Gamma, he carried false identification as "Martin" (below). Some Army generals suspected Marasco was a CIA agent planted inside the Green Berets, but they had the wrong man. (Photos courtesy Robert Marasco)

The arrival of South Carolina lawyer George Gregory in Saigon created a media circus. Against the Army's silence he was the only person connected to the case willing to talk. The *New York Times* was paying Gregory's hotel bill, but that failed to give bureau chief Terence Smith (left) exclusive access to the lawyer. *(Photo courtesy George W. Gregory, Jr.)*

George Gregory arrives in Long Binh to see his client Tom Middleton (right) and take on the Army. Gregory had just learned that Army intelligence agents all across Vietnam were making discreet calls to the legal offices, expressing fears that they too would be prosecuted for carrying out assassinations under the CIA's Phoenix Program. *(Photo courtesy George W. Gregory, Jr.)*

General George L. Mabry, commander of the U.S. Army in Vietnam, arriving at the headquarters of the 5th Special Forces Group. Mabry was a strict disciplinarian, believing that spies should be turned over to the South Vietnamese for prosecution, regardless of the security problem. The case sparked a bitter division between World War Two officers like Mabry and younger men who had experienced only Vietnam's messy counterinsurgency. *(Photo courtesy Eulena Mabry)*

General Creighton Abrams, supreme commander of American forces in South Vietnam. The Green Berets were convinced that Abrams was "out to get them" because of a longstanding prejudice against the Special Forces. But Abrams was enraged that the suspects had covered up the truth about Thai Khac Chuyen. *(U.S. Army photo, National Archives)*

CIA Director Richard Helms was called on the carpet by President Nixon, who read about the case in the newspapers and demanded to know what "termination with extreme prejudice" meant. Helms dispatched a CIA lawyer to find out what was going on in the Green Beret mess. Another CIA agent was sent to spy on him. *(CIA photo)*

A B-52 lifts off from Guam, en route to a bomb run over Southeast Asia. The secret raids on Cambodia were concealed from regular Air Force targeting officers, who worried that White House officials were tampering with the FAILSAFE system of controlling the nuclear-capable bombers. The raids would have been exposed by a trial of the Green Berets. *(Photo courtesy National Archives)*

Army detective Frank Bourland, who with his partner Bob Bidwell cracked the Green Beret cover story. Bourland was deeply distressed by having to investigate the highly decorated men. He advised against putting them in solitary, but was overruled. *(Photo courtesy Frank Bourland)*

Army detective Bob Bidwell at first thought it was impossible that the Green Berets had murdered Chuyen. "That's not the Green Berets I know," he insisted to his partner. Bidwell had served with the Special Forces in Iran. *(Photo courtesy Bob Bidwell)*

The Navy sent minesweepers from Pearl Harbor to search for Thai Khac Chuyen's body. Here Army detective Bob Bidwell prepares to board the USS *Woodpecker. (Photo courtesy Bob Bidwell)*

Col. Robert Rheault (center), commander of all the Green Berets in Vietnam, awaiting a courtmartial decision with his men at Long Binh. Rheault was born into a socially prominent Boston family and attended the elite Phillips Exeter Academy and West Point. "Getting rid of double agents," he maintained, "was as old as time." *(Photo courtesy George W. Gregory, Jr.)*

The Army flagged the promotion of Lt. Col. Ken Facey, Rheault's deputy, and kept him in Vietnam until he testified against his boss. In earlier days he had better luck, landing a bit part in John Wayne's movie, *The Green Berets*, and escorting Marilyn Monroe around Korea. *(Photos courtesy Ken Facey)*

Secretary of the Army Stanley Resor, donning fatigues during a Vietnam visit, was the lightning rod for Congress's outrage about the Army's handling of the Green Beret case. Resor backed General Abrams and believed that communist spies were due the same treatment accorded regular prisoners of war. *(U.S. Army Signal Corps photo courtesy Stanley Resor)*

The Army and General Abrams, especially, were roundly ridiculed for their handling of the Green Beret case. *(Copyright 1969 by HERBLOCK in the* Washington Post*)*

A Viet Cong suspect, one of the more than 20,000 Vietnamese killed by the Phoenix Program's Provincial Reconnaissance Units. Nixon wanted more money for the PRUs, but the assassinations were political dynamite. *(Photo courtesy Paris Theodore)*

Nixon and advisors at Camp David. During dinner one night, H.R. Haldeman (second from right) and John Ehrlichman (in tan jacket, left) began to suspect that Defense Secretary Melvin Laird was monitoring phone calls from the presidential retreat, in order to find out what the White House was thinking about the Green Beret case. *(National Archives photo)*

Nixon and his national security advisor Dr. Henry Kissinger ran the secret Cambodian bombing from the White House. Kissinger had his own channel of information on the Green Beret case. *(National Archives)*

Nixon and his chief of staff, H.R. Haldeman, with stacks of pro-war telegrams that were in many cases generated by his own speechwriter, Patrick Buchanan (inset). "The case is hurting us," Buchanan told Nixon. *(National Archives)*

CIA regarding the double agent. They decided on murder. Next day CIA eliminated murder from the alternatives. CIA supposedly feared "a moral flap." Abrams heard about it -- said to "clean up" the Special Forces. Questions remain according to NBC's Goralski: Why make such a big thing out of this particular murder and why did the CIA give the options on the agent's future and then change them?

CBS' Gary Shepard called the case "one of the most significant events of the war" with the entire concept of the killing of a person believed to be an enemy on trial. Footage of military attorneys for the defense.

The editors of the White House Morning News Summary tried to persuade Nixon that the Green Beret case was causing a public relations debacle for the administration, but the president seemed more interested in blaming the affair on CIA Director Richard Helms, as his note to Henry Kissinger in the margin shows. *(National Archives)*

Nixon with Defense Secretary Melvin Laird, Henry Kissinger (far left), and White House spokesman Ron Ziegler (far right) outside the Old Executive Office Building as body-guards look on. Ziegler initially denied Nixon had any role in the Green Beret affair, but later took credit when the decision proved to be popular. *(National Archives)*

MEMORANDUM

THE WHITE HOUSE
WASHINGTON

π - 4
9·29·69   9AM

① Agenda   UAC
② Meat — continue quota 3 mo
③ Coretta King — garment zing lier

①
EK ──→ see Al Haig — CIA letter —
              Rts of Defs prejudiced —
CIA Executive Privilege — Cong. Hearing

② Meat prices down —
    Do w/in 3 months —

③ Sar. Leadership Mtg —
    Richard Lyons — Wash Post
    initiatives
    (Scott) hit this — debate it —

H.R. Haldeman's notes from the morning staff meeting with President Nixon on September 29, 1969. Nixon ordered Haldeman to have White House aide Egil Krogh ("EK") see Alexander Haig, Kissinger's assistant, and arrange for the CIA to write a letter saying it would refuse to cooperate in the Green Beret trial. That would force the Army to drop the charges and thus abort a Congressional hearing on the affair. *(National Archives)*

Phan Kim Lien, the widow of the spy at the center of the Green Beret case. Lien went to the U.S. Embassy to protest when she heard the charges were dropped. As she wept, the Green Berets were happily flying home to heroes' welcomes. *(AP/Wide World Photos)*

smoothed over and that the generals would be satisfied with an explanation thereof?"

Bidwell considered the question again. He and Bourland did tell Marasco they *thought* the matter would be smoothed over. But they had been careful never to say that *if* he made a statement it would be dropped.

"No, sir, I didn't."

Young tried a new tack. "Isn't it further a fact that you told Captain Marasco that the charge, if any, that would be lodged against Captain Marasco would simply be a technicality which would be voided?"

"No, sir, that is not true."

"And finally, is it not true that as a result of Captain Marasco giving a statement, that you could not really deliver on your so-called promises or inferences?"

"Sir," answered Bidwell, "I did not make those promises or inferences."

Young sat down. All the defense lawyers had gotten the same story from their clients, that the detectives had suckered them into making statements. It was always worth probing. Maybe something would shake loose.

Steve Berry took his turn, sarcastically jabbing at Bob Bidwell for bringing up General Abrams's "interest" in the case.

"Do you think," he said, "from your experiences as an investigator, that the mention of the fearful name of General Abrams would tend to induce people to speak more readily than they might otherwise have done?"

"I imagine it would," Bidwell conceded.

"How many witnesses, prior to questioning them, did you mention General Abrams's 'interest' in this case to?"

"Knutson," Bidwell answered, "because he thought I was just up there to conduct a whitewash. And Ishimoto. The rest of them I can't say. I don't know. It is possible that I did." Or Frank.

Berry moved on to the events of the day that Lee Brumley was picked up for questioning. Boyle and Marasco were already in custody, Berry recounted, setting the scene. He suggested that the detective had manipulated Brumley by telling him that others had confessed and that a refusal to talk would make his situation worse.

"Didn't you say that?"

"No, sir, I told him he had an absolute right to remain silent."

Bidwell was offended by the question. He certainly had told Brumley he had a right to remain silent. Well, not right away, but as soon as they had him in Long Binh.

"You didn't suggest in any manner that he would be well advised to contact Captain Marasco before making up his mind?"

"I don't recall that I did," Bidwell said. He tried to remember when he told Brumley he should read Marasco's statement. "If I did, it would've been after I advised him of his rights."

"Don't you think it would weaken him by saying, 'You have the right to remain silent, but you had better find out if anybody else talked before you do'?"

Bidwell repeated his denial, but Berry was already walking away, turning the witness over to Steven Shaw. The counsel for Budge Williams stood up at the defense table.

"Didn't you tell Captain Williams that others had made statements?" he drawled.

Bidwell said he had, yes.

"Didn't you tell Captain Williams he wouldn't be confined if he made a statement?"

"I can't recall," Bidwell said. The pounding was getting heavy. "But if I did, I made it perfectly clear that it was not within my bounds to decide whether or not he would be confined. I think I made that clear to all the suspects."

Shaw snorted and sat down. Now it was the turn of Richard Brown, military lawyer for the forlorn Alvin Smith. He opened with a hard punch.

"Do you remember being given a typewritten statement by Sergeant First Class Alvin Smith?"

"Yes, sir, I was," Bidwell said.

"Do you also remember telling him, before the statement was sworn, that there was nothing in it to involve self-incrimination?"

Bidwell hesitated. He knew this was a troublesome area. It had been the Army's decision to treat Smith as a witness for three weeks and then prefer charges. The detectives had done what they had been told.

"I don't recall using those exact words, sir. When I questioned Smith, I questioned him as a witness."

Brown slowly turned around and looked the detective in the eye.

"I did not warn him of his rights," Bidwell conceded.

"You did not?" he echoed.

"No, sir, I did not."

"Therefore, the statement taken from Smith was a witness statement?" Brown continued.

"Yes, sir, it was."

"Did you say afterwards"—Brown picked up his notes—" 'So help me Smith, you will *not* go to court, nor will *anybody* go to court involved in this case'?"

"No, sir, I don't remember saying that at all."

Brown slowly shook his head.

"That's all I have," he said, and he walked back to the defense table.

The traces of CIA agents wafted over the case like the cigarette smoke and half-finished glasses of hastily departed guests.

Williams, Crew, and Brumley had persuaded Berry that at least three CIA officers had condoned, if not encouraged, the execution of Thai Khac Chuyen. The defense lawyers knew their argument would be problematical: On the Army charts, no official lines of authority connected the CIA to the Special Forces.

To solve that problem, the lawyers needed to show that a web of CIA money and influence permeated B-57's operations. To begin, they attempted to show that CIA witnesses were not only improperly missing from the hearing but had blocked the CID's inquiry into their own role in the affair. Lee Brumley's inside sources at MACV had given Steve Berry a lead.

"Is the CIA involved in this investigation in any way?" Berry asked Bidwell.

"Sir?"

"The CIA."

"Yes, sir, I believe they are."

"Did you receive any instructions from Captain Scrymgeour or Lieutenant Colonel Enking involving these operations or this investigation?"

"No, sir, I did not."

"What instructions did you receive from the CIA, if any?"

"Sir, I wouldn't classify them as instructions. I attended a meeting. A Mr. Shackley from the CIA was there. . . ."

Bidwell thought back to his confrontation with the arrogant CIA boss. It was get-even time.

"He read four or five reasons why his people would not be permitted to be interviewed in the course of my investigation," the detective went on, "and he made the educated guess that they would not be called to appear in court, by executive immunity. He cited a couple of federal court cases, things along that line. I was instructed by him that his people would not be available to me to give any statements."

"So," Berry boomed, opening his arms, "from the exalted offices of the CIA, your position was going to be, that if there was a scapegoat, it could only be the military. It couldn't be anybody from the CIA?"

Bidwell had to be careful. "All I know is where the line was drawn," he said.

"That was the halls of the CIA," Berry roared again. "Is that correct? To which this investigation has *not* reached—is that correct?"

"Yes, sir," Bidwell answered quietly. "That's correct."

Berry's pyrotechnics subsided, and Budge Williams's lawyer Steven Shaw rose. In a soft, back-country southern accent, he asked Bidwell to take him through CIA agent Enking's remarks at the MACV meeting on July 13. Slowly, exactly.

"He said," Bidwell stated, " 'I talked to Crew and I told him that we could not sanction the elimination of the agent, but that it was probably the best solution, or the best possible solution.' Or words to that effect."

Shaw politely asked him to continue. What happened next?

"After the meeting was over," Bidwell went on, "I approached Colonel Enking. I said, 'Sir, I believe that statement is vital to my investigation. I would like to have that in the form of a sworn statement.' "

Shaw hunched his shoulders in a question.

"He said he'd have to check back with headquarters," Bidwell responded.

"In other words," Shaw said deliberately, "he told you he recommended elimination but refused to make a sworn statement, is that correct?"

Bidwell wanted to be precise. "No, sir, I don't believe that's correct at all. He said, 'I talked to Crew and told him that we could not sanction the elimination of the agent, but that unofficially it is the best solution, or possibly the best solution,' or words to that effect."

Shaw peered softly at the detective. He had picked up subtle signals in his answers. Bidwell, perhaps, was trying to help them.

"No further questions," he said.

Martin Linsky grew up in the Bronx and went to law school at Fordham. Broad-shouldered, contemplative but ruthless, Linsky was a slashing courtroom advocate. His client was Bob Rheault, whom he had come to admire. In some ways, they were much alike.

Linsky was thinking of staying in the Army, maybe as a military judge. He listened to Bidwell's testimony with growing disgust. When it was his turn, he stood and leaned forward on the defense table like a bull pawing the dirt before a charge.

"I would just like to make a point for the record," he said. "Mr. Bidwell, an experienced criminal investigator, suspected Sergeant Smith of having committed an offense under the code. At that point, he was bound to advise that individual of his rights."

He approached Colonel Seaman. "This was not done. I submit that the statement of Sergeant Smith therefore should not be considered.

"Further," Linsky went on, "on the basis of the statement of Sergeant Smith, which was illegally obtained, Mr. Boyle made a statement. I submit that his statement itself was illegally obtained as a result of Sergeant Smith's statement.

"Following that along to its obvious conclusion, Captain Marasco made a statement. Based on the illegal evidence obtained from Sergeant Smith's and Mr. Boyle's statements, Captain Marasco's statement itself was an illegal statement."

Linsky curtly smiled.

"I don't think that there is *any* statement," he said, "that can be used by *anybody* that's been brought out at this investigation." He gave Colonel Seaman a look of disgust.

Linsky moved back from the detective, turned around, and appeared to be in deep thought. He decided to take a detour.

"Mr. Bidwell, do you have any real evidence in this case, any material, meaning objects, weapons, et cetera?"

"Yes, sir, I have a .22 caliber pistol with a silencer on it."

"Is that all you have?"

"I have some possible suspected blood, and one suspected human hair that was found on the boat that allegedly was used in carrying out the attack."

There was movement at the defense table as Booth and Berry caucused in whispers. Booth asked Seaman for a brief recess. "I have some information that concerns his client, sir," he said. He took Berry aside when Seaman granted the recess.

"Sir," Berry announced when they were finished, "as a result of our conversation, I would request a Major Bender, along with Mr. Bourland. They will show that the one piece of real evidence, the pistol, is not usable for any purpose, it cannot be offered into evidence."

"Who is Major Bender?" Nixt asked, rising.

"Assistant S-2, Fifth Special Forces," Berry said.

"What knowledge does he have?" Seaman asked.

"Sir, I am simply making an offer of proof to use these two witnesses to show that the pistol may not be offered into evidence for any purpose. I want to put them under oath for that purpose."

Seaman made a note and Berry sat down, as did Nixt. The pistol, Berry hoped to prove, was inadmissable because Brumley had handed it over before his rights were read. Brumley wasn't really worried. "What will they match it to?" he asked. The slug was at the bottom of the sea.

"Any more questions?" Seaman asked. Linsky said he wanted to continue from where he was.

"Now you mentioned this hair and blood. . . ."

"Well, sir, I suspect it was blood," Bidwell said. "It did not test negative, that's all I can say, so it could be blood. Whether or not it's human blood or not, I don't know." He was embarrassed.

"What about this hair?"

"It was a hair, a black hair, about this long," he said, spreading his hands about eight inches.

"It's human hair?"

He fudged. "No, sir, I have not heard from the laboratory yet." He wanted one more go-round with the Tokyo labs.

Linsky was quietly astonished at the lack of real evidence.

"Let me ask you another question," he said to Bidwell. "In your opinion as an experienced criminal investigator, do you feel that your investigation was hampered by the fact that Mr. Shackley told you that you could not talk to his people?"

Bidwell exhaled. "Sir, I will put it to you this way. The only reason I conduct an investigation is to establish the facts. To me, it is important whether or not the CIA had any involvement in this case. And when I was told that I could not establish this, I would have to say, yes, that hampered my investigation. As a matter of fact, it could stop it completely."

Roger Nixt was staring blankly from the prosecution table.

"And you would have to admit," Linsky bore in, "on the question of just basic fairness, that the accused should not be similarly hampered by being refused permission to interview, to consult with, and if need be, to interrogate members of the CIA?"

It was the kind of leading question allowed in an Article 32 investigation.

"Certainly, sir, if I can't complete my investigation, that is where it will have to stop. . . ."

"And that would be unfair to you, and these men. . . ."

"Sir, I don't know whether it would be unfair to me. It might certainly be unfair to the suspects," Bidwell said. "In my own mind, throughout the investigation, that was one point I felt I had to establish before I could complete my report. Until then, I would just have to file it the way it is, uncompleted."

He paused, searching for the right words.

"I cannot conduct an investigation in this manner," he added matter-of-factly.

Berry mumbled into folded hands. *Thank you Jesus!*

Linsky paced once again, stating the obvious.

"I feel that Mr. Bidwell has been hampered in his investigation," he said slowly. "It would be a gross miscarriage of justice if this Article 32 is continued, if the charge is not dismissed, unless the CIA is brought into this thing completely."

He looked at Seaman, then walked deliberately back to his seat.

Berry pushed back his chair, stood, and leaned on the table.

"Many of these questions will simply be a foundation for motions," he said. "But I would submit that if there is no corpse, there is no crime."

He tapped on the stack of CID interviews in front of him. "This is a flimsy case. Nobody would have the nerve to take it into court. The international implications would be disastrous.

"It is obvious that these men have committed no crime, in any way. However, if there is some reason for continuing this Article 32, and not simply dismissing all charges, if there is some reason for reconvening, if there is some reason for calling in all these other people, then I would like to add some names to the list."

He tore a single piece of paper from his yellow legal tablet and passed it to the front desk. Colonel Seaman read down the list.

> Theodore Shackley—CIA, Saigon
> Lt. Col. Enking—CIA, Saigon
> Capt. Scrymgeour—CIA, Saigon
> Mr. Almy—CIA, Nha Trang
> Mr. Chipman—CIA, Nha Trang

At the bottom was William Colby, followed by two words, "Operation Phoenix."

The rain had finally stopped. The hearing was recessed.

42

Lt. Col. Harold Seaman dodged mud puddles as he rushed to the Long Binh Chapel, arriving late for the morning session on August 2. Inside, he walked hastily to his desk at the front of the room, took off his green plastic poncho, and gave it a shake. The MP standing at the entrance made sure the door was locked. A bright red Secret sign was posted on the wall.

The defense lawyers waited anxiously as the presiding officer took his seat, opened his briefcase, and took out a sheaf of documents. Without preliminaries, he began reading.

Five of the CIA agents whose testimony had been requested by the defense, he said, were "not essential" for the hearing. "I am not calling them," he declared, peering over his reading glasses and listing the names: Colby, Shackley, Almy, Scrymgeour, and Enking.

At the defense table, Steve Berry began to object, but Seaman raised a cautionary hand. He wasn't finished with the subject.

Harold Chipman, the CIA agent who allegedly consulted with Lee Brumley and David Crew in Nha Trang, Seaman said, would be "requested" to testify at the hearings. His appearance was being handled "through channels."

Now it was time to proceed to other matters, Seaman said.

Steve Berry was on his feet. "Sir, the purpose of these particular people, this list, is to suggest that if in fact anyone was killed, if in fact there was a killing of any kind, if it is ever established that there was a crime, the guilt or innocence of these people may hinge on the total environment, the total flow of circumstances under which any particular act may have been done."

It was essential, he argued, for the court to understand "the total authority, instructions, customs of warfare, military necessity, and other instructions of higher-ups" involved in the acts that had been alleged. If the CIA men involved in the case wanted to claim executive immunity from testifying, he said, then let them come into the Long Binh Chapel and assert their special privilege. They can't just hide behind the skirts of the Army.

"If we are bureaucratically office-covering, then I would like to know whose office we are protecting and why," Berry demanded. "This is very important to the legal theory of the defense."

What was the basis of Seaman's ruling? he inquired. Did he consult with anybody on his decision?

"I have not," the colonel responded curtly. After the silence that followed, he amended his statement to say that he did receive "guidance" on the witness list from an Army legal officer before the hearings began.

Marty Linsky stood up, the *Manual of Courts-Martial* open in his hand. It didn't say anything about witnesses being "essential," he lectured.

"It says that 'all available witnesses including those requested by the accused, who appear to be reasonably necessary for a thorough and impartial investigation, will be called and examined in the presence of the accused and his counsel.' "

Linsky put the manual on the table. "I submit, sir, that you should reevaluate whether these individuals should be called, in light of the test of 'reasonably necessary,' in the interest of justice."

Seaman looked past Linsky to the defense table. "Are there any other statements?"

Linsky dropped slowly to his seat.

"I might comment . . ." said Capt. Michael Burke, a new addition to the defense team. He addressed Colonel Seaman with great care. "The purpose of an Article 32 investigation is two- or threefold," he said softly. "Obviously the government has an interest in proving its case. The defense has an interest in finding out what the government has available to it. And thirdly, the United States Army has an interest in finding out both sides of the story."

Burke walked across the room, pensive. "An Article 32 investigation should be as wide open as the parties wish it to be. The investigating officer should want to dig into all areas. And while we can't reveal the theory of the defense, it is obvious that if any crime was committed here, or if a killing did in fact occur, it was sanctioned by higher officials, officials who are almost one step below the president." He paused to sum up. "They can hardly be irrelevant, or not 'reasonably necessary' for the inquiry."

Burke faced the colonel. "Why," he asked Seaman, "should the *instruments* of these officials, the ones who actually carried out the alleged acts at *their* direction or indirection, bear the brunt while these officials get off scot-free?"

Seaman appeared to be listening closely.

Burke continued. "Now it may be that these CIA men have already put on record that they don't intend to say anything. But this fact is in itself essential. They must be brought here and say, under oath, that they aren't going to say anything. This fact in itself would reveal a great deal about what has gone on in this case."

Burke had frozen the hearing room with the soft eloquence of his appeal. Now, Steve Berry picked up the tempo.

"Yesterday," he declared, "I asked Mr. Bidwell about his meetings with the generals. I tried to get from him whether there was any indication, anywhere, by any of the generals, that loyalty ran downhill as well as uphill. I also asked him, Was there any indication, at any of the meetings, that any of these generals were upset by what Colonel Enking or Mr. Shackley had to tell them about this case? Was there one spark of courage in that room? Was there any indication that loyalty and justice were as important as another star on their shoulders?"

Berry moved out from behind the table. "Of course, detective Bidwell remembered nothing of that." Disgust drooped at the corners of his mouth.

"We have here the makings of a colossal whitewash," he said, his voice dropping, "something just short of a conspiracy on a very high level.

"Unless this hearing is opened up wide, unless these people are brought in here and forced to say, 'I ain't going to talk because I am going to cover my own office,' then the truth isn't going to come out."

He walked around the room. A fair trial, he added softly, was what separated Americans "from the people we are fighting over here. A whitewash," he closed, "is a vicious, unconstitutional thing." He returned to the table and took his seat.

Seaman looked toward the defense table. He had been prepped that the lawyers would try to open a philosophical inquiry into the nature of the war, of counterinsurgency, and of ties between the CIA and Green Berets. Likewise, he had been advised that all those things were irrelevant to the case. His duty was merely to weigh testimony concerning the events on or about June

20, when, according to the Army, the eight men sitting before him conspired to drug, shoot in the head, and drop one Thai Khac Chuyen from a boat into the South China Sea.

"Do other counsel desire to make a statement?" he asked.

Bill Hart and the other lawyers rose one after another to echo the arguments of Michael Burke and Steve Berry. A fair hearing, they insisted, was impossible without all of the requested CIA witnesses.

Linsky returned to his feet with the *Manual of Courts-Martial* in hand. This time he tried not to lecture.

"I would again refer, sir, to paragraph 34, with reference to what your duties are. It says, and I quote, 'He is required to conduct a thorough and impartial investigation and is not limited to the examination of witnesses and documentary evidence listed on the charge sheet . . .' " He snapped the manual shut.

"Sir, unless all these individuals are made available, you cannot have 'a thorough and impartial investigation.' It would be a gross miscarriage of justice. If they want to cloak themselves in the un-American privilege of executive immunity, let them do so; let them have the courage to do it right in front of the accused, right in front of their counsel."

Linsky waited for a response, but Seaman merely gave him a curt nod and picked up another document. "I would like to proceed to my determinations with respect to the documents you requested."

Linsky, dejected, slowly sat down.

"Three are not in existence," Seaman went on. "Captain Berry asked for CID statements by Lieutenant Colonel Enking and Captain Scrymgeour. I am informed there are no such statements. Another item was the CID report of investigation. There is no report yet. There may be at some future date."

Grumbling came from the defense table. Berry threw a pencil down. Bidwell had *testified* about Enking's statement! It was in the record. It had to be written down somewhere—that's the way detectives worked.

Seaman picked up another piece of paper. "Now, the following are documents which I have determined are not essential for the purposes of this investigation and therefore, I do not intend to get: the CID file on the alleged victim, the B-57 case file on the alleged victim, a list of agents in Muc Hoa and Thanh Tri, a passenger list of the Mirabelle in 1954 . . ."

The eyes of the defense attorneys began to narrow.

". . . a report of NVA or VC affiliation of these individuals, memos between the CID and CIA concerning the alleged victim, Vietnamese government files and dossiers on the alleged victim, his wife, and sister. Two operations plans, one identified as Thanh Tri and one identified as Blackbeard. A list of terminations with extreme prejudice in unilateral operations since 1961, a list of all terminations with extreme prejudice in bilateral operations since 1961, a list of all terminations with extreme prejudice in multilateral operations since 1961, and"—Seaman looked over his glasses—"documents which were not specifically identified but were listed generally as messages from Nha Trang to Saigon and vice versa, regarding the alleged victim."

Seaman put down the list expecting an immediate response. None came.

The attorneys appeared to be immobilized by the ruling. Seaman started to call the next witnesses, two sergeants who had watched the boat being loaded. He was interrupted.

Thomas Young, the lawyer for Bob Marasco, was on his feet. "I just want to state my feelings for the record," he began. He paused to gather himself, standing behind the defense table.

"There may be some repercussion," he began slowly. "I hope not. But this entire proceeding has been a fiasco."

He paused to clear his throat, thinking.

"After being subjected to this type of proceeding on the part of the government," he resumed, "and its decision-making, I would sincerely say here that I have lost complete respect for the military."

He started to sit down, flushed. Seaman watched him, angry.

"For the record," the colonel shot back, "I would like to point out that the determinations made here, as the investigating officer, are mine, and not those of the government."

Young slumped into his seat. Steve Shaw, the counsel for Budge Williams, finished a whispered conference with his client and stood up, a scribbled note in his hand.

"Sir," he drawled, "if I may at this point, should there be a reconsideration of the request for documents, I would like to make an addition, if I may, at this time."

Seaman nodded.

"We've had a request for a list of all terminations with extreme prejudice, under three different types of arrangements. If and when those are made available to us," Shaw went on, "we'd like to add another few.

"We'd like a list of the same type of terminations with extreme prejudice in Laos, since 1958, and under the same conditions in Bolivia, in 1968."

"Bolivia?" Seaman asked, looking baffled.

"Yes, sir. Bolivia. 1968." He paused.

"The elimination of Che Guevara."

PART V

Showtime

43

George Gregory turned the last page of the hearing transcript and sat back in his chair in the air-conditioned office.

Jesus, it was freezing! That goddam colonel who grilled him about security must've turned up the cold for the hell of it. He rubbed his arms and looked at the piles of documents on the table that he had just finished reading.

Pretty good work, he had to admit. There were about twenty-five interviews by the Army detectives. They told the whole story: the suspicions about Chuyen, his arrival and departure from Saigon, the injections of morphine and sodium pentathol, the visit to Camp Goodman by Chuyen's wife and her sister. There were the confessions by five of the suspects, including the grisly accounts of Chuyen's death in the boat by Brumley, Williams, and Marasco—all ably challenged by the defense lawyers, he thought. But the Army's self-appointed judges, Gregory knew, tended not to have the same appreciation for legal niceties as the American Civil Liberties Union.

There was Wayne Ishimoto's recollection of his cover flight to Tay Ninh, transcripts of Chuyen's interrogation, and Horton's summaries of the polygraph results. There were copies of Rheault's false messages to General Potts. The paper trail wound all the way back to May, when Alvin Smith plucked the captured photograph from the pile of pictures in the darkroom in Nha Trang.

Gregory picked up the famous captured photo, the start of all these troubles, and peered at it. Was it Chuyen?

All those smiling teeth in a row of Viet Cong. Who knew? They all looked alike to him. It could be, and it couldn't. He looked at Chuyen's ID photo and back at the grainy black-and-white photograph. He held them side by side, the ID and the soldiers. He couldn't be sure. Who could?

Gregory tended to agree with that major's assessment—what was his name,

Thrasher? He pawed through a pile of documents for the memo—that the drawstring on the floppy hat made it impossible to tell for sure. You couldn't see the ears. The nose looked a little different, too.

Smith saw what he wanted to see, that's what Gregory thought. And then they all got caught up in it. Cloak-and-dagger—he could tell they all liked that stuff.

But was Chuyen a double agent? He doubted it. It didn't look that way. Even the interrogation reports were inconclusive, although it struck him as odd that not all the transcripts were there, only a couple hundred pages. From what there was, Chuyen didn't admit to a thing, except maybe contacting his brothers. Big deal; it's a civil war over here, families fight on both sides. Even Brumley's own memorandum for the record, dated June 20, said no proof existed that Chuyen was a Communist agent. But maybe he was.

He had to admit some things were intriguing—all the other agents quitting in Muc Hoa, for example. Maybe he was selling to both sides. But that hardly made him a high-level spy, a dangerous rogue agent.

So why did they kill him? Gregory reached into the pile and spread out some of the statements of the Green Beret sergeants who had guarded Chuyen. One theme was consistent: Chuyen had started to climb the walls. After eight days of interrogation, sleep deprivation, and drugs, he had turned completely against them. He was making noise, banging on the door. *He was one pissed off sumbitch*, Gregory thought. *And who wouldn't be?*

If they'd let him loose at that point, he probably *would* have joined the VC. Or held a press conference in Saigon. Jesus, Gregory thought, *I would have.*

And then all hell would have broken loose. Ted Kennedy and William Fulbright would've taken an overnight flight from Washington to hold field hearings on the secret war in Cambodia, the bombing, the outrageous flouting of human rights by interrogating a Vietnamese citizen with drugs and sleep deprivation. Thai Khac Chuyen would have been the star witness, along with Lee Brumley and all the others, summoned by subpoena.

Gregory understood it now; the Green Berets had simply run out of time. The CIA wouldn't take him. His wife was asking questions. So they made up a story and killed him to keep him quiet. Forever.

But they hadn't counted on Alvin Smith.

The role of the CIA was interesting. It was clear that the Green Berets *thought* they had encouragement, if not authorization, to kill the guy. Enking—he had to remember that name. He hoped to get a shot at the CIA man at the next Article 32 hearings, scheduled to resume in a week.

These things always unravel, Gregory thought, just like our mothers told us. There's always a loose end somewhere. Alvin Smith was theirs. But if it hadn't been Smith, it could've been somebody else. Chuyen's wife and sister-in-law—they weren't going to let go, that's for sure. What were the Green Berets going to do, smoke them, too? Or hadn't they thought that out?

Jesus, what a mess. So this was the ultrasensitive operation Tommy Middleton had written him about. No wonder he didn't go into the details.

At least there was a silver lining: The Army didn't have a lot on his own client. Middleton helped with the cover story, Gregory thought—maybe there's a count of obstruction of justice, and that can be whittled down. Maybe for an exchange of testimony.

But conspiracy to murder? No way. Like Facey had testified, Middleton just sort of held the door for people coming and going in Rheault's office.

That was the heart of the matter, Gregory thought: Rheault lied to Abrams.

Good lord! He tried to imagine what that scene was like, how Abrams must have reacted when he found out. *I bet that ole boy ain't used to some chickenshit colonel coming into his office and giving him a line of bull like that,* Gregory thought. *Not General Abrams, not a tanker. Boy! That Rheault must have balls of steel.*

Rheault, Gregory thought, would have been a stronger man for saying no, don't kill Chuyen, or at least handing the problem over to Mabry or Abrams. Rheault reminded him of Robert E. Lee, who survived annihilation by superior Union forces so long that he began to think of himself as invincible until he hit the wall at Gettysburg. Pickett's brigade was destroyed there, and now, it looked like, so would be the Green Berets. Or at least these eight men.

Abrams had a right to go after Rheault, Gregory began to think. You can't have your colonels lying to you, can you? At least not once you've found out they've broken the rules. Not when it's right in your face. That's like letting the dog dump on your rug; he has to be punished.

Gregory could be philosophical in private, but he had a client to defend. Time to get back to Saigon, he thought. The sun had long gone down. And he was freezing. He banged on the door to summon the security guard. A few minutes later, he walked out of the staff judge advocate's office and into the sweltering night air. It cloaked him like a warm blanket.

Now, walking down a dark lane, he was sweating in a torrent. Goddam, this is going to be torture, he thought: Cold, heat, cold, heat. *No wonder they had itchy trigger fingers in Vietnam. I feel like killin' some sumbitch myself.* His glasses slipped down his nose. He wiped his forehead. His shirt was soaked. *Where's the goddam gate?* He saw it in the distance. *Jesus. There it is. Thank God. Get me off this base.*

Gregory walked through the main entrance, lazily waving at the guards. Somebody was waiting by a car in the shadows.

Gary Shepard of CBS News smiled and stepped forward, and offered Gregory a ride back to Saigon. The lawyer happily accepted.

The highway was clogged with cars, trucks, soldiers setting up their nightly roadblocks. Ordinary Vietnamese rode their bicycles or walked along the shoulder in the darkness, hurrying home before curfew. You could hardly see them until you were right on top of them, men and women with blank faces and charcoal eyes, floating ghostlike through the night. They looked right through you, Gregory thought.

Moving among the Vietnamese at night rattled a lot of Americans, especially when they first arrived in-country. You looked at all those people around you and wondered: Which ones are ours, which ones the Viet Cong? Any one of them could pull a pistol or toss a grenade in your lap. You looked at them and saw nothing, or everything.

And that was what this case was about. How the hell, Gregory wondered, is a soldier supposed to know who to shoot over here? He had thought about that theoretically, but now here he was riding along a dark highway where any one of those unreadable people could reach out and kill him.

Who's the enemy here? he wondered. How do you pick him out of a crowd? Are there full-time VC and part-time VC, free-lancers, people working both sides? Only the North Vietnamese Army, encamped in the far-off jungles, seemed to wear uniforms, and we couldn't find them half the time, either.

The Green Berets had tried to figure it all out in this case. They had tried to cut a Communist agent out of the crowd. In their pursuit of the real Thai Khac Chuyen they had drowned in Vietnam's thousand-year history. What they did with Chuyen was the Vietnam War in a nutshell, Gregory thought. You couldn't tell who was on our side and who was on theirs. Hell, you didn't know who our side was!

The Army's Code of Conduct didn't adequately define counterinsurgency, this wading into an unfathomable civilian population, this vast indecipherable country and its people, and telling who the enemy was. And the code didn't begin to deal with the irony of Project Gamma, an intelligence program expressly designed to be kept hidden from America's putative Vietnamese allies. Article 106 of the Uniform Code of Military Justice provided that spies caught behind the lines and not in uniform could be punished by death—but not before trial and conviction. But where were the lines in Vietnam? And who would conduct a trial? Who had the ultimate authority to judge a Vietnamese suspected of treachery in a unilateral American intelligence organization? How could such a trial be realistically conducted in secret with the rights of the defendant protected?

Soldiers aren't lawyers. It was unfair, Gregory thought, to put them into a position where they had to calibrate the degree to which a Vietnamese person was loyal or disloyal without realistic judicial options. And loyal to what? To us? To the revolving cliques of South Vietnamese generals who spent half the time plotting against each other and the rest of the time making themselves rich? In the middle of a thirty-year-long civil war, exactly who was the enemy? It was damn hard to tell.

Gregory looked out at the crowds of Vietnamese hustling along the sides of the dusty highway, and something long buried began to stir in him. Not quite outrage, more a disdain. How arrogant it was, he thought, that American generals thought they could come into this family dispute with their napalm, their tanks, their B-52s, and their lumbering army of teenage southern whites and northern ghetto blacks and expect them to do political surgery in Vietnam's tiny villages—these small-town boys who hardly knew which fork to use, much less decipher this alien society and its thousand-year-long feuds.

Ah, but the CIA thought it could tell the black hats from the white, another arrogant notion. Now he recalled what Richard Booth had told him about the anonymous phone calls to the Army's legal office, the Army men assigned to something called Operation Phoenix. He remembered the mention of Phoenix in the Article 32 transcript.

Jesus. The proverbial light bulb went on in his head. *How could he be so dumb?*

"The most effective course of action," the CIA man had said, "might well be to get rid of him. We can't sanction it, but that may be your best course of action." Gregory had seen the quote in two places, Budge Williams's statement, and the CID agent's report. He had scribbled it on a piece of paper and stuffed it in his pocket.

Operation Phoenix. That was something to hold on to.

Gregory and Shepard pulled up to the Caravelle Hotel, parked, and walked through the art deco doors into the lobby. He was exhausted. A few reporters spotted him, came forward, and began asking questions. What the hell, Gregory decided. "C'mon up for a drink."

Settling into his suite, Gregory poured a vodka and tonic and said he'd have a press conference in the morning. He had a lot to digest.

"Listen, George, you can't wait until the morning," Terry Smith protested. "You're on the other side of the world. It's morning there. If you wait, you'll miss the East Coast deadlines."

Gregory stood for a moment, considering the *New York Times* bureau chief. The *Times* was picking up his tab. Sweat streamed down the edges of his new sideburns. The other reporters looked anxiously toward him. The thought of that arrogant lieutenant colonel who had given him the security lecture at Long Binh flitted through his mind. Obviously, the Army wanted to keep the whole case wrapped in secrecy. He had to give them a wake-up call.

"Okay," he said, "give me an hour to get my thoughts together."

It was near ten o'clock when Gregory arrived at the top of the hotel. A gentle breeze nudged the colorful lanterns hung around the dining area, the bar, and the dance floor. Beyond the rooftop, the lights of Saigon twinkled like diamonds on black velvet. At the city limits, at the bridges where major highways led into the capital, sentries lofted flares into the night sky. On the western horizon the rumble of artillery and air strikes could be faintly heard, and occasionally a red ember appeared in the dark.

The Caravelle had once been one of the favorite watering holes for correspondents, military officers, CIA agents, and a smattering of Vietnamese officials and stylish Saigonese women, who, taken together, constituted what there was of polite society in the capital. Now it catered to more out-of-town visitors. The bar was rarely empty. Secrets were told, favors traded, wartime affairs begun and ended. "Other people had unhappy childhoods," one of the correspondents had written. "We had Vietnam."

A circle of reporters formed around Gregory. In a moment the television lights snapped on. His face looked pale and fleshy in the white light and glistened with sweat. He grinned nervously and traded a few off-camera quips as the TV people set up their microphones.

George Gregory was learning a lot about this business. From the remarks of the reporters in his room a little while ago, he could tell they were desperate for stories. *Hell, he owned the damn story.*

He had a short statement to make, he said, when the technicians were ready. The cameras began to roll.

First, he said, his client was being held without justification, in "subhuman conditions" in a secret section of the Long Binh jail. He described the sweltering five-by-seven-foot cells, the bare light bulbs, the solitary confinement, and the slits in the doors. The prisoners were subjected to degrading strip searches, he said. They couldn't exercise.

"This is how the North Koreans treated the men of the *Pueblo*," he said, alluding to the disgraceful episode of the previous year when a Navy spy ship was captured and its men subjected to a Communist show trial. The reference struck a broad chord. The Navy had court-martialed the *Pueblo*'s skipper, Lloyd Bucher, for surrendering his ship before destroying its sophisticated electronic gear. Many Americans thought Bucher was made a scapegoat for the Navy's own failure to protect the *Pueblo* when it was sent into dangerous North Korean waters.

"It's outrageous," Gregory went on. Solitary at the LBJ was inappropriate for any U.S. Army officer, especially for ones with no criminal records. In fact, the men hadn't even been charged; they were only suspects, Gregory said, entitled to treatment accorded any American citizen. He planned to file a petition to have his client released immediately on his own recognizance.

"Major Thomas C. Middleton has never been charged with a crime. Major Middleton does not have a criminal record, and he is not a criminal—even under the, uh, wonderful system of military justice we have here. He is no danger to anyone else, nor is he likely to flee."

Gregory's shirt was soaked through. He called for a congressional investigation of the case "to insure that in the future people with my client's caliber will not be sacrificed." He accused "the highest military authority in Vietnam"—that is, General Abrams and his staff—of pressing "these most unwarranted charges" against his client "to improve their interests."

"Certain varied and high commanders," he added, were so afraid of international and political repercussions "that it became necessary to sacrifice the life, the career, of my client." But there was something more intriguing, Gregory said.

The Vietnamese man at the heart of the mystery, he said, was "a dangerous Communist double agent" who was threatening to expose the lives of thousands of Americans in Vietnam.

"If it is proven that someone reached his demise," he went on, being careful not to admit there had been a killing, "I believe you will find that he will be a dangerous Communist double agent hired by the best financed agency of the United States of America."

"Let's put the finger right on where it should be," he went on. The reporters scribbled furiously. The cameras churned. "You will find that this agent was wrongfully entrusted with such valuable information that hundreds and thousands of lives of American agents and fighting men were saved in a most necessary manner."

The reporters were intrigued. Here, finally, was a keyhole into the "shadow war," the assassinations and torture long rumored to be employed in the twilight struggle against the Viet Cong. To some, it held promise as the best story of the war, with much larger dimensions, a metaphor for how America had mortgaged its moral standards to win in Vietnam.

What could illustrate that better than a tale of Green Beret thugs interrogating the shit out of some hapless Vietnamese, shooting him in the head, and dumping him in the ocean? And then the Army tries to cover it up.

Gregory, of course, had a different slant on it. He wanted the public to be outraged over the Army's treatment of the Green Berets—not Thai Khac Chuyen.

The reporters pressed him for more details. What more could he say about who was to blame? Was he blaming the CIA?

The portly lawyer hesitated. He wanted to say more, he said, but he was bound by the strict security agreements in which the Army had unfortunately smothered the case. "Other agencies," they would soon see, were at the heart of the affair.

Bud Merrick, a correspondent for *U.S. News and World Report*, did not like what he was hearing. Middle-aged and as conservative as his stodgy magazine, Merrick was a defender of the war effort and had friends at the CIA. He lashed into Gregory for his unsupported statements against the agency and demanded proof for his wild charges.

Gregory sensed he had the crowd with him. "I assure you that I know what I'm talking about," he said. "I just can't get into the details. If you don't believe me, why don't you ask the CIA or the Army?"

The press conference eventually dwindled to a close. *Washington Post* reporter Bob Kaiser wandered away, checking his notes. It was a skillful performance, he thought. Gregory was clever, putting himself forward as a country lawyer. But Kaiser knew that Gregory was a hell of a lot smarter than that. He had managed to define the case on his own terms—*Thank God the victim was eliminated*. It was no small accomplishment.

But it also left him feeling that the whole tale had yet to be told.

Kevin Buckley, along with a gang of other reporters, accepted Gregory's invitation to come down to his room for drinks and more talk. As a weekly magazine correspondent, he had a more leisurely deadline than many of the others. He could gather string for another day or two, feeding tidbits along the way to his friend Kaiser, whose paper happened to own *Newsweek*.

The reporters arrived in Gregory's suite and gleefully ordered up drinks from room service. After a while, the crowd thinned out, but Buckley hung around hoping to get a chance to talk to Gregory alone. Eventually, the room emptied, and the two men sat down by themselves to talk.

It was well past midnight when Kaiser typed the last sentence of his story at the *Post* bureau, a cramped studio apartment in an old building near Le Pagode, a local watering hole. He thought it would be a good idea to double-check a few details with Buckley before sending it to Washington. Suddenly, the telephone rang.

"Come over here right away," Buckley whispered.

Come over? Kaiser asked. It was 3 A.M. He was exhausted.

You've got to get over here, Buckley insisted. *Gregory's talking.*

Kaiser groaned. Give me a few minutes, he said.

The reporter walked through the dark and empty streets, faint with yesterday's heat and the moist oncoming dawn. Only an occasional jeep of "White Mice," the Saigon police, passed by. A curfew kept everyone else inside.

When he got to the Caravelle, the hotel was locked up like a bank, its metal doors rolled down and the watchman sound asleep. The hell with it, he thought, and turned back to walk to his apartment. When he got there, it, too, was sealed like a can of sardines, the metal doors locked and the watchman asleep inside. Finally, with a few urgent calls, he roused the unhappy sentry and went upstairs to bed.

Before turning out the light, he called Buckley. He had given up, he said. The hotel was locked up.

"Get over here," Buckley said again, even more urgent this time. "I'll go downstairs and get the guard to let you in."

Kaiser trudged downstairs and nudged the watchman awake.

"Again?" the guard asked. *Encore?*

"*Oui, oui, on m'a téléphone de Washington, très urgent,*" Kaiser explained. He slipped out and walked back to the Caravelle.

The hotel watchman was waiting at the front door to let him in this time. Upstairs, Buckley cracked open the door with a smile. The bourbon was gone, but Gregory was still there.

Kaiser sat down. Buckley persuaded Gregory to go through his story one more time.

The Saigon sky was pink when Gregory finished. He had given them nearly the whole story—the suspicions about the agent, the captured photo, the fears the Green Berets had of what their agent knew, the interrogation with sodium pentathol, and the killing in the boat off Nha Trang.

But what really piqued the reporters' interest was the accused men's dealings with the CIA. According to Gregory, the Green Berets had sought advice from the agency about what to do with their man. And the answer the CIA gave was to "terminate him with extreme prejudice."

That, he insisted, meant orders to kill the agent, and they carried it out.

But then the CIA sent a second order, Gregory said, revoking the first. It was unclear why, he said, but it was too late. The CIA then angrily told General Abrams what had happened. Abrams, who didn't like the Green Berets anyway, ordered the unit "cleaned up." An overeager underling apparently interpreted that as an order to have the Green Berets arrested, and there the case stood. It was a classic Army screwup. And the CIA was getting away clean.

Kaiser listened closely. No wonder Buckley had insisted he come over. *Nobody* had stuff like this. As usual, however, his steady eyes gave away nothing.

"George," Kaiser finally said, "we've got to figure out a way to get some of this information out of Vietnam and into our papers and magazines. To help your client," he added, "without getting you in trouble."

Gregory quickly agreed, but he suddenly seemed alarmed about the enormity of what he'd just told the reporters. He'd given them the whole thing only hours after signing a security agreement with stiff federal penalties for disclosing *anything* about the case. The reporters sensed his embarrassment and worry. They began to discuss how to handle it, calming him down.

Finally, they decided to draft a cable to their editors with a skeletal outline of the case that would say only, "suggest you pursue this theory." Gregory would not be mentioned, not even hinted at, as their source. Privately, they decided to send a second, complete account of their conversations to their editors. But they had to make sure it didn't fall into the hands of the CIA or South Vietnamese intelligence services, who they knew wiretapped the telexes of foreign correspondents. (In one of the more amusing episodes, a *Newsweek* cable from Saigon that merely suggested a story on impending changes in the South Vietnamese government had been intercepted and denounced by President Thieu before it even got into print.) Kaiser and Buckley decided to ask a CBS film courier to pigeon their story out of the country.

The sun was rising when Kaiser and Buckley walked into the offices of Reuters, the British news agency with which they had arrangements to transmit their dispatches. Terry Smith was there filing his story to New York. He looked at his two rivals and immediately figured out what had happened. He snatched a telephone and called Gregory's room.

"The lid is off now, huh?" he said sarcastically. The *Times* thought they had an understanding. After all, he had gotten Gregory a room. He had bought his liquor. And what did Gregory do? He handed an exclusive to the fucking *Washington Post*.

Smith angrily rushed off. He was going to drag that goddam cracker out of bed and squeeze him for everything he had.

Gregory's press conference generated dramatic television coverage and front-page headlines in American newspapers the next day, August 14. Most led with some version of the account by the Associated Press or United Press International quoting George Gregory's declaration that the "the alleged victim was a double agent who imperiled the security of thousands of Americans." Gregory's lurid description of the wretched conditions of the Long Binh stockade was also given prominent play.

Terry Smith had caught up with Gregory in time to file a fresh story to the *Times*. Quoting "sources close to the investigation," Smith wrote that the affair had been triggered by a captured enemy photograph of the double agent, whose "termination with extreme prejudice" was "suggested" by the CIA.

"For reasons the sources are unable to explain," the account continued, "the CIA directive was reportedly revoked. A new order directed that he was to be spared." Smith had also filed a colorful "Man in the News" profile, which was syndicated to hundreds of newspapers, recounting Gregory's humorous tale of beating the Army physical by forging his test scores. In the *Charlotte Observer*, the story appeared under a banner headline: "We're Not Going to Sacrifice These Good South Carolina Boys, Lawyer Says."

Bob Kaiser's trek to the Caravelle, meanwhile, turned out to have been a waste of time. His editors had passed on his second dispatch. Thinking about it later, he thought it was probably a good idea. The paper had already carried one account of the killing from anonymous sources in Washington, which pretty much told the same story Gregory did. One of those was enough. He still felt there was a lot more to be told.

Kevin Buckley, meanwhile, stayed at his hotel, drafting the outlines of his story. *Newsweek* was planning a cover. So was *Time*.

George Gregory was pleased. Nothing like the network news and the front page of the *New York Times* to wake a general up, he thought, riding happily out to Long Binh with Richard Booth on August 16. The media had become part of his team now, loaning typewriters and secretaries to help him type up his legal appeals for Middleton's release. Which was great, except that Middleton was still locked in the deep recesses of the stockade.

Whatever he was charged with, Gregory argued, Middleton didn't deserve to be squirreled away in that cage. He'd never been arrested for anything before. He was a respected, decorated officer with a spotless record. He should be released pending trial or, as Gregory hoped, the dropping of charges. He needed better access to his client to prepare for the Article 32 hearings.

The Army should be feeling the sting of publicity by now, he thought. People back home were outraged about the prison conditions Gregory had described. Telegrams were flooding the Pentagon, White House, and Congress. Well, there's more where that came from, he thought. The Army better wise up.

They bounced along the baking highway in Booth's jeep, weaving through the pedicabs, the motorbikes, the peasants trotting along the road with their baskets, sucking up the exhaust of Army trucks. The fighting was out there somewhere, Gregory mused, gazing at the far treeline. It was somewhere out in the jungle and rice paddy, where another two hundred American soldiers had died last week, many by stepping on mines.

Still, Vietnamese soldiers at their roadblocks at intervals on the highway looked nervous. They were checking the papers of the peasants and taxi drivers closely. In their dark glasses, Marlboros dangling from their mouths, M-16s on their hips, ordering the peasants around, they didn't look like anybody Gregory wanted to tangle with. Jesus, with allies like this, he thought, who needs enemies? No wonder people helped the Viet Cong cut this highway at Tet.

Gregory and Booth swung through the gate at Long Binh and drove to U.S. Army headquarters. Inside, they were directed to the conference room. Walking into the room, they found General George Mabry flanked by his staff judge advocate, Col. Wilton Persons. Another colonel sat off to the side, monitoring a tape recorder. Gregory introduced himself, to a stony silence. He was directed to a seat.

"I have read your petition, and I understand you have some additional oral arguments to present," Mabry said evenly, his eyes fixed on the civilian lawyer. "I am prepared to listen."

Gregory didn't expect a bear hug from the general, but he thought it would be warmer than this, at least, lawyerly civility.

"Could I ask what the judge advocate's recommendation was?" he finally asked. "Then I'll know how to proceed."

Mabry ignored Gregory's question. "I have read your petition," he repeated, "and I understand you have some additional oral arguments to present. I am prepared to listen."

Gregory was taken aback, but he was still feeling pretty cocky about his progress, the reception by the press.

"You know, General," he started, "I have been a United States Army officer, an officer in the Judge Advocate Corps. The confinement of my client Major Thomas Middleton, solitary confinement in that tiny cell, is unheard of."

Mabry did not respond.

"The commanding officer is in a house trailer," Gregory said. "I am very happy with that, but the treatment is inconsistent."

Mabry merely stared at Gregory. Now the lawyer didn't know what to say. He turned to Booth with a quizzical look. Booth returned it with a shrug and whispered to Gregory to let him give it a try.

Army regulations, Booth explained, showed that maximum security confinement was neither necessary nor required in the present circumstance. Middleton had an unblemished record during eight years in the Army. He was no danger to anyone. There was no question he would be present for trial—in fact, Major Middleton welcomed a trial to clear his name.

In comparison, Booth said, the preferential treatment accorded Colonel Rheault was "highly irregular." Why should Rheault be in an air-conditioned house trailer while the others were in solitary?

"I'm also having trouble conferring with my client," Booth added to Mabry's stolid visage. "It is true that we have been told we can use the chapel, but the chapel is not always available." An office had been provided for all the lawyers and their clients, but the noise and lack of privacy made it unsatisfactory.

"I feel I cannot as a military defender of my client adequately discuss matters with him," Booth said. "I feel I am being harassed."

Still Mabry remained silent.

Booth, glancing at Gregory, pressed on. "The first time I asked for Major Middleton, all was hush-hush. Then I had to ask for 'Number Two.' Since the Army's press release, I can ask for Major Middleton. But I still cannot adequately confer—"

Gregory interrupted. "Wasn't he also strip searched when he was put in jail?"

Booth nodded. They were having a conversation with themselves. Mabry remained silent.

"I cannot understand," Booth resumed, "why Colonel Rheault is in a house trailer. I would like to ask the reason for it." He waited for an answer.

The general stirred. "I am listening," he finally said. "I have the petition. I prefer to listen."

Gregory shook his head. This was the strangest judicial experience he'd ever had.

"I have a question," he said.

"I am prepared to listen to anything you have to add," Mabry responded stiffly.

Gregory shook it off. "The house trailer is interesting," he went on. "I realize that Colonel Rheault has been under a strain. I am happy the Army used good judgment in that case. In the case of Middleton, I realize you have a tremendous amount of discretion. As Booth stated, the question is, Will the person try to escape? We have no reason to fear a court-martial."

He looked to Mabry for a response. None came.

"This is not a murder-type case," Gregory went on, growing frustrated. "There is a great deal of speculation as to what it is."

He flashed a hint of things to come. "As a practical matter, I have documentary evidence that more than a hundred people have been extinguished, apparently as a result of lawful orders."

The threat bounced off Mabry like a rock thrown at a wall. Maybe he didn't even understand what Gregory was talking about. Shit, he thought, don't waste that stuff here. The lawyer looped back to his main argument.

"The original confinement was harassment for a failure to spill the beans the way Facey did," Gregory said. "He was put in the Long Binh stockade under the worst conditions I can imagine, except for hardened criminals. It depresses him. It is obviously punitive. It is making it extremely difficult for this man to participate in his defense. He has been in there since—what was it?—the twentieth of July. I reject any theory that he will escape. If the original confinement was for the purpose of extracting a confession, it no longer exists. We feel it is unlawful to extract a confession in that manner. There is no lawful reason for his continued confinement. If it is of overwhelming national interest, he can be restricted to the post."

Gregory paused. He had run on for a while. Mabry still just stared at him.

"Well, General," Gregory said with a bewildered smile, "I certainly appreciate your *listening* to our arguments. We would of course appreciate a decision on this at the earliest possible time." He looked down at his briefcase, and then back up, preparing to leave.

"When," he smiled sarcastically, "by the way, might that be, that we would know of your decision?"

"I have your petition," Mabry said. "I will advise you as soon as I can."

Well Jesus Christ, Gregory thought. What kind of a hearing is this? The session was over. He drove back to Saigon, his rage growing.

I'm just going to have to give these generals another smack across the forehead, he decided.

The press eagerly gathered around George Gregory when he returned from Long Binh. They knew he had been out to argue his client's release with General Mabry.

The Army had refused comment on the session, so they came in droves, expecting fireworks. But Gregory was not the colorful country lawyer of previous nights. He launched into a slashing, bitterly passionate attack on the Army and General Mabry in particular.

Mabry and his legal advisers, he said, had not just denied the petition for his client's release, they had ignored it. The Army apparently didn't recognize such modern legal concepts as pretrial release and habeas corpus. They had kept Major Middleton and the others—honorable soldiers, decorated soldiers, officers and gentlemen all—in the most deplorable conditions, the kind of inhuman conditions used rarely with even the most hardened criminals.

The case was a frame-up, Gregory charged, starting at the top. He left no doubt who he was fingering: Gen. Creighton Abrams, the top man in Vietnam. He would go over their heads, he said, to the secretary of defense, and if necessary, the president of the United States, to secure justice and reasonable treatment for these men.

Gregory elaborated on his conspiracy theory. The case was poisoned by a rivalry among the CIA, the Army, and the Green Berets, he proclaimed. The jailed men were scapegoats in a vicious conspiracy of top Army officers to rein in the Green Berets, abetted by the CIA.

As Gregory went on, some of the reporters began to grow restless. The press conference had degenerated into a tirade. Gregory was flinging charges this way and that with little or no substantiation. In the terms of the trade, the lawyer was failing "to advance the story" with facts, to add something new.

The relationship between reporters and a news source is like a courtship. The reporters are in full thrall, the source loves the attention. Then comes the moment of truth. *Give it all*, the reporters say. *I can't*, the source says. The romance starts to cool. The press starts to move on. The source grows desperate, fearing the loss of attention.

George Gregory was at that point in the Caravelle dining room, which had been requisitioned for the press conference. The reporters were losing interest in his tirade. TV crews began to dismantle their equipment. The klieg lights were starting to go off. The spotlight was moving away. Gregory had gotten a free ride for a couple days, now they wanted facts. Their questions were taking on a harder edge.

How did they know any of what he said was true? they asked. Where's the proof of the conspiracy? Who was the agent who supposedly worked for the Green Berets and the CIA?

That was the week's newest question. Exactly who was the victim? The Army refused to say.

Gregory reached into his briefcase. He pulled out the charge sheet. The victim in the case, he said, was a man by the name of Chu Yen Thai Khac.

The reporters fell silent and began to scribble again. He had them back.

Bob Kaiser had been hanging on the edge of the crowd. Now he challenged Gregory: Read from the rest of the document, he said. If he could read part of it, he could read the rest of the specifications. Everyone was entitled to know what the men were charged with.

Gregory slipped it back into his briefcase. He refused. It didn't matter anyway, he chortled to the throng, the victim's name was probably false, a cover.

Grabbing another sheaf of papers, he then went on to say that the military code permitted the execution of secret agents under certain circumstances.

This is a circus, Kaiser thought, packing up his notebook. The victim was or was not a man named Chu Yen Thai Khac. Take your pick.

Well, it was something to work with, he thought, walking away. Not much, but something. The press's love affair with George Gregory, though, was over.

George Gregory returned to his room alone and took a long cool shower, washing off the dust from the ride to Long Binh. He replayed the press conference in his mind as the water washed over him. There was no doubt his stature with the press corps was waning. What had he done wrong? He had handed up the story on a silver platter—what more could he do? The reporters seemed mad at him because he hadn't given them *everything*. Why didn't they dig up the rest on their own?

As he was toweling off, there was a soft knock at his door. "Just a minute," he said, and quickly pulled on a pair of clean slacks.

When he opened the door, he found two Vietnamese women standing in front of him. One shyly asked if he was the American lawyer, Mr. Gregory. Yes, Gregory said, he was. The three of them stood awkwardly in the doorway, until Gregory finally invited the women into his room. He asked them to take a seat while he put on a shirt.

When he returned, one of the women handed him a small, black and white photo. "My husband," she said, tapping it. "Thai Khac Chuyen."

Gregory studied the picture, and the woman began to dab at her eyes. Meanwhile, the other woman explained in awkward English that her sister-in-law's husband worked for the Green Berets and had been missing for many days. They had read about Gregory in the Saigon newspapers. Could he help them find her husband?

Gregory hesitated; his conflict was obvious. As the lawyer for one of the men accused of conspiring to kill her husband, he could not in any way admit that he knew anything about Chuyen's fate. Not to her, certainly. But the human face of the drama had suddenly shown itself. The woman silently weeping before him, whom the Green Berets had assumed was Chuyen's accomplice, certainly didn't fit the portrait of a hardened North Vietnamese agent. After all, what was she doing here? If she was a spy, why hadn't she fled by now?

"I can't help you," he said, pocketing the picture. "What you should do is talk to the journalists." They didn't seem to understand, so Gregory found a piece of paper and a pen. He wrote down a name and an address and handed it to her.

Bob Kaiser had dinner guests the next night when a slim young Vietnamese man appeared out of the darkness at his door. Vu Thuy Hoang was his assistant at the *Washington Post* bureau. Foreign news organizations hired scores of English-speaking Vietnamese to help out on interviews, translate the local press, and keep up with the constant rumors of coups in the Saigon coffee houses. They were an indispensable element in running a bureau.

Hoang was a cut above most. He was a good reporter on his own. He had worked in the Defense Ministry, and his contacts were uncommonly wide.

Kaiser excused himself from his guests. Hoang said he had some news. A man had showed up at the bureau looking for more information on the name mentioned by the American lawyer in a story printed in the local press. If the name was Thai Khac Chuyen, and not the other way around, as it had been reported, then that might be his brother, the man said. He said his brother had been working as an interpreter with the Green Berets when he disappeared on June 13. No one had seen him since. Chuyen's wife was distraught, the man said, can you come and talk to her?

Hoang told Kaiser that he had visited the woman at her house on Phan Thanh Gian Street. She was very nervous, he said. She emotionally denied her husband worked for the Communists. He was only a low-level interpreter for the Green Berets, she insisted, he was not a big-time spy. She also said that her husband had complained of being interrogated by the Berets while sitting in "an electric chair," just before he disappeared.

Hoang showed Kaiser something else—a note she claimed her husband had written when he left Saigon on the thirteenth, saying he was going away on a mission.

Kaiser and Hoang went back to the office. Throwing themselves into a crash story to meet the next deadline, they patched together the first story on the victim's family since the announcement of the arrests on August 5. Vu Thuy Hoang, as Kaiser's editors had urged, had "talked to the Vietnamese." On August 18, the story appeared on page 1 of the *Washington Post*.

SLAIN VIET A LOW LEVEL INTERPRETER
By Robert G. Kaiser
Washington Post Foreign Service

SAIGON—The apparent victim in the Green Beret murder case was a 31-year-old native of North Vietnam known to his family as an interpreter for U.S. Special Forces, it was learned early today.

Unless descriptions offered by the victim's wife and brother are wildly misleading, the dead man was almost certainly not a major U.S. intelligence agent or an important Vietnamese official. Instead, the picture that emerges is of a relatively low level operator.

The victim, apparently, was Thai Khac Chuyen. A garbled version of his name was released Friday night by George Gregory, an attorney for one of the men accused of murder in the case. . . .

The story attributed the information to Chuyen's brother and wife by name. After running in place with George Gregory for the past few days, Kaiser found it a pleasure to write a story without anonymous sources, putting a story right out there in the open where people could judge for themselves.

Further, Kaiser believed it was solid. There was always something wrong with Gregory's version, he thought. The notion of Chuyen being a superspy who "imperiled the lives of thousands of Americans" never rang true. Kaiser had grown up around spooks; his father was an American diplomat. Superspies tended not, Kaiser thought, to be in the employ of Green Berets.

But Vietnam—what a weird place. Who knew for sure? His favorite GI slang was "the world," as in any place outside Vietnam, particularly America. There was "the world," and then there was Vietnam, which was on a different planet. Anything could happen here.

Kaiser sat down to try and make sense of the rush of events, to pull everything together in a carefully reasoned piece of analysis. By nature, the dark-haired Yale man was thoughtful, not given to sensationalism. He tended to shy away from conspiracies. He believed the simplest explanation was often the right one. It was reflected in his weekend dispatch, based on a melding of the versions Gregory and Chuyen's wife had told and a discreet sounding of his own military and diplomatic sources.

There were three explanations for the curious arrests of the Green Berets, he wrote. One, it could have been "a catastrophic mistake" by an overzealous Abrams underling. Although he didn't attribute it to Gregory, it was one of the lawyer's early assertions, and in a way it made sense.

A second possibility was that the Army had no choice but to remove Rheault and his men because they had committed an incident so serious that it demanded swift and decisive attention.

Maybe.

"There is a third explanation," Kaiser concluded, "but it is one which nobody this reporter has talked to is willing to accept.

"It is that the Army simply will not tolerate murder."

He was right. Nobody would ever believe that.

44

Through some odd combination of soaring temperatures, careless politicians, and bored reporters, summer always seems to erupt in scandal and calamity. The summer of 1969 was turning out to be no different. First there was the death of Mary Jo Kopechne in Ted Kennedy's car. Now the Green Beret case, with its hints of international intrigue and a power struggle between the CIA and the Army, began to move to center stage. By mid-August, the affair reached Congress, propelled by the frantic efforts of the defendants' wives to get their men out of the Long Binh stockade.

At the heart of the burgeoning scandal was a flurry of speculation over the identity of the mysterious Thai Khac Chuyen. Few reporters could accept the idea of the Army wrecking the Green Berets over a low-level interpreter.

There had to be something else to it. A succession of wildly speculative stories quickly flowed from Saigon. In one version Chuyen was "authoritatively" said to be a "triple agent" working for the United States, Saigon, and Hanoi. In another he was killed when he got in the way of an investigation into corruption in the South Vietnamese army. In yet another, he was linked to the operations of French intelligence.

Most of the stories had some root in George Gregory's decision to pump Chuyen up into a mythical figure, a dangerous double agent who "had to be eliminated to save the lives of thousands of American servicemen." But there were other hands at work now. "Sources identified as Central Intelligence Agency officials have given a version of the Green Beret mystery in South Vietnam that gives the CIA 'a clean bill of health,' " an Associated Press story began.

"The sources say the dead Vietnamese was working as an undercover agent for the Green Berets. After he was suspected of being a double agent, Special Forces men asked CIA 'friends'—who were also engaged in undercover work—what to do. The friends reportedly said the man should be turned over to South Vietnamese authorities.

"Later, according to the sources, the Green Berets told their friends the man had been killed."

The story went on to emphasize: "The CIA agents recommended the true story be told" to General Abrams.

Saigon reporters didn't buy it. Why, it was asked around the bars where correspondents gathered, if Chuyen were a nobody, would the CIA bother to go to Abrams, and why would Abrams go public, risking a major security breach, to prosecute the commander of the Green Berets? The idea that the men had been arrested simply because the Army forbade the execution of secret agents was roundly ridiculed. There had to be an arcane political angle to it all, a hidden entity at work. This, after all, was Saigon.

Compounding the challenge of figuring it all out was the eruption of yet another spy scandal that week, this one right inside the South Vietnamese Presidential Palace. A circle of top officials, including some close aides to President Thieu, had been uncovered as Communist spies and arrested. There were rumors of dozens more arrests to come. Although the scandal was comparable to the arrest of half of President Nixon's cabinet as Russian KGB agents, it garnered only a few paragraphs in most American papers and thirty seconds on network television—this despite five hundred thousand GIs and two million dollars per hour in American aid to prop up the Saigon regime. The Green Berets and Thai Khac Chuyen—that was the story.

Inevitably, the two spy scandals got tangled up.

"The arrest of eight Green Berets," reported the *Washington Star*'s correspondent, "may reach into the fabric of the entire complex relationship between the United States and Vietnam. That single conclusion emerged this weekend from the maze of rumors and reports, charges and countercharges emanating from the U.S. Army's investigation. . . ."

But there was more than that at stake, he wrote: "The case now appears directly related to President Nguyen Van Thieu's own struggle for survival in the uncertain atmosphere of war and peace talks."

Thieu himself, the account went on, was acquainted with Thai Khac Chuyen: "He was a leading intelligence figure close to Thieu's own staff in Saigon." Another Kim Philby? A high-level Communist mole at the center of the alliance? The two spy scandals of the week were getting blurred.

Murray Sale, the sardonic Australian correspondent for the *Sunday Times of London*, surveyed all the rumors and speculation and concluded that the blossoming scandals were just what the sordid, depressing war capital needed. Sale concocted his own lurid version of events and then whimsically admitted to friends it probably wasn't true.

"What does it matter?" he sighed. "The truth will never come out."

Karen Brumley was frantic. Like the other wives of the accused men, she didn't know what to believe. The stories kept exploding in Saigon, one after another, gluing her to the radio and TV. She rushed out for the morning paper each day and snatched up copies of *Newsweek* and *Time*. Each day brought a new, shocking bulletin, some troubling new development on the fate of her husband.

If the Army had given her just a shred of information, something to hold on to, she might not have been so worried. But two weeks after the startling announcement of his arrest, no one had called.

The hardest blow had been that South Carolina lawyer's account of the awful conditions at Long Binh. She'd had no idea the men were being held in solitary, under bare light bulbs, in five-by-seven cells, until his press conference. It sounded like a prison camp in Russia or Red China—how could the Army treat its own men this way?

Her husband had said nothing about that in a letter that had finally come a few days later. He had only said he was in trouble, a political thing. Don't worry, he said, because it would all soon be ironed out. Colonel Rheault was taking care of things.

The petite dark-haired schoolteacher was in a quandary. At night, in the little frame house in Duncan, Oklahoma, she would hug her six-year-old daughter and try to explain the unexplainable, that Daddy was in trouble with the Army but it would all be over soon and he would be home. But she could hardly be sure.

One day in desperation she went to the Western Union office and sent off a telegram to General Abrams, begging him for information, asking him to sort out the facts. That, too, went unanswered. Then came George Gregory's startling charges of a CIA frame-up, and suddenly she found herself in the middle of an international scandal.

Reporters' calls continued to plague the house night and day. At first, accustomed to keeping all her husband's activities secret, she had hung up. Now, however, she was beginning to look to them for information. Finally, in total frustration, she turned to her congressman. She hoped he could give her a hand.

Carl Albert could do more than that if he wanted to. The Oklahoman was the second-ranking Democrat in Congress, next in line to be Speaker of the House.

In Baltimore, Dorothy Boyle angrily slammed down the kitchen telephone and burst into tears.

"He kept asking me what did *I* know?" she exclaimed to her friends, frustrated by another wasted talk with an officer at the Pentagon. Her coworkers at the trucking company didn't know what to say. A traffic accident, a death in the family, those were the sorts of things they knew how to deal with, not an arrest by the Army on charges of murder. And it wasn't even a crime—not in the ordinary sense. Ed Boyle was charged with killing a Vietnamese spy, in Vietnam—since when was that a crime? The war was impossible to figure out.

Like many Army intelligence wives, Dorothy Boyle didn't know exactly what her husband did. He was an investigator of some type, she thought, working on a case with the Green Berets. It sounded pretty exciting, hush-hush, until now. He had written that he would be home in a few weeks when it was all wrapped up. Then Vietnam would be behind them, somebody else's war. They would get on with their lives. She had planned a big party.

Instead she spent two weeks barraging the Pentagon with desperate telephone calls, trying to find out what had happened, what condition he was in, whether he was one of the men in solitary. The Army either couldn't or wouldn't tell her a thing. Most of the time she spent on hold, being passed from one smooth-talking officer to another, being put off. None of them, they finally began to tell her, knew what was going on. They began to ask her what she had found out from the reporters who called.

"All I know is what I see on TV!" she finally screamed.

Double agents, triple agents, the CIA—Each day brought new and puzzling headlines. She didn't know where to turn. Finally, in exasperation, she picked up the telephone.

"Who the hell is our congressman?" she asked one of her friends.

All politics is local, goes the Washington maxim. And so it was that the Green Beret case soon caught the attention of Congress.

Representative Peter Rodino read the latest story out of Saigon with its description of the prison conditions at the Long Binh stockade and decided he had to do something. He had tried to investigate the information in Bob Marasco's letter quietly, but the Army had rebuffed him. Now it was a big story.

Like any congressman facing reelection every two years, Rodino paid close attention to the voters in his northern New Jersey district—and especially to the concerns of a fellow Italian with a son in Vietnam. But the case of Capt.

Robert Marasco had now gone well beyond a simple constituent service. It was on the front page of the *New York Times*. That might be bad for Marasco, but it held interesting possibilities for Rodino. Depending, of course, on how things turned out.

Newark had changed a lot since 1948 when Rodino, a World War II veteran who had gone to Seton Hall Law on the GI Bill, was first elected. Then it was a thriving city of nearly a half million people, the financial and manufacturing center of northern New Jersey. The immigrants who had passed through Ellis Island on their way to Newark were prospering. The pollution was so thick on some days that the skyscrapers of Manhattan, only eight miles away, were blotted out in a brown haze; but to the city's working people, the smog had the smell of money.

Rodino set up a small practice in the North Ward, home of the city's tightly knit Italian community. His first run for Congress was a cake walk, and he returned to Congress ten times more over the next two decades, a feisty, outspoken liberal in the mold of John Kennedy and Lyndon Johnson.

But slowly, the political ground began to crack beneath Rodino. Manufacturing jobs were evaporating. Whites were moving to the suburbs. Blacks, who had just begun to make inroads with jobs and housing, were hit particularly hard by the recession. With unemployment came crime and drugs, along with radicals seeking to turn Newark into a laboratory for revolution. The city simmered with racial tension. When Leroi Jones announced plans for a Black Muslim community center in the heart of the Italian North Ward, the whites left behind reacted with anger, then hate, then violence. Vigilante groups were formed. The city was out of control.

Rodino had been the floor manager of the 1965 civil rights bill in the House of Representatives, but his laurels had turned into an albatross. Faced with the growing repudiation of all his liberal ideals back home, and with the Nixon administration fanning white resentment of school integration, Rodino began to avoid the painful trips back home. A strong challenge, possibly even defeat, faced him in 1970. Suddenly, however, the Marasco case offered an opportunity to recoup.

It hadn't started out that way. After he received the letters from Frank Marasco, Rodino had quietly asked the Army for an explanation—a routine kind of service for a constituent. He was still waiting for an answer when the case surfaced on August 5. Then came that South Carolina lawyer's pyrotechnics in Saigon, which publicly dragged the CIA into the case. Now, what had started out as a delicate errand on behalf of a constituent had erupted into a national sensation.

Rodino wasn't eager to take on the Army or the CIA, but he had taken some discreet soundings in his district that encouraged him to go ahead. There was a lot of bitterness against the Pentagon, he found. The patriotic people of his district had sent a lot of their sons to Vietnam who had returned in metal boxes. And for that they blamed the politicians and generals, not for fighting an immoral and unwinnable war, as the protesters had it, but for being too chickenshit to go all out and end it. Putting any one of their neighbors on trial for killing a Viet Cong would be too much.

Rodino called a staff meeting. They were getting out front on the Marasco case, he said.

Jerry Zeifman, a lawyer for the House Judiciary Committee, sat in his small office on Capitol Hill, thumbing through the folder of newspaper clippings and his boss's correspondence regarding Capt. Robert Marasco.

Zeifman felt very fortunate. A few days before he had been toiling on state tax codes for a minor House subcommittee headed by Peter Rodino. Then the Green Beret case burst into the news. Rodino's administrative assistant had apparently remembered Zeifman's background as a public defender in the Bronx, and had drafted him to work on the case.

Zeifman studied Captain Marasco's letter, sifting for clues to the origin of the Army's baffling prosecution.

"We went through all the channels," Marasco had written, "including civilian intelligence agencies." Zeifman checked the newspaper clips. The lawyer Gregory had tied the victim of the case to the CIA. Zeifman went back to Marasco's letter.

"For some unknown reason," he had written, "the generals are pressing this thing."

Zeifman thought for a minute, then picked up the telephone. A while back, he had met a CIA man in the agency's congressional liaison office. Maybe that man could make more sense of it.

Zeifman had come to respect the agency people; a close friend worked for the CIA, and Zeifman had met other CIA men during a congressional junket overseas. Compared to the tepid diplomats and self-seeking military attachés, he thought, they were often the most impressive people in the embassy, a credit to the federal government. He expected a straighter answer from the CIA than he'd gotten at the Pentagon, where his Army contacts professed to know nothing.

The CIA officer quickly agreed to visit on the understanding that the meeting would be off the record. No problem, Zeifman said. It meant no notes would be taken, no attribution given later. In exchange, he would be "backgrounded" on what the case was all about from the CIA's perspective. In Washington parlance, it would be a meeting "that did not exist."

Settling into a chair in Zeifman's office a few hours later, the CIA man cautioned that he could not, of course, comment on the case in any official capacity. He would just give the Zeifman a few thoughts off the top of his head.

Understood, Zeifman said. What's it all about?

The Green Berets were involved in covert activities on the Cambodian border, the CIA man said. Very sensitive stuff.

Zeifman nodded. So why was the Army prosecuting them? he asked. Why risk exposing the operations, making them an object of attention?

The CIA man began cautiously. "General Abrams," he explained, "is an old-line, World War Two tank commander. He doesn't have any understanding of the exigencies of modern warfare."

Zeifman listened.

Like a lot of generals of his era, the CIA man continued, General Abrams didn't appreciate the "other side" of the war in Vietnam. It was the first pure guerrilla war the United States had fought. The methods were different—had to be. But he didn't understand that.

This kind of war also required the close cooperation of the Green Berets and the CIA, he went on, which Abrams and his ilk also resented, because it meant they didn't have control over everything. The Green Berets were involved with operations with the CIA in Cambodia, and Abrams didn't like it.

Zeifman listened closely. Here was the inside spin, the bureaucratic politics that he had always suspected were driving the case. But the CIA man wasn't through.

General Abrams, he continued, lowering his voice, was also suffering from some . . . "problems." Those . . . "problems," unfortunately, had influenced his handling of the affair.

"Problems?" Zeifman asked.

"Severe psychological problems," the CIA man said, "apparently something to do with some kind of religious crisis. You know, of course, that the general was converting to Roman Catholicism?"

Zeifman pulled back. Abrams was off his rocker? A religious nut?

The CIA man's eyes were full of pity.

Zeifman sat wordless for a moment, assessing what was going on. He looked back at his visitor, figuring it out. Finally, it came to him: He had just been flashed a green light to attack the sanity of the commander of U.S. forces in Vietnam. By the CIA.

Jesus, Zeifman thought, this is like the Bronx. The knives are out. As soon as the CIA man left, he called Rodino's secretary for an appointment with the boss.

Carl Albert had represented the southern district of Oklahoma since 1946. A tiny man who carried himself with the vacant optimism of a small-town haberdasher, Albert was a product of the "get along, go along" school of congressional seniority, the second-ranking Democrat in the House, soon to become Speaker. But the long wait had only made him more cautious. He had become a congressional timepiece.

On Vietnam, Albert was an "Okie from Muskogee" attuned to the prairie patriotism of the oil-patch roughnecks and dirt farmers of southern Oklahoma. He had always been an open cash register for the Pentagon's new weapons, but when Karen Brumley pleaded for help, there was no question of what he would do. Constituents, after all, were what got him elected. The Army didn't have a single vote at election time.

On August 15, the tiny congressman joined with Peter Rodino in demanding the release of Lee Brumley and his comrades from solitary confinement.

Oklahoma's two senators, Fred Harris and Henry Bellmon, quickly followed. And they, too, had questions about the Army's policies on handling double agents.

Congressional delegations from the other states of the accused men quickly fell in line, from Massachusetts to Maryland, Georgia, Florida, Iowa, and South Carolina. Considering the divergence of ideology on Vietnam among them, the unity of the antiarmy coalition was remarkable. Sen. Edward Kennedy released a letter to Defense Secretary Melvin Laird saying that "whatever may be the charges against these men, they are entitled to humane treatment under our concept of our democratic system of government."

Far more threatening to the Army, however, was the mobilization of Rep. Mendel Rivers, the silver-haired chairman of the House Armed Services Committee. Rivers had a well-known fondness for bourbon and could often be found tottering about the halls of Congress with a policeman trailing behind to catch the ashes from his smoldering cigar. But he also controlled the purse strings of the entire Defense Department. Although he seldom saw a weapon system he didn't like or a military base that couldn't be built, especially in South Carolina, confronted with a choice between soldiers and the generals, Rivers usually chose the soldiers. Faced with the pleas of his constituent's wife, Mrs. Tommy Middleton, it was no contest.

"Simple justice requires that these persons who are under investigation should be released in order to prepare their defense," he wrote Laird formally. Quietly, he let it be known his artillery would be raised if he didn't get quick answers to his questions.

South Carolina's other Democrat and promilitary stalwart, Sen. Ernest Hollings, also chastised Laird but went beyond the demand for the men's pretrial freedom. "These were soldiers who were doing a job that had to be done," he said in a press release, adding that he had information about the case that had not been made public, but "I am not at liberty to divulge it."

That was going too far for Jerry Zeifman, who thought it was important to stay away from the particulars of the case. At the end of the week, he convened a meeting of senior aides to congressmen who had been activated by the desperate families of the accused Green Berets.

Stick to procedural issues for now, he urged, stay away from the guilt or innocence of the men, a murky issue at best in intelligence operations. The first item to focus on was the Army's "inhumane" treatment of the men in solitary. That will paint the Army right away as bogeymen, inherently predisposed against the accused men.

That established, we can begin to agitate for moving the case out of Saigon, Zeifman urged, taking it out of Abrams's tainted hands. Widening the issues to what the Green Berets were accused of doing, and whether it was justified, he said, would muddy the waters.

Confine your attacks to Abrams and Resor, he advised, which would allow Defense Secretary Melvin Laird, a former Wisconsin congressman attuned to the political winds, to step in and "save the day."

The important thing was to nip the case in the bud, before it went to trial.

At the end of the meeting, they decided to put together an ad hoc Green

Beret caucus that would include the staffs of a dozen congressmen from eight states. A similar group of sixteen senators was forming on the other side of the Hill, liberals and conservatives, hawks and doves.

Walking back to his office, Zeifman was amused when he thought about it. He could never have imagined the staffs of Ted Kennedy and Mendel Rivers agreeing on anything about Vietnam.

The fragile coalition couldn't last for long, he knew. After all, what had they really agreed on except to sidestep the facts, shift the blame and hope the case would go away?

My God, he thought, it was like the war itself.

Nan Rheault might have called Ted Kennedy, but, as she acidly observed, he was tied up with other matters. That's why there was such a large crowd of reporters on Martha's Vineyard to pester her. As soon as they left, she took down the Rheault family sign on the wooden fence out front.

Nan Rheault was accustomed to privacy as the daughter of a wealthy New York investor. She had been raised on estates on Long Island and Connecticut and educated at the Chapin School and Vassar. Her father did not quite approve of her marrying a military man. Nor did Bob's father approve of her as an Episcopalian. She was alone to deal with her crisis.

Working the telephone from the gray-shingled island house late into the night, she found most of her husband's friends in Washington had turned to stone. So she turned to his closest pal, Bill Simpson, whose career had been twinned with her husband's since they graduated from West Point together in 1946. At the moment, he was in Okinawa, commanding the 1st Special Forces Group.

Simpson and Rheault had gone through infantry and airborne training together, circulated through the Army War College and staff schools in tandem, and then leapfrogged through a series of Special Forces assignments. Over the years their families had grown close, often spending part of the summers together on the Vineyard.

Simpson had been the reason Rheault joined the Green Berets, enticing him from a teaching assignment at West Point with tales of the free-swinging paramilitary group. They linked up in Germany in 1962. While Rheault played hide-and-seek with the 7th Army, Simpson roamed the Austrian frontier, putting in place war plans for guerrilla action against a Russian invasion. A few years later, when Rheault was at the Joint Chiefs of Staff, his friend was deputy commander of the 5th Special Forces, as Rheault had been. In August, when the emergency call came from Nan Rheault, Simpson threw his career to the wind and immediately left for Vietnam. Two weeks later, he arrived on Martha's Vineyard with a disturbing story.

Landing at Ton Son Nhut with his sergeant major on the pretext of an inspection tour, Simpson said, he was met by a delegation of Green Berets who told him they had tracked down their commander in a house trailer at Long Binh.

That night, he said, he slipped onto the post, talked his way past the guards, and found Rheault in the trailer. The two friends talked late into the night, Bob laying out the events of June and July, the backdrop of Chuyen's demise, the unexpected flight of Sergeant Smith. He was certain that Creighton Abrams was directing their prosecution.

Simpson didn't need to be persuaded of Abrams's visceral feelings for the Green Berets, nor did he need to elaborate on them to Nan Rheault. Through the years they had all encountered the Army establishment's disdain. No one was worse, they agreed, than a tanker. If there was any doubt of that, Simpson related, it was dispelled by the events that followed.

He had left the trailer at midnight with the purpose of justifying his trip to Vietnam by checking into a unit up-country. The next day, the Army released the news of the arrests, and he rushed back to Long Binh.

At the runway, Simpson said, he was intercepted by two MPs and taken into custody. Without explanation, he was detained for hours. Finally, after threatening the provost marshal with an official complaint, he was freed. That night, openly challenging the Army, he visited his friend again in the trailer, this time arriving with a bottle of scotch and two steaks.

Nan Rheault smiled at the thought of the two friends drinking and reminiscing late into the night, surrounded by MPs—a typical *up yours* response. They were both classic Green Berets in the old mold, romantic outsiders.

Simpson continued his story. It wasn't over, he told Nan. He tried to see Abrams before he left Saigon, but he was shunted off to a deputy. Then an incident happened that left no doubt in his mind that Abrams had mobilized the Army to keep tight control over the case.

Convinced he was being shadowed, he had disappeared into the maze of Saigon alleys, thrown off his surveillants, and eventually made his way to a Special Forces safe house. Waiting for him by prearrangement was his sergeant major. They waited until dark before leaving the house and heading for the airport.

At Ton Son Nhut they boarded a midnight flight to Okinawa. Just as they were belting into their seats, however, a pair of MPs stormed aboard, claimed a flimsy excuse to arrest them, and took them off the plane. They spent the night under guard in a trailer. In the morning, without explanation, they were driven back to the airport and put on a flight. The message was clear: Stay out of General Abrams's backyard.

"What do we do next?" Nan Rheault asked.

"I'm going to Washington," Bill Simpson told her. He was going to see Al Haig, Henry Kissinger's deputy.

He looked her in the eye. "You'd better get a lawyer."

"When Bob Rheault was born," the account by Bob DiOrio in the *Boston Herald* began, "his name was entered in the Boston social register.

"Now it's also on the register of the Long Binh stockade."

Tracing the well-born defendant's family tree, DiOrio found a classmate of Rheault's from Phillips Exeter Academy. "He was a very straight-laced sort of guy who played it right," the classmate recalled. "A top-drawer guy from the right side of the tracks."

"Now," DiOrio cracked, "the bright military career of the 'top drawer guy from the right side of the tracks' is in danger of being derailed."

More than a bright career now—the charge was murder one, a capital crime.

Bob Rheault had brushed off his wife's queries about hiring a lawyer. If everybody would just keep quiet, he insisted, the thing would go away. The letters flew back and forth. *Give Abrams room to maneuver*, Rheault said. *He'll soon feel the heat. Everything's under control. My Army lawyer is fine.*

Nonsense, his brother Charles argued, this was a murder case, a homicide, for God's sake. He could be executed for that. It was indeed serious. Charles, an executive with the printing division of Houghton Mifflin, was the only businessman in the family.

Bob's other brother André agreed. He had spent time with the CIA, including a tour of Vietnam in the 1950s. He had "hung up his star," as he put it, to pursue a passion for collecting antique cars, and he had even carted up and brought home an ancient Bugatti from Vietnam. The old CIA gang had a sense of humor, André thought, but the war had brought in a new group of guys. The waters were treacherous, swimming with sharks. Bob should have a civilian lawyer, the best.

On a bright blue day in mid-August, Nan and Charles flew to Nantucket. They were going to meet Edward Bennett Williams.

The criminal lawyer's barrel chest, wavy hair, and cunning smile were instantly familiar. Williams was not only a world famous trial attorney, he was a classic Washington insider—private adviser to Presidents John Kennedy and Lyndon Johnson, a pal to political columnists and sportswriters, part owner of the Washington Redskins. His clients included Teamsters Union leader Jimmy Hoffa, New York Mafia don Frank Costello, and Joseph McCarthy, the Communist-hunting senator from Wisconsin. "We wanted to be a very powerful firm," a partner said, "for people in deep, deep trouble."

A Williams defense meant a "scorched earth policy," he once said. Every case was "a contest of living. You're either churning up earth or you're standing still." Williams's rages were legendary; his secretary kept a "mood meter" at her desk in the red brick building a block from the White House.

Williams's entry into any case had "a ripple effect," a U.S. senator once remarked. His reputation was no doubt enhanced by being the *Washington Post*'s lawyer and a close friend of its executive editor, Benjamin C. Bradlee.

Charles Rheault figured that hiring Williams would balance the scales against the Army and the CIA. He would give the case "marquee value." The government would hear the heavy artillery being drawn forward and back off.

Williams led Charles and Nan Rheault to a table on his backyard patio. The sloping green lawn gave way to a sparkling blue vista of Nantucket Sound. Polite sandwiches and iced tea were served.

He had three simple rules when he took on a case, he said: that his clients give him total control, that they tell him the truth, and that they pay him his fee. He bit into a sandwich and smiled.

"You know that he's guilty as hell, right?" Williams said. He had already made a few calls.

Nan Rheault was stunned. Later, all she could remember asking was how much it was going to cost.

A hundred dollars an hour, Williams said, still smiling. And expenses, of course. He'd have to go to Saigon.

The mood of the Green Berets plummeted. In the dim corridor of the stockade, they passed around newspaper clips of George Gregory's latest press conference, groaning with every wild accusation. Now even congressmen were making speeches.

Their strategy was shot. They had planned on keeping things quiet, allowing time for the transcripts of the Article 32 hearings to percolate upward to the Pentagon and for General Abrams to be reined in. But George Gregory had destroyed any chance of that with his flamboyant nightly press conferences. One day, embarrassed by his dramatic depiction of the stockade conditions, they had apologized as a group to its commander. The jail was bad, they said, but not *that* bad. They were tough; they could take it.

Bob Marasco complained about Gregory in a letter to his parents on August 12, blaming the South Carolinian for their unwanted fame. "He's hurting us with his big mouth and publicity-seeking. We are trying to shut him up. I'm afraid he wants the personal publicity."

From a routine execution in a small boat off Nha Trang, "The Mysterious Case of the Green Berets" had mushroomed into an international sensation, splashed on magazine covers from New York to West Berlin. Hundreds of reporters were flying into Saigon for a courtroom showdown and an anticipated peek into "the war in the shadows." The Green Berets now grimly accepted the prospect of a long, drawn-out battle in which their acquittal was not assured.

Steve Berry surveyed the smoldering wreckage of his strategy and decided it was time to break the glass on the fire alarm. In only a week, the Article 32 hearings would resume under a cloud of disturbing recent developments.

Bob Rheault had told him that his wife had hired Edward Bennett Williams over his objections; despite the colonel's assurances that no deal would be cut, Berry took it as an unsettling sign. The unity of the defendants was threatened, putting his own client and the other two captains in deep legal water. If Rheault, Crew, or Middleton defected, the others were red meat.

A few years earlier, Berry had met Henry Rothblatt at a legal convention. Tall and thin, with his pencil mustache, beady black eyes, and characteristic bow tie, Rothblatt was a well-known New York criminal lawyer. A graduate of Brooklyn Law School and a professor at NYU, Rothblatt had cut his legal teeth in the Bronx County courthouse. He was also chairman of the criminal law section of the American Trial Lawyers Association and the author of such nuts-and-bolts books as *The Complete Manual of Criminal Forms* and *Defending Business and White Collar Crimes*.

Berry wrote to Rothblatt and asked him to represent three of the Green Berets—Boyle, Crew, and Brumley—"with no possibility of ever receiving a fee."

"This case will be unique in legal history, Mr. Rothblatt," Berry promised, hoping to pique the lawyer's interest, "and I promise you that if you do come, your skills and talents will be taxed to their utmost."

Berry stuffed the letter in an envelope and wrote "privileged and confidential" on the outside. Then he signed his name across the flap. After that he covered his signature with Scotch tape. Maybe he was being foolish, maybe not. There had been a lot of strange things happening with their mail. Most of it had been opened.

45

From his spacious austere office on the second floor of the Pentagon, Stanley Resor could crane his neck and see Arlington National Cemetery in the far distance. Rows of bone-white headstones filled the grassy hillside. Nearly every day in the summer of 1969, caissons carrying the caskets of soldiers killed in Vietnam arrived there, winding mutely through the shady paths.

The secretary of the Army was unavoidably moved by the grim processions. Most were his responsibility, after all. He was third in the Army's civilian chain of command, below the president and the secretary of defense; his black-and-white picture hung in countless Army mess halls, and every recruit had to memorize his name.

With his degrees from Groton and Yale, his Pillsbury flour heiress wife, and long service with an old-shoe Wall Street firm, Stanley Resor seemed like a typically Republican presidential appointment. His close-cropped gray hair and reserved manner reinforced the image of a wealthy New York lawyer taking a political fling in Washington.

Most of those assumptions were wrong. Resor, a liberal Republican, had been brought to Washington by Lyndon Johnson, whose administration was looking for bipartisan support for the war. But unlike many presidential appointees to the office over the years, he took his job seriously, avoiding the weapons plant ribbon cuttings and ceremonial tours of foreign bases that could keep him aloft on a constant global cocktail tour. He cared deeply about the institution—working thirteen hours a day, taking lunch at his desk, recruiting top people from law schools and the ranks, appealing to their patriotism at a time of national distress. He listened closely to his aides, keeping copious notes in an Army-issue notebook he carried in his suit pocket.

"He wasn't a wink-and-nod guy," a close aide observed. "He was always concerned about doing the right thing." Defense Secretary Melvin Laird renewed his appointment over Nixon's objections.

Resor projected a kind of fastidious rectitude that hid his close regard for the troops. Few knew that he had won Bronze and Silver Stars at the Battle of the Bulge. Surrounded by Nazis at Bastogne with the 10th Armored Division, along with his contemporary Major George Mabry and a certain Private Kenneth Facey, Resor had been rescued by the tanks of a young jut-jawed officer named Creighton Abrams. Twenty-five years later, they were bound by the shared values of an earlier time, men of a certain age.

Resor had been planning an inspection tour of Vietnam for some time, but the Green Beret case gave the trip a new urgency. Congressional brickbats were already hitting him from every direction, demanding he take over the case. The second phase of the Article 32 hearings would be convening in a few days, Resor had learned, and he wanted to talk to Creighton Abrams about the case before letting it go on much longer.

He had not been sitting on his hands. Given the extraordinary publicity the case was generating, he had sent two of his lawyers ahead to look into the facts. Everything was in order, they reported back. They had also consulted with the head of the Justice Department's Criminal Division, Assistant Attorney General William Wilson, who had reviewed national security precedents and given a green light to the prosecution. Creighton Abrams, Resor felt confident, would not go off on a witch-hunt, but he wanted to see for himself.

As Resor was packing his briefcase on August 17, Melvin Laird strolled into his Pentagon office. The defense secretary was not really one of the president's men, although his was certainly a political appointment. For starters, his beady eyes seemed surgically augmented with a perpetual twinkle, setting him apart from Nixon's apparently humorless aides John Ehrlichman and H. R. "Bob" Haldeman. Compared to them, Laird was an elf. He was a creature of Congress, a Washington insider, a genial deal maker and moderate Republican who had represented Wisconsin in the House of Representatives for 18 years. Laird liked politics, which he played like a contact sport. But to Nixon's men, politics was an extension of war.

Which was exactly why Nixon made him his secretary of defense, posting him like a radio tower on the far foothills of the administration where he could broadcast signals of the administration's intent to wind down the war in Vietnam.

Laird was amused by the unfolding Green Beret affair, insofar as he could imagine Nixon glowering at CIA Director Richard Helms and demanding to know how the CIA could botch the execution of one Vietnamese spy. Neither he nor Nixon had been fans of the aloof, socially connected Helms, and Laird knew Nixon had ambitious plans for the U.S. intelligence community.

Still, Laird was worried that the emerging fuss would soon muddy the Nixon administration's boots on Vietnam. Laird hadn't been talked out of a safe seat in Congress to look out his Pentagon windows at another war protester dousing himself with gasoline. He wanted the United States out, and he believed Nixon and Kissinger did, too.

Laird noted, however, that some reporters on the Green Beret story were beginning to ask questions about CIA activities in Laos, Cambodia, and Thailand. The dangerous subject of assassination was in the wind. Before long, the Green Beret case could become their albatross, weighing them down with Democratic-era misdeeds.

All the secrecy was unnecessary, Laird thought. Why not get out front of the thing and just lay out the facts? The American people would understand. The secrecy was just fueling the press. After years on the Hill, he knew how they worked.

He felt the same way about the bombing of Cambodia. Why keep it a secret? The eastern part of Cambodia had been occupied by the North Vietnamese Army for years. By trying to keep secrets, Laird thought, you risked a cataclysm when they inevitably leaked. The secrecy became the issue, instead of the war.

"What's your game plan?" Laird casually asked Resor. His convivial style caught the Connecticut Yankee off guard. The question momentarily confused him. He had never heard the term "game plan" used like that before.

"You know, with the Green Beret thing," Laird prompted.

"Oh, just to talk to Abrams," Resor said.

Laird waited for him to continue, and Resor recognized the silence.

"I have an open mind about it," Resor said. "I'll get the facts from him and then make my recommendation." General Westmoreland, he added, had persuaded him to have the accused men moved from solitary confinement to less harsh quarters. Otherwise he had kept hands off, he said. He trusted Abe's judgment.

"Fine," Laird said. Abrams was a hell of a good man, he added, and he meant it. If there was any general who could manage to get the troops out of Vietnam with a minimum of problems, it was Abrams.

Laird wished Resor a good trip and left. For now, he thought it was enough to let Resor know he was concerned that the Army's handling of the case not go from bad to worse. The press was giving them a beating. "An informational Dienbienphu," Washington Post Pentagon correspondent George Wilson had just called it.

Stanley Resor's military jet lifted off from Andrews Air Force Base outside of Washington on August 18, the first leg of a twenty-four-hour, thirteen-thousand-mile flight to Saigon. High over the Pacific, Resor reviewed a draft statement on the Green Beret case prepared by his legal aides, Stephen Sachs and Robert Comeau. Despite the intense public pressure, the young lawyers advised, Resor should resist the temptation to release any details on the case. They offered a draft statement for Resor to read when he deplaned in Saigon.

"While the Army would like to explain the basis for its actions," it read, "we have an obligation to insure that the rights of the eight individuals to a fair trial are fully protected. Therefore, despite the public's great interest, we cannot comment additionally on the case at this time."

Resor was mobbed by reporters when he touched down in Saigon and decided to repeat the statement verbatim at Ton Son Nhut before motoring off to see Abrams. Then he disappeared into a waiting limousine, leaving behind a press corps shaking its collective head over the Army's continuing public relations debacle.

Creighton Abrams was waiting for Stanley Resor at the door of his bungalow. The motorcade pulled in, and the general greeted his old friend with a wrinkled smile. Classical music boomed from his study as he led him through the doors. An immense security contingent was posted around the grounds.

Abrams knew what was on Resor's mind beyond the combat situation. He had the CID reports of Frank Bourland and Bob Bidwell waiting in his study for Resor to read. If the Department of the Army was going to take the case away from him, he wanted Resor to see the raw reports.

The Army secretary had already brushed off the scuttlebutt that Abrams was "anti–Special Forces," carrying on a vendetta against the Green Berets. Privately, even other influential Special Forces alumni had begun to agree. One of them, Jonathan Ladd, had commanded the 5th Special Forces in 1965 and had been invited by Abrams to look at the file. As a result, Ladd became Abrams's most influential booster around the water coolers of the Pentagon.

It was true, Ladd conceded, that Creighton Abrams didn't have the same interest in Green Beret operations that Westmoreland did. But he deeply appreciated their valor.

Abrams visited him often in Nha Trang, Ladd said. "He'd take a shower, sit in his underwear and get three or four martinis in him. He'd play with my German shepherd—the dog loved to chase beer cans—then he'd have coffee. He just wanted to sit and chew the fat once every two or three months."

One thing that did perplex Abrams about the Special Forces, though, was their fetish about uniforms: the berets, the pants tucked into jump boots, the black-and-yellow "tiger" fatigues some of them wore. Their need to be different annoyed him. He thought it was an affectation, not wholly masculine.

Underlying Abrams's uneasiness about some Green Berets, Ladd felt, was a conviction that they didn't really want to be in the same Army. And for that, he had no patience. There was only one Army in Vietnam, Abrams said, and he was running it.

That's where Rheault went wrong, Ladd thought. Abrams went after Rheault because he had been lied to. "He blew his stack. He said, 'Get that whole goddamned lot of people and bring them down here to Long Binh and lock them up.' "

Why Rheault even bothered to get involved with the problems of B-57 perplexed Ladd: As far as he knew, it wasn't under the command of the 5th Special Forces Group.

On the night of August 18, Resor and Abrams sat together on his couch, quietly reading the statements of Smith, Marasco, Brumley, Williams, and Boyle. They reviewed Rheault's handwritten denials. Any reservations Resor once held about Abrams's handling of the case peeled away with each page. The right to prosecute the men now seemed clear.

"When I read those statements about killing this man," Resor remembered later, "it seemed to me unnecessary." From his perspective at the top of the Pentagon, he concluded, "there was no threat of being hurt by him."

Abrams defended himself. After the statements were taken by the CID, he said he had acted on the advice of his legal officer. With the admission of the killing, he was doing the only thing he could under the circumstances. On the face of it, it was murder. They had executed a prisoner of war. If the press was howling now, imagine what they'd say if he let them go!

Resor quietly agreed. There was nothing else Abrams could do.

As to the CIA's role in the affair, Abrams mumbled an expletive, took a puff on his cigar, and stared straight into his courtly visitor's eyes. Resor got the message: *Fuck 'em.*

Resor's inspection trip required making the rounds of the Army commands. On his second night in Vietnam, he was having dinner at II Field Force headquarters near Saigon when an aide whispered in his ear. A Mr. Shackley of the CIA was outside, the aide said. He would like a word.

Resor hid his surprise, excused himself from his dining companions, Gen. Michael Davison and Deputy Ambassador Charles Whitehouse, and stepped outside.

He saw the man waiting in the light. They shook hands and then walked a few steps away into the shadows. Shackley rushed through the preliminaries in a low voice, then got to the subject of his nighttime visit.

Richard Helms, he said, was very disturbed about the ongoing press coverage implicating the CIA in the Green Beret affair. He would appreciate it if the Army could issue a statement "clarifying" the situation. The CIA, Shackley said, did not of course "order" any murder.

Resor assessed the tough CIA man. His eyes were unreadable behind his thick glasses. Taking quick measure of Shackley, Resor wondered why the head of the CIA station had come all the way to Bien Hoa at night to make such an unusual request. *Strange.* Why would Richard Helms ask his station chief to lobby him in this fashion? Helms must be having problems in Washington, he concluded, getting the White House and Laird on his side. The CIA was obviously being pinched by stories that it had given the Green Berets advice on killing Chuyen, and no one had stepped forward to bail the CIA out.

Too bad. Resor couldn't possibly clear the CIA before the case got to trial. The facts were too murky.

"I think that it would be unwise," Resor said. "There is conflicting testimony, you know, between your agents and the two Special Forces officers who met with them before the killing."

Shackley's face twitched with the rebuff.

"I'm awfully sorry," Resor said, and bid Shackley good night. The CIA man slipped off into the darkness as quietly and oddly as he had arrived.

＊　　＊　　＊

Henry Rothblatt settled into a chair in his suite at the Caravelle Hotel, drink in hand, his bow tie neatly fixed under his pointed chin. Reporters gathered around.

"I am here to inject reason on *both* sides of the issue," he said. A palpable sigh of relief swept the room. They had noted the lawbooks that had been unpacked and put on the shelves. Several were criminal law primers Rothblatt had coauthored with F. Lee Bailey, another high-profile defense attorney.

The reporters scribbled quietly. Here, finally, was a voice of moderation. The week with George Gregory had been wild, crazy, a roller-coaster ride.

In the far corner, Steve Berry watched Rothblatt smoothly stroke the press. He beamed and turned to his legal sidekicks Marty Linsky and Bill Hart. "This guy," he whispered, "is pure velvet."

Berry hoped there was enough time left to hammer down the tent flaps in the two days before the Article 32 hearings resumed. The time was past when they could beat the Army into a quiet retreat. They were in the middle of a three-ring circus now, thanks to George Gregory. Rothblatt, Berry hoped, just might be able to sit down with Mabry and his staff and talk sense, bring some rational discourse back into the case.

The reporters left impressed. A new calm seemed to have infused everyone. The young military lawyers were in awe, and Rothblatt reciprocated by showing complete calm about the case, assuring them of a satisfactory outcome. He would sit down with a few of these generals and talk sense to them. They'd work something out.

"What about Gregory?" Berry asked. "He's got to be controlled."

Rothblatt asked where Gregory was staying. Only a few floors away, the lawyers told him. Rothblatt got up and excused himself. On the way out the door, he told the lawyers to relax and enjoy the drinks and food.

A little while later, he returned. "I assure you that you'll have no more trouble from Mr. Gregory," he declared. They went off on a tour of the city.

George Gregory was at the hotel bar the next day, mocking Henry Rothblatt for a small group of reporters.

"Mis-tuh Rawth-blatt," he drawled, "has come to the wah zone, to bring ree-son into this affayuh." Gregory slapped his thighs and broke into gales of guffaws. "What a silly sumbitch! He doesn't know shit about the Army."

Gregory turned serious—he could flip in and out of the country lawyer routine as fast as a light switch. He denied the rumors that he'd been taken to the woodshed by the silky New York lawyer.

"That's bullshit," he said. He also scoffed at the news that Rothblatt had dined with a few generals the night before, that perhaps a settlement was in sight.

"Look," he said, "this is not the kind of courthouse where you can go down to the coffee shop with the DA and plea bargain your client. This is the goddamn Army, and only one general is running things here, and his name is Abrams."

He tried to explain to the reporters how a man like Abrams thought. "The general," he said, "is not interested in who I am, and he certainly doesn't give a fuck about Henry Rothblatt. The general is in the habit of running his own fucking army. And he is not going to have either a southern yahoo or a New York Jew coming in here and telling him how the fuck to do it."

Abrams wants Rheault's hide, Gregory said, and he'll do everything he can to get it.

Gregory sipped his vodka and tonic, the small group of reporters listening without comment.

Gregory knew that he had become second banana now that Rothblatt had arrived and Edward Bennett Williams was getting into the act. The reporters had taken to following Rothblatt around, hanging on his every word.

"This case is a dead cinch," Rothblatt had pronounced after a visit to Long Binh, showing, Gregory thought, some signs of stress. How was that "bringing-reason-to-both-sides"?

Rothblatt had also said, "They have no evidence. This case should be won without a trial." He predicted the men would be released "within a couple days after the investigation opens Wednesday."

Gregory scoffed at that, too. The Army has plenty of evidence, he thought. Plenty. And denying that is not the way to get these guys off. He'd planned a few fireworks for the hearings, set to resume the next day.

46

C ol. Harold D. Seaman tapped the hearing to order at 9 A.M., August 20. As in the last session, two metal fans pushed the close hot air around the sealed room. The lawyers wrung sweat off their hands and wiped their pants. George Gregory felt like he might pass out, having just come from the frigid air-conditioned JAG office, through the blinding tropical sunshine, and then back into the fetid chapel.

The first order of business, Seaman said, was the material that had been requested by the defense at the last session. The presiding officer was reading from a prepared text. The following documents will not be provided to the defense, he said. "The dossier on the North Vietnamese intelligence school . . . a listing of terminations of extreme prejudice in Laos . . . a listing of terminations of extreme prejudice in Bolivia . . ."

Henry Rothblatt sat at the defense table, thumbing through the case file like a luncheon guest about to give a speech. The Army's denial of the documents didn't surprise him. There would be opportunities later to get the message across with discovery motions and demands for depositions, if it got that far.

He calmed his restless young colleagues. The object now was to attack the government's evidence, he reminded them.

Rothblatt sat in the middle chair behind the long green table with Steve Berry, Bill Hart, and Marty Linsky around him. The defendants and the other lawyers filled out the rest of the table. Tom Middleton, looking chagrined, had been moved to the edge of the crowd to sit with his attorney.

George Gregory studied Rothblatt with wry amusement. *That silky sumbitch thought he could just whisper in the ears of a few generals and they could all go home, didn't he? They'd all have some wine and they'd throw up their hands and say, "Okay, you win." But here you are, sittin' here sweating' with the rest of us in the Long Binh Chapel.*

From across the room, Roger Nixt, the government prosecutor, unhappily contemplated another session of the hearings. Privately, he had confided to his colleagues that he had little heart for the case. It seemed so picayune compared to what was going on in the war. U.S. forces were launching a stepped-up campaign against Viet Cong strongholds in populated areas. Under the command of General Abrams, battalion-size operations had increased nearly fifty percent in the past ten months. Some of the results were predictable. In the Mekong Delta province of Kien Hoa, unrestricted shelling and bombing had caused the death or forced relocation of thousands of peasants. At least five thousand civilians had been killed in the effort to "pacify" Kien Hoa, Kevin Buckley reported in *Newsweek*. From the perspective of the Long Binh Chapel, the case of Thai Khac Chuyen seemed like an empty, cynical exercise.

At 9:30, Nixt called his first witness, Sgt. James Parris. The Special Forces radio operator was sullen and hostile as he took the witness chair. Under Nixt's prompting, he could remember only that he had seen "something put on the truck" on the night of June 20.

"I think his name was Chuyen. I am not sure," Parris said.

Steve Berry took the first, bloodying swipe at the obviously reluctant prosecution witness.

"You are not certain, are you, that it was a person on that litter?"

"It could have been a duffel bag, couldn't it?"

Parris hunched his shoulders. "I don't remember."

Berry: "It could've been any number of things . . ."

Parris: "Right."

Berry turned the witness over to the new leader of the defense team.

Setting down the transcript of the first hearings, Rothblatt rose and deftly finished off the NCO. He suggested that it was the detectives who had put Chuyen's name in his mouth. Until then he didn't really know who it was, did he?

"Let me put it this way. You were approached. They said, 'We are investigating the disappearance of this person, Chuyen,' or whatever name they used. Is that correct? They introduced the name to you?"

"That is true," Parris agreed, suddenly brightening. "I didn't know this person . . ."

"Thank you, Sergeant Parris. Nothing further."

Rothblatt handed the witness back to the government. Both sides had hardly worked up a sweat over the skirmish.

Seaman began to read from a document, but the whack-whack-whack of an approaching helicopter soon drowned him out. It was apparently landing right outside. Then, just as quickly, the noise began to subside. With a whistle, the engine spooled down and fell silent. There was a commotion, and then the door opened. It was Harold Chipman, a gun belt and holster strapped to his thick waist.

The appearance of the witness, Colonel Seaman announced evenly, had been approved "by the appropriate authorities in Washington." His testimony, he said, "shall be confined to the limited area of what transpired in contacts with defendants concerning the Chuyen case."

Seaman proffered a memorandum for the inspection of the defense. It was signed by Theodore Shackley, "Special Assistant to the Ambassador, Embassy of the United States of America, Saigon."

Steve Berry scanned the document and immediately stood up to enter a protest.

"He may state his immunity and refuse to answer," Berry said, gesturing at Chipman, "but we don't intend by proceeding at this time to waive any of our earlier statements." He stopped to gather his thoughts and continued.

"The government has its choice between either opening up this entire operation—customs of warfare, the manner in which this war is being fought, and the entire flow of circumstances surrounding this alleged event," he said, "or dismissing the charges.

"We don't intend to waive any of this, sir, but we are willing to proceed at this time." He took his seat.

Seaman merely nodded. "I call Harold Chipman."

The CIA officer lumbered to the witness chair. A few strands of thin yellow hair fell on the sides of his glistening forehead. He raised his palm, took an oath to tell the truth, and sat down.

The accused soldiers stared at the witness. Chipman was not the key CIA player in the case. He was important, but they really wanted Enking and Scrymgeour, the godfathers of the alleged crime. Both had vanished to the States.

The steel fans pushed the fetid air around the tiny room. Henry Rothblatt gathered his papers. Before Seaman could ask a question, Chipman made a request. "I would like to read a chronology of my contacts with Special Forces and my knowledge of this case," he said, gesturing to the presiding officer with a handful of index cards, "in order to put this in the proper perspective, if this is agreeable. Then you can all ask questions."

Seaman and the defense counsel, surprised, agreed.

*   *   *

Chipman spoke for nearly an hour. The CIA agent told a story that was sharply at odds with the version Crew and Brumley had relayed back to their comrades during the week of Chuyen's interrogation. In his version, the Green Berets were bumbling amateurs who had been warned and warned again not to take Chuyen's life. His concern for their problem with Chuyen, he emphasized, was personal and informal: "As far as intelligence operations are concerned, we have neither control nor command over what Special Forces does."

The events began on June 17. "I recall that Major Crew and Captain Brumley brought some papers in with them," Chipman said of their first meeting, "and they were unable, or Major Crew was unable to answer the questions I asked. He apologized. He said, 'Well, I am relatively new; I am not read in on the case,' or, 'I am not fully familiar with the case.'"

Chipman turned to Colonel Seaman. "I didn't know whether he meant he was new with respect to knowledge of the operation or new to Vietnam. I didn't ask him."

He turned back to his index cards. "When he could not answer a question, Captain Brumley did. But frankly speaking, his answers were not satisfactory, as far as I was concerned, to make any judgment at that time if it was a double agent case."

Chipman's sarcasm grew as he recalled his efforts to help the Green Berets. The home address Brumley supplied for Chuyen, he said, was out-of-date. Chuyen's sister-in-law worked at CORDS, not the U.S. Embassy. Biographical data on his other relatives was "scanty." Even their polygraph techniques were faulty: "blips" did not translate automatically into lies, he said. Even their concern for what Chuyen could compromise was blown way out of proportion.

"Their first point was that he knew Special Forces were running unilateral operations into Cambodia using Vietnamese nationals. I said, 'Hell, that's no secret. I saw that on TV about two weeks ago.'"

That was goddam clever, Budge Williams thought. *Of course* there were "exposés" about U.S. operations in Cambodia. Who the hell did the leaking—the CIA! That was part of it, a deception to make the North Vietnamese think U.S. recon teams were everywhere while drawing the press's attention away from the real stuff, the bribery of Cambodian army officers, the plans to assassinate Sihanouk. None of the "exposés" ever revealed real names, dates, and locations—as turning loose Chuyen would have done—or what this case might do. Without names and dates, or a murder trial, though, they were one-day stories.

Goddam, Williams thought, *what a beautiful fucking frame-up. Just beautiful.*

Chipman was plunging onward.

As to Chuyen's knowledge of cover units at Muc Hoa, he had told Brumley and Crew, "Well, he has already blown them" to the Vietnamese Green Beret captain Chu. All the Green Beret concerns were melodramatic, he said—Chuyen's knowledge of their radio procedures, their targets in Cambodia, the address of a Saigon safe house, the identity of other agents in Muc Hoa, and the fact that Special Forces used polygraph exams on potential agents.

"I said, 'There are a lot of terminated Vietnamese, ex–Special Forces agents, that know that Special Forces used polygraphs on employees. This is a well-known fact.' " As for safe houses, he told Seaman, "After you take an agent there one time, you figure the thing is blown. You have a high rate of turnover for safe houses." And as for exposing other spies, well, Chuyen had stopped working before any of his subagents had been sent into Cambodia, Chipman said. Thus, technically speaking, they were recruits, not agents.

Chipman turned to Seaman. "I told them all this."

"Really," he recalled saying to Crew and Brumley, "based on what I've seen, he doesn't look like he would do you any damage. He doesn't look like a double agent at this point." Chuyen, he had concluded, was an "intelligence bum" who latched onto American spy units to stay out of the South Vietnamese draft.

One thing *had* "disturbed" him, he said—the imminent departure of Chuyen's sister-in-law for the United States. She had a scholarship at Columbia University.

"I thought, Jesus, this is bad news, because if there is any connection here, any North Vietnamese control, we had better do some investigation first, because it is not the best thing to have foreign agents in the United States." It was known that Hanoi's spy service worked closely with the Soviet KGB, he said. Until their investigation was complete, there was also a possibility that a friend of Chuyen's brother, who had also come down from North Vietnam, as well as his father, were Communist agents.

"I pointed this out. They said, 'Fine, we won't take any action.' "

Well, shit, Gregory thought, you could drive a truck through that. First he says he's not a dangerous agent—"an intelligence bum"—then he's all worked up about his sister, brother, and father. *He's worried more about Communists in New York than right here in the goddam war zone!*

The Green Berets, Chipman was going on, repeatedly inquired about sending Chuyen to a CIA-controlled island. Despite his advice, they seemed determined not to turn him loose.

"We can zap him," he recalled Brumley saying. "Take him on a one-way mission or some kind of patrol."

"I got up from my chair, and I walked to the window," Chipman recalled dramatically, making the hearing room still. "I said, 'Jesus, don't get involved in that, because that means trouble.'

"I said, 'The individual who does that is going to get caught here, just like they do in the States when they are involved in something like this.' "

Muffled expletives came from the defense table. Chipman's eyes darted to the Green Berets as he pushed on.

"I said, 'We don't get involved in that because there is no need to.' I said, 'The Soviets did some years ago and maybe some of the other services do, but we don't.' "

"You fucking liar," Budge Williams grumbled. The other defendants pushed back their chairs, twisted in their seats, shook their heads. Rothblatt, keeping his eyes on the witness, patted Brumley's elbow.

"I pointed to Captain Brumley and Major Crew," Chipman pushed on, "and I said, 'If *you* do it and *he* knows about it, sooner or later one of you is going to talk. Loyalty between people is very short. If one of you gets promoted faster, you will have a falling-out. There will be a fight. It will blow the whole thing.'

"I said, 'If an officer in our organization ever proposed such a thing, he would find himself on the next aircraft home. . . .' "

Bob Rheault snorted through his steepled hands.

"You would never," Chipman insisted, "get anybody in our organization to sign off on something like that. I said, 'It's better to let the guy go and take your lumps rather than ruin your career and yourself by some low-level type that is not worth it.' I said, 'If you handle your agents—if you select your agents correctly and handle them right—you won't have to go through this.' "

Budge Williams groaned. This was too much. The CIA's record of handling agents wasn't so hot. How about Ngo Dinh Diem and his brother? Those guys were ours until they got out of control. Then the CIA killed them off. And then what happened? Revolving cliques of corrupt generals were propped up as the Republic of Vietnam. Forty thousand American lives and billions of dollars later, all the United States had in Vietnam was a cup full of misery.

Now *that*, they thought, was a fuck-up.

Rothblatt and the other lawyers counseled them to stay quiet.

Chipman turned another index card. He related how Crew had asked him for an aircraft and either Crew or Brumley had asked him if the CIA could doctor the flight logs. Technically it wasn't a problem, he said, but it planted a doubt in his mind about their intentions. "I thought at the time, if you are going to fly the guy to Saigon, why do you need to doctor an aircraft? . . . I said, 'Don't take any action until we have got traces back from Saigon.' "

Chipman turned to Colonel Seaman as if looking for confirmation of his logic. "I said, 'Bring over what material you have. Let me study it and maybe I can come up with some recommendations.' "

Late on the nineteenth, he went on, Crew and Brumley came back with more files on Chuyen—his handwritten autobiography, dates on the opening and closing of the Muc Hoa operation, and some personal data on the suspect agent and his relatives. But even then, "the documents did not contain all the biographic data needed," Chipman said. "There were no places and dates of birth other than on Chuyen and his wife. They did give me the names of about seven relatives. It was still insufficient. For the next half hour we tried to reconstruct again how he came to Vietnam and certain points I noticed in the polygraph examination. . . ." Finally, Chipman said, he dismissed the soldiers with the promise that he would study the documents further.

"All right, I had the documents," he told the hearing room. "It was six o'clock and it was my judgment that the case did not look like a double-agent case, and Special Forces promised not to take action until I had time to look at them and get traces back from Saigon. So I studied that night from about seven to eleven o'clock and wrote about a six- or seven-page cable to Saigon outlining everything we discussed. That cable left for Saigon—left my office—on the nineteenth." He made sure to include Brumley's threat of "taking the guy on patrol," Chipman said. He requested a priority answer.

By late the next day, the twentieth, no answer had come. It was clear that time was running out.

"First Captain Brumley, then Major Crew came over" to see if Saigon had answered yet, Chipman said. When he told them no, Crew exclaimed, "Jesus, we have got to do something fast," he said. They came back again later and talked to his boss Dean Almy, who had just come back from Saigon. Almy asked them about "the possibility of turning Chuyen over to the MSS," Chipman said, and the soldiers exploded.

"I think Captain Brumley—one of the two men—said in essence, 'Jesus Christ, I thought we just went through this exercise two days ago!' " The question was again broached about a doctored aircraft. Almy flatly turned them down.

"Okay, forget it," he recalled Brumley or Crew saying. But Almy had started worrying about what the Special Forces might do, too. "You will wait for traces from Saigon?" he said Almy asked the two men. "And they said, 'Yes,' " Chipman said.

As soon as they left, Chipman got on the telephone to Saigon "to try and find out what the hell was going on down there. They said they were working on it." He urged them to hurry. Early the next morning, he tried again, without result.

Finally, at 10 A.M. on the twenty-first, Shackley's cable arrived telling him to advise the Green Berets that they should "return the agent to duty" or answer to General Abrams and Ambassador Bunker.

And that, Chipman said, was where he left it.

Henry Rothblatt leaned forward on his bony knuckles, opening the cross-examination of Harold Chipman. Chipman's dramatic account had portrayed the CIA in a flattering light, compared to the reckless, fumbling Green Berets. And it gave a rational, bureaucratic explanation for the agency's ten-day delay in answering their desperate queries. Its greatest value was in sidestepping the issue of Enking and Scrymgeour's original suggestion of executing Chuyen. Rothblatt had work to do.

"I noticed that as you were testifying, you were referring to some brief notes and what appeared to be three-by-five cards," Rothblatt said. "Is that a fair description of the cards?"

"Yes."

He waltzed around the defense table to the witness.

"May I see those cards?"

Chipman cautiously handed the stack to the lawyer.

"May I ask," Rothblatt said, "whether these are a summary of other records or reports that you made concerning your conversations and actions on this matter, this Chuyen matter, that you had concerning all of these dealings and communications with these accused officers and with your office?"

Chipman was wary. "No. On some occasions just a letter to remind me. There is no summary written."

"Was any record kept after each conference—"

"Yes, sir."

"—or of your conversations with the persons involved?"

"Yes, sir."

"I see." For the next several minutes Rothblatt led the CIA man through the dates and durations of his meetings with Crew and Brumley, as well as the record of cables from CIA headquarters in Saigon. The information would be useful for preparing discovery motions and deposition questions later on. But more importantly, Rothblatt wanted to elicit a pattern of CIA responsibility for the handling of Chuyen as demonstrated by Chipman's repeated meetings with Brumley and Crew. It was a relationship that Chipman had sought to minimize in his morning monologue.

"They came to you on the eighteenth to get the assistance and cooperation of your agency, did they not?" the courtly lawyer asked.

"True."

"And upon that request, you sent this urgent, twelve-hour-response cablegram consisting of the number of pages you described before, setting forth all the facts?"

Chipman shrugged. The Green Berets wanted an island and an airplane, that's all, he said. So he relayed their requests to Saigon by cable.

"Didn't they ask for advice on what is to be done and how do we do it?" Rothblatt pressed.

"They were open to suggestions."

"Suggestions from your agency, that had more expertise in these matters, isn't that correct?"

Chipman flicked his palms. "Possibly."

"And you asked to see their files, their polygraph examinations?"

"No." He stiffened.

"Didn't you ask for their polygraph examinations?"

"I asked for information."

"Specifically, what did you ask for?"

"I said, 'I will need additional biographic data and anything else you might have—Let me study the case.' "

"And what did they furnish you with?"

"They gave me some name traces. . . ."

Rothblatt waited for more. Chipman's mouth turned down.

"They gave me the polygraph examinations," he conceded, "and the handwritten autobiography of the agent."

"Did you indicate in your cablegram what they required, what assistance they were asking for?"

"I believe I did."

"Did they get that assistance or response to that request for assistance on the nineteenth?"

"Of course not."

"Did they get it on the twentieth?"

Chipman caught on. He dodged the question. "The assistance they requested we could not possibly provide."

"Didn't they ask for advice and guidance as to what was to be done? 'Will your agency take over?' Didn't they ask for that?"

"No."

"At no time they said, 'Will you take him?' "

"No."

"You are sure about that?"

Rothblatt slowly paced back and forth in the steamy chapel, grilling Chipman for the next half hour. Like a veteran actor in a well-practiced part, he seemed oblivious to everyone else but himself, the witness, and the hearing officer. He continued to hammer the CIA man on the urgency of the Green Berets' request and their expectations, based on Chipman's continuing consultations, of a CIA solution to their dilemma.

"You say it wasn't urgent?" Rothblatt asked. "Is that what you are telling us?"

Chipman was contemptuous. "Does it indicate it is urgent just because they don't want to hold him? I wouldn't imagine."

"Well," Rothblatt countered, "you told us this morning that there were conversations about a life being sacrificed, isn't that so? About a life being sacrificed?"

"Yes, they said that was one of the options," Chipman said. Periodically, he glanced at his watch.

"This was discussed as one of the alternatives, a life being sacrificed, isn't that right?"

"I don't know about that."

Rothblatt picked up his legal pad.

"Wasn't that your testimony this morning? You said, 'We don't go in for that; even the Russians have avoided that'—or words to that effect. Didn't you say that?"

"No."

Rothblatt stopped short. He was incredulous. He had never encountered a government official trying to deny his own testimony, at least not when it involved words taken down only moments before. That was the dodge of low-level Mafia types, wise guys playing to a courtroom full of their friends. Who did Chipman think he was? Was this the way they did things in the CIA?

"Well," the lawyer asked politely, "what did you say about that?"

Chipman snarled, "You will have to read from the record."

"Well, you tell us," Rothblatt answered.

The CIA man stared at the lawyer with contempt. "I am a voluntary witness," he said.

Rothblatt studied the man. He was clearly uncomfortable in the unfamiliar position of being closely questioned. "Well, Mr. Chipman, I assume we all have the same interest in this case. All we are interested in is the truth of what took place. Whether a person is brought here voluntarily or involuntarily, all I want to know is what happened."

It was a lawyer's standard ploy. But who knew what would happen with

Chipman? Rothblatt thought it might work. He turned to face the witness directly. "Don't you think that is a reasonable request?"

"What is the question again?" Chipman asked.

Rothblatt stood in front of him. "Wasn't a life going to be sacrificed if your information wasn't forthcoming? Didn't you consider that urgent?"

"I thought it was so outlandish, they wouldn't do something like that," Chipman said.

"Now Mr. Chipman," Rothblatt said, sensing another opening, "can you be objective? These officers have been living with this case for months. They worked very intensively on this case. They were dealing with the problem at hand, directly with the person. Do you think your judgment in a one-hour conversation was superior to theirs, with their intimate knowledge of the case?"

Through the afternoon Rothblatt continued to pummel Chipman, raking him over the events of 17–21 June, piling up evidence that the CIA man had assumed de facto jurisdiction over the defendants.

The witness was obviously unprepared. The CIA lawyers in Washington had probably been confident that Chipman would stay on the path by himself. Obviously they didn't have much experience with wide-ranging cross-examinations. Chipman probably thought he would just read his statement and leave. The CIA hadn't even bothered to send a lawyer to protect him. Amazing.

Rothblatt continued to saw away on Chipman, exposing new areas of CIA polygraph techniques, radio procedures, and the proper management of secret agents. The witness dodged and sulked, but he nearly always seemed to feel compelled to retort with an answer that fed more raw material into Rothblatt's expert maw.

"Mr. Chipman," Rothblatt asked, "doesn't this whole case reduce itself down to who made a mistake in judgment—you or they—by not getting an answer when they were seeking an answer fast?"

"That is not the issue."

"They were seeking an answer fast, weren't they?"

"Not just on traces."

"They were seeking an answer to their problem, yes or no?" Rothblatt repeated, moving closer.

"The answer wouldn't necessarily be in the traces."

"They were seeking an answer to their problem *fast*, yes or no?" "Yes."

"And you didn't give them the answer in time, did you?"

"We didn't have the answer."

Rothblatt's voice rose.

"Your agency didn't give them the answer *in time*."

Chipman appealed to Colonel Seaman. "Do I have to put up with that, Colonel?"

"Weren't you basically," Rothblatt thundered, "by your testimony this morning, trying to show that you and your agency were not at fault, but rather the fault lay with these officers?"

"No," Chipman answered, his teeth baring. "I thought I made it clear this morning. We have no command or control over the Special Forces."

Seaman pounded the questioning to a halt.

Ten thousand miles away at San Clemente, California, Richard Nixon was also thinking about Cambodia. The bombing reports suggested that the B-52 raids were not having their intended effect. The Keyhole satellites stationed in geosynchronous orbit over Southeast Asia, the U-2 spy planes flying out of Vietnam and Thailand, and the electronic intercepts of the National Security Agency told the same story: Not only was the Communist headquarters for the war in South Vietnam functioning as smoothly as ever, the bombers couldn't find it.

Nixon had vowed not to sink into the Vietnam morass as his predecessor had. Vietnam was chickenshit, he often said, compared to managing the superpower relationship with Moscow and opening a new door to China. That was one thing on which he and the antiwar protestors implicitly agreed: Despite all the blood and treasure expended in the war, Vietnam was not that important. It was a backwater, a fifth-rate rice bowl of bicycle-peddling, fish-eating peasants. Who gave a shit? Domestic politics, that's all it was, some-thing for the John Birchers and VFW to chew on. He, more than most, knew that. Vietnam had served his purpose years ago when he was a young con-servative on the make. But Russia, Europe, and now China were really im-portant, not Vietnam. That's why he was bugging out.

But the way out was through more bombing, and Cambodia. That was the only language the Communists understood. He could not keep drawing down American troops with the Communists building for another all-out assault on South Vietnam just forty miles from Saigon. The bombing had to be kept secret, along with everything else the United States was doing in Cambodia. If the bombing leaked, other things might. If the bombing unraveled, they could not threaten Hanoi with it anymore. It would be an empty pistol.

There had been a security scare in March. The *New York Times* had reported that the United States was bombing just over the border in Cambo-dia. The story missed the full extent of the raids, as well as the deeper impli-cations of the secret operations—that the White House had taken control of nuclear-capable strategic bombers.

The White House came down hard on the story, denying it in the strongest possible terms. Off the record, officials ridiculed it and cast aspersions on the capabilities of its author, Pentagon correspondent William Beecher. To the mild surprise of the White House, the rest of the press corps failed to follow the story up, confirming the Nixon men's view that most reporters were lazy slugs more interested in the respect of their peers than going out on a limb with a scoop. They also knew they had tightly compartmentalized the bombing with threats of a ruined career to anybody who leaked.

But the story was enough to send tremors through Nixon and Kissinger, who scrambled to find the leaker. In April they had the FBI put wiretaps on the telephones of several officials in the National Security Council and the Pentagon, including Defense Secretary Laird's aide, Col. Bob Pursley.

Cambodia had to be protected at all costs—

Which is exactly what the Green Berets had thought all along. Wasn't that why there was a big red Secret sign on the wall of the Long Binh Chapel?

In mid-afternoon, Steve Berry rose to examine Harold Chipman on the importance of U.S.-only espionage operations in Cambodia.

"Can you educate me a little bit?" Berry asked, hunching up his fatigue pants with sweaty palms. "Just what happens when a unilateral net is compromised? What does that mean exactly?"

"They are blown," Chipman answered.

Berry considered the words. "They are blown," he echoed.

"Friendly forces to enemy forces," Chipman continued. "In other words, it could mean it had come to the attention of the newspapers, or conversely, it had been compromised intentionally to friendly forces, or to enemy forces."

"So," Berry said, pacing the room, "would it be a fair statement to say that a compromise of a net can cost the lives of Americans and friendly Vietnamese?"

Chipman curtly nodded.

"And this Chuyen, this Vietnamese in question, was the man who was responsible for that, is that correct, sir?"

"Yes."

"And this was a unilateral net, an American intelligence net not operated with the cooperation of the Vietnamese, correct?"

"Right."

"Also, sir, there is the question, is there not, of some international delicacy, isn't there?"

"Yes."

"So when these nets are blown, would it be safe to say it is bad, not only from the standpoint of the GIs or the allies who are killed, but also bad from the standpoint of international relations with the government of Vietnam?"

"It is possible," Chipman said. "It depends on how fast it is blown." He was tiring of the tutorial.

"So," Berry said, turning his bulk toward the witness, "potentially, it has two forms of harmfulness, let's say. Tactical and diplomatic?"

"It is possible."

"Is it correct to say you felt their only alternative was to turn him over to the Vietnamese if he turned out to be a double agent?"

Chipman sighed. "The one alternative I did have—the only alternative I had was, I said, 'Based on what we've got here today, turn him loose.' "

Berry's eyes flashed. "At any time during the discussions, was it ever mentioned that if this man is loose and he talks, if he tells on us, if he exposes nets, Americans might be killed and Vietnamese might be killed? Did this general area of conversation ever come up?"

"No."

"It did not?" the lawyer asked, incredulous. He turned and picked up his legal pad, then faced Chipman again. "Sir, you stated under oath this morning, 'We don't assassinate.' Does this imply that the CIA does not assassinate?"

"Yes."

Berry's arms were akimbo, sweat drenching the sides of his wrinkled green fatigue shirt. He towered over the witness.

"And you will state under oath then, sir, that the concept of assassination, of rubbing people out, is something that is never practiced by the CIA, is that correct?"

"That's right," Chipman declared.

George Gregory had been studying Harold Chipman all day, occasionally taking a note, most of the time just sitting back with his legs stretched under the table, hands locked behind his head.

Rothblatt was smart, no doubt about it. Excellent on cross-examination. He had really tripped Chipman up on his testimony. And he had masterfully elicited a whole catalog of CIA documents to subpoena—messages, cables, notes. He had surfaced a new CIA name from Chipman, Dean Almy.

But Gregory thought the CIA man was pretty smart, too, as far as intelligence matters went. Chipman was certainly more astute, better educated, better trained, and much more experienced in the business of spying than these poor defendants, these brave-to-a-fault soldiers now in the dock for murder. He could see how they had bungled.

But who had helped put them in this room? Harold Chipman and his CIA. And the way things sounded, the CIA would just as well let these men go down the tubes now, these men who did nothing more than try to do the right thing for their country.

Who the hell did the Army and the CIA think they were putting out in the field to run these tricky operations, Gregory thought, a bunch of John le Carrés? If the CIA was so good at it, why aren't their agents out there in the jungle themselves, instead of these poor guys sitting at the defense table. Who the hell in the U.S. government, Gregory wondered, could stand up, after ten years of war, and say with pride, "I know what I'm doing in Vietnam, I know what the right thing to do is, I know who the Viet Cong are, and who the innocents are"?

The CIA and the Army couldn't even agree on how many Viet Cong there were. They couldn't agree on where the supplies to Cambodia were coming from. The CIA had been consistently wrong in its more basic analyses of the war, Gregory concluded.

The CIA failed to make sense of two hundred and fifty thousand armed Communist troops creeping into the suburbs of Saigon and thirty other cities on the eve of Tet 1968, the result of which was a military and political setback even more devastating than Pearl Harbor, for it flattened America's will to stay the course in Vietnam.

Who could stand up now and claim they knew what they were doing in Vietnam? Nobody. Not a goddam person in the government would stand up and take credit for Vietnam. Not now. They were all on the run. Which was one of the reasons these poor Green Berets were on trial for their lives in Long Binh. Scapegoats all.

Gregory thought back to his first snickers about Tom Middleton and the other Green Berets. He felt a little shame. *These guys aren't lawyers, for Chrissakes, they're just soldiers with fancy French hats. They've been put in an impossible situation, like every other grunt pounding through Vietnamese villages and praying to Jesus they didn't wipe out a whole family before getting killed by their ten-year-old kid. It's the fault of the Army and CIA for putting them in this position,* Gregory thought with growing disgust, *and now they're trying to cover their ass.*

Gregory believed Chipman when he testified that he suggested to Crew and Brumley that they should turn Chuyen loose. He believed that. Chipman's general lament that "I knew this damn thing would unfold, as they always seem to do" had the ring of truth.

But that wasn't the point. The point wasn't what Chipman suggested. He never *told* them not to do it. No one in the CIA *told* them not to do it except for Shackley—and that came too late. Quite the opposite, they had entertained the idea all along. Or they had been silent. So the point was whether, based on these discussions, assassination was routine. That's what it sounded like to George Gregory.

Chipman had made a big mistake, Gregory concluded, when he said the CIA didn't know anything about assassinations.

Gregory's turn to question Chipman came, and he rose to his feet.

"Do you know a Lieutenant Colonel Enking?" he drawled. It came out "Inking."

"Yes," Chipman replied.

Gregory moved to the corner of the defense table.

"And is he with the CIA?"

"I can't discuss that."

Gregory pursed his lips and nodded.

"Is he in a supervisory capacity over you or are you over him?"

"No, he is over me," Chipman said.

Gregory turned away. He had to keep himself from smiling. Maybe Chipman is a dumb shit after all—why'd he answer that if he couldn't answer the first question?

He picked up the detectives' report of the July 13 meeting at MACV headquarters and then walked toward the CIA man, pushing his glasses back up his glistening nose.

"Do you know whether Colonel Enking—*Inking*—felt that elimination of the agent was the best course of action? Do you know that?"

"Beg your pardon?"

"Do you know that Colonel Enking stated that elimination of the agent was the best course of action?"

"I tend to doubt that," Chipman declared. "I saw his—first of all, something like that just isn't done."

"Yes."

Chipman seemed agitated again. "Something like that just isn't done, number one. Number two, Enking has no authorization to tell anybody that—and he'd be a fool if he did."

God bless 'im, Gregory thought again, resisting a smile. Chipman just unlocked the gates to Enking's deposition and testimony. There's no way to keep him out of court now.

"This sort of thing just isn't done," Gregory summed up. "And Russia doesn't do it either."

"I don't know . . ." Chipman said, weary.

"And you know of no power or country that does do it, is that correct?"

"Okay, they do it."

"They do it?" Gregory asked, sounding surprised. "Where?"

"I have heard—I don't know of any specific cases that I can mention," Chipman said.

My god, Gregory thought. *This is a bonanza.* "And do you know if this has ever been part of the Vietnamese war, on either side?"

"Not to my knowledge." Chipman looked up. "Execution of agents?"

"Yes."

Chipman frowned and shook his head.

"Neither side has engaged in this?" Gregory asked again.

"North or South Vietnamese?" Chipman asked.

"I am asking you. You are the expert."

"The Viet Cong do on occasion."

"Do you know how frequently?"

"No—I know of one case."

Gregory went back to Bob Bidwell's progress report and informed the presiding officer he would read from the detective's account of the July 13 meeting at MACV.

"It says '. . . Bourland, Enking and myself. Enking stated that he had talked to Crew and that he had told Crew that, of course the CIA could not arrange the elimination of Chuyen, but that it was the most efficient course of action.' "

Gregory turned to Chipman. "Do you know of anything like that?"

"No, sir," Chipman declared.

"The CIA never knows anything!" Gregory said, smiling in mock wonderment. He walked a few steps, enjoying the moment, and then turned back to Chipman.

"Do you know what the word 'Phoenix' means? Do you know anything about a Phoenix operation?"

Chipman shifted in his chair. "It is a program."

"What kind of program?"

"It is run by MACV."

MACV? Gregory wondered. The CIA hid the Phoenix program under MACV? Oh, sure, so it could get the free use of American soldiers, he supposed.

"And what is the purpose of this program?"

"To arrest VCI."

"VCI being what?" Gregory asked, prompting the CIA man to explain it for the court.

"I don't know whether I should talk about this. It is classified," Chipman said.

Gregory turned his palms up. "This is a classified hearing."

"But I don't think this should reach the . . ." He paused as Seaman leaned over and told him he could decide for himself whether Phoenix was beyond the limits of classification for the hearing.

"It is not top secret, no," Chipman said. Seaman nodded for Gregory to continue.

"Do you know whether or not," he resumed, "Viet Cong agents are tracked down in this Phoenix operation?"

"Agents?" Chipman obviously sensed a way out.

"Agents or . . ."

"I would rather not discuss it," Chipman said. "I don't think I should."

"Are you aware of assassinations connected with this program?" Gregory continued.

"Not assassinations." He was going to quibble over definitions, Gregory saw.

"Okay, are you aware of any killings, or anything of that nature?"

"Not from our side," Chipman declared. "Not from the American side."

Gregory cocked his head. He hadn't heard such brazen lying since a real estate deal he had brokered in Cheraw.

"I know," Chipman added sarcastically, "that the Viet Cong have come in and assassinated people."

Gregory started to push further, but he stopped. There'd be more time to chase that later. The issue of assassinations had to be carefully honed into a two-headed ax. This was not the place to do it.

"That's all I have," he said to Colonel Seaman. He turned to walk back to his seat.

"You just don't shoot an agent," Chipman insisted at Gregory's retreating back.

As the long afternoon wore on, the other attorneys took their whacks at Chipman. The CIA man remained alternately defiant and pliable, holding to his story that he had taken every step possible to keep the Green Berets from executing their agent. Their operation didn't call for such extreme measures anyway, he insisted.

"The Vietnamese know that Americans run unilateral operations, this is no secret," he said.

Marty Linsky, grilling Chipman on behalf of Bob Rheault, spun around at the remark.

"It isn't a secret?"

"No."

"Why do you think all this stuff is stamped secret?"

"I can't answer that," Chipman shrugged.

"Why, because your answer is secret?"

"I don't know why you stamped it secret," Chipman snapped.

"This stuff is classified," Linsky said, raising a dossier from the table, "because obviously we would not want the Vietnamese government to know about this unilateral operation."

"While an operation is *going on*," Chipman insisted.

Linsky let the remark float across the hearing room.

"Exactly," he said.

Henry Rothblatt rose for a last swipe at Chipman.

"Did you tell Major Crew that Mr. Shackley had been responsible for two hundred and fifty political killings in Laos?"

"I can't answer that."

"Is that classified secret?" Rothblatt inquired.

"Really," Chipman said, appealing to Seaman, "I don't know whether this is in the purview of the Chuyen case."

Seaman quickly agreed it was not, and in any event, it was the end of the day. Harold Chipman, he said, was excused. He gaveled the hearing to a close.

The only thing left to decide now was whether to send the cases forward to a general courts-martial.

47

It was a typically hot and muggy August afternoon when CIA lawyer John Greaney, his wife, and their six kids finally arrived on the Delaware shore for the start of their summer vacation. Already tired and restless from the traffic-jammed trip down Route 50 from Washington, they pulled into Bethany Beach with a tire going flat. It was a bad omen.

After unpacking the car, Greaney drove back to the local garage for the repair work. As he waited, his wife tracked him down with a dreadful message: His boss, CIA general counsel Lawrence Houston, had just called. It was urgent, she said coldly.

Mary Frances Greaney had endured her husband's emergencies through the years, the many abrupt departures for CIA "jobs" somewhere in the world. Broken dinner engagements, vacations alone, the uncertainty of knowing exactly where he had gone or what he was doing came with being a CIA wife. Not even longtime neighbors and non-CIA friends could be counted on for solace; most of them knew only that her husband worked "for the government." The spy agency was a graveyard for marriages and a garden of alcoholism, but that wasn't a problem for the Greaneys. In fact, they had forsaken the clandestine life just so their children could have a more normal routine in Washington. After fifteen years abroad, the last three in Taiwan, John Greaney filled a slot as a CIA lawyer and settled his family in Chevy Chase, a leafy suburb of Washington.

That didn't bring an end to the travel. When there was a CIA man in legal trouble somewhere in the world, or if the agency was being dragged into court, the curly-haired, easy-going lawyer packed his bags.

Greaney checked in with Larry Houston, and the news was indeed bad. The CIA's chief lawyer wanted him to go right to Saigon on the Green Beret case: "Something needs fixing."

"My God," Greaney said, "I just got to the beach. When?"

"Now," Houston said. "Very sorry. Come to headquarters first."

It was early evening by the time the lawyer turned off Route 123 in northern Virginia and drove the hundred yards to the main CIA gate, where he stopped to show his ID. An armed civilian guard checked his photo and waved him through.

The CIA offices were located in a forested campus-like setting backed up against thick woods overlooking the Potomac River. Except for the National Institutes of Health, it was the only major federal agency with a privileged suburban sanctuary. The headquarters building, a seven-story smoked glass and concrete structure, had been completed in 1962. Old hands remembered the irony of John F. Kennedy dedicating the new building, which consolidated CIA offices scattered around Washington, at the same time he was thinking about breaking up the agency in the wake of the Bay of Pigs disaster.

Greaney took the elevator to the seventh floor and walked down the cool, quiet executive corridor. Houston had already gathered together a few of his other legal deputies.

Tall and thin with intense narrowly set eyes and a beaked nose, Houston was a member of Washington's Old Guard, one of the gray insiders who hold real power but whose names are rarely, if ever, in the newspapers.

Houston's father had been the president of Texas A & M University and held two cabinet posts in the administration of Woodrow Wilson before becoming president of Bell Telephone Securities Company and later the president of the Mutual Life Insurance Company of New York. Young Lawrence went to Milton, Harvard, and the University of Virginia Law School, graduating as Europe plunged into war. He resigned from the prestigious law firm of White and Case and volunteered for combat, but there was only one job suitable for a man with his poor eyesight, strong academic background, and political pedigree: lawyering for the OSS. He was assigned to the Middle East.

The wartime commando and spy service was disbanded quickly by President Truman at the end of hostilities in 1945, its functions divided up by the military services and State Department. To wartime intelligence veterans, the arrangement was clumsy and inadequate. They began lobbying for a new service that would meld espionage and paramilitary missions into one central agency. In 1947, the CIA was born as part of a total reorganization of the military services. Houston wrote the CIA's charter, which included the artful phrase permitting the agency to "perform such other functions and duties relating to intelligence affecting the national security as the National Security Council may from time to time direct." He soon became a legend in the secretive corridors of the spy service.

One of Houston's first tasks was to fashion a web of corporate disguises for the CIA's far-flung network of airlines and shipping companies. As the agency's chief counsel, he was also kept busy keeping the CIA out of court. Espionage, with its associated activities that ranged from illegal mail openings to the payment of bribes, foreign currency manipulations, coups d'etat, and assassination, required full-time monitoring by the CIA's lawyers. There was also the vague congressional testimony of CIA directors to vet and defend.

Houston was, in effect, the CIA's long-range legal radar. From his spacious corner office on the agency's executive corridor, he wryly told visitors, he could look out on the Virginia horizon and spot summer thunderstorms heading toward Washington. He'd call home and warn his wife to shut the windows.

Houston briefed Greaney on the nettlesome Green Beret affair. A lengthy cable from the CIA station in Saigon lay on his desk, summarizing the Article 32 hearings, and in particular Harold Chipman's testimony. It was causing everybody a headache.

Chipman had gone too far, Houston said; he had left the agency vulnerable to a fishing expedition by the Green Berets' defense lawyers. CIA director Richard Helms, who had reluctantly authorized the testimony, was furious. The White House, no less than Nixon and Kissinger, was making inquiries too. From the news accounts out of Saigon, they thought the CIA might have ordered the Green Berets to kill the Vietnamese agent. Of course it wasn't true, Houston said, but "they are very annoyed."

Greaney's mission, Houston said, was to scout out the Army's intentions in the affair, find out what CIA people and documents the defense lawyers were after, and advise station chief Ted Shackley on whatever legal problems might be coming down the road. The point, of course, was not to have any.

"Take care of it," he said dryly.

Greaney gave his wife the bad news and at 6 P.M. Tuesday night, August 22, boarded a flight at Baltimore-Washington Airport for Saigon. There were no shortcuts to the war zone, which was literally on the other side of the world. With Pan American still on strike, he hopscotched across Europe and the

Middle East, passed through the international dateline, and finally landed in Saigon thirty-one hours later.

Greaney deplaned at Ton Son Nhut at 12:30 Thursday afternoon, local time. Dry mouthed and aching from the aircraft cabin, sagging with jet lag, he stepped into the wet, superheated air. Ed Brooks, the Saigon station's chief of support, was waiting for him. They sped off to the Duc Hotel, where Greaney dropped his bags, and then went straight to the embassy, where over the lawyer's protestations, Ted Shackley wanted to go right to work.

Greaney said he was exhausted. He had been in sandals at the beach only the day before. He had just flown through twelve time zones.

Shackley waved off his complaints. He wanted Greaney on the case now.

Greaney knew Shackley mainly by reputation, although they had met briefly a few times over the years. Greaney had worked in operations on Taiwan during the early 1960s that supported paramilitary groups of exiled Chinese. He had also worked on the Laos desk, but he had never set foot in Vietnam.

Over the exhausted lawyer's resistance, they began combing through the case. Finally, six hours later, Greaney begged off and returned to the Duc Hotel's coffee shop for dinner. He fell asleep before the hamburger was served.

The next day, they started in again. Shackley kept saying he wanted "this case off my back."

Greaney suppressed a smile. All the operators came running to the seventh floor when they got in trouble. They didn't care about the intricacies and requirements of the American legal system; they just wanted the lawyers to make their problems go away.

Greaney's main objective was to batten down the manhole covers protecting CIA operations. The agency's usual defense against legal assaults was to assert that everything was related to the CIA's "sources and methods," the particulars of agent names and locations and specific systems of operations. It was a catch-all defense that linked even the most innocuous piece of information to "national security," and from the beginning of the cold war judges usually went along with it. Vietnam, though, was beginning to open things up. Some judges were deciding that "national security" was sometimes an excuse to cover up crimes and incompetence.

Shackley wanted Greaney to provide detailed reports on his findings and what the defense was after. Lawyers for the Green Berets, Greaney quickly found, had thrown everything at the CIA's wall to see what would stick. The Article 32 transcripts left no doubt of the defense's strategy to switch the tables and put the CIA on trial. The lawyers wanted to open a general debate on assassinations that their clients implied were widespread in Vietnam and elsewhere. If the Green Berets got Ted Shackley into the witness chair, the attack could also very well reveal his operations in Berlin, Laos, Miami, and Cuba.

Despite Shackley's stony demeanor, Greaney saw that he was worried. According to Shackley's deputy, Joe Lazarsky, the station chief had turned over his daily administrative chores to focus on the case. He insisted Greaney meet with him every night to go over the case. He wanted exact reports on the lawyer's interviews with CIA personnel, and judgments on the potential fallout from testimony and defense motions. It was vintage Shackley, everybody saw: total, all-out war.

One day Greaney signed out one of the Ford Falcons from the CIA motor pool and drove off to Long Binh. The Viet Cong had blown up a key bridge along the highway, however, which made him miss his scheduled meetings. The next day, he requisitioned a blue-and-white Air America helicopter. With Shackley's backing, the eyebrow-raising perk was no problem. In any event, Greaney figured that a noisy dust-beating arrival at Long Binh would raise his stature in negotiations with Army legal officers.

The counsel for MACV, Wilton Persons, had been cordial and cooperative in their initial meetings. But there was trouble ahead, he warned. Gen. George Mabry was making it clear to everyone, including the CIA, that he didn't "give a rat's ass" about the CIA's problems with the case.

"Murder doesn't fit in my book anywhere," the general declared to one and all. "I was not raised that way." He was going forward with the prosecution, by God, wherever it led.

Greaney and Shackley hunched over the case, trying to figure out which locks to change first.

The defense lawyers, no doubt, would fire their hardest shots in the few weeks remaining before a decision on courts-martial, upping the ante for the Army and CIA to go forward. The main targets for depositions would be Clement Enking, Bruce Scrymgeour, Harold Chipman, Dean Almy, and of course, Shackley himself. Greaney gently suggested to the station chief that he might have to take the stand.

"Jesus Christ, you Benedict Arnold," Shackley exploded. "What are you trying to do to me?" He was appalled. How could Greaney even consider allowing more documents or testimony into the record, especially after Chipman's debacle on the stand? Particularly from himself. Where would it stop?

Greaney could only guess at the true depth of Shackley's apprehension. He knew the station chief's career was intertwined with some of the agency's most jealously guarded secrets—the pact with Mafia hoods to get rid of Castro, operations in Berlin, Laos, and now Vietnam. Then there was the Phoenix program. Everybody knew there were "excesses."

The files were not pretty. They were, in fact, the family jewels.

Shackley wasn't ashamed of his record of government service; quite conversely, like others fighting in the trenches of the cold war, he felt he had served his country proudly and well on the orders of four presidents. He had done what they asked against ruthless, immoral foes in Moscow, Cuba, East Germany, Laos, and now Vietnam. Who would trade sides with that bunch of thugs?

Not many, he thought. But Vietnam had soured public opinion. One of the great frustrations for CIA professionals was the notion, fashionable among liberals lately, that our side was just as bad as theirs. At first it was limited to radical journals like *Ramparts*, which had exposed secret links between the

CIA and the National Student Association, and "alternative" papers in such predictable places as Berkeley, Cambridge, Madison, and Ann Arbor. But as the war had gone on, the notion of a parity of evil between Moscow and Washington had gained currency among intellectuals, and even some congressmen. GI coffee houses and draft-resistance organizations were popping up on the edge of military bases, seeding the idea that if our side was bad in Vietnam, the other side had to be good. The Viet Cong, it was said, were hardly more than Jeffersonian peasants.

Men of Shackley's generation were appalled and amazed by such developments. *Hell, we are the liberals!* they protested. *Has everybody forgotten Joe Stalin? About the gulags? About Soviet tanks in Poland, Hungary, and Czechoslovakia?*

For God's sake, they said, *we saved Western Europe with a little quiet help to democrats in the Communist-controlled trade unions. We helped freedom-minded bureaucrats in Africa, Asia, and Latin America. What's so bad about that?*

Phoenix is liberal! We are trying to get the Viet Cong out of the crowd, one by one, so the Vietnamese can have their revolution without the Communists. Would you prefer the Army and Air Force keep leveling villages with their tanks, artillery, and air strikes? If we had stuck with things like Phoenix, the CIA man said, *instead of bringing in the Army, maybe we all would have been home by now, and Vietnam would be history, instead of a mess.*

The bloody stalemate, however, had tipped the scales against everything to do with Vietnam, and everybody knew it. The CIA had many enemies, Shackley knew, including liberals who could not, or would not, accept the hard methods sometimes used to keep the third world in the American column. Everything was politicized now. All hell could break loose if he ever were forced to take the stand. It would be a propaganda holiday for the Viet Cong and their radical admirers.

The Green Berets' fishing expedition had to be sunk, but how and where? Shackley's own "return-agent-to-duty" memo, now part of the record thanks to Chipman's undisciplined testimony, had given the Berets a big hook. The CIA was inextricably bound to Thai Khac Chuyen's fate. With Shackley's memo the defense lawyers had at least a good chance of breaching the wall of "executive immunity" that the station chief had temporarily erected to block questioning by Bob Bidwell. After all, military judges would be unlikely to refuse the attempt of eight heretofore honorable soldiers, facing a firing squad or life in prison for doing what they thought was their duty, to question the practices of the CIA in Vietnam.

John Greaney, however, believed that Shackley's testimony could be restricted to the events specifically at issue. When he examined the paper trail, Shackley's position looked pretty good: He had ordered the agent returned to duty, after all, had warned the Green Berets of a "moral flap," and had gone to General Abrams and Ambassador Bunker when the soldiers stonewalled.

There were plenty of precedents for limiting testimony: Over the years, many military intelligence personnel, and occasionally the CIA's own agents, had tried to entangle the agency in their renegade escapades. The

CIA had beaten back almost every defendant's maneuver to drag it into criminal court.

One precedent was the case of Green Beret captain John McCarthy, who had been court-martialed in 1968 on the charge of murdering a Cambodian agent. The court, deliberating in secrecy, rejected McCarthy's protestations that he did not shoot the agent and his arguments that he was operating under CIA control. He was doing twenty years in the federal prison at Fort Leavenworth, Kansas—albeit with his salary and benefits intact.

In another precedent, a group of Cuban exiles had been unable to implicate the agency in their 1967 trial for organizing a private invasion of Haiti, a violation of U.S. neutrality laws. That verdict could certainly be cited to limit CIA testimony in the Green Beret case.

All of which gave Greaney grounds for optimism in the case.

But there was another problem, he found, for which there was no easy solution: the CIA dossier of Sgt. Alvin P. Smith.

Smith's file contained his recruitment by the CIA in 1957, his assignment to a phony Army reserve unit in Washington, his training in Virginia, and, of course, his undercover stint as a State Department consular officer in Port Said. Any one of these elements posed a multitude of problems.

The Army, Greaney had learned, was planning to offer Smith immunity and compel his testimony against the others. The quirky sergeant was being groomed as the Army's star witness.

That would not do, Greaney knew; as soon as Smith took the stand, his former employment by the CIA would become fair game. The revelation would cause all sorts of political and diplomatic headaches. The press would go wild. Smith had fingered the others, after all. Had he done it at the behest of the CIA?

Who would not assume that Smith had been a CIA agent all along, a sleeper in the ranks, a cog in some unfathomable CIA-Army scheme to frame the Green Berets? In the supercharged atmosphere surrounding the case, the mere suspicion of Smith's true allegiance and motives would shift the spotlight to the CIA.

But not only the press would be suspicious. There were much wider implications to the release of Smith's CIA history. Greaney found that Smith had left the CIA without warning during his brief stint in Port Said. Reading through Smith's dossier, Greaney concluded Smith had "flipped out." The Army would rightly ask why that hadn't been part of his file.

And how many other former CIA agents, the Joint Chiefs of Staff might want to know, were planted in the military services—beyond those officially accounted for? An official inquiry was certain, perhaps even a congressional investigation.

Smith's file would open another old sore. American diplomats were forever fending off accusations stoked by the Soviet KGB in third world newspapers that they were all CIA agents. The dossier of Alvin Smith would only aggravate their woes. The State Department would mount another campaign to purge its ranks of the CIA.

But the dossier was also fodder for a diplomatic crisis that would dwarf the parochial concerns of Washington bureaucrats.

Egypt, its relations with Washington already strained by its defeat by Israel in the 1967 Six Day War, might feel compelled to respond to revelations of Alvin Smith's CIA posting to Port Said. Cairo was certain to lodge a diplomatic protest, maybe something stronger. The Port Said consulate, strategically located on the Red Sea, would be a lightning rod for demonstrators shouting "Down with the U.S." As the scandal played into the hands of Marxist radicals and Muslim fundamentalists, the Egyptian government could well be forced to shut down the consulate and declare the staff persona non grata. A break in relations was not even out of the question. A tilt toward Moscow was possible. At the very least, the exposure could foul U.S.-Egyptian relations for months, if not years.

All this because of Sgt. Alvin P. Smith. Maybe it wouldn't turn out that badly, but who wanted to gamble? Why risk wrecking American policy in the Middle East for the sake of fixing guilt for the death of one Vietnamese?

All in all, the Green Beret case gave Greaney an awful pain. The defense lawyers had already demonstrated an affinity for running to the press. Greaney confidently expected appeals on every withheld document, every rejected request for a deposition, right up to the Ninth Circuit Court in Hawaii, or even the Supreme Court in Washington. The case would become even more of a circus than it already was, cheered on every step of the way by a chorus of delighted reporters. And every time George Gregory and the others were thwarted, Greaney was confident they'd hold a press conference on the courthouse steps. Or leak their documents to the press.

And now he had Edward Bennett Williams to contend with.

Alvin Smith. The family jewels. The Middle East. Edward Bennett Williams.

The case was not just a headache, it was a cancer.

Langley was in an uproar.

John Greaney's findings had made their way back to CIA headquarters. The operations section, officially the Directorate for Plans, wasn't about to leave the case in the hands of seventh-floor lawyers. Messages from Ted Shackley complaining about Greaney had already filled the in-basket of Thomas Karamessines, head of the directorate. The lawyer didn't understand how things worked in Vietnam, Shackley said. He was in over his head.

"Tom K," as he was known, decided to have his own man keep an eye on things. "Wild Willy" Wells was dispatched to Vietnam.

William O. Wells was the number-two official in the Far East Division. An intense, yet forgettable-looking man with thick black hair, Wells was said to have begun his love affair with Asia by peddling kerosene lamps to Chinese peasants for Standard Oil—an apocryphal story perhaps, maybe not: Wells was that kind of guy. He could've done it.

With the outbreak of World War II, Wells joined the OSS, which made him a charter member of the CIA's "China hands" clique and, not long after, a trusted aide to Karamessines, head of what was increasingly becoming known as the "dirty tricks" division.

Wells and Greaney knew each other. They had clashed once when Greaney, citing family problems, successfully appealed over Wells's head to block a transfer from Taiwan to Saigon. Another time Wells had complained about one of Greaney's operations. Wells, a gruff, determined personality on the model of Ted Shackley, had apparently never forgotten the incident. From the moment he arrived in Saigon, sparks flew, and not just with Greaney. Wells rubbed everyone raw.

The China hand quickly opened his own back channel to Langley, prompting Greaney to complain that Wells was looking over his shoulder. Wells's reports that Greaney was insufficiently sensitive to operational concerns found a ready ear with Karamessines and his boss Richard Helms. All were lifelong operations men to whom lifting the slightest lid on the agency's secrets was heresy.

The Wells mission involved more than guarding the operations directorate's prerogatives, however. The decision to involve him in the Green Beret case was prompted by the White House: President Richard Nixon wanted to know what the hell was going on.

Nixon had followed the case through the White House morning news summaries. It hadn't interested him much at first; it was just one dead Vietnamese, some soldiers arrested. And he was busy with much bigger things. He was in Communist Romania when the case broke, riding through Bucharest in a tumultuous motorcade, the end of a seven-nation tour. There had been a meeting with Nguyen Van Thieu in Midway, and a state visit by Golda Meir was in the works. A new relationship with China and a summit in Moscow were on the horizon. As for the war, there was the bombing to monitor, and a secret opening to the North Vietnamese in Paris. And that was just the foreign agenda. The domestic calendar was full, too, with inflation, taxes, and integration cases.

Nixon noticed the one-paragraph item on the Green Beret arrests in the August 6 White House morning news summary. "When did this happen?" he scrawled on the margin. "During LBJ?" But a quote by George Gregory a week later drew the President's attention: "termination with extreme prejudice."

What the hell was that? Nixon asked Helms, calling him on the carpet. What was this goddamn mess all over the papers and the nightly news? Couldn't the CIA get rid of one goddamn Viet Cong spy? He told Helms to find out what was going on.

Nixon loved to tweak the well-tailored, piranha-jawed CIA director. He loathed the CIA crowd in general. They were Ivy League, Georgetown, smart-asses born with silver spoons in their mouths, he thought. Liberals, he suspected. Soft. Worse, he thought they were all Democrats. The Kennedy crowd.

Helms, a graduate of Williams College in Massachusetts, had a dry wit and a cool patrician style that reinforced Nixon's prejudices. The president probably didn't know that Helms was a career government employee who had lived on his salary in a plain house in Chevy Chase, distinguishing himself in secret operations long before the election of John F. Kennedy. Nobody had ever heard Helms voice a partisan political opinion.

It didn't matter to Nixon. Helms was a Johnson appointment. He was not loyal. He would have to go, eventually. But Nixon had to avoid anything that could damage his Vietnam policy for now. Everything else he had in mind for the next three years depended on getting rid of the Vietnam albatross.

Nixon would not be an LBJ, he vowed, imprisoned in the White House by war protestors, blood thrown at his cabinet officials by campus bums. The antiwar movement was already showing signs of new life—Nixon had his people closely watching that. In the meantime, though, the president thought he might learn something about the CIA and assassinations that he could hold over Helms's head. That's what "termination with extreme prejudice" meant, wasn't it?

How, Nixon wondered, could the execution of a goddamn Viet Cong spy get to be such a big deal? How could the CIA screw that up?

Helms, urbane and unruffled, the loyal servant of the president, told him he didn't know. It had to be something the newspapers made up—the CIA didn't *use* such a phrase. "Terminate with extreme prejudice" wasn't in the CIA's vocabulary.

Nixon snorted. "Find out what the hell's going on out there," he told Helms. "Fast."

Greaney had already found it. It was in Project Blackbeard, the Green Beret operations plan for Cambodia. There it was: "terminate with extreme prejudice."

In the military intelligence system, every operations plan included descriptions of the mission, the personnel, the secret communication arrangements to contact agents, and the "termination plan," or scenario for disposing of agents when an operation was completed or compromised. Generally, there was "termination without prejudice," and "termination with prejudice." The latter meant that the agent had been fired and put on the "burn list" of unreliable agents. In Project Blackbeard, the phrase "terminate with *extreme* prejudice" was used.

Greaney had never heard of the term. He wondered if it was something unique to the Green Berets, something akin to "terminate with prejudice." Or did it mean more? He simply didn't know. The Green Berets, he thought, tended to overdramatize their importance to the future of the free world. Maybe this was just another example. In any event, he had put his finger on the origin of the term in George Gregory's press conferences, and it had nothing to do with the CIA. He reported his findings.

Willy Wells, meanwhile, was conducting his own interviews with the CIA officers who had dealt with the Green Berets. One of them, Nha Trang base chief Dean Almy, quickly became agitated by the covert bureaucrat from Langley.

The trouble started when Wells decided to take the occasion of his first Vietnam trip as a senior Far East Division official to summon the regional base chiefs for a briefing on the war. Not long into the embassy meeting, Wells remarked offhandedly that Vietnam "was not really important" to the United States, compared to other parts of the world.

Almy inwardly stiffened. Wells turned around and searched for a spot on the map of East Asia on the wall behind him.

"That's where the action is," he said, tapping China, a pink blob on the map. "Or Moscow."

Wells warmed to his subject. He got up and located a particular spot on the Sino-Soviet border where fighting had broken out between Russian and Chinese troops in recent months.

"That's really where it's at," he said, peering at the spot. "That's where war three will begin." He tapped the map confidently and sat down. "That's important," he repeated. "Not Vietnam."

Almy was disgusted. To him, Wells and the other China hands were a bunch of phonies who watched China from afar and called it espionage. Strictly sidewalk engineers. They never got closer than Hong Kong or Japan. None of them knew anything about operating *inside* a hostile environment, in places like Indonesia, Laos, or Vietnam where a mistake could cost an agent's life, or where a career could go up in flames in the time it took some ambitious colonel to surround the presidential palace with his tanks.

China was bullshit, Almy thought. Try Indonesia. Or Laos. Or Korea. Or Vietnam. He couldn't stand to hear Wells prattle on.

"Well, Jesus Christ, thanks a hell of a lot," he finally exploded. "We've come all the way over to Vietnam, where we happen to be in a shooting war. A lot of us are volunteers on a second or third tour. And we think we're doing a pretty good job. And our ass is on the line here. And you're telling us what we're doing isn't even important."

"Fuck you," he wanted to say, but it wasn't in his nature. After a stiff silence, the meeting resumed without further discussion of what was more important—China, Moscow, Vietnam, or some pissant border post on the Sino-Soviet border to which neither Wild Willy Wells—nor any of his other "China hands," Almy was sure—had likely gotten an agent closer than a thousand miles.

"Why didn't you make more of it at the time?" Wells asked Almy about the Green Berets' handling of Chuyen. "If you suspected they were going to kill that guy, why didn't you blow the whistle harder on it?"

Almy was nonplussed. How could he explain Vietnam to someone who'd never been there? It was like describing the other side of the moon.

"It happens all the time! There's a war going on over here!" he told Wells.

Young military intelligence operatives came to the CIA all the time for help with solving their problems, he related. Apparently they thought the CIA was where you went if you wanted to bump off somebody. They read too many spy novels.

"An MI guy came to me not long ago and asked for an airplane to drop somebody out of. I said, 'You're a nice guy, but you've got the wrong people. Leave now and I'll forget we ever had this conversation. I'll forget I ever met you.' "

Almy's point wasn't that the CIA was just writing term papers on the Viet Cong. Hardly. There were joint CIA-Vietnamese interrogation centers around the country where the rough stuff was routine. There were the infamous "tiger cages" of Con Son Island. Everyone knew that Viet Cong suspects just disappeared from time to time, probably taken around a corner and shot. Snuffing enemy spies was as old as time. But that wasn't what was involved here. They had killed one of their own. The Green Berets should have taken care of it themselves, not come knocking on the CIA's door. Or in the way it usually worked in Vietnam, the local province chief is tipped off that there's a VC agent living in his village. Bang, he's dead.

"When I came back to Nha Trang from Saigon," Almy told Wells, "I talked to Dave Crew and Lee Brumley and told them we didn't do that sort of thing. They were astounded."

Almy said Harold Chipman was really to blame for the fiasco. "It never would have happened if I had been there, or Ed Splain," his deputy. "These guys would have been turned off fast." It went unspoken that Chipman was a Shackley protégé from the days in Berlin and Miami.

What happened to the repeated cables from Nha Trang to Saigon? Wells wanted to know. Why had it taken so long for Chipman to get an answer?

A bureaucratic screwup, Almy guessed. The messages had "gotten lost" in Saigon. He turned up his hands.

"What about Enking and Scrymgeour?" Wells asked. "What were their roles in this thing?"

"Those two are not CIA men," he reminded Wells. They were military guys who had been grafted onto the agency in Korea and stayed there. They served a function, liaising to the military units. But they didn't have the same level of training and professionalism as CIA men. They weren't as good.

"They screwed up," Almy said. They must have said something the Green Berets took the wrong way.

Shackley was furious at Harold Chipman. With Wells and Greaney crawling all over Saigon and defense lawyers and press pummeling the CIA, he was outraged to read in the Article 32 transcript that Chipman had cracked to Crew and Brumley, "Shack won't mind—he's killed two hundred and fifty operatives in Laos."

"Did you say that?" he demanded, calling Chipman to account with Dean Almy in attendance. Steam was nearly coming from his ears.

Chipman blanched. He quickly denied anything of the sort.

Shackley stared at his underling, outraged by the picture Chipman had drawn of him as some kind of gangster, popping Communist agents. Sure, Pathet Lao agents got killed, sometimes by the CIA's guys. There was a war going on in Laos, a counterinsurgency struggle even more blurry than Vietnam's. And he was the field general. That didn't make him some kind of Mafia don, ordering rubouts, particularly rubouts of the agency's own assets.

Chipman's squirming denial, however, made it obvious to both Almy and Shackley that Chipman had indeed mouthed off to Brumley and Crew. He was finished, which pleased Almy no end.

Sam Halpern fielded the report from Willy Wells at CIA headquarters and took it to Karamessines. Halpern, a wiry short man with a dry sense of humor, was part of the old covert action crowd. He seemed to know everyone in the building and had a prodigious memory for names, dates, and places. His recall made him a good executive assistant for the deputy director for Plans.

Halpern flipped through the detailed fifteen-page report, a who-struck-John on the CIA's role in the Green Beret mess. Wells had written off the culpability of any CIA officer in the execution of Chuyen. The Green Berets had "misinterpreted" their meeting with Enking and Scrymgeour, Wells concluded, who in any case were not career CIA employees. Likewise, he found, Chipman's extended counseling of the Green Berets was "misguided" but "well-intentioned."

The CIA connections to Alvin Smith, Wells said, weren't worth worrying about. He had left the CIA more than ten years ago and hadn't had any contact with the agency since. The record would show that. Let the press and the Army howl. The facts were the facts. As for Egypt, that was the State Department's problem.

Wells concluded that the Green Berets had gone off on their own and killed this man, and now they were desperately trying to entangle the CIA in their mistake. The way was open to a speedy trial, as long as it was kept secret.

Greaney had come to a similar conclusion on the legal facets of the case. He was far less sanguine, however, about the scandal that could erupt over Smith's dossier. That would be trouble.

Halpern was amused by the whole thing. Seldom had he seen such a major flap over a minor event, the screwed-up killing of one Vietnamese agent. As Almy had said, it was a comedy of errors.

Halpern handed the report to Karamessines, who read it, marked a copy for Helms, and told Halpern to send a copy to Nixon at the California White House.

As it turned out, the CIA had no direct scrambler line to San Clemente, so Halpern hand-carried the report to the White House for transmission to Nixon. The communications room was in the basement, just off the Situation Room, crisis center for the National Security Council.

Halpern peeked in for a look. He was unimpressed: There wasn't even much of a world map on the wall. A few clocks told the time in Tokyo, London, and Moscow. Not much of a war room, he sniffed.

He handed the report to the two Navy enlisted men manning the crypto-graph machines, who began punching it into the system. Normally the clerks hardly took notice of what they were typing. But this time they were paying attention. The Green Beret case was hot stuff.

Halpern stood behind the sailors as they typed on the awkward keys. Slowly, he noticed they were smiling. Finally, they turned around and laughed.

"Is this all there is to it?" one asked.

"That's it," Halpern said.

As the CIA report made its way to the California White House, George Gregory and Henry Rothblatt were boarding a Pan American jet at Ton Son Nhut. They were going home. In a few weeks, the Army would announce whether the men would be court-martialed for murder. There was nothing more to be done for now in Saigon.

"Weighing the evidence," Rothblatt told reporters as he left, "there is just no case. I would be surprised to see how any objective law officer could bring this case to trial."

Gregory, for once, bit his tongue. He was saving his remarks for the home front. He was going to wrap the Phoenix program around the necks of both the Army and the CIA.

48

With her quail's egg face, matchstick arms, and tiny figure under a white cotton blouse and black pants, Phan Kim Lien moved with the delicate beauty for which Vietnamese women were famous. But her frail appearance was misleading. Thai Khac Chuyen's widow was a relentless, determined woman.

Raising the banner of martyred husbands was a powerful motif in Vietnam-ese history. Nearly every city had a street named after the legendary Trung sisters, who rallied the armies of their fallen husbands against Chinese invad-ers in A.D. 40 and established a popular, if short-lived, reign. Vietnam's epic national poem, Kim Van Kieu, learned by every schoolchild, is a tragic woman's tale. Military heroines and other female patriots were sprinkled through Vietnamese history. If men seemed to run the country, a woman was never far behind the throne, raising the children, keeping alive the family honor.

In the days that followed the Green Berets' arrests, Lien had been carried along like a piece of cork in the swirling mystery. Unable to learn for sure whether he was alive or dead, she had become a reluctant bystander in her own tragedy, following the newspaper accounts and rumors of an international scandal in the making. In the second week of August, however, hearing that political pressure might force the Army to drop the investigation into her husband's disappearance, she decided to act.

First she hired a lawyer, who helped her draw up two letters, one to the U.S. Army and one to the U.S. Embassy, asking for confirmation that the man who had been killed and her husband were the same. No one, after all, had told her officially whether the missing interpreter was her husband.

Normally a spouse is the first stop for detectives on a homicide case. She can supply useful facts about his last hours, his movements up to the moment he disappeared, his fears, his state of mind, any notes or other evidence he left behind. She usually knows, in fact, who probably killed him. Yet in the two months since Chuyen's disappearance, no official had talked to her—no Vietnamese policeman, not the detectives Bourland and Bidwell, nor any representatives of the South Vietnamese or American governments. She was at the center of a murder investigation but oddly not part of it.

Unknown to her, the detectives had been dissuaded from making any contact. Lien, the generals at MACV had warned, could not be ruled out as an espionage accomplice to her husband. Anything they told her could find its way to Hanoi.

It was another of the odd contradictions in the case, the detectives thought: If Lien was a spy, why hadn't she been arrested? And why, in its public statements, was the Army still refusing to identify the victim of the Green Berets?

But circumstances had changed. The Article 32 hearings had revealed the weakness of the government's case: The prosecutors had not found a body; the suspected murder weapon was worthless without a matching slug from a corpse; the confessions had all been challenged on procedural grounds. Now, circumstantial evidence had assumed a greater importance. On the basis that they would not divulge any information on the case, the detectives received permission to interview Lien to establish the last time she had seen her husband, and with whom.

But that's all they did. They did not take a detailed statement on her efforts to track her husband's whereabouts or who she talked to. On August 15 they took a statement that she had last seen her husband on June 12, and then they left.

The days passed slowly. Lien drew her children around her, brushing their hair, rocking them to sleep, trying to give comfort. Their father would be home soon, she whispered. He was on a mission in the war. At bedtime, they cried. Lien turned to her father-in-law for solace. Thai Khac Qui had lived through the Japanese occupation, two wars against the French, and seven years of the American offensive. People often just disappeared, he knew, vanishing in the jungle. After thirty years, the Vietnamese missing in action numbered in the hundreds of thousands.

Lien went to the American embassy again on August 18 after reading in the paper that the Army had "no case." She took her two children with her, gave her name, and took a seat in the waiting area.

For an hour, she sat and waited. The children played on the tile. No one, it became clear, was going to see her. Finally, she left an envelope with the receptionist.

Inside was a note for Ambassador Ellsworth Bunker that asked for help in clearing up the mystery of her husband's disappearance. Attached to it was a copy of a petition asking the Saigon government to open its own investigation into the case. It was addressed to the prime minister of South Vietnam.

This time, the embassy took notice.

The next day a political officer was dispatched to find Lien at her house in the alley near the river. Thai Khac Qui met him at the door. No longer taking chances on odd Americans who showed up unexpectedly at their house, he stiffened at the visitor's request to see his daughter-in-law. Lien was not feeling well, he said; she was resting elsewhere under a doctor's care. He refused to answer any questions.

The anonymous visitor said he would like to pass on a message. Qui assented and let him inside.

"Tell her," the young man said, "that the American embassy sympathizes with her concern over the lack of news from her husband since June 13.

"But since her husband was employed by Special Forces," he added, "she should direct her inquiries to the American military authorities in Vietnam, and specifically to the staff judge advocate, headquarters, MACV."

Qui wrote down the essentials. The diplomat quickly departed and vanished down the alley.

That night, Ambassador Bunker sent an "Immediate" top secret cable to Secretary of State William Rogers in Washington with copies to General Creighton Abrams and the U.S. delegation at the Paris Peace Talks.

Bunker detailed Lien's visit to the embassy, her retention of a private lawyer, and his subsequent dispatch to her home of a foreign service officer who advised her to redirect her concerns from the embassy to the Army.

"Mrs. Chuyen [sic] has asked the prime minister," Bunker reported, "in case that the alleged victim of the Green Berets was indeed her husband, to consider her letter an official accusation of homicide against the eight U.S. Special Forces personnel."

Bunker added, "Mrs. Chuyen said the men should be brought to justice for their 'illegal, immoral, and barbarous activities.' "

Bunker closed drily, "Mrs. Chuyen insisted her husband was not a Communist spy."

New York Times reporter James Sterba had been hustling to match Bob Kaiser's exclusive story identifying Chuyen by name and describing him as a low-level interpreter. He dropped by Lien's home when she returned from the embassy.

"I am sure my husband could never make a good agent," she told him, "because he was so hot-headed, so straightforward, and he would lose his temper easily." She added, "He is not the type of man who can keep secrets or get secrets."

Lien went on to tearfully describe her marriage to Chuyen in 1966, her husband's "several missions with the Special Forces along the Ho Chi Minh Trail in Laos," and his distressing return from the interrogation at Camp Goodman at 11 P.M. on the night of June 12.

That night, she remembered him saying, "I am worrying why I am required to pass another polygraph test. They asked me questions like I was a VC."

It was the last time she saw him, she said. She showed Sterba the note Chuyen had sent from Camp Goodman: "To my darling and my cherished children, I have to go on a mission for a few days. Don't worry. I want to wish all of you good health and happiness."

Sterba noted that Lien had learned of the Army's investigation through the newspapers. No one had talked to her despite her own inquiries at Camp Goodman. She was running in circles.

The Army's handling of the case, Sterba thought, had been bizarre from the beginning. The secrecy had been like a red flag, taunting the press to find out what had really happened. Now in its clumsiness, the Army had incited the victim's widow to plead for her own government's assistance, adding a diplomatic dimension to the case.

The missing man's family, Sterba reported, was not going to let the Americans settle the matter in secret.

"If the Army drops the charges against them," Chuyen's brother told him, "the family would seek the help of the South Vietnamese government in bringing the eight Special Forces officers to trial before a Vietnamese court."

Ten thousand miles away in South Carolina, Phyllis Middleton poured out her bitterness to a reporter from the *Charlotte Observer*, her hazel eyes flashing. In the two weeks since learning of her husband's arrest on television, she said, no one in the Army had tried to visit or even call.

"I talked to one of the generals at Fort Jackson," she said. "I told him, 'By damn, if my husband had been a casualty, they would have been right here on my doorstep with a notice. And I think, by damn, the living are more important than the dead.'

"He said I shouldn't be bitter. No, I should just smile sweetly and say thank you for not letting me know anything. I asked him what, just what, if I had a heart condition? 'Well,' he told me, 'that would have been your problem.' "

Her patience with the Army had run out, she told the reporter. It was absurd for Tom Middleton to be charged with murder anyway—everybody knew he wasn't a killer. And now she had to endure the agonizing suspense about the court-martial decision.

"It is the waiting that is nerve-racking," she said, as her three young children played at her feet. "The children don't understand. They asked a little while ago if Daddy is dead."

Friends and neighbors, she said, "have all been behind us one hundred percent," in stark comparison to the Pentagon. "I have heard from people we had long lost contact with. I haven't had one prank call. No peace freaks," she noted, "have bothered us."

*   *   *

Readers of the *Duncan Banner* anxiously awaited every troubling development in their hometown hero's plight. Karen and Lee Brumley had been an
ideal couple, high-school sweethearts, regular members of their Methodist
church. He had been a grocery boy, an Eagle Scout. The newspaper rarely let
an issue go by without some bulletin on the distressing case. On August 23,
another black headline streamed across the front page of the Oklahoma paper.

MRS. BRUMLEY RECEIVES LETTER FROM HUSBAND
HE'S ALL RIGHT, HAS LEGAL AID

"He says he is all right, but he gave no details about the case," the twenty-
six-year-old brunette told the paper. "Apparently he is in good spirits."

Karen Brumley had spent "a quiet day," the paper reported, but she had still
not heard from the Army. Only the Red Cross, she said, had let her know how
he was. Reluctantly, she said, she had taken steps to involve her congressman,
Carl Albert.

In Athens, Georgia, Budge Williams's embittered father released two of his
son's letters to a reporter from United Press International.

"I guess you are wondering why we were charged with murder," he had
written. "I have asked myself the same question a thousand times. I can't help
but think we are being held here on political reasons only."

The letter went on to describe the conditions the prisoners had endured in
solitary confinement. "You wouldn't treat a dog this way."

The family, Frank Williams said, had hired its own lawyer to look into the
case.

"We are writing to him every day," Emily Marasco told the *Newark Ledger*,
"trying to keep his spirits up."

Breaking her silence on the case, the mother of the captain accused of
pulling the trigger in the murder said she first learned of the arrest from a
friend who heard about it on the radio.

"We called the station," she said, "and they confirmed it." Nothing was said
of the letter her son had written home on July 23, pouring out his shame at
being arrested for an operation that had gone awry.

"He's been a good boy," said Emily Marasco. "He's a very dedicated
boy. He volunteered twice. He didn't have to go over there. He's very dedicated."

Privately, Bob Marasco's uncle Robert worried about the publicity. The
good press "can go the other way," he warned.

*   *   *

Nan Rheault sat behind her house on Martha's Vineyard, watching the gulls whirl and screech over the lagoon, talking to a reporter from the *New York Times*. She was smoking "far too many cigarettes," she said, and flinched at every ring of the telephone. Her twenty-year-old daughter, Suzanne, screened the deluge of calls.

"I'm afraid if I say anything I will jeopardize my husband," she said. "I'm afraid if I don't say anything, I will jeopardize him. But he is innocent of the charges that were made."

But not innocent of stepping on General Abrams's toes, she was sure. She knew that some of the stories suggesting a bitter Army–Green Beret rivalry driving the prosecution were true. She was also certain that her husband's aloof disdain for the Regular Army, combined with his near religious belief in the Special Forces, might have propelled him into a fatal clash with Gen. Creighton Abrams.

Her husband had been so anxious to get ready for Vietnam that he had skipped his mother's funeral, refusing to make the flight home from Okinawa.

"Why do I need to do that?" he said when she urged him to go home for the funeral. "What difference will it make if I'm there or not?"

As a full colonel with his own Green Beret unit and air wing, Rheault could have requisitioned an executive jet and flown to Boston and back in two days. But the 5th Special Forces job was too important for that; nothing could get in the way of getting to Vietnam and taking command.

Nan Rheault was shocked; Bob's mother had been the most kind and giving person, she thought, a nurturer, an anomaly in a family of remote, austere men. The fruit doesn't fall far from the tree, she concluded.

The Bradleys were cool New England patricians, but Bob's father was even more rigid, a French Canadian Catholic who had refused to come to their wedding. Bob brushed it off; his father was a man of another generation, he said. In fact, he was an aloof raconteur given to fireside chats about his exploits with the Mounties. He didn't talk with people so much as at them.

There was a lot of that in her husband, Nan Rheault thought, a kind of Victorian ideal of male suffering in the outdoors that was inflated by enlisting in the Green Berets. He certainly disdained the requirement of paying obeisance to Regular Army generals—they were so plebeian—while he was a warrior *and* an intellectual.

He always thought he was above them, she knew, going back to their time in Germany. He was a man in total control of his own destiny, not just another faceless colonel in a huge organization. The flip side of it was that he was the most natural leader of men she had ever seen.

He was lean, smart, aloof, nearly stoic, impatient with rambling philosophical discourse. Things were simple, black and white, good and bad. He had a way of grinning wide that gave him a messianic aura, his men thought. His remoteness, combined with a kind consideration for his men's welfare, created a fanatical devotion among his troops. "Ma'am," a sergeant volunteered to Nan Rheault one day out of the blue, "I'd follow him to hell and back."

Bob Rheault was never more happy than when he was with his men in the field. He hated stateside duty on an Army post. He had to be in the mountains or jungles leading a small team of Green Berets. He was good at suffering, his wife thought, to the point of masochism.

"Nothing is worth having," he would lecture his children, "unless it's hard to get." Yet he detested a lack of control in others. One night a gas oven blew up in his wife's face and she ran screaming from the kitchen. He slapped her across the face.

"Why did you do that!" she cried, shocked, her eyebrows and eyelashes singed.

"Because you were hysterical," he said.

She could imagine the difficulty he would have in suppressing his disdain for Abrams. She was particularly apprehensive about his assignment to Vietnam after he told her of a tense encounter he had had with the general.

He had lobbied Abrams not to take the Green Berets out of Vietnam ahead of regular Army troops. The general had dismissed him with hardly a word. Rheault later told the story to Nan to illustrate Abrams's intractability and blind prejudice against the Green Berets. But she drew a different interpretation from the account. When, in June, she got a letter from him saying "I've just made the most important decision in my life, which will affect you and the children," she felt a wave of apprehension.

Now she knew why.

"Mrs. Rheault," the New York Times reported, "is nothing like the movie stereotype of an Army wife." The paper recounted her schooling at Chapin and Vassar, her stints as a painter and fashion model. The Rheaults were married in an elaborate wedding at St. James Episcopal Church in New York, with a reception at the Cosmopolitan Club. "Daddy wanted it," she said. "I was his only daughter."

What she didn't tell the reporter was that her father had turned a cold shoulder to her when the case broke, appalled by the conduct alleged against her husband. So had Bob Rheault's own father, but for a different reason; he was ashamed of his son for disgracing the family name by his arrest. Even their Army friends had abandoned them, afraid for their careers.

Once they were the toast of the town. Now they were just toast.

She didn't want to be "pushy," she told the reporter, but she had visited the summer home of Republican senator Edward Brooke to enlist his support.

"Well, here I sit," Eddie Boyle wrote to his parents, "waiting to find out if we will have to go to trial for the alleged killing of one gook."

In the three weeks since the end of the hearings, Boyle had jogged daily, played cards, and written countless letters home. At night, he drank smuggled beer with his comrades and watched reruns of "Combat" on Armed Forces TV, hooting "War crime! War crime!" every time a Nazi soldier was gunned down by a heroic GI.

"The CIA screwed up the whole operation," Boyle wrote home. "Now they deny their part, of course.

"All of the key defense witnesses have disappeared. One CIA witness appeared at the hearing. That bastard actually *lied* under oath. His lies were ridiculously obvious, and my lawyer Henry Rothblatt shot holes in his story. Other than this shithead's phony story, the government has no evidence that can be used against us."

If the case went forward, he vowed, the Army would have hell to pay. "If we go to trial, it will be the messiest affair in the history of the army. We know enough nasty stuff to shake everything from international affairs to the price of cigarettes on the black market.

"We will go all out to drag the army, not to mention the CIA, through the mud. If push comes to shove, we will put out enough dirt about the army and the CIA to make the Bay of Pigs look like a Sunday school picnic."

Just that morning, he told his parents, he had read about a VC terrorist attack that had left fourteen children dead.

"Will they be tried for murder? I don't think so. The U.S. has lost its first war due to its own idealistic standards of morality. The VC used these standards to beat us. The U.S. used these standards to charge us with murder. They trained us and sent us to Vietnam to fight a war. When we used our training, they decided to call it murder."

Boyle mused about American bombing and strafing in Vietnam, which had produced thousands of civilian casualties: "I wonder if the bomber pilot and artilleryman will be put in jail? I think that we have been pretty good about it so far. We have been loyal to the government. Believe me, they had better start showing some loyalty in return."

It was time, he told his parents, to write to their congressman. "Tell him we are not all bad guys, that we don't hate kids and dogs and that we like apple pie and baseball.

"You know," he quipped, "jazz it up a little."

More than most people, CIA agents accepted the fact that Americans were ambivalent about the necessity of a spy establishment. The public liked the idea of a medieval order of knights fighting for their honor in the back alleys of the world, but they preferred not to know the details.

Now, with the fickle winds of public opinion beginning to shift against the elite secretive agency, CIA officers fanned out to provide unusual background briefings for selected editors and reporters on the Green Beret case. One of the chosen outlets was the New York Times.

"Since the CIA was formed in 1947," an anonymous "reliable source" assured the newspaper, "the agency has followed a strict policy of neither ordering, suggesting, or condoning assassinations."

"The CIA," the source declared, "is a member of the U.S. Government's intelligence community, and subject to very strict control by a special White House team of presidential advisors. It does not go in for assassination."

A Newsweek summary of the CIA press offensive began with the headline, "Who Killed Thai Khac Chuyen? Not I, said the CIA."

Amid reports that agency officers had indeed "advised" the Green Berets to kill Chuyen, CIA headquarters was concerned enough to send out a memorandum of "guidance" on the case to its employees in Saigon and other global outposts, advising them that assassination was strictly against regulations.

The memo was received with relief by some, especially the more recent recruits who had joined the agency with the belief that intelligence gathering was an honorable profession in a nuclear-armed world. One was Frank Snepp, a bright young political analyst who had arrived for a second Saigon tour just as the Chuyen affair surfaced. The son of a North Carolina judge and a graduate of Columbia University's School of International Studies, Snepp's specialty was managing North Vietnamese spies. He believed he had a highly developed ethical compass.

Immoral acts were hard to define, Snepp thought. Like pornography, you knew them when you saw them. He considered Operation Phoenix a distasteful but necessary tool of guerrilla war, as long as it was conducted as designed with legal arrests and interrogations. He attributed its "excesses of violence" to criminal or inept South Vietnamese. Sometimes the excesses were retaliatory: The Viet Cong were routinely carrying out assassinations in their elaborately staged "people's revolutionary courts," in which a hamlet chief would be dragged out of his home in the middle of the night, denounced, and executed on the spot in front of a crowd of cowering villagers. The guerrillas would leave his bloody corpse on the street as they faded back into the dark.

Phoenix was an inevitable response to guerrilla war, Snepp believed, but assassination as a policy was something else. That was over the line, Gestapo tactics.

He was disturbed by what he heard about the Chuyen case. When a memo came from CIA headquarters specifically prohibiting assassinations as a matter of policy, he shrugged with cautious relief. He wouldn't want to be part of an organization that did that sort of thing.

Another who read the memo was Jim Ward, the desk officer for Vietnam operations at Langley. A graduate of Boston College, Ward had studied ethics under the Jesuits. He had been concerned about the moral quotient of warfare ever since he joined the Army as a private in 1940. His whole career had been spent in the paramilitary ranks, going back to the OSS's Detachment 101 in Southeast Asia during World War II. After that he joined the Green Berets, serving with the 10th, 3rd, 6th, and 7th Special Forces Groups in Europe and Asia.

On one occasion with the OSS, he intervened to stop Burmese Kachin tribesmen from beating to death a Shan tribesman who had led them into a Japanese ambush. That was forbidden, he explained; they had to have a trial: That was what the war against the Fascists was all about.

"Okay," they said. "We have a trial, then we kill him."

Ward had run a Phoenix team in the delta before taking up a desk in Langley.

There were abuses, he conceded. At first, the PRUs were killing far more than they were capturing. He struggled to bring the team into line, weeding out the extortionists and other bad elements among the Vietnamese who filled the ranks. Then it started to turn around. Somewhere along the way he asked

CIA headquarters in Saigon to send him the rules of land warfare to distribute to the team. He asked again. And again. He never got it.

Ward was troubled by the Green Beret case. He strongly felt that no Americans should be running around Vietnam willy-nilly eliminating people. But he thought these men had been singled out for special punishment by General Abrams, because he was very worried about being brought up before Congress on a "dirty war" charge. Considering what else the U.S. military was doing under Abrams's command, Ward thought, the prosecution was hypocritical. When he made his thoughts known around Langley, he was severed from any connection with the case.

In the last week of August, "The Case of the Green Berets" made the covers of *Time, Newsweek,* and *U.S. News and World Report.* The pace of the coverage was intensifying daily. Creighton Abrams, dubbed "too good a general to waste on Vietnam" when he succeeded William Westmoreland in late 1968, had become an object of ridicule. One cartoon showed him taking aim with an ax on a Green Beret's neck only to slice off his own head on the backstroke.

It was a public relations disaster.

"Details will leak out of a secret trial," the *Washington Post*'s George Wilson had observed. "The legal preliminaries certainly have demonstrated that. The Army has maneuvered itself into a position on the murder case that it cannot hold or get out of unscathed."

At the White House, the Pentagon, and on Capitol Hill, mailbags piled up with thousands of letters protesting the Army's treatment of the embattled defendants.

The case had touched a raw nerve, but polls showed few Americans felt that a dubious ethical threshold might have been crossed in Vietnam. Many thought the case showed how hard it was to tell friend from foe among the Vietnamese. But the overwhelming majority of Americans, to judge from mail flowing to Washington, saw the arrests as a symbol of the high-level politicking that had hamstrung the fighting men from the beginning.

"I am a supporter of the U.S. policies in Southeast Asia," one man wrote to Congressman George Bush, "but my confidence is greatly shaken when organizational bungling is 'straightened out' by murder charges against American troops. The CIA and particularly General Abrams are not representative of America, what we stand for and fight for in Vietnam or anywhere else."

Another man wrote to Texas senator John Tower: "I deplore and protest what seems to be an increasing effort to make sacrificial goats of our combat personnel. Our men are fighting a particularly vicious enemy who assume the role of peaceful civilians to infiltrate and destroy at will, and under such circumstances mistakes can occur."

A Virginia man protested in *Newsweek:* "At a time when everyone from the Vietcong to the Israelis is emphasizing clandestine military operations as an integral line of defense, we hamstring our own effort, the Special Forces."

Only a minority thought that the alleged acts of the Green Berets might signal a broken moral compass in Vietnam. "The nation has lost its sense of shame," one man wrote to *Time*, for condoning "the murder of an unarmed civilian, who should have been imprisoned if indeed he was guilty of anything."

The case was "a nauseating introduction to the realities of our 'conflict' in Vietnam," wrote another. The name of the Special Forces, she said, should be changed to "what it is—the American SS."

Under a broiling sun at Fort Bragg, North Carolina, a ceremony was held to rename the Special Warfare Center, home of the Green Berets. From now on, the assembled dignitaries were told, it was to be called "The John F. Kennedy Center for Military Assistance."

"The new name," its commander proclaimed, "emphasizes the positive things we do. We are 'assisters'—a constructive force."

"In a way, we're a kind of Peace Corps," the center's training officer told reporters later.

Unfortunately, the Green Beret case had put a pall over the festivities.

"They have made us look like a bunch of Mafia characters who sit around fingering people to kill," one colonel grumbled to a *Washington Post* reporter. "And that is a goddamned lie. We don't have any Al Capones in this outfit."

William Westmoreland was outraged over the bad publicity the case was giving the Special Forces. One morning the Army chief of staff called an old friend, Gen. Ted Clifton, to discuss the case. Per usual, his secretary listened in and took notes.

"That Green Beret thing is unfortunate," he said. He had conducted his own investigation and discovered that only Colonel Rheault could be legitimately called a Green Beret.

"All the others are intelligence types," he said. "The captain from New Jersey," he mused, "is CIA"—apparently confusing Bob Marasco with Alvin Smith's former CIA employment. He wondered about the possibility of changing the way the Pentagon referred to the affair. Instead of "the Green Beret Case," he suggested, why not start calling it "The Double Agent Case"?

"Do you think the CIA will stand for it?" Clifton asked. "They came out pretty burned on this thing."

"I think so," Westmoreland said. "The military can have double agents, too." He said he'd take it up with Stanley Resor.

The conversation turned to golf. Neither man had apparently thought of the difficulties the name change would have with the Army's version of the case. In the official scheme of things, Thai Khac Chuyen was still an innocent civilian.

"I don't know how long they're going to drag this thing out," Tom Middleton wrote to George Gregory as August gave way to September.

"I am just glad that Col. Rheault is involved. If not, I wouldn't be a bit surprised if they didn't try to hang us. He is so big and has so many friends that he could, and probably will be, our ace in the hole."

PART VI

Flap

49

Richard Nixon sat at his Oval Office desk, swelling with irritation and disgust as he read through the White House morning news summary. "Ho gets better notices than Dirkson," the president scribbled in the margin. It galled him that Ho Chi Minh, with whom the United States was effectively at war and who was the nemesis of five U.S. presidents going back to Harry Truman, had died to respectful American notices on September 3. In comparison, Everett Dirkson, the longtime Illinois Republican leader in the U.S. Senate, had earned only faint praise as a legislative technician.

Nixon had served in Congress for years with Dirkson, a mellifluous orator who had backed Nixon's many campaigns and anti-Communist crusades, one of which was Vietnam. Nixon had made an issue of Vietnam as far back as 1954 when Ho's guerrilla armies were defeating the French at Dien Bien Phu. In some ways, the careers of Nixon and Ho mirrored each other with their alternating triumphs and detours. When Nixon entered the Oval Office in January 1969, each was at the height of his power, facing off, dominating the world's stage.

The obituaries on Ho Chi Minh were a bad omen. They signaled that the honeymoon was over for Nixon; the press had given him a grace period to launch his "secret plan" to end the war. Now they wanted results. The antiwar movement was restless, showing signs of new life after a dormant winter.

Nixon was convinced the media was hopelessly liberal, but he railed at it nevertheless. Unlike his predecessor, who had installed a bank of television sets in his office so he could monitor all three nightly news broadcasts, Nixon thought it was a waste of time. Not that he didn't care what the networks and columnists said about him. He cared deeply; he knew they carried the power to make or break his administration. But Nixon, an avid reader, preferred to pore over a daily digest of the national and regional media, both television and print, which he could read in a matter of minutes. He had hired a brash young conservative, Patrick Buchanan, to run the operation and put a compilation of excerpts on his desk by 9 A.M. It was called the White House morning news summary.

Buchanan had impressed Nixon with his tough, take-no-prisoners editorials in the St. Louis Globe-Dispatch, with his outspoken support for the Vietnam

War, his opposition to busing, and his excoriation of weak-kneed liberals on a variety of other subjects. It didn't hurt Buchanan's standing with Nixon that he had infamously slugged a liberal student during an argument at Columbia Journalism School.

Buchanan further ingratiated himself with Nixon by putting a conservative spin on the items in his news summary, which seldom failed to get a rise out of the boss. On the morning of September 9, Buchanan put the needle in deep with lengthy excerpts from the media's respectful treatment of Ho Chi Minh's life.

Buchanan also noted that students at Boston University had announced plans to hold memorial services for the North Vietnamese leader. Condolences were flowing to Hanoi from antiwar groups around the world. "The voice of the hawk is hardly heard in the land," he lamented.

Buchanan also reported that the Viet Cong had already violated the three-day cease-fire proclaimed in honor of Ho's death, which the United States said it would also observe. Viet Cong rockets had been launched on eighty-three allied bases in South Vietnam, killing twenty Americans, thirty South Vietnamese soldiers, and eight civilians. The U.S. command claimed a body count of one hundred forty enemy killed.

A report on the Green Beret case noting that the Army was expected to announce its courts-martial decision soon appeared further down in the news summary.

For Nixon, the juxtaposition of the three events—American citizens mourning Ho Chi Minh while Viet Cong rockets killed GIs and the U.S. Army prosecuted its own soldiers for killing a North Vietnamese spy—was galling.

"Get twenty letters on this," he scrawled in the margin. By day's end Buchanan had inspired twenty letters to the editor from "ordinary citizens" protesting the media's "biased" coverage of Ho's death. Most of them were manufactured in Buchanan's office, which had compiled a list of phony names and addresses for just such a purpose. The list was salted with the names of real Nixon partisans who could be called on to fire off a letter on any given subject at the request of the White House.

The Green Beret case only reinforced Nixon's resentment of college students: They had it easy, he bitterly complained. They were far from the lines. They were spoiled. They were bums.

Nixon, a Navy supply officer in the Pacific in World War II, would often rail against the students, pacing the Oval Office in his dark suit and heavy shoes while John Ehrlichman, H. R. Haldeman, or Henry Kissinger murmured agreement.

Something needed to be done about the antiwar movement, Nixon would grouse. *Yes, sir.* The Communists and their fellow travelers in the universities and Congress had to be neutralized. *Yes, sir.* They were even infecting the military services. *Right, boss.* There were too many leaks. *Goddam right.*

But the gloves were coming off. His illegal wiretaps, which had started with Kissinger's own aides after the Cambodia bombing leaked partially in March, were expanding weekly to officials at the Pentagon and the State Department and to the homes of reporters who covered foreign policy in Washington. The problem was, nothing much had come of the taps beyond the usual capital gossip—typically, office chitchat and the price of real estate.

Haldeman sensed his boss's frustration. The CIA was useless, they thought; despite a million-dollar CIA investigation, Richard Helms had failed to find proof of ties between the antiwar movement and Moscow. That was ridiculous, the Nixon men thought; of course the KGB was fueling the protest. To satisfy his boss's gut instincts, Haldeman had scheduled a meeting for the president on September 11 with Egil Krogh and Tom Huston, ambitious young White House assistants who had formulated a broad new strategy for infiltrating and disrupting the antiwar forces.

Much to Nixon's distress, Vietnam was taking too much of his time. The week was nearly devoted to the war. Ambassador Bunker and General Abrams were due at the White House on September 12. FBI director Hoover, CIA director Helms, Defense Secretary Melvin Laird and Secretary of State William Rogers were scheduled for special Vietnam strategy meetings. How could he find time for his grand new initiatives with Moscow, Peking, and the Middle East?

Nixon vowed he was going to get out of Vietnam, and he didn't want anything to interfere with that. He needed to deemphasize Vietnam, he told his aides, to get it out of America's daily consciousness. But all of a sudden, things like the Green Beret case were getting in the way; he was considering taking over the case, he told John Ehrlichman, and dismissing the charges.

Good idea, the pugnacious Seattle lawyer quickly agreed. The Berets were heroes, not villains. They shouldn't be treated like criminals for doing their job. Damn right.

But there was a roadblock, he said: Melvin Laird. Laird was backing General Abrams on this thing.

Laird had been picked to run the Pentagon because of his clout on Capitol Hill, but he was already thinking of going home to Wisconsin and running for the Senate, Ehrlichman said. Wisconsin, of course, was strongly antiwar, politically beyond the pale. To soften up the voters back home, Laird was constantly leaking stories that distanced himself from the "hawks in the White House."

Laird had actually opposed the bombing of Cambodia, enraging Nixon and Kissinger and forcing them to go around him to the Joint Chiefs of Staff. Laird soon found out about it, but he didn't mind Nixon's deception on the bombing so much; he could disown the operation when it inevitably flapped.

There was already plenty of dissent churning among the small circle in the Pentagon privy to the bombings, some of whom worried that the secrecy tampered with the command and control of the Strategic Air Command's nuclear weapons.

Laird was "a sneak," Nixon railed. That's why they had to bug his aide's telephone. Ehrlichman readily agreed.

The other problem was Stanley Resor, Nixon grumbled. Nine months had gone by and Resor still had holdovers from the Johnson administration working for him. Resor was a decent man, but he was an LBJ appointment. What the hell was the problem? he demanded. Couldn't they find any Nixon people to hire?

Ehrlichman scribbled a note to himself to begin looking for replacements for Resor. He would have to work through Laird—it was the defense secretary's bailiwick. But Nixon wouldn't deal with Laird himself; it wasn't his style. He'd deal through Henry Kissinger.

As it turned out, the "Resor problem" had been kicked around the White House already. Nixon had asked his political operative Peter Flanagan to get Kissinger involved. It was typical of the president to put three different people on something like this and not let any of them know.

Flanagan had dropped a memo on Kissinger on August 22.

"When Stanley Resor was retained as Secretary of the Army, it was agreed that his retention would be for only one year. When I suggested to the president that he remind Secretary Laird of this, he asked that I ask you to discuss this with Laird instead. For your background information, Resor has not been particularly cooperative in restaffing the Department of the Army."

Good, Ehrlichman thought, let Kissinger handle it. In Ehrlichman's estimation, Kissinger was nauseously duplicitous, goading Nixon into escalation in Vietnam while presenting himself as a dove to the liberals at Harvard. Kissinger wouldn't want to leave any fingerprints on a move against Laird, Ehrlichman thought. So he was surprised one morning in mid-September when he found Resor sitting in Kissinger's office.

Ehrlichman had been auditing a perfunctory meeting between Nixon and Joseph Blatchford, director of the Peace Corps, when Kissinger called him out of the Oval Office. He had Stan Resor with him, Kissinger said collegially. They were discussing the Green Beret case. Since there were legal issues involved, maybe the White House counsel should hear what he had to say.

Ehrlichman was amused; Kissinger was loath to involve other senior aides in anything he considered to fall within his national security portfolio. Ehrlichman suspected Nixon had ordered Kissinger to include him. He also guessed Nixon was using Kissinger to make an end run around Laird to Resor on the Green Beret case.

Kissinger had already established his own back channel around Laird through David Packard, a California industrialist and heavy Nixon contributor who had been appointed assistant secretary of defense. Packard had confidentially reported to Kissinger on the deliberations of the President's Foreign Intelligence Advisory Board on the Green Beret case.

The PFIAB was composed of heavy hitters recruited from the highest circles of the military-industrial complex. Set up by President Kennedy following the Bay of Pigs disaster, it was publicly praised as a panel of towering figures in American finance, industry, and the military who could give the president independent advice in the midst of a pressing national security crisis. In reality, PFIAB members usually just sucked their pipes and rubber-stamped decisions the president had already made. When it sat down in secret to take up the Green Beret case in August 1969, it was composed of such men as New

York governor Nelson Rockefeller; William O. Baker, the chairman of Bell Labs; Edwin Land, the founder of Polaroid; Frank Pace, the chairman of General Dynamics; and Franklin D. Murphy, chairman of the board of the Times-Mirror Company, publisher of the *Los Angeles Times*. Others around the table were Adm. George W. Anderson, a former chief of Naval Operations; retired Gen. Maxwell Taylor, Kennedy's military adviser and former ambassador to South Vietnam; and Gordon Gray, a onetime secretary of the Army.

The board met in an unremarkable red brick building on Jackson Place across from the White House. Chairing the meeting was J. Patrick Coyne, a ranking former FBI official. Coyne explained the absence of the customary yellow pads and pencils in front of the members with the instruction that no notes were to be taken for the special session. The topic was too sensitive.

The board heard two separate briefings, one from Army counsel Robert Jordan, one from CIA counsel Lawrence Houston. The events of the case were briskly reprised with emphasis on the nature of the Green Beret spy mission in Cambodia in support of the secret bombing. The identity and mission of the dead agent per se was not important, the board was told. What was important was the extent and means of the bombing, as well as other sensitive intelligence operations in Cambodia. Plus, the board was informed, "over-aggressive" defense lawyers in the case were attempting to broaden the inquiry into other areas that were "inappropriate" for public discussion.

The Army and CIA versions of the incident were "generally in agreement," Packard informed Kissinger, except for some minor recriminations on who was responsible for orders to kill the agent. The board recommended the president bury the case. Too much was at stake.

Ehrlichman walked down to Kissinger's cramped suite adjacent to the Situation Room in the White House basement. Nine or ten assistants worked at desks outside his office.

When Ehrlichman entered, Resor was summarizing the facts of the case and his belief that the case should go to trial. The men would be exonerated, he believed, but the principles of law must be upheld. General Abrams felt very strongly about it.

Ehrlichman sat back to listen. He had never met Resor before. The courtly lawyer was not his image of a secretary of the Army, he thought. He expected someone different, a little rougher around the edges, perhaps, someone more blunt, more military. Resor seemed a little sensitive in Ehrlichman's estimation. He even sounded squeamish about the details of Chuyen's execution.

"To quash the court-martial of these men," he would remember Resor saying, "would, in my view, be both immoral and political dynamite. It is bad enough we are over there fighting an immoral war." Resor vehemently denied such sentiments later.

Kissinger soothed the Army secretary. Yes, yes, he said with a deep sigh, his eyes drooping, wagging his head slowly. He, too, thought it was an immoral war.

Ehrlichman was amused. Kissinger was a master of this act, which he usually employed with antiwar delegations from Cambridge. All the professors came away thinking their former Harvard colleague was the only hope among the warmongering Nixon crowd. Little did they know Kissinger was hand-picking targets in Cambodia and reading wiretap summaries of their favorite reporters' gossip.

"The CIA and the United States Army," Resor went on, "simply do not do business as the men in this case did. Spies are not taken out and killed without due process of law."

Kissinger nodded. Ehrlichman made a note on his legal pad: "Who'll believe that?"

Indeed, that very morning's White House news summary included a CBS report from Saigon that "three hundred South Vietnamese have been assassinated by the Green Berets over the past seven years."

"The Army," the report went on, "which does not like the independence of the outfit, would like to see it destroyed. But the sordid nature of the exposures could be damaging to all concerned. The assassinated supposedly include high South Vietnamese officials, whose death has been made to appear the work of the Viet Cong."

Patrick Buchanan had noted that the expanding attention to the Green Beret case by the media served "no other purpose than to show an administration in disarray."

Ehrlichman agreed with that. Nixon had been enraged when the idea had been floated of cutting the budget for the Phoenix program. He wanted "more assassinations" of Viet Cong, he demanded, not fewer. He had ordered Kissinger to have the Pentagon study the option of assassinating Cambodia's Prince Sihanouk, an operation code-named Dirty Tricks. Not even Laird knew about that.

The Green Beret case was posing a dilemma for the White House, Ehrlichman thought. General Abrams, with Laird's backing, was intent on courts-martial. If the White House called off the case, it risked his wrath, maybe even resignation, as well as the denunciation of liberals who could be counted on to make a cause célèbre of the case. If the White House let the Army go forward, all sorts of other garbage could percolate to the surface.

Who would have thought putting cement boots on one Viet Cong spy could have caused all this?

Ehrlichman mentally flipped a coin. Nixon would want the case dropped, he was sure. The question would be how to cover their tracks.

The telephone rang at Camp David, the presidential retreat in the Maryland mountains. A steward took the message and entered the room where Nixon was dining with Ehrlichman, Haldeman, Kissinger, and Bryce Harlow, Nixon's old friend and congressional liaison. Melvin Laird was on the telephone, the steward said. He wanted to speak with John Ehrlichman.

Ehrlichman raised an eyebrow. The others around the table were equally mystified. Why would Laird be calling *him?* Kissinger was Laird's contact at the White House.

The stocky White House counsel left the room to take the call.

Stanley Resor was with him, Laird said. Resor had just talked to General Abrams and Adm. John McCain, commander in chief in the Pacific. Both of them, Laird said, felt it was absolutely necessary for the Green Beret case to proceed to a court-martial.

Ehrlichman wondered why Laird was calling Camp David at night to relay such a message.

Well, Laird said, he wanted the president to know that the top two military men in Vietnam believed the Green Berets would be absolved and that it was important for a trial to proceed to such a verdict.

Ehrlichman waited for more.

"Unfortunately," Laird said, "a great many people think the Berets *are* assassins; an acquittal would clear the record."

Ehrlichman grunted assent. He said he would relay the message and hung up.

He wondered again why Laird had chosen him to talk to. When he returned to the table, he recounted the strange conversation.

Harlow, a longtime Republican political operative, mentioned that he knew McCain well. He doubted that the admiral felt that way about the case. He suspected Laird was playing politics with the affair, looking for some kind of an advantage. He had probably picked up a rumor that the president might dismiss the case and was already paddling away from it. Harlow wondered what his old friend McCain had really told Resor and Laird.

The men chuckled. At Nixon's urging, Harlow picked up a telephone at the table and tried to call McCain. They all listened as Harlow learned the admiral was not available; he was flying to his office in Hawaii. Harlow hung up and they went back to their meal.

An hour later, Ehrlichman was summoned out of the room for another call. It was Laird again.

Why was the White House trying to reach McCain? the defense secretary wanted to know.

Ehrlichman started to refer him to Harlow, but Laird stopped him. A Pentagon reporter, he said, was going with a story that the White House had decided to quash the court-martial.

A typical Laird gambit, Ehrlichman thought. Laird was trying to flush out what they were doing on the case.

No decision had been reached, Ehrlichman assured Laird. He hung up and returned to the table.

"Mel knows Bryce tried to call McCain," he said, smiling. "How do you suppose he knew that?" Ehrlichman put on a Cheshire cat's grin as Nixon and his aides chewed on the riddle.

Finally, there were chortles all around. They knew how Laird found out: All of Camp David's telephones went through an Army Signal Corps switchboard. Laird obviously had his spies keeping track of who they were calling.

Haldeman made a mental note to change the communications system and to expand the taps on Laird and Kissinger's staff.

Nobody could be trusted.

At 9:40 the morning of September 12, Nixon convened a special meeting on Vietnam in the White House cabinet room. All the major players in the war were seated around the long shiny table. There were Ambassador Bunker and General Abrams from Saigon, Admiral McCain from Hawaii, and from the Paris Peace Talks, Ambassador Philip Habib. Gen. Earle Wheeler came over from the Joint Chiefs of Staff. Laird, CIA director Richard Helms, William Rogers, Kissinger and his military aide, Colonel Alexander Haig, and even Vice President Agnew, filled out the room along with assorted note takers and assistants.

The administration had been facing sharp political and military setbacks in Vietnam. Nguyen Van Thieu, already nervous about U.S. troop withdrawals, was paranoid about Nixon and Kissinger going behind his back to make a deal with the Communists. There had been troubling reports of deepening friction between U.S. and Vietnamese troops, in the field, at General Staff levels, and in the streets of Saigon. Hanoi, meanwhile, was showing no signs of allowing the United States a "decent interval" to get its troops out. Casualties were up in a series of sharp attacks.

Nixon's first announcement was his intention to resume B-52 raids over North Vietnam, which had been suspended for three days as a peace initiative. The generals smiled.

But there were other items on the agenda. The withdrawal of another thirty-five thousand U.S. troops from Vietnam would shortly be announced. With students returning to campus, there would also be an announcement of a dramatic reduction in the draft call.

Next up for discussion was the long-range prospect for withdrawing American troops from Vietnam. Nixon was well attuned to the American fatigue with Vietnam. He had campaigned on ending the war with a "secret plan." He told the assembled group he was putting the finishing touches on a televised address to the nation on September 16.

"The time has come to end this war," he would say. "The time for meaningful negotiations has arrived."

It was an elaborate deception, as some of the men in the room knew. Privately, they were planning for a series of violent spasms to end the war. Unknown to the public, the press, the Congress, and many administration officials, the White House had decided to invade Cambodia and Laos. Going around Laird, Henry Kissinger was minutely involved in the planning with military officers.

None of this, of course, was openly discussed in the cabinet room meeting, which was adjourned at 1:45. The participants left thoroughly implanted with the notion that Nixon was ending the war through negotiation and conciliation. The way Washington worked, the message of Nixon-as-statesman would be making the rounds of Georgetown dinner parties by sundown.

Twenty minutes after the meeting ended, Nixon gathered together Kissinger, McCain, Bunker, and Abrams in his hideaway office in the Old Executive Office Building next to the White House.

This time the topic was Cambodia, and everything related to it. The meeting began at five minutes past two.

When Nixon emerged an hour later, he quickly returned to the Oval Office. He summoned John Mitchell to discuss a touchy legal problem.

"Dear Mom and Dad," Bob Marasco wrote on September 13. "We have been told unofficially, by unofficial sources in D.C., that everything will be taken care of, but we have been hearing that for a month now. It is my understanding that the decision is being made in the White House."

Tom Middleton, like Marasco and the other men, was impatient with the long delay. They had been transferred from solitary into a guarded barracks, but they were still in jail. Altogether, they had been locked up for almost two months.

"Not a damn thing is happening here," he wrote to George Gregory, who was back in South Carolina making speeches on behalf of the Green Berets to the local Lions and Rotary clubs. There was talk of running the celebrated lawyer for a seat in Congress.

"I don't know how much longer they are going to drag their feet," Middleton complained. "I have a bad feeling the brass here want to push it. If they do, it could be bad. There are many other leads that they could hustle up if they were sharp. I wrote to Phyllis and told her some things she could release."

Middleton told Gregory to make sure South Carolina's congressional delegation was working together "to quietly put pressure on the secretary of the army."

Rheault is "our ace in hole," he wrote once again, because "he is so big and has so many friends."

Not far away, alone in his trailer, Rheault agonized over his men's fate and what he could do about it. He still believed Abrams was the cause of their problems, and Abrams still held the key.

In the past few weeks, he had rallied his men again. He had touched their deep competitive nerves, their natural instincts to fight back, to escape from impossible situations. He had inspired them, telling them that the country backed them, that the people of America knew they had acted honorably in defense of their country.

He assured them the government would inevitably come to its senses, that they would end up the heroes they truly were. The Army, he promised, would be forced to drop the case.

The men had responded, believing once again in their charismatic leader, forgiving him for the difficult times during the investigation. As Budge Williams said, "Shit, I would probably have done the same thing." Now they were together again. They were going to beat the rap—or take everybody down with them on the way.

Privately, however, Rheault knew their situation was dire. The rumors from his friend Bill Simpson had been bad, very bad.

Nixon and Abrams had argued over the case, his friend reported.

Abrams had won. It looked like they were going to trial.

50

B ut gentlemen," Stanley Resor said again, "the Army simply cannot condone murder."

The secretary of the Army sat patiently in the corner of Rep. Peter Rodino's office, responding to the tirades of a half dozen congressmen gathered together to denounce his handling of the Green Beret case. For the third time, he attempted to explain the rules of military justice and the Geneva Convention. Even a spy had the benefit of trial under the rules of the Geneva Convention, he said. Even in Vietnam.

It was a bad time to be the civilian head of any one of the military services. Stanley Resor's army, the army of his own youth, had found its character at Anzio, Normandy, and the Battle of the Bulge. It was an army that had stood atop the ashes of Nazi Germany and imperial Japan, proud symbols of American courage, decency, and democracy, a cross section of all America. And it was rapidly passing from the scene.

In its place was a far different corps: professional systems men, management types, cautious bureaucrats, and politicians. The army raised for Vietnam was racked by poor training, slack discipline and, as the conflict wore on, drug addiction, race riots, and the poison of "ticket-punching career hops." Even old-fashioned corruption was eating at the ranks, as an indictment of a group of sergeants major for controlling a racket of Saigon slot machines amply demonstrated.

No wonder Americans were disenchanted or hostile toward their military services. Even the Army's gross IQ had been lowered under a notorious scheme of Robert McNamara, LBJ's defense secretary, who relaxed mental standards to fatten the draft-call rolls. Juvenile delinquents were being given the choice of jail or jungle, while college students were exempted. The average age of American soldiers chasing Viet Cong guerrillas, meanwhile, was nineteen. In World War II it was twenty-six.

The Army and Vietnam were inextricably bound. The longer the war went on, the more dramatic the military's slide from its honored place among American institutions. The soldiers were the first to know it, shunned by their peers, ridiculed when they came home. "Baby killers," they were called as they exited the gates. Lately an alarming phenomenon had developed: The soldiers themselves began to agree that they had done something terribly wrong in Vietnam.

America deserved a better army, Resor thought. Nearly ten years of fighting in Vietnam had corrupted its standards. Civilians had been bombed, villages razed, prisoners slapped and beaten, often on TV. Such practices were as predictable as war itself, but not to an American dining at home, watching the news. And to Stanley Resor, the excesses could not be accepted as policy.

The Army's partnership with the CIA had also been subversive. Secrecy, the mother's milk of intelligence work, was too often the handmaiden of deceit. The lying bred arrogance. Congress had been misled too often in recent years. It was not the proper conduct for an army in a democracy.

All these things had happened, and were continuing to happen, because of Vietnam. Against such crimes, the summary execution of a lone suspected enemy spy might seem inconsequential. But there were consequences, Resor thought: the Code of Conduct, which stitched the Army together with discipline and honor.

A civilized army, an army bound to international conventions composed as a result of history's record of atrocities, does not approve of shooting prisoners, he believed. Even in a guerrilla war, where the identity of civilians and soldiers was blurred. That, he thought, was what made us different from them.

The Army's salvation, Stanley Resor believed, lay in raising its standards, not debasing them. In that, he was one with his contemporaries, Creighton Abrams and George Mabry, who had learned the rules of ground warfare in an earlier era, fighting Nazi tanks.

But the congressmen who now flailed at Resor saw none of that. What they saw was a patrician Wall Street lawyer, educated at Groton and Yale, married to a Pillsbury flour heiress. A dilettante who couldn't possibly understand Vietnam.

The congressmen scoffed at Resor's case for courts-martial. That might have made sense in World War II, they said, where the battle lines were clearly drawn. But in Vietnam, half the civilians were helping the enemy. How could the soldiers reasonably be expected to distinguish between the Viet Cong and the civilians? They had done their best. If the Green Berets did wrongly kill the man, so what? Was the proper punishment life in jail?

Rodino held in his hand the letter from Bob Marasco, citing "coordination with civilian agencies." And from the news accounts of the case, it was clear the CIA had been consulted and had given its advice. He had also obtained a secret memo from Army intelligence to the judge advocate general on the relationship between the Green Berets and the CIA.

"Members of Special Forces," it said, "are not subject to orders promulgated by CIA or any non-military agencies of the United States."

Rodino read further: "In the case of intelligence, sensitive operations are coordinated with the representative of the Director of Central Intelligence as required by National Security Council Directives."

He gave the Army secretary a puzzled look. The Army wanted it both ways. What was the difference between "orders" and "coordination"?

But Rodino's attention was drawn to the next sentence of the Army memo: "It is unknown to this office if any of the suspects involved in this case were subject to any order outside of the military chain of command in connection with the incident that gave rise to the alleged murder."

"Unknown?" Wasn't that the crux of the case? he asked Resor. The memo was signed by Col. Richard L. Ruhle, director of operations for the Army's General Staff. To Rodino, it smacked of bureaucratic ass-covering by the Army.

Suddenly, Rep. John Culver of Iowa stood up, red-faced and furious. A rugged blond-haired former marine, Culver had fought in Korea. But he hated the war in Vietnam, which gave him all the more sympathy for the boys who had to fight it. Especially a constituent from Cedar Rapids, Major David Crew.

Culver thrust out an arm and pointed a finger at the elegant Army secretary sitting in the corner.

"How the hell can you judge these men!" he roared. "You have no goddam idea what they are going through. You have no idea what Vietnam is all about."

Culver moved across the room and stood directly over Resor.

"Hell, this isn't murder," he shouted. "This is the killing of a goddam spy. Vietnam is full of spies." Culver trembled with rage, looking like he was about to lift Resor out of his seat by his pin-striped lapels and punch him in the mouth. A few of the other congressmen moved forward and gently pulled him back.

William Westmoreland was grumbling about the Green Beret mess, too. He had been unhappy about Creighton Abrams's handling of it from the beginning.

Part of it no doubt stemmed from pique, even jealousy, toward his former subordinate. Abrams was getting the credit that should have been his.

With his silver hair, clipped speech, and chiseled features, Westmoreland once seemed like a general from central casting. That was before he ran smack into the unimagined resilience of the Viet Cong and North Vietnamese. Four years later, his career went up in flames with the massive surprise attacks at Tet, the shocking coda to a slow-motion disaster ten years in the making. With the Nixon election, he had been kicked upstairs as Army chief of staff, but the albatross of Tet would always sit on his neck.

Westmoreland was a paratrooper by training and inclination. He was outraged by the confinement of the Green Berets in solitary and told Abrams so. Three weeks went by before they were moved. In the ensuing weeks he fruitlessly lobbied Abrams to release the men pending the filing of formal charges. Later he pressed for their parole pending courts-martial, again without results.

Westmoreland was convinced that Abrams's bias against Special Forces troops in general was influencing his harsh handling of the case. And he had no illusions about Abrams calling the shots. One morning in September he called his vice chief of staff, Gen. Bruce Palmer, to complain about it. As usual, Westmoreland's secretary listened in, taking notes for posterity.

"They threw them in the worst part of the jug," Westmoreland groused. "This is not the normal handling of an officer when the case hasn't even been investigated formally. You normally don't confine a man until he's tried, convicted and sentenced. You don't demean him. They treated the company and field graders like common criminals."

Palmer let Westmoreland vent his rage. He had listened to the general's frustrations for many years in Saigon, where he had also been Westmoreland's deputy.

"Naturally the press picked it up immediately," Westmoreland went on, "and that's why they were forced to release them."

Courts-martial would raise all sorts of problems, he exhaled. "There are so many defenses that can be used that I'm not sure the confessions are admissible."

He had talked to Stanley Resor about it the night before, he told Palmer. "Normally, the secretary is concerned about the rights of the individual. Here he says we can't condone this. I think he's afraid to fight Abe on this."

Bruce Palmer grunted agreement. He could remember conversations with Abrams about the Green Berets a few years back. Abrams was the vice chief of staff then, the job Palmer held now.

The Green Berets, Abrams had remarked, were "prima donnas" who went airborne to get the jump pay and "show off."

Abrams often stated his aversion to "off-line" outfits in general; they detracted from the regular units, particularly the infantry and tank corps who bore the brunt of the fighting—and the casualties.

Palmer had no doubt such prejudices were still influencing Abrams, though he'd heard through the grapevine that Bob Rheault had lied about the incident. There was no faster way to play to Abrams's bias against the Green Berets than that, he thought. Or to any general's. That was a no-no.

"I think we have to look at it in broader terms than MACV has from the beginning," Westmoreland was going on, "and disagree with the way it has been handled." Resor's own deputy, Thaddeus Beal, had told him that no one at the top of the Pentagon or CIA was in favor of going forward, he said.

"Beal told me that Laird and Packard and Helms all don't want it to go to trial, and I know Wheeler doesn't either," he said, speaking of the chairman of the Joint Chiefs of Staff.

"The other point I made," Westmoreland said, returning to his conversation with Resor, "is that you have a chain of command involved here, and some of their defense is that they carried out their orders.

"If you use the illegal order theory," he went on, speculating on the prosecution's argument that the men should have ignored CIA advice and disobeyed Rheault, "the whole Army will start thinking twice about this. Particularly the intelligence people, who are risking their lives all the time on this."

Palmer listened without comment.

"It's a sticky one to handle," Westmoreland said. "The public will raise some flak for a day or two—a few sob sisters. It's almost disappeared in the press now, but it'll come back if they're tried."

Stanley Resor had never felt such pressure, on any issue, since he came to the Pentagon in 1964. On one side was General Abrams and the law, on the other the Congress and CIA—an odd alliance. In late August he had asked Lawrence J. Fuller, the Department of the Army's acting judge advocate general, to find a middle way out of the mess.

Fuller reported back that Article 43(e) of the Uniform Code of Military Justice empowered the Army secretary to certify to the president that a court-martial for criminal acts during a time of war may be detrimental to national security.

Resor considered the matter: What is "national security?" Is it avoiding a trial that may embarrass the Army? Is it sidestepping a legal spectacle that the Communists could exploit for propaganda purposes? Or is it something else?

There was, in fact, an odd symmetry between the accused men's developing defense and Communist propaganda: Both maintained that assassination was a routine tool of the CIA in Vietnam.

Did guerrilla war, did winning in Vietnam require a new set of rules? As Resor considered his options, he ordered a study done on alternate methods of disposing of the case.

The findings came back from the Army's lawyers: Anything less than a court-martial would leave the impression that the United States, and the U.S. Army in particular, "condoned the murder of troublesome agents."

"The resulting adverse effect on the image of the Army could have Congressional repercussions, impair recruiting, increase draft resistance, lower Special Forces morale and reduce its effectiveness," the study maintained.

Dismissal of the charges would also "subject the U.S. to the charge that it has violated the principles of the Hague Convention regarding the treatment of spies (a trial required) and/or the Geneva Convention regarding treatment of civilian non-combatants (a war crime to kill)."

Finally, the Army lawyers wrote, freeing the accused men "would provide Hanoi some basis for justifying its maltreatment of our prisoners, on the theory that the action taken amounted to a whitewash."

The sound of the reports being thrown against office walls resounded around the Pentagon. North Vietnam is already torturing prisoners! Dropping the case will *adversely* affect morale? What a joke!

But the Army could survive a trial, Resor believed. The question was whether it could survive *not* having a trial. The case had become a metaphor for the moral dilemma America had been drawn into by the war: How much was winning worth?

The Green Berets "have been out in the rain too long," Abrams told his wife, Julie. It was time to show who was in charge. He had no problem with the Cambodia bombing: The president put those orders in writing. Nobody in the Army gave Bob Rheault the authority to summarily execute a Vietnamese civilian—spy or not.

Without orders—orders from the Army—it was murder. Those were the rules. Bob Rheault worked for him, not for the CIA.

Abrams read the newspapers, he saw the cartoons heaping ridicule on him. An avalanche of back-channel cables from Washington queried him on the details of the case. On September 15, he asked Melvin Laird, breezing through Saigon on an inspection tour, what he should do. Should he back off, let it go? What did the president want him to do?

Do what you think is right, Laird told him. It's your decision—officially, of course.

The defense secretary's answer was small comfort. Abrams knew Laird didn't want to touch it himself.

The irony for them was that the Green Beret affair was a tiny thing, all in all. It had gotten blown way out of proportion. They had a much bigger problem coming down the road: There had been an apparent massacre of Vietnamese civilians by American troops in a village called My Lai. Although it had happened over a year ago, all the soldiers involved had covered it up, including the commander of the division.

That was a problem, not a small bunch of outlaws in the Green Berets. But there was no way to let them off now. Not with My Lai about to break. General Westmoreland had commissioned a private study: Anyone was liable for war-crimes prosecution, it said, from the MACV commander on down.

Privately, the Army's case was falling apart. In early September the Military Justice Division forecast serious roadblocks for the prosecution. Its report was stamped Secret.

"Proof of the actual killing is rather weak," it began. "Other than the perpetrators, there were no eyewitnesses to the actual killing."

"Colonel Facey's two statements and his later testimony at the Article 32 investigation," the analysts drily noted, "may result in his becoming the best defense witness the prosecution has."

Facey was therefore useless as a government witness, the study concluded, and without him "it may be impossible to establish the complicity of Colonel Rheault and perhaps Major Crew."

That left Maj. Thomas Middleton as a potential government witness on the conspiracy charge, it said. He had attended meetings in Rheault's office on June 17, 18, and 19 when Chuyen's disposal was discussed. That, of course, was why he was charged as a conspirator.

But Kenneth Facey, the analysts noted, testified that Middleton had been essentially passive during the discussions. He hadn't really been involved, and he had no command responsibilities within 5th Special Forces Group. Middleton had also refused to confess.

"He might be acquitted if tried," they concluded. "Consideration should be given to a grant of immunity"—in order to force him to testify against Rheault and Crew.

Who else could testify that Rheault and Crew gave the order?

The three captains: Brumley, Marasco, and Williams. But only Brumley, they noted, was present at one of the planning sessions. In any event, giving any one of the captains immunity to testify, when they had actually killed Chuyen, would be "particularly inappropriate," the analysts noted, "except as a last resort."

The conspiracy charges against Rheault and Crew were in deep trouble.

Nor, the analysts said, could the captains be compelled to testify against themselves. The case against them, too, would rely on circumstantial evidence, and only Boyle and Smith could supply that.

Edward Boyle "could testify with assurance that the victim was loaded aboard the boat, that it departed, and that the victim was not aboard when the boat returned with a red liquid at the bottom," the analysts noted. Boyle had also been the first suspect "to abandon the cover story and reveal the truth to the CID."

Therefore, Boyle should also be given a grant of immunity to force his testimony against the others.

Smith presented a greater problem, the analysts concluded, if only because "the CID investigation resulted from his first statement before he was even considered a suspect."

Smith was involved in the cover story to explain Chuyen's disappearance, having obtained his signature and fingerprints on the contract sending him off on the bogus mission to Cambodia. But "the sole other facts of which Smith had firsthand knowledge were, (1) he secured dry clothes for the captains after their return, and (2) Captain Williams made an incriminating statement to him. Smith did not accompany Crew, Boyle, and the captains to the boat launch."

As a result, Smith's testimony would amount to little more than hearsay. He would not make a good witness anyway, the legal analysts concluded, because he could very well appear paranoid to the court.

"Smith is credited by his associates with an over-vivid imagination," they wrote, "and this is buttressed by his stated fear of an assassination plot against him." His background, they added vaguely, was also "somewhat suspect."

For all those reasons, "no useful purpose would be served by granting him immunity." Even the admissibility of his statement to the detectives, they noted, would be problematical: Smith had not been given a warning that he could be a suspect in the case. The question would revolve around whether he had been in protective or criminal custody when they questioned him. If he had been "deprived of his freedom of action in any significant way" during the questioning of 1–2 July, then his statement might very well be inadmissible.

The Army's secret study was a remarkably accurate echo of defense lawyer Martin Linsky's argument in the Article 32 hearing: Since the detectives' questioning of Smith led to the interrogations of Boyle, Marasco, Williams, and Brumley, the Army's whole case was built on sand.

Suddenly, Stanley Resor faced a quandary: One set of his analysts was saying that the case couldn't be dropped. Another set said the case couldn't be won.

Stanley Resor had another problem: the CIA.

According to the Army's own lawyers, the Green Beret defense motions were on solid ground: The defendants had a right to see relevant CIA documents and question Clement Enking, Bruce Scrymgeour, Dean Almy, Theodore Shackley, and any other CIA personnel who could be ruled material to their case. The Army could probably not keep them out.

There was a precedent, his legal experts had warned. The case involved an airman accused of cutting wires in the wheel wells of a B-52 bomber slated for "Sortie No. 1" upon receipt of the "Emergency War Order," a nuclear attack on the Soviet Union. The airman was charged with intentionally damaging military property to interfere with the national defense, a serious offense that could result in a long prison term at hard labor.

But the airman's lawyer, attempting to show that the aircraft could have accomplished its mission even with the wires cut (thus demonstrating that the offense was relatively insignificant), started to question a government witness on the aircraft's mission. The president of the court-martial stopped the questioning and admonished the lawyer that the information was top secret, could not be divulged, and was irrelevant to the issues of the case.

The airman was convicted, but the decision was overturned.

The appeals board ruled that "the fact of classification does not have any bearing on whether the evidence should ultimately be admitted."

Although "the precise mission of an aircraft [was] not relevant to the technical elements of the offense," the court added, it had become relevant in the case at hand because of the seriousness of the offense charged.

Understandably, the government did not want to reveal the B-52's mission, but it could not have it both ways, the court said. It could not keep the targeting information secret *and* prosecute the airman.

The government declined to retry him.

The ruling was relevant to the Green Beret case, the Army's lawyers wrote.

"In order to try the case, the Government must waive its evidentiary privileges and permit the defense any witnesses or evidence which may be relevant or material to a rational theory of defense or mitigation."

That was exactly what Steve Berry and the other Green Beret lawyers had argued. That was what John Greaney had advised a furious Ted Shackley. But they all had been rebuffed. Now, however, the Army's own lawyers agreed with them.

How, Resor wondered, would that play with the CIA now? He sent Robert Jordan, the Army's top civilian lawyer, to find out.

* * *

Bob Jordan drove up the George Washington Parkway and turned off where the sign said Federal Highway Administration. At the CID gate, he showed his government ID and waited while the sentry checked his picture against the visitors list. After a telephone call inside, the guard returned his card and waved him on through.

Jordan was no stranger to the CIA. He had been to Langley twice, once during an earlier stint at the Pentagon and another time when he was a lawyer for a division of the Treasury Department responsible for intelligence activities. He knew his way around Washington. After graduating from Harvard Law and working in the Pentagon's civil-rights office, he had moved to the U.S. attorney's office for the District of Columbia, the largest and most politically sophisticated regional office of the Department of Justice before being appointed counsel to the Army.

Stanley Resor and Bob Jordan had decided that the CIA could not be fully trusted to cooperate in the Green Beret case. There had already been a pattern of transferring witnesses out of Saigon on the eve of the Article 32 hearings. In the past few weeks, there also had been grumbling from the spy agency that it didn't intend to cooperate any further.

Resor was stuck. Mabry and Abrams were insistent on prosecuting, but without CIA witnesses, the case would have to be dropped. If the Army didn't drop it, the defense lawyers would eventually force them. If it was found out the Army proceeded knowing that its case was faulty, making a spectacle of the men, it could find itself under investigation for prosecutorial misconduct.

But there was another, more basic reason for persuading the CIA to cooperate, Resor thought: fairness. After reading the case file, he and Jordan felt the CIA did have some responsibility for what happened—a lot more, in fact, than the agency had asserted. The Green Berets had gone to Enking and Scrymgeour because they were a lot less experienced in intelligence matters than the CIA—"they were the pros." The detective Bidwell, meanwhile, had given sworn testimony at the Article 32 hearing that Enking had admitted saying "elimination might be the most efficient course of action."

It was only fair, Resor and Jordan felt, that a panel of court-martial judges hear that straight from Enking. His testimony would be given a lot of weight. It might even be exculpatory; the judges might feel the men should go free.

Jordan's mission to Langley was designed to strike a firm deal on CIA witnesses with Lawrence Houston: yes or no. It would be better to know now rather than later, Resor thought, if the CIA intended to cooperate or stonewall. If the agency backed out in the middle of a trial, they'd all be damned. They'd be in mud up to their armpits. There would be congressional investigations. It would be ruinous.

And wrong.

Jordan was escorted through the spacious foyer of CIA headquarters. He walked past the wall of bronze stars, an anonymous honor roll of dead and missing since 1947, and around the CIA's eagle-headed seal and motto set in tile in the stone floor. He waited for the elevator, which eventually deposited him on the seventh-floor executive corridor.

Lawrence Houston was waiting, along with his deputy John Warner, in a small conference room. The men shook hands and sat down around a handsome wooden table.

Jordan had some idea of what the CIA counsels had been through in the past several weeks. The operations people, from Ted Shackley on up through the CIA director himself, Richard Helms, had strenuously opposed cooperating with the Army, especially after the debacle with Harold Chipman at the Article 32 hearing.

Helms was loath to open the agency's conduct to public scrutiny. He, like the half dozen directors who had preceded him, earned the faith of their presidents by taking secrets to their graves. He was impatient and irritable when the CIA lawyers gingerly approached him about the case.

"His whole attitude was 'make it go away,' " John Warner remembered. "A lot of people in clandestine services thought that way."

Warner and Houston sat down with the Army's lawyer. They listened as Jordan made the purpose of his visit clear: He and Stan Resor didn't want to get out on a limb with this case and have the CIA saw it off. They knew the CIA had been uneasy about the case. They knew the CIA had transferred witnesses around to avoid making them available before. They had visions of that happening again. If it did, the case would collapse in midstream. It would not be fair to the defendants, or to the Army. It could lead to serious repercussions.

The CIA lawyers quietly assented.

Jordan pulled out his list: He wanted to make sure the following witnesses were available: Clement Enking, Bruce Scrymgeour, Dean Almy, Harold Chipman, and Theodore Shackley.

Helms, of course, had been subpoenaed by Henry Rothblatt. That was the CIA's concern, not the Army's. The Army wanted to confine testimony to the facts at dispute, too.

The CIA lawyers agreed with that. If testimony could be focused on the subject of who killed Thai Khac Chuyen, and Chuyen alone, the Army could have its witnesses.

No problem, Jordan said, somewhat surprised. It's a deal.

Stanley Resor walked down the long Pentagon hallway to Melvin Laird's cavernous office the next day and explained the problem.

Despite Bob Jordan's negotiations in Langley, he had been picking up rumors that Richard Helms was lobbying the White House to block any CIA witnesses from cooperating with the Army. The Army was about to make an announcement and he wanted to make sure the agency would make its witnesses available.

Could he help?

Laird picked up the telephone. Resor sat by his side, listening.

Helms came on the line.

"Just wanted to nail this thing down, Dick, about those witnesses for the Green Beret trials," Laird said.

He nodded as Helms talked.

"I know. It's got a lot of people mad. But Stan and I wanted to make sure before we went through with this thing. Otherwise it would be a waste of time."

Laird listened.

"Then he hung up and turned to Resor.

"You've got your witnesses," he said.

On September 17, Laird notified Henry Kissinger that the courts-martial were going forward, "of which you were given advance notice."

"The Secretary of the Army has concluded that the cases should be permitted to follow the usual military justice procedures in the field," Laird wrote, "with actions being controlled by the convening authority, Major General George Mabry, Jr." Mabry had decided to make it a noncapital case, Laird reported. The penalty upon conviction would be life in prison, not a firing squad.

The trial announcement was scheduled for 10 A.M., September 18, Washington time.

"Since the decision in this case is basically that of the convening authority," he added, "we could be put in a difficult position if word of the impending announcement were to leak to congressional or other sources in advance."

51

The teletype machine in the Long Binh communications center began clattering at 1:23 A.M., September 18.

A secret cable addressed to Gen. George Mabry was retrieved from the back-channel terminal. It was from Gen. William A. Knowlton, secretary to the General Staff of the United States Army.

Mabry had stayed up late waiting for the reply to his recommendations for courts-martial. An aide handed him the pale yellow telex and stood by for instructions. The telex read:

> 1. THE COURSE OF ACTION PROPOSED BY YOU WITH RESPECT TO THE RELEASE OF INFORMATION CONCERNING YOUR DECISION IN THE CASE OF US V. RHEAULT ET AL IS APPROVED AND YOU MAY PROCEED WITH YOUR MODIFIED PRESS RELEASE ON THE MATTER SET FORTH BELOW.
>
> 2. THE DEPARTMENT OF THE ARMY HAS OBLIGATIONS TO NOTIFY CERTAIN CONGRESSIONAL COMMITTEES AND MEMBERS OF CONGRESS IN ADVANCE OF THE RELEASE OF YOUR DECISION TO THE PRESS.
>
> IN ORDER TO ACCOMMODATE NECESSARY SCHEDULES WITH RESPECT TO CONGRESSIONAL PRESS NOTI-

FICATION IN WASHINGTON, RELEASE SHOULD BE MADE
AT PRECISELY 2200 HOURS, 18 SEPTEMBER 69 SAIGON
TIME. DEPARTMENT OF THE ARMY RELATES THAT A
STATEMENT WILL BE MADE BY SECRETARY OF THE
ARMY A FEW MINUTES AFTER YOU RELEASE YOUR
STATEMENT, AND A TEXT OF THE SECRETARY OF THE
ARMY STATEMENT WILL BE SENT TO YOU.

Mabry was pleased. The next paragraph was only a minor disappointment.

3. PURSUANT TO PARAGRAPH 53E OF THE MANUAL OF
COURTS MARTIAL, THE SECRETARY OF THE ARMY HAS
ISSUED THE FOLLOWING DIRECTIVE: "WITH RESPECT
TO THE CASES OF THE UNITED STATES V. COL.
RHEAULT ET. AL., I DIRECT THAT ALL TRIALS WILL BE
OPEN TO THE PUBLIC EXCEPT WHEN IT IS NECESSARY
TO PROTECT THE DISCLOSURE OF CLASSIFIED MATE-
RIAL TO UNAUTHORIZED PERSONS."

Ridiculous, Mabry snorted; you couldn't open and close a classified trial like
a cereal box.

But it was a pissant matter. What counted was that all of those men would
soon be in the dock, including Maj. Thomas Middleton—over the objections
of Colonel Seaman and the lawyers, who thought he was only a bit player in
the murder decision.

"Misprision of a felony, hell!" Mabry said again and again. Middleton was
there through the whole thing. He could've stopped it if he'd spoken up. He'd
also had a chance to come clean with the detectives later. Instead, he played
it like it was all a big joke.

Well, by God, Major Middleton had failed as a United States Army officer,
and he was going to pay for it. He was going to stand in the dock for murder
with the rest of them.

Or become a witness.

Facey—there was another sorry excuse for an officer. He was a zero for the
prosecution, maybe even worse. Based on his Article 32 testimony, they
couldn't put him on the stand as a defendant or a witness.

But Mabry could make Facey's life miserable; he had signed orders flagging
Facey's promotion. And as far as he was concerned, Facey could stay in
Vietnam until the end of the war, or at the very least until the end of the
courts-martial—many, many months away.

As for Smith and Boyle, the Pentagon had approved his recommendation
that both be given immunity and forced to testify.

Mabry didn't care one whit about the Army lawyers' caution that Smith
would be a problem. Nor did he care what the CIA thought. Hell, Smith knew
about the whole thing, didn't he? He cooperated. If Smith embarrassed the
CIA, so what?

Mabry dictated a reply to Washington that he had received the message. He handed it to his aide. Then he went to bed, satisfied that the case was finally on track. He would be glad when it was over. There were a lot more things to do in Vietnam than chase a bunch of renegade Green Berets around a courtroom.

Col. Wilton Persons, MACV's staff judge advocate, sent separate messages to the defense attorneys Monday night, summoning them individually to his Long Binh office. Just after nine o'clock, they all showed up together.

"An announcement will be made within the hour in Washington," Persons said evenly.

The lawyers were confident of what that announcement would be. One of Lee Brumley's spies at MACV had gotten hold of the Army's own legal assessment of the case. There was no way the Army could go forward now.

"There will be two trials," Persons said, prompting a few jaws to crack open. "Captains Marasco, Brumley, and Williams will be tried first. No date has been set, but it will be soon, probably early October. Following that, Colonel Rheault, Major Crew, and Major Middleton will be tried together."

He looked around the room, which was thick with tension and anger.

"Sergeant Smith and Warrant Officer Boyle will be presented with offers of immunity from prosecution," Persons continued, "pending the completion of the other courts-martial."

Persons looked up. "Do you have any questions?"

The lawyers were in shock.

"When will the announcement be made?" Steve Berry asked.

Persons looked at his watch. "In about an hour."

Berry was still smoldering from the instructions, which he had quickly ignored, not to tip off his comrades about Person's request to see him.

"Sir, there is a brief period of time now. I would like for my client to be able to advise his family that these charges are being preferred, prior to their finding out by the media. The media will release it soon. I would like a head start."

Persons shook his head. "I'm sorry, but that's not possible."

A shocked silence.

"Look, this shouldn't come as a surprise," Persons impatiently told them all. "There were two eyewitnesses, three confessions, and a wealth of corroborating evidence."

More stunned silence.

"And there's no legal right for them to be notified in advance," he added.

Berry's rage came unhinged. "Sir, I am not talking about legal rights. I am talking about basic elements of human decency."

Marty Linsky, the unflappable lawyer for Bob Rheault, suddenly reached his own limits. The events of the past two months flew through his head. The Article 32 hearings had been a joke. The investigation had been a joke. The confessions were a fraud, tainted from Smith on down. The defense had been denied key CIA witnesses and documents. The prosecution was a waste of all their time. From the beginning, he thought, the case had been a cynical bureaucratic exercise.

An image flashed through the lawyer's mind: American soldiers dying in droves at "Hamburger Hill" just so a general could make the point that his marines could take a mound of dirt from the NVA. In an act of stunning profanity, the hill was quietly abandoned a few weeks later.

Linsky suddenly lashed out at Persons. "Why are you hounding these men?" he shouted. "If you want someone to prosecute, go lock up the commander at Hamburger Hill. That man was just as guilty of murder, maybe even more so, than these men."

It was a shocking leave of decorum. Yet the ongoing carnage around them put the prosecution in a bizarre light. Just the day before, U.S. helicopter gunships had opened fire on a group of civilians fleeing a battle between South Vietnamese troops and the Viet Cong near a delta village called Bac Lieu. According to the official tally, seven villagers had been killed and seventeen wounded. The *New York Times* was also reporting that U.S. soldiers were backing up Laotian troops in a recent offensive in the Plain of Jars in direct contravention of a congressional prohibition. In the midst of all that, the prosecution of the Green Berets on first-degree murder charges seemed cruelly out-of-place.

Everything's upside down in Vietnam, Linsky thought. He confronted Colonel Persons directly. "For what did they die at Hamburger Hill? For what? And for what have these brave Green Berets risked their lives only to have the Army turn its back on them? What kind of Army is this," he roared, "that will do this to its own men?"

Linsky steamed on. "Vietnam is *all about* body counts. The prosecution is a joke. You don't have a shred of evidence that will stand up in court. The confessions are bogus. The prosecution is bogus. It's a railroad job. You're going to take this to the end and destroy these good men even though you know the whole thing will be thrown out in the end.

"Why? To make a point? So General Abrams can get his rocks off about the Green Berets? What a goddam fraud!"

The lawyer's face was red. His fists trembled. Linsky's colleagues surrounded him, pulling him back before any more damage could be done.

Outside, a few minutes later, Linsky, Bill Hart, and Steve Berry quickly made up their minds on their next steps. To hell with the Army, they decided. They jumped into a jeep and headed for Saigon.

It was time to hold their own press conference and let the American people know what a travesty of justice this was.

On the morning of September 18, Stanley Resor faced the bright television lights in the packed Pentagon briefing room. He said he had a prepared statement to read.

"After careful consideration," he said, "I have concluded that it would be unwise, and unjustified, for me to interfere with the normal course of proceeding in this case."

A few wire service reporters fled from the room with the press release.

"As a lawyer and as secretary of the Army, I believe firmly in the efficiency of the traditional process and in the fairness of our basic procedures under the Uniform Code of Military Justice."

Resor looked up into the bright lights.

"Historically, we have placed great faith in our system of criminal trials as a fair and effective way of resolving disputed questions of fact and law, and of assuring justice to all," he continued.

"A court-martial will provide a chance for the full exploration of matters bearing on the innocence, guilt, excuse, justification, mitigation, and extenuation."

The trials would begin in October, he said. He would take no questions on the specifics of the case.

"Has there been any change," a reporter asked, "in the orders to Army commanders that their mission is the pursuit and destruction of enemy forces?"

"No," Resor replied.

Patrick Buchanan scanned the media's handling of the courts-martial announcement. He was dismayed. The case was killing them. Why wasn't Nixon getting rid of it?

The White House speech writer had been unhappy with the case from the beginning. The antiwar types and the professional Nixon-haters in the media were using it to hammer the administration.

Beginning with the television networks' coverage of the announcement from Saigon, Buchanan devoted several pages to the case in the White House morning news summary:

> CBS's Gary Shepard called the case "one of the most significant events of the war," with the entire concept of the killing of a person believed to be an enemy on trial.
>
> Footage of military attorneys for the defense. One said there won't be many issues dealing with the war that won't be dealt with; another spoke of the "morale" problem. He said for the first time such questions have come up among the troops—Who are we fighting for; Who are we fighting against—and Who is fighting for *us*?
>
> Also mentioned was the refusal of the Army to let the men communicate with their families. The attorneys said the Army has abandoned these men.
>
> CBS footage of wife of one of the men calling for return of trial to US because Abrams's role as instigator of trial will prevent fair treatment in Saigon.

"CBS said the future of the case was undecided until Abrams met with RN," the summary went on, referring to the president. "He threatened to resign if trial wasn't conducted and apparently got his way. Footage of very noncommittal General Abrams on both CBS and NBC."

The analysis switched to Washington. Eight congressmen led by Rep. Peter

Rodino of New Jersey had held a press conference and demanded "that the Army take the case out of the hands of the generals in Vietnam."

Rodino had read his statement into a forest of microphones and a jammed room of reporters at the Capitol. "To date, this case has been characterized by intraservice rivalries, bureaucratic mismanagement and an irresponsible regard for the rights of the accused persons," he said, "as well as for the serious adverse effects of the proceeding on the morale of the servicemen."

Patrick Buchanan surveyed the mounting furor with dismay. Nixon had been pushing his news summary staff to put more analysis into the morning report. Now Buchanan reached back and let loose with his feelings about the Green Beret case.

The paragraph was titled "TROUBLE AHEAD."

"We view with general alarm the Green Beret decision, which offers us nothing that would benefit the administration, the Green Berets, the US Army, or the American effort in Viet Nam, and has great potential for damage to all four."

The recent trend of Vietnam-oriented mail to the White House had been ominous, Buchanan also noted.

"Volume, including the heaviest number of telegrams, increased slightly over the previous week, with opposition continuing at a high level. A few letters applaud the President's decision to bring more US troops home."

An attached sheet added up the dire numbers: Only 12 letters favored administration policy in Vietnam; 706 opposed it.

Nixon read the mail report and scribbled a note to Kissinger on the margin: "K—have your staff analyze a couple weeks to see how much is inspired." A lopsided toll like that, he thought, had to have been manufactured by the antiwar movement.

The reverberation from the court-martial decision continued the next day.

"What may be the first round of a systematic bombardment of the US military command in Vietnam," the White House news summary reported, "began on ABC with film of Henry B. Rothblatt, the civilian attorney retained to defend the first group of GB officers to go on trial.

"He told the press upon his arrival in Saigon that the court-martial was the result of 'people in high places making a mistake and refusing to admit it—a typical bureaucratic blunder.'

"Rothblatt indicated he may call Abrams as a witness," the news summary continued, "and he will insist upon an open trial—'I don't intend to compromise the democratic rights of these great officers.' He predicted an acquittal."

The White House media office summarized the effect of Rothblatt's filmed press conference: "Effective footage of an articulate, smooth criminal lawyer who knows the important jury in this case doesn't wear uniforms."

It went on: "(ABC-TV anchorman) Howard K. Smith noted that several of the accused officers met the press today and said their treatment has 'shattered the faith of their families in the military.' Their 'betrayal' theme will be a big one throughout this case.

"Both CBS and NBC spent about 5 minutes on the case. NBC reported that the two men not going on trial don't intend to serve as stool pigeons either. Footage of Colonel Rheault 'maintaining some of the mystique of his command even in the humiliating circumstances in which he finds himself.'

"NBC 'has learned' what really happened in the murder. Berets were given three choices by CIA regarding the double agent. They decided on murder. Next day CIA eliminated murder from the alternatives. CIA supposedly feared 'a moral flap.' Abrams heard about it—said to 'clean up' the Special Forces.

"Questions remain, according to NBC's Goralski: Why make such a big thing out of this particular murder, and why did the CIA give the options on the agent's future and then change them?"

Nixon finished reading the summary. The CIA was hopeless, he told Ehrlichman. Annoyed that such a minor incident was threatening to spill over on the White House, Nixon scrawled a note to Henry Kissinger in the margin.

"K—I think Helms should be made to take part of this rap."

52

Peter Rodino's voice was naturally raspy, but when he rose in the House of Representatives on the morning of September 19, his throat was abnormally raw and dry. He had stayed up late deciding exactly what to say.

Everything he had heard left him convinced that Bob Marasco and the other men were being railroaded: There was Marasco's own letter from Vietnam to his wife, which said that the CIA had given approval for the agent's execution; there was Jerry Zeifman's CIA source, who blamed the case on General Abrams's rage against the Green Berets. There had also been convincing stories of pressure by the South Vietnamese government to try the men.

Then there was the role of General Mabry, who had appointed himself chief detective, judge, and jury during the investigation. That, Rodino thought, was a classic example of the failures of military justice.

Rodino had invested deeply on the outcome of the case. He had kept in close touch with Marasco's family, issuing press releases after each meeting or exchange of letters with the Army on their behalf. He had become their champion. His cause and theirs were one. Failure now to pry Marasco loose would be an embarrassing defeat, one that he could ill afford back home.

But it was no longer just a political issue. Rodino had grown close to the Marascos. The jailing of their son touched a nerve that lies just below the skin of many second-generation immigrants: the resentment at having to play by different rules than the establishment. In Rodino's mind, the soldiers were being punished for the sins of the generals.

"Mr. Speaker," Rodino began, "I rise to speak of a terrible injustice being dealt one of my constituents by the United States Army. I am speaking of those heroic Green Berets serving our country so well in Vietnam, putting their lives on the line each day so we can live so well here in this great country of ours."

The House chamber was unusually quiet as Rodino stood on the thick red carpet summarizing the developments in the case, including the previous day's announcement that the Green Berets would be court-martialed for murder.

"Mr. Speaker, there is a gross lack of civilian control over the Army," Rodino went on, growing hoarse.

The Green Berets "are being sacrificed simply to protect the image of career military commanders and CIA officials."

Under military law, he argued, the secretary of the Army could take jurisdiction of the case himself rather than leave it to field commanders. But despite the conspicuous evidence of prosecutorial bias and repeated congressional urging, the Army secretary had refused.

"His shirking of personal responsibility and bowing to the will of Army bureaucrats and pressure from the Vietnamese government is inexcusable," Rodino declared. "The mishandling of the case from the beginning has been so flagrant that it is impossible for the field commanders, who themselves have been involved in the rivalries and jealousies that have given rise to this case, to act impartially."

The diminutive congressman had unleashed a rare personal attack. At the rear of the chamber the handful of congressmen who had been milling about stopped to listen. Even those not directly involved had been deluged with mail from angry constituents. The Green Berets had become a national cause célèbre, the absentee heroes of radio talk shows across the nation.

"Mr. Speaker, the secretary's position that the case has not been mishandled to date is astounding," Rodino went on. "Let's not forget that the confinement in five-by-seven-foot cells was inhumane and a violation of the Code of Military Justice."

Rodino moved to the side of his desk and raised his hands in frustration.

"The fact that the secretary now wants a trial in the field, which will be 'open to the extent consistent with security requirements,' is a further indication that these men are being made scapegoats."

Congress was due "a full explanation," Rodino said, his voice rising, for why the Army "deliberately withheld from members of Congress crucial information which indicates the Green Berets were acting under orders."

Rodino returned to the side of his desk, smoldering with anger. He wasn't finished. He wanted answers, he said.

Without them, "I believe we should demand the resignation of those civilians in our government who have been concerned more with their own prestige than with our nation's objective in Vietnam."

As Rodino took his seat, the House gallery broke out in applause.

Jerry Zeifman walked back across Independence Avenue after listening to his boss's speech. It was hot and hazy, typical for a late-September afternoon in Washington.

Zeifman was pleased with the reaction to the speech, which he had written. No doubt the press coverage in Newark the next day would be enthusiastic. Everybody'd had a good ride with the Green Berets so far. Rodino was back up in the polls.

But something was off-kilter. He should be feeling great, Zeifman thought, but he wasn't. He felt like a piano player in a whorehouse.

The queasy feeling had first crept over him during one of the early meetings with Rodino's staff to discuss the Marasco case. At first everybody was pumped up. It was a great issue for Newark, especially Rodino's key constituency, the Italians who had defected from him on the race issue. The prospects for getting Marasco off and bringing him home to the district arm-in-arm looked good. Reelection could be a cakewalk.

Getting out from under the drudgery of the tax subcommittee hadn't felt so bad, either, in the beginning. Taking on the CIA and the Army was a hell of a lot more fun than wrestling with state tax codes.

The trouble was that he hated everything about Vietnam. So did Rodino. They were all liberals. So what were they doing defending these guys?

One of the women on Rodino's staff forced them all to face the question one day as they sat around planning another assault on Stanley Resor. Joyce Judson still had some of the flower child in her. She had come to Congress to work for breakfast plans for ghetto kids, decent housing, education—the entire litany of the Great Society that was being chipped away by the budget for Vietnam.

"What are we doing backing this guy?" she asked. "So he took orders from the CIA—so what? Does that make it right? Is that what we're supposed to be doing in Vietnam, executing people like the Nazis did?"

The room fell silent. Nobody dared to be glib. Zeifman knew she had struck a nerve. Finally, somebody mumbled an explanation of political realities, about the practicality of defending a constituent, about the frame-up the Army and CIA were hanging on the soldiers.

Judson would have none of it.

The fact was, the Army made it easy to defend Marasco. Zeifman had learned a lot of what was going on in Vietnam in the past two months— napalm, Agent Orange, the Cambodia bombing, the Phoenix program, CIA operations in Laos and Cambodia. One day Henry Rothblatt stopped by the office and suggested there was an even bigger scandal brewing in Saigon.

"The Army is sitting on a massive hot potato," Rothblatt had intimated. "It will break in the news soon. I can't discuss the details." It was My Lai, Zeifman would learn later.

General Abrams's indignation over the Green Berets reminded Zeifman of an incident just after he was admitted to the bar. He was doing pro bono defense work in the Bronx. His clients were drug addicts and sundry vicious killers. One day he was assigned to defend a member of the Avengers, one of the gangs that controlled Spanish Harlem. The man had been charged with slitting the throat of a rival gang member who made a pass at his wife.

When they met at the arraignment, Zeifman reviewed the guy's rap sheet. It was as long as a city sewer.

"Okay, no bullshit, tell me exactly what happened," Zeifman said.

His client beamed. The cops got it wrong, he said. He never used a knife.

"Talk to anyone on 116th Street," he bragged. "Never a knife, always a gun."

That was Creighton Abrams, Zeifman thought. Never a knife, always a gun. Bombing was okay, shooting a spy in the head was wrong. Abrams signed more death warrants with his B-52s, artillery, and napalm in one day than the Green Berets had shot in a decade, he mused. More bomb tonnage had been dropped on tiny Vietnam than the Allies dropped in four continents in World War II.

So Rheault had lied to him. Big deal. Who does Abrams lie to? Wasn't Abrams in on the Cambodia bombing—a deliberate deception of Congress and the American people?

Zeifman went back to his nook on the second floor of the Rayburn Building and looked out the window to Independence Avenue, thinking.

In the beginning, they had avoided specifically defending Marasco, focusing instead on procedural issues like solitary confinement and pretrial release. That was the right thing to do. They were right to bash the Army for that. But now things had changed. Their position had changed. Meanwhile, the Green Berets had become martyrs, even national heroes.

To what end? What was their position on Marasco now? He'd seen the Army's rap sheet on the Berets: Marasco put a bullet in the guy's head after a week of interrogation, truth serum, wrapping him up in chains and tire rims. How would Americans react if a story came out that terrorists had done the same thing to a "suspected" CIA agent?

Zeifman had skirted the issue in Rodino's speech. He had stayed focused on the Army's "mishandling" of the case. He knew where Rodino was going with it now, and he understood the pragmatic defense of a constituent's son, but he wasn't sure he could follow. He doubted he could call Bob Marasco a hero, a martyr.

A victim.

That was a bit much.

But it was a tough call in other ways. Zeifman had been looking into the subject of government-sanctioned assassinations. He had picked up an interesting piece of information: In the last years of the Eisenhower administration, the CIA and Justice Department had negotiated a secret agreement virtually absolving the CIA from prosecution for illegal criminal acts committed in pursuit of "national security." Under the terms of the agreement, the decision to refer an incident for prosecution would be made at the discretion of the CIA, not the federal law-enforcement agency.

Not much had changed, he thought, since the murder of Beckett in his cathedral. Like Henry II, American presidents wanted an agency to do the dirty work for them. "Rid me of this turbulent priest"—"Do it but keep it away from me." An ageless story. Nothing was new.

But the Green Berets had a problem, even if the CIA "ordered" the killing of Thai Khac Chuyen, Zeifman thought. There was nothing in the secret executive agreement between the Justice Department and CIA that mentioned the Special Forces. It was a CIA pact. The Green Berets were left out in the cold, assassins without portfolio.

Maybe that's what Resor's point was, Zeifman thought, and Abrams's as well: They didn't want the Army mucking around in the CIA's brand of murder. And maybe, he began to think, that wasn't a bad idea after all. Maybe one secret agency was enough.

There were other things he had heard recently that suddenly clicked in his mind. The Kennedy assassination, for one. Hale Boggs, a Louisiana congressman and good friend of the late president, had been whispering that there was much more to the president's murder than what the Warren Commission had reported—murky connections to CIA operations in Cuba and secret pacts with organized crime to kill Fidel Castro.

And why was Nan Rheault's visit suddenly bothering him so much? Zeifman wondered. Was it because when she visited Rodino one day, she made a point of saying how much she "liked and admired the Italians"? It stuck in his mind.

It was a harmless affectation of the well-to-do, he thought, that's all. She was beautiful, intelligent, charming. Sincere.

Or was there some thread, just now forming in his mind, that tied together all of this—the Kennedys, the CIA, the Green Beret case, and assassinations? Was it that people like that thought they were above the rules?

The night was growing long. Why was he brooding so much? Outside, the streets were empty. The office was dark. He was hungry. Maybe that's why he was getting so morose.

His mind switched back to the meetings with Stanley Resor.

"But gentlemen," the Army secretary had said over and over, "there is no way the Army can condone murder."

Zeifman felt embarrassed now. He had missed the whole point.

"This is a war," he had lectured Stanley Resor, joining in the hectoring. "This isn't murder, this is killing a spy."

What did *he* know about war? He was a Bronx lawyer. Until a few weeks ago, a tax guy. Stanley Resor, he had subsequently learned, had distinguished himself in combat. So had Creighton Abrams and George Mabry.

Zeifman reached up and plucked a book from the shelf. A few weeks earlier, when he began to have second thoughts about the case, he had seen a copy of T. S. Eliot's *Murder in the Cathedral* in a Capitol Hill bookstore and bought it on an impulse. It had been years since he first read it.

He opened the book to the first page.

At dawn, he finished reading. The king's reign had collapsed after the archbishop's murder.

"My God," he thought, alone in his Capitol Hill office. "I'm on the wrong side."

53

Bob Rheault sat in his trailer, scanning the confidential list of officers whom Mabry had selected for the court-martial board. The document had been slipped to him from a source inside Mabry's staff.

His optimism grew as he read through the names. Almost all of the men on the list had commanded platoons, rifle companies, and battalions. These men were not desk jockeys and horse-holders for Abrams and his staff. These were men who had seen hard combat in the hamlets and jungles of Vietnam. They knew what the war was all about. None of them, he was certain, would vote to convict them for killing an enemy spy.

For the first time in weeks, he was buoyed. The past month had been like free-falling through the darkness on his first night jump, tumbling in a black void, waiting for the chute to open, the ground to come up. The ground had come up, but he had landed in the trees, in the Long Binh Chapel.

It was as if he had been blown off course. When he had looked around the hearing room, all the faces were strange. Who were these men, these fellow "conspirators" who now shared the dock with him? He hardly knew them. They hardly knew each other. They had arrived at the 5th Special Forces for only days before the Chuyen problem came along—six days, to be exact, between his assumption of duty on June 4 and the first CIA meeting in Saigon. He had hardly gotten started. The system of musical chairs in Vietnam— rotating men in and out of the war zone on one-year tours instead of keeping units intact through the duration—was exacting a very literal price.

If there *was* a conspiracy, Rheault thought in the first weeks after his arrest—it was composed of their predecessors, the men who had dumped Chuyen on him before they went home: Colonel Aaron and his staff. They had had two months to solve the problem before he arrived, but they had passed the buck. He had solved the problem as best he knew how—*how it had always been done!*—then, like gunfire, came Shackley's cable, Abrams's call, Smith's defection, the investigation, the arrests, and the storm of publicity.

It seemed like a nightmare. It *was* a nightmare, but here, finally, was a glimmer of good news.

He was surprised the case had gotten this far. He had counted on friends calming Abrams down and setting them loose. But the publicity had made that impossible. Now they were going to trial.

Shortly after the courts-martial announcement, Rheault drew his men together in the guarded barracks at Long Binh. Oddly, he felt calm. This was territory he knew, fighting like a guerrilla.

What they had done, he told them, was no different than shooting down an enemy soldier who had crawled through the wire. Forget all the talk about "assassination"—getting rid of Chuyen was nothing more than self-defense, killing an intruder. But if the Army wanted to put it in those terms, he said, they had plenty of ammunition to shoot back.

*   *   *

The defendants threw themselves into their research. Lee Brumley and Budge Williams sat down to write an exposé of CIA and Special Forces operations around the world, as well as abuses under the Phoenix program. The fifteen-page report was intended for Mendel Rivers, chairman of the House Armed Services Committee, and Carl Albert, who would soon be Speaker of the House.

The "opus," as they called it, was wide-ranging, and politically lethal. It was not limited to activities in Vietnam.

One section outlined a standing plan at SOUTHCOM, U.S. military headquarters in the Canal Zone, for the Green Berets to assassinate Panamanian leftists in the event of an anti-U.S. coup. Williams had learned of it during a 1968 assignment there. Code-named Key Cities, it called for "definite hits on selected Panamanians," Williams wrote. "Select SF teams would 'eliminate' left-wing politicians, labor leaders, known communists, and Marxist reporters."

Budge Williams also had been privy to the role the CIA had played in helping Bolivian Rangers track down and assassinate the peripatetic Cuban revolutionary Che Guevara in 1968. Williams's knowledge of the incident was only tangential from his time there, but it had been a highly sensitive operation. One of the CIA agents on the operation, using Special Forces cover, was a Cuban exile named Felix Rodriguez, who had also been involved in the Bay of Pigs. Other Cuban exiles had been sent to Vietnam by the CIA to work on the Phoenix program, he knew.

Another section concerned the activities of Col. Mike Healy, who was the adviser to the Vietnamese Green Berets in November 1963, at the time of Ngo Dinh Diem's overthrow and assassination.

But it was the Phoenix program that they focused on. Phoenix particularly galled Lee Brumley in light of the circumstances in which he now found himself. He threw himself into a project of documenting its abuses. "The individuals who were attempting to portray us as barroom thugs," he wrote, "were the very people who were engaging in an indiscriminate, murderous campaign against mostly civilian targets."

Brumley and his comrades quickly built up a cache of classified documents slipped to them by friends. Mixed in with their own knowledge and anecdotes supplied by friends, they found:

• From 1965 through 1968, U.S. and Saigon intelligence services had created and maintained an active list of Viet Cong cadre marked for assassination.

• The Phoenix target for 1969 called for "neutralizing" eighteen hundred civilian Viet Cong cadre a month.

• Approximately one-third of the Viet Cong targeted for arrest had been summarily killed, belying U.S. claims that Phoenix was nothing more than an aggressive police program.

- "Security committees" were set up in provincial interrogation centers to determine the fate of Viet Cong suspects, outside the judicial controls bally-hooed by U.S. officials.
- Green Berets and Navy SEALs were the most common recruits for the Phoenix program, under direct CIA supervision.
- As it did for Project Gamma, Detachment B-57 provided administrative cover for other intelligence units. One was Project Cherry, tasked to assassinate Cambodian officials suspected of collaborating with the North Vietnamese, and in some cases, the Soviet KGB. Another was Project Oak, targeted against suspected South Vietnamese government collaborators. They were controlled by a top secret section of the Pentagon, the Special Assistant for Counterinsurgency and Special Activities, which worked with the CIA outside of General Abrams's control, and often without his knowledge.

SACSA, of course, was where Bob Rheault had worked. He knew where all the secrets were buried.

"We have been writing friends," Tom Middleton confided in a letter home, "and asking them to beat the bush quietly and round up things and people who might have something that will help the defense or who would be willing to testify.

"Colonel Rheault has high-ranking friends everywhere," he added. "We hope some of them will step forward."

Three-fingered Louie was among the first to answer the call.

Lou Conein had worked in the shadows during the 1963 overthrow of South Vietnamese president Ngo Dinh Diem, carrying messages between the CIA and the coup-plotting generals. A swarthy, sharp-witted Corsican with two fingers missing from his left hand, Conein was nominally a U.S. Army lieutenant colonel, but he had served so long with the CIA that the distinction was irrelevant.

On the night of November 3, 1963, Conein had signaled the conspirators that Washington would not oppose them, a crucial element in their decision to go forward. Tanks rolled into the streets and surrounded the Presidential Palace. Diem was captured by rebel soldiers after he escaped from the palace through a secret tunnel. He and his brother were executed on the spot. The murder was said to come as a surprise at the White House, which in any case denied any role in the affair.

Conein knew better. That Ambassador Henry Cabot Lodge had favored Diem's removal was no secret, but the degree of the CIA's complicity in getting rid of him was. The Kennedys clamped a tight lid on the affair, which continued after the president's own assassination. Some in the White House who knew about Conein's activities first theorized that Dallas might have been retribution for killing Diem.

Conein would be a useful witness in knocking down the CIA's assertion that it did not condone or engage in assassination. Other calls, meanwhile, went out from the barracks at Long Binh, asking other agents to testify on the U.S. government's activities in Cuba, Chile, the Congo, Honduras, the Dominican Republic, Iran, Syria, and Brazil, or in advising a dozen regimes' secret police.

Operatives began arriving in Saigon from all over the world. It began to look like a soldiers-of-fortune convention.

Bob Rheault was out leading his men on a jog around the post one day in late September when an old friend pulled up alongside in a jeep. It was Larkyn W. Nesom, a former Green Beret master sergeant he had worked with in Germany.

"Whoa, there, podnah. Slow down a bit," Nesom said, smiling.

Rheault stopped and grinned, breathing heavily under the searing sun. He waved his men on. They had gotten used to the five-mile jaunt every day, along with his "officer's call" for cocktails every night. They even had a "blue movie" night, with the colonel standing sentry at the door. Morale, finally, was good, bolstered by packets of fan mail.

"Rocky" Nesom was one of Rheault's favorite soldiers, a career Green Beret with a taste for guerrilla war and a fondness for quoting Kipling. By trade, he was a "kicker," a man who shoves equipment out of the back of a low-flying airplane. In the mid-sixties Nesom had left the Green Berets and signed up with Air America, the CIA airline. Along the way, he had also gotten his pilot's license.

He had an idea, he told Rheault. They went back to the colonel's trailer and locked the door.

Nesom told Rheault he was willing to be a defense witness on the CIA's relations with Special Forces. No problem. He was well versed in Special Forces's operations with ex-Nazis in Germany back in the late 1940s and early 1950s that he was sure the government wasn't eager to have publicized. But he had a better idea: a breakout.

Rheault listened and smiled.

Most of the troops at Long Binh, Nesom argued, were lightly armed, if at all, and assigned to clerical and supply duties. Pushovers. It would be easy to freeze them in their boots.

Nesom said that he had recruited a band of Montagnards, whom he would land in a small Dornier aircraft right outside the Long Binh barracks. He'd also stockpiled enough food and supplies for the men to survive in the jungle.

"I'll take you anywhere you want to go," he told Rheault, looking him in the eye. "Cambodia, Laos, wherever."

The colonel was amused. And touched. He had no doubt Nesom could pull it off.

Budge Williams wasn't putting his faith in any "friendly" court-martial board. He'd seen and heard enough of the Army in the last two months to convince him he was going to get screwed. Just in case, he'd stockpiled hand grenades, a Browning automatic rifle, and a false passport for an escape.

He had also taken to slipping out of the barracks on nighttime practice jaunts to the bars in Saigon. No one, he swore, was going to put him in jail for killing a goddam dink—fuck *that* shit.

In the meantime, he was flouting the Army's prohibition on contact with the press.

Very close contact: One night he smuggled an admiring female reporter into his room, "a long-legged, big-titted thing," he cackled. She got her story. An aide to General Abrams happened to be walking by when he was escorting her out the door. The officer recognized them both and threatened Williams with new charges.

"Just tack them on the list," he said.

"I understand it's really hitting the fan back there," Bob Marasco wrote to his parents September 27. "I am glad that you want to talk to the press. You have my permission to tell them anything you want to.

"We played the army's game for awhile, but now that's over. We gave them a chance and now they've blown it. I am taking off the gloves. Tell everybody to write their congressmen."

Mail was flooding Washington. A nerve had been touched; the Green Berets had become symbols of decent American boys left to fight an unwanted, unwinnable, and, with the onset of troop withdrawals and the draft lottery, a largely forgotten war. Most people blamed both General Abrams and the CIA for making the Green Berets "scapegoats" for the failures of Vietnam. A thousand letters and telegrams arrived at the White House alone in the third week of September.

One woman with a son in Vietnam wrote to President Nixon, "The mothers I have talked to have all agreed that the boys in the field are the ones who need bolstering. . . . The court martial of the Special Forces men is a disgrace."

Another, identifying herself as a Republican committeewoman, wrote, "I have never been so horrified and disturbed over an incident. . . . Our poor son is serving in Vietnam, a voluntary infantryman. Am I to understand that he is in jeopardy of being accused of murder?"

From Wisconsin, the father of a young man who had died in a Viet Cong ambush wrote that an enemy spy like Chuyen had probably caused his son's death. Give the Green Berets "a medal for gallantry in action," he urged.

"I'm an American mother who lost my beloved 23 year old son," one woman appealed to Nixon. "If you let this trial continue, it is a disgrace to American justice." Another mother asked, "What do we mothers who have sons over there, and some of us who have lost our sons, and mothers who have sons yet to go and be trained to kill or be killed, have to look forward to? Tell me why the Green Berets have to be charged with murder. You know and I know this was what they were trained to do."

A widow with two of her boys buried in Arlington Cemetery as a result of Vietnam bluntly asked President Nixon: "Which side are you on?"

It was a letter to Melvin Laird, however, that squarely framed the dilemma for U.S. troops and their commanders in America's first modern guerrilla war.

"Special Forces are given a dirty job to do," wrote a man who had been in the OSS. "In intelligence or counterguerrilla warfare, they can't use the same methods we'd expect to use in a civilized nation."

In Saigon, one woman disagreed. On September 20, Phan Kim Lien wrote to Arkansas senator J. William Fulbright, a liberal member of the Senate Foreign Relations Committee, asking for help.

54

Mendel Rivers evenly welcomed Stanley Resor to his ornate office on the second floor of the Sam Rayburn Building on the eastern side of Pennsylvania Avenue. The inner sanctum was a shrine to the chairman's nearly thirty years in Congress. Photos of aircraft carriers, fighter jets, and missiles lined the walls. But what caught any visitor's eye were the pictures of the now seventy-two-year-old congressman shaking hands with a half dozen presidents.

The spindly Dixiecrat had served on various House military committees since his election in 1940, beginning with the Naval Affairs Committee and continuing through his elevation, twenty-five years later, to the chairmanship of the Armed Services Committee. Along the way he had stocked South Carolina with military contracts and bases, including a Marine air station, three Air Force installations, and a Polaris submarine base in just his own district. Defense-related industries accounted for thirty-five percent of the payroll in Charleston.

Along with the committee's seven senior members, Rivers had a hammerlock on military budgets. Together they were not-so-jokingly known as "the junta." Presidents crossed any of them, especially Mendel Rivers, at their peril.

The chairman had no inclination to offer Resor a customary whiskey as the Army secretary took a seat by the huge mahogany desk. He asked his counsel, John Blandford, a former marine, to wait outside.

Rivers got right to the point. He had wasted too much time on the Green Beret case, he said, writing letters to Melvin Laird and issuing warning statements through the press. Persuasion had failed. This time, he'd have to use a different vocabulary.

Sitting just outside the door, John Blandford heard voices raised in anger.

"The Army's handling of this affair is disgraceful," Rivers was saying. "It is a disgrace to the Army in particular, and the country in general." He threatened to hold hearings on the case.

Resor started to protest. Rivers waved him off.

"The Army seems to have gone out of its way to blunder and bungle," he continued. "This stupidity and incomprehensible inanity has to stop."

He lifted two documents and held them in his hands. One was the administration's antiballistic missile construction bill, the other, the annual military authorization bill.

"I am warning you bluntly and explicitly," he said, "that unless the Army drops the case or shifts the trial to the U.S., the Army will grievously rue it. This is not an idle threat. I mean every word of it, and you know damn well I can make good on every word I'm saying."

He dropped the two thick bills with a thud.

A few minutes later, John Blandford watched Stanley Resor walk grimly out through the office.

The next visitor, White House liaison Bryce Harlow, was due in a half hour. After that he had scheduled a special event.

"I wish I could give you a cigarette, hon, but they don't let me smoke cigarettes anymore," Mendel Rivers smiled, holding Phyllis Middleton's hand.

"Would you like a cigar?" he minced, leading her to a seat in front of his massive desk.

"No, thank you," she smiled, demure in a navy blue tailored suit, navy heels, and a simple strand of pearls, all bought for the occasion. Her light brown hair had just been cut in a stylish bouffant. She was nervous and excited to be meeting the silver-haired chairman of the Armed Services Committee, a legend back home in South Carolina. Phyllis Middleton would never forget this day. September 19 was her birthday, and meeting Mendel Rivers was the high point of an already tumultuous week.

There had been interviews with the *New York Times*, the *Washington Post*, coffee with syndicated columnists, appearances on CBS, ABC, NBC. She had been on Huntley-Brinkley and Walter Cronkite. There had been more drama in a week than a small-town school teacher could expect in a lifetime. She had really made a splash.

"You're a beautiful woman," Rivers said, taking his seat and picking a cigar from the ashtray. The chairman was a connoisseur of power and beauty, in that order, and the uncomplicated woman sitting before him had some of both. She had gotten more television time in a week than he had in a year.

Phyllis Middleton tittered, her hazel eyes twinkling.

The chairman reminisced about his campaign visits to Jefferson County for a few minutes, and then he turned to the matter at hand.

"Don't you worry, honeybun, I'm going to get that husband of yours the hell out of jail," Rivers said, drawing on his stogie.

He buzzed the intercom. "Get me the president," he said.

Phyllis Middleton was stunned. *The* president? President Nixon? She eyed the telephone as Rivers bantered about her choice of lawyers.

"I believe you were wise to pick that good ole boy George Gregory," he mused. "That New York Jew Rothblatt may be good for the others, but not for you. No, you were wise to pick that country boy." Of course, he would have said the opposite had she hired Rothblatt.

A separate red telephone on the corner of his desk rang, and Rivers picked up the receiver. Cupping the mouthpiece, he motioned for her to pick up an extension and put a finger to his lips.

"Mr. President," he drawled. "I'm so happy to talk to you." They traded pleasantries.

"I have Mrs. Middleton here with me," he finally said. "You know, the wife of one of those wonderful Green Beret soldiers in Vietnam."

Nixon was noncommittal. "Yes, Mendel."

"Well," Rivers continued, "she's come here to Washington, you know, to tell us her story, and to let us know how badly she wants her husband home." Rivers paused.

"There's a lot of us up here in the Congress, you know, who think she's right, that her husband should be home with her, and her children."

Nixon thinly chuckled. "Well, Mendel, I truly agree with her, and with you. But, you know, this is a difficult situation. She's got to go home and let us deal with it up here. She's stirred up a lot of trouble over this thing, and I'm not sure it's helping. We can handle it here, I'm sure. Tell her not to worry— the men will be released. Don't tell her that, of course. It's all very sensitive."

"Well, I'm very glad to hear that, Mr. President."

"So if you can persuade her to leave it to us, I'm sure we'll get it settled. Quietly."

"That's good news, Mr. President. Thank you."

"Thank you for calling, Mendel. You always have my ear."

Rivers put down the telephone and smiled at Phyllis Middleton.

"Well, you heard the president yourself," he said. "Now you go on home and let us take care of it."

"Oh I will, Congressman. Thank you so very much." She sprang to her feet.

"But one more thing," he added. He slowly got up and walked around his desk, cradled her arm, and began to escort her across the room. At the door, he stopped.

"We can't do anything if you cause more of a stir right now, you know." She wagged her head.

"So you must keep this all very secret—no word of talking to me, and not the president. You just keep this quiet, leave it to us."

Like a great tank battle, with huge armadas wheeling into positions over the horizon, lawyers for the Green Berets and the U.S. Army prepared to face off for an unprecedented courtroom test of the extralegal methods of the shadow war. Reporters were pouring into Saigon for the expected spectacle, antici-pating a massive leak of U.S. intelligence secrets.

On ABC's "World News Tonight," anchorman Howard K. Smith called the looming contest "one of the big show trials of the decade, pitting the country's top criminal lawyers against the entire leadership of the U.S. Army."

In Washington, Edward Bennett Williams announced plans to leave for Saigon. In Boston, famed criminal defense attorney F. Lee Bailey called a press conference to say he was entering the case on behalf of Robert Marasco. In San Francisco, Henry Rothblatt, boarding a jet for a third trip to Saigon, declared, "We can call literally two hundred and fifty witnesses who will testify that this was a normal military operation."

Rothblatt also said that he had subpoenaed the entire chain of command over Green Beret operations, starting at the top with Nixon and going on down the parallel lines of Army and CIA authority. His targets included Melvin Laird, Stanley Resor, Creighton Abrams and the MACV staff; for the CIA, Richard Helms, Ted Shackley, Dean Almy, and Harold Chipman. No high official, Rothblatt said, would escape responsibility for the events under trial.

In Athens, Georgia, Guy Scott, an attorney retained by Budge Williams's father, prepared his own subpoenas for Helms and Resor. He demanded the Army secretary appear for a deposition at the Pentagon on October 1.

And he added an instruction to the subpoena duces tecum. "This notice," he said, "is also to be deemed as a notice to produce the following specified document or documents."

First on the list was Defense Intelligence Agency Manual 30-18. It was classified Secret-Noforn.

Double agents, it said, "may be terminated according to approved plans."

George Gregory was having some odd experiences. Plainclothes agents, he discovered, had been prowling through Cheraw and trying to dig up dirt on him. They had been to his high school, the courthouse, questioned his friends and neighbors. They had asked whether he was a radical, an alcoholic, corrupt, or a homosexual.

A neighbor across the street from Gregory's restored 1790s home came over one day and said one of the gumshoes had interviewed him, too.

"I told him," the neighbor said with a wry squint, "that you took a drink now and then."

Gregory chuckled. All in all, he thought, the arrival of the agents was good news. It meant he was "puttin' the hurt on 'em." The defendants' families were trading similar stories. Their mail had been opened and clumsily resealed, there were clicks and echoes on their telephone lines. One of Nan Rheault's neighbors discovered men in an unmarked truck working on her telephone pole. In Connecticut, Eddie Boyle's brother-in-law was laid off from his longtime job at a Connecticut defense plant after his sister criticized the Army.

If the Army was watching, the families had certainly earned its attention. All of the defendants' families were now in harness with their congressional delegations, giving press conferences, appearing on talk shows, lobbying Washington to drop the charges.

George Gregory had been beating the Pentagon over the head ever since he got back to South Carolina, where anti-Washington messages struck with a particular resonance. In Camden County, people boasted of ancestors who had fought for the Confederacy. The Federal government had always been the enemy; in the past decade, Strom Thurmond and Mendel Rivers had done well by setting up a wall of "massive resistance" to racial integration. Backing the heroic Green Berets against Washington was a natural thing. What was the life of one gook compared to valiant American boys?

Gregory had given several forceful talks on the case to local civic and fraternal groups, saying the CIA was running a virtual Murder, Inc. in Vietnam, and what was the Army doing picking on a few Green Berets? He was becoming a sought-after speaker, his name raised as a candidate for Congress. His message was always the same: The boys were engaged in a brutal war for survival in Vietnam, where body counts were the measure of success; the Green Berets were being singled out for punishment. "It's unfair to send soldiers over there and expect them to be lawyers in a guerrilla war, saying you can kill this person but not that one," he said. "They thought they were honestly protecting us. Now we're destroying them, taking them away from their families."

Privately, he thought the Green Berets might have been inept, but they weren't criminals. Especially his own client, Tommy Middleton, who the Army's own files showed had been on the periphery of events. Gregory kept hammering away on the scapegoating theme with the aim of building a wave of public pressure in South Carolina that would give Mendel Rivers the down-home support to move against the Department of the Army. Quietly, if that failed, he prepared to separate his client from the others in the case.

The problem was, Tommy Middleton had changed his mind. On September 27, he expressed his fears that the three captains, who were scheduled to be tried first, would turn on him if he cut his own deal. They were still mad at Middleton for hiring Gregory in the first place.

Middleton no longer wanted Gregory to come over to Saigon, he wrote; he wanted Richard Booth to handle the case in Vietnam and Gregory to stay in the background, working the case at home. Now he wanted "togetherness" with the other defendants.

"As you know," Middleton wrote Gregory on September 27, "we thought there would be a damn good chance that the charges against me would be dropped. Actually, it's probably good that they weren't, because it would have put me in a hell of a position. . . ."

Colonel Seaman, he had discovered, had recommended he not be included in the murder indictments, but Mabry had overruled him. Despite that blockbuster, "I don't want this news released *under any circumstances*," he wrote. "It could hurt me with the press and for damn sure the Army, not to mention getting me in hot water with the other seven who could later testify against me." The threat of retaliation against anyone who turned state's evidence was real, Middleton wrote.

"All eyes," he said, "are on Smith and Boyle now, and it is not going to be too healthy for them if they rat."

Gregory pondered that. "Not too healthy to rat"? Jesus, when will these guys learn? They read too many spy books. Maybe Smith was right after all; maybe they were going to kill him.

All in all, a vainglorious gesture, Gregory thought. Didn't his client know he was playing adolescent games with a life sentence? The only reason the Army hadn't dropped them all down the trapdoor of a sealed courtroom by now was because of the ruckus he had raised. He was certain of that. Now his client wanted to go back being buddy-buddy with his pals.

Or maybe it was prudent self-protection.

The lawyer was in a quandary. Go to Saigon or stay home? There wasn't much he could do about it for now. When Middleton walked into a court-room facing life in prison, Gregory guessed, he'd rethink his lone heroics. The main thing now was to keep digging into Phoenix, following up those calls to the JAG office.

Anyway, he thought, the *New York Times* was suddenly balking on picking up his Saigon hotel bill.

Eddie Boyle was furious. He had never asked for immunity, he told the officer who served the papers on him, and would refuse it now.

"I've got two words for you," he said, "and they aren't good morning."

Henry Rothblatt rushed to put out the brushfire. Hearing the Army an-nouncement that charges against Smith and Boyle were being "held in abey-ance" pending the outcome of the courts-martial, he quickly talked to Boyle and confirmed his intention to refuse to testify under any conditions. Then he arranged for Boyle to repeat it to the *New York Times*.

Boyle called the Army announcement "foul play," the latest in a string of Army outrages that included opening their mail and listening in on their telephone calls.

"I got a medal down in Saigon last year when me and another guy pulled a lot of people out of a fire," he said. "I showed it to my wife and she made a big thing out of it. She said I was a hero and all this junk. It's kind of interesting to note that the Army gives me a medal for saving a hundred and fifty Vietnamese people, and then this."

Privately, Boyle now planned retaliation. Before coming to Vietnam, his specialty was DAME and DASE, acronyms for Defense Against Mechanical Entry and Defense Against Surreptitious Entry—euphemisms for lockpicking and wiretapping. From his assignments in Washington and Germany, he knew that the CIA and FBI routinely broke into foreign embassies to photo-graph documents and plant bugs. Now he was ready to let loose if he ever got on the stand.

Alvin Smith had long ago been removed from the barracks for his own safety. Now he brooded over the offer of immunity, debating whether to accept it. Little did he know he was at the center of an intense CIA effort to quash his dossier.

His wife had emptied his savings account of six thousand dollars to retain a lawyer, George Lattimer, a former military appeals court judge. What's the difference if I cooperate or not? he thought. I'm in a no-win situation.

Smith harbored dark suspicions of what would happen if he ever took the stand. The other men would surely kill him this time, he mused. Maybe not now, maybe sometime years later when he was walking down a street in Florida. He kept to himself, replaying the strange chain of events that had brought him to this place.

Who, really, was Chuyen? he wondered. And who were his helpers in Saigon. He began putting his thoughts together for the president of the United States.

Edward Bennett Williams arrived in Saigon on September 28 and set up camp in a plush suite at the Caravelle Hotel, complete with a bar and an exercise bicycle. The admiring young defense lawyers gathered around the famous criminal defense attorney, whose well-tailored, short-sleeved tropical walking suit nicely showed off a barrel chest and fireplug arms.

"I have a message from Vince Lombardi," he said. Williams had hired the legendary football coach for his own Washington Redskins. Lombardi had also coached at West Point. "These men," he said Lombardi told him, "were just good soldiers who have been hamstrung from doing their duty. They are heroes. Give them my best."

True to his advance billing, Williams's presence sent ripples through the case. That night, he took all his young charges to dinner at La Cave, one of Saigon's most fashionable bistros. The waiters cooed like mourning doves around the attorney, further enchanting the military attorneys.

The spell was broken the next day in Long Binh, though, when Williams asked Steve Berry to leave the room while he talked to Bob Rheault.

Berry was nonplussed; the implication was obvious. Williams had no special regard for the Special Forces, or the group as a whole. He was here to represent his client, Bob Rheault; Berry rightly suspected that Williams might well try to persuade Rheault to go his own way. With begrudging acceptance, he left the room.

Rheault had a good defense on his own, Berry had to admit. But the colonel had repeatedly signaled the men he was with them to the end. Berry fervently believed that. Now Edward Bennett Williams was threatening to rewrite the script.

Walking away, he doubted Rheault would desert them, but the scales had dropped from his eyes. He had to reconsider. All these high-powered civilian lawyers were entering the case, and their reputations were on the line. He had to be careful. He'd worked hard to present a unified defense against the Army, and it had worked pretty well so far. It was, he believed, their only hope of getting all the defendants off, and not just his client. If he thought it was right for just the three captains to get off, he would've copped a plea long ago. But he had no taste for a "good Nazi" defense. He was convinced they should stick together. The government had to prove that someone had been killed. Without a body, and without anyone testifying, he believed, they'd have a hard time doing it.

Smith, he didn't worry about; the guy's insistence that he was being plotted against made him useless as a witness. Boyle, meanwhile, had come into line.

If Edward Bennett Williams fashioned Rheault into a loose cannon, though, anything could happen.

The Washington lawyer further put Berry's nose out of joint when Lee Brumley called to alert him that Williams had tried to talk to him alone, too.

"What should I do?" Brumley asked.

"Don't talk to him," Berry said. "I'll handle it."

Berry found Williams later and walked up to him with a blunt message: "Go fuck yourself." He told him to stay away from the captains.

Back in Washington, the Army lawyers had their own new headache:
Phan Kim Lien wanted money.

Ignored by the U.S. Embassy, Chuyen's widow had simply deduced that the Army's decision to bring murder charges meant that her husband was indeed dead. Now she demanded death benefits due to the widow of a U.S. government employee.

Her letter was forwarded to Col. Wilton Persons, the legal adviser to General Abrams. It was a sticky problem, he conceded in a conversation with a Pentagon lawyer.

"No claim is payable without a formal admission by the United States that his death was caused by U.S. acts." In short, the Army couldn't take responsibility.

But something had to be done, he agreed. You couldn't let the widow wander the streets of Saigon with her children, complaining about the Americans, turning into a martyr.

Mixed signals began popping up all over the Pentagon's legal radar.

It began on September 19 with a telephone call to deputy Army Counsel R. Kenly Webster from a White House lawyer on the staff of John Ehrlichman. Henry Cashen told Webster he had been contacted by Guy Scott, a civilian lawyer for one of the Green Berets.

"The president is not interested in touching this matter," Cashen explained. "Where do I send it at Defense?"

Webster checked with his superiors, then called Cashen back. Tell Scott to file his petition with the military judge assigned to the court-martial, he said. If necessary, the judge advocate general's office at the Pentagon could expedite it.

Four days later, however, Scott's petition arrived on Webster's desk, sent by Henry Cashen.

"What gives?" Webster asked Cashen, calling him back at the White House.

Scott had delivered the petition in person, Cashen said, asking that it be given to Nixon.

"And what did you say when you took it?" Webster asked.

"It would be given appropriate consideration."

"No good," Webster said. He told Cashen not to leave Scott "under the misimpression that the petition was pending in the White House" because it smacked of command interference.

Webster hung up, wrote a memo on the matter for the judge advocate general, and prepared to channel the petition to the Army, as he had tried to get Cashen to do.

Within moments, however, his confusion deepened. Len Niederlehner, chief counsel for the secretary of defense, had a new set of instructions.

The president, he was told, "wants all copies of Green Beret petitions sent to him."

Something was happening, but what? As far as the Army knew, the prosecution was still on track.

Oblivious to the flurry of messages between the White House, the Army, and Saigon, Congress prepared to take up the Green Beret case.

"Mr. Speaker," Peter Rodino began, standing at the rostrum in the House of Representatives. "One of the weirdest—and probably cruelest—trials in the military history of this nation is about to unfold in far-off Vietnam.

"So great is my indignation, and so deep my dismay over the handling of the Green Berets, that I must speak out."

A half dozen congressmen milled in the rear, waiting to speak in the Green Berets' defense. The chamber was unusually full, moving toward a vote on the ABM bill, the Nixon administration's request to fund an antiballistic missile system. Critics were gaining momentum, claiming it increased the chances for a nuclear war, and it looked like the bill would go down in defeat.

On the Senate side, the scene was the same. The Green Beret case, which had begun as a parochial issue, had ballooned into a national debate. On the afternoon of September 27 it preoccupied both houses of Congress. Standing on the deep blue carpet beside his desk, Sen. Ernest Hollings denounced the Army's handling of the case. His deep South Carolina drawl boomed over the busy chamber as he raised his long arms in anger.

"No good can come from this procedure," he declared. "Standing trial with these six officers will be the reputation of the Green Berets and, as a consequence, their effectiveness in the future."

The world was a dangerous place, he said, with PLO hijackings and hostage-takings that required men with special skills.

"Our intelligence system will be tried, and any way you view it, covert activities will be jeopardized merely by being put to trial," he said. "We are being asked to believe that career soldiers did conspire and commit common murder."

He stood at his desk, slowly forming his words.

"I personally don't believe that is the case. Action against an enemy agent is by no stretch of the imagination murder. In war, the primary objective is to destroy the enemy."

The chamber was subdued.

"A trial for murder," Hollings concluded, "doesn't do anyone any good."

He sat down to a flurry of applause from the gallery.

*   *   *

Stanley Resor sat at his desk reading the classified back-channel message from Long Binh.

That's odd, he thought. The CIA had just told its liaison officer to "stand down" from assisting the Army in preparing for trial.

In addition, the CIA was still "reluctant to afford access to evidence in the possession of the agency," according to the message from Wilton Persons.

Resor sensed something terribly wrong. Was the CIA backing out of the case? After all this? After the CIA negotiations with Bob Jordan and Laird's call to Richard Helms? After a million-dollar investigation, two minesweepers sent to sea, a summer of horrendous publicity, and the lives of eight defendants and their families turned upside down?

Not to mention a dead man and his widow.

A few minutes later, he had a visitor.

It was Len Niederlehner, the longtime chief counsel for the Department of Defense. The courtly southerner had a big smile on his thin face.

"I've come to he'p you out," he drawled. In his hand was a letter from Lawrence Houston, Niederlehner's counterpart at the CIA.

Resor read it.

There would be no CIA witnesses, it said. The CIA wasn't going to show up.

55

General George Mabry reached for the telephone and snapped on his bedside light. It was nearly dawn. The soft boom of outgoing artillery could be heard in the distance.

"The case has been dropped," the voice said. "The CIA backed out. There'll be an announcement in a few hours." He hung up.

Mabry was shocked. He had been assured of the CIA's cooperation in the court-martial only the day before.

They're dropping it? Just like that? Nobody had even asked his opinion—he was supposed to be in charge of the case.

General Abrams, he was shocked to learn, had accepted the decision with a shrug. The old tanker had apparently churned up enough earth to make his point and had withdrawn, crushing the Green Berets under his treads.

Shortly before 2:00 P.M. on September 29, reporters hanging around the Pentagon press room were notified that the secretary of the Army would be making an important announcement. They rushed to the auditorium, crammed into the seats and set up their cameras.

A few minutes later a solemn Stanley Resor stepped up to the podium in a gray pin-striped suit, dark tie and white shirt, and faced the blazing lights.

Without preliminaries, the secretary read slowly from a two-page statement. He looked distinctly uneasy.

"I have been advised today," he began, "that the Central Intelligence Agency, though not directly involved in the incident, has determined that in the interests of national security, it will not make available any of its personnel as witnesses in connection with the pending trials in Vietnam of Army personnel assigned to the 5th Special Forces Group."

A few reporters noticed the slight shift in language; the defendants were no longer Green Berets, they were "Army personnel assigned to the Special Forces."

"It is my judgment that under these circumstances the defendants cannot receive a fair trial," Resor continued. "Accordingly, I have directed today that all charges be dismissed immediately. The men will be assigned duties outside of Vietnam."

Wire-service reporters rushed from the room, copies of the statement in hand.

"While it is not possible to proceed with the trials," Resor said, now looking directly into the cameras, "I want to make it clear that the acts which were charged, but not proven, represent a fundamental violation of Army regulations, orders, and principles.

"The Army will not, and cannot, condone unlawful acts of the kind alleged."

The secretary left the stage without taking questions.

The reporters were perplexed, even stunned. They gathered around Pentagon press officers for an explanation.

Why were the charges being dropped if there had been "a fundamental violation of Army regulations, orders, and principles?" Which was it—was there enough evidence to prosecute or not? Why did that depend on the CIA's cooperation? Were the Green Berets guilty or weren't they? The Army seemed to want it both ways, dropping the charges but calling the Green Berets guilty.

The press officers just shook their heads. They couldn't add anything to what was said.

Had Resor's statement been cleared by the White House? the reporters pressed. Did President Nixon, as had been rumored, order the charges dropped?

"This is strictly the Department of the Army's affair," a Pentagon spokesman insisted.

CIA deputy counsel John Warner was driving to work when he heard the announcement.

"What a crock," he laughed to himself. The CIA legal section had been perfectly prepared to go to trial. Arrangements for limiting the testimony of CIA witnesses had been worked out with Army lawyers right up until yesterday.

Somebody backed out, he thought, but it wasn't the lawyers of the CIA. It had to be Helms and Shackley, with the help of Richard Nixon.

*   *   *

Steve Berry stepped out of the shower. Somebody was banging on his door.

"Hey, Captain." It was his driver. "I'm supposed to drive you to Long Binh. Get your gear and let's head out."

What was it, he wondered, more trouble with Edward Bennett Williams? He pulled on his rumpled fatigues and scuffed boots. A few minutes later he was heading up the bumpy road from Bien Hoa to Long Binh.

As he drove up to the barracks, he heard "The Ballad of the Green Berets" blasting from a window. Then he saw Marasco, Middleton, and Brumley rushing toward him.

"It's over!" they yelled, grabbing him by the arms. "The Army dropped the charges!" They all hugged as a horde of photographers surrounded them.

David Crew followed, his cheeks glistening, a Bible in his hand. Budge Williams sauntered forward with a bottle of beer. Eddie Boyle pulled up in a jeep and ran over.

A mob of reporters with cameras and notebooks, many of whom had been staked out near the barracks for days, engulfed the now-freed defendants.

Off to the side, Bob Rheault was crouching by a fire, grinning tightly as he ceremoniously fed a sheaf of documents into the flames. The reports on Operation Phoenix and Ngo Dinh Diem, Cambodia and Laos, Key Cities, Che Guevara, and the Congo curled into flaky black sheets.

A reporter asked, "Did your men kill Thai Khac Chuyen, Colonel, and if so, why?"

"I feel we are still under the restrictions they have placed on us, so I'll have no comment," he said.

"Was the outcome ever in doubt?" another reporter asked.

"The only question," he said, "was how long and how difficult it would be to prove the point." Later, he said, he might elaborate on the case. But questions about Thai Khac Chuyen were "classified."

"Captain," Robert Marasco was asked, "you were charged as the trigger man in the execution. Do you feel you did anything wrong?"

"No I don't. The charge is absurd. I have done nothing wrong or that I am ashamed of. I have never done anything that has not been with the purest of motives and with the best interest of my country in mind."

"Was Thai Khac Chuyen executed," another asked him, "and was he executed in the line of duty as a double agent?"

Marasco hesitated. Finally he said, "You are aware there are special operations here in Vietnam, and I have no comment on that."

At a signal from Rheault, the men cut off the questions and retreated to the barracks. Within a few hours, they were all flying out of Saigon together—all except Alvin Smith, who was shunted to a separate flight home.

As the World Airways jet banked over the green Mekong Delta on the flight back to America, the pilot came on the intercom and announced the presence of their famous passengers. A loud cheer went up.

*   *   *

Peter Rodino stood quietly at the Speaker's podium on the floor of the House of Representatives as a wave of shouts, cheers, and applause washed over him. He had just announced the Army's decision, setting off a fifteen-minute standing tribute.

"I am deeply gratified . . ." he said. A roar broke out again, forcing him to stop. He soaked up their cheers once more, then gestured for quiet.

"I am deeply gratified that the secretary of the Army has finally addressed himself personally to all the issues in this case . . . and has taken a fair and just position."

Scattered applause.

"These dedicated servicemen have finally been released. However, nothing can undo the suffering experienced by them and their families."

He paused.

"I pledge to these men and their families that I, for one, shall continue to do everything in my power to undo the damage that has been done, and to ensure that never again will servicemen be exposed to the abuses and miscarriages of justice that have characterized this case," he said.

The House sprang to its feet again for another long tribute. As Rodino stepped from the podium, he was surrounded by two dozen colleagues who pressed close to pat his back or shake his hand.

After he finally exited the House, he went back to his office and thanked his staff for working "very, very hard" on the research for the case.

Edward Bennett Williams was thronged by reporters outside the Caravelle Hotel. He had expected the charges to be dropped all along, he said. "It was a terrible miscarriage of justice."

In San Francisco, Henry Rothblatt, who had made a last-minute trip back to San Francisco, said, "Thank goodness reason prevailed. This is what I predicted—they had to drop it. How can you charge men with crimes for doing their duty? How stupid could they be?"

In Boston, F. Lee Bailey said he welcomed the decision and had not relished the prospect of "gambling with a jury."

"I didn't look forward to it—the damage we would have had to do to the intelligence network to demonstrate why these men did what they did. The CIA would've been in a terrible position if the defense had started putting them on the witness stand. . . . The only victor would have been the North Vietnamese."

The Marascos were besieged by a throng of reporters on the lawn of their suburban Newark home. Emily Marasco clutched a handkerchief to her face as her husband put a comforting arm on her shoulder. "My boy is free, my boy is free," she cried. "I'm so happy."

In Duncan, Oklahoma, Lee Brumley's mother, Vera, wept and told the local newspaper she had baked his favorite cookies and cake.

In Baltimore, Eddie Boyle's friends stocked the refrigerator with a week's worth of beer. His wife planned a huge blow-out.

In Georgia, Budge Williams's father said matter-of-factly that he held no grudge against the Army. "They had to do what they had to do. We're just glad it's over."

Nan Rheault was stopped by a CBS reporter as she hurried into her apartment in Brookline, a suburb of Boston.

"Did you ever doubt the results?" the reporter asked. A radiant smile spread across her face.

"No, I had faith in my husband and in all the American people who stood up for him," she said.

"How did you hear about it?"

"On the radio." No, she said, no one had called from the Army. Ever. Did she think the case would affect her husband in any way?

Mrs. Rheault stopped, momentarily thrown by the question.

"Why don't you ask him?" she said. "I've got to go."

As reporters scrambled to record the reactions of the freed men's families, an impromptu press conference was unfolding outside the gate of the United States Embassy in Saigon.

Phan Kim Lien, dressed in mourning white, holding her infant son in one arm and a two-year-old boy by the hand, burst into tears.

"My husband came south looking for freedom and democracy and the help of the Americans," she sobbed. "The Americans killed him and won't take the responsibility."

Her mouth was stretched in agony, tears cascading down her cheeks. Someone tried to comfort her, but she tore away. A large group of reporters stood around her, uncomfortable with the spectacle. As she fell to the ground, Marine guards watched silently from inside the closed embassy gates.

"They must either take responsibility for his death, or my death," she screamed, and threatened to commit suicide on the spot.

As the horrible scene unfolded, her children burst into loud wails. Finally, she collapsed into the dust, heaving with sobs.

"The soul of my husband," she cried, "will follow all those who killed him."

The World Airways jet flew west through the night, to Hawaii and then on toward San Francisco, carrying the men home. As they slept, speculation about the abruptly suspended sensation began to grow. The story had led all three network newscasts. Huge black headlines had announced the dropped charges on the front page of the *New York Daily News*.

BERETS FREED!
CIA Balks, Army Cancels Trial

But more questions had been raised than answered by the Army's abrupt dismissal of the investigation.

Who made the decision to drop the case? NBC said it was the Army, CBS said it was the CIA. ABC said it was the CIA and the president, acting together.

A CBS correspondent listed the lingering mysteries:

"The CIA's refusal to provide witnesses settled the matter," he said, "although it leaves many questions unanswered:

"Why that agency became involved in the case of Thai Khac Chuyen, other than through regular military channels;

"Why Chuyen was not turned over to the South Vietnamese Army when his involvement with the enemy was discovered;

"Whether he was in fact secretly serving as a South Vietnamese agent, as well as working for the Green Berets and the North Vietnamese;

"Perhaps more to the point, whether the case will lead to the destruction of the Special Forces, or strengthen them against those in the regular Army who would like to do away with the Green Berets."

Twelve hours later, floodlights washed the fuselage of the World Airways jet as it pulled to a stop on the tarmac of Travis Air Force Base north of San Francisco. A huge crowd of reporters and camera crews was on hand waiting for the Green Berets when they walked into the terminal.

Reluctantly, Bob Rheault stepped to a bank of microphones. His men stood in a row behind him in their fatigues and berets, blinking in the bright lights. The first question came from the front.

"There has been a lot of rumor and speculation about exactly what happened, Colonel," a newsman asked as camera crews pressed in for close-ups. "To start with basics, did you personally, was it your decision, to execute the Vietnamese man, the so-called double agent?"

Rheault cleared his throat, considering the question.

"There has not been any substantiation that such an individual ever existed," he said.

The reporter hesitated, incredulous. "Are you denying there was a slaying at all?" he asked.

"That's correct."

A clamor broke out with other questions, but Rheault said he could not discuss anything that was classified, and as far as he was concerned, the whole matter was over and done with. He picked up his bag to leave. The other men followed suit.

"Can you tell us then, Colonel, just what it was all about, in general terms?"

Rheault turned, impatient.

"War is a nasty business," he said, "with a lot of high-minded objectives, like freedom and fighting the aggressor, to justify killing people."

He paused.

"All this would best be forgotten," he added grimly, "so long as people remember we were exonerated."

More questions were shouted, but the colonel cut them off.

"If you'll excuse us," he said, "we'd like to get on to see our families and pick up our lives."

They walked off through the terminal.

56

MALIBU, CALIFORNIA

October 2, 1969

D aniel Ellsberg lay in bed reading an account of the Green Beret case in the *Los Angeles Times*. Outside his window, the azure waters of the Pacific knuckled on the white sands of Malibu. As he read on, drinking his morning coffee, he began thinking how hard it would be to give all this up.

A wiry, intense intellectual with piercing blue eyes, Ellsberg was one of the very few real experts on Vietnam. He had made several trips to Saigon in the early 1960s as a State Department officer, studying counterinsurgency at the feet of Edward G. Lansdale, the legendary CIA agent fictionalized by Graham Greene in *The Quiet American*. A former marine, he often went off by himself into the villages to ask questions. Despite his growing doubts about the war, he wrote the doctrine on pacification for the U.S. Embassy, which to his horror a few years later, formed the basis for the Phoenix program.

In 1964, working for the assistant secretary of defense for international security affairs, Ellsberg had also become a recognized expert on the dynamics of force and negotiations, particularly relating to the effect of American bombing on the old-line Communists in the politburo in Hanoi. Threats of escalation, he concluded, never worked with the North Vietnamese. Instead, they had the paradoxical result of propelling the United States into an ever-deepening quagmire to maintain its credibility.

Ellsberg's skepticism about a satisfactory solution to the war expanded with every new combat brigade and bomber squadron hurled into Vietnam. In 1965, he happened to be in Saigon when Dr. Henry Kissinger visited on a fact-finding trip and asked the embassy for an off-the-record briefing by resident Vietnam experts. During the afternoon talk in a shaded house on Cong Ly Street, Ellsberg told the Harvard professor that Lyndon Johnson's secretary of defense, Robert McNamara, had been repeatedly misled by senior military officers. Go talk to the younger men in the field, he urged Kissinger. Go without an embassy escort. Talk to the lieutenants and captains. Talk to some Vietnamese outside the system.

Kissinger came back deeply pessimistic about the chances for victory in Vietnam, believing then that the Saigon government was not worthy of support. The U.S. negotiating strategy, he confided to friends, should be designed to create "a decent interval" between a U.S. withdrawal and an inevitable Communist takeover.

He was grateful to Ellsberg. "I have learned more from Dan Ellsberg," he told one group during a lecture, "than anyone else in Vietnam." A few years later, however, the invitation from Nixon to be his national security adviser prompted Kissinger to revise his views. He now thought more bombing could work.

Ellsberg, meanwhile, had undertaken an unusual assignment. A team of national security experts had been put together at the Pentagon to compile a diplomatic, military, and political history of the Vietnam war. Ellsberg was invited to join it.

The Pentagon vaults revealed a top secret record in deep contradiction to the official version of events. As Ellsberg waded into the boxes of classified cables, back-channel messages, embassy reports, and CIA memorandums going back twenty-five years, he discovered that deception had been piled on deception all through the U.S. years in Indochina. The paper trail reached back to 1945, when Ho Chi Minh was an agent of the OSS, helping the allies defeat the Japanese in Indochina. The documents recounted Ho's requests to the American agents for a copy of the Declaration of Independence, and his plans to use it as a model for Vietnam. They recorded President Truman's reneging on the pledges of Roosevelt to keep the French from reclaiming their colony.

From the spurious election of Ngo Dinh Diem as president and U.S. complicity in his assassination, through the secret CIA wars in Laos and North Vietnam and the implementation of the Phoenix program, the vaults disgorged an ugly, disturbing history of official deceit in Vietnam. What particularly stunned Ellsberg, though, was the record of events surrounding a clash in the Gulf of Tonkin in 1964, an incident that provoked the bombing of North Vietnam and led to the introduction of the first U.S. ground combat units into the war.

President Johnson's explanations for the incident were completely false, Ellsberg found. In the White House version, Communist patrol boats fired on innocent U.S. destroyers on station in international waters off North Vietnam. But in the top secret files, Ellsberg discovered that the warships were encroaching on North Vietnamese waters at the time in support of classified Green Beret sabotage missions in North Vietnam. Even the much-ballyhooed "attack" on the destroyers was doubtful; the captain of one of the ships had misinterpreted radar "shadows" as torpedoes; no other evidence of an attack existed. Lyndon Johnson and the Pentagon had manipulated the incident to stampede Congress into passing an open-ended resolution of support for the war. A tragedy of immense proportions, in Ellsberg's view, followed.

Ellsberg was no stranger to lying, having served at high levels in the government related to secret operations in Vietnam. But this particular deception shocked and depressed him. The Tonkin Gulf lie was directly responsible, he believed, for forty thousand American deaths and two million Vietnamese casualties, as well as untold treasure and grief. Had the U.S. Senate Foreign Relations Committee known about the deception, he thought, Congress never would have granted Lyndon Johnson carte blanche to wage war in Vietnam. And the American people would have known that Johnson's pledges of peace during his presidential campaign against Barry Goldwater were a fraud. Johnson had been planning to escalate all along, just as, Ellsberg knew from his contacts in the White House, Nixon and Kissinger now were, too. The parallels between the summers of 1964 and 1969 were striking. Nixon's pretext for trying to bomb his way out of the war would be Cambodia. But Ellsberg found no one in Congress willing to believe him.

Threads of the Green Berets wove all through the secret history of the war, from the early raiding parties in North Vietnam through the creation of an "armée clandestine" in Laos, their curious background role in the Diem assassination, and now, the scandal surrounding Col. Robert Rheault and his men. As Ellsberg read through the long account of the case in the *Los Angeles Times*, his revulsion and anger grew. Reading between the lines of the *Times* account, he concluded that the cover-up began at the bottom and moved up, from the three captains to the major to Colonel Rheault. Rheault then lied to General Abrams; Abrams then lied about the motives for his prosecution. And the grand finale was Army secretary Stanley Resor's sleight of hand about why the case had been dropped. Of course the CIA men could be compelled to testify, Ellsberg knew; all the president had to do was order them. It was all a tissue of lies.

The thought went through his mind, and not for the first time: "This is a system I have served for fifteen years. It is a system that lies automatically from top to bottom to protect a cover-up murder." His attention drifted to his own copy of the secret history of the war, thousands of pages locked in a safe in his office.

As Ellsberg brooded, Richard Nixon sat down at his Oval Office desk and scratched out a handwritten thank-you note. After a mysterious week-long delay, the House of Representatives had finally passed the military authorization funding bill.

> Dear Mendel,
> I need not emphasize the importance to our country of the issues involved. You know them as well as I do, and you acted as you always do where the good of the nation is at stake.
> Thank you,
Richard M. Nixon

Nixon had solved the Green Beret case just as Daniel Ellsberg suspected. And for good reason, Nixon believed: to protect national security secrets, particularly relating to Cambodia.

Every president who had dealt with the war thought he acted reasonably. Nixon had come into office, as had his predecessors, determined to project an image that the war was winnable without great domestic sacrifice. Each had been forced to discard bits and pieces of his strategy along the way while maintaining an aura of normalcy. Unable to provide a satisfactory explanation for the mounting American commitment, Nixon, like Johnson and Kennedy before him, had been forced to rely more and more on secrecy.

Nixon had vowed not to be consumed, as they had, by Vietnam. He would be engaged by much wider horizons: arms-control agreements with Moscow, an opening to China, the unity of Europe, peace in the Middle East, welfare overhaul, crime. Vietnam would not bog him down, as it had Kennedy, Johnson, and Hubert Humphrey.

To liberals in and out of Washington, Richard Nixon's campaign message had been comforting, that Vietnam was already in his rearview mirror. The war was going to be ended, the agony of a long decade brought to a close. There would be peace in the streets. Parents could talk to their children. Students would go to class. Draft resisters could come home from Canada. Everyone could go back to normal.

The image of impending tranquillity was intended to translate differently in Hanoi, however: With the war only one item on a much larger administration agenda, with American public opinion under control, Nixon would be free to carry on the fight on his own terms. That's what the Nixon men wanted Ho Chi Minh to know.

Then came the Green Beret case. It was a piddling matter in the larger scheme of things. But the letters had come pouring in, threatening to reignite a debate on the morality of the war, the conduct of the troops, the methods of counterinsurgency, and in a worst-case scenario, the wide range of activities pointing toward an American invasion of Cambodia and the toppling of Prince Sihanouk. The Green Beret case, in short, threatened to make the war his.

As the case came to a head in late September, Nixon had feigned disinterest in Vietnam. There were long days at Camp David and sailing on the *Sequoia*. He played golf at Burning Tree with Bob Hope. He hosted Israeli prime minister Golda Meir at a glittering White House dinner. But beneath the projected calm, Richard Nixon was as consumed by Vietnam as his predecessor was.

On the morning of September 25, as Edward Bennett Williams announced his imminent departure for Saigon and Rep. Peter Rodino took to the House rostrum for another speech on the Green Beret case, the president convened a breakfast meeting with all his top generals: Earle Wheeler and William Westmoreland from the Army, Marine Corps general Leonard Chapman, Air Force general John D. Ryan, and Navy admiral Thomas Moorer. Melvin Laird, Henry Kissinger, and congressional liaison Bryce Harlow filled out the long mahogany table in the White House Situation Room.

The basement meeting was unheralded and officially characterized as routine. But on the docket were secret plans to invade Cambodia and Laos, resume the bombing of North Vietnam, and mine Haiphong Harbor. But as the president was beginning to learn, these were subjects on which the Green Beret defendants also were conducting related research in Saigon; copies of lawyers' subpoenas for the testimony of Richard Helms, Stanley Resor, and Melvin Laird relating to years of illegal operations in Indochina were arriving daily at the White House. So were defense petitions for the president to intervene and dismiss the charges. And then came the call from Mendel Rivers.

Nixon had promised to do something about it, but he curiously hadn't. Was he still trying to burn Helms with it? Bob Haldeman, Nixon's chief of staff, suspected that was the case. But by week's end, he knew he had to force the boss to pay attention to the case. He made a note to himself, "Green Beret— Mon." They had to get rid of it.

Nixon seemed less interested in the Green Berets than anti-Vietnam college students, who had just returned to campus spoiling for a fight. Radicals had invaded the Harvard Institute of Government and beaten up a handful of professors holding a forum on the war. Two hundred other Harvard students had occupied the dean's office and demanded the school break all ties with the Pentagon. As the "Chicago Seven" trial opened, Columbia radical Mark Rudd boasted that "the violence is just beginning."

A major Nixon worry was a march on Washington scheduled for October 15. White House aide Charlie McWhorter was dispatched to meet secretly with its organizers, Sam Brown and David Hawke. He reported back that the protest would be big, "a most satisfactory result from the standpoint of its sponsors." He cautioned the White House to not antagonize the antiwar movement more with inflammatory statements.

Nixon brushed the advice aside. "It is absolutely essential that we react insurmountably and powerfully to blunt this attack," he instructed Haldeman in a lengthy memo. Nixon proposed that Pat Buchanan mount one of his phony letter-writing campaigns against Ted Kennedy, who had recently charged that the slow pace of troop withdrawals and negotiations was a cover for more escalation.

"Get a major mailing out to editors and columnists in Massachusetts and perhaps even nationally," Nixon wrote, suggesting they reprint a quote from Radio Hanoi approving of Kennedy's speech. "The best place from which this could be mailed is, of course, Boston." The *Chicago Tribune*, he added in a later meeting with Haldeman, "should hit Percy," the liberal Republican senator from Illinois, "if he's tied in with peace groups."

But that wasn't enough. Nixon wanted to throw a tougher punch at the antiwar forces. On the morning of September 28, as lawyers for the Army and the CIA worked out final details in the Green Beret prosecution, Nixon told Haldeman to hire Charles Colson, a staffer responsible for White House liaison with special interest groups, for the job of discrediting liberals.

"One of the best follow-up men," Haldeman wrote in his notes of the meeting. "Dirty tricks. Take him out of this job—onto the attack. He's competitive, restless, not a grey p.r. type. We need an S.O.B."

Colson, a conservative New Englander, shared Nixon's visceral hatred for the Kennedys. He had an ex-CIA man, Howard Hunt, working to discredit them. Hunt, a CIA case officer during the Bay of Pigs era, was dispatched to Martha's Vineyard to see if he could dig up any more dirt on the accident at Chappaquiddick. In Washington, Hunt began quiet research on the Kennedy administration's involvement in the overthrow of Ngo Dinh Diem and recommended they fabricate diplomatic cables tying Kennedy personally to Diem's assassination.

"K—full report on this week's bombing of Cambodia," Nixon also ordered from Kissinger. The national security adviser had been selecting the targets and ingratiating himself further with Nixon by sharing the fruits of FBI wire-taps on newsmen and his own aides.

Kissinger's fall from grace distressed Daniel Ellsberg, who was keeping abreast of events through old friends on the national security council. The Nixon men, he had heard, were worried about what he knew about the bombing plans and might try to hurt him. The deceit that had long governed the conduct of the war inside Vietnam, he surmised, was coming home to roost.

Nixon was finally forced to focus on the Green Beret case during the daily 9:00 A.M. staff meeting on September 29. The morning network news shows had been filled with film of the civilian lawyers and the press pouring into Saigon for "the biggest show trial of the decade." The case had turned into a circus.

It was time to get rid of it, Nixon said, sitting at his desk in the Oval Office. Richard Helms's feet had been held to the fire long enough. Haldeman and Ehrlichman listened. There had been rumors that Helms had used Attorney General John Mitchell to lobby Nixon to intervene in the case. The CIA wouldn't be worth a damn in Vietnam, Helms had allegedly said, if the case went forward.

The president and his staff considered alternatives. Haldeman suggested using Egil Krogh, a lawyer on Ehrlichman's staff responsible for Howard Hunt and Gordon Liddy, to work on it. Krogh was trustworthy; he had been helping Colson on Dirty Tricks.

Kissinger's people would have to be involved, too, Haldeman noted. It was, of course, a national security case.

"Have Krogh see Al Haig," Nixon said, as Haldeman scribbled notes. "Get a letter from the CIA saying they will refuse to provide witnesses for the Green Beret trial—executive privilege." The details could be worked out with CIA counsel Larry Houston.

"Without CIA witnesses," Nixon declared, playing the lawyer, "the rights of the defendants will be prejudiced."

No witnesses, no trial. Creighton Abrams? Tough. We can't sink the whole ship because the general hates the Green Berets. Let him take out his rage some other way. Stanley Resor? Let him get the message from the CIA. What can he do? He'll have no other choice but to go along.

That would end it, Nixon thought, and there would be no White House fingerprints.

Daniel Ellsberg read Stanley Resor's explanation for dropping the charges and put his newspaper aside. His thoughts again went to his safe full of top secret documents. If he leaked them, he knew his whole life would change. He'd certainly go to jail for many years; his security agreement was quite specific about that. He'd no longer have the rambling house on Pacific Coast

Highway. After that, who knew? He'd no longer be employable as a government consultant, and who else was interested in his arcane skills?

But another vision of devastation, less personal, came into his mind: Thousands of dead and maimed American soldiers for years to come. A million dead Vietnamese, Laotians, and Cambodians. Villages in flames, peasants wailing. It was a trail of carnage that stretched over and beyond the horizons of his imagination.

The lying had to stop, but it wasn't just any kind of lying. It was a question of what the lying was about. The papers in his file were not just about cost overruns and weapons that didn't work, they were about aggression, about secret and unjustified escalations of the war, and about killing. The murder of Thai Khac Chuyen was just one more death, but it was one too many. It was the last straw.

The documents in his safe were the solution to "a mass murder mystery," Ellsberg thought. They explained why two million Vietnamese had died on America's cold war chessboard. They explained how four American presidents had secretly, and fruitlessly, escalated their war *before* Nixon was elected. Now a new chapter in the history of crime was about to be opened.

Only if Congress and the American people saw the secret documents themselves would they be persuaded to believe what Ellsberg knew: that Nixon and Kissinger were planning another escalation while professing peace. That they were bombing Cambodia despite the forceful and successful denials by the White House last March. That the United States had been mucking around in Laos and Cambodia for a long, long time. That the United States was running death squads under the cover of a police program called Phoenix.

If Congress understood the past, Ellsberg thought, it might be persuaded to consider the bloody future.

Ellsberg called Anthony Russo, a colleague at the Rand think tank in Santa Monica. Russo had worked on the secret history project, and like Ellsberg, he had once been a Pentagon consultant and Vietnam believer.

"Do you know where there's a photocopying machine?" Ellsberg asked.

Russo did, and he was ready to go. He could start copying the papers that night, he said.

"Let's do it," Ellsberg said.

How wonderfully ironic, Ellsberg thought as he hung up, that Nixon thought he could keep the secrets forever by sweeping one more murder under the rug.

Not this time. Nixon had just triggered the biggest leak of them all, the whole secret, sordid history of the war. The Pentagon Papers were on their way.

57

WASHINGTON, D.C.

October 4, 1969

Robert B. Rheault walked across the Pentagon parking lot in the bright autumn sunshine, wearing his Army tunic and tie, shiny black boots, and green beret. He was rested but nervous, heading for a meeting with Gen. Richard Stillwell, the Army's deputy chief of staff for special operations. It was time to discuss his future.

The future of Phan Kim Lien had just been decided in the same office. A financial officer for covert operations had authorized a secret payment to Thai Khac Chuyen's widow for $6,472, equivalent to three years of Chuyen's salary. The money would be paid in cash from the Pentagon's "black bag," a classified operational fund, thus skirting the need for an official acknowledgment of U.S. responsibility for his death, or even that he worked for the Green Berets.

The decision to pay Lien a "death gratuity" had reopened the debate over Chuyen and who he really was. If he was an innocent victim of a murder plot, then the Army clearly owed his family money—and maybe a lot more than six thousand dollars. But if his allegiance lay with Hanoi, the government owed them nothing.

In the end, the Army settled the debate with the same ambiguity in which the case had begun. It cut a check but attached a note that said, "He was the double agent the Green Berets were accused of killing." On October 2, a secret courier sped down the alley to Lien's simple house and delivered the cash in exchange for her signature on a promise never to talk about the case or contest the award in court.

But the fact was, there never was a unanimous verdict on the true allegiance of Thai Khac Chuyen. The CIA assessment was at a polar opposite from the Green Berets'. A dozen Army officials who read the file likewise couldn't agree.

But that was no longer Bob Rheault's business. He was looking to the future now, his general's star, maybe more: certainly a return to normality. The charges, after all, had been dropped.

Rheault bounded up the concrete Pentagon steps and into the harshly lit corridor. It was a routine business day, the long waxy hallways awash with uniformed generals and admirals and civilians in their white shirts and muted suits, security badges dangling from small chains around their necks. Small tractors pulling wagons full of documents hummed through the crowds.

Rheault walked into Richard Stillwell's office. Also there were Gen. William DePuy, Gen. William Knowlton, and Gen. Richard Fulton. Their greeting was cordial but awkward. They exchanged light banter.

"What do you want to do now?" Stillwell eventually asked.

Rheault looked at him as if the answer were obvious.

"I'd like to go back to Vietnam," he said, "to the 5th Special Forces. There's still a big job to be done." If the Army had truly vindicated him by dropping the charges, he wanted them to show it.

The three men stared at him, nearly exhaling as one.

"That's not possible," Stillwell finally said. "I don't think General Abrams would stand for that."

Rheault hesitated, letting it sink in, disappointed but not surprised. He had already made up his mind. If he could not have the Green Berets again, a cloud would follow him wherever he went. And he didn't want to sit at a desk with a do-nothing assignment.

"Then it's time for me to go," he said.

With quiet, reluctant assents, the three generals agreed. There was nothing else to say. With a round of murmured apologies and handshakes, the meeting was over. So was Bob Rheault's career.

The colonel left the Pentagon and drove directly to Walter Reed Army Hospital for his retirement physical. The hospital commander met him at the door. Two hours later, Robert Bradley Rheault walked out a civilian, twenty-six years after he had entered West Point.

Tom Middleton sat in the hot sunshine on the fifty-yard line of Fulton County Stadium, an honored guest of the Atlanta Falcons football team. It was October 8.

George Gregory sat at home watching TV as the halftime festivities began.

"We'd like to welcome some special guests," the public address announcer began. The names of prominent people were announced and they stood—the mayor, a few congressmen, and Georgia governor Lester Maddox—to scattered applause.

"Ladies and gentlemen," the announcer then said, "We have another special guest, a Green Beret officer whose name will be familiar to you all. He has just come home to South Carolina after a grueling ordeal in Vietnam . . ."

The crowd began to applaud.

"and we are particularly glad to honor him. . . ."

The crowd began to roar. . . .

"Won't you please welcome . . . Major Thomas A. Middleton!"

The roar built to a crescendo as Tom Middleton stood and waved at the sixty thousand applauding fans crammed into the stadium.

At home, George Gregory watched, a smile wrinkling his mouth.

The telephone rang. It was Gregory's sister, a civil-liberties lawyer. She was watching the same scene at home. "You know, George," she drawled, "I'm really glad you got Tommy off, but this is ridiculous." He chuckled, said he'd call her back, and hung up.

As he watched Tommy Middleton bask in the cheers, a feeling of immense sadness crept over him. Of course he was glad that the Green Berets were freed; they shouldn't have to pay with their lives for policies that were designed by men high above them long ago.

But with the dismissal of charges, he thought, a chance had been missed to open the crypt of Vietnam and look inside. The White House had nailed it shut by stopping the case from going forward.

For a while. But that won't last, he predicted, thinking of all the anonymous calls to the JAG office from the worried Phoenix program operatives.

There will be another case, he knew, and another, and another. They can't stop them all.

Mark my words, he thought, this isn't over. Not by a long shot. It's just begun.

Aftermath

58

D aniel Ellsberg gave copies of the Pentagon Papers to a succession of antiwar congressmen and senators during 1969 and 1970, all of whom declined to release them to the public. In 1970, U.S. forces crossed into Cambodia, Prince Sihanouk was ousted, and the Khmer Rouge arose to battle the cabal of right-wing generals who had taken his place. The peaceful nation, which had managed to stay out of the war in neighboring Vietnam and Laos under Sihanouk's adroit maneuvers, was plunged into civil war, and eventually a nightmare of genocide. The secret bombing, meanwhile, was extended into North Vietnam under the cover of "protective reaction" strikes. Laos was invaded by U.S. and South Vietnamese forces in early 1971 in a disastrous move resulting in a hasty retreat with heavy losses. The bloody tragedy that Ellsberg had foreseen when he decided to copy the secret Pentagon history of the war had become reality.

Ellsberg finally found a willing customer for the documents in Neil Sheehan, a reporter for the *New York Times*. When the *Times* began excerpting the papers in June 1971, the Nixon administration desperately sought to quash their publication, thus prompting the most serious confrontation between the American press and the government in modern times.

A lower court issued a restraining order against the *Times* until the larger issues of national security could be settled. As lawyers for the newspaper prepared to challenge the ruling, the *Washington Post* and then the *Boston Globe* obtained their own copies of the papers and began publishing them in defiance of the court order. The Nixon Justice Department pursued them as well, with the threat of ruinous litigation and damages. Finally, the Supreme Court overturned the lower court's decision and the newspapers were free to publish without fear of prosecution.

Daniel Ellsberg, however, was apprehended and indicted for theft of government property, as well as for violations of his security oaths. He went on trial in California in 1972, facing a long prison term. During the trial, however, revelations surfaced that White House operative E. Howard Hunt and a team of Cuban-born burglars had broken into the office of Ellsberg's psychiatrist to gather embarrassing information on the former defense consultant; the government was forced to drop the case.

The publication of the Pentagon Papers was the opening chapter of the Watergate era. Revelations eventually surfaced that Nixon and Kissinger had illegally wiretapped White House and Pentagon officials and journalists in search of the Cambodian bombing leak. Congress called for the president's impeachment. The secret bombing itself was weighed by the House Judiciary Committee as an impeachment charge.

George Gregory continued to give speeches accusing the United States of sponsoring Phoenix "death squads" in South Vietnam, but without documentation his charges fell on deaf ears. Finally, in 1970, former Army intelligence sergeant Kenneth Barton Osborne came forward and told the story of Phoenix to a congressional committee. Osborne's vivid accounts of assassination and torture prompted front-page headlines in the *New York Times* and full-throated congressional outrage over the practices of Army intelligence and the CIA.

William Colby, testifying before Congress in 1973 during his confirmation hearings to be CIA director, conceded that twenty-one thousand Vietnamese had died as a result of Phoenix operations. Many observers felt the figure was far too low; other experts, writing in later years, felt that the true figures would never be known; many killings were undocumented, on the one hand, or, on the other, inflated with combat casualties by Phoenix bureaucrats.

The battle for the future of the Green Berets was waged well past the time when Gen. Creighton Abrams left Saigon in 1971. After the charges against the Green Berets were dropped, operations of the 5th Special Forces were severely circumscribed with Army intelligence officers brought in to ride herd on the group. Its colors were struck in early 1972, well ahead of the end of all U.S. military operations in South Vietnam. For the next decade, the Green Berets were relegated to the back lots of the John F. Kennedy Special Warfare Center at Fort Bragg, North Carolina, eclipsed by other paramilitary units. Their star lay low until the advent of the Reagan administration, which began assigning Green Berets to Central America as advisers to Salvadoran intelligence units and the CIA-backed Nicaraguan Contras.

The Army of the Republic of Vietnam, meanwhile, had collapsed in pandemonium in 1975. As American helicopters escaped from the roof of the U.S. Embassy in Saigon, according to the account of former CIA officer Frank Snepp, the CIA abandoned thousands of its loyal Vietnamese agents and employees in a "moral flap" of horrendous proportions. Left to the mercies of the victorious Communists, most were imprisoned and shot.

The widow of Thai Khac Chuyen and her two children were among those left behind. Today they live in abject poverty in Saigon, ignored by the

Communists her husband allegedly served and harassed by former South Vietnamese soldiers.

The body of Thai Khac Chuyen was never found. In August 1991, his son wrote to the author and asked whether it was true his father had died in the war. "It is difficult to live all these years not knowing for sure," said Thai Quoc Viet.

Others in the case, on the whole, fared better:

THE GREEN BERETS

Colonel Robert B. Rheault divorced his wife, retired to Maine, and began a new career with Outward Bound, where he launched a special program for disabled Vietnam veterans. In 1988 he led an expedition of Vietnam veterans and Soviet veterans of Afghanistan to into the mountains of Soviet Central Asia. Many of them were former Special Forces and Soviet *spetsnaz* troops.

Major Thomas A. Middleton retired from the Army in 1978 after several more intelligence assignments. He now sells real estate in suburban Washington, D.C.

Major David E. Crew stayed in the Army and attended the Army War College. He is now retired and employed in the security industry in southern California.

Captain Leland J. Brumley transferred to Armor after he returned from Vietnam but later served with the Defense Intelligence Agency as an expert on Soviet tanks. He retired in 1989 and lives on his sailboat near Houston.

Captain Robert E. Marasco was seriously injured in an automobile accident within days of his return from Vietnam. He fully recovered and now owns a kitchenware store with his wife in New Jersey.

Captain Budge Williams stayed in the Green Berets and returned to Vietnam in 1972 to strike the flags of the 5th Special Forces Group. After a fling at owning and running liquor stores with his father, he began to write war novels in Bogart, Georgia.

Warrant Officer Edward J. Boyle resigned from the Army after returning from Vietnam and joined the Baltimore Police Department. As a security consultant to the Maryland gubernatorial campaign of Marvin Mandel in 1972, he uncovered several electronic bugs. He died in 1986 at age forty-five from prostate cancer thought to be connected to Agent Orange.

Sergeant Alvin Smith continued on to a series of foreign assignments with Army intelligence before retiring in the 1970s. In 1972, he wrote a report of his suspicions that Army intelligence in Saigon had been infiltrated by the Communists and gave it to a secretary to Vice President Spiro Agnew. He is an investigator in the Florida State Department of Professional Regulation in Orlando.

Lieutenant Colonel Kenneth Facey finally got his full colonel's eagles. Now retired, he runs Turner House, a home for disabled veterans, in Augusta, Georgia.

Captain John McCarthy's 1968 conviction for murdering his Cambodian agent was reversed shortly after the Green Beret case was dropped. The Army declined to try him again, and he was released from prison.

THE LAWYERS

F. Lee Bailey is a criminal lawyer in Miami, Florida.

Captain John Stevens Berry is a criminal defense lawyer in Lincoln, Nebraska, and active in the Baker Street Irregulars, a Sherlock Holmes fan club.

Captain Richard Booth is in private law practice in Conway, South Carolina.

George Gregory is a lawyer in private practice in Cheraw, South Carolina, where he and his wife also raise horses.

Captain John W. (Bill) Hart is a lawyer and businessman in Burley, Idaho.

Major Martin J. Linsky stayed in the Army and became a chief administrative law judge in Washington, D.C.

Henry Rothblatt went on to national fame as a lawyer for some of the defendants in the My Lai massacre, which surfaced a month after the Green Beret case was dropped. Later he defended some of the Watergate burglars. He died in 1980.

Edward Bennett Williams practiced law in Washington until his death in 1987. He had sold his interest in the Washington Redskins, but bought the Baltimore Orioles.

THE DETECTIVES

Warrant Officer Robert Bidwell is director of security for Douglas Community College in Georgia.

Warrant Officer Frank Bourland left the Army to become a special agent with the Oklahoma State Bureau of Investigation.

THE ARMY

Stanley B. Resor resigned as secretary of the Army in 1970 and returned to his New York law firm of Debevoise & Plimpton.

Robert A. Jordan practices corporate law in Washington, D.C.

General Creighton Abrams succeeded William Westmoreland as Army chief of staff in 1972. He died from cancer in 1974.

General George L. Mabry was transferred from Vietnam to the Canal Zone in early 1970, where he headed the U.S. Army Southern Command and became a close adviser to Manuel Noriega, chief of Panamanian military intelligence. He died in 1990.

General William Potts is a defense and intelligence consultant in Arlington, Virginia.

Colonel Wilton B. Persons eventually became judge advocate general of the Army. He is retired in Savannah, Georgia.

Colonel Harold D. Seaman, who presided over the Article 32 hearings, is retired in Kill Devil Hills, North Carolina.

General William Westmoreland retired in 1972. Over a decade later a CBS News documentary charged that in 1968 he had ordered intelligence estimates skewed to downplay the strength of Communist forces in Vietnam. Westmoreland sued for slander but settled the case out of court.

THE CENTRAL INTELLIGENCE AGENCY

Dean Almy went on to become CIA station chief in Jamaica in the mid-1970s, among other assignments. Now retired, he is a member of the city council in Bath, Maine, and active in environmental affairs.

Harold Chipman retired from the CIA in 1974 and died in 1988. An obituary in the Washington Post described him as a cryptographer for thirty years with the Army Security Agency.

Clement Enking retired in 1980 and died in 1986. His daughter said "he had always been with the CIA" and was "pardoned by President Nixon" for his role in the Green Beret affair.

John Greaney, former CIA deputy counsel, is retired in Chevy Chase, Maryland.

Richard Helms was appointed ambassador to Iran by President Nixon in 1972. In 1977 he pleaded guilty to withholding information from Congress in connection with his testimony before a U.S. Senate committee concerning CIA bribes in Chile. He is a private business consultant in Washington.

Lawrence Houston, former CIA chief counsel, received the agency's highest medal of honor when he retired in 1972. He lives in Washington.

Bruce Scrymgeour retired in 1972 and died in 1980. An obituary in the Washington Post described him as an Arab language specialist and Middle East analyst who transferred from the Navy to the CIA in the mid-1950s.

Theodore Shackley became Western Hemisphere chief for the CIA in the early 1970s and was later promoted again as the agency's liaison with other U.S. intelligence agencies. He is now a consultant in international trade based in Arlington, Virginia.

John Warner, former CIA deputy counsel, is retired in Texas.

THE WHITE HOUSE

John Ehrlichman is a novelist in Santa Fe, New Mexico, having served a prison term for his role in Watergate.

Alexander Haig became chief of staff under President Nixon during the Watergate crisis and secretary of state in the Reagan administration. He is writing a book of Vietnam memoirs.

H. R. Haldeman lives in Santa Barbara, California, having served a prison term for his role in Watergate.

Henry Kissinger became the Secretary of State in the Nixon and Ford administrations. He is an international business consultant and national news media commentator.

Charles E. Colson went to prison for his role in the break-in of the office of Daniel Ellsberg's psychiatrist. He is now active in Christian prison ministries.

Gordon Liddy went to prison for his role in the Watergate break-in. He is a writer and talk-show host.

E. Howard Hunt went to prison for his role in the Watergate burglary after leading a team that broke into the office of Daniel Ellsberg's psychiatrist.

Egil Krogh is a lawyer in Seattle.

Richard Nixon resigned the presidency in August 1974.

CONGRESS

Carl Albert was Speaker of the House during 1971–1976.

Tom Gettys practices law in South Carolina.

Mendel Rivers died in 1971.

Peter Rodino became chairman of the House Judiciary Committee, which weighed the impeachment resolution against President Nixon. He is retired in Newark, New Jersey.

Jerry Zeifman is a lawyer in private practice in Washington, D.C.

THE PRESS

Kevin Buckley is a writer in New York and the author of *Panama: The Whole Story* (Simon & Schuster, 1991).

Robert Kaiser is managing editor, the *Washington Post*. His most recent book is *Gorbachev*.

Terence Smith is a Washington correspondent with the CBS program "Sunday Morning."

James Sterba is a correspondent for the *Wall Street Journal*.

Gary Shepard is an ABC Television News correspondent based in Los Angeles.

Juan Vasquez is a Miami-based correspondent with CBS Television News.

Daniel Ellsberg now lives in the San Francisco Bay Area and is active in efforts to shut down nuclear-weapons factories.

A Note on Sources

T his is a story about spies, war, murder, and the bureaucratic intrigues of several U.S. government agencies. It is based on thousands of pages of U.S. government documents declassified under the Freedom of Information Act, including the entire U.S. Army criminal investigative file on the case, formally known as *United States v. Col. Robert B. Rheault et al.* or the *Green Beret Murder Case of 1969.*

The documents were supplemented by my repeated interviews with all the major and many of the minor participants in the story, including the defendants, their lawyers, the detectives and Army prosecutors assigned to the case, senior Army officers, and a score of civilian officials in the Department of Defense, White House, and Central Intelligence Agency. Altogether, over a hundred people were interviewed for this book.

Not all of those individuals can be thanked, or even acknowledged, here. My attempt to footnote each chapter separately quickly became bogged down in the difficulty of segregating information that was partially or wholly provided on a confidential basis from that which was freely and openly provided. Readers, however, deserve to know the sources of the author's information, analysis, and conclusions to the fullest extent possible. Therefore, the following documentation is offered as a guide.

The key element of the documentary evidence is the Criminal Investigation Detachment file on the case (69-CID448-38250), which consists of the detectives' reports of investigation, their working case notes (informal conclusions and impressions compiled on a daily basis), and their in-depth interviews of witnesses and subjects, which include verbatim questions and responses.

The reports were written by CID detectives Frank Bourland and Robert Bidwell. When I interviewed them twenty-one years later, their memories of the case were remarkably fresh. They generously spent hours reconstructing and amplifying their official reports in taped interviews and several exchanges of correspondence. Without their recollections and insights, the story would have been impossible to tell with its necessary detail and complexity.

All in all, the detectives took statements from thirty-seven witnesses and eight suspects and gathered twenty exhibits—internal Special Forces memoranda and transcripts on the interrogation of Thai Khac Chuyen, polygraph reports, and forensic evidence—that were included in the Army file released to me under the Freedom of Information Act.

The reader will note the extensive dialogue between interview subjects and the detectives. It has been reconstructed from the detectives' question-and-answer reports on their interviews, their working case notes, plus my multiple interviews and correspondence with the detectives and the defendants during 1989–91. Five of the defendants gave signed statements to Army detectives that covered their roles in the affair from beginning to end. Two stopped short of sworn statements, but their remarks under interrogation by Army detectives were recorded in the working case notes. Col. Robert Rheault wrote a statement in his own hand that became part of the Army file. All of the defendants' statements were released to me under the Freedom of Information Act, along with the detectives' impressions of the interrogation sessions in their working case notes.

Dialogue among the defendants is taken from their own detailed statements to the CID and supplemented by their extensive interviews with me. Dialogue between the two detectives, as well as with their Army superiors, is taken from their reports of investigation, oral histories of senior Army officers at the Army War College, and personal interviews with the parties concerned. Warrant Officer Floyd Cotton also gave a 5,000-word statement to the detectives that became for me an essential connective tissue for reconstructing the events during Chuyen's interrogation in Saigon.

I repeatedly interviewed six of the defendants during 1989–91. Lt. Col. Ken Facey, the executive officer of the 5th Special Forces Group but not a defendant, also talked with me at length and loaned me important personal correspondence and photographs—as did many of the defendants. In addition to his interviews and correspondence with me, Col. Robert Rheault gave me permission to read his confidential oral history on file at the Army War College despite an oft-expressed view that he wished the book would not be written.

Many of the defendants' wives, friends, and relatives also agreed to be interviewed; particular thanks are due to Dot Boyle, Mary Boyle O'Hara, Karen Brumley, Phyllis Middleton, Nan Rheault, Tom Riley, and Suzanne Shackley. Letters home from the defendants, quoted liberally in the text, were supplied by the defendants or their families.

The defense lawyers, in particular John Stevens Berry, Richard Booth, and George Gregory, each spent scores of hours independently reconstructing their knowledge of the case in interviews and correspondence with me. Steve Berry's own memoirs of his service as an Army lawyer in Vietnam, *Those Gallant Men* (Presidio Press, 1984), also provided valuable insights into the thinking of the defense team. George Gregory spent days recollecting his role in the case for me, and his memory of the events, when checked against documents and transcripts that became available later, turned out to be phenomenally accurate.

There were sharp disagreements between Gregory and most of the military defense counsel on how best to handle the case. Any apparent conclusions on which methods were "better" are the responsibility of the author and will no doubt be debated forever.

The moral ambiguities that were intrinsic to the Army's prosecution of the men, among other subjects, were ably recounted for me by former Army secretary Stanley Resor, who spent countless hours helping reconstruct the events and the reasoning behind them. Former defense secretary Melvin Laird was also helpful in this area, as was counsel Len Niederlehner. Any errors of interpretation on this subject are, of course, mine.

Negotiations between the Army and Central Intelligence Agency to provide for the testimony of CIA witnesses in the looming courts-martial were helpfully fleshed out to one degree or another by several individuals, including former Army counsel Robert Jordan, former CIA director Richard Helms, then–CIA counsel Lawrence Houston, and then–CIA deputy counsels John Warner and John Greaney. Oral histories given by General Abrams's staff to the Army War College also dealt in depth with the subject of the CIA.

The exact role of the CIA in the events, of course, was one of the most contested issues of the entire affair. Pieces of the puzzle were supplied by over two dozen sources from the CIA and the Army, lawyers on both sides of the issue, and the defendants themselves. But the story quickly took on a Rashomon effect; everyone tended to see the CIA's role in the events from their own perspectives. What I have tried to do is to take the reader through the case from each participant's point of view.

Under the terms of several interviews with CIA personnel, I am not able to identify exactly who said what on various points of the agency's conduct. Some sources would not agree to be identified at all. In general, however, I can acknowledge the assistance of the following former CIA officials—and some of their relatives who must remain anonymous—for their time and patience in talking with me, either in regard to their personal knowledge of the events and/or the overall history of the CIA in Vietnam. They are (in alphabetical order): Dean Almy, Paul Belford, Douglas Blaufarb, Bob Brown, William Colby, Sam Halperin, Richard Helms, Joe Lazarsky, Bernard MacMahon, Alan Paul, Tom Polgar, Charles Timmes, Jim Ward, and David Whipple.

Other documents released in the file include a collection of forty-seven highly classified "back-channel" messages exchanged between the Army command in Vietnam and the Joint Chiefs of Staff in Washington on the progress of the case, which enabled me to reconstruct the thinking of the high command as it planned its various moves in the prosecution of the Green Berets. The cables were supplemented by my interviews with most of those who wrote them, including the staff of then–Army secretary Stanley B. Resor; Gen. George Mabry, commander of the United States Army in Vietnam (USARV); Gen. William Westmoreland, the former Vietnam commander who at the time of the events was Army chief of staff; Gen. Bruce Palmer, Westmoreland's deputy; Gen. William Potts, the J-2, or chief of staff for intelligence for the Military Assistance Command, Vietnam (MACV); and Col. Wilton B. Persons, the chief legal officer for USARV. Former major Bob Comeau, who as chief of the Special Actions Branch of the Army's judge advocate general's office wrote or was privy to much of the message traffic, also helped me interpret the actions and intent of the high officers involved in the case.

Another key element of the file was the tall stack of legal memoranda produced by lawyers in the office of the Army's judge advocate general, as well as the staff of Army secretary Resor, which analyzed precedents and weighed the pros and cons of the prosecution. These, too, were supplemented by interviews with many of their authors. Robert Jordan, the Army's civilian counsel, was particularly helpful in explaining some of the most sensitive aspects of the case to me.

For insights into the thinking of MACV commander Gen. Creighton Abrams, who died in 1974, I am particularly indebted to his widow, Julie; his former aide, then-major James Anderson; Gen. William B. Rossen, a close friend and adviser to General Abrams on special operations; Generals Westmoreland and Palmer; and Gen. William McCaffrey, a former deputy commander to General Abrams at USARV.

These interviews were supplemented by the taped recollections of key officers on Abrams's staff, which have been compiled by the Oral History Project of the Army War College in Carlisle, Pennsylvania. Most of the officers discussed the Green Beret case in detail in their oral histories since it was a major event of Abrams's tenure as the supreme U.S. military commander in Vietnam. These included the reminiscences of Gen. Elias C. Townsend, Abrams's J-3, or operations officer; Gen. Frank T. Mildren, former USARV commander; Gen. John K. Singlaub, head of the U.S. Military Assistance Command's Special Operations Group; and Col. Jonathan Ladd, a former commander of the 5th Special Forces Group in Vietnam.

Also on file at the Army War College were the telephone logs and notes of telephone conversations between General Westmoreland and other officers regarding the Green Beret case. They are quoted verbatim in the text.

The Army conducted four days of secret hearings on the case in a sealed converted chapel in Long Binh, South Vietnam, during July–August 1969. Known as an Article 32 investigation, the proceeding amounts to the military's version of a civilian grand jury and preliminary hearing rolled into one: The Army presents evidence and witnesses, which defense attorneys are able to challenge and cross-examine. I was able to obtain complete transcripts of the hearings under the Freedom of Information Act, and they are quoted verbatim in these pages, with minor editing for redundancy, clarification, and continuity.

The hearing record was immeasurably enhanced by my interviews with key personnel present at the hearings, including the defendants, many of their lawyers, and Col. Harold Seaman, the presiding officer. On the defense side, the recollections of former Army captains John S. Berry, Richard Booth, Bill Hart, Martin Linsky, and civilian defense attorney George W. Gregory were particularly valuable, allowing me to recreate the atmosphere and hidden intentions behind their questions.

The Presidential Papers Project of the National Archives held important evidence on the thinking of President Richard Nixon and the White House staff regarding the Green Beret case. The president himself made several jotted notes about the case on the margins of the daily White House morning news summary, which are explicitly referenced in the text.

The papers and daily diaries of Nixon's chief of staff, H. R. "Bob" Haldeman, and White House counsel John Ehrlichman also revealed the clinching evidence of how the case was eventually settled. Interviews with Haldeman and Ehrlichman, as well as other former White House staffers, filled in the blanks.

I am particularly grateful to John Ehrlichman, whose memoir of his White House duty, *Witness to Power: The Nixon Years* (Simon & Schuster, 1982), also included a colorful passage on the Green Beret case, which, when supplemented by his generous interviews, painted a convincing picture of the hidden factors and considerations that lay behind President Nixon's handling of the case.

I am also indebted to former Bell Labs chairman Dr. William O. Baker, a member of the president's Foreign Intelligence Advisory Board, for confirmation of the board's handling of the Green Beret case.

Daniel Ellsberg, the former Vietnam expert at the State and Defense departments, also gave valuable time in explaining how the resolution of the Green Beret case provoked him to leak the secret history of the Vietnam War, famously known as "The Pentagon Papers."

Of all the principal players in the executive branch, only President Nixon and Dr. Henry A. Kissinger, his national security adviser, declined to be interviewed for this book.

Congress also played a key role in the affair, pushing President Nixon to intervene in the case. Former New Jersey congressman Peter Rodino, who led the charge against the Army in the House, generously granted me an interview and pointed me to important documents in the case. One of his former staff attorneys who worked on the issue, Jerry Zeifman, supplied both interesting anecdotes and a thoughtful philosophical framework in which to consider the affair.

The late Rep. Mendel Rivers, the then-powerful chairman of the House Armed Services Committee, played the climactic cards that forced President Nixon to intervene in the case. I am indebted to several people for their recollections and insights on Congressman Rivers, particularly his son Mendel Rivers, Jr., and John Russell Blandford, former chief counsel of the Armed Services Committee. Lee Bandy, the veteran congressional correspondent for the South Carolina *State* newspaper, provided an authoritative account of Mendel Rivers's showdown with the White House and the Army.

I would be remiss in not crediting the work of other journalists and scholars for their work on the Green Beret case in particular and Vietnam in general. First among these is Robert Kaiser, now managing editor of the *Washington Post*, who covered the unfolding case in Saigon. Kaiser dug up his diary from the period, which contained a vivid (and often humorous) account of his and other reporters' efforts to get to the bottom of the Green Beret mystery. Kevin

Buckley, a Saigon correspondent for *Newsweek*, Terence Smith, then Saigon bureau chief of the *New York Times*, and James Sterba, then a *Times* reporter in Vietnam, also provided lively recollections of the affair.

Vu Thuy Hoang, an assistant to Kaiser in the *Washington Post*'s Saigon bureau and now a research librarian with the newspaper in Washington, not only provided his valuable recollections but helped me correspond with relatives of Thai Khac Chuyen in Vietnam and Canada.

Hundreds of books and countless articles deepened my understanding of the Vietnam War and intelligence operations. A complete bibliography is impossible here, but some works deserve special mention for the information and inspiration they provided.

For an overview of the tortured history of Vietnam and the United States, nothing touches Stanley Karnow's reissued *Vietnam: A History* (Viking Penguin, 1991). For brilliant insights on the idealistic but misguided attempts of Americans to change Vietnam's destiny, Neil Sheehan's *A Bright Shining Lie* (Simon & Schuster, 1990) is incomparable. On the United States in Cambodia, William Shawcross's *Sideshow: Kissinger, Nixon and the Destruction of Cambodia* (Simon & Schuster, 1979) was invaluable. Seymour Hersh's monumental work *The Price of Power: Kissinger in the Nixon White House* (Summit, 1983) brilliantly lit up the dark corners of the Nixon strategy on the war.

On intelligence matters, I am grateful to former CIA officer Frank Snepp, whose 1977 classic on the CIA in Vietnam, *Decent Interval* (Random House), was a constant companion. For a wider understanding of the personalities and policies that drove the CIA during the 1960s, I found myself turning repeatedly to *The Man Who Kept the Secrets: Richard Helms and the CIA* (Knopf, 1979) by Thomas Powers and *Wilderness of Mirrors* (Harper & Row, 1980) by David C. Martin. In his *Lost Victory* (Morrow, 1990), former CIA director William Colby put forth provocative arguments in defense of the Phoenix program.

The history of the Green Berets in Vietnam was most reliably and soberly recounted by Shelby Stanton in his *Green Berets at War* (Presidio Press, 1985). As a tutorial of how to combine a strong narrative with investigative reporting, I am completely indebted to Robert Lindsey for writing *The Falcon and the Snowman* (Pocket Books, 1985).

And finally we come to the alleged murder victim at the center of the case, one Thai Khac Chuyen. Throughout the events portrayed in this book, Chuyen remained largely a mystery.

The defendants themselves never agreed on his exact identity. The press, relying largely on unidentified sources, variously described him as a double, triple, even quadruple agent (for the CIA, the Green Berets, South Vietnam, and North Vietnam). Twenty years after the event, it was not easy to reconstruct his life, and impossible to assess with certainty his true allegiance.

Nevertheless, several clues to his personal history were gathered together for the first time here, some from the transcript of Chuyen's interrogation by the Green Berets, part of which was obtained by the author. Other clues were supplied by the Green Berets themselves in their signed statements and interviews with me, particularly former sergeant Alvin P. Smith, Chuyen's spy handler. Other glimpses into his shadow life were supplied by Chuyen's widow and his two children, whom I located in Vietnam in 1990, and a brother, who now lives in Canada. Another brother, who surfaced with the North Vietnamese army in Saigon in April 1975, has not been available to be interviewed.

In the end, it will be up to the reader to judge whether Thai Khac Chuyen was a North Vietnamese double agent, as most of the Green Berets believed. He never confessed. Only he knows whom he served for sure, and he took the truth with him to the bottom of the South China Sea.

Index

INDEX

About the Author

When the Green Beret case broke in 1969, Jeff Stein was himself an Army intelligence case officer in Vietnam. He remained fascinated with the affair and was determined to write about it once declassified documents were available. Over the years, he has written for such publications as the *Washington Post*, the *New Republic*, *New York* and *Esquire* magazines; served as foreign news features editor at United Press International; and authored *The Vietnam Fact Book*. Stein was recently filmed for a fifteen-part BBC series on the CIA. He now lives in Washington, D.C.